Credit
Management
Handbook

Also by Cecil J. Bond

CREDIT AND COLLECTIONS FOR YOUR SMALL BUSINESS

HANDS-ON FINANCIAL CONTROLS FOR YOUR SMALL BUSINESS

Credit Management Handbook

A Complete Guide to Credit and Accounts Receivable Operations

Cecil J. Bond

McGraw-Hill, Inc.

New York St. Louis San Francisco Auckland Bogotá
Caracas Lisbon London Madrid Mexico Milan
Montreal New Delhi Paris San Juan São Paulo
Singapore Sydney Tokyo Toronto

Library of Congress Cataloging-in-Publication Data

Bond, Cecil J.
    Credit management handbook : a complete guide to credit and
accounts receivable operations / Cecil J. Bond.
        p.   cm.
    Includes index.
    ISBN 0-07-006564-0 :
    1. Credit—Management—Handbooks, manuals, etc. 2. Accounts
receivable—Handbooks, manuals, etc. I. Title.
HG3751.B67   1993
658.8′8—dc20   92-28307
                                            CIP

1 2 3 4 5 6 7 8 9 0   DOC/DOC 9 8 7 6 5 4 3 2

ISBN 0-07-006564-0

*The sponsoring editor for this book was David Conti, and the production supervisor
was Donald F. Schmidt. It was set in Baskerville by North Market Street Graphics.*

Printed and bound by R. R. Donnelley & Sons Company.

This book is printed on recycled, acid-free paper containing a minimum of 50% recycled de-
inked fiber.

Special Thanks to . . .

Linda Smith, specialist in foreign trade and foreign trade services and a good friend during and since our days at Dysan Corporation. Linda contributed addresses, publications, regulatory guidelines, telephone numbers, and information pertaining to key areas of Export.

Part 5 has an abundance of good material because of Linda's willingness to share sources and material.

My daughter, Coralyn Bond, for monitoring more than 1000 pages of manuscript with the avowed goal of curbing the number of dangling phrases, midsentence changes in thought—and her father's lifelong proclivity to insert an inappropriate punctuation mark at an appropriate place.

Contents

2. Operating the Department   49

3. Gathering Credit Information   73

Part 3. The Uniform Commercial Code   353

15. When and How to Use UCC Filings   357

16. Secured Transactions (Division 9)   387

17. Creating the Security Interest   405

Part 4. The Bankruptcy Act   489

22. When a Debtor Files for Protection   497

23. The Bankrupt's Obligation to Creditors   521

24. The Many Costs of Bankruptcy   539

Preface

The goal of *Credit Management Handbook: A Complete Guide to Credit and Accounts Receivable Operations* is to provide credit grantors with a guideline source to which they may turn for help in coping satisfactorily with all aspects of credit management. *Credit Management Handbook* takes the reader through the defining of a company's credit policy objectives, through the writing of the credit policy, and subsequently through the confronting and the solving of problems in specific areas, and in areas of more general impact. It gives credit grantors the tools they must have to arrive at solid answers and solutions—and it offers them in a format that ensures speedy access to material relevant to answering a specific question or solving a specific problem.

Credit Management Handbook: A Complete Guide to Credit and Accounts Receivable Operations addresses all areas, topics, and subtopics that might impact the establishing of a credit function or department; the managing of the company's credit accounts; the solutions to problems that relate to the successful managing of credit accounts; and the managing of all peripheral areas having an impact on the credit function. Here are a few of the many areas that are covered via explanations and examples:

- Does the credit department deliver the level of financial support required to minimize bank borrowings? If not, why not? What, or where, is the specific area of weakness? What must you do to correct the problem? (Cash trickle in lieu of cash flow is the most obvious result of a credit function that is not doing its job.)

- Does your company's accounts receivable represent a solid, responsive "quick asset"? Is receivables aging in line with the average for your industry? With one, both, or neither? (Industry average is fine, but it may not do the job for your company. Your receivables may be required to perform at a turnover rate faster than the industry average.)

- Does your firm sell to overseas accounts? Do you understand the rules of export sales as administered by the Department of Commerce? Do you know when and how to apply for an export license? If your company gets one, what must you do with it? What is a "documents package" and why must it be complete and accurate? Should your company accept payment in a form other than an irrevocable letter of credit? Do you know when a letter of credit is properly prepared? Why must the instructions in a letter of credit be followed without deviation?

- What is the purpose of the Uniform Commercial Code? Is the Code a security blanket or a potential source of loss for many manufacturers and distributors? Are you capable of making a proper UCC filing? What is the difference between a "perfected filing" and an "imperfect filing"— and how can you avoid the "imperfect"? What is a continuation filing and when is it used? What must you do when your company's security interest in a creditor ends?

- Who may file a petition under Chapter 11 of the Bankruptcy Code? What is the guideline difference between a voluntary and an involuntary petition in bankruptcy? What are the duties and responsibilities of the trustee? What is the purpose of a creditors' committee? What is a continuation plan? A plan of arrangement?

These are a few of the major areas covered in *Credit Management Handbook*. The book has a great many guideline examples that illustrate how *Credit Management Handbook* material can be applied in daily decision making. There is extensive cross-referencing among sections, subsections, and topics to assist the credit grantor in his or her effort to focus relevant material on a question or problem. Whether the question or problem is specific or general, *Credit Management Handbook* offers a format that provides answers and guideline solutions.

Credit Management Handbook offers the credit grantor a comprehensive volume of guideline information that includes examples of problem situations and appropriate solutions. There are extensive exhibits (forms of all types, including form letters, letters for special or unique situations, a guideline credit policy, etc.) and a back-of-the-book appendix which will enable the reader to pinpoint a page or pages that relate to a section, subsection, or topic of interest. There are also "how-tos" for short- and long-term contingency planning against the effects on your company's receivables of inflation or deflation, as well as strategies for hedging credit exposure against the short- and long-term effects of recession or depression.

Readers who have one or both of my recent books—*Credit and Collections for Your Small Business* and *Hands-On Financial Controls for Your Small Business* (both published by McGraw-Hill's Liberty Hall Press)—will find that *Credit Management Handbook* offers a much more extensive and in-depth approach to the problems and solutions of credit management than *Credit and Collections*. This book is a comprehensive approach to credit management, but it is written with the goal of providing in-depth assistance to credit grantors ranging in experience from "very limited" to credit administrators whose companies have annual sales into the tens of millions of dollars. *Credit Management Handbook: A Complete Guide to Credit and Accounts Receivable Operations* puts management tools between two covers and in a format that makes "self-help" a correct and a welcome phrase.

Cecil J. Bond

Credit
Management
Handbook

PART 1

The Credit Department

The single most important contribution that a credit department can make to the success of a company is to have a credit policy that is tailored to the needs of the company, and to so effectively implement that policy as to ensure the achievement of its stated goals.

There are any number of ways to sum up a credit department, to administer a credit function, and to arrive at a specific goal. The primary consideration for any credit manager, or entrepreneur who also functions as the credit manager, is to take the most effective and appropriate route for the requirements of a particular company. A credit policy that does not provide the credit department with guidelines appropriate for what it must do to maximize its value to the company is falling short of the goal. A credit plan that details what is expected of the credit department of one company may be totally inappropriate for the needs of another. Imagine the frustrations of trying to apply a liberal credit and collections policy to the cash-flow needs of a cash-poor company. The result would be catastrophic in both the short and long term.

A sound credit policy must reflect the needs of the company for which it is designed. It must reflect those needs not only in the short term (from start-up through early sales of a product), but also into the long term. Nothing, however, is cast in stone. Conditions, or combinations of conditions, may make it necessary to revise sections of the original credit policy while the company is still very young. Economic conditions, competitive pressures, changes in customer product preferences, or the introduction of new technology may have an impact on the credit policy of a specific company. There must be room in the credit policy for flexibility in the interpretation and application of it, for minor changes when they are called for, or for something as drastic as a reevaluation of the company's original criteria for authorizing credit account sales and for collecting receivables balances.

A good credit policy has its best chance to be an effective and a productive tool when it is coupled with a competent credit manager or credit administrator. One cannot be totally effective without the other, although I must add that a good credit manager can, because of his or her experience and expertise, overcome the shortcomings of a faulty or an inadequate credit policy. The chances for success are not as good, however, when that same "good credit policy" is coupled with an inexperienced credit manager, or with a credit manager whose level of experience is not adequate for the size and scope of the department he or she must manage.

When the credit manager's experience and skill level are not compatible with the level of his or her responsibilities, there is danger in many areas that are credit management's responsibility. There is danger that accounts will be approved for credit lines that do not fall within the guideline criteria of the company's credit policy, or within any acceptable standard of safety. Inexperience in evaluating data and inconsistency in applying evaluated data can be hazardous to the health of a company's accounts receivable and cash flow.

In the context of the company's financial welfare, no facet of the credit department's responsibility is more important than its contribution to the company's monthly cash-flow requirement. Accounts that have not been evaluated against the yardstick of the company's credit policy will not make the contribution expected of them. The amount of cash generated from receiving such an irregular quality will fall far short of the company's needs and expectations. And when cash generated from accounts receivable fails to contribute a major share of the company's monthly requirement for cash, the cost of doing business rises by the cost of the money borrowed to supplement that received from receivables.

A credit department should contribute favorably to the company's public image. There are times when "straight talk" is in order; certainly, a customer who cannot be persuaded to fulfill his or her payment obligation to your company is a prime candidate for straight talk. But in the larger context of the credit manager's and the credit department's relationships with customers, the general public, other suppliers, and other departments of the company, a tone should be set and projected that is consistently cordial. It is unacceptable for anyone who has contact with the department to be subjected to an attitude that calls up a hostile or negative image.

The credit department is a highly visible area of the company's image. If the manner in which the department's image is being projected is unflattering to the department and the company, corrective measures must be taken immediately. Credit people can, without being weak or allowing themselves to be manipulated into unacceptable credit decisions, be a potent public relations force for their company. Helpful, innovative credit arrangements based upon sound financial and experience data are one of the most effective ways to help your company build a strong customer base, and to let the company's customers know that the credit department is as sales-oriented as the sales department itself. The era of the credit manager who grouched his or her way through the day may never have been "in," but I can assure you of one thing: it is definitely "out"!

Progressive companies are "goal-" or "objective"-oriented, and to attain company goals or objectives demands the same orientation of individuals and departments. Is your company projecting an annual growth rate of 10 or 15 percent? The credit manager must lift the level of his or her performance and that of department associates to a corresponding level. This does not mean that you and your associates must increase your personal work load by the same percentage; it has nothing to do with personal work load. What it means to you, as the person charged with credit and accounts receivable responsibility, is that your capacity for handling new and/or more complex responsibilities must grow more rapidly than the company's rate of growth.

Growth normally takes a company into new marketing areas and more complex supplier–customer relationships, puts more dollars into individual receivables accounts, and increases the total of accounts receivable dollars. A company that has been selling within the boundaries of its own state may become a regional or a national manufacturer or supplier. There may be agreements for consignments of product to new customers, for an increase in the number of in-state and out-of-state distributors, or for a dramatic increase in filings under the protective cover of the Uniform Commercial Code. Your company may find also that its products are generating interest in countries overseas; welcome to the wide, wonderful, and somewhat complex world of Export Trade.

Unless the credit manager grows at a rate faster than his or her company, the company will not benefit from the level of management skills essential for the protection of accounts receivable balances. The successful management of these areas is vital to the financial health of every company. No company can afford to retain a credit manager who is unwilling or incapable of making the personal effort necessary to ensure that his or her professional growth is never less than half-a-step ahead of the company's growth. Given that commitment, the credit manager and the company should do well together.

What is the most important contribution that the credit department can make to a company? Financial officers will concur that the number one contribution is an accounts receivable collection effort that delivers a high percentage of the company's monthly cash-flow requirement to the company's cash-flow pipeline. Other contributions are important, but the bottom line for a credit manager is good amounts of cash generated from accounts receivable that consistently have a high level of liquidity. A credit manager will be forgiven if he or she falters occasionally in other areas of the department's operation, but not if he or she fails to do a professional job selecting and monitoring accounts, or collecting receivables balances. It is a monthly challenge, a challenge that is renewed endlessly.

Credit management is business management. It is the management of a particularly important area of the company's assets, an area that has the potential to impact the company favorably or unfavorably. When credit management is effective, the benefits to the company can be considerable. If incompetence or inexperience is allowed to blunder its way into a multitude of problems—most of which will not be resolved satisfactorily—the negative impact on the company can be devastating.

Do not be intimidated by the magnitude of the challenge. Many of us have gone before, and some of us have lived to put words of advice and encouragement between the covers of books. Take pride in your profession and let your work reflect that pride. Make a strong contribution to the success of your business or company, and do not forget to work constantly to upgrade your skills and the skill levels of department associates.

Is the Credit Department Meeting Its Obligation?

If your company has a credit policy (and if it does not, I hope you will take steps immediately to put one in place), it is not difficult to measure the performance of the department against that yardstick. And because the credit department is responsible for what the department does or does not accomplish, the manager should have no difficulty determining the strong and weak points of his or her personal performance.

The question of whether the credit department is meeting its responsibility to the company can be answered in many ways. Some of the "if" statements that require a "yes" response are the following:

1. If applicants for credit are being processed and evaluated in a professional manner and in accordance with the company's credit policy.
2. If the department is making every effort to find a mutually acceptable way to sell every credit applicant.
3. If accounts receivable aging is (a) in line with the company's credit policy and (b) compatible with account aging averages for the industry.
4. If department personnel is interfacing effectively with customers and other departments and individuals in the company.

5. If receivables balances are being collected in a timely manner.
6. If slow-pay accounts are being contacted for payment frequently and effectively.
7. If the department is projecting an image that enhances the public image of the company.
8. If the level of knowledge within the department is high enough to cope effectively with growth.
9. If company growth and knowledge within the credit department can be focused successfully on out-of-state sales, filings under the Uniform Commercial Code, servicing certain distributors with innovate credit arrangements, and potential export sales.

These are some of the important statements that can be affirmative if the credit department is making a strong contribution to the company. If you manage a credit department that is handling successfully most or all of the responsibilities listed above, you are to be congratulated. If, however, an evaluation of the department indicates that the department—although delivering results that are well within the criteria for a satisfactory rating—should correct some minor misdirections in its total focus, those elements should be addressed promptly and corrective measures taken immediately.

What does the credit manager do when an evaluation of the department's performance reveals a laundry list of problems, some of a magnitude strong enough to reduce the department's effectiveness to a level below that set in the company's credit policy? The manager should look first at his or her own performance. How effectively is the department being managed? Is the credit manager trying to do too much by trying to retain control of areas that could be assigned to people who are ready to assume responsibility that is more complex? There is also the possibility that the manager has overestimated the capabilities, or the readiness for additional responsibility, of one or more individuals. Perhaps an employee has been assigned a level of responsibility that is beyond that person's present capabilities. If so, the manager's ability to judge the readiness of department members could be faulted. Be sure that the people who make important decisions and have important responsibilities have the knowledge and experience to handle them in a satisfactory manner.

A credit department must maintain a level of performance consistent with the company's requirement for cash. The performance of the credit department must be one of the strongest links in the company's financial chain because the ongoing financial requirement of most companies offers almost no latitude for a level of achievement that delivers less than its projected goal. The department must generate, from receivables, a flow of cash consistent with the company's monthly requirement and consistent with its projected costs of borrowed money. When there is a major increase in the projected requirement for funds to supplement internally generated cash flow, it pumps an unanticipated cost (interest dollars) into projections that ultimately become guideline figures in an annual budget. Dollars that under other circumstances would find their way into the "bottom line" of the company's financial statements become instead an unproductive addition to the company's overhead expenses.

If your company's credit department or credit function is not meeting its obligation to the company, do something about it. A faulty or a deteriorating situation will not improve of its own volition; corrective steps must be initiated if the problems are to be resolved successfully. Check the criteria being used to evaluate new applicants for credit, and evaluate the data received in response to your requests for credit experience data. Monitor all accounts on an ongoing basis, and do not hesitate to make downward adjustments in credit lines when experience (yours and that of other suppliers) warrants it. What is needed is an experienced hand and a flexible rein on the "when, where, and how" on the amount of credit granted to the company's accounts. Of equal importance is a consistent, constant, and firm hand on the collection of the company's accounts receivable balances. If your company is enjoying this level of credit and receivables control, the credit department is doing its share to maximize the flow of internally generated cash.

Never allow your credit department to function at less than the professional level expected of it. Make whatever changes may be necessary to attain the required level of professionalism, and make them promptly! Your company expects it of you, and you owe it to your company.

How to Improve Performance and Results

Start with the basics of how credit data is gathered and evaluated, and what personnel evaluate it. Do you include yourself in this analysis of the department at work? You certainly do! Review departmental procedures with staff members and how those procedures are applied to the processing of credit applications, the references given by applicants, the responses given by the applicant's references, and how you and your associates evaluate and use that information.

Did the person who evaluated specific reference data and approved an order or set a credit line use criteria appropriate for the account situation? What about the experience of the person who made the initial credit decision, monitored the account on an ongoing basis, and collected receivables balances in a less than timely manner? And if you are the credit manager, how well have you handled your management responsibility? Have you been giving too much authority to people whose professional experience cannot support it? Even more stifling to the growth of the department is giving too little authority to people who are qualified to handle more.

If the credit department is doing anything to earn its keep, there will be occasional mistakes or errors in judgment. They will occur regardless of how diligently the manager or supervisor monitors the work of associates, but good management skills will minimize the magnitude and frequency of those mistakes. When a mistake does occur? Hope that it can be identified as a growth step rather than an act of carelessness or incompetence. Every mistake has a price tag, but the tag on one that can be identified as a growth step can be prorated over and absorbed into an impressive number of positives.

1
Organizing/ Reorganizing the Department

This chapter contains the tools necessary to set up or to reorganize a credit department that will work for you, not against you. A credit department should be lean, an area in which each member knows his or her assignment, has the experience to do a job effectively, and is able to work with a minimum amount of supervision. It should be a department that is geared to handle growth (the company's and that of individual members of the department), and must be capable of making important credit and receivables decisions.

Whether your company is large or small, has a part-time or a professional credit management person, and is or is not poised for rapid growth, capable credit management is an essential if the company or business is to maximize its chances for healthy, financial performance.

The Business Plan

If you are an entrepreneur, my hope is that you prepared (or had prepared) a solid business plan well in advance of the morning when you opened the company's doors for business for the first time. You should know what a business plan must contain, and if it doesn't, what should be done to correct it. What about the credit manager who is not an entrepreneur and has no aspirations to be one? He or she should still be aware of what belongs in a business plan, and especially what to look for in a customer's business plan.

9

Customers who have planned well will usually be happy to discuss their business plan with a supplier's credit manager. Although it is not a tool that is routinely requested of a customer, it is the type of information that reveals a great deal about the individual(s) who founded the company or business. What goals were set for the company and how do the owner/managers intend to achieve them? If the company has been in business for one or two years, is it on target with what was projected in the business plan? Is there a reasonable explanation for any major delay in achieving planned goals? Has there been any reluctance on the part of the customer's management to make available to you a copy of the business plan? Have you asked to see the business plan and been refused?

The business plan can say a great deal regarding how well organized the company's management seems to be. Does the business plan include time frames that are too narrow for the attainment of certain levels of results? This might be indicative of a dangerous level of impatience at the top management level that could be unleashed in an ill-timed attempt to accelerate growth that is less than was projected in the business plan. Dangerous levels of impatience have a way of translating into ill-conceived decisions—decisions that then stretch the demands on the company's cash flow well beyond what it is capable of handling. Receivables balances begin to stretch deeper into past-due columns as more and more of the company's suppliers see smaller and less-frequent payment checks.

It is in your interest and in the best interest of your company to be familiar with what should be included in a well-written business plan. A long, rambling piece of writing is not an acceptable substitute for a shorter, more concise, all-inclusive plan. It should cover all of the major areas: "Goals," "Risks," "Organization," "Financial," and "Exit Option." The essentials should be there—spelled out very clearly—but nothing should be in minute detail.

The following is an example of what guidelines to look for in each of the stated categories:

The Business Plan

1. *Goals.* This category includes projected timetables, an outline of products, personnel requirements (short-term and long-term), facilities, market area(s), etc. These are the essential ingredients in the how, where, and when of your company.

2. *Risks.* Explain the risks as you know them and what you have built in for coping with the expected and the unexpected. Define the major and secondary risks in terms that can be understood by people who are the primary investors or the key employee targets.

3. *Organization.* Detail what type of organization you believe it will take to allow the company to reach each plateau of growth, and how you

intend to provide guidance on your own and with the assistance of qualified help. Think it through carefully and revise it until the business plan becomes a living guideline document.

4. *Financial.*   It is important to accurately project the company's need for financial support at every early level of its growth. What amount are you, the entrepreneur, going to invest? Is your investment money in stocks, bonds, or other negotiables, or must it be repaid to a second party from company earnings? In addition to your investment, what funds will be needed at the start-up level, at the first level of growth, etc.? If you expect to attract private investors or venture capitalists, do not divulge any numbers that allude to the percentage of stock you might be willing to assign in any prospectus, business plan, etc. Instead, state your long-term projection for either taking the company public (a public offering of stock when there is SEC approval) or allowing it to retain its initial identity as a closely held corporation (yourself, family members, or a few carefully selected investors who will not pressure you to position the company for a public offering).

5. *Exit Option.*   Spell out the terms and chart the procedure for getting out of your business whether it is a sale to another company, a merger with a larger and/or stronger company in your industry, or a sale to a large company that is allegedly diversifying for the ultimate benefit of both parties. Reasons for selling the business might range from an offer you cannot refuse, a need for time when the business becomes too consuming to properly supervise other investments or properties, or a profit margin that is less after one or two years than had been projected.

6. *Spell it all out*—everything from *A* to *Z*. If your experience at putting together a business plan is limited, take your outline and ideas to a professional business consultant, a successful business acquaintance who has built his or her business within the parameters of a written, clearly defined business plan, and take the final revision of your plan to the attorney who handles the company's (or your) legal affairs. Only then will you have the feedback to ensure that you have written a good, comprehensive business plan. Don't settle for less than a plan that fits what you intend for the company to do, is realistic in its goals, and gives you a real chance to accomplish those goals.

If what I have just said about writing and administering a business plan is causing some credit managers to wonder how they can judge the effectiveness of a plan, ask yourself the following questions:

Is the business making the progress that it projected for itself?

Has there been a noticeable loss of direction and/or momentum?

Is the trade wondering whether the company is less competitive or less service-oriented than it should be?

Is the company borrowing more money than the strong level of sales indicates is appropriate to pay the company's monthly bills?

What about the company's budget? Is there good financial control over company expenditures?

The answers to these questions will be enormously helpful to any credit manager who is looking to compare key areas in a company's progress. If the answer to one or more of these questions is ambiguous to the extent that it leaves almost as much unanswered as there was before the question was asked, it could be a warning that there are problems—problems that might be difficult to recognize if the company's business plan is not available to use as a yardstick.

If after 18 or 24 months there is an update to the business plan, the motivation for the update could be a need for a substantial increase in the bank line to expand existing production and warehouse facilities. This is of interest to the credit managers of the company's suppliers because it says that the company is increasing sales. It does not say that the company is properly screening and monitoring its accounts, or that it is collecting receivables balances in a timely manner. It does say, however, that there is current and anticipated growth. How should a supplier's credit manager react? When all of the signs are good—trade reports and suppliers', banks', and your own experience with the account—your company should not be slow to react favorably to any reasonable request that this customer might make. You have seen the company's first-rate business plan, and the steps being taken to expand the business are on target for the timing and the size of expansion. Do not let another company steal this customer's business from you. Your company could be doing business with a real winner!

Types of Growth

Cynics might be guilty of oversimplification when they demand to know at what point planned and unplanned business growth replaced profitable and unprofitable business growth. Neither of the two phrases has been replaced. Strong financial control has been inserted to contain unplanned growth and keep it from becoming unprofitable growth. Unless unplanned growth is the recipient of strong financial controls, "unprofitable" becomes the unwelcome synonym for unplanned business growth.

Steady Growth.   Of the various types of growth, none is more rewarding in the long term, or less troublesome to credit managers, than steady growth. It offers the lowest number of unexpected, growth-related challenges. It is also the rate of growth that should most nearly approximate the timetable set forth in the company's business plan. Credit managers must still monitor these accounts, but the category produces very few failures.

Steady growth should translate into a financial statement that reflects the progressive pattern of the company's growth. Profits should be commensurate with the quality, discipline, and opportunism of management's skills and should not fluctuate wildly from one quarter to the next. There is always the acceptable (but rare) extenuating circumstance to explain an uncharacteristically poor quarter, but the explanation should not be rooted in substandard or uneven management. Any momentary hesitation in the company's progress should be the result of a downturn in the industry, a downturn in the economy, or because a large order was canceled or deferred to another quarter. Any hesitation in the company's progress should not be attributed to a weakness in management's ability to foresee problems as they arise and deal with them before they disrupt the company's pattern of growth.

Sporadic Growth. Sporadic is the lurch-, slowdown-, spurt-, and hesitate-type of growth that does not speak favorably for the company's long-term planning or day-to-day management skills. When a business is very young there can be legitimate reasons for growth that does not trace a textbook-steady upward line. Breaking into a target market area is often not without its joys and disappointments, each of which might leave an imprint on the growth line.

The type of business and the strength of the competition strongly influence the growth of a business. The majority of your customers might have well-established businesses, but unless there is some form of utopian business situation (very little competition, a product line that is in great demand, a very strong regional economy, etc.), the businesses of your customers will not be immune to the shock effects of bumps, shudders, and hesitations. The big plus is that if a company has been around from some time and it has been well managed, it should be somewhat less vulnerable than newer companies or companies that have not been well managed.

Owners and managers often don't handle success very well. They may have worked hard to bring the company to its current level of success, but they then succumb to the temptation of complacency. They begin to spend more time away from the business; the result, particularly in a smaller company, is a dangerous drop-off in the quality of day-to-day decision making. Most owners and managers don't jeopardize the future of their company by taking unreasonable liberties with its success. They remain as conscientious about the company's financial and business operations and controls as they were in its earliest days. This is management at its best and most responsive level. Whatever the future may hold—recession, industry-threatening changes in products or technology, changing customer requirements, or increasing levels of competition, the well-managed company will not fall into any of the traps of sporadic growth.

Volatile Growth.   There is no more unattractive business scenario than that of volatile growth—most of which is unplanned. There are so many negatives and so few pluses to this type of growth. There is rarely enough in-house talent, money, production, or distribution capability to begin to keep pace with the demands of a volatile or runaway growth. The business finds itself struggling with what looks like an overload of success, or with a level of business that could be a major success if it could be controlled. When a company's growth puts too much distance between itself and the projections of its business plan, it is in grave danger of becoming a statistic rather than a success. Suddenly the entire support system is too small and too far behind growth to save the company from pushing itself into the quagmire of multiple financial and production problems.

When a credit manager is approached by a company that is plunging headlong into a pattern of unplanned and uncontrolled growth, the evidence should be clear cut. Suppliers will not uniformly have good things to say regarding how the account is being handled, particularly if the frantic pattern of growth has been going on for several months. Cash will be in increasingly short supply, so payments to suppliers will be slowing. The bank may still report a satisfactory relationship, but inquiry will usually bring an admission that credit lines have been drawn virtually to zero. Repayment schedules may still be acceptable, but there is also a gradual slowing—an obvious struggle—to stay close to the repayment schedule.

This is not the type of risk to give a credit manager any comfort. From the moment a supplier takes on a customer of this type, the certainty is 99 percent that the account will go down as fast or faster than it went up. Short of a miracle—a buy-out or a takeover by a company with a large supply of cash—there is no profitable future for the supplier who allows himself or herself to be drawn into volume sales with an account whose future has the indelible imprint of a Chapter 11.

If a credit manager decides to sell such an account or is instructed by top management to do so, monitoring the account will involve a disproportionate amount of the credit manager's time. Unfortunately, the disproportionate amount of time spent monitoring this account (or accounts of this type) will only heighten the awareness of the credit manager to the dangers involved in selling it at more than a minimal level; it will do nothing to guard against the potential for the loss of a substantial number of dollars if there isn't tight, watchful credit control.

How can management slow the runaway momentum of an account that is experiencing volatile growth? It must first slow runaway growth without destroying all forward momentum. New orders must be minimized while the company does its best to fill the enormous backlog of orders as rapidly as the company's production capacity will permit. If managers and/or owners are able to show the bank that they are taking appropriate steps to regain control, the bank will probably go along with any realistic proposal. Even secured creditors need salable assets to realize some return on their investment.

The Foundation

The primary incentive for putting your credit department on a solid foundation is "dollars." When the credit department puts varying amounts of the company's assets at risk, the degree of risk depends largely on knowledge and experience, especially the professional knowledge and experience of the credit manager and his or her knowledge of the accounts and experience with conditions in the industry. When an account is new to your company, the degree of risk hinges not only on the customer's references, but also on the level of experience the manager and his or her associates bring to the evaluation process. The manager must be qualified to evaluate data received from supplier and bank references, and to weigh the quality and the importance of the financial statements, and must be competent in analyzing reports from reporting agencies such as Dun & Bradstreet, the National Association of Credit Management (NACM), etc. Accept the idea that there is never too much information available for any decision-making process. Realize that your most dangerous area for retroactive regret involves what should be rare areas or situations where information is scarce and reliability is questionable.

The less complex the system for dealing with credit and credit-related matters, the more efficient the department is destined to be. Unless a credit manager is uncommonly fortunate, the skill levels of the department's employees can vary from almost none (a trainee) to some knowledge of credit procedures (six or eight months in the department) to a level of experience that enables the employee to make the routine decisions (those within prescribed parameters) for the accounts assigned to him or her. A system (or procedures) that does not allow people to do their work in a timely and an efficient manner should not be used. If you inherit such a system, you must either make the necessary changes or gradually rework the system to the point where it is time-efficient and effective. Plan major changes carefully. Do not make hasty changes or move to throw out existing procedures until new ones are in place. Unless existing procedures generate a high level of chaos, eliminate them gradually and only after new procedures have become operational and need only some additional fine-tuning.

Your company deserves credit procedures that require a minimum of management time and produce quality results. When planning is inadequate or faulty, the unsatisfactory aging of accounts receivable balances speaks all too eloquently regarding the quality of credit decisions. Every company needs a strong credit policy, one that is supported by good credit procedures that are applied properly. No company should put sizeable amounts of its assets at risk in any area of the business spectrum unless every tool necessary for safeguarding that investment is in place. That philosophy should be at the core of any credit and receivables operation.

Overhauling the Department

How do you determine whether a credit function or department needs to be reorganized?

- When you process an account one way, then vary the procedure the next time.
- When too many loose ends exist before the reference data is in place and you are ready to evaluate it and make a decision.
- When there is no pattern and no consistency to the gathering, processing, and evaluating of the reference data.
- When you do not have the forms that make it easier and faster to gather data and put it in a useful form.

Take a hard look at the procedures you currently use to process new accounts, to assign credit limits, to monitor accounts receivable, to control credit limits, and to follow up on in-house and third-party collection efforts. If a review of your current procedures indicates that you need to reorganize them, now is the time to begin.

Begin with a simple physical layout which includes the amount of space that will be allotted to the credit department based upon the number of people who currently occupy or will occupy the space, and the size, type, and variety of the equipment. The next step should be an evaluation of the present system for processing data. If it isn't a computerized system, incorporate into the thinking and planning the question of how soon an appropriate system can and should be installed.

Credit Policy
(Three Basic Types)

The size of a company or a business is irrelevant to the indisputable fact that a written credit policy is a must for any business whose sales program includes selling on credit terms. No company can expect to collect for sales within a time frame appropriate for the specific company or business if the company's credit policy doesn't fit its requirements. The question of whether credit decisions will be made by an experienced professional, by a less experienced professional, or by an entrepreneur has obvious relevance as it relates to expectations for the quality of the results. What is not addressed in the above statement is how the absence of a company credit policy can lead to credit decisions that are inappropriate for a company whose standard for acceptable credit accounts should be based on a primary criterion of good liquidity.

Credit policy is a key financial management guideline that should be prepared under the guidance of the company's financial vice president, the treasurer, the director of finance, an experienced credit professional, a qualified firm of accountants, or an entrepreneur who has the necessary business and financial background. It should incorporate the company's goals, the criteria and timetable for achieving those goals (as they relate to the credit function), and the type of accounts that will be required to achieve the anticipated requirement for internally generated cash (but leave the implementation of that plan to a credit management professional).

Credit policy may be influenced by the amount of capital that a start-up or fledgling company receives from the venture capitalist. If it is the goal of management to minimize the number of dollars borrowed from venture capitalists, the credit department must build an accounts receivable base that has a high percentage of within- or near-terms liquidity. Including these two key requirements in the credit policy sends a clear message to the credit manager: the company's management expects accounts receivable to be the major source of cash flow; the quality of receivables must be high to ensure a rapid turnover; the procedures for evaluating and accepting credit accounts must be compatible with the company's reliance on a strong base of internally generated cash; and the credit department must function in a professional, knowledgeable, responsive, and diligent manner. The company's requirement for cash leaves no latitude for less than a maximum level of professionalism applied to a well-directed effort.

An effective credit policy combines current and projected financial requirements with the need to compete effectively in a particular industry or geographic area. A credit policy should be written in the most concise, all-inclusive format that good business sense indicates will help the company meet its objectives. Literary style? Forget it. Unless the words can be translated into guidelines for everyday credit decisions, it will be of little value.

Credit decisions must be consistent with guidelines incorporated into the company's credit policy. If changes in business or economic conditions make it obvious that your credit policy is too restrictive, the written credit policy should be changed to reflect the changes in the parameters for acceptable accounts. Some flexibility must be written into every credit policy or plan. No company should lock itself into policies and guidelines so rigid that there is no provision for servicing an account that is credit worthy, but doesn't fall totally within the guidelines. Too much rigidity and too little flexibility offer the probability that the effectiveness of the credit department will be constrained to a point where its effectiveness is impacted adversely. Plans and policies—for all departments and areas of a company or business—will help to focus people, time, talents, and energies into a work pattern calculated to offer the company its best chance for success.

The three basic credit policies are restrictive, moderate (middle-of-the-road), and liberal. Each type of policy involves a different mix of ingredients, a somewhat different business philosophy, different goals, and different financial needs, or a combination of the three policies (something from one, a few things from another, and one or two guidelines from the third). A credit policy tailored for a company from one or more of the basic categories of policies is acceptable. The test of a credit policy is not how many guidelines you use from how many separate and different sources; the test is whether it does a good job for a specific company. If it meets that criterion, then the policy is sound.

Restrictive Credit Policy

This is the credit policy of a company that has no plan to grow at a rate that is more than minimal. The company is unwilling to take risks that are more than minor, preferring instead to do business with customers whose paying habits almost never vary from discount and/or within terms.

Receivables of this type represent the thinking of a management that is ultraconservative toward business and business practices. The company or business is almost invariably on a solid financial footing; it intends to remain there, and it uses little or no bank support to augment the adequate supply of cash generated from fast-turning receivables. More aggressive companies do not understand this level of conservatism, but many very conservative businesses have survived long after more aggressive companies have failed.

Although an ultraconservative credit policy is intended to protect the business, it is not without its own elements of risk. A policy of restrictive growth can stifle all growth to the point where the momentum necessary to maintain the company's position is lost. When a business is not aggressive enough to replace lost accounts, the receivables base will erode to a dangerous level. A restrictive policy should never be allowed to stifle "normal growth," which varies with individual companies. (Example: a small manufacturer supports cash-flow needs from fast-turning receivables. A potential customer, who has been in business for several years, who is marginally profitable, and whose volume of business and slower-turning receivables require suppliers to wait 40 to 55 days for payment, asks the company to set up a credit line—a credit line that would make it one of the manufacturing company's largest accounts. The manufacturer's decision? After evaluating payment information received from the potential customer's supplier references, the manufacturer decides it cannot handle the potential customer's credit requirements. It is not an account that falls within the parameters of the company's credit policy. Payment of receivables would not be prompt enough to meet the credit policy and cash-flow requirements of the manufacturer. Under other financial circumstances, and with a credit policy that afforded latitude for some slower-turning receivables accounts, the manufacturer would probably have granted the credit line. But in this example, the request for a credit line did not fit the company's credit policy or the company's monthly financial requirement.)

Moderate Credit Policy
(Middle-of-the-Road)

The moderate credit policy mixes good accounts with average accounts, and accepts some accounts that are always up to 30 days slow. It is a more conventional mix of credit risks than the conservative or the liberal approaches to credit. There is a somewhat greater risk with this policy than there is in a policy that sells only to accounts that are well-established and pay within terms; it is, however, a much safer policy than that of the credit grantor whose liberal policy could easily become reckless. Some bank support is usually combined with monthly receivables collections to provide an adequate flow of cash.

The financial strength of these companies may be more shallow than companies whose policy is restrictive, a fact that can translate into a pattern of payables payments that rarely includes the discounting of invoices. Many customers take advantage of the higher percentage discounts and let the accounts of other suppliers drift from a few days past due to 20 or 30 days. Suppliers who have this experience with an otherwise strong account might equate the payment policy to that of their own company. This experience with an otherwise strong customer is an inconvenience rather than a concern; the concern only become major when the monthly payment response becomes less and less prompt. (Example: a potential customer has asked a small manufacturer for a credit line. The applicant has been in business for several years, has established a good reputation in the trade, has been growth oriented, and has paid trade accounts consistently between "prompt" and 30 days past due. Profit and loss statements and the applicant's bank indicate that the business is well-managed; there is no unusual risk involved. Suppliers are not always paid within terms, but that is because profits are being put back into the business. This small manufacturer has adequate cash flow and financing to support the company's credit policy, and the prospective customer meets the criteria for the requested credit line. The manufacturer goes into the relationship knowing that payments will not always be within terms, and that is acceptable.)

Liberal Credit Policy

This is the most dangerous of the three credit policies because it forces the credit manager to walk a decision-making tightrope over a pit filled with the bones of companies that failed. These bones represent companies so eager to go forward that they propelled themselves well beyond the point of sound business judgment before they stopped, realized where they were, then went straight into the pit with other Chapter 11 victims. A liberal credit policy is a high-risk policy; risks are high, the loss of receivables dollars can be heavy, and the danger to company survival can be real. When any creditor company loses a major customer to a business failure, it can be a serious problem; when a company that has a liberal credit policy loses a major customer to business failure, it can be a catastrophe. Unlike the preceding two credit policies, many companies who have a liberal credit policy are big risk takers in every area of their operation. They expand much too rapidly for the size and worth of the company, and this often dictates accepting accounts that are not strong enough for the credit line they receive. Liberal credit grantors are frequently incapable of handling any combination of major losses and established, slow-turning receivables.

In addition to the above problems, two other negatives often plague companies that promote a liberal credit policy: undercapitalization and sporadic cash flow. When the delicate balance is working, these companies can project an exciting image of success. When the apparent success begins to unravel, major crisis can build upon major crisis until the company or business collapses under the weight of its own uncontrolled drive for success. There is always the rare company that can walk multiple tightropes and succeed—a liberal credit policy, a high-profit product line that finds instant marketplace acceptance, and bank balances strong enough to support runaway growth. It is, however, an extremely rare company that can overcome the multiple problems of uncontrolled growth, just as it is a rare credit manager (or a credit manager/owner) who can handle the pressures of constantly performing on a tightrope. (Example: the small company is committed to rapid growth. Whether the company can afford the awesome risks inherent in receivables that range from current thru slow [60/75 days] is apparently of little concern to management. The aggressive, chance-taking manufacturer is focusing first on growth in sales and second on quality of accounts. The manufacturer is accepting accounts that other suppliers report experiencing slow pay of 40 to 60 days past due—and then only after a number of calls. What we have here is a liberal credit policy extended to the point where it has become "liberal-foolish.")

Figure 1-1 shows a sample company credit policy. It is concise, covers all areas, and should be helpful when you tailor one to your own company. Remember, however, to shape the credit policy to conform to the require-

pays when there are no step-by-step procedures to build a case for or against the granting of an applicant's request for a credit line. Good credit procedures involve a conscious effort to repeat successful and sequential procedures until the person who makes credit decisions is aware immediately when any step in the process is missing or incomplete. Procedures should interface comfortably with your company's credit policy and should result in a contribution to the company's goals as stated in the credit policy.

Can a credit department be effective with a policy and no procedures— or procedures and no policy? Your credit department needs the disciplined approach to credit management that a good sequential approach will give you. Safe shortcuts are not available. You cannot eliminate one or two of the fact-gathering or fact-evaluation steps and still expect to arrive at a sound decision. Do it the sensible way; administer your credit accounts by plan, not by chance.

The following are two planned, sequential procedures. The first gives you the step-by-step method for how to obtain credit information from an applicant, how to evaluate the information, and when to assign the credit line or approve a first order:

- Send the credit applicant a New Account Information Form and include a self-addressed, stamped return envelope.

- Attach the New Account Information Form to a cover letter and ask for a current financial statement.

- Contact credit references (from data on the New Account Information Form) by telephone or letter.

- Enter information gathered from the applicant's references (suppliers and banker) on the Credit Investigation Form.

- Consolidate and refine the information on the Account Information Sheet.

- Compare the dollar total of the applicant's pending first order or requested credit line with the experience of the suppliers, banker, and financial statement information. If the supplier and banker experience continues to be good and is at or above the high credit amount you are being asked to carry, then the account should qualify for the requested credit line. If the accumulated data indicates a slow-pay account with trade payments becoming increasingly slower, the account could be sliding into serious trouble. This account should not be sold on credit terms.

- Send the customer a letter stating that you have approved a credit line for the requested amount or a lower amount. If the amount is lower than the amount that was requested, your explanation should not reflect unfavorably on the new customer. Cite the fact that your company is a grantor of minimum credit amounts until you have accumulated more experience with the company. Mention that you feel sure the customer company is equally prudent in its approach to credit matters; express your appreciation for the opportunity to be of service, and close with the statement that you are available to help if there is ever a problem—in your area or another area.

The second example moves forward to the point when account balances have been appearing on the Accounts Receivable Aged Trial Balance Report for several weeks. The oldest open balance has now moved into the past-due column (1 to 30 days), and at 10 days past due, you begin the following collection sequence:

- Make the first reminder telephone call to the payables person who handles your account.

- If there is no payment response, make a second call to the same person seven to ten days after the first call. Get a firm payment commitment (check to be released the day you call, the day after you call, Friday of that week, or some specific near-term date).

- When the account is 20 to 30 days past due, confirm that the person who processes your company's invoices has written the check or has forwarded payment data to the data processing department for the weekly or twice-monthly writing of checks. If he or she has done that, or has taken the next step of contacting the controller and has been told that the check is being held for a few days, ask to talk with the controller. Make your case for the prompt release of the check; nail it down to a specific release date (within seven days of your call). You also might tell the controller that you will be unable to ship his or her company any products until they have paid the past-due balance (state the amount).

- If the check does not arrive within two or three days after the promised date, notify the company by letter (attention of the controller with a copy to the purchasing manager) that you will be unable to favorably consider offering credit terms on future orders if the past-due balance is not paid within 10 days of the date of your letter.

- If there is no response and no satisfactory explanation, decide what final action you must take. You can assign the account for third-party collection (to a collection agency or to an attorney who specializes in collection matters), or if the balance is less than $1500 you can sue for a judgment in a Small Claims Court. At this point, there is no interest in again selling the account on credit terms. Your only concern is to collect your company's money and move on to other customer relationships of a better quality.

Credit policy and credit procedures are blood relatives in the context of interlocking guideline material for every company, every management executive, every credit manager, and every entrepreneur-manager who wants the best and the most effective credit function for his or her company. It is a very attainable goal, a goal that will keep accounts receivable dollars out of the bad-debt account and put them where they belong—in the profit figure on your financial statement.

The Department Budget

To prepare a budget for the credit department involves a combination of internally generated cost figures (both estimated and real) plus certain other costs (assigned costs and indirect labor) that come from the office of the controller, the finance director, or, if the company is large enough, the budget director.

A department budget is prepared by the department manager and reviewed by higher management. A budget should be realistic, should be completed within the time frame allotted, and will be the yardstick against which the financial operation of the department is measured. Get it right before budget figures have been approved because future adjustments must be approved by the next higher echelon of authority—and an increase in funding will not be easy to sell.

The following instructions should enable a credit manager who is unfamiliar with the process to complete an acceptable budget. The three major parts are:

Part 1—Assumptions

Part 2—Preparation of Departmental Labor and Expense Budget

Part 3—Fixed Asset Budget

The preliminary phase of budget preparation is planning. This involves an objective evaluation of your department to determine the priority of the various needs that must be funded within the number of available dollars. The key questions are: What is needed to continue to handle the present function plus fund the department's objectives for the coming year? Does the department have what it needs (without frills) to do the essential things effectively and efficiently? Are the highest priority items or requirements budgeted accurately?

(The following *Instructions for Budget Preparation* [Figure 1-2] were put out to the various departments in the company by the office of the controller for a major electronics equipment manufacturing company. They are quite comprehensive and when combined with the *Assumptions— Annual Budget* form, and a preapproval copy of the annual *Departmental Expense Budget* with supporting data for each account number, they should enable credit managers with limited experience to budget accurately.)

Figure 1-2. Instructions for budget preparation.

Instructions for Budget Preparation

These instructions are intended to provide a uniform basis and format for preparation of the annual departmental budgets (see Figure 1-3).

You are being requested to prepare your departmental budget, for you are the one most able to evaluate your requirements. Should business conditions or management desires necessitate a revision, you will be consulted regarding any and all changes.

All budgets will be reviewed by management. You can save everyone concerned a great deal of time by preparing realistic, complete budgets the first time.

This budget will become the basis for evaluating the financial operation of your department. Adjustments to the budget for changing conditions, etc., will only be possible with management approval.

General

1. The Annual Departmental Budget is composed of two major parts:
   Part I—Assumptions
   Part II—Departmental Labor and Expense Budget (see Figure 1-4)
      Specific instructions for preparation of each of these parts are contained in this procedure as follows:
      a. Assumptions—See below.
      b. Departmental Labor, Expense, and Capital Budget. See next page.
2. Completed budgets are due to Cost Accounting no later than _____(date)_____.
3. Budgets not properly completed per this instruction will be returned for correction. A budget will not be considered complete until the assumptions and the departmental labor, expense, and fixed assets are properly prepared per this procedure.
4. Budgets need not be typed, but must be neat and legible. Use dollars only; do not show cents. Handwritten budgets should be completed in pencil rather than pen. Care should be taken to total the budgets correctly both horizontally and vertically.

Part I—Assumptions

The preliminary phase in the preparation of any budget is planning. This involves the objective evaluation of your operations to determine the priorities of requirements which must be funded within the affordable dollars. The key questions to assist in establishing the priorities in your department are:

Figure 1-2. (*Continued*) Instructions for budget preparation.

1. What is essential to accomplish our present function as well as our objectives for the coming year?

2. Are the essential things being done effectively and efficiently?

3. Are the highest priority requirements budgeted to indicate that priority?

Your assumptions should cover but not be limited to the following major items:

1. Major cost reductions.

2. A brief outline of the requirements which are not included in your budget due to the lack of dollars.

This summary must indicate all assumed conditions having a significant effect upon your proposed budget and will become the basis for management evaluation of your budget request (see Figure 1-5).

Examples of the type of information required are as follows:

Administration and International

1. New programs or functions requiring additional equipment or personnel?

2. Availability and extent of automated data processing for relief of clerical effort?

3. Relocation or expansion of facilities contemplated? When?

All Departments

You are encouraged to coordinate with other departments who utilize your services to determine their estimated requirements for __(year)__.

Your assumptions become the basis for evaluation of your requested Departmental Expense Budget. Incomplete or inadequate Assumption Sheets will result in the budget being rejected.

You should therefore ensure that your assumptions are complete and that requested budgets are compatible.

Part II—Preparation of Departmental Labor and Expense Budget

To assist you in the preparation of the Labor and Expense Budget, the following data is available for your department:

1. A current report indicating:
   a. Personnel presently on census.
   b. Dollar amount of current payroll.

(*Continued*)

Figure 1-2. (*Continued*) Instructions for budget preparation.

2. A budget report indicating actual labor and expense for this past year reflecting current accounting procedures.
3. A sample budget.
4. The budgeted occupancy cost for your department.

To Budget Labor Requirements

1. Review the Payroll Report which you have been furnished, making any adjustments necessary for terminations, raises, new hires, etc.
2. Detail additional labor requirements for the budget year. Indicate month required.
3. Determine your overtime requirements as a monthly dollar amount. The straight time is treated as regular labor. Direct labor is the time charged to jobs, work orders, and projects only.
4. Outside contract labor is not treated as payroll labor. This should be budgeted under subaccount _____ .
5. Compute all labor transfers into and out of your department from other departments.

Summary

Upon completion of budgeting labor you will have the following information for submission:

1. Your current census updated for changes and pay increases by month.
2. Labor allocated to the proper subaccounts (Direct Labor—012, Indirect Labor—103, Payroll Burden—243, Vacation, Holiday, and Sick Pay—255).

To Budget Direct Expenses

1. Determine what subaccounts will be utilized by your department in __(year)__ and enter the account title and account number, if it does not appear, on the Departmental Expense Budget.
   a. You must budget any allocation or cost transfer accounts. Departmental allocation and transfer accounts such as occupancy, depreciation, etc., will be budgeted by Accounting.
   b. Do not budget items amounting to less than $100 per year. A provision may be made in a subaccount (Miscellaneous—Other Expenses) for the sum total of these items.
   c. Round to the nearest five dollars.

Figure 1-2. (*Continued*) Instructions for budget preparation.

d. Expenses which will occur at a rather constant rate throughout the year may be entered only in the total column. Accounting will then allocate the charges to each month at a constant rate of expenditure based on the number of weeks in the month.

e. Expenses which will occur in specific months must be budgeted in those months with the total cost indicated in the total column.

f. Compute labor transfers into and out of your department. Be sure and coordinate all transfers with the Receiving Department. All labor transfers not approved by the Receiving and Transferring department managers will not be allowed.

Summary

Upon completion of budgeting direct expenses and a fixed asset budget, you will have the following information for submission to Financial Planning:

1. Expenses indicated by subaccount.

2. Breakdown of labor and overhead transfers.

Approvals Required for _____ Budget

All proposed budgets are to be reviewed by the Area Directors prior to submission of the budgets. The approving individual must indicate his or her approval by initialing each departmental submission.

Components to be submitted:

1. Payroll Budget

2. Labor and Expense Budget

3. Labor and Overhead Transfers

4. Assumptions

The foregoing instructions for preparing a credit department budget—and the examples that accompany them—is a guideline package that should not be difficult to follow. If your company is quite small and the credit function is just one of several duties of the entrepreneur, the company's manager, or a designated employee, the foregoing material can be scaled down to accommodate a smaller operation. It may also be put on hold until the company's growth reaches the point where it is ready for a credit manager, a separate credit function, and a separate budget.

(*Continued*)

Figure 1-2. (*Continued*) Instructions for budget preparation.

Items on the Departmental Budget are detailed on work sheets. Travel and Entertainment (listed as Acct. 206 on the budget recap for the 12-month period) is budgeted at an annual figure of $885; the breakdown sheet lists the various items that total the $885. Collection Expense (Acct. 716 on the budget recap) is budgeted for $4135; the breakdown sheet for these services (D&B, NACM, UCC Filing Fees, and Third-Party Collection Fees) totals $4135. Other items on the budget recap are similarly supported with worksheets.

It is a rare company that differentiates between the budgeting process and the forecasting of cash from receivables. Both are perceived to be a part of the credit manager's job, and it is expected that both will be done well.

This summary must indicate all assumed conditions having a significant effect upon your proposed budget and will become the basis for management evaluation of your budget request.

Examples of the type of information required are as follows:

Manufacturing (4XX numbered departments)

1. What effect from:
   a. New Products
   b. New Processes
   c. Automation
2. Is any major relocation or expansion of facilities contemplated? When?
3. Any major transfer of activity to an international operation? When?
4. Any interaction with other divisions that will effect your department?
5. What will be the impact on your budget throughout the year?

Engineering, R & D, and Equipment Laboratory (5XX and 7XX numbered departments)

1. What major programs are contemplated which will require additional equipment and/or personnel?

2. What will be the level of Research and Development effort? Increase or decrease?

3. Will manufacturing require more or less production engineering?

4. Relocation or expansion of facilities or addition of equipment contemplated? When?

5. Processing and customer demo requirements in the lab?

Figure 1-2. *(Continued)* Instructions for budget preparation.

Marketing & Customer Service (6XX numbered departments)

1. Will increased efforts be required to maintain or increase percentage of market? What area?
2. Policy on commissions, sales meetings, etc., to be changed?
3. What level of advertising? What products?
4. Relocation or expansion contemplated? When?
5. What shows will we attend and what equipment will we show?
6. What support will we need from the demo lab?

Administration and International (8XX and 9XX numbered departments)

1. New programs or functions requiring additional equipment or personnel?
2. Availability and extent of automated data processing for relief of clerical effort?
3. Relocation or expansion of facilities contemplated? When?

All Departments

You are encouraged to coordinate with other departments who utilize your services to determine their estimated requirements for the budget year.

Your assumptions become the basis for evaluation of your requested Departmental Expense Budgets. Incomplete or inadequate Assumption Sheets will result in the budget being rejected.

You should therefore insure that your assumptions are complete and that requested budgets are compatible.

Parts II and III—Preparation of Departmental Labor and Expense Budgets and Fixed Assets Budgets

To assist you in the preparation of the Labor and Expense Budget, the following data is available for your department:

1. A current report indicating:
   a. Personnel presently on census.
   b. Dollar amount of current payroll.
2. A budget report indicating actual labor and expense for this past year reflecting current accounting procedures.
3. A sample budget.
4. The budgeted occupancy cost for your department.

(Continued)

Figure 1-2. (*Continued*) Instructions for budget preparation.

To Budget Labor Requirements

1. Review the Payroll Report (Schedule A) which you have been furnished, making any adjustments necessary for terminations, raises, new hires, etc.

2. Complete Form A detailing additional labor requirements for the budget/fiscal year. Indicate month required.

3. Determine your overtime requirements as a monthly dollar amount. Only the premium time is entered under subaccount 113. The straight time is treated as regular labor. Direct labor is the time charged to jobs, work orders, and projects only.

4. Outside contract labor is not treated as payroll labor. This should be budgeted under subaccount 165.

5. Compute all labor transfers into and out of your department from other department. Use Form B-1 for this.

Summary

Upon completion of budgeting labor you will have the following information for submission:

1. Your current census updated for changes and pay increases by month, Form A—Payroll.

2. Labor allocated to the proper subaccounts also, such Direct Labor— 012, Direct Labor, Parts—022, Indirect Labor—103, Premium Time—113, Payroll Burden—243, Vacation, Holiday, and Sick Pay— 255.

To Budget Direct Expenses and Fixed Assets

1. Determine what subaccounts will be utilized by your department in (budget year) and enter the account title and account number, if it does not appear, on your furnished Schedule B. The budget report of (year) actual charges, which is furnished, can guide you in this. Additional accounts and information on the purpose of each account is available through the Cost Accounting Department.

   a. You must budget any allocation or cost transfer accounts. Departmental allocation and transfer accounts will be budgeted by Accounting such as occupancy, depreciation, etc.

   b. Do not budget items amounting to less than $100 per year. A provision may be made in subaccount 526 (Miscellaneous—Other Expenses) for the sum total of these items.

   c. Round to the nearest five dollars.

Figure 1-2. (*Continued*) Instructions for budget preparation.

    d. Expenses which will occur at a rather constant rate throughout the year may be entered only in the total column. Accounting will then allocate the charges to each month at a constant rate of expenditure based on the number of weeks in the month.

    e. Expense which will occur in specific months must be budgeted in those months with the total cost indicated in the total column.

    f. Compute labor transfers in and out of your department. Be sure and coordinate all transfers with the Receiving Department. All labor transfers not approved by the Receiving and Transferring department managers will not be allowed. Overhead follows labor with 325 percent for assembly and shop labor, 100 percent for Engineering labor, and 150 percent for R & D labor.

2. Fixed Asset—Expenditures

    a. Purchased Assets—purchase amount and any costs of installation.

    b. Built asset—total material, labor, and proper overhead costs. Remember assembly and shop overhead is 325 percent, engineering is 100 percent, and R & D is 150 percent of respective labor.

Remember to coordinate the facilities requirements for a new asset with the facilities manager early in your planning.

Summary

Upon completion of budgeting direct expenses and a fixed asset budget, you will have the following information for submission to Financial Planning:

1. Form B—indicating expenses by subaccount.

2. Form B-1—indicating labor and overhead transfers.

3. Form C—indicating a fixed asset budget.

Approvals Required for (Year) Budgets

All proposed budgets are to be reviewed by the Area Directors prior to submission of the budgets. The approving individual must indicate his or her approval by initialing each departmental submission. Forms to be submitted:

1. Form A—Payroll Budget

2. Form B—Labor and Expense Budget

3. Form B-1—Labor and Overhead Transfers

4. Form C—Fixed Asset Budget

5. Form D—Assumptions

Figure 1-3. Credit department budget.

	19__ Departmental Budget _____
Department Title ___Credit___	Department Number _811_
	Revision Number _____ Dated _____
Department Manager ___L. Garvin___	Schedule Number _____

Account Title	Account Number	Total	4 Weeks November	5 Weeks December	4 Weeks January	4 Weeks February
Indirect Labor						
Indirect Payroll—Labor	103	28,806	2,051	2,729	2,219	2,219
Vacation, Holiday, Sick Pay Expenses	243	2,849	203	270	220	220
Expenses						
Payroll Burden Expense	255	3,482	248	330	268	268
Travel/ Entertainment	206	885	30	30	30	155
Dues/ Subscriptions	316	110	10	10	9	9
Collection Expense	716	4,135	165	165	164	2,329
Publications/ Related Expenses	357	54	4	5	4	5
FICA (Annual Premium) (Pay Quarterly)	756	6,800	1,700	—	—	1,700
Dun & Bradstreet (Pay Quarterly)	756	1,400	—	450	—	—
NACM (Pay Quarterly)	756	800	200	—	—	200
Assigned Costs						
Occupancy	398	2,240	186	186	186	186
Telephone/ Utilities	558	2,100	175	175	175	175
	Total	53,661	4,972	4,250	3,275	7,466

Figure 1-3. (*Continued*) Credit department budget.

19___ Departmental Budget _____

Department Title ___Credit___   Department Number _811_

                                       Revision Number _____ Dated _____

Department Manager ___L. Garvin___   Schedule Number _____

5 Weeks March	4 Weeks April	4 Weeks May	5 Weeks June	4 Weeks July	4 Weeks August	4 Weeks September	4 Weeks October
Indirect Labor							
2,775	2,219	2,219	2,275	2,260	2,258	2,824	2,258
274	220	220	274	223	223	279	223
Expenses							
335	268	268	335	274	273	342	273
30	180	30	30	30	30	180	130
9	9	9	9	9	9	9	9
164	164	164	164	164	164	164	164
4	5	4	5	4	5	4	5
		1,700			1,700		
350			350			350	
		200			200		
Assigned Costs							
187	187	187	187	187	187	187	187
175	175	175	175	175	175	175	175
4,303	3,427	5,176	4,304	3,326	5,224	4,514	3,424

Travel and Entertainment Account <u>206</u>	**Amount** <u>$850</u>
Four One-Day Trips to Los Angeles Basin Area	
(Customer calls and Credit Management Association	
of Southern California business/lunch meetings.	
Round trip via air and compact car rental at airport.	
Possibly necessary to stay over one or two nights.)	$600
Fall Credit Conference (San Francisco—one day and	
one night)	$150
Foreign Trade Club Meetings (San Francisco—nine a	
year—travel by company car)	<u>$135</u>
Total (Account 206)	$850
Collection Expense Account <u>716</u>	**Amount** <u>$4,135</u>
Dun & Bradstreet Service (Subscription)	$1,610
Dun & Bradstreet Service (International)	$ 620
Collection Expense ($150.00 a month)	
(Covers costs of commercial collection agency	
assignments, attorneys fees, etc.)	$1,800
Filing Fees (Uniform Commercial Code, etc.)	<u>$ 105</u>
Total (Account 716)	$4,135

Figure 1-4. Travel and entertainment (budget).

Hiring a Credit Manager

It is not possible to offer one set of guidelines and expect that set to be broad enough to become the criteria for the requirements of credit grantors both large and small. There are too many factors that have relevance—or do not have relevance—in the screening of candidates for a specific job. Before the qualifications of individual candidates can be considered, questions must be asked regarding the company or business. What is the current size of the company, including the figure for annual sales? What is the total number of the company's active accounts? What is the average monthly total of receivables balances? Of the average aging (days of sales) of receivables accounts? What is the company's plan for growth? Is growth projected as something that will be accomplished slowly, at a moderate rate of speed, or rapidly? What is the anticipated rate of annual growth?

Perhaps the most important consideration relevant to the requirements of the company and the qualifications of the respective candidates is the

Figure 1-5. Assumptions (budget preparation).

Assumptions—19__ Budget
Department ____

Instructions: Complete each of the questions below. If the space provided is not adequate, additional sheets referenced to the applicable item should be attached.

A. The major or primary function for the existence of this department is:

_____

_____

_____

_____

B. The ____ budget for the above department is based on the following assumptions:

　1. Changes in responsibilities, organization, volume, and/or operating conditions for this department are as follows:

_____

_____

_____

_____

　2. Major costs reductions, effect of automation, new products, processes, and other data which will assist in substantiation of requested budgets are:

_____

_____

_____

_____

　3. Relocation (internal or external) or expansion of facilities as follows are contemplated:

_____

_____

(Continued)

Figure 1-5. (*Continued*) Assumptions (budget preparation).

4. Number of shifts being operated and any changes being planned:

_____

_____

_____

5. If your department is primarily responsible for providing a service, please indicate those areas or departments who are recipients of your services and the percent that they should incur:

_____

_____

_____

_____

_____

6. Indicate any conditions which may affect your ability to meet the 19__ Sales Forecast or the performance of the goals in your area of responsibility:

_____

_____

_____

_____

7. Indicate those requirements which are not included in the requested budget due to the lack of dollars:

_____

_____

_____

_____

8. List of major projects in which your department has major responsibility:

_____

_____

_____

current size of the company and the projected rate of annual growth. A company that is already doing annual credit sales in the millions of dollars cannot afford to hire a person who is not an experienced, capable professional. If that same company is on a fast track—one calculated to show growth of at least 20 or 25 percent per year—add "aggressive, innovative, and a strong capacity for work and personal growth" to the basic requisite of "an experienced, capable professional."

The qualifications and the levels of experience that qualify a credit manager for one job might not qualify that person for the top credit job at a bigger company. Many credit managers come to small growth companies from the credit departments of major area or industry players. This is good for the individual and good for his or her new employer. Given the benefit of several years in an environment of company growth, this credit manager will increase his or her experience, knowledge, and capabilities to the point where no job challenge will be too complex or too intimidating.

In a company that has sales of 50 to 100 million dollars a year, an accounts receivable base of 2000 to 3500 active accounts, and an average receivables dollars base of 10 to 20 million dollars, the credit manager must be a trained professional. The company's current and future success is tied directly to the capable management of the credit and receivables function, so this is not an environment in which the credit manager should be doing on-the-job training.

The credit manager of this company (several credit department employees, data processed reports, etc.) should have an accounting or a financial background, good knowledge and experience with data-processed reports (and what it takes to produce them), and a personality that allows him or her to interface effectively with all levels of company personnel and with customers at all levels of dollar exposure. This credit manager must have the experience, knowledge, and ability to make good, timely credit decisions, to know when (and how firmly) to press a delinquent account for payment, to recognize and implement within-department changes before the need impacts the department's performance, to use experience as the base to make perceptive credit decisions that will allow the company to avoid the vast majority of potential Chapter 11 accounts, and to be active in promoting credit groups and the exchange of credit experience information at monthly or quarterly meetings. The benefits, short- and long-term, will be enormous.

A fair generalization is the statement that smaller companies do not need a manager who has the same level of heavy credit management experience and expertise that is required of managers at larger companies. Most smaller- to medium-size companies concentrate their sales efforts in local or a regional areas. A customer base might be located within a radius of 100 or 200 miles of the firm's plant and headquarters, and because the company's efforts are directed toward in-state customers, there is limited necessity for filings under the Uniform Commercial Code or for concern with the complexities of sales to customers in foreign countries. The credit manager at a company with annual sales of 10 to 50 million dollars can be younger and less experienced than a peer at a larger company, but the manager at the smaller company should have the same potential (and capacity) for growth that the manager at the larger company had at a similar point in his or her career. What about the capacity and the capability for growth? They're essential. Each is a "must have."

An entrepreneur or a partner in a start-up business or small company often doubles as the credit manager. It's a matter of necessity, and qualifications may have very little to do with the choice. The start-up or small business isn't doing enough business to be able to afford an experienced credit manager, so the owner/manager or a designated employee becomes the decision maker. If the designated person realizes from the start the importance of a strong receivables base, the arrangement can be successful. It will, however, not be a success if there is too strong an emphasis on sales to the detriment of the quality of the receivables.

The person who assumes the responsibility for credit and receivables decisions must do a certain amount of on-the-job learning, and unless it is handled cautiously, it can be costly. The owner/manager or designated employee should adopt the procedure of sequential information-and-data gathering that is detailed in Chapter 3, then proceed to evaluate the data as detailed in Chapter 4, and finally cautiously assign credit lines to credit-worthy accounts as detailed in Chapter 5. It is imperative that the neophyte credit and receivables administrator should proceed cautiously along lines that are spelled out in minute detail. You will find that level of help in Chapters 3, 4, and 5. Other relevant help (such as receivables management, etc.) can be readily found in the text of Part 2, "Accounts Receivable." The guidelines you need in order to get a handle on your credit and receivables responsibility are clearly indexed in these pages.

Support Personnel

If your business or company is small, the term "support personnel" may refer to the assignment on a part-time basis of an office clerk to a specific number of "support" hours each week (typing collection letters, sending out requests for supplier information, filing report data, filing copies of outgoing correspondence, telephoning suppliers for their experience with a prospective customer, etc.).

The "support personnel" in your small company or business could be a few hours each week of one person's time—a person who may wear several hats in support of many of the company's activities—or, perhaps, the full time of one person. Unless growth is quite rapid, the business will probably not be in the market for a full-time credit manager for at least one year or possibly two. But whatever the time frame, use the help of a support person when, and as, needed to ensure that account records and the credit file data you use to monitor the company's credit accounts is providing a reference source that is as good as good credit procedures can make it.

When your company is an "in between" (not small but not large), the reasonable assumption is that a professional credit manager is heading the company's credit and receivables department. The dollar levels of individual accounts and the cumulative total of receivables balances involve a higher percentage of the company's assets than of a small company. The possibilities of a costly mistake are more numerous when individual risks average a higher per-order dollar total. Because risk factors are higher and more constant, there is an increased level of danger to the company's receivables asset as the "in between" company begins to move itself forward. The credit manager's professional growth is tied directly to companies in this category because so many of them are on the move. So many are on a transitional road from small to big, with all of the pitfalls, chances, and dangers that lurk between those two points. Unless it is a semistatic, slow-growth company—one that does not respond well to opportunities and challenges—the credit manager must be committed to a program of professional and personal growth. He or she must be ready to exploit opportunities for growth as they present themselves in the current company, or move forward in response to a new and more challenging offer from another company. Growth is essential, and it comes first; opportunities will come when essential growth is in place.

Bigger companies are not exempt from the need to live with department budgets, but justifying a growth-induced need for additional help to expedite the processing of new accounts, to clear pending orders, and to accelerate the collecting of receivables dollars is strong motivation for approval of the request. Applicants for clerical support positions should be screened with the goal of working them into the full range of credit and receivables duties. It is as easy, more cost-effective, and much more satisfying to hire a person who has the intelligence and the capacity for growth.

Data Processing Systems

The basic question for most companies or businesses is not whether the firm owns and uses computer equipment to process data, but which of the many types of hardware and software does it use? Or perhaps your computer-processed data is done on in-house equipment that is leased, is on a lease-purchase agreement, or is on a time-share basis (an in-house key-punch operator inputs data but the data processing equipment is located elsewhere). Or does your company have a contract with a data processing service?

Companies or businesses ranging in size from moderate to quite large have available a broad selection of electronic hardware and software to meet their various requirements. The needs, requirements, and preferences of one company may not be comparable or compatible with those of another, but the marketplace can accommodate the needs of any member of any industry. If the company is large, it may be looking at one or more of the high-speed, enormous capability and capacity mainframes. A smaller company has its own broad variety of options from among the products of manufacturers whose targeted customer base includes companies that are one, two, and three steps below the majors in business and industry.

Is your business or company small, perhaps quite small? Size is no excuse for not giving your small enterprise the benefit of advanced technology. The availability of good, inexpensive electronic technology makes it possible for even the smallest business to access some form of data processing equipment. There are inexpensive word processors that produce excellent spreadsheets and reports; there are laptop, semiportable and desktop computers that are capable of storing and processing surprisingly large quantities of data of various types. These units deliver requested report data on small, fold-up screens, on separate desktop monitors, or as printouts when coupled with a printer that is compatible with the data processing unit. Data processed in this manner can save a company an enormous amount of time while producing reports that are more attractive, more comprehensive, and more meaningful.

The small size of your company does not validate the idea that modern equipment (data processors, copiers, conventional and laser printers, etc.) is not affordable. Price alone is never a valid answer. How many hours and dollars of management and clerical time will your company save if it uses computerized data? Not data prepared on a piece of high-tech equipment for which your company may be ready in five or six years, but affordable equipment that is right for the present size of your company, and will be right for the next two, three, or five years. Consider also the intangible benefits to your small company of reports, letters, and reproductions that reflect the type of image your company should project in this era of highly competitive marketplace situations. Furthermore, bear in mind the need for modern equipment that is compatible in size and cost with the needs and the budget constraints of a growing firm. When chosen wisely, it is an investment in growth, not just cosmetics.

Example: the Accounts Receivable Aged Trial Balance Report, referred to in these pages as an "aging report," is an ongoing list of all accounts that have open balances. It reflects the aging of those balances as it relates to the terms of sale (balances that are current, 1 to 30 days past due, 31 to 60 days past due, 61 to 90 days past due, and 91 days and over past due). Appropriate dollar amounts are listed by invoice date, number, and amount under the appropriate category of aging.

The status of the various accounts (amount owing, aging, etc.) changes daily or periodically with the payment of a portion or all of the account balance or the purchase of more product(s) or services. But how rapidly does the person charged with responsibility for the credit accounts see those changes? What is the time lag between a credit sale or a payment on account and the date the credit manager receives an aging report that reflects such a change? It is obvious that the shorter the time frame between account activity and a report reflecting that activity, the more informed the credit manager is going to be regarding the status of the company's credit accounts.

When aging reports are prepared manually, the time lag between reports is usually longer than when report data is prepared electronically. The credit manager can be more effective when report data reflects account activity that is quite current. Between the saving in clerical hours and the potential for a reduction in bad-debt losses, the low cost of relatively unsophisticated electronic equipment (a word processor with spreadsheet and other capabilities) is an expenditure that cannot be faulted.

Support Services

When a company has hundreds or thousands of active accounts in one or more geographic areas of the country, it may be wise to consider subscribing to a credit rating and report service such as Dun & Bradstreet or The National Association of Credit Management (NACM). A brief description of the two services follows:

Dun & Bradstreet (D & B)

This company provides a service of variable scope that is tied to an annual contract with a minimum base of reports (100) per year to an unlimited number on the high end. The subscriber has a choice of many services, but the "Reference Guides" for regions of interest (Pacific Coast, Rocky Mountain States, East Coast, etc.), for a combination of regions, or for the entire United States and Canada have long been the most practical products for most credit managers.

Reference Guides (available on a bimonthly, quarterly, or semiannual basis) list nonretail businesses and companies by their state, county, and nearest town headquarters. An Industrial Classification Code Number identifies the year in which the business was established or incorporated (if less than 10 years), and D & B includes a rating of the account. The Reference Guide will show no rating (a "blank rating") if appropriate, currently applicable data to rate the account is not available.

A report states whether the company is a sole proprietorship, a partnership, a company or corporation, a division, or a subsidiary, and the name of the parent company. Reports also include the date of the report, the number of employees on that date, supplier payments experience data, and the bank's comments regarding the firm. Data regarding the founders of the company, their successors, the current active founders, and the backgrounds of the founder's successors—purchasers of the company and key management people—is also included. Such a broad variety of antecedent data is not readily available from other sources.

An annual contract for Dun & Bradstreet's Basic Service will involve a memorable number of dollars, and the more you build into the contract the more indelible the imprint on your memory and on the company's checkbook. Should your company subscribe to the service? If your business is growing at a steady rate (currently 200 or more active accounts whose levels of purchase range from "no impact if lost" thru "a big impact if lost") and has several accounts which are slow pay or increasingly slow pay, you are a candidate for the service. You should weigh carefully whether the annual cost is currently within your company's financial capability versus the benefits of the service. If you decide to try it, the basic service for your geographic area of business interest is usually enough. It is always possible to increase the number and types of services in your present contract or add them to the next contract.

National Association of Credit Management (NACM)

The Association offers a service similar to that provided by Dun & Bradstreet, but it offers a different format. The Association's National Business Credit Report does not attempt to assign credit ratings. The Payment History section of the report draws ledger experience from NACM's member companies on a regular basis and includes member numbers, business categories, years businesses were started, the months and years of the information in the reports, the last purchase activities with each respondent supplier, the high credit with each supplier, the amount owed to each supplier, the aging of accounts payable balances, payment terms, and any comments by suppliers or banks.

There are sections that summarize totals of reported trade experience in both dollars and percentages, a record of inquiries on the subject business during the preceding 90 days, and bank data pertaining to credit history and the average balances maintained in commercial accounts. Historical information is included on all aspects of the business, including principals, past and pending lawsuits, SBA loans, attachments, and bankruptcies. NACM's reports are available by telephone and mail and via a link between your computer and its National Automated Database Center in Houston. To be eligible for these services you must, of course, join the National Association of Credit Management.

One of the Association's major benefits is the number of industry credit groups. Most of these credit groups meet for lunch on a monthly, semi-monthly, or quarterly schedule. Members submit questions regarding certain customers; the Association compiles that information, distributes it at the start of the luncheon meeting, and it is then discussed under the watchful eye of an Association representative. The representative is present to ensure that the discussion does not get into the mine field of antitrust laws and regulations. Group members discuss old accounts, new accounts, recurring and new problem accounts, the bold or peripheral return of a notorious industry jackal, and sudden negative changes in the payment pattern of struggling or established accounts. The number of participating members is important to the volume and scope of the information they exchange, but it does not negate the possibility of an important exchange among as few as three or four members.

The worth of NACM and D & B reports hinges on the number of firms who furnish experience data on a regular and timely basis (for an effective update of reports), the skill levels of field and in-office reporters and analysts, and the depth and reliability of information received regarding suits, bulk transfers, attachments, tax liens, Small Business Administration (SBA) loans, bankruptcies, and other recorded data.

Do not back away from a reporting service because you have limited credit management experience and are uncertain whether the service is for you. It is for you if your company's level of activity is adding bigger balances and more accounts to the receivables aging report. Never let yourself slip into a "no professional growth" cop-out. Reports are easy to read and easy to interpret. Guideline instructions are a part of your subscriber kit and should help you phase quickly and effectively into the evaluation process.

Credit Groups (Regional and Area)

For the small business that is unable to stretch its limited budget to include the cost of membership in a national credit organization, there is the option of a local group. These meetings are often sponsored by the local chamber of commerce and although they are not directed exclusively toward credit management problems, they offer a helpful alternative to the industry meetings sponsored by national credit organizations.

Locally organized and locally directed meetings usually address the general business needs and problems of the community of small businesses, and that's fine. If you are a credit manager and your community is not large enough to have an industry credit group, the next best thing is a group that includes a mix of businesses and industries. Do you have a credit problem with some of your accounts? So do they. Do you solve your problems with one technique or another? So do they. Wouldn't it be interesting, and of mutual benefit, to find out how these other people—many of whom are not professional credit managers—handle some of their credit problems? You may be a pro with years of experience or a neophyte who still faces a career-load of decisions, but you can always learn something from the way others handle their problem accounts.

Sample Credit Policy

The Lambert-Cartright Electronics Company is committed to a growth pattern that is moderate in terms of our industry's standards. We do not propose to take unusual financial risks. We also do not propose to undertake growth at levels beyond our financial capabilities, beyond the capabilities of our present plant facility, or beyond our ability to add good, productive employees. Our company is dedicated to a pattern of solid, steady growth, and to a company policy that incorporates the highest standards of personal and business ethics in our relationships with fellow employees, all segments of the general public, our customers, and our suppliers.

It is our commitment to manufacture products of the highest quality for the targeted market and to act responsibly and positively in our relationships with other members of our industry. We do not intend to become a major player in our industry, but it is our goal to make the Lambert-Cartright Electronics Company a positive factor in how the consumer perceives our industry. In a phrase, we are not a "fast buck" company. We are in business for the long haul, and we expect this attitude to guide and motivate employees' interactions with each other and with the public, and every decision-making and production area of our company.

The following guidelines will help the Credit Department to channel its efforts toward making an appropriate contribution:

Credit terms should not be offered to accounts that do not meet the criteria for a low-risk receivables base.

Figure 1-6. Sample Credit Policy.

Figure 1-6. (*Continued*) Sample Credit Policy.

Account evaluation procedures shall be geared to an annual bad-debt loss (percentage of sales) that is not in excess of the average for our industry.

The Credit Manager's decisions regarding any sales or credit line situation may be reviewed by the Treasurer (or Vice President [VP] of Finance) if so requested by the Sales Manager (or Vice President of Sales).

The Credit Manager shall work effectively with all departments and levels of company management to ensure a continuity of company objectives.

Any question that the Credit Manager might have regarding the application of this credit policy to a specific account is to be discussed with the Treasurer.

Credit policy will be reviewed periodically by senior management to ensure that the company's goals remain unchanged as they impact the credit department.

Credit department personnel should, whenever possible, be a positive force in our effort to build strong customer loyalties and relationships.

The Credit Department shall expedite the process of credit decisions within the context of an appropriate input of necessary data and an appropriate time frame in which to evaluate that data.

The Treasurer (or VP of Finance) will monitor the effectiveness of methods used by the credit department to achieve its goals.

_____   _____
  (date)   (title)

The foregoing Sample Credit Policy (Figure 1-6) is a moderate one. If the same credit policy were to be modified to accommodate the needs of another company for a more restrictive policy, all elements of the policy would be tightened to reflect that goal. Account evaluation procedures would remove any latitude for accepting accounts not of the highest quality. This would, or should, ensure that the company's bad-debt loss for a business year is well below the industry average, while also maximizing the flow of internally generated cash. In a liberal credit policy, the receivables base would include more slow-pay accounts, more accounts that offer a higher level of risk, more borrowed funds to augment the slower flow of internally generated cash, and a higher annual percentage—and dollar total—of bad-debt losses.

Credit Department Procedures include procedures for a variety of duties. Figure 1-7 is an example of one procedure.

Processing a Credit Application

Department members will use the following procedure when processing a request for approval of a pending order, an in-house order, or a credit line.

a. Mail the credit application form, with a cover letter, to the applicant. Include a self-addressed, stamped envelope.

b. When the completed application has been returned, call the applicant's supplier and bank references for experience data. Review the customer's currently applicable financial statement, requested as part of the credit application.

c. Enter the experience data (from the suppliers and the bank) on the Account Information Analysis Sheet.

d. Evaluate the body of the reference data (including report data from D & B, NACM, or other) to approve or decline an order and/or to set a credit line.

e. Assign a credit line. Write the assigned figure in the upper right-hand corner of the Account Analysis Sheet.

f. Notify the customer first by phone and then by confirmation letter that an order or a credit line has been approved, has not been approved, or has been approved for a lesser amount.

g. If the original request cannot be approved as submitted, tell the customer the amount of opening line credit you can assign. Suggest that a favorable account relationship should enable you to gradually increase the amount of credit available to this customer.

Figure 1-7. Processing a credit application.

2
Operating the Department

It is possible for a company to have a good credit policy, solid credit procedures, an excellent product, competitive pricing, and good marketplace acceptance, yet discover over a period of time that, in areas such as internally generated cash flow, the credit department's performance is not good. If business is so good, why is cash flow just a trickle? If sales are in an upward curve that has top management's eyeballs rolling, why is payables getting heat from suppliers who have unpaid balances ranging from 40 to 50 days past due? Are there contradictory circumstances that defy explanation? Not really.

Unless the person who is charged with the management of credit and accounts receivables is effectively utilizing the various tools and aids that the company provides (a good credit policy, computerized data, a credit reporting service such as D & B or NACM, etc.), and unless that person is properly focusing the experience and qualifications that he or she brought to the management position, the department is going to fall far short of the contribution expected of it by the company. Are there too many deviations from the credit policy? Are there too many attempts to shortcut the department's procedures? Is it just a failure to shorten the aging of slow-turning receivables? Taken individually, each has the potential to be a major operational problem. When they are lumped together, these and other failures can combine to cripple the effectiveness of a credit department or function.

Every credit manager owes a company or business, regardless of its size, age, or financial strength, a job performance of superior quality—one that ensures the quality of results that good credit management should deliver. There are individuals and departments that do not deliver at a level that coincides with the rightful expectations of the company. No credit manager should settle for less than an optimum level of achievement for him or herself, for the department, and for the company, whose survival may be influenced greatly by the quality of the work done in the credit department.

If you cannot state unequivocally that your credit department is meeting its responsibility to the company, do a step-by-step review of the department's procedures as they should be applied. You may be surprised to learn that some of the department's most critical procedures no longer have the square corners and well-defined edges that made them effective. Over a period of months or years, they have been rounded in the interest of an expediency that, if not corrected, can become self-destructive to the department and to the company. How should you manage your company's credit responsibility? Work smart, work intelligently, work effectively—and stay focused!

Establishing/Maintaining High Standards of Efficiency

The financial officer, working with and from the input of other top-echelon officials, formulates a credit policy that is based on the goals and the financial requirements of a particular company. The director of finance (or VP of Finance) may also oversee the implementation of the company's credit policy, but it is the credit manager who breathes life into the words. It is the credit manager who has the responsibility to write the credit procedures, put them in place, and set and maintain standards of efficiency that ensure compliance with the requirements of the policy.

It isn't the job of the credit manager to be a cheerleader, but he or she should be an effective motivator. The challenge of having to "establish and maintain high standards of efficiency" among employees, who may or may not be working at their full capability or potential, is not just a routine challenge—it is a motivational challenge. The department's standards have been in a noticeable decline (less attention to important details, failure to follow up with customers and other departments of the company, sluffing off the need for answers to questions regarding the slower payment pattern of some accounts, incomplete credit evaluation data, etc.). This is not the type of change in attitude—or work ethic—that should be allowed to gain momentum. It is essential that the credit manager, by his or her own example, set the appropriate efficiency standards for the department. No member of the credit department staff should have to look at the department's manager and wonder why he or she has the job. There should be no question concerning the manager's high personal standard of efficiency.

Please understand that no job spec for a credit manager would ever contain any statement to the effect that he or she must exhibit personal competence and a high standard of efficiency to fellow employees. It is never stated, but I can assure you that it is always there. The manager's level of daily activity demands a high level of controlled personal energy, and the ability to juggle several major account decisions at one time, while answering questions for various members of the department's staff. Is the company big enough to have an assistant credit manager (or more than one)? In that setting, the energy of the credit manager is focused generally on major accounts: setting, extending, or curtailing credit lines, taking care of problems relating to payments, goods, or services, finding a major job in a financial crisis that is impacting the customer's ability to pay a large receivables balance, etc.

Regardless of the size of the company or the scope and variety of tasks undertaken by the credit manager, it is imperative that the person who has the primary responsibility for managing credit and accounts receivable is aware of the necessity to establish and to maintain high standards of efficiency in the department.

The account screening procedure (which also includes the evaluation of an account and the assigning of a credit line) is the key to everything that follows. A good procedure that is applied efficiently provides a business or company with a consistently good base of high-liquidity accounts receivable. This allows a credit person to handle effectively a larger number of accounts; it reduces the number, the dollar amounts, and the aging of slow-pay balances; it reduces the number and the total dollars of bad-debt accounts; and it substantially increases the internally generated contribution to cash flow. The cumulative effect is to further reduce the cost of doing business, a fact that is readily visible in the low total of dollars charged to bad debt losses. The increase in "bottom line" dollars is the direct result of good credit and collection procedures applied efficiently and effectively.

Example: Company A has five people in the credit department: a credit manager and four credit assistants. Each assistant is responsible for a block of active accounts that ranges between 600 and 700 on the accounts receivable aging report. This responsibility includes the processing of all new account applications within the assigned alphabetical block, the setting of credit lines (reviewed above a certain limit by the credit manager), the collecting of receivables balances, and the monitoring of accounts for changes (such as a change in ownership, a change in the product or product lines, the loss of a key executive, the slowing of payments to other suppliers, etc.) that might have a bearing on the stability of an account. The credit manager handles the company's major accounts, interfaces with department heads and customers, maintains an active relationship with peer industry credit managers, and is responsible for supervising the work of the four assistants. Because the screening procedure for new accounts is good, and is applied consistently by all members of the department, the quality of accounts receivable is consistently good. Accounts pay their balances within or close to terms, the credit assistants have more time to monitor effectively a larger base of accounts, and a more consistent flow of converted receivables dollars enters the company's cash-flow pipeline.

The credit function at Company A is helped also by the fact that Company A is committed to a program of steady, carefully controlled annual growth. The business philosophy is reflected in the language and the goals stated in the company's credit policy, which enables the credit department to operate in an atmosphere conducive to producing better results.

Company B is an entirely different case. Its credit department has the same number of people as Company A's (a credit manager and four assistants), has credit procedures, and operates under the umbrella of a company credit policy, but delivers results that are much less impressive than those of Company A. What's the problem? What are the reasons for two companies of similar size (companies that manufacture and distribute a product of similar quality and price, and who operate in the same industry and in the same general marketplace area) to get dramatically different results from their credit departments?

There is no one-word or one-reason fix to change the level of the results that Company B's credit department is delivering. Each credit assistant at Company B is assigned a block of active accounts that never exceeds 550 to 600 (50 to 100 less than at Company A), but because of the higher percentage of slow-paying accounts, the assistants at Company B are generating less cash from their accounts, while constantly involved in a game of catch-up. The credit manager at Company B handles the company's major accounts less effectively than his or her colleague at Company A because Company B's manager must devote more time to advising and supervising the department's assistants.

The screening procedure at Company B is good, but it is not being used effectively. Short cuts are taken in the interest of expediency, and expediency delivers, as its major product, a much higher percentage of slow-pay accounts. These accounts are given credit lines, not because the credit manager and the credit assistants don't know how to follow guidelines, but because the management of Company B is committed to a company program of accelerated growth, with the goal of an early public offering (or a second offering). This policy puts additional pressure on the credit department to deviate from a sound credit policy and credit procedures in order to accomodate the overriding demands of top management for an accelerated rate of growth. And what, in this instance, is an "accelerated rate of growth?" It is a euphemism for the language used to tell the credit department to accept too many accounts that do not fit the criteria of the company's original credit policy—one that has been changed by verbal edict rather than by written amendments. No company can expect its credit department to contribute at the level of which it should be capable when the company creates situations (accelerated growth, etc.) that force variances from good account selection and management techniques.

How to Measure the Department's Effectiveness

Measuring the effectiveness of a company's credit department can be done in a number of ways. The measurement of primary importance, however, must always be the one that rates what a department does against the standard required of it by the company. All other measurements are relevant only as they relate to whether a department is or is not doing for the company what the company needs and expects of it.

Some of the standards that are used to determine whether a company's credit department is below, equal to, or in excess of the performance level of others in the same industry, involve the use of ratios, the comparison of average number of days sales outstanding on the accounts receivable aging report, and a comparison of a company's figure against one figure that is alleged to be the "industry standard." It may be compiled by the industry's credit group, the National Association of Credit Management, a manufacturers' or distributors' group, or some other industry group that has asked for figures from a broad representation of the industry.

The phrase "broad representation of the industry" is used purposely to alert credit managers to the variations that are built into a figure that might rightfully be termed an "industry average." There is a problem, however, when a credit manager at a small company (annual sales of $5 million or less) tries to compare his or her figure with an industry figure that is compiled from data supplied by companies whose annual sales are $50 million, $100 million, and more. There may also be a broad variation in credit granting policies (and the question of how many participating companies are on course with a program of controlled growth and how many have their eyes on the stars and are racing to become as big as they can as fast as they can). Each of these factors—company size, growth philosophy of the company or business, quality of the credit manager and the credit management team—is relevant to the figure submitted by individual companies.

There is the ever-present danger of complacency—of becoming satisfied with the current level of performance. Is it enough that a department seems to be doing a satisfactory job, based on the cash-flow requirements of the company, what is expected from receivables, and the absence of any glaring over-age balances? No, it isn't enough. The department may not be doing as good a job as it could or should be doing. Some companies are well-established and, over a period of years, have developed a customer base that meets the company's requirement for internally generated cash. Could that translate into a more laid-back credit department? Or a credit department that is less aggressive in collecting past-due balances from accounts that chronically take an extra 15 or 20 days, simply because they are not asked to pay? Many of these accounts pay other suppliers within terms or within a few days of terms. They would probably do the same thing with every supplier, if asked to do so.

Credit managers who supervise directly the department's credit assistants should review with them on a weekly basis the status of their accounts. The status of past-due accounts should be discussed, including a review of what has been done (telephone calls, collection letters, personal visit, etc.), any specific payment commitment(s), and the course of action to be taken during the coming week. Giving associates enough time and latitude to do their job is an important concession for a credit manager. It should be uppermost in the credit manager's mind when problems, actions, and the timetable for completing those actions is established. There should be a level of trust and confidence in the credit manager's attitude toward the credit assistant that is commensurate with that person's experience, proven ability, and growth capability. The first two are givens; the last—growth capability—is a judgment call that can't be turned into a "bankable," until the person challenged has the opportunity to succeed.

The Credit/Sales Relationship

It was not many decades ago that the usual relationship between sales and credit was confrontational. Credit people regarded sales and sales management people with a high degree of suspicion. On the other hand, sales managers were convinced that the goal of credit managers was to destroy them, both professionally and economically. The almost universal absence of professional or personal regard between these two key elements of the business offered little or no room for rational discussion or the most minor of compromises—an attitude for which, unfortunately, companies and businesses were the losers.

The more recent relationships between credit and sales are the more enlightened ones (see Figure 2-1). Had credit and sales not been forced to change their attitudes and begun to bury the hatchet in something other than each other, the marketing success enjoyed by many of our biggest companies would not have been possible. If the levels of suspicion and infighting that had marked these associations in the pre-World War II era had been allowed to dominate into the high-growth period that followed, many of this country's biggest companies would not have become major players in the areas of domestic and international trade.

(Company Letterhead)

August 4, 199X

To: Sales Managers—Outside Sales Offices

From: Cecil Bond, Credit Manager

Re: Credit Authority and Responsibility

The following program has been designed to give outside sales offices the maximum amount of credit clearance control in the processing of first orders, and orders that must be expedited. Sales managers should find that these guidelines provide enough latitude for them to clear many of their first orders, thereby expediting the flow of orders to the order desk and to the shipping department.

This procedure does not eliminate the sales manager's responsibility to obtain bank and supplier reference information in first-order situations where the customer has indicated that he or she will need a credit line in excess of the $300 minimum. It is important to promptly forward all New Account Information Forms as rapidly as possible with the ultimate goal of a mutually realistic credit line.

Please contact me in any situation or circumstances where there is a question not covered by the attached procedures.

C. Bond

Distribution:

VP Finance/Financial Officer
VP Marketing/Sales
(Copies to Sales Managers,
all Outside Sales Offices)
Order Desk
File Copy

Figure 2-1. Credit authority and responsibility (sales managers and outside offices).

A sizeable share of the credit for this change should go to the top management of companies with hot products and the dedication to fast growth who knew—and passed the word—that there was no room in a company's business projection for credit and sales to indulge in the type of bickering, infighting, and general hard-headedness that had been prevalent in past eras. When the word from the top to the managers of credit and sales is to make every effort to see that the company doesn't lose a single sale that fits the company's criteria for what is an acceptable credit risk, many more accounts find their way onto the sales report and the accounts receivable aging report.

Sales (And How It Relates to Credit)

It is the job of the sales executive to push for the highest monthly, quarterly, and annual sales figures that the department can deliver. This is in response to the constant pressure on the sales department to maximize the dollar total of sales, not to just meet sales quotas and goals, but to push to exceed those goals by the largest margin possible. Under most business and growth scenarios, the company's expectations from the sales department are the key to whether the budget for the fiscal year will be funded and, in the larger spectrum, whether the business plan will succeed as written. This level of pressure to deliver projected results makes it mandatory that sales are supported as strongly as possible by a credit department that will go to great lengths to find a way to finance a good piece of business.

Most companies offer commissions, bonuses, and other incentives when sales quotas or sales projections are exceeded. These commissions or incentives may be offered at various levels or tiers, and they represent an important source of income to sales personnel. They are motivational factors in that they help to push sales personnel to higher and more lucrative levels of accomplishment—and financial reward. Although it should never influence a credit decision, it is important for the credit manager to remember that any sale that he or she does not approve is a blow to the salesperson who carried the piece of business, to the sales manager, and to the sales department. Regardless of how good the basic relationship between the two departments may be, the loss of a sale because the authorization for credit was denied hits the salesperson and the sales manager in their pocketbooks. What might have been a commissionable sale (or a sale that might have pushed the sales total of the individual and the department to or above quota) is lost, and with its loss may go the work of several days, weeks, or even months. It is understandable that the salesperson is upset, the sales manager is upset, and the company's top management has questions regarding the reasons for not approving the request for a credit clearance.

A sales manager should never be pleased when he or she loses an order for a potentially profitable piece of business because the credit department could not find an acceptable way to finance the order. The sales manager may accept the credit department's reason(s) for not granting the requested amount of credit, but the fact that what might have been—an order that was obtained at the right price and for a quantity of product that would have ensured a good profit—is a major disappointment for people who worked hard to get the order.

Any sales manager (or salesperson) who does not exert every ounce of reasonable, rational pressure on the credit department to find a way to accept the order is not doing a complete job for the company, the customer, or the sales department. And if the credit manager's reasons for not giving an order credit clearance is not clearcut—if there is any reason to believe that the credit department's effort to approve the order was less than total—then it is the sales manager's prerogative to take the credit clearance problem to the director of finance, to review the order and the quality of the credit department's effort to approve the credit request.

The credit manager, however, is not alone in bearing the responsibility to protect the quality of the company's accounts receivables asset. The sales manager also has a responsibility to the company in that same area. He or she must recognize and accept the fact that, dependent on the credit policy of the company, there are accounts that cannot meet the qualifications for a credit sale or a credit line with that particular company. The parameters and guidelines that are an integral part of a company's credit policy allow only so much latitude before the customer must be considered an unacceptable credit risk; perhaps a customer is acceptable at a very low opening limit, but is not acceptable at the much higher limit that would be required to accommodate a specific order.

Sales departments need the sympathetic cooperation of a credit department that is sales oriented. Both departments must work together, not only for the good of the company, but also to provide an atmosphere of respect and harmony between the two of them. It is an approach that, fortunately, is no longer unique. All types and sizes of businesses and companies are benefiting as the result of this greatly improved level of cooperation between their sales and credit people.

Credit (and How It Relates to Sales)

The mandate of every credit department, regardless of whether there is or is not a written credit policy, is generally clearcut as it relates to the acceptance of credit risks: the rapid-growth company wants every account that isn't flashing neon warnings of impending "Chapter 11" or "Bad-Debt Account" doom; the medium-growth company wants a strong base of within- or near-terms accounts; the restrictive company wants accounts that unfailingly deliver an "on-time" payment experience. Nothing that the credit department does to implement the company's written or suggested credit policy should represent more than a variation of minor magnitude from good credit procedures as they relate to the company's policy.

Where does that apparently unbending approach leave the credit department in its relationship with sales? In very acceptable shape if both departments accept the premise that they're working for the Yeper Company, not the Zyder Company or the Xinflat Company. The three companies compete in the same marketplace area with product lines of similar quality and price, but with three different approaches to what is an acceptable credit risk. Zyder is gung ho for growth and is willing to take more chances with the quality of its receivables base; Xinflat wants growth, but wants a more measured growth that has a financial base of receivables that deliver a consistent, high-level of internally generated cash flow. Yeper? It wants a minimum amount of tightly controlled growth, virtually no debt, and a policy of supplying the monthly cash-flow requirement from fast-turning receivables.

So you're with the Yeper Company. Your sales manager is not new to the company, but since new owners took over the company eight months ago, he has been having difficulty accepting a credit policy that has gone from moderate risk to very little risk. Orders are lost to the more liberal credit policies of the Zyder and Xinflat companies; this bothers you too, but the decisions made by your department are within the parameters established when the new owners took over the company. Although you always make it a point to give the sales manager an explanation for orders and accounts that cannot be cleared for credit (or more credit), there is a mutual sense of frustration when a particularly attractive piece of business must be declined because the customer doesn't meet your company's credit guidelines.

The most productive thing any credit manager can do for the company's sales department—regardless of the strict, moderate, or liberal nature of the company's credit policy—is to be a sales-oriented credit person. Do your best to qualify the applicant for the credit line or order clearance. Help the company to build its success on the criteria for success that it has chosen, and make it clear to sales department personnel that your department is doing everything it can to support their efforts.

There will be moments when both of you will know and appreciate what the other has tried to do; there will also be moments when frustration will color the judgment or the remarks of one or both. Never—absolutely *never*—allow the remarks, the actions, or the reactions to be acrimonious in content, nature, or sound. The nature of your work brings the two of you together on an almost-daily basis and, granting the assumption that both the sales and credit managers are intelligent, diligent human beings who are not always the masters of what they must do, you must respect each other for what you are able to accomplish under conditions and mandates that are always less than idyllic.

The following is an example of a credit department that is working in close cooperation with sales. The employer is a manufacturer and distributor whose floor tile, cove base, and adhesive were specified for use on a large development of expensive oceanside condominiums. The manufacturer's customer is a progressive, well-managed, floor-covering contractor, who has enjoyed an excellent reputation with the manufacturer and distributor. The problem follows.

The floor-covering contractor has the contract to supply and install floor-covering materials for the general contractor. Unfortunately for the floor-covering contractor, the general contractor has mismanaged the project and is virtually out of funds. By the time payments begin to come due for the floor-covering materials installed (including labor charges for installers), plus an additional amount for materials not yet installed, there is very little money. This transfers the payment burden for the materials purchased, in the amount of $100 to $125 thousand, onto the back of the flooring contractor. The contractor must tell the manufacturer of the problem with the general contractor, and ask the manufacturer for an extended payment arrangement on the material furnished for the condo. In the absence of any extended payment plan, the flooring contractor's cash flow would be so severely impacted that other jobs—ongoing and soon to start—could not be financed, short of incurring some large and expensive new debt.

The floor-covering contractor has protected its interest and the interest of the supplier by filing the appropriate material men's liens. Although payments from the general contractor will be slow, the size and diversity of the general contractor's activities minimize any thought that the general contractor might be forced into a Chapter 11 filing. The situation does, however, call for understanding and payment relief on the part of the manufacturer's credit department, which adds new strength to an already strong relationship between the manufacturer/distributor and the floor-covering contractor.

When the manufacturer's credit manager and the floor-covering contractor work out a payment agreement satisfactory to both parties (one that will enable the floor-covering contractor to separate the problem job from the regular account relationship), the sales department is then able to move forward with the floor-covering contractor on other jobs, for which the manufacturer's products are either specified or are one of several acceptable. At this point, the floor-covering contractor's gratitude may show itself in the form of using the manufacturer's products on several jobs that might otherwise have been split among two or three suppliers.

The manufacturer/distributor, the sales department, and the floor-covering contractor benefit greatly from the fact that the credit manager knows the customer and has a high level of confidence in the customer's integrity, business ability, and resilience in handling a problem of this magnitude. The credit manager is able to work out a mutually satisfactory payment arrangement for materials supplied to the problem job, which neutralizes any adverse impact to the cash flow of the floor-covering contractor's business.

What about the future relationship between the supplier and the customer? Because of the credit manager's efforts, it will be stronger than ever. There will also, within the credit manager's own company, be an appreciation for the work done to protect a receivables asset, to help a good customer over an unforeseeable financial hurdle, and to continue to supply the customer's ongoing need for a product(s). And what about the sales manager? He or she may not buy lunch, but the good work of the credit manager will not go unrecognized.

Interfacing with Customers/ Other Suppliers/ Other Departments

An effective credit manager never forgets that he or she has a responsibility to the company or business that is not restricted to the managing of credit and accounts receivable. The credit manager is also a public relations person for his or her company, a highly visible person who is constantly interfacing with the company's customers, and who realizes the need to develop and maintain good relationships with peer-credit managers. And lastly, the credit manager must interface effectively with the people and the departments in his or her own company. These relationships can, at times, be the most challenging of all the relationships. Tempers can flare between people in the same company over issues and problems that would be handled quickly, effectively, and dispassionately if dealing with a customer. But in the context that employees of a company or business are members of the same family, so these family members may do and say things to each other that would never be said to an outsider.

Interfacing with Customers

Every credit manager has an obligation to create goodwill for the company with the company's customers. Differences in personalities and backgrounds make it impossible for a credit manager to have the same type of rapport with every customer, but a level of understanding is possible that can translate into another positive in the intercompany relationship.

Does this mean that a customer whose account has an overdue balance should not be contacted for payment? Of course not. Your obligation—and the obligation of every other credit manager—is to collect the company's receivables balances in a timely manner. Unless the account is deteriorating rapidly, or has deteriorated to the point where it is beginning to look like a potential bad-debt loss, your contact with the owner, manager, or person who has payment authority should be cordial and helpful.

Present your company's case for prompt payment of the past-due invoices, and do it by using language that conveys your desire to clear past-due invoices from the receivables aging report. Your manner should include nothing that is threatening, derogatory, defamatory, or objectionable in tone, demeanor, or language, but you must still ask for a specific number of dollars and a release date for the check. No pressure and no hassle. You will have handled the problem in a nonconfrontational manner—one that the customer can accept as appropriate, given the past-due status of the receivables balance.

As a general rule, it isn't wise for the credit manager to develop close friendships with the company's customers. Such friendships always hold the potential for distorting judgments that might adversely impact credit decisions, the aging and totals of receivables balances, and the effort to collect past-due balances. Let me hasten to add that this should not be interpreted to mean that a credit manager cannot establish business-oriented friendships with customers. An occasional lunch, a round of golf, or a game of racquetball when the credit manager visits the customer's city are reasonable pleasures that business friends can enjoy. These are the types of business friendships that lead to exchanges of business-related information over lunch or golf, exchanges that would not be possible if time and association had not built a strong rapport between two individuals. The credit manager benefits because the customer tells him or her more about his or her business than the credit manager could ever assemble from conventional sources—and the customer knows that the credit manager is sincere when he says, "George, give me a call before anything has a chance to become a problem. Our two companies have had a long and an excellent relationship, and I know that you're a man who has an enormous sense of business and personal integrity. If you need some help or a favor, call me. I'll do everything I can to make it happen."

Interfacing with Other Suppliers

The rivalry for local, regional, and national market share that exists between businesses and companies in the same industry does not extend to their credit managers. Although credit managers are close-mouthed regarding the product and marketplace plans of their company, they freely (or should freely) exchange credit experience information, as it relates to current and/or former customers (see Figure 2-2). And whether the information is exchanged at a monthly or quarterly luncheon meeting, arranged under the auspices of The National Association of Credit Management or some other national or local organization, the confidentiality of the source is of primary importance. Credit groups have been destroyed because one credit manager quoted the source of information that was being used to leverage a customer into paying a past-due balance.

(Date)

To: **Re:**

The above-named firm has given your name as a credit reference to assist it in establishing an account with us. We greatly appreciate your help and pledge that any information given to us by your company will be treated in strictest confidence.

Sold from: _____   **Method of payment:**

Highest Credit: _____   Discounts _____

Owing: _____   Prompt _____

Past-Due: _____   Slow _____

Terms: _____   Pays by Note _____

                                         Pays on Account _____

Remarks: _____

_____

_____

_____

Sincerely Yours,

Credit Manager

Please complete and return to:

Figure 2-2. Request for supplier credit experience.

Credit managers depend on each other to share their account experience and to share it in a disclosure that is complete and truthful. Such information can be very helpful in providing an explanation for why a company wants urgently to buy your product(s) after months or years of buying nothing at all. When data from other industry accounts confirms that the account has been slow to pay other suppliers (so slow that the credit line has been reduced to the point where it is not high enough to meet the company's requirements), then the knock on your company's door is much easier to understand.

A credit manager might also alert peer credit managers of the return to the area of a company or an individual who had, some years before, been a major problem for area and regional suppliers, costing them tens of thousands of dollars before the bankruptcy court dissolved the business. A protectionist mindset develops in a good credit group that embraces all members, and although the first priority of every member is to look out for the interest of his or her company, there is, immediately below the primary layer of responsibility, a strong secondary interest that addresses itself to the welfare of the entire group. Credit reports, bank experience, and financial statements are essential sources of information pertaining to the history and the payment habits of an account, but data that has been obtained from peer credit managers tells a much more focused and personalized story.

Interfacing with Other Departments

When the credit manager (or a member of the credit department) interfaces effectively with the manager and members of another department, it should be an experience that benefits both departments. Perhaps the credit department has some questions regarding accounts receivable reports that were received earlier in the morning. The credit manager contacts the manager of data processing, points out to the manager that one day of payments and one of shipments was omitted from the reports, and asks for a rerun that will include everything through the preceding day's work. The data processing manager agrees that an error has been made and that new reports will be run and available by 10:00 the following morning. Credit is assured of an updated receivables report in time for calls to the east coast regarding past-due balances, and data processing has been left with the pleasant feeling that credit is not insensitive to the unexpected problems that can impact its production schedule.

Interfacing with a number of the company's departments is something that occurs daily. There is daily contact with the sales department (a problem clearing an order, or a new order that requires some creative credit work), shipping and receiving (the customer returns several units of defective product for credit), accounting (receivables personnel often work under the supervision of the controller or chief accountant), purchasing (it is time to order a budgeted piece of office equipment), personnel (hire authorization and job description for a new credit assistant), plus the contacts with other departments and functions of the company.

When you and your department interface at maximum effectiveness with others in the company, the work of your department should be easier and more effective. Efficiency should improve because a smoother working relationship between departments allows department members to focus their attention on the customers and the rapid turnover of high-quality receivables. Acts or attitudes that reflect feelings of pettiness between individuals and departments work to the detriment of everyone.

When there is a legitimate difference of opinion between the managers of two departments—a difference that defies a mutually satisfactory solution—agree to take the problem to a management executive who has no supervisory responsibility to either department. Give a straightforward presentation of the credit department's version of the problem and the preferred solution(s); sit back while the manager of the other department presents the problem, and the potential solutions preferred by his or her department. Whether the problem is weighed quickly or lengthily, and regardless of which department receives the response of choice, there should be no residual frustrations between the two managers and their departments.

Good managers should rarely need the services of a third party to judge or to arbitrate a decision or a course of action. Two managers, both people of goodwill with the best interest of the company overriding thoughts of department advantage or preference, should be able to arrive at a compromise that does not adversely impact the work load of either. This should be accomplished in an atmosphere that is nonconfrontational and without recriminations. Every individual or department is charged with working for the common good. In that context, "the common good" is what is best for the company, not what is best for one department over another.

Forecasting Internally Generated Cash Flow

The accurate forecasting of cash flow generated from accounts receivable is one of the most important services that a credit manager can perform. When there is accurate forecasting of accounts receivable collections for one, two, or more weeks, the problem of funding the company's cash-flow requirement becomes more manageable. Given a known figure for a specific time frame of the company's cash-flow requirement, plus the credit manager's solid forecast of internally generated cash from receivables, the financial officer is left with the relatively easy decision of how much to borrow from the bank and at what point in the month to borrow it.

Financial officers need a level of accuracy that, with good knowledge of the accounts and a few weeks of practice, is very attainable. A successful forecaster must know the payment patterns of most of the company's credit accounts, with emphasis on the payment patterns of the major accounts. The integrity of the forecast demands a high degree of accuracy in projecting the amount and the time frame of payments made by major accounts. No forecast is meaningful unless it is within five percent of the receivables payments with a decreasing, but meaningful level of forecast accuracy for weeks three, four, and five. Results that fall below this level of accuracy fall short of providing the quality of income information needed by the financial officer.

A dependable method for determining the accuracy of your cash forecasting involves the use of two forms: a weekly cash forecast and report. The forms impose the one requirement that has just been mentioned—that you are thoroughly familiar with the payment patterns of the company's volume accounts. If your knowledge of accounts and analysis of balances on the receivables aging report is good, you should have very little trouble developing cash forecasts that meet the criteria for reliability.

To use the worksheet for weekly cash forecasts, list alphabetically, from the receivables aging report, those major accounts whose open balances you project will be paid during one of the weeks from one through five. If payment of one or more invoices will be delayed because of a price problem, quantity invoiced versus quantity received, etc., back those totals out of your projection for Week 1, and probably Week 2, unless there is a strong ongoing effort to resolve the matter.

List some of the small accounts and projected payment totals below the list of major accounts. Add a heading for miscellaneous small/smallest accounts, and under that heading, forecast a figure for each of the five columns. Add each of the five columns and enter totals at the foot of each column.

Fill in the requested information through Collectible A/R total on the Cash Forecast Summary Sheet. Bring the worksheet totals forward and enter in Week 1 through Week 5 under "Collections by Week."

The other headings—"Projected," "Actual," and "Difference"—will be your personal report card. At the end of each week you should enter your projected totals against the total accounts receivable dollars collected during that week.

Forecasting your internally generated cash flow is not difficult. The key to successful projections is how well you know the payment patterns of your accounts and how accurately you break receivables balances down into your weekly forecast figures. You'll be surprised at how rapidly your forecasts will reach the point where they're "on the money."

Example: The Winkleman Food Processing Company has grown during the past five years from a start-up, doing specialty food items for small distributors, into a company with 55 permanent employees and annual sales in excess of $15 million. The founding partners took the company public when annual sales reached $10 million, and growth has continued at the projected rate.

A financial director has been hired to initiate company-wide financial controls. She has directed the credit manager to begin to forecast receivables receipts on a weekly basis and over a projection period of five weeks. The credit manager has not had cash forecasting experience and is apprehensive that his forecasts will be inaccurate, to the point of being worthless.

The credit manager makes his forecasting inexperience and his concerns known to the financial director. She gives him samples of the appropriate forms (see Figures 2-3 and 2-4), explains how they are used, and suggests that he do three weeks of practice forecasts before they begin to phase his work into the projection for the company's weekly cash-flow requirement.

Before he does the first forecast, the credit manager reviews receivables aging reports for the preceding six months. He does a month-to-month recap of the payment patterns of the major accounts, adds a figure for the smaller accounts, and adds a third figure for the smallest accounts. Before doing the second forecast, he goes again to the six months of aging reports, familiarizes himself with the payment patterns of the smaller accounts, combines that figure with one for the major accounts, and adds a third figure for the smallest accounts. Forecasting for the third week consists first of fine tuning the average age of major and smaller account balances when they are paid, adding an educated figure for the small accounts, and then putting a forecast figure on report. This forecast delivers a variance from receipts of four percent.

Confident that he can deliver a credible figure, the credit manager prepares his forecast for Week 4 and delivers it to the financial director. She reviews it, reviews the averaging of account payments he did from receivables aging reports of the preceding six months, and then agrees that the figure he has given her looks good. To summarize the example, the figure was good, his forecasts continue to be within acceptable parameters, and the financial director is able to save a substantial number of interest dollars by borrowing only the amount the company needs to supplement internally generated cash flow.

If you are not currently doing a weekly forecast (and a five-weeks projection) from accounts receivables balances, your company is being denied the benefits that accrue from this type of report. Most companies require that their credit managers do receivables forecasting as a standard part of the department's work. It is not an intimidating forward step if, for the first three or four weeks, it is done as outlined in the preceding example—as an

Cash Forecast

For Current Week and 2 Weeks Ending _____

	Prior Week Actual	Current Week	2d Week	3d Week
Receipts:				
Receipts—Trade				
Other				
Total Receipts				
Disbursements:				
Accounts Payable				
Payroll				
Payroll Taxes				
Deposits/Contracts				
Other				
Total Disbursements				
Cash Generated (Used)				
Beginning Cash				
Cash Generated (Used)				
Transfer to Europe				
Transfer to _____				
Transfer to _____				
Bank Borrowing (Payback)				
Ending Cash				
Borrowing YTD				
Available Credit				
Cash Available to Borrow				

Figure 2-3. Cash forecast.

Cash Forecast Summary Sheet

Month of _____

Accounts Receivable Balance _____
    (at end of preceding month)

Less:
    Credits to Be Issued _____
    Current Balances _____
    Disputed Balances _____
    Samples, Etc. _____
Collectible A/R Total_____

Collections by Week (Available Total)	Projected	Actual	Difference
Week 1 _____	_____	_____	_____
Week 2 _____	_____	_____	_____
Week 3 _____	_____	_____	_____
Week 4 _____	_____	_____	_____
Week 5 _____	_____	_____	_____

Figure 2-4. Cash forecast summary sheet.

exercise only. When the day comes that your forecast for the coming week (and projections for Weeks 2 through 5) is phased into the company's projection for the cash-flow requirement, the credibility of your forecasts and projections will be on the line. But if you know your accounts and how their payment history should be used, you should have very little reason to be concerned.

Applying Payments/Credits/ Credit Memos

The prompt and accurate application to a customer account of a credit balance in any of the above categories should be an elementary act in the process of enlightened customer relations. In too many companies, however, the words "prompt" and "accurate" become lost in a maze of unprocessed or carelessly processed paperwork. There may be continuity in the processing of account payments, but frustration is the lot of the customer whose account is overdue to receive a credit for items returned, etc.

Applying Payments

A company does not have to be large to have a standard procedure for processing account payments. One procedure has accounts receivable personnel taking checks from envelopes, listing them on a combination deposit slip and receivables record, then hand-carrying a copy of the receivables/payment record to the credit manager. The credit manager reviews the list of payments, makes appropriate notations and/or comments on his copy of the receivables aging report, and passes the payments list on to an assistant. When a credit department is big enough to have accounts broken into four or five alphabetical sections, a copy of the payments list is given to each person who has supervisory responsibility for one of the sections. The payment date and amount is noted on the appropriate customer area of the receivables aging report, and the processing cycle is complete.

There can be no acceptable excuse for the failure of a business or a company to systematize the application of payments to accounts receivable balances. It is unacceptable as a business practice, creates any number of unnecessary problems with the customer, and invites a form of internal chaos that defies understanding.

Applying Credits

The failure to issue or to process credits promptly can have an adverse domino effect on your relationship with a customer. From a seemingly simple and promptly correctible failure to issue a credit in a timely manner, the customer may escalate the incident into a refusal to pay the part of the invoice total that is not involved with the pending credit (see Figure 2-5). Some customers may take a giant step beyond that level of protest, refusing to make any payment to the account until the one isolated problem has been resolved.

Is the customer being unreasonable? Is the customer using your company's failure to issue a credit in a timely manner as a ploy to avoid making any payment? A look at the payment history of the account will give you the answer to that one. Does the account traditionally pay balances within terms or close to terms? Then there is no denying the fact that you have a very unhappy customer, one that calls for you to move quickly to eliminate the problem before a good customer is lost. The customer does not do business with your company to endure the aggravation of putting up with inconvenience and the absence of consideration. When a customer

Dysan CORPORATION

CREDIT MEMO REQUEST

CUSTOMER NAME: _____

CUSTOMER NUMBER: _____

RE: CUSTOMER P.O. # _____   DYSAN S.O. # _____

DM # _____   INVOICE # _____

SM # _____   INVOICE DATE _____

RMA # _____

REC. RECORD _____

TO CREDIT YOUR ACCOUNT FOR:

☐ MERCHANDISE RETURNED   ☐ MERCHANDISE NOT RECEIVED

☐ INCORRECT PRICING   ☐ OTHER (SEE BELOW)

DESCRIPTION/COMMENTS	QUANTITY	UNIT PRICE	AMOUNT	CREDIT
		FREIGHT:		
		SALES TAX: YES ☐ NO ☐		
OTHER:				
		TOTAL CREDIT DUE:		

INITIATED BY: _____ DATE: _____

APPROVED BY: _____ DATE: _____

APPROVED BY: _____ DATE: _____

WHITE: ACCOUNTING   PINK: FILE   BLUE: INITIATOR

Figure 2-5. Request for credit memo. (*Form courtesy of Dysan Corporation.*)

reminds a department (sales or credit) that an overdue credit has not been issued, the customer deserves immediate attention.

Put an end to the problems and frustrations that feed on such situations by seeing that credits are issued promptly. It could be an overcharge for an item, an error in the quantity billed versus the quantity received, or a problem with size, color, or style. These are negative situations that can erode the customer's feelings of goodwill, unless prompt and effective action is taken to correct the inconvenience. An incident that is allowed to drag on only leads to more confusion, increasingly frequent and intense telephone calls, and a level of customer anger that can only lead to the customer terminating the relationship.

The possibility that a seemingly simple invoice adjustment could become your longest-running project of the year is more than enough incentive for you to see that the appropriate department or individual authorizes the issuing of a credit (credit memo) as soon as the need for one surfaces.

3

Gathering Credit Information

The quality of the information that goes into the evaluation of a credit application is crucial to the quality of the credit decision. Whether an experienced credit manager will be evaluating information received from the applicant and the applicant's references is also very important. The experienced credit manager might suspect the credibility of certain information received from the applicant, and proceed to determine whether it was incomplete, purposely inaccurate, or otherwise flawed.

Should a credit manager attempt to clear a first order or assign a credit line if data furnished by the applicant (or the applicant's references) is incomplete or flawed? No credit manager should assign a credit line or release an order of more than minimal size if appropriate experience data has not been received from the applicant's suppliers and bank, and a currently applicable financial statement has not been prepared internally. What about a Dun & Bradstreet or a National Association of Credit Management (NACM) report? Either is extremely helpful and should contain enough historical and other information to confirm whether there is an ongoing problem, a problem in the recent past, or a problem in the distant past from which the business did not recover fully. Information regarding a change in ownership or management is helpful in determining whether there may be a change in the company's attitude toward its suppliers, and in its ability to pay those suppliers.

If there is one nonnegotiable in the chain of action and information that leads to a decision regarding the release of an order or the granting of a credit line, it is good information, good credit information received from sources with whom the applicant is currently (or has recently) had a credit account. It is the basis for the subsequent evaluation of the risk factors in any sale on credit terms—and it is totally nonnegotiable! Never settle for less information than you need to make an informed credit decision. Do not be unduly influenced by pressure from the applicant or from your own sales or marketing department. And if you are an owner/manager, put your entrepreneurial drive for new business on a back burner and do not succumb to the thought that just this once you might waive getting a financial statement from the applicant, or back away from persisting until the bank gives you some meaningful information. Do not take shortcuts. Do not allow yourself to accept the absence of essential documents, report data, or supplier information in the step-by-step process of gathering decision-making tools.

Your goal is to add as many good accounts as you can, while avoiding costly mistakes in judgment. Most applicants are honest, but be alert for those applicants who will give you ambiguous statements, managed data, and slanted facts. When you have been evaluating account data for a number of years, it is generally not difficult to recognize the presence of one or more of the elements of deceit. Your warning might be an unusual variance between a piece of data supplied by the applicant and data from sources you know to be reliable. It might also be the proverbial "gut feeling" that credit people develop after years of examining the business and credit histories of prospective accounts. Whatever it is that raises a question in your mind, resolve it satisfactorily before you find that you have committed some of your company's receivables assets to a troublesome, slow-pay account.

When the credit information that you receive from all sources is not strong enough to approve the requested credit line, first tell the marketing department what (if anything) you can do for the account. If it isn't much, be candid about it. A company that is committed to a plan of well-managed growth has no room on its receivables aging report for problem accounts of such questionable quality that they would be potential bad-debt items from day one of the association. Special terms are always a possibility when it's a one-time order, but the safety of your company's receivables asset is always the primary criteria.

The Credit Application (and Cover Letter)

In the introduction to this chapter, I emphasized the importance of a good supply of reliable account information. The credit application is the window that provides a credit management person with the opportunity to get the quantity and variety of information that is essential for a quality decision-making process. If a company offers you a window so smudged with incomplete or ambiguous responses that its value is almost negligible, insist that the applicant do a job on the smudged window with the business equivalent of Windex—full, complete, and truthful answers to every question on the credit application.

Every line of the requested information is relevant to your evaluation of the account and to your subsequent relationship with it. If information is missing, call the business or company and ask for the person who signed the application. If you are unable to reach that person, leave a message that explains the reason for your call, and ask for a prompt return call. If you do not receive a return call by the end of the next business day, notify marketing that you cannot proceed without the requested information. Will marketing do a follow-up call? Put the application on hold. What if marketing is not interested in doing a follow-up call? Return the application to the applicant with an appropriate cover letter.

The reasons for insisting that all information relevant to an evaluation of the account must be available to you are virtually without end. Your applicant's receivables and payables departments may be located at different addresses, and those addresses may be within the same city or sometimes a city or state apart. Your invoices should not wander in company limbo because information on the credit application failed to clearly state that each of the two functions (payables and receivables) has its own address. You also must know whether your company is dealing with a corporation, a partnership (general, limited, etc.), or a sole proprietorship. You also need to know whether the customer is a company, a division, or a subsidiary of another company. Bank and trade references are vital to your pool of pre-evaluation information. Let me repeat this warning: you should not assign any applicant a credit line if you are not completely satisfied as to the applicant's relations with its bank and suppliers.

Your company's major competitors, and firms you may never have heard of, are among those that will surface on an applicant's list of references. When you contact competitors for reference data, some will give complete responses, others will give responses that are less candid (not untruthful, but lacking much of the experience detail). Take what you can get from that reference and expand your base from information given to you by other references. Most credit people will give you the benefit of their company's experience with an account. Be appreciative of that information and always be as generous in your response when asked by another supplier, bank, or credit reporting company. Statements that come from what might have been a good or a head-knocking experience are welcome information—information that is not available from other sources.

This section includes three samples of credit applications (see Figures 3-1, 3-2, and 3-3). The primary difference among the three forms is an obligations agreement which, on one of them, requires the signature of an authorized person. The agreement details obligations that the customer company must perform under specified circumstances, and invokes certain

Figure 3-1. Application for credit.

Pyramid Credit Application

Name of Firm: _____ Kind of Business: _____

Address: _____ Date Firm Established: _____

City: _____ State: _____ Zip: _____

Annual Sales: _____ Employees: _____

Contact Regarding Payment: _____

   Type: ____Corporation ____Individual

Phone Number: _____   ____Partnership ____Subsidiary

Firm Listed in Dun & Bradstreet ____Yes ____No

   D&B Number: _____   Fed ID Number: _____

Does Firm Pledge or Borrow against Receivables/Inventory? _____

(If Yes, with Whom? _____)

If a Subsidiary or Division

Name of Parent Company: _____

Dun & Bradstreet Number: _____

Address: _____ Does Parent Guarantee Debts? ____Yes ____No

City: _____ State: _____ Zip: _____

Banking Information

1. Name: _____ Savings Account Number: _____

   Address: _____ Checking Account Number: _____

   City: _____ State: _____ Zip: _____ Loan Number: _____

   Contact: _____ Phone: _____

2. Name: _____ Savings Account Number: _____

   Address: _____ Checking Account Number: _____

   City: _____ State: _____ Zip: _____ Loan Number: _____

Figure 3-1. (*Continued*) Application for credit.

```
Contact: _____ Phone: _____

Trade References:

        Name        Address     Phone Number     Monthly Purchase

1. _____  _____  _____  _____

2. _____  _____  _____  _____

3. _____  _____  _____  _____
```

By affixing their signatures below, the undersigned (or if a Corporation, the Corporation authorized Officers/Agents) agree 1) That the information contained herewith is warranted to be true and correct, 2) to pay when due, all invoices from Pyramid Graphics Corporation, 3) that in the event of default of payment when due, all costs of collection, including Attorney's fees and Court costs, shall be paid by the Applicant, 4) to authorize Pyramid Graphics Corporation to investigate any references herein listed or statement or any other data obtained from any person pertaining to the credit worthiness or financial responsibility of the applicant.

Signature _____ Title _____ Date _____

Signature _____ Title _____ Date _____

(Please attach a copy of latest Financial Statements)

penalties in the event the customer defaults on payments, falsifies statements, or interferes with the investigation of the applicant's relationships with bank and trade references. One application attempts to deal with every default/collection related contingency. The second and third applications contain no statement(s) of liability, requesting only the signature of the person who furnished the information.

The signature of a corporate officer (or an authorized signature) on the credit application adds leverage when some form of third-party collection effort is necessary, and no Chapter 11 filing has been made or appears imminent. If the company has slid into a Chapter 11 filing, or is in a bankruptcy liquidation, an authorized signature won't help a bit. You are at that point where you are either mud wrestling for pennies, nickels, and dimes with other unsecured creditors, or you are one of several secured creditors whose position is much more clearly defined.

Account Information Sheet

Date _____

Company Name _____

Billing Address _____

Shipping Address _____

Person to Contact
Phone Number _____   Regarding Payment _____

Type of Business _____   Annual Sales _____

Corporation   Partnership   Sole Proprietorship   Resale Number _____

Year Business Established _____   Present Ownership Since _____

Is There a Parent Company? _____

_____ Is This a Division? A Subsidiary?

Company Pledge or Borrow Against Receivables? ___   Inventory? ___

Bank References:

Bank Name _____   City/State _____

Person to Contact _____   Telephone _____

Bank Name _____   City/State _____

Person to Contact _____   Telephone _____

Trade References:

Company Name _____   City/State _____

Person to Contact _____   Telephone _____

Company Name _____   City/State _____

Person to Contact _____   Telephone _____

Company Name _____   City/State _____

Person to Contact _____   Telephone _____

Information Furnished by:

_____   _____
(Name and Title)   (Date)

Figure 3-2. Credit application (another version).

Account Information Analysis Sheet

Company Name:_____   Credit Limit: _____

Mail/Billing Address:_____   Date Assigned:_____

Supplier References:	Number 1	Number 2	Number 3
Years Sold			
Recent High Credit			
Current Balance			
Past-Due Balance			
Terms			
Disc/Ppt/Slow to–			

Supplier Comments: _____

Bank Reference:

Savings (Date opened/average balance) _____

Checking (Date opened/average balance) _____

Loans (Equipment, land, buildings, revolving) _____

Credit Line (Including loans) _____

Comments _____

Financial Statement:

Date(s) _____

Audited or Unaudited _____

If Audited, Auditor's Comments _____

Dun & Bradstreet, NACM, or Other Credit Report:

Name of Reporting Company _____

Date of Report   If D&B, What Rating? _____

Additional Comments _____

Figure 3-3. Account information analysis sheet.

Cover Letter

Unless the situation is something that is not routine, you should generate most of your cover letters from form letters. They are time-savers; they can be altered to fit a variety of circumstances and situations, and they may be more effective than a letter written to be used one time. Form letters may be better organized, because they are carefully reviewed and edited before the final draft is added to the list of available letters. In the context of this particular usage, the purpose of a form letter is to serve as a cover letter (an explanation) for an attached form that must be signed and returned (see Figure 3-4).

Cover letters are appropriate when sending application forms to customers, for sending the applicant's bank and supplier references a request for their experience, sending some credit memos (many require a letter of explanation), notifying an account of a past-due balance, and many other

---

(Date)

Mr. Leonard Carter, Controller
The XYZ Company
1348 Sherman Way
San Francisco, CA 94120

Re: Credit Application and Financial Statements

Dear Mr. Carter:

We can expedite the processing of credit reference date if you will complete the attached Account Information Sheet and return it, with a copy of your most current financial statement, at your earliest convenience.

We appreciate the confidence your company has expressed in our products by giving us a first order. It is our hope that this is the beginning of a long and a mutually satisfactory business relationship.

Sincerely Yours,

Credit Manager

Figure 3-4. Cover letter (credit application).

purposes. You must be careful, however, to use form cover letters only when it is appropriate. Never use one as a substitute when a personalized letter or a telephone call is the appropriate way to communicate.

Many credit managers fail to give themselves and their company the benefits that their unique position in the company/customer relationship makes available to them. They seem unaware that from the beginning of the relationship, they can build a rapport with the customer that will be separate from the relationships developed by the company's sales people or the customer's purchasing people. The benefits are the same whether you are an entrepreneur who handles credit matters for your business or you are the credit executive for a company whose annual sales run into the hundreds of millions of dollars. Yours is a unique position; you have an ongoing opportunity to promote a long-lasting relationship between your company and the customer company. When you enjoy a first name relationship with the customer company's controller or vice president of finance, your good relationship with that person will enable him or her to discuss more candidly a receivables problem with one of its major accounts. When you have the facts, giving a customer, whose good faith and integrity is unquestioned, the extra time necessary to pass through the cash crunch is no major decision.

Your first letter to the credit applicant will be the cover letter for the Credit Application and Resale Card (see Figure 3-5). It should focus on your need for information—bank and supplier references and financial statements—while extending your company's appreciation for the order, a brief explanation for your company's requirement of C.O.D. terms for the first order or two (this is determined on an individual basis), while reference data is being processed, and your request that the applicant return the Credit Application and Resale Form (with a copy of the customer's currently applicable financial statement) as promptly as possible in the enclosed, stamped, self-addressed envelope. The letter is a straightforward request for the information and data that will allow you to promptly process the applicant's request for a credit line or an order clearance.

A cover letter is an opportunity for the credit manager (or the credit department) to begin to lay the groundwork for what might become a mutually attractive commercial relationship. If later there are payment problems, some of the luster may disappear from the relationship, but at day one or two of the relationship, the odds should strongly be in favor of it becoming a success. So you mail a credit application and a resale card (if required in your state), and you tie it all together with a cordial cover letter. At this point, there is nothing more you can do to get the relationship started in the right direction.

The credit department is in an excellent position to project a good image for the company. Remember that all correspondence to the company's cus-

---

(Date)

Company Name
Street Address (or P.O. Box Number)
City, State, Zip Code

Attention: ___Addressee's Name___

Dear Mr. (Ms.) _____

A review of our files indicates that we do not have a completed Resale Card (Sales Tax Exemption Number) for your account.

To avoid having California State Sales Tax charged to your invoices, please complete, sign, and return the enclosed Resale Card.

We appreciate your prompt attention to this request.

Sincerely,

Credit Manager

Figure 3-5. Cover letter (resale card).

tomers deserves your best and clearest thinking—never downgrade the importance of those early "first impression" letters in determining the direction the supplier/customer relationship may take.

The Importance of Financial Statements

A financial statement is a vital link in the chain of information you should have to properly evaluate the credit worthiness of an applicant. It is a key piece and if there is no positive response to the first request, do not hesitate to ask again. You may find, at that point, that the applicant is one of the individuals, partnerships, or close-held corporations that does not release financial data—not to you, not to credit reporting agencies, not to anyone. But before your request draws the "we don't release financial statements" response, pursue the subject until you are comfortable with the thought that it is a long-standing policy of the applicant to withhold financials, and not a relatively recent change. And if it is a recent policy change? There may be good reason for it, but accept the change as a reason to be especially watchful of input data received from suppliers and the bank. Responses from these sources should reinforce the applicant's statement that there is no problem; otherwise they may reveal information that poses some serious questions for you.

It is important to remember that financial statements come in two varieties: internally prepared and externally prepared. Externally prepared financial statements are usually the work of the company's accounting firm. They may be prepared from audited or unaudited figures, which have bearing on the credibility that should be attached to each. Other financial statements may be internally prepared (by the applicant company's own in-house financial person or people). These should be regarded as "for information only," with credibility discounted heavily, because no outside source monitors the figures or procedures that are used to produce the statement.

Too many accounts who have their own internally prepared financials slant them for the purpose of favorably impressing bankers and suppliers, particularly in businesses where there is instability or a downward trend—a trend due, perhaps, to faulty management decisions or techniques. If the account slants information, you must assume that the business ethics of the company slanting that information are equally shoddy.

There will be times when the unaudited financial statement of an applicant firm is signed by the owner, a partner, or a corporate officer. If you later suspect that there was misrepresentation with intent to defraud—and it can be shown that the financial statement was persuasive in the granting of a credit line or in increasing an existing line—the signature of an owner, partner, or corporate officer can give you additional leverage. You don't, however, want your hopes for a recovery of receivables dollars to be dangling from such a slender thread. The customer company could be out of business before your attorney gets a trial date.

Credibility is generally conceded to increase greatly when a financial statement is prepared by a CPA. This is very encouraging until you remember that many CPA-prepared financial statements are prepared from unaudited figures. These financial statements are essentially the product of information stemming from in-company practices, procedures, and controls. Need I cite the frequency of allegedly unexpected business failures, and media reviews of those failures, to remind you that there is never a guarantee?

It is not necessary for a person to have a strong accounting background to get help from the financial statement. What you're looking for is ratios and how to interpret and use them. For the safety of your company's receivables, you must understand the meanings of current ratio, liquid ratio, and net worth ratio. When the meanings are clear, you should then apply them to the financial statement of the customer or applicant. Here are some definitions and comments:

- *Current Ratio.* The current total of cash, securities, inventory, and accounts receivable (current assets) versus all indebtedness due within one year (current liabilities). You should not feel comfortable with a current ratio of 1.1. Under most conditions, 2.1 is satisfactory.

- *Liquid Ratio.* Cash and accounts receivable versus current liabilities. If the ratio is less than 1.1, it is unsatisfactory. (1.1 means $1 in liquid assets to offset $1 in current liabilities. This figure is not strong enough.)

- *Net Worth Ratio.* Owner's investment versus creditor's investment. There is concern when the number of dollars (or total investment) of the owners (sole proprietor, partners, venture capitalists, and/or stockholders) is substantially less than the amount supplied by creditors (bank, suppliers, etc.).

Following are some other ratios relevant to the evaluation of an account or an applicant:

- *Current Debt/Net Worth.* Current debt should be a small percentage of net worth. If it is heavy, there is a strong possibility that total debt will exceed net worth.

- *Total Debt/Net Worth.* When total debt exceeds net worth, there is a deficit net worth. When the deficit increases from year to year, or when it is not decreasing, beware!

- *Inventory/Working Capital.* Inventory levels should never be higher than necessary to properly service customers. Excess inventory levels tie up working capital and restrict liquidity.

- *Long-term Debt/Working Capital.* Long-term debt should fit comfortably into the total financial picture. It should not take a disproportionate amount of working capital to service it.

- *Net Profit/Net Worth.* Net worth should increase from year to year. Is the account's net profit going back into the business or is it being absorbed in bonuses, etc., for the owner, partners, or key executives? Unless the business is exceptionally strong financially, business worth should increase each year.

The Balance Sheet (Financial Spread Sheet) that is shown in Figure 3-6 will accommodate as many as five annual financials. You will be doing exceptionally well if you can obtain copies of the three most current ones, but try for more. Consolidating financial statement data onto the one form makes it much easier to identify favorable trends and/or abnormalities, and that can only improve the overall quality of your company's receivables.

Balance Sheet **Financial Spreadsheet**					
Assets	199X	199X	199X	199X	199X
Cash	35,990	16,140	14,147	27,244	41,667
Accounts Receivable					
(Net)	52,148	67,184	121,414	138,797	140,816
Inventory	66,850	99,345	114,149	140,895	138,054
Prepaid and Others	2,971	9,774	7,532	21,308	6,339
Total Current Assets	157,959	192,443	264,421	328,244	326,826
Net Fixed Assets	109,082	122,564	139,390	160,312	198,231
Noncurrent Assets	-0-	7,564	5,300	4,218	4,478
Liabilities	199X	199X	199X	199X	199X
Trade Accounts					
Payable	57,992	62,742	51,101	72,360	63,025
Other Current					
Liabilities	-0-	-0-	-0-	21,596	23,108
Current Portion of					
Long-Term Debt	21,784	41,243	59,829	131,007	134,139
Total Current Debt	80,210	110,769	170,127	231,715	237,112
Long-Term Debt	87,224	88,572	63,704	48,829	35,487
Total Liabilities	167,454	199,341	233,831	280,544	272,599
Net Worth	98,527	123,230	175,280	212,230	256,936
Total Liabilities					
and Net Worth	265,981	322,571	409,111	492,774	529,535

Figure 3-6. Balance sheet (financial spread sheet).

Contacting Supplier and Bank References

Credit managers routinely contact credit references by telephone to clear an order or a credit line for an applicant. The telephone is faster and frequently more cost-effective than a form letter (see Figure 3-2). This statement isn't one that, to get proof, requires a battery of accountants. Anyone who tries to justify the extra time necessary to type and mail form letters is not destined for one of the higher rungs on the corporate ladder. Today's business environment demands that you get and process information as quickly and as accurately as you can. The telephone gives you immediate access to the appropriate information base, and it allows you to deal immediately with responses or statements that require clarification or elaboration.

This does not mean that forms should never be used. There are, in fact, situations where a form is the only way to ensure a response. Many banks will not give experience or account information over the telephone. A telephone call and a request for information is frequently countered by a response that asks the caller to submit the request on a letterhead that identifies the caller and his or her company. Some banks will take your number, call their customer for authorization to give you the bank's experience, and then follow through with a return call. Others are inflexible regarding the requirement for a written request.

You are not without some leverage in the "telephone versus written request" problem. Ask the applicant to contact the banker, and suggest that it is of mutual interest to have your firm (the new supplier) approve a credit line as rapidly as possible. Your product line may be what the applicant needs to increase marketplace share to an appreciable degree—a statement that should motivate the bank to waive the usual written request for information.

Contacting supplier references is generally a very straightforward response to your telephone or written request. Suppliers are in the position of needing the support of experience data from people such as yourself, which makes them more forthcoming with information than some banks. Unless a supplier has had a particularly bad experience with an account—an account that should not have been allowed to run up the receivables balance that it did—the embarrassment of having to tell other suppliers is offset by the desire to see other suppliers take a more restrictive approach.

There is always the rare supplier who does not seem to understand the value of exchanging experience data with other suppliers. This attitude usually begins to erode when the company that is reluctant to divulge information suddenly finds itself needing the experience data of others. When this occurs, and you receive a call from the reluctant one, remind the credit person that you are happy to give his or her company the benefit of your experience, but you do so with the expectation that the future will see a two-way exchange of information between your two companies.

Unless there is a mindset in the other company that is not compatible with twentieth-century management, you and other credit-management colleagues should have no future problem getting the company to share its experience.

An example of a telephone conversation with a credit manager, who does realize the mutual benefits that can be derived from sharing trade experience, follows:

"The Carver Company. May I help you?"

"This is Randal Clarkson, credit manager for the Parmalee Aluminum Products Company. I'd like to speak to your credit manager, but I'm embarrassed to say I don't know his or her name."

"Our credit manager is Harvey Nettleton, Mr. Clarkson. I'll ring him for you."

"Thank you."

(The phone rings three times before a male voice answers.)

"Harvey Nettleton."

"Harvey, this is Randal Clarkson, credit manager at Parmalee Aluminum Products Company."

"Yes, Randal. Didn't we bump into each other at an NACM function a year or so ago?"

"Yes, I think we did." Randal moves on. "I'm calling, Harvey, because an applicant for a credit line has given your company as a reference. I'll appreciate it if you can share your company's experience with me."

"No problem. What's the name of the company?"

"Barnstrom Products. They're located in Denver."

"Oh, sure. We still sell them." There is a pause while Nettleton brings the account up on his monitor. "Yes, they're currently showing an open balance of $9500 with $5700 current and $3800 past due to 35 days."

"How long have you been selling the account?"

"About four years—probably the last two years at this level."

"Have you had any problems?"

"No. In fact, they usually pay within our terms of net 30 days. You've called at one of the few times when there's a past-due balance."

"So, at your sales level, it's a satisfactory account?"

"Absolutely. I'd like to trade a few of my less prompt accounts for some more like Barnstrom."

"I appreciate the information, Harvey. Give me a call if I can return the favor."

"You're welcome, Randal. Let's keep an eye open for each other at the next NACM regional function."

"Fair enough. Goodbye, Harvey."

"Goodbye, Randal."

This conversation is typical of what is said when one credit manager requests the account experience of another supplier. Exchanges of account experience may occur between members of the same industry or members of unrelated business or industry groups. When the call is to a banker, the dialogue may not get beyond the point where you introduce yourself and your company, state the reason for the call, and are then told that, one, the bank releases no account information, unless the request is submitted on the company's letterhead, or, two, the bank will contact the customer for permission to release the information.

Try to avoid any delay in getting the information you need to make an evaluation of the account. If there is a delay, and it will have an impact on the time frame within which you must make a credit commitment, try to work around the missing information. There may be enough good experience data from the other references (suppliers and bank), plus the financial statement, to clear the first order or to grant a credit line that is useful.

Consolidating Credit Information

The systematic consolidating of credit information is essential, if you are to have any chance to give your company an accurate evaluation of a credit applicant. Experience data from banks and suppliers, report data from reporting firms, such as Dun & Bradstreet and NACM, and financial statements from the applicant (audited or unaudited, and prepared from figures that were audited or unaudited) are the ingredients that must be brought together in a useful form—one that will point the way to an appropriate credit decision.

If gathering good information is the basic step in the sequence leading to a solid credit decision, then the knowledge of how to use it properly is of equal importance. Unless you know how to take data from various sources, and systematically assemble it into a helpful bank of quality reference data, it will not be useful to you.

It surprises some people when they realize that the "gather, evaluate, and decide process" includes nothing of insurmountable complexity. The credit manager must, of course, have a level of training and experience commensurate with the responsibility of offering four-, five- and six-figure credit lines, but that is only common sense. No person whose experience is limited should expect to walk into a decision-making situation, and begin immediately to make decisions of good and professional quality. Owners, who make credit decisions for their small companies, must be especially careful during the early stages of their learning and growing experience; credit assistants, who are promoted or leave one company to head the credit department at another, must also be especially careful during their learning and growing experience. Over a period of time knowledge and experience will grow to the point where complex problems will appear more routine—more to be taken in stride than to be worried about before a decision is made.

Do not, however, make a decision in haste that is at the outer edge of your decision-making capabilities. You will become more comfortable with the decision-making process as your experiences prepare your analytical and judgmental skills for applications that are new and more complex.

Consolidating credit information is the core procedure leading to an evaluation of the account, and, subsequently, deciding to assign a credit line (and how much) or to decline the account (and why). There is a sequence of forms and guidelines that must be used to consolidate information, so it can be used to make sound credit decisions. Whether your credit management experience is limited, or whether you have years of big-dollar experience at a major corporation, there is a need to bring information together within a framework that moves the decision-maker toward good and practical credit decisions.

Account Information Analysis Sheet

This form (see Figure 3-7) is used to bring together the bits-and-pieces of information that have been gathered from suppliers, the bank(s), and the financial statement. The data is consolidated in such a way that the credit manager can make side-by-side comparisons of the experience of the three supplier references, get a clear understanding of the bank's experience and comments, and note the strengths and weaknesses of the applicant as revealed by the financial statement; if there is access to reports prepared by a credit reporting agency (Dun & Bradstreet, NACM, etc.), these may be added for comparison with the other data. All the information and data that is necessary to evaluate the account is together on the one form.

When an Account Information Analysis Sheet has good supplier data on every line, the decision-making process cannot be far behind. Interpreting the various areas of key information should pose no problem. Have the three suppliers each sold the applicant successfully for periods in excess of one year? Are high credit, open balances, and past-due figures in line with sales terms? Then any credit manager would have good reason to be pleased.

The bank's experience with the credit applicant may not be the same as that of most suppliers. Companies and businesses make every effort to take

---

Credit Investigation

Company Name: _____   Date Opened: _____

Financial Statement: _____   Credit Limit: _____

D & B Rating: _____   Limit Updated: _____

Bank: _____   Comments:

Checking

Savings

Loans

Reference: _____   Comments:
Contact _____
Years Sold _____
Terms _____
Recent High _____
Current Balance _____
Past-Due Balance _____
Prompt _____   Slow _____

Reference: _____   Comments:
Contact _____
Years Sold _____
Terms _____
Recent High _____
Current Balance _____
Past-Due Balance _____
Prompt _____   Slow _____

Reference: _____   Comments:
Contact _____
Years Sold _____
Terms _____
Recent High _____
Current Balance _____
Past-Due Balance _____
Prompt _____   Slow _____

Figure 3-7. Credit investigation (consolidating information).

good care of their relationship with the bank. Because of this attitude, the bank may report that its customer always pays within the terms of loan agreements. If there is a monthly cash-flow problem, the company is not going to jeopardize its borrowing position by failing to make on-time payments. It would, therefore, be very surprising if the endorsement the bank gives to the customer is not as strong or stronger than the payment experience of suppliers. It is very unlikely that a banker would endorse a relationship with the customer (your applicant) beyond a level that the facts of their relationship would support. Where you should exercise conservative judgment is in the weight given to the bank's position as the supplier of your applicant's primary raw material: money. Supplying money to a customer is a privileged position. It is one not equalled by a major supplier. That position should cause you to assign a little less weight to the bank's experience than you do to supplier relationships, a good Dun & Bradstreet report, or a credible financial statement.

An applicant's request for a credit line is bolstered when reporting agencies such as Dun & Bradstreet and the National Association of Credit Management offer reports that substantiate data received from other sources. If it does not make that type of quality contribution, examine the credit request in the context of reference data received from suppliers and the bank, less report data that may serve to decrease the attractiveness of the credit risk.

Credit Rating and Report Services

Very few people, who have been in business for any length of time, are unfamiliar with Dun & Bradstreet's service (see Figures 3-8 and 3-9). It is the rating and report service with the most recognizable image, and the one that offers its customers the most comprehensive variety of options. It is a service of variable scope that is tied to an annual contract—a contract that offers service from a minimum base of 100 reports per year to an unlimited number on the high end. The subscriber (D & B's term for those who use the service) may also select Reference Guides for regions of interest (Pacific Coast, Rocky Mountain States, East Coast, etc.), for a combination of regions or for the entire United States. Reference Guides list nonretail businesses and companies by state, county, and nearest town. An Industrial Classification Code Number identifies the company's primary type of business; a single digit identifies the year in which the company was established or incorporated (if less than 10 years); Dun & Bradstreet includes a rating for the account. If sufficient current data is not available to rate the account, the Reference Guide shows no rating (a "blank rating").

Figure 3-8. Dun & Bradstreet (consolidated statement). (*Report courtesy of Dun & Bradstreet.*)

Dun & Bradstreet offers many additional services, including the International Reporting Service, which reports on firms in many countries throughout the world. Information is gathered from sources that Dun & Bradstreet has found to be as reliable as the uncertainty of the international marketing scene can make them. When combined with reports from the Department of Commerce, the international department of the exporter's

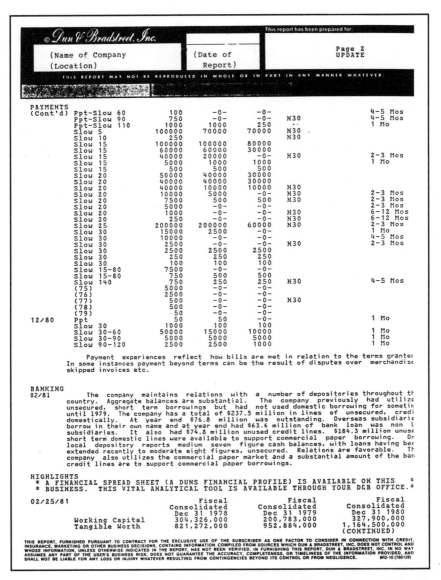

Figure 3-9. Dun & Bradstreet (creditor's experience report). (*Report courtesy of Dun & Bradstreet.*)

bank, and overseas sales representatives (guard against too much sales-oriented enthusiasm), D & B's information can be quite helpful.

Antecedent data, regarding the founders of a company or business, their successors, the currently active founders, and the backgrounds of the founder's successors, is just one type of information not readily available from other sources. There is data regarding recent or past Chapter 11 filings or bankruptcy problems in the recent backgrounds of any partner, managing owner, or key executive. In addition, there is information on suits and liens filed against the company by the IRS or a State Board of Equalization, or brought about by a civil proceeding involving the company's product(s).

Whether your company should subscribe to D & B's service, or one of its services, is something you must decide. I do suggest that, if your business or company is growing at a steady and/or a rapid rate and currently has accounts whose levels of purchases run from "no impact if lost" thru "a *big* impact if lost" (and several are slow pay or increasingly slow pay), your company is a candidate for one level or another of the service. Probably, the majority of credit professionals feel that the report data—base reports, continuous service updates on most accounts, and information pertaining to personnel or internal/external changes—makes it a worthwhile service for many companies below, at, or above the activity range mentioned previously. The service is not cheap. Be prepared to spend a memorable number of dollars, but, if you decide to try it, the basic service for your geographic area of business interest (the area your company services) is usually enough. Experience, and the amount of money available for extending the service, will determine when to increase the number of reports, reference guides, or other services. It is possible to increase the number of services during the term of a current contract or when the contract is arranged for the next year.

The National Association of Credit Management

NACM's service is an alternative to the service provided by Dun & Bradstreet. The formats have some similarities, but each has certain features not offered by the other—or not offered in as much detail as the other.

The large member base of NACM enables it to draw from the credit and receivables experience of members in all areas of the country and in all types of businesses (manufacturing, distributing, service industries, wholesalers, etc.). The door to membership in NACM is open to all commercial companies and businesses (with the exception of retail) that sell on credit terms. Experience data is solicited from all areas of NACM's membership; all members agree, as part of the membership agreement, that they will share their credit and receivables experience with members of the Association. There is usually input on a regional and national basis that comes together in a report that maximizes the amount and the value of the information.

Other sections of the NACM report summarize totals of reported trade experience in both dollars and percentages; an inquiry record lists previous inquiries on the subject business during the preceding 90 days; bank data includes customer history and loan information, plus information on SBA loans, attachments, bankruptcies, and other categories. NACM's National Business Credit Reports include information that is somewhat similar to that included in Dun & Bradstreet's Basic Credit Report. Reports are available by telephone, mail, or direct link between your computer terminal and NACM's central National Automated Database Center in Houston. To access these services, your company must be a member of the National Association Of Credit Management.

A major benefit of membership in the Association is the availability of membership in a broad range of regional credit groups. These groups usually meet for a business lunch on a monthly or quarterly basis. Members submit discussion information to their area office where it is compiled and printouts distributed at the start of the meeting. Later in the meeting, there is discussion of problem accounts, mutual and individual problems, and a general exchange of information. This is conducted under the monitoring eyes of an Association representative to ensure that there is no area of discussion that might be in violation of antitrust regulations. There is discussion regarding old accounts, new accounts, the return of a notorious industry jackal, recurring and new problem accounts, any sudden negative shift in the payments pattern of an established account, etc. The number of members who participate is important to the volume and scope of the information exchanged, but it does not negate the possibility of a meaningful exchange among as few as three or four members.

The worth of NACM and D & B reports hinges on the number of firms that furnish experience data on a regular and timely basis (for an effective update of reports), the quality of the skills of field and in-office reporters and analysts, and the depth and reliability of information pertaining to suits, bulk transfers, attachments, tax liens, SBA loans, bankruptcies, and other recorded data. D & B's ratings come down to the net worth of a company (a high of *AAAA* through a low of *E*) and the manner in which a business or company handles its bank and supplier obligations (1 is High, 2 is Good, 3 is Fair, and 4 is Limited and/or Poor). NACM lists all of the data it can gather, but does not make an effort to assign a credit rating. The judgment of risk is left to member credit managers.

Do not back away from a credit reporting service because you have limited credit management experience and do not know if the service is for your company. It is for your company if your company's sales and credit volume warrant it. Never allow yourself to slip into a "no professional growth" cop-out. Reports from both services are easy to read and easy to interpret. Guideline instructions are a part of your instruction kit, and should help you to phase them into the evaluation process quickly and effectively.

Credit Groups and Associations

Many regional or area businesses are unable to stretch limited budgets to accommodate the cost of membership in a national credit organization. For these firms, there is the option of a local, small-business group. Such groups are often organized and sponsored by the local chamber of commerce and, although they are not directed exclusively toward the problems of credit management, they offer a helpful alternative to the industry meetings sponsored by national credit organizations.

Locally organized and locally directed meetings usually address the general business needs and problems of the community of small business, and that's fine. When a credit manager is in a community that is not large enough to have an industry credit group, the next best thing is a group that includes a mix of industries and businesses. Do you have credit problems with some of your accounts? So do they. You solve your problems with one technique or another—and so do they. It would be interesting, and mutually beneficial, if you found out how these people, who are not professional credit managers, handle some of their credit problems. You can be a professional with years of credit management experience, but you can still learn something from the way others handle their problems. There is always the possibility that what you sometimes learn is that you never want to make a credit decision of such poor judgmental quality as the one you have just heard described. That fact in itself is worth the price of admission to almost any group meeting.

Whether the group is large or small, local or affiliated with a national organization, or more nearly represents a pickup group, confidentiality is the key admonition. At all levels of such meetings, the universal admonition should be that, whatever is heard or discussed during the meeting—or between credit management people at any other time—information received in confidence must never be repeated to a customer. A violation of this need for confidentiality not only has legal implications, but also is the most effective way imaginable to destroy the willingness of group members to freely discuss account experiences. Years spent nurturing a group, to the point where there is complete candor among members, can be destroyed with one careless comment.

Many industry credit groups will not accept owners who double as credit managers. When a credit group accepts an owner/manager as a provisional or probationary member, the question is whether his or her interest in belonging to the organization is the exchange of credit information and account experiences for credit management purposes, or the availability of information that he or she will try to convert into a sales tool or advantage. The question of motivation is so strong in the minds of many credit managers, that many groups and associations will not allow a firm to join a credit group, if the firm does not have a full-time employee credit manager.

The free exchange of credit information among members of a specific industry is extremely helpful. It is impossible for any one manager to be aware of every potential or emerging trouble spot in the company's business area. Every company or business should be a member of a local, regional, or national credit group or association—one whose primary focus is in your industry or area of business. If there are several similar businesses in your area or region, but there is no credit group, take the initiative. Contact other industry credit managers who would benefit from such a group and try to bring them into a formal, bylaws type of organization. Every member should benefit enormously from such a group.

Get all the help you can for yourself and for peer credit managers. Why should you be interested in helping the credit managers of competitor companies? You help them because, by doing so, you broaden the scope of the help that is available to yourself. When you are one of six, eleven, or twenty members of a credit group, you give information and experience data to others, but you have five, ten, or nineteen members of the group from whom you can obtain information. That is not a bad ratio of return.

When you first come together as a group, there will be doubts and apprehensions as to whether it will work. Fortunately for the members, the great majority of industry groups develop into long and mutually satisfying experiences. When there is the recognition that it takes time to build confidence in the integrity of your peers, any group can be a success.

Account Experience Form

The percentage of telephone calls to supplier references to get their input, versus the use of a cover letter with an attached form requesting credit experience, is probably no contest. It makes good business sense that it is heavily shaded in favor of telephone calls. Telephone charges are minimal when questions are organized, responses are short, but informative, and the call is well-managed. Not only is the cost of obtaining reference data minimized (telephone charges and the time of a credit department employee), but also the cost to the supplier is minimized. Preparing and mailing letters (and forms) of inquiry is a surprisingly expensive way to handle inquiries. The cost of labor is higher to prepare form letters, address and stamp two envelopes (one for a return reply), and seal and post them—and the foregoing does not take into consideration the additional number of days it takes to receive information when requests are handled in this manner.

It should be recognized that certain situations require the use of a form request. Offices in which there are very few employees or in which there is no designated credit person may not be able or willing to leave other duties to answer a telephone request for credit experience data. When the tone of voice of the person contacted makes it obvious that he or she is unwilling to respond orally or that your request will be handled at a time convenient to the person with whom you are talking, thank the person for his or her time and tell them that you will put an inquiry in the day's outgoing mail.

The cover letter (see Figure 3-10) and the form (see Figure 3-11) are shown as examples of how this procedure can be handled. When the Account Experience Form is returned to the sender's office, it should include all or most of the information requested. Whether the accuracy in reporting past-due balances—days past due, etc.—is as good as you expect will depend on the quality of the records from which the data was obtained, and the experience level of the person who is supplying it. A relatively inexperienced person may not know that three months before your request for information, the customer suffered the loss of a major receivable via the bankruptcy of one of his customers. The discount/prompt relationship reported by the supplier is diminished only slightly by the entry of open-credit balances at 30/40 days past due. These responses give no hint that the account may be about to pose a major collection problem—if not for the responding supplier, then quite probably for new suppliers who may extend credit.

This form has an additional plus. Whether it is or is not mailed to the applicant's suppliers, it is an excellent guide when information is gathered via the telephone. Start with the company's sales terms, then move down the list of sections until you have everything that the respondent can give to you. If that is 80 percent or better of what is on the Account Experience Form, consider the telephone call a success.

This form, when used in a sequence appropriate with others to be discussed, offers a well-balanced menu of what is needed to assemble all elements of the reference data into the form most useful for evaluating the credit worthiness of an applicant. What is the use for good credit information, from a variety of sources, brought into a manageable and useful form? Given the additional input of an experienced person to evaluate the data, there should be a high percentage of good credit decisions (see Figures 3-12 and 3-13).

Account Prospect List

Should you decide that Dun & Bradstreet's service(s) can benefit your company, your D & B Reference Guide offers a dimension that goes beyond its more obvious purpose of screening and evaluating the history of a credit applicant. It can be used to provide sales and marketing with lists of new account prospects whose credit ratings and years in business indicate that there would be no credit problem at a credit line compatible with the finan-

---

Account Credit Experience Form

Name of Account _____

Address_____   Contact_____

City and State_____

Sales Terms_____

Credit Balances:

   High Credit_____

   Open Balance_____

   Past-Due_____   Number of Days_____

Payment Experience:

   Discounts_____

   Disc/Prompt_____

   Prompt to Slow_____

   Slow _____ to _____ Days

   Slow _____ Days and Over

Evaluation of the Account:

   Excellent _____

   Good _____

   Satisfactory _____

   *Unsatisfactory _____

*If unsatisfactory, do you plan to continue selling the account?

_____

If the answer is "yes," will sales terms be on a secured rather than an open-account basis? _____

Your cooperation is greatly appreciated. Please contact the undersigned if this company can return the favor.

_____   _____
 Credit Manager   Date

Figure 3-10. Request for credit experience.

Attention: The Purchasing Manager

Ladies and Gentlemen:

This office forwarded via cover letter dated _____ one of our New Account Information forms. I expressed our appreciation for your order, and asked that the completed reference data be returned to this office at your early convenience.

We have not received the reference information, which could pose a problem with future orders in that we are unable to extend open-account terms until reference information has been combined and evaluated with other data.

In the not unlikely event that the first letter did not reach your company, another copy of the New Account Information form is attached.

Sincerely yours,

DYSAN CORPORATION

Cecil Bond
Credit Manager

enclosure

CB/dd

Figure 3-11. Cover letter.

cial strength of the company. A preliminary list of this type is not conclusive, nor is it a promise to your sales department that every account on the list could or should be sold to the level of the D & B rating. It is, however, a good indicator of which accounts should be acceptable credit risks, and at what approximate dollar figure a credit line might be set.

The same rules of confidentiality apply when dealing with the information in written reports that applied in the earlier scenario of a luncheon meeting involving a number of credit managers in an industry group. Under no conditions should any part of a report be repeated to the business or company about whom the report was prepared.

(Date)

Mary Carter, Credit Manager
The Bonilla Corporation
16531 Crenshaw Drive
San Francisco, CA 94120

Dear Ms. Carter:

This office forwarded an Account Experience Form to your attention
on __(date)__ with a cover letter asking the benefit of your experience
with __(company name)__.

Your company's position as one of __(company name)__ major suppliers is, as you can appreciate, a valuable source of information as we prepare to evaluate the account for a credit line.

If it would be more convenient to give us the requested information by
telephone or fax, please call the undersigned collect or use the fax number listed on this letterhead.

Your assistance is greatly appreciated.

Sincerely,

Frank Hanneford
Credit Manager

Figure 3-12. Request for return of new account information form.

The use of Reference Guides to prepare a list of prospective customers
for use by the subscriber's sales department is not a breach of confidentiality. Under this circumstance, it becomes a tool that is helpful in determining whether the subscriber company is getting the maximum amount of
business from its present sales territory. This is very important before there
is serious talk of expanding into a new territory. And when the timing is
right for moving forward with plans for extending the company's marketing area, the capability to preselect and prequalify prospective new customers is enormously helpful.

Prospect List

SIC (Standard Industrial
Classification) Code Numbers
51–41 Groceries, General Lines
51–49 Groceries and Related Products
51–82 Wines and Distilled Alcoholic
     Beverages
51–81 Beer and Ale

SIC Code	Name of Business	Location (City/County)	Business Established	D & B Rating

Figure 3-13. Prospect list.

To compile a prospect list that is similar in quality to the one shown in Figure 3-13, turn to the Reference Guide and the county, state, or region where your company indicates it would like to see growth. Determine, from the tables at the front of the Reference Guide, which of the standard Industrial Classification Code Numbers cover the types of firms who are, or who should be, interested in your company's products. Go down the columns of listings, pick out the applicable ones, and list them on the Prospect List form (including those firms whose ratings do not seem to qualify them for credit). Make an appropriate mark opposite the names of companies whose ratings seem to offer the strongest credentials (financial and longevity), then pass the list along to the sales manager for his or her information (if your company is large, send a copy to the financial officer).

This is an excellent way for a company or business to prescreen the pool of potential customers in a given area before there is any type of commitment. If the D & B review of potential accounts does not measure up to the number required to develop a successful territory, the time to know that fact is before money has been spent or human power has been committed. The Prospect List also has value in any company, large or small, where one salesperson covers a territory that is too large for one person and too small for two. A salesperson, who barely has enough time to see the company's established accounts, is not able to prospect the territory for additional accounts. The credit manager, or a member of the credit department staff, can use D & B's Reference Guide to check the territory for new account prospects. If the territory is fairly populous and commercially active, D & B's Reference Guide could supply enough new prospects to expand the current territory so it could be split into two. It might also confirm that the potential for opening a new territory is there for the taking.

Partnership

It is important to the security of a company's accounts receivable that the credit manager knows the type of business entity that the company is selling. Do you doubt that it would pose much of a problem? Look at this list of potential questions:

1. Is it a sole proprietorship?

2. Is it a partnership?

3. If it is a partnership, is there also a silent partner who might have liability in the event of business failure?

4. Is it a general partnership or a limited partnership?

(Date)

Mr. Leonard Carter, Controller
The XYZ Company
1348 Sherman Way
San Francisco, CA 94120

Dear Mr. Carter:

Let me first thank you for the order your company has placed with us. We appreciate the confidence in our products that this order represents.

It is our policy to process the first order or two from a new customer on a C.O.D basis. This is not a reflection on the creditworthiness of customers who are new to us. It is simply a recognition of the fact that we are new to each other and must be as prudent in our approach to open-account terms as we feel sure you are.

Please complete the attached Account Information Sheet (also the Resale Form), attach a copy of your most recent financial statement, and return the documents to this office in the enclosed stamped self-addressed envelope.
When the reference data has been processed, we hope to offer a mutually acceptable credit line on our standard terms of 2%/10 days/Net 30.

Sincerely,

Credit Manager

Figure 3-14. Thanking customer for first order, etc.

5. If it is a limited partnership, are the claimed limitations allowed by the statutes of your state?
6. If the business uses a "trade style" (also commonly known as a "fictitious name"), how do you penetrate the trade style to get partnership or company information?

7. Is your customer a division or a subsidiary of a parent company?

8. If it is one of these two, what should you know and/or be doing about customers who are in these various business formats?

9. What are the variables among the various types of partnerships and company structures that a credit manager should be aware of to give his or her company's receivables asset the appropriate level of protection?

If you have survived this flurry of questions, be relieved to know that they will be answered in the paragraphs that follow. Know the who, what, and where of a credit applicant or a customer who has a balance on your receivables aging report. Available protective devices are not uniformly applicable. This important area of credit and credit management is too frequently overlooked in the push to ship merchandise or to move too quickly into other areas of credit.

General Partnership

Do not spend a disproportionate amount of your time trying to memorize secondary points relating to partnerships. It is enough that you remember certain major differences and guidelines, and know where to get answers to the others. Most credit people have neither the time nor the legal training to seek answers to questions that can best be resolved by the company attorney, or as you become familiar with it, the National Association of Credit Management's *Credit Manual of Commercial Laws*. The manual is not a substitute for your company's attorney, but as you become more experienced in the credit management process, it should enable you to extract and apply various types of useful guideline material. With the help of this book, an appropriate level of experience, and the sources mentioned previously, you should have no difficulty gathering enough data regarding partnerships to make responsible decisions for your company.

Following are some of the responsibilities, benefits, and liabilities that are a part of general partnership:

1. It involves two or more people and is the most common form of partnership.

2. The Uniform Partnership Act defines rights, powers, and liabilities to general partners in a business or company.

3. It is a relationship of interlocking restraints, obligations, and ramifications.

4. It is not a valid partnership unless it includes everything that is in the definition of a partnership. It isn't a partnership—and there isn't partnership liability—if one or more of the ingredients is missing.

5. General partners generally have unlimited liability for the firm's obligations.

6. A general partner who withdraws from a partnership cannot terminate his or her liability until all people, companies, and businesses with whom the firm does business have been notified. The withdrawing partner must give appropriate notification to all interested parties.

7. "Silent partners" are silent only in the context of not identifying themselves with the firm or the general partners. They have the same unlimited liability for the firm's obligations as the general partners.

8. The acts of one general partner are the acts and the responsibilities of all the general partners.

9. They share equally in the profits (unless otherwise stated in their business agreement), and, unless the agreement states otherwise, they share equally in the liability for expenses and losses incurred by the firm.

10. Most states require the filing of a partnership certificate and also a fictitious name certificate if the firm name doesn't include one or more names of the general partners.

11. Individual assets of general partners are not exempt from creditor action if creditors have proceeded against the firm's property to satisfy liens and judgments and, after proceeding, there are still unpaid balances and obligations.

12. The death of a general partner means that the partnership is at an end, although surviving partners must then settle the affairs of the partnership.

13. Prior agreement among partners allows surviving partners to buy the deceased partner's interest in the firm at a previously-determined price (or one tied to a current evaluation of the firm's assets and liabilities).

14. Agreement for a buyout may be funded by a life insurance policy on the life of each partner.

15. The buyout agreement puts no constraints on cash flow, as it would if the surviving partners were using company money to partially fund the buyout. (The business is able to continue, but without the deceased partner's contribution of particular business, sales, or technical expertise. This loss could prove to be a problem and is something that the surviving partners, and the company's creditors, will want to monitor. Meanwhile, the deceased partner's estate receives the benefit of a full-value buyout of his or her share in the firm.

Limited Partnership

A limited partnership is virtually self-explanatory; there is no active role in the business, no contribution to partnership capital, and no personal liability for debts. The limited partner's liability is limited to the amount he or she invests in the partnership and, on the same plane with all partnership property, it is subject to creditor claims.

To assist creditors and other persons and businesses of interest to determine whether general partners also have one or more limited partners, many states require the filing of a limited partnership certificate. The certificate is signed by all parties, contains the firm name, its principal place of business, the type of business, the names and addresses of partners (which are general partners and which are limited), the amount of capital put up by each, and the period of the partnership. There are other requirements and nuances, all of which you can get from your company's attorney or in NACM's *Credit Manual of Commercial Laws.*

Other points of interest regarding limited partnerships are as follows:

1. A limited partnership, unlike the liability of general partners, continues only for the period stated in the limited partnership certificate.

2. Limited partners do not usually participate in the management of the business.

3. Their pay is interest on the money they have invested, plus a percentage of the profits.

4. If the firm loses money, the limited partner's liability is the amount of his or her capital investment.

5. The death of a silent partner usually does not terminate the partnership.

6. To determine whether a general partnership has one or more limited or silent partners, include a question regarding that issue on the New Account Information Sheet.

7. Include also a question (on the New Account Information Sheet) regarding the existence of a buyout agreement in the event of the death or incapacity of a general partner, and how the agreement is funded: life insurance, treasury certificates, company stock, etc.

Some of these questions and statements may seem unimportant as you gather information pertaining to a firm that is well-established and has no obvious financial problems. What you cannot know, unless you take the time to investigate, is the particulars of the partnership—the questions that suddenly take on enormous importance if there is a problem or a death within the partnership. A credit manager must know in advance the particulars of the partnership and that the company's accounts receivable balance will not be in jeopardy because there was insufficient advance planning.

Parent Firms/Divisions/ Subsidiaries

Of the many firms that your company sells, do you know which of them are divisions, subsidiaries, or parent firms? It is extremely important that you know the type of business entity your company is selling—or is about to sell. If you do not make a conscious effort to get that information—and use it during the credit evaluation—your company could eventually face an entirely different sales and collection situation from the one you thought it was getting into.

A parent firm is a company that stands alone. It is solely responsible for all of its actions and decisions. There are no "deep pockets" from which it can get money to support itself when business declines. If the company has financial problems and the banker turns away (often the only "deep pocket" to which the firm can turn), then the problem can be critical for the parent, the divisions, and the subsidiaries. If the parent company fails, or makes a Chapter 11 filing, the assets of divisions and subsidiaries, along with assets of the parent firm, become hostage to credit claims.

A division is a part of a company, and is not a company in its own right. It is a specific part of the whole. It might be the ball bearing division of an automobile manufacturer, or it might be the dairy products division of a food chain, but it is not a company in its own right. It does not have control over its own destiny.

Many divisions handle their own payables. It is cause for concern, however, when a division that has paid satisfactorily becomes increasingly slow in processing payments. The supplier should look for indications that the parent is syphoning too much money out of the division. This may be because the parent is losing money in its own operations, or there may have been a change in ownership of the parent, with the result that there is a new attitude toward the division and the suppliers who service it. Before your company sells a division, do your homework on the company's relationship with its suppliers. It could save your company a great deal of trouble down the road.

Selling a subsidiary can be an excellent piece of business, or it can be a tricky and dangerous relationship. A well-prepared report from a commercial reporting firm should alert you to the fact that your potential customer company is a subsidiary. The report should also include the parent company's name, headquarters' location, and principal type(s) of business. A possible problem is that you may not be able to get financial information (bank, financial statements, etc.) on the subsidiary company. Many parent companies incorporate the figures from subsidiaries into the parent company's financial statement. Many parent companies also have a policy of not divulging financial information on their subsidiary companies.

If you have determined that the prospective customer is the subsidiary of a financially strong company, remember that this financially strong parent could turn its back on the subsidiary in its time of financial need. A parent company may not be legally obligated to come to the financial aid of a subsidiary. Some parent companies accept responsibility for the debts of their subsidiaries, and others do not. Whenever there is a question regarding the financial stability of a subsidiary, inform the subsidiary that your company is unable to offer credit terms unless the financial officer of the parent firm furnishes a letter to your company stating that the parent company either accepts payment responsibility for all obligations incurred with your firm by the subsidiary or accepts such obligations to a specific dollar limit and termination date. If the parent company's financial status is good, such a letter will give "deep pockets" protection to your receivables interest in the subsidiary company. A parent company should have no corporate or legal problem with your request for a letter of guarantee. When a parent company gives such letters in support of a subsidiary's customary business activity, rulings on the legality of such letters have been almost uniformly positive. Such letters normally qualify as being "in support of the subsidiary's customary business activity."

A letter, such as the one just described, does not give your company the same level of protection from other claimants as does a Uniform Commercial Code Filing, but this letter is a different type of protection for a different type of problem. The letter from a parent firm is intended to ensure that a financially strong parent will not abandon a failing subsidiary, and that the parent will accept responsibility for monies owed by the subsidiary.

Assumed or Fictitious Names/ Trade Styles

A trade style should not be a screen created by an owner or a company for the purpose of deceiving suppliers and other creditors. The people who operate under a trade style or a fictitious name should know that they have specific legal obligations to those individuals, partnerships, or business firms with whom they do business or might do business. Following is a look at the more important aspects of dealing with "assumed or fictitious" names.

1. People who transact business under partnership or assumed names (trade styles, etc.) are required to file a certificate detailing that information.

2. The statutes of most states provide for fines and/or imprisonment for failure to comply with this legislation.

3. The designated place for filing the certificate varies from state to state. Some states designate the office of the Clerk of the county in which the company has its principal place of business. Others specify the County Recorder, Office of the Town Clerk, Clerk of the Circuit Court, etc.

4. Partners in a business operating under a fictitious name should check for filing requirements with the County Clerk or the County Recorder of the county in which the headquarters of the business or firm is located.

Compliance is a simple matter of completing and filing the appropriate form. Any person who does not accept that responsibility is not worthy of the trust that suppliers must have if they are to offer credit terms to the customer.

Statutes That Regulate Trade and Antitrust

Congress has, for many decades, attempted to limit the wrongful concentration of economic powers in the hands of the few to the competitive disadvantage of the many, who are smaller in size, marketing capabilities, and financial strength. To summarize quickly: Congress passed its first legislation to control these matters with the Sherman Act in 1890; this was extended in 1914 when the Clayton Act became law. Robinson-Patman was enacted in 1936 as an amendment to the Clayton Act, and those of us in Credit have been guided by it as we have attempted to avoid any brush with "restraint of trade."

Between these pieces of legislation and amendments to existing legislation, Congress has been able to do a decent job of regulating trade or business practices through its use of constitutional powers to regulate interstate commerce and foreign trade. A level playing field for all participants has always been the goal of record; nothing is ever as perfect as it could be, but the goal has a high percentage of attainment.

The Sherman Antitrust Act—1976

The purpose of the Sherman Act is to eliminate the elements that contribute to the restraint of trade—any collusions, conspiracies, etc., that can be used to monopolize trade among the states or with foreign countries. The Sherman Act does not attempt to regulate or restrict legitimate growth; it is not in place to penalize the entrepreneur who, through hard work and more efficient production and distribution methods, can sell a comparable product for less than his or her competitors. The Act does not attempt to tell an entrepreneur that the excellent service provided to customers by his or her company is an element of unfair competition because it exceeds what competitors are giving their customers. It is not growth-restrictive, when growth is the result of everybody competing fairly and openly in the same marketplace.

No penalties can be invoked unless there is a violation involving inter-state commerce; a climate of free and unrestricted trade is the essence of the Sherman Act. Given the premise that your company is not interested in trying to create a monopoly, restrain trade, or engage in other practices for-bidden by the Act, it is free to sell to whomever it can. If, however, a person or company is charged under the Sherman Act and found guilty (it is a felony), an individual may be assessed fines up to $100,000; corporate defendants may be fined to $1,000,000. Although the pockets of some defendants may be deep, there is also the matter of a possible sentence of three years in prison.

(Antitrust and trade regulation laws are extensive, complex, and are the province of attorneys who specialize, or who have an appropriate level of expertise, in this and related areas. The Sherman Act goes on and on—page after page after page—so what has been outlined here is a very super-ficial skimming of the deep water represented by this and other regulations pertaining to the various Acts that comprise this area of law.)

The Robinson-Patman Act

This Act addresses the legality of any attempt by a person, company, or busi-ness to discriminate in price between purchasers of commodities of like grade and quality when one or both is engaged in interstate trade, when commodities are sold for use, when consumption or resale is within the United States, or where discrimination might have the effect of decreasing the amounts and levels of competition.

The Robinson-Patman Act seeks to protect businesses and companies against the acts of individual competitors whose discriminatory practices might injure competitors and restrict or affect the climate of free competi-tive trade, and give small businesses a level of protection adequate to pro-tect them from the sometimes questionable tactics of larger competitors.

Price Differentials

It is customary in many types of business for the seller to offer buyers dis-counts for quantity purchases, the rationale being that there is almost always a lower per unit cost to the seller when the buyer orders 100, 200, or 500 units of an item versus 5 or 10. The delivered cost per unit of a large order is usually substantially less than for a small one, so a quantity purchase generally entitles the purchaser to a unit price that reflects the seller's lower costs. A seller might also have one price structure for sales to manufacturers or processors, another to wholesalers, another to retailers, and still another to consumers. Neither prohibited nor expressly approved under Robinson-Patman, the conditions under which these discounts are granted must be monitored on a continuing basis.

Sellers may demonstrate a "good faith belief" that they are offering a customer a price concession to meet the same price offered by a competitor. It is a legitimate defense to the seller if the method(s) used or quantities bought by a purchaser create a saving for the seller in the cost of goods sold. The seller is entitled to reflect part or all of that saving in the price he or she charges the customer. The basic rule is that not all differences in costs (manufacturing, sales, shipping, etc.) can be used to justify a discrimination in price among different purchasers of the same goods. Cost savings are applicable in prices offered only as those differences result from differing methods or quantities of sale or delivery.

Federal Trade Commission Act

This Act adds additional substance to the Sherman Act, the Clayton Act, and the Robinson-Patman Act, in that it is the broadest of the antitrust and trade regulation laws. It gets into areas such as false advertising (of food, drugs, etc.), or any other advertising practice which operates with the intention of deceiving the public.

Violations not covered in any of the Acts listed previously are covered by the FTC Act, such as false representations, the disparaging by one seller of the products of another, and other acts of unfair competition. The FTC will take action against one or more practices of a company, and file suit to stop those practices and to indemnify groups or classes of people who have been injured or charged unfairly over a period of time. This may result in a negotiated settlement in which the alleged offender does not admit guilt or wrongdoing and is allowed to stop the challenged practice without penalty or prejudice. Other violations may, as mentioned above, become charges filed in federal court by the FTC against the alleged offender for a finding (guilty or innocent) and punitive or other damages. The Federal Trade Commission has the exclusive authority to move to enforce the FTC Act and to seek damages for alleged violations.

The Commission must determine, before issuing a complaint charging unfair competition, whether the person, business, or company is using methods that constitute unfair competition. If the determination substantiates the charge, the Commission is still not authorized to proceed unless the interest is specific and substantial, and the proceeding would be in the public interest. When a set of circumstances does not fit the criteria, it falls short of being an actionable cause for the Commission.

Another act that can be related to the daily activities of credit management people is the Antitrust Procedures and Penalties Act, which attempts to decrease the number of "consent degrees" for antitrust complaints with a public statement outlining the proposed settlement, followed by public commentary before there is disposition of the case. Others acts include:

1. The Antitrust Act of 1976 (This Act attempts to control mergers of companies whose combined size would threaten to create a monopolistic situation. It permits a state attorney general to file suit for damages and gives the federal government additional powers of disclosure in litigation over antitrust matters.)

2. State Antitrust Laws (These laws attempt to sort out the areas of authority of state and federal antitrust laws. They help to prevent an overlapping of powers or an assumption by state or federal authorities of powers that do not belong to them.)

3. Fair Trade Acts (This legislation allows the federal government to move against price fixing by manufacturers or processors of products, resale price maintenance agreements, general maintenance of fair trade practices within the various states, and federal law for interstate transactions, etc.)

The Exchange of Credit Information

This is such a volatile area for credit management and department personnel that it demands special attention—particularly as antitrust laws apply to credit groups or to the exchange of credit information between two or more credit grantors.

The exchange of credit experience data among credit management personnel plays a key role in decisions that are made as to when and how much credit a company might extend to a prospective, new, or current customer. But as credit information is being exchanged (over the phone, at a one-on-one lunch, at a credit group meeting, etc.), there are rules that must be observed to ensure that what should be a simple exchange of experience and/or information does not become something that takes on elements of restraint of trade. There can be no "group agreement" (explicit or implied) to withhold goods from a customer(s) whose account is delinquent with all members of the group or whose account has been placed on cash or C.O.D. terms. Credit managers will certainly be influenced by the combination of their own knowledge and experience and that of other credit managers in the same trade group—and that's fine. That is individual judgment made on the basis of the best and widest base of information available to the credit manager. Nowhere in the scenario of a decision that has been reached independently is there a shred of restraint of trade.

Competitors or members of a credit group may not set or maintain uniform prices, discounts, or terms or conditions of sale. Practices of this nature fall under the jurisdiction of the Fair Trade Act and carry the potential for some very heavy fines. Your credit group must also recognize the potential for trouble if a qualified applicant is refused membership in the group, although questions regarding the integrity of the applicant and whether the applicant could be expected to adhere to the rule of confidentiality, as it relates to information shared at meetings with all or some members of the group, is a relevant concern when considering an application for membership.

Some excellent credit groups have been severely damaged because the rule of confidentiality—the cornerstone upon which every exchange of information pertaining to customers or potential customers is based—was violated by a member in a moment of anger or thoughtlessness. No person who seeks information from other credit managers regarding the paying habits, reputation, etc., of a customer or prospective customer should repeat any of that information to the subject. Credit management people must know they can trust other credit managers, as individual managers or as members of a credit group, to protect the confidentiality of information and the sources of information.

When the fabric of individual or group trust is shredded, the effectiveness of the group is gone. In my own experience with credit groups, I have seen one area group of 27 company members become apprehensive, tentative, and, in many instances, unwilling to share anything derogatory about an account—all because one relatively new member had thrown a piece of negative information at a delinquent customer that could have had only one supplier source. Did the group survive? It was almost a year and a half before the group approached the earlier level of trust that had made it so mutually effective.

Credit organizations may protect themselves and their membership by requiring that applicants for membership are members of a credit association, that the applicant business or company is actively engaged in selling product or goods to customers in the territory or industrial/business classification represented by the credit group, that the applicant has good standing in the business community, and that the applicant company does a gross annual business in excess of a qualifying floor-figure. There is also the very important requirement of an experienced, full-time credit management person—one who can be expected to understand and to protect the confidentiality of sources of information.

Remember that lists of delinquent accounts, which are frequently exchanged or discussed at credit group meetings, must not include persons, businesses, or companies whose normal payment pattern is within terms or on an acceptable basis, and whose only current problem may be a disputed charge or charges. These customers do not belong on a list of past-due or delinquent accounts, and any negative or disparaging remarks about a charge or a balance that the customer views as a valid problem is totally out of line.

It is important that meetings of credit groups—whether a regularly scheduled monthly luncheon meeting or some other format—should have an agenda for each meeting. A staff member of the sponsoring organization (National Association of Credit Management, local Chamber of Commerce, etc.) should take minutes of the meetings, which will serve as a reference source should a question or a challenge from an outside source threaten to evolve into a legal action against the group or an individual member.

The confidentiality that members of a credit group agree to maintain as group members and individual credit professionals is applicable also to credit reports available to members from commercial credit reporting organizations such as Dun & Bradstreet, the National Association of Credit Management, etc. Reports offered by these organizations are compiled from data furnished voluntarily by subscribers, nonsubscribers, members, and nonmembers. Reports issued to a subscriber on request are considered to be privileged information; if, however, these reports are given general circulation, any negative or defamatory information must be verified before the report is issued. Can credit groups revoke the membership privilege of a group member? If there is a provision in the bylaws that relates to specific situations, membership can be revoked for a violation of that bylaw. The key to the legality of the provision is that it must be applied uniformly.

When there is an alleged violation of antitrust laws, there must be provable or demonstrable evidence to substantiate the allegation. The plaintiff must be able to prove that an agreement existed among group members before the subject information was shared either orally or in written form. What about a group acting in unison? The allegation must have legs to stand.

A Challenge for the Securities and Exchange Commission?

An example of the dilemma that can immobilize a credit manager is the scenario of a hypothetical company, Celebrity Games, Inc. Founded by three men who left other companies in a related industry, Celebrity Games received 42 percent of its start-up and support funding from a firm of venture capitalists. The company product incorporates various elements of advanced technology, has been aggressively promoted in the media, and has enjoyed strong, early-market appeal. So what is Celebrity Games' most obvious and self-destructive problem? The company did not go into the marketplace battleground with a credit manager. In fact, they did not hire one until accounts receivable had reached $8 million—with more than half of that total ranging from 45 to 90 days past due!

Fred Fuller is an experienced credit manager who has come to Celebrity Games from a semiconductor company that has sales in excess of $100 million. His first day at Celebrity is a shocker. There are only 17 credit files on the 132 active receivables accounts. Perhaps the most startling fact is that past due accounts—some of which have past due balances of $100,000 to $250,000—are still being sold on open account terms, despite the fact that no payment has been received for weeks! Has anyone been attempting to contact these accounts for payments? And why hasn't someone had the good sense to stop open account shipments to these accounts until, one, a substantial payment has been received and, two, credit references (bank and supplier) have been received and evaluated? The answer is that management has placed the lowest priority possible on the quality of customer accounts (accounts receivable) and the highest priority on increasing sales and shipments.

After two days of evaluating the situation—trying to get a handle on what is in the files versus the enormous amount of essential bank, supplier, and credit reporting agency information that isn't there—Fred picks up his yellow-ruled pad and takes his problems to Bill Sharp, Vice President of Finance.

"Bill," Fred tapped his forefinger on several pages of notes. "This is a disaster. This is the most out-of-control operation I've ever seen!"

Sharp had known Fred when the two were in the semiconductor industry. He leaned back in his chair.

"Come on, Fred. You've only been here two days." He shook his head. "That isn't enough time to brand us an out-of-control company."

"Oh, I differ with you on that one, Bill." Fred turned several pages, glancing at the notes on each. "I've been able to find 17 file folders out of a possible active account total of 132." He looked up. "Seventeen file folders, Bill, and not one of them has anything in it that pertains to the evaluation of the account as a good or a poor credit risk."

Sharp leaned forward.

"That's why you're here, Fred. We need to get a handle on these accounts to help prepare us for a public offering of the company's stock."

"How can you be thinking of a public offering when the biggest chunk of the company's assets are in such terrible shape?" Fred shook his head. "I didn't have to be here more than an hour to know that you aren't generating more than a trickle of the company's monthly cash-flow requirement from these receivables."

"We have $7 million from the venture capitalists that we're using to help us in that area." Sharp nodded. "But you're right about the monthly contribution from accounts receivable."

Fred put the note pad on Sharp's desk.

"I want to put a hold on shipments to accounts that are past-due 30 days and over—or at least until we can get some credit experience data from suppliers, banks, and a credit reporting agency."

"I don't think we subscribe to a credit report service."

"No, and I want to subscribe to one today, preferably to both D & B (Dun and Bradstreet) and NACM (National Association of Credit Management)."

Bill nodded.

"I don't have a problem with that. Order what you feel is necessary." He paused. "A hold on past-due open accounts is something else, something I'll have to clear with the CEO."

Fred's eyes widened.

"There aren't any acceptable alternatives, Bill! If we don't hold orders, or go to a $2 for $1 or a $3 for $2 "cash versus merchandise" formula for reducing past due balances, those balances are going to get bigger and older."

"I hear what you're saying, but approval for anything that would slow the company's rate of quarterly sales growth is beyond my authority." Sharp glanced at his watch. "I've got a meeting in five minutes, Bill. I'll get back to you later today or tomorrow on the accounts receivable problem."

Fred stood up.

"I don't like to put it this way, Bill, but I need the backing of the company to do the job that I was hired to do." He turned toward the door. "If I'm to be denied the authority necessary to apply the most basic controls to the management of the company's credit accounts, then the company is wasting its money on me, and I'm sitting here spinning my wheels."

Bill nodded.

"We'll work it out, Fred." (End of scenario.)

It is obvious that Fred Fuller must have the support and the authority to do his job. The question that immediately arises is how far down the road toward financial gridlock has Celebrity Games gone? If there is full-and-accurate disclosure regarding the state of the company's receivables, will the SEC approve a public offering? If there is no approval for a public offering, how long can Celebrity Games continue the charade of a strong and a healthy growth pattern, when it is based upon sales to customers who provide receivables of limited liquidity? And how long can Fred Fuller accept a situation in which solid principles of credit management are questioned by, or even unacceptable to, the very executives who should be most responsive to his recommendations?

Unless Celebrity Games Company reverses its philosophy suddenly and dramatically, it is inevitable that the company will peak quickly, then slide into a pattern of declining sales and increasingly strong pressure from creditors. There will be an increase in past-due balances, a continuing decrease in the liquidity of accounts receivable, the inevitability of a Chapter 11 (a buyout of a badly faltering company), and the potential for substantial investor losses. Too bad.

Entrepreneurs should be rewarded for their willingness to take risks, but creditors and investors should not be put in the position of losing their money because owners and venture capitalists are unwilling to shackle greed and build instead a company based on sound business principles, not excluding personal and corporate integrity. The credit manager? In situations of this type, he or she is destined to be an ineffective, helpless pawn in a game that is driven by a syndrome of questionable personal and corporate ethics. Fortunately, the majority of entrepreneurs, managers, and corporate CEOs are working to build their companies, not to put them on the road to self-destruction. In that conventional environment, the credit manager (small business, entrepreneur, large company) can make strong and meaningful contributions to the success of the business or company.

4

Consolidating and Evaluating Credit Information

It has been said that gathering good information is the basic step in the sequence leading to a solid credit decision. If that is true, and experience confirms that it is, then knowing how to use that information is of equal importance. You can be a world-class collector of information and data, but if you cannot interpret and apply it, then collecting it is pointless. If it is to be useful, you must be capable of taking data from various sources and systematically assembling it into a helpful bank of quality reference data.

There is no insurmountable complexity in the gathering, evaluating, and decision-making process. A person should have some experience before he or she begins making credit decisions, but owners of small companies are not experienced and have no experienced person to guide them. Circumstances force them to make decisions for their small companies, just as credit professionals are making bigger-dollar decisions for the larger companies. People at every level of the decision-making spectrum must, however, be capable of taking information and data from various sources, systematically assembling it into a helpful bank of quality reference data, and using it in an effective manner.

The title of this chapter goes to the core of what must be done with information that has been gathered. There is a sequence that must be followed, if there is to be a point where all of the decision-making tools are in place. This chapter provides the format for taking and refining credit information to the point where a person with a reasonable level of experience should make good credit decisions.

The "Right to Know"

A prospective customer, who is unwilling to give your company the reference data necessary to properly evaluate the account, should not be offered a credit line—or offered more than a token amount of credit. If the requested information is finally received, evaluate it and make your credit decision. Do not, however, succumb to pressure from the applicant or from your sales department to make a credit decision that cannot be justified on the basis of reference data received and verified. If a large order is released before credit information has been received and evaluated, the company's exposure is an unjustified risk that, on completion of the evaluation, could quickly elevate itself into the category of high risk. It is irrelevant that the applicant seems to be doing well, which makes the image of stability very tempting. Do not be lulled into compromising your standards for credit approval or your procedures for qualifying an account. Unless the expected level of purchases is so low or so infrequent as to make the normal evaluation procedure a costly and somewhat meaningless procedure, the application should be rejected.

Example: The focus of this hypothetical example is on a person who has had three high-volume floor-covering dealerships in various parts of a state or region over a period of 10 or 12 years. He is notorious for impacting each market area with prices so low that he has made a competitive shambles of regional or area marketplaces for legitimate members of the floor-covering industry. He buys large quantities of carpeting, gradually builds up large past-due balances, strings his supplier accounts to unacceptable aging limits, liquidates heavy warehouse inventories for cash, files for bankruptcy under Chapter 11 of the Bankruptcy Act, and ultimately is discharged as a bankrupt. He then disappears for a year or more.

Nearly two years after the last bankruptcy, a new floor-covering retailer surfaces in another section of the same region or area. The front man for the company is not the person mentioned previously, but he has experience; he has been associated with successful and unsuccessful companies; he has been known to engage in some borderline practices; he offers an aggressive style of merchandising that contrasts with the slower pace of others in the area. A major manufacturer, who has been looking for an aggressive outlet in the dealer's area, accepts the account with a minimum of background checking and risk evaluation. (A major manufacturer can occasionally take this risk; a small company cannot.)

About this time, your company is approached for a credit line. You know the business is two months old, but you send a copy of the New Account Information Form and ask for a copy of the company's opening financial statement. There is an in-house order for what would be a substantial dollar amount for an established account, and there is pressure from the applicant for you to release the order. You are not swayed by telephone assurances that "we've got plenty of money to handle our accounts. There's no problem." You don't release the order on that type of self-serving assurance. The applicant's spokesperson is urged to complete the application and return it promptly.

The next day, a friend in the trade calls and mentions that his salesman called on the account. As he was leaving the office he saw "the person" drive around to the back of the warehouse. He immediately asked the man, who had represented himself as the owner, if "the person" was involved in the company. The reply was to the effect that "he's a friend and he's helping set up some things, but he has no interest in the company." You contact the agency in your state that handles the approval and monitoring of corporations, find that "the person" is not listed as a partner or a corporate officer, and you wait for the New Account Information Form.

The form finally arrives with a copy of the opening financial statement. Supplier references are the previously mentioned major supplier, and one other (both sold for less than two months), with the major's account ten days past due and the other six days past due. The bank says that the company's opening-and-average balance has fluctuated between a "high 4 and low 5 figures" (something between the low side of eight-to-ten thousand and ten-to-twenty thousand on the high side). The bank has extended no line of credit and the account has leased all vehicles, warehouse equipment, and office fixtures. The internally prepared financial statement indicates that the business was started with a net investment of $19,000.

Does your company bite? You do not! Trade talk becomes increasingly persistent that "the person" is spending more time at the store and, although there is nothing to link him with the company, his involvement is evident. Three times he engineered a bankruptcy that bilked his suppliers of hundreds of thousands of dollars, but he was clever enough to provide no hard evidence upon which a district attorney could build a case. When will the fourth bankruptcy occur? At some point down the road after "the person" assembles all of the pieces for a fraudulent bankruptcy—one that cannot be proved.

Don't allow your company to be victimized by a seasoned scam operator such as "the person." Your company might make a few dollars in the early stages of his game, but if you allow receivables totals to become bigger and older, your company's ultimate loss will be "the person's" gain.

A different interpretation of "the right to know" involves what you should know or consider before you sell one or more of the biggest firms in the country, or an agency or department of federal, state, or local government.

It seems incongruous to say that selling one or more of the biggest companies in the country could present problems, but problems are a possibility when the level of sales to one or more major companies would represent a substantial percentage of your company's total sales. It isn't a question of whether the giants will pay; the question is, "When will they?" Your smaller company would be justified in welcoming one of the huge corporations to your aging report; you could not afford, however, to allow that corporation to be casual with payments for your product(s). Forty-five or fifty days from invoice date might not be a problem for a major supplier who has no cash-flow problem, but your company might have a serious cash-flow problem if payments from your casual giant did not arrive until 15, 20, or even 30 days after the due date. Take a close look at the promptness record of the giant company before you commit the liquidity of your company to it.

Payments from government agencies can range from prompt to sporadic to very slow, and the flow of bureaucratic questions, delays, and red tape can be very testing. Unless your company's product(s) or service has the potential for nothing more than a minimal problem situation (not high tech, etc.), locking a high percentage of your business into a relationship with an agency of the government could lead to some new and potentially unwelcome business and financial experiences.

Can any kind of a case be made for a small business to take on a relatively high percentage of government business? Of course. A company with a strong cash flow and a product profit margin that would not be unfavorably impacted if receivables payments were to extend 15, 30, or 45 days beyond terms might do quite well. The concern is not whether the receivable will be lost, but how soon will it be paid? If payment within or close to terms is not a cash-flow consideration, and profit margins are good, then a strong case can be made for taking on some government business or some business with one of the giant corporations.

The Account Information
Analysis Sheet

This form is used to bring together the bits-and-pieces of information gathered from the suppliers, banker, and the financial statement. It consolidates the data in a format that allows a side-by-side comparison of the experience of three suppliers, the bank's experience and comments, the financial strengths and weaknesses as indicated by the financial statement, and data from credit-reporting agencies.

When there is good supplier data on every line of the Account Information Analysis Sheet (see Figure 3-3), the next step is the evaluation and decision-making process. If the credit analyst (usually the company's credit manager) has a level of experience that corresponds in scale with the material he or she is being asked to evaluate, the resulting credit decision should be solid. When references one, two, and three on the Account

Information Analysis Sheet have each sold the account successfully for one or more years, and when high credit, open balances, and past-due figures are in line with sales terms, there is good reason to be satisfied. Add to the above a good bank relationship and a financial statement that has no obvious flaws, and the person evaluating the account data should be able to grant an appropriate credit line.

If those are not the facts, and the person doing the evaluation is looking at supplier reports of balances 25 to 50 days past due, that is not good. Add to the supplier reports a bank report that reflects chronic past-due loan payments, and the credit manager or analyst is faced with an account that might be acceptable for a small first order and a small credit line, or perhaps no credit line at all.

Assigning a credit line is the culmination of a process of evaluation and utilizes an important section of credit procedures. Everything relevant to the gathering, consolidating, and evaluating of information is important. No segment of the account evaluation process should be slighted; each segment or step is equal in its importance to the others. The first step, after the reference data has been consolidated, is to look for a payment pattern in the responses received from the applicant's suppliers. Each supplier sells a customer to a credit high that might be higher or lower than others, but the customer should pay all suppliers on a reasonably equitable basis, regardless of whether they are large or small. If one or two suppliers are the majors and they have reported account payments as "prompt to slow 30 days," you (the owner or manager, or the credit manager or analyst) must determine whether the prospective customer pays other suppliers within a similar time frame as it relates to their sales terms.

If you find that there is no consistency in payment treatment from major suppliers to other suppliers, it means that your applicant keeps major suppliers happy by paying them within their terms (or past due a very few days), while paying other suppliers much more slowly. If sales to this prospective customer would put your company in the "slow pay" group, it could be a major factor in determining the direction of your credit decision. It is not unusual for a customer who is experiencing tight cash flow to first take care of the major supplier(s), but the accounts of other suppliers should not be abused to support this policy.

There may be a considerable difference between the bank's experience with your credit applicant and the payment pattern reported by most suppliers. Some suppliers may report a pattern of slow payments, while the bank is reporting that the customer pays within the terms of loan agreements. Businesses protect the source of cash to supplement internally generated cash flow. Most companies need occasional or frequent help from the bank to meet their monthly cash-flow requirement. To ensure that there is no problem, they take good care of the banking relationship.

Without ongoing bank support, the cash shortfall could trigger problems that might quickly deteriorate into a crisis of survival. It follows that the endorsement the bank gives this customer should be as strong or stronger than the endorsements of supplier respondents.

An applicant's case for a credit line should be bolstered with CPA prepared financial statements (preferably from audited data) and should show an acceptable level of profit from sales. Report data from a credit reporting agency (Dun & Bradstreet or NACM) is usually very helpful, but not always available. An experienced credit manager will, at times, question whether an assigned rating is justified by the report data. You might not have the experience of a seasoned professional, but your knowledge of an applicant company might give you good reason to question the rating.

The offset to this question, regarding the accuracy of a rating, is that you give weight to your own knowledge of the business or company. Mentally deduct something from the higher rating and add something, if your knowledge of the account tells you that it is too low. Information available to the analyst may not be as complete or as current as it should be, so the quality of his or her rating could be impacted adversely. When you know the companies to whom you sell—their backgrounds, the history of their owners, and their reputation in the trade—and your decision does not agree with Dun & Bradstreet's rating, you are not automatically wrong. Evaluation of data is a matter of interpretation, experience, and judgment. Two people could use the same reservoir of information and arrive at surprisingly different ratings. There should, however, be no major difference in the decisions, unless one of the people evaluating the data has more or less experience than the other, overlooks something, or makes a judgmental error.

You should have a high interest level in any account that, over a period of a year or more, shows a supplier payment record of within or near terms. When you are evaluating such an account, be sure that the average high-credit experience of the reporting suppliers is within the range of the credit line requested from your company. If the figure is comparable and there is nothing derogatory in the input from the bank, suppliers, credit reporting agencies, or financial statements, you should offer the applicant a credit line adequate for his or her needs, but somewhat below the high credit reported by other suppliers. You do this because you prefer to begin a credit relationship by offering a new account a credit line or limit that your best judgment tells you is not close to your company's maximum for the account. Unless the first order is going to immediately push the limit to or above your "best judgment" maximum, try to open it below the highs being sold by others. Only when the first order represents a unique opportunity to develop what your company hopes will become a solid account should you consider giving the applicant a credit line as high or higher than the highs reported by other suppliers. It is also prudent to remember that you are not, and probably will not be, a major supplier of the applicant firm. Unless your product(s) fill more than a support gap in the activities or in the product lines carried by the applicant, there should be no valid reason for the credit line you authorize to approach those of the applicant's major suppliers. If the requested credit line is unusually high, let the applicant know that you are pleased to have the opportunity to process the application, but you are surprised at the size of the requested credit line, since your product line is a support product (if, of course, this is correct), rather than one of the major product lines. Why, you might ask, do you need an opening credit line that seems more suited to what fits your needs from a major supplier? Press diplomatically, but firmly, for a satisfactory answer. Your company wants to sell your product, but any major deviation from what you can easily or immediately understand should not be allowed to pass without some questions.

A "Credit-Worthy" Customer

The ingredients that qualify a customer (or a prospective customer) as "credit worthy" should provide a good, strong balance. A minor weakness here or there that is offset by one or more strengths should balance out an acceptable credit risk, if the requested credit line is appropriate to the total worth of the input from all reference and reporting sources. A checklist of the ingredients follows:

- Is the business well established?
- Is it a growth, static, or declining situation?
- Is new technology, or technological development, a threat to the product line(s), services, etc.?
- If technology is important to the continuing success of the business, is there an ongoing and effective program of R & D?
- Does the customer operate in a growth-oriented area, an area of limited growth potential, or an area in economic decline?
- Is the business well managed? Are management and support people experienced and competent?
- Is cash flow adequate for the level of business?
- Is there strong short- and long-term bank support?
- If the business extends credit to its customers, does the credit management person have the experience for his or her level of responsibility? (Remember that your receivables are only as good as theirs.)

- If there is a heavy investment in inventory, is it justified by geographic, market, or other conditions?

- Is receivables aging in line with sales, sales terms, and the company's need for internally generated cash flow?

- Is internally generated cash (receivables collections) adequate for normal business requirements, or is an abnormal level of bank support used to supplement cash-flow needs?

- Is there a good balance of management, financial, manufacturing, and marketing skills?

- Is there enough depth in the various areas of management so that the loss of one person would not adversely impact management's strength?

- If the business is a sole proprietorship or a partnership, what is the age (or ages) of the owner(s), and what is their health and probable (if older) retirement? These are all important factors. If the death of one partner removed his or her area of expertise from the business, would it run as effectively? Could the surviving partner afford to buy the level of expertise or skill provided by the late partner?

- Is there a surviving partner buy-out arrangement, funded usually by life insurance or a combination of a life insurance policy and a form of deferred payment program to the widow, widower, or the estate?

- Is there supplier continuity, and do suppliers generally express satisfaction with the relationship?

- What does the banker say about the customer? If the banker has granted loans for capital equipment and operating funds, is he or she satisfied with the agreement and the customer's performance?

Take a close look at any negative or questionable responses before you assign a credit line, but accept the fact that an overwhelming majority of favorable answers to the above questions is about as good as most credit accounts will get. The list of questions is comprehensive enough to flush out almost any major flaw in the applicant's business.

How Much Weight to Growth/ Stability Potential?

One of the intangibles that should be included in the criteria for passing judgment on the risk factors that encumber any applicant for credit (one order or an ongoing line) is the potential for growth—and the question of stability.

When a business or a company is very young, there may be very few tangibles (money, inventory, property, etc.) to commend it to a prospective grantor of credit. The owner, partners, or owner/managers in a close-held company may be qualified to run the business, and they may have a product that is innovative, inexpensive, has marketplace appeal, and is a non-luxury item, but owner equity in the business is very low when compared with the investment of creditors (bank, suppliers, etc.). There is, in this venture, a stronger element of risk because the company must rely heavily on borrowed money (the bank) and the forbearance of creditors, whose account balances will remain consistently in the past-due categories of 30 to 60 days.

If your company is a supplier (manufacturer or distributor), is in a highly competitive, low-profit-margin industry, and is being subjected to its own problems of growth, the primary question is not whether your company should accept the risk factors posed by the account. The question is whether you can afford to accept the account. Regardless of how bright the future may look for this particular applicant, if the purchase level would put a strain on your company's cash flow, could your company afford to assume the extra risk, plus the possible reduction in the flow of cash versus the strong probability that this well-managed prospective customer will become a long-term major winner?

This is opportunity in its embryonic stage. Your company is looking at what is a ground floor opportunity to become a key supplier in the customer's pattern for growth. The potential is exciting, a bit awesome, and more than a little intimidating. So much depends on the business plan and the business philosophy of your own company. If it is slanted toward a pattern of steady but conservative growth—a growth that does not involve more than basic risk taking—then this applicant's needs may not be a fit for your company. If, however, your company is well-funded and cash flow would not be impacted to the point where it would affect payment patterns (payables, etc.) or the cash-flow requirements of short- and long-term planning, the carefully monitored risk posed by accepting the account could be manageable.

Risk should always be minimized. In the above situation, the risk should not be considered acceptable unless other factors in the process of evaluation and decision-making have been clearly defined and are above question or reproach. Only if the company's financial position and business philosophy are compatible with the applicant's requirements should the supplier accept the account.

The "He's All Right" Syndrome

Many people learn, to their dismay, that the charismatic man or woman who was so successful at getting investors to hand over large sums of money was totally dishonest. Every credit grantor must realize, too, that personal and business vulnerability can be even more serious and damaging when the talk is about relationships with people who are much closer to us than strangers.

The terms "acquaintance, friend, good buddy" are not synonyms for the term "good customer." When a credit manager lulls himself or herself into thinking that procedures can be bypassed—checking bank and supplier references, etc.—because he or she is dealing with a friend or an acquaintance, the painful fact is that these people have the potential for being very hazardous to the health of a company's accounts receivable. As a credit manager, when you ship that one-time order, or when you set the account up on a continuing credit line that allows it to get several smaller orders before individual balances begin to become past due, the story has already taken a familiar turn. Acquaintance, friend, good buddy? Perhaps. An opportunist who is using a personal relationship to his or her advantage? It isn't pleasant to contemplate such a situation, but it happens frequently enough to warrant a warning.

Do not skip any procedural steps. Check the credit references of friends or acquaintances as thoroughly as you would the references of an out-of-the-blue stranger. The one time that you fail to follow your procedures could be the time you set the company up for a serious collection problem —or a loss. The only way you can have presale knowledge of how a business or company handles supplier relationships is supplier information, credit reports, and banker's comments. If "he's all right" or "she's all right" is indeed a solid article—a good friend in every sense of the term—then asking him or her for some preshipment reference data will be applauded as good business practice. If your request prompts seemingly uncharacteristic grumbling and testy asides, a look at your friend's relationships with suppliers could make you very happy that you did not exclude any of the customary steps from your account evaluation.

To illustrate how evaluated credit information might be applied to three hypothetical account situations, the following three examples will give the reader an insight into how three different but basic accounts might be handled.

New Account Situation—Example 1

Your company is a small supplier and your maximum credit line is $2500. The subject credit applicant has been in business for three years and releases no financial information.

First Reference: Sold two years to a high credit (H/C) of $1500. The customer consistently pays 30/40 days slow with recent slowing of payments to 45/50 days. $980 is open with $390 current and $590 slow to 48 days.

Second Reference: Sold two and one-half years to H/C of $850. The customer, until recently, paid 20/30 days slow, but is now paying 30/45 days slow. $720 is open with $340 current and $380 past due to 42 days.

Third Reference: Supplier of primary product line. Sold three years to H/C of $2300. $2300 is open with $640 current and $1660 past due 30/46 days.

The Banker: Speaks somewhat guardedly regarding the account and its prospects. Has a medium five-figure credit line secured by accounts receivable, merchandise, and capital equipment. Facilities (land and buildings) are leased. Says the account has had sales and management problems that, to date, do not seem to have been resolved. The banker has been working with the account (restructuring loan agreements, etc.) to ease the considerable strain on cash flow.

The Questions: You are asked to approve an order for $380 with additional orders to follow over the period of the next two weeks. The requested credit line is $1500, based on projected product requirements.

- Do you approve the $380 order on credit terms?

- How do you evaluate the request for a $1500 credit line given the input of suppliers and the bank?

- If you decide not to sell the account on open terms, or at a credit limit below the requested $1500, under what conditions might you sell the account? If you do sell the account on open terms, what is your rationale?

The Answers:

- You do not approve a $380 credit sale.

- Each supplier reference reports slow to slower pay and a deteriorating account situation. The banker's report strongly supports the experiences of the suppliers and offers nothing to encourage thoughts of a turnaround. No incentive is strong enough to involve your company at a credit level of $1500. This account would be a collection problem from the moment your products left your warehouse.

- If the order would involve special purchases of materials or ingredients, special packaging and labeling, etc., get an advance payment large enough to cover your costs of manufacturing the special product; perhaps utilize the alternative of 50 percent of the dollar amount of the order if that percentage will cover your manufacturing costs. Then what about the balance? Instruct the freight company or your driver to get the balance that is still due (cashier's check or bank money order if there has been any report of a problem with company or personal checks), and be sure to notify the customer to have payment ready in the amount and form you specified when the delivery is made. Should you accept payment later that afternoon, the next day, or the next week? No way! The driver (yours or the freight company's) is to get the customer's payment in the specified form and amount when the delivery is made, or they are to return the order to your company.

The thought uppermost in your mind should be that this is not a customer situation that you can develop into something good, profitable, meaningful, or relatively safe. When a prospective customer who has these types of problems is not favorably inclined to play your game by your rules, don't touch the account.

To convert Example 1 into an acceptable credit situation would necessitate changes in the input of the suppliers and banker. If the past-due figures submitted by the three suppliers were to each lose 20 days, the resulting past-due average of 10 to 20 days per account (down from 30 to 48 days past due) would be acceptable. Changing the banker's input to indicate that the account handled loan obligations as agreed—and with no apparent sales, financial, or management problems—would effectively eliminate that problem area.

With no derogatory reports from the suppliers or the banker, your decision on the $380 credit sale would change to a "yes," and you would give your approval to the applicant's request for a $1500 credit line.

New Account Situation—Example 2

Example 2 directs your attention to a credit application from a two-person partnership. It is a close-held corporation with each partner owning 50 percent of the stock. Because it is not a publicly held company, the partners do not choose to release financial information. The applicant firm is well known in the trade and has been in business for approximately nine years.

Your firm is not the same small one profiled in Example 1. It is larger, offers sales terms of Net 30, and extends credit in the area of $5000 to $7500 to several accounts.

First Reference: Sold for years to a H/C of $3600. The customer usually pays within terms, and never more than 10 days past terms. $950 is open and nothing is past due.

Second Reference: Sold for about a year to a H/C of $5200. Customer pays within terms. There is an open balance of $2840, and nothing is past due.

Third Reference: Sold for approximately four years to a H/C of $4480. Supplier states that there have been a couple of slow-pay situations, but those were the result of some problems with merchandise. The account usually pays within terms to a maximum of 10 to 15 days slow. $2100 is open and nothing is past due.

The Banker: States that he helped the account with a capital equipment loan of $150,000 when the business was started nine years ago. Payments have been as agreed and the bank has subsequently provided the company with a standby "cash-flow" credit line of $50,000 (not currently being used). The banker is very satisfied with the relationship and expresses a high regard for the ethics and business skills of the two partners.

Additional Information: One partner is the company president. He handles administrative matters, financial and company planning, is 46 years old, married, and spent 15 years as general manager of a large regional company in the same business. His personal record is clear.

The second partner is the company's vice president of sales. He is 41 years old, also married, and had 12 years of related experience (as a division sales manager in the same business) before the current partnership was formed. His personal record is clear.

Questions: The first order is $1480. The customer expects to buy between $2000 and $2500 worth of product each month.

- Will you approve the $1480 order on credit terms?
- How do you evaluate the request for a $2500 credit line?
- If you decide to assign the account a credit line of $2500, what is your rationale?

Answers:

- You will approve the $1480 order on credit terms.
- An evaluation of the supplier reference data and the banker's statement make it clear that you will approve the $2500 opening credit line.
- The applicant firm is obviously solid and well managed. In addition to the excellent supplier and bank reports, your $2500 credit line is well within the maximum offered by other suppliers.

New Account Situation—Example 3

This example uses the same set of facts as those outlined in Example 2. The two partners and their close-held company are unchanged—unchanged until a major problem occurs that periodically confronts managers in the real world of credit situations.

The facts as they relate to your company, the credit grantor, are the same as stated in Example 2. Your challenge is how to deal with a radical change in the internal structure of the customer company.

The Facts: Health reasons make it mandatory that the company president (one of the two partners) sell his 50 percent of the business. The other partner agrees, with the bank's support, to buy his partner's share of the business for $200,000—$75,000 to be paid immediately from bank-advanced funds and the other $125,000 in the form of a secured note (UCC filing) against the business. Payments are to be $2500 per month for a period of approximately five years (including interest charges, etc.).

The Questions:

- What, if anything, will this do to the business?

- What are some of the potential dangers that did not exist prior to the dissolution of the partnership?

- What is the major danger? Is it financial, or is it in the balance of experience and skills, now greatly diminished via the loss of one partner?

- The business has been netting between $35,000 and $40,000 a year for the past three years. Will a payment of $2500 a month ($30,000 a year) put too severe a strain on it?

- How would this change (these changes) influence your thinking regarding your credit line for this firm?

- Would you immediately downgrade the credit line? Would you continue the same credit line, but monitor the account more closely? Would you decide that the succeeding partner must know what he is doing, so you assign the account no more attention than you previously gave to it? Would you panic, leave your company, and take a job in a distant state under an assumed name? (If the latter, please consider another line of work.)

- If account balances slowly begin to stretch out on your aged trial balance report, what do you do to protect the interest of your company? Do you do any of the options mentioned in the above paragraph? What other suggestions or options do you have?

The Answers:

- Obviously, the banker does not think that the combination of the above problems poses a major danger to continuity of the business, or he would not advance $75,000 to enable the surviving partner to gain control of the business.

- If the business has been experiencing steady annual growth, and the projection for continued growth is good, the question of whether one partner can continue to successfully operate the business has been partially answered.

- The second part of the answer is not as obvious as the first. There will be no replacement for the partner who was the company's president—its financial and business planner. How will the purchasing partner deal with the absence of these very necessary strengths as he attempts to project financial needs and plan steps and plateaus of growth consistent with the capabilities of what is now a different company? How will he avoid the dangers that could result from stretching beyond the capabilities of the business to handle these situations?

- You would probably not downgrade the credit line, but you would monitor it carefully for at least a year after the departure of the one partner (the company's president). You would definitely not increase the credit line until the company's performance under the surviving partner's management indicates a level of continuity that spells survival first, growth second.

- If the account begins to lose ground and balances begin to slip into new and unacceptable aging areas, you will want to contact the account (before it has slipped more than a few days), discuss the transitional problems with the surviving partner, check with peer supplier credit managers for their input, and decide whether to reduce the credit line. Also decide whether you should go to some formula for account balance reduction (have your driver pick up a check for one and one-half times the value of each new order when he or she delivers it, or hold orders until the account pays the oldest open balance(s), etc.).

Never make a premature, panic-induced decision. Unless account balances begin almost immediately to stretch into new past-due aging, take no precipitous action. First, do a rapid evaluation of what might be only a temporary situation. If your discussions with peer credit managers indicate the beginning of a downward trend, that is the time to reduce your credit line and move for faster collection of past-due balances. What do you do if the decline becomes more rapid? You must then go to a program that requires lump sum payments at short intervals, plus C.O.D. payment for current deliveries of product or services.

The decisions that are made after credit information has been consolidated and evaluated are among the most important of your responsibilities as a credit management person. Credit decisions do not have to involve thousands of dollars to be major decisions; the size and the financial condition of a company will dictate whether the decision is a major one. A credit decision that involves an order for two, three, or five thousand dollars worth of product is as important to the financial welfare of a small company as is the two, three, and five million dollar order to the financial welfare of a bigger business or company. At their respective levels of business, neither company can afford to misjudge the quality of a new account, or the ability of an older customer to suddenly (and successfully) become more aggressive while seeking to grow more rapidly. Each company could suffer the same percentage of receivables loss if the customer failed to pay.

Is such a loss more difficult for the small company to handle or for the larger one? It depends on the financial strengths of the two companies. A large company that is overextended because of a management-driven desire to grow could find itself with a serious cash-flow problem. The small, well-financed company, for whom the two or three thousand dollar order is a large one, could be in a better position to absorb such a loss with no loss of momentum or sudden cash-flow problem. Individual company situations will dictate the seriousness and the ramifications of these types of losses.

5

Assigning/Reviewing Credit Limits

A cross section of input from a variety of sources has been gathered and evaluated. That input has been consolidated on the Credit File Control Sheet (see Figure 5-1) and the final step in the evaluation process is at hand. It is now time to reject the applicant or to write a figure in the Credit Limit box on the upper right-hand corner of the Analysis Sheet.

Pause a moment before you write that figure, and as a part of your future pattern for analyzing and assigning credit lines, refer again to the Check List form (A "Credit-Worthy" Customer—The Ingredients). Compare the information compiled on the Account Information Analysis Sheet against the Check List form guideline questions. If the check list of what you should be looking for versus what the applicant has to offer is on target, a credit decision should not be difficult.

The process of reviewing credit lines is an important step in the process of acquiring and maintaining accounts that will provide receivables of acceptable quality. Reviewing credit lines is an ongoing process. When accounts are new to a company, the credit manager should monitor them more closely than accounts with which there has been a continuing and satisfactory relationship. Experience with new accounts should be updated no later than 90 days after an opening credit line has been assigned, and updated a second time at six months after the opening date. Unless there is a change in the payment pattern of an account, or something is brought to the credit manager's attention during a conversation with a sales rep, another credit manager, or the account's banker, the cycle of reviewing credit lines can be extended to intervals of six months.

The previously mentioned time frames are suggestions only, not inflexible rules. Individual accounts will dictate when and where there is a need

Figure 5-1. Credit file control sheet.

Credit File Control Sheet

Identification

Name (and/or trade style): _____

Billing/Payments Address: _____

Documents in File

Credit Application (Date) _____ Application Received _____

Contacted _____

Security Documents _____ UCC Filing: Date _____

Location _____

Credit Reports   (Report Date) (Update Requested) (Update Received)

D & B _____

NACM _____

Other _____

Bank Reference _____

_____

Trade Reference _____

_____

Financials, Business Plan, etc. _____

_____

Comments (Territory Representative) _____

_____

Authorization

Credit Requested:

First Order _____

Anticipated High Credit _____

Figure 5-1. (*Continued*) Credit file control sheet.

Credit Line:

Amount _____ Special Instructions _____

_____

_____

by _____ date _____

Experience Analysis at _____ : _____

_____

_____

Experience Analysis at _____ : _____

_____

_____

for closer supervision and more frequent updating of experience and reporting agency data. Be sure to include a call to the banker when reviewing an existing credit line or evaluating the account for a requested increase in the line. An update of the bank's experience is important, as is any change in the customer's payment pattern, a decrease or an increase in the bank's loan limit for this customer, or any other change in the bank's attitude or relationship with the customer. Most bankers can be quite helpful to the customer's suppliers which, unless there has been a dramatic downturn in the business and financial fortunes of the firm, should enhance rather than diminish the quality of the risk.

One of the best reasons for a review or update is when an account wants to increase purchases of a product to a figure above the present credit line. Your company (or any company) should be receptive to new business or more business from good, current customers. The one thing you do not want to do is to step back from the legitimate needs of an account on the upswing, when every indicator points to a well-managed growth cycle. These accounts offer the best opportunity for safe, solid growth for your company and theirs. To abandon a promising new account relationship would also be foolish, unless the current update indicates that your company is the only supplier whose account is not being handled properly. If the business is experiencing a problem, but there is no indication that it has or will slip into a serious down trend, you still might successfully sell the account. Monitor the gradual loss of business over several months with the emphasis on maintaining close payment control of all open balances, including the open balances of other suppliers.

The Credit Limit Update Form (see Figure 5-2) is designed to recap data currently applicable to accounts. It deals with the aging of receivables balances during the three or six months of your experience with the account, the most current D & B rating, and the date of the most recent financial statement. Base your comments on aging and payment experience described previously, then add the amount of the credit limit requested and the reason for the increase. The core for any consideration of a credit line increase is this reason. A properly managed firm will not offer a frivolous reason. If the reason is not related to growth, a special customer order, an expansion into a new territory, or some equally good reason, then you must question seriously the motivation for an increase in the credit line. If account balances are beginning to string out across the receivables aging report and most of the original or current credit line is already represented in current and past-due balances, do not add new dollars to those already extending deeper into the past-due columns of your aging report. Never allow your company to be put in the position of a secondary source of financing for any customer, unless it is a prearranged, short-time or one-time agreement. Should you give a qualified account a credit increase for a good reason? Absolutely. Should you give an account a major credit line increase for much less than a good reason? It is not a good idea.

Temporary Opening Credit Line

There are a number of reasons why an account should be assigned a credit line that, in your cover letter, should be identified as a "temporary opening credit line." Some of those reasons are as follows:

1. A first order for the applicant is in-house and must be shipped before credit experience data can be received and evaluated. Although the order is several hundred dollars in excess of the limit occasionally released before credit data has been received and evaluated, the company has been in business for several years. In this instance the procedure would be to make two or three calls to suppliers, and check the D & B rating. If the rating is good and the one or two suppliers have sold the account for a year or more, have sold at or above the amount of your company's order, and have had a satisfactory experience, you will probably release the order on standard credit terms. Send the customer a letter to thank him or her for the first order, and set a temporary credit

---

Credit Limit Update

Customer Name _____ Account Number _____

Present Limit $_____ Aging as of _____

Date Approved _____ Current $ _____

Approved by _____ 30–60 $ _____

                                       60–90 $ _____

                                         90 Plus $ _____

D & B Rating _____ Balance $ _____

Date of Last Financial _____ Last 6-Months Sales $ _____

Terms, Aging, and Pay History _____

_____

_____

New Limit Requested $_____ By Date _____ By Whom _____

Reason for Requested Change _____

_____

_____

Recommendation _____

_____

_____

Amount   **Approval**

_____ By _____ Date _____

_____   _____   _____

Next Review Date _____

Input to System by _____ **Date** _____

Figure 5-2. Credit limit update form.

line/limit for the amount of the order. Let the customer know that the credit evaluation will be completed promptly and that your company will try to accommodate the credit line requested. If the applicant did not request a specific amount, let him or her know that your goal is a mutually realistic figure.

2. The credit department is not able to complete a credit check before a small in-house order is due to be shipped. The company has been mentioned favorably at industry credit meetings, and the size of the order is well within the dollar limit for first-order credit releases for which a credit line has not been set. Notify the customer by telephone (and a letter similar to Figures 5-3 and 5-4) that you are releasing the order and setting a temporary credit line (of the amount), and that it will be adjusted when the credit evaluation has been completed.

(Date)

Name of Account
Street Address (or P.O. Box Number)
City, State, Zip Code

Dear Mr. (Ms.) _____

This is to confirm the temporary credit line for your company of $5000, which I mentioned during our telephone conversation earlier today.

The processing of account data is not complete, but there is enough good information so that I am able to offer your company this credit line. When processing has been completed, I expect that the opening line will be somewhat higher than $5000.

Your order for $825 worth of products has been cleared and should be delivered on the date specified in the purchase order.

Please contact me if there is ever a problem.

Sincerely,

Credit Manager

Figure 5-3. Temporary credit line.

(Date)

Company Name
Street Address (or P.O. Box Number)
City, State, Zip Code

Dear Mr. (Ms.)_____:

Thank you for your prompt response to our request for credit references and credit reference data.

We have assigned your account a temporary credit line of _____ on our standard sales terms of _____. Our account experience will be reviewed at the end of 90 days, and if our experience and your product requirements indicate the need for an increase, we will hope to do it at that time.

Your interest in our products is greatly appreciated. We anticipate a long and a mutually rewarding relationship.

Sincerely,

Credit Manager

Figure 5-4. Temporary credit line (different format).

3. The applicant has placed an order for $15,000 worth of product or services. A credit decision must be made almost immediately if the arrival date requested by the applicant is to be met. Your company's temporary credit limit for accounts whose screening process is incomplete is $2000 to $2500, with variations based on the obvious quality of the account or the presence of questions that could diminish the quality of the account.

　　Contact the customer by telephone. Explain that you do not have enough experience data from references to clear the full amount of the $15,000 order. Ask if the first order can be shipped in three increments of approximately equal size and at intervals of seven to ten days. (This will enable you to receive and evaluate more experience data from suppliers before the second part of the order must be released.) The customer accepts this temporary opening line.

4. The credit policy of your company is based on rapid growth. Maximizing sales is the priority of your company's top management, which means that the standards by which your department judges applicants for credit are much less stringent than those at companies whose business plan is much more conservative.

A floor covering company has been in business for less than one year. They have opened four stores during the past nine months and are running full-page, price-slashing weekly newspaper ads. You question how they can be making a profit. They contact your company with an opening order for $25,000 worth of floor-covering products, with talk of future monthly purchases in the area of $35,000 to $50,000. The firm is moving so fast that there is no accurate handle on their current financial status and some cloudiness regarding the handling of current trade account balances; if scattered reports of slower payments become a trend, will the account become a collection problem before the end of another six months?

The pressure for sales forces the credit department to approve the $25,000 order on Net 30 terms. To provide some protection for the company's receivables balance, you tell the customer that the release of the $25,000 order is a temporary credit line. Whether it can be continued will depend on how promptly the customer pays the open balance. If the evaluation of the account reveals that the credit limit can be raised to a figure above $25,000, it will be done as the need arises and if accounts receivable balances are not allowed to go beyond a maximum of 30 days past due. If the evaluation indicates that the temporary credit line of $25,000 is several thousand dollars above what experience and the facts of the business warrant, then you must make your case for tightening credit standards with the company's top management.

Rapid growth may be the goal of some companies, but even the most driven of company executives pales at the thought of a receivables loss (a bad-debt loss) that is large in the context of the company's annual sales and net profits. And when the company executive is reminded that a major bad-debt loss reduces profits, even the most aggressive CEO has been known to have second thoughts regarding certain accounts.

Notifying the Customer

Enough good customers is the indispensable ingredient that can make a business a success. If your company does not have enough customers, the fact that your company would have been brilliantly managed is irrelevant. If customers are not there in adequate number, no combination of management skills can do more than sustain a struggling firm for longer than a minimum length of time.

The treatment a credit customer receives from the person who handles credit decisions has an important impact on how he or she perceives your company. Every company can use as much good customer relations input as it can get. The credit manager or a credit department associate can help the company's image in the way problems are handled and by the cooperation and spirit of helpfulness in other areas (sales, shipping, etc.) that could adversely effect the company's relationship with the customer.

The customer should be notified promptly when there is a pending in-house order that is tied to the processing of a New Account Information Sheet. When the order has a release or a shipping date that does not allow enough time for the credit department to receive and process experience data from the applicant's suppliers, every effort must be made to expedite enough information to make an informed decision. Contact the applicant company or business by telephone, then confirm what was said in the telephone conversation with an appropriate piece of correspondence (see Figure 5-5). It is particularly important for the credit manager to make every effort to save the account if he or she has been unable to approve the credit line as requested. If the credit evaluation indicates that your company can offer a $5000 line of credit instead of the $8000 requested, your public relations and negotiating skills must be focused to arrive at a mutually workable credit line. Perhaps the customer did not realize that a $5000 credit line, when combined with prompt payment of outstanding balances and a well-planned and monitored program of shipments, is adequate for current needs. It is one of the credit manager's responsibilities to work with the customer and the company's sales department to create workable options in lieu of an inflexible "No."

When credit lines have been assigned, you should enter them on a Credit Lines control sheet (see Figure 5-6). The sheet provides for the account's assigned number, name, and location of the account, the date the credit line was first assigned, the amount assigned, the date of the last review, and the amount of the current credit line.

This document enables the credit manager (and credit department personnel) to determine quickly and easily which accounts are due for a review, how long it will be before others should be reviewed, and, in the instance of an account that seems to be experiencing a change in the pattern of payments, whether the present interval between reviews of three or six months is too long. This form—Credit Lines—is the efficient way to maintain data relevant to the monitoring of your customers' credit lines.

(Date)

Name of Account
Street Address (or P.O. Box Number)
City, State, Zip Code

Dear Mr. (Ms.) _____ :

It is my pleasure to advise you that we have set an opening credit line of $5000 for your account. This should not be construed as a maximum figure for use over the long-term, but rather an opportunity for our two firms to become better business acquaintances before we consider increasing the line.

Please call if I can assist you in any way. We greatly appreciate your interest in our product(s) and anticipate a mutually successful long-term association.

Sincerely,

Credit Manager

Figure 5-5. Permanent credit line.

The Data— Reliable and Complete?

When a credit manager reaches the point where a credit decision is about to be made, there must be more than just an assumption that the reference data, the bank information, the financial statements, and the credit reporting agency reports are reliable and complete. There must be a level of confidence in the data that is equal to, or surpasses, the total number of the company's asset dollars (receivables)—dollars that will be committed on the basis of the collected data. The credit manager must know, however, that dollars are being committed not only on the quantity of the collected data, but also on the quality of that data (see Figure 5-7).

How does a credit manager determine whether data is reliable and complete? What does he or she do to determine the quality of the data? There are no precise standards for making such a determination, but there are reasonable criteria for determining the reliability and completeness data you are about to use (see Figure 5-8). Ask yourself some of these questions:

Credit Lines					
Account Number	Name and Location	Date Originally Assigned	Date Originally Assigned	Date Reviewed	Current Credit Line

Figure 5-6. Credit lines.

dy/an Dysan CORPORATION

CREDIT DEPARTMENT
(REFERENCE VERIFICATION DATA)

DATE: _____

CUSTOMER NAME: _____

ADDRESS: _____

BANK REPORTS: _____

_____

_____

_____

SUPPLIER #1: _____

_____

_____

_____

SUPPLIER #2: _____

_____

_____

_____

SUPPLIER #3: _____

_____

_____

_____

D&B RATING: _____

NEW ACCT. INFO. SHEET REC'D: _____   DATE PROCESSED: _____

PROCESSED BY: _____

FOR INTERNAL USE ONLY

Figure 5-7. Reference verification data. (*Form courtesy of Dysan Corp.*)

Intradepartment Memo

To: Department Personnel

From: Credit Manager

Subject: Processing New Account Information

1. Review your holding file every Friday afternoon.
2. Pull all file folders that are 10 days or more older than the date on the New Account Information form.
3. Pull all file folders for which you have received either *(a)* a bank response and one supplier reference response or *(b)* no bank response but two supplier responses.
4. Give me the file folders in the category covered by paragraph 2 (above) each Monday morning. Give me the file folders in the category covered by paragraph 3 (above) as rapidly as they meet minimum processing requirements (*a* and *b* in paragraph 3).
5. Credit references are to be contacted by telephone whenever possible, and as rapidly as possible. If telephone numbers are not listed on the New Account Information form, but street and city information is given, reference requests should be mailed promptly to the listed companies.
6. If you receive a New Account Information form that includes reference names, but no telephone number or city or street information, contact the sales representative and have him or her obtain the missing information.

These instructions are to be followed without change unless change is authorized by me.

_____   Date _____
(Credit Manager)

Figure 5-8. Intradepartment memo (processing new account information).

1. Does the information received from one supplier seem more negative (slower pay, etc.) than that received from other suppliers?

2. Is the supplier who furnished the negative information a competitor of your company—one who might lose some or all of the business it does with the customer if you assign the account a credit line?

3. Have you had difficulty getting specific High Credit information ("I'd have to go back and check. It varies a lot from month to month."), Open Balance information ("The open balance includes some pending credits—and I don't think this aging report includes one payment and a couple of invoices."), or Past-due information ("We've never had any really serious problems with the account.").

4. Do you know the company's credit manager? If your two companies are part of the same industry, does the other company belong to the credit group for your area or region? Does he or she contribute experience data and share with other credit managers information regarding accounts of mutual interest to members of the group?

5. If you received an incomplete response to a mail inquiry from one of the applicant's references, were you able to get the missing information with a follow-up telephone call? If not, did the reference give an acceptable reason for withholding the information, or was a reason given for why the information was not available when you asked for it before?

6. Having stated that the information you use to set credit lines and to make other credit decisions must be totally reliable and complete, are you satisfied that every reasonable step has been taken to ensure the integrity of the information? That for purposes of making credit decisions, the information you have is reliable and complete? If you are at that point, then make your credit decision.

The Data—Incomplete and/or Suspect?

When the above heading is put in the form of a question, there is a certain amount of overlap between data that is "incomplete and/or suspect" and data that is "reliable and complete." Data is quite often not in one category or the other, which can cause any number of problems for the person who needs to rely on it as the cornerstone of a decision or as the key part in a decision-making process. Although a credit manager must ultimately go with his or her belief that data is either acceptable or unacceptable ("reliable and complete" or "incomplete and/or suspect"), there is, in the final analysis, the need for data that is reliable.

(Date)

The XYZ Company
1400 No Such Boulevard
Anywhere, California 00000

Ladies and Gentlemen:

A review of the information in our credit file indicates a need to upgrade our decision-making data.

The following list pinpoints information that was either not requested when your account was opened or has become outdated. In order that we may do the best possible credit job for your company and ours, it is important that we promptly receive the indicated information.

_____ Current Financials (Statement of Income/Profit and Loss)*

_____ Trade References (three major suppliers with whom you are currently doing business)

_____ Bank Reference (name, location, telephone number, and bank officer most familiar with your account)

_____ Business Plan

*This important information will be treated in strict confidence.

Please address the requested information to the attention of the undersigned.

Sincerely,

Credit Department

Figure 5-9. Upgrade information in credit file.

Information or account data that is incomplete and/or suspect can pose a variety of questions and problems (see Figure 5-9). Data from one supplier is incomplete? If that supplier is unable or unwilling to give you the missing information, will you be able to flesh out your requirement with data from one or more of the other suppliers? How reliable is your experience data from the applicant's suppliers if the business has changed hands within the past one to three or four months? The experience that suppliers had with the previous owner(s) is of no value in the context of how new owners may handle the company's obligations. The new owners may have extended themselves to the financial limit to acquire the business, and servicing interest and mortgage payments will be their first priority for a long period of time. What about the company's suppliers? They are probably much closer to 30- to 60-days past due than the pattern of payments within or near-terms under the former owners.

The credit manager who finds himself or herself suspecting that data received from one or more sources is inaccurate—whether somewhat or grossly—has a serious problem. Data that is suspect cannot be used as a cornerstone upon which to build a decision, and it cannot be blended with reliable data without risking a flawed base upon which to make the credit decision(s).

What to do? What is there about the data that makes it suspect? Is there one specific item to which you can point or is it a combination of things? If the person or company that furnished the possibly flawed data to your company has no reason for doing so, try to isolate the error or the basis for your suspicions. If, after reexamining the data and comparing it with data reported by other suppliers, you find that there is a major inconsistency or a pattern of inconsistencies, call the credit manager. Do you have legitimate concerns regarding the experience data that has been given to you? Relate your concerns regarding the variance(s) among the payment pattern this supplier reports and the more current payments experience reported by the other suppliers. Does this supplier give the customer special terms on certain items or types of products? What about special terms on the purchase of seconds, overruns, or discontinued items or lines? Is the pattern of slower pay with this supplier the legitimate result of a variation from regular terms? Is it actually a special agreement between the supplier and the customer that does not constitute a variance from an acceptable payment pattern?

These are some of the legitimate reasons why experience data might indicate major variations in the way a customer handles two or more supplier accounts. Unless a credit manager searches for an explanation of the obvious differences by probing beneath the surface, serious question relating to the quality of the data could remain unanswered.

Data that is incomplete should not be accepted without question or without an effort being made to get the source to provide appropriate corrections or additions. A business or a company that should be a source of information is occasionally uncooperative. Nothing that the credit administrator may say or do will move the recalcitrant company to share its credit experience with another company; this is an 1890's mindset in a 20th century world. When this happens, rely on data supplied by other sources.

And what if you have data that is suspect, but the reasons for the suspicions cannot be clearly defined? Work on it. Approach the problem from every angle, and try to come up with some good answers.

Remember that the quality of almost every credit decision is tied to two things: the depth of the credit administrator's knowledge and experience plus the key ingredient of "reliable and complete" evaluation data.

Credit Limits—Improperly Assigned and/or Reviewed

To assign a credit line or a credit limit is the proverbial "piece of cake." Anyone can do it. Anyone? Of course. The problem surfaces almost immediately, however, when the person who assigns credit lines does not have enough experience to do the job properly. Receivables balances that should represent no problem (because they were properly screened and a realistic credit line was set) begin to slide into past-due columns during the third and fourth months. The number of past-due balances begins to escalate and aged trial balance reports begin to take on the appearance of a jungle—a jungle of potential bad-debt accounts. And as the company's receivables picture becomes darker and darker, the company's cash flow decreases from a flow to a trickle.

Can all of these dire happenings be the products of some improperly assigned—or reviewed—credit lines? Absolutely. Any company that finds itself sinking into the type of morass described above should take immediate corrective action. Does the person who has been assigning credit lines have a level of experience appropriate for the size and credit activity of the company? The percentage of good credit decisions should be high, but the person who assigns credit lines and monitors the receivables balances must be prepared to handle his or her company's level of credit activity. Unless there is excessive and unrealistic pressure from the highest echelon of management, a review of the credit administrator's credit line assignments should show that virtually every account falls within acceptable parameters for receivables safety.

Improper credit lines (too high or too low) can be the result of inexperience, excessive caution in the decision-making process, and/or a very conservative company credit policy. On the high side, credit lines might be dictated by top management as a means to enhance sales and the public image of a successful and volatile growth company.

Entrepreneurs who must wear most of the administrative hats in their company or business have perhaps the most difficulty living the role of credit administrator. It is their desire, as the entrepreneur and founder, to nurture the company's growth—to do nothing that will in any way inhibit it from becoming the success that was visualized when the business was started. To be in the position of having to decline some credit sales is both difficult and essential, and although the entrepreneur should always be protective of the quality of his or her company's receivables, saying "No" to a customer who dangles the possibility of a substantial amount of business is not easy. It is not easy to separate the need for caution from the need for growth, but it is essential that the entrepreneur learns very quickly to turn away from business that can be damaging to the financial health and future of his or her company.

The credit manager or credit administrator of a company or business that has sales in the millions of dollars per year has the same problem as the entrepreneur, but it is on a much larger scale. He or she is making credit decisions that range from a few hundred dollars to tens of thousands of dollars. The company may be in high tech, hard goods, food products, or any one of many other categories, but the person who makes the company's credit decisions must have the level of knowledge and experience necessary to determine which accounts are financially capable of handling four-, five-, or six-figure credit lines. When that basic premise has been established, a minimum commitment of effort on the part of the supplier's credit department should be necessary for things such as monitoring the account, making or writing reminder calls and letters, etc.

Corporate credit managers at the larger companies may have several assistants. Their jobs might vary from directing and/or monitoring the work of credit managers in the branch offices to working with division managers (product, etc.), with subsidiary company managers, to working on a variety of special assignments for the corporate credit manager or credit administrator. In big corporations, receivables balances and credit clearances will often be in the millions of dollars, and the pressure to be 100 percent correct in the assessment of each risk is enormous.

Three companies or businesses are in the same industry. The first company has sales in the range of $100 to $500 million a year—and it can lose millions of dollars in one Chapter 11 bankruptcy filing. What can a $5 million to $25 million a year account lose? It may suffer a loss that is proportionate to the bigger company's, perhaps a receivables loss in the area of $100,000 or $150,000; because this supplier's financial base (cash flow) is smaller and narrower than that of the larger firm, the smaller firm may, under comparable conditions, feel a greater impact on its financial strength than the larger firm.

The basic strengths (financial, management, and product) will vary greatly from one company to the next, so the impact imposed by a loss of similar or proportionate size will vary in the effect it has on supplier companies. Are credit limits assigned and reviewed at figures completely out of touch with the reality of customers' business and financial situations? This is the heart of "bad debt" country. The probability of a financial loss, with the potential for it to become a major financial disaster for the credit grantor, is almost inevitable.

Selling on Terms Other Than Credit

There are other options for selling a customer whose request for a credit line has been turned down or approved at a figure that the customer says is not adequate for the needs of his or her business. It is quite true that none of the options comes close to being as appealing or as practical from the customer's point of view as a line of credit. Powers of persuasion and the customer's need for your product(s) become, at this point, very crucial as you attempt to sell the customer on one or a combination of the following:

- Cash—synonymous with a personal check, certified check, cashier's check, bank money order, post office money order, or other money order.

- C.W.O.—Cash with Order. Many of the other cash payment options are acceptable here.

- C.B.D.—Cash Before Delivery. You may modify sales terms to a specific percentage of the total amount of the order. The time frame in which one or more of these C.B.D. payments is due depends upon the specific agreement between buyer and seller. (Example: The seller might insist that payment, if it is to be in the form of a check, must be in the seller's hands a minimum of 10 days before delivery (or release) of the goods. This early receipt will enable the seller to deposit the check and allow time for it to clear before it releases the product.)

- C.O.D.—Cash On Delivery. This term is not a particularly popular sales term with most companies. You should use it only if the customer is not credit worthy at the level of the order or if you have not received and processed credit information. Some customers prefer to pay on C.O.D. terms; however, this practice is rare. Remember the risks involved in accepting company or personal checks about which you have little or no reliable information. Remember also that if the customer refuses to accept the merchandise on C.O.D. terms (even after agreeing to do so), you might have to pay two-way shipping charges. Get your shipping costs up front or be sure the customer knows that you will be sending the shipment C.O.D. Make sure that he or she is willing to accept it on those terms, and that he or she knows the dollar amount of the shipment and the date on which you intend to ship the product(s). (The shipping date is particularly important if the customer must pay for the shipment with a cashier's check or money order.)

- 2%/10 Days/Net 30—This sales term offers a 2 percent discount if the customer pays the invoice within 10 days from the invoice date. Net 30 days means that the customer has 30 days from the date of the invoice to pay the total amount.

- Net 30 Days—This term is about as bare bones as terms can get. The supplier does not offer a discount and the customer has 30 days from the invoice date to pay the invoice total.

- E.O.M.—End Of Month. Payment is due by the end of the month following the month in which the buyer purchases the merchandise. The supplier does not offer a discount if the sales term is stated in this language. The seller might, however, link this term with a discount if he so desires.

- 2%/10th Prox/Net 30—The seller offers a 2 percent discount if the invoice is paid by the 10th of the month following the month in which the purchase is made. If the discount is not taken within this time frame, the full amount of the invoice becomes payable prior to the last day of the month following the month in which the buyer purchased the product(s).

- R.O.G.—Receipt Of Goods. This term is a different approach to defining the point when the discount period starts. In other sales terms, the discount period is calculated from the date of the invoice. When R.O.G. becomes a part of the sales term, the discount period does not begin until the customer has received the merchandise. When consideration is given to the distance between seller and buyer, and the direct or indirect nature of freight service, the buyer could gain several days with R.O.G. over date of invoice.

There are sales terms that require a minimum of part cash with the order before any action will be taken to process the order. This is especially useful when a supplier must manufacture, process, or package the product or item in a manner that would make it unsalable to another customer. Such an order might involve the purchase of special ingredients and/or packaging materials, rearranging production schedules, and straining warehousing capabilities. The order might also involve some in-house research and development, and levels of quality control that could impact the scheduling of other products.

Under conditions that commit time, money, and effort to a custom product, a minimum payment of 50 percent of the total value of the order should be required before there is any commitment to it; a payment in excess of 50 percent should be required if costs are projected to exceed that figure. The balance that is still owed will be paid when the order is delivered. If there is enough latitude between production costs and the customer's cost, the manufacturer or processor might, under certain circumstances, accept an arrangement of 50 percent, 25 percent, and 25 percent; this translates into an agreement for 50 percent of the customer's cost for the order when the order is accepted, 25 percent of the order total when the order is delivered, and the final 25 percent within 30 days of the delivery date or the invoice date.

If a customer wants to place a special order and has a credit line with the supplier, but the supplier's standard terms (Net 30, etc.) are a tighter time frame than the customer can handle, a discussion might ensue between the supplier's sales and credit managers. Why does the customer need special terms on this order or special dating on the invoices that cover product shipments? The customer will not be receiving his or her payment for the product(s) until 30 days after the supplier's standard credit terms. To protect the customer's credit relationship with the supplier, the customer has wisely come to the supplier with the request and an explanation for the request.

The final decision in this and other similar situations should be in writing. The person who has the responsibility for sales should complete the Request for Special Terms form (see Figure 5-10), go over the acceptable payment options with the credit manager, then relay that information to the customer. Credit manager and sales manager arrive at terms that are acceptable to the customer, the completed Request for Special Terms form is filed in the customer's credit file, and there can be no future question regarding the circumstances that prompted the decision. This is an example of a procedure used properly, used at the right time, and used under the right circumstances.

Revolving Letter of Assignment

It is best described as the domestic version of an International Letter of Credit. The Revolving Letter involves a written agreement (initiated by the supplier) among the customer, the customer's bank, and the supplier, whereby the supplier submits invoices for material or products to the customer's bank for payment. The bank pays invoices against the customer's credit line for the period of months and maximum dollar amount specified in the assignment letter.

If the Revolving Letter of Assignment is for $100,000, the dollar value of unpaid invoices should never exceed that figure. As the bank pays invoices, that amount is freed again for use under the agreement—hence the term

Request for Special Terms

Date _____

To Be Completed by Sales:

Customer Name: _____

Customer Address: _____

_____

Terms Requested: _____

On (P.O. or Invoice Number): _____

Reason: _____

_____

_____

Requested by: _____

- -

To Be Completed by Credit Department:

Date Account Opened: _____

Financial Statement (Date): _____

D & B Rating: _____

Our Payment History with This Company: _____

_____

Comments and Recommendation: _____

_____

_____

Approved: _____   Approved: _____

Figure 5-10. Request for special terms.

Revolving Letter of Credit. The supplier is able to sell a customer who might be difficult or impossible to carry under other conditions. The customer is able to purchase the supplier's goods—perhaps a particular type or brand of goods specified by an architect for a development of expensive oceanside condominiums—under material release and payment conditions not acceptable to the supplier under any other form of secured position. A unique situation often calls for an equally unique or innovative solution. Although it is used infrequently, the Revolving Letter of Assignment can be a very effective way to save a good piece of business.

A word of caution: do not become involved in an ongoing control situation of this type unless you have the background and experience to properly handle it. The banker monitors the dollar amount of unpaid billings in his or her office at any given time versus the dollar amount stated in the Assignment. He or she is taking care of his bank's position only, not yours. You must know, at all times, the dollar value of invoices submitted and unpaid and the amount of credit still available between the total of unpaid invoices and the credit line figure in the Assignment. Closely monitoring the status of this type of arrangement is your responsibility—the responsibility of the supplier's credit manager. It is, therefore, a responsibility that must be handled with care to ensure a satisfactory and a profitable experience for your company.

The preceding outline of sales terms is applicable primarily to accounts that do not qualify for a credit line. It also applies to accounts that qualify for a credit line, but whose purchases occasionally stretch that line to the limit and beyond. When that occurs, some form of cash terms must be used to pay for the amount(s) above the credit limit. One or more of the non-credit sales terms can be selected to handle the problem.

6
Your Credit Decisions

The most difficult part of some credit decisions is not when the decision is made, but when a credit manager and his or her company must live with it. *Risk*—hopefully reasonable and manageable, but still spelled with a capital *R*—is the ever-present challenge to the success of all credit judgments and decisions. Even in a work environment where the full scope of decision-making tools is available—supplier references, the banker's data, commercial credit agency reports, financial statements, peer information with a trade group, and an experienced professional to analyze and evaluate the data—the resulting decisions will be imprecise judgments that include varying amounts of risk.

There are too many unknowns and intangibles for the credit manager or the owner and credit manager, regardless of his or her experience level, to expect only infallible judgments. How can the credit manager know that an applicant or a current customer is not concealing personal, health, or business problems? How can you, as the guardian of your company's receivables balances, be sure that an apparently successful business partnership is not being bent and twisted from within, to the point where it is no longer very stable? Do you like what you've seen of the small company that is asking you for a sizeable credit line? Is the founder going to tell you that he or she is about to retire, or that he or she is quietly reducing his or her interest and activity in the company, and that future management control will be in the relatively inexperienced hands of a son-in-law? You will probably not hear a word of warning from any of the above in any of the given situations. Is there risk? Believe it!

There are things you can do to give your company the strongest level of protection from bad debt losses. One of the best things you can do is to load

159

the evaluation and decision-making process with procedural uniformity. It has a nice ring, but the truth is that nobody cares how it sounds if it doesn't contribute something. Fortunately, it does. It can help to minimize the number and potential effects of risk-prompting variables, while improving the effectiveness of the credit management process. It can be one of your strongest allies in helping you to make a higher percentage of good credit decisions. Do everything in sequence. Make the sequential approach your guideline for dealing with applicants from the first contact through all the years of your association with a company that becomes a customer. You will take your accounts through other sequences in the credit management process, but nothing will make your work easier, your hours of credit management more productive, or your credit department more effective than adopting as your everyday guideline the one phrase—procedural uniformity.

Look constantly for the hedge against the unknowns, the intangibles, and the imprecise. Experienced credit managers look also for evidence of stability in a company's financial depth and in the quality of its personnel. They look also for well-planned growth and the potential for trouble-free longevity. The hedge against risk should be a combination of the depth and experience of a company's management, the high-profile recognition factors of the product line(s), the company's financial stability, and the unique geographic nature of the market area (a semiprotected market with little or no competition). Try to hedge your risks—those that are unknown, intangibles, and imprecise. Try to assemble the greatest number of plusses and the smallest number of minuses before making a judgment that puts some of your company's assets at risk.

Can you live with your credit decisions? Of course, but you must remember that an occasional one will turn sour; never let yourself forget that all decisions are sprinkled liberally with ingredients and factors about which you have no knowledge and over which you have no control. This doesn't mean that, when you sit down to make credit decisions, you are putting your hands on the throttle of a runaway train. You must always be in control of your decisions and of the decision-making process. You are the one who controls the approval of orders and credit lines.

When your decisions are the result of a good input of information, sound evaluation and judgment, and procedural uniformity, your hand— the one that is on the always-in-motion affairs of the credit department— will ensure as steady a ride as most credit professionals could give your company. Every credit administrator regrets the loss of a receivables balance, but you should not waste time and energy faulting yourself for the loss. If you did a solid job with the account, save the self-chastisement for a situation where you really should have seen the emerging problem before it was too late.

The Good, the Fair, and the Ugly

The credit decisions you made yesterday, and the yesterdays before that, will ultimately settle into one of these three categories. Unless you change the guidelines for a particular account (see Figure 6-1), or something happens that impacts the account itself, your continuing experience with the account should reflect little or no measurable change. From that earliest point when you relied solely upon the experience of others, your experience with the account gradually will become the experience of primary importance. What your peer credit managers are doing and experiencing will always be relevant to your decisions, but they will be secondary to your own experience. Your evaluation will become the determining factor in any decision to continue selling on the terms and dollar level you first assigned; your company's account experience will indicate that you should make an upward or downward adjustment.

(Company Letterhead)

Corporate Guarantee

The XYZ Company _____(address)_____ agrees to guarantee payment for purchases made by its subsidiary, _____(name and address)_____ , from the _____(creditor/supplier company's name and address)_____ , during the period from _____ thru _____ inclusive.

Should the _____(subsidiary company)_____ fail to make payment or payments within the Net 30 Days sales/credit terms of the _____(creditor/supplier company)_____ , the _____(parent/guarantor company)_____ will upon notification received in writing from the _____(creditor/supplier company)_____ , and upon receipt of invoices for which the payment claim is made, promptly pay the submitted past-due invoices as covered by this agreement.

It is understood that payments for invoices are subject to verification of the quantities ordered and received, the prices quoted and billed, and such other obligations and requirements as may be a part of the agreement between the _____(subsidiary/purchaser company)_____ and the _____(creditor-supplier company)_____ .

Dated _____ by _____
                                              Treasurer, XYZ Company

---

Figure 6-1. Corporate guarantee.

Avoiding the losers has always been the name of the credit management process, but no person who manages credit for any period of time succeeds in avoiding every loser. Rid yourself of any preconceived notions regarding the infallibility of a professional, in his or her own credit environment, or in your seat, where you make the decisions for your company. The professional will lose one now and again just as the less experienced person does. The difference between the professional and the inexperienced manager, however, is that the good professional will not make the same judgment mistake a second time. You must do the same thing. Take each negative experience and turn it into a learning one—one that you can use successfully in your future efforts to reduce the toll taken by the intangibles and by *risk*. If you are an entrepreneur, your incentive for doing a good job of managing credit and receivables should exceed the motivation of a salaried professional. A professional's pride in his or her work should ensure a good performance, but pride isn't the only thing that motivates an entrepreneur. You, Mr. or Ms. Entrepreneur, have to be interested in what happens to the "bottom line" because, if you are the owner, that bottom line is yours! How much additional incentive does a man or a woman need? Probably none.

Large and small companies find themselves doing scenes from the same scenario. The premise is the same for both categories of companies. If, each year, the credit managers for a small and a large company routinely handle comparable numbers of new and existing accounts, and bring to these account situations a level of competence and experience appropriate for the level of his or her decisions, each manager will have an occasional bad-debt loss. It is not possible to be infallible, and it is unrealistic to expect it. An account relationship begins with as many verified facts as possible, and those facts are constantly updated; yet certain intangibles, when combined with the normal flow of business problems, make it impossible for any credit manager to always come up with winners.

How can you maximize your chances of picking a high percentage of winners for your company? In addition to the controls and self-restraints previously discussed, let me suggest that you do not give away the store. Who would do such a foolish thing? When you develop a friendship with a customer, never let that relationship influence your business judgment as it relates to the amount of credit extended to the customer or the credit terms. You cannot allow a personal relationship to interfere with a business relationship. Never allow the personal relationship to inhibit you from insisting that the customer make his or her account payments within the parameters of good credit management and of your company's credit policy. An account that becomes a bad-debt loss because of poor judgment is as damaging to your company's financial statement as the common theft of money or merchandise. Face it. The customer is not always right and not always honest. The customer's abuse of the credit privilege is the same as that customer having a hand in your till. You don't need that kind of help or that kind of business.

Good credit decisions? These are the decisions that add a good account to your accounts receivable aged trial balance report, that results in the customer paying the invoice within terms or within an acceptable time frame, and that gradually build the confidence, knowledge, and overall expertise of the credit manager, until that manager is a fully qualified professional; finally, these are the building blocks that enable a credit professional to move into a decision-making role that involves more accounts, bigger accounts, and many more receivables dollars, and to move on to the top plateau of the credit profession.

Example: The Ransome Company has been in business for nine years, is a major area wholesaler in plumbing and garden supplies, and has recently notified the trade and the public of its intention to open a large branch store and warehouse in a community some 50 miles from its present location. Ransome has never bought product(s) from your firm (a manufacturer of sprinkler fittings, couplings, etc.), but has decided to drop another line to add your company's line of quality products.

Ransome's expansion program has put a temporary strain on cash flow. You are being asked to give Ransome additional invoice dating of 30 days beyond your normal credit terms on the initial stocking order, plus an additional 30 days on subsequent orders over the period of the next 90 days. If, at the end of that period, Ransome's cash flow is still somewhat restricted, you are being asked to agree to an extension of the "30 days of additional dating" for another 90 days. At the end of that period, it is agreed that credit sales will revert to your company's standard terms.

Ransome's three major suppliers report payments within terms to an occasional slow 10 to 20 days. The bank reports that all loan arrangements have been and continue to be handled as agreed with commercial account balances averaging a medium to high five figures. A credit report agency gives the account a strong credit rating (net worth and creditor payments), and lists antecedent data that addresses favorably the strengths of the company, its principals, its business reputation, and its product lines. CPA prepared financial statements have been forwarded for the preceding three years; they reflect good growth and a profits trend that continues upward.

Do you have any problem with this package? You do not. This is obviously a well-managed company that has planned carefully for a move into an area that has no real competition. There is one regional supplier who has been doing a half-hearted job of serving what has become an area of strong growth (many new homes, industrial construction, etc.); it is nothing comparable, however, to the variety of products, pricing, and service capability that Ransome will be offering. Ransome is not without some name identification in the area because of a stepped-up program of sales and service over the preceding 12 months.

This is opportunity knocking. If your company delivers the type of product(s) and service that Ransome obviously expects from you, the relationship should become increasingly lucrative and extend over a long period of time.

Fair credit decisions? These are the accounts that will not make their way onto a bad-debt list. These are accounts that require more telephone calls to get account payments and more monitoring to ensure that their strengths remain adequate for their levels of activity; they are accounts that, because of their mix of ongoing problems, contribute heavily to the broadening of credit management skills; they are accounts from which credit managers can bank significant experience to draw on in future parallel situations throughout their professional careers.

Example: The facts outlined in the previous example (the Ransome Company) are going to be changed to make the decision more difficult for the credit manager and offer a less secure account for his or her company.

Assume that the Ransome Company has been in business for four years, has encountered some difficulty in its effort to build a strong customer base (a major area competitor and an economic recession that has only begun to ease within the past 12 months). In spite of these early problems, Ransome sees an opportunity to open a branch store and warehouse in a community 50 miles from the home location. Your company is pleased that Ransome has dropped one line to take on your company's line of fittings and couplings. Unfortunately, rumor has it that the supplier dropped Ransome because there was concern that Ransome is not ready for a major expansion.

Internally generated cash flow is frequently augmented from a revolving bank line. Opening the new store and warehouse will put additional strain on a cash-flow bank line that has been increased twice during the past 14 months. The bank will not increase it again, and suppliers are being asked to extend invoice payment 30 to 45 days beyond regular terms for the next six months. If, after six months, the new location is not operating at a level that is close to break even, there is the distinct possibility that the Ransome Company's debt structure could endanger the survival of the firm.

Major suppliers have expressed their concern. Account payments are already 20 to 35 days past due and, with the opening of a second store, can be expected to slip to 35 to 50 days past due. Suppliers and the banker agree that there is an opportunity for a company such as Ransome to expand into this area, but the consensus is that for Ransome the timing is not right.

What is your company's reaction to this package? Are you comfortable with the idea of stocking both stores with product and subsequently supplying more product before you can expect the first payment? There is also the question of whether this proposal is compatible with your company's credit plan. If it is not, top management should tell you that it wants the business, understands the risks, and is willing to accept them. Your reaction? You cannot be comfortable with Ransome's payment proposal. This can either be a good piece of long-term business or it can be a relatively short and expensive ride into a Chapter 11. If you decide to accept Ransome's account and its request for an additional 30 to 45 days beyond normal terms, what measures can you take to protect your company's receivables asset?

Without jumping ahead into a discussion of the mechanics of a Uniform Commercial Code Filing (see "Part 3—Uniform Commercial Code"), you will examine your company's protection under a Security Interest filing; get a list of the UCC filings that have priority over yours; examine the filings and decide whether your company's protection under a UCC filing would be acceptable, and, if you ship product, monitor all shipments and receivables balances on the accounts receivable trial balance report. Keep the account aging as short as possible, and watch for any sign of business and/or financial deterioration.

What about ugly credit decisions? These are the decisions that, when they are made, seem destined to find their place among the good and the fair. These are accounts that, for one reason or another, go downhill until they find their way into a Chapter 11 filing and/or a bad-debt loss. These are the accounts that permanently change a credit administrator from one who might previously have spent less time on account evaluation data than the seriousness or the complexity of the decision-making process deserved to one who is transformed into a procedure-oriented professional.

Example: The Ransome Company is again used as the basis for this example. The solid facts that were used to provide the example of a good decision, and then were weakened to provide the basis for the examination of a fair decision, will be further weakened to provide the scenario for an ugly decision.

In this scenario, the Ransome Company has been in business for four years, is struggling to operate at a break-even level, and hopes that opening the new store in the community 50 miles from its home location will give it the additional base management feels it must have to become profitable. The bank and suppliers are skeptical. They feel that the new store and warehouse will put too much strain on cash flow that requires monthly help from the bank line. Internally generated cash is bogged down in receivables that are paid an average of 49 days from invoice date on sales terms of Net 30 days. Suppliers are being paid 30 to 45 days beyond terms, with an occasional supplier holding orders until the account reduces aging from a past due of 60 to 65 days to 45 to 50 days.

Several major suppliers have refused to extend invoice payments 30 days beyond regular terms for a period of six months to stock and resupply the new store and warehouse. Your company has not sold to Ransome in the past, but the loss of certain key suppliers has brought Ransome to your door. Their proposal to your company is the same as the one they have offered their current suppliers: invoice dating 30 days beyond regular terms for stocking and resupplying the original and the new store, an arrangement which is to continue for six months.

Is this proposal within the scope of your company's credit policy? As the company's credit manager, are you comfortable with Ransome's proposal? The answer to both of the above questions is "No!" You are an experienced credit manager and Ransome's current relationships with its suppliers and the bank serve to point up the additional factors of risk if Ransome goes ahead with the second store and warehouse. This is currently a business that is surviving, rather than a success story. Your analysis of what the financial burden of a second store and warehouse can do to Ransome's chances for survival are in agreement with the evaluation of those major suppliers who have refused to grant Ransome's request. After discussion with your company's top management, you decline to sell Ransome. The risks are too great. The Ransome Company does not fit your company's criteria for an acceptable credit risk.

Credit managers do not expect that their credit decisions will become losers. The credit professional takes every precaution to ensure that his or her experience, the quality of data received and evaluated, and good procedural practices come together in the acceptance of credit worthy accounts. None is more dismayed than the credit professional when a credit account that has been properly screened and carefully monitored suddenly develops problems that ultimately become terminal.

The Consequences of Weak or Hasty Decisions

The products that come from decisions of poor quality are found in slower moving receivables, internally generated cash flow that is well below the level that would be expected from receivables, and an accounts receivable aging report that has too many slow-turning account balances in the 30- and 60-days past-due columns. There are too many accounts that fail to pay within or near sales terms, with the consequence of too much expensive bank borrowing to augment the shortage of internally generated cash flow.

Weak Decisions

The causes are many. These dangerous decisions can be the result of an inadequate supply of good credit data. They might also be the product of a credit administrator who has been put in a position for which he or she is not adequately prepared; perhaps he or she has too narrow a range of experience for the size and demands of the credit granting company. If not properly controlled, weak credit decisions will infiltrate and undermine the quality of the receivables base to the point where cash flow becomes a cash trickle. The receivables aging report may be loaded with accounts that owe varying numbers of dollars to the supplier company, but if many of those balances are the result of weak credit decisions, the provision for bad-debt losses may be understated by a sizeable sum.

Any credit manager, who finds himself or herself in the position of making credit decisions that push the limits of the decision-maker's experience and knowledge, should "proceed with caution." An account that, because of the size of the order or unusual circumstances relating to the order, must be evaluated from many angles in order to arrive at an acceptable credit decision is not the situation for a weak decision. If there is weakness in the levels of knowledge and experience that the credit manager brings to a difficult evaluation and decision, the quantity and quality of the data (experience, financial, and reference) that is available to determine whether risk factors are within parameters that meet the supplier company's standards must be maximized. It may be reassuring if risk factors are within industry parameters, but the primary criterion is that they are acceptable within the standards for receivables risk set by your company.

The bottom line of a company's financial statement is the ultimate victim of weak credit decisions. An accounts receivable total that contains an especially high percentage of potential bad-debt accounts is decreased by a high-dollars provision for bad-debt losses. The company's financial statement is the victim, and it is a scenario that does not reflect good credit management. It is the type of correctable situation that must be addressed by the credit manager or the credit administrator via the processes of self-education (books such as this one, D & B's correspondence courses, seminars, monthly or quarterly industry credit meetings, or any process or opportunity for self-education that will broaden the scope of the manager's knowledge, and provide that person with the tools and the confidence to turn the decision-making process from one of *weakness* to one of *strength*).

Hasty Decisions

Decisions made in haste may have the same negative impact on receivables liquidity that weak decisions do. The primary difference is that their origin is not the same. A hasty credit decision might be made by an experienced credit manager who is being pressured to release an order or to raise a credit line before the "gathering and evaluating" cycle is complete. The person making the decision might bring a depth of experience that would seem to immunize this individual from a pressured or a hasty decision. Unfortunately, no one is so experienced that circumstances cannot conspire to put even the professional with long-term experience in a position where a good decision is almost too much to expect.

A credit management person, who does not have the background of experience and knowledge necessary to cope with some of the more complex decision-making situations, is rarely going to err on the side of a hasty decision. This person is probably going to worry the problem from all angles, cope successfully with areas where experience and knowledge give adequate support, and attempt to make sense of certain more complex areas that are a step or two beyond experience, knowledge, or both.

The results from hasty decisions can be as costly as those from weak ones. Certainly a company's bottom line does not differentiate between the negative impacts of a weak decision or a decision that was made in haste. When a bad-debt loss is the result of a decision that was made in one of these two categories, the dollar impact on the company's bottom line is equally severe. Questions may be addressed to the experienced credit manager who knew better than to make the hasty credit decision; there may also be questions regarding the qualifications and/or experience level of the credit manager who is making too many weak and costly decisions.

Getting the experienced credit manager back on track should not be a long-term problem. He or she must simply resist any future pressure to make a premature decision when the base of experience data is not adequate for the magnitude of the decision. And if a decision must be made? The credit manager must make the company's financial officer aware that the credit decision will be made on less-than-adequate experience data for a decision that commits such a large number of dollars—and the financial officer must concur in writing (initials, etc.) with the credit manager's opinion.

What about the credit manager who is making weak and costly decisions because he or she is not qualified by experience or knowledge to deal with everything that comes to the manager's desk? If it is a weakness in knowledge that can be corrected within a relatively short period of time (via the suggestion given earlier in this section), the financial officer should help to work a talented person through this period of growth. If the problem is rooted in an inadequate experience level and the volume and complexity of the company's credit decisions demand an immediate and appropriate level of experience, a change may be necessary. But before there is a change, every effort should be made to help a promising young professional augment his or her skills. This could be done by briefly bringing a skilled credit management consultant in to work with the young professional. Such an arrangement would, as a goal, fill the gaps in the manager's knowledge that have been highlighted by a recurring pattern of (in some areas) decisions of questionable quality.

No company should allow itself to be put in the position of having to cope with the consequences of weak or hasty decisions. There must be a level of credit management proficiency and professionalism that meets the criteria for a particular company or business. A credit manager who does a good job for a company at one sales level might or might not be qualified to meet the requirements of a company doing a more diversified business. The presence of large numbers of interstate and overseas customers demands expertise in protecting receivables under the Uniform Commercial Code and in handling transactions that involve Letters of Credit.

A credit manager who has spent most of his or her professional experience selling intrastate accounts faces an entirely new and hazardous challenge when a sizeable percentage of a company's accounts are interstate and/or foreign.

Fine-Tuning the Decision-Making Process

In addition to the common decision-making format that should be followed by credit grantors, there are the tangible and intangible ingredients that companies use to modify and/or fine-tune the process to fit their own needs. What one company must have from its accounts receivable may differ greatly from what is required by other companies. The nuances and the special cash requirements of individual companies make it mandatory that there are appropriate areas and levels of fine-tuning. Expand those differences to the requirements of companies in different industries, whose size and goals are not compatible with a "ready made" rather than a "tailored" decision-making process, and you have the need for fine-tuning.

Fine-tuning the decision-making process is not to be confused with dismantling it. What if the goal is to maximize the flow of cash from receivables? Then the key point in the fine-tuning process is to select carefully the accounts that will form your company's receivables base. They must be good, fast-turning receivables if the company's goal is to minimize the borrowing of bank funds to sustain cash flow. Given the above criteria, you will try to avoid accounts that have a questionable payment record, that have not been in business long enough to have an established business and payments trend, or that do not conduct their business in a manner that is compatible with the standards set by your company.

The process of fine-tuning should be sufficiently pliable, so that your company doesn't find itself locked into positions so inflexible that corrective movement or adjustment is virtually impossible. The following are examples of areas that might require fine-tuning to meet the target of your company's financial requirements:

1. If a strong, consistent flow of internally generated cash is essential (to minimize interest charges), do not rely too heavily on payment informa-

tion received from the applicant's major suppliers. (If your company will not be a major or a key supplier, your receivables experience with the customer may be entirely different from that of major suppliers.)

2. Your company has been in business for approximately two years, is having difficulty attracting enough of a market share to become more than borderline profitable, and must maximize the flow of internally generated cash. The bank will not increase the revolving credit line and supplier payments are becoming a problem. (You must have fast-turning receivables. Fine-tune your decision-making process to favor accounts that pay within terms or close to terms. Although your company needs more business, it cannot accept customers whose payment pattern is not in synch with your terms. Slow pay accounts will only magnify the company's problem with its suppliers—and the bank.)

There are degrees of fine-tuning. Work on yours until the decision-making process is a fit with your company.

Slow-Pay Accounts—
Gamble or Prudent Risk?

Carefully selected slow-pay accounts—if they are a fit with your company's credit policy and cash-flow requirements—can be profitable business. Slow-pay accounts might be categorized in one of three ways: occasionally slow, chronically slow, and terminally slow. Avoid the latter group, but if your credit policy is a middle-of-the-road (moderate) policy, take on the well-established account that pays never later than a few days beyond terms. If you select them carefully, there should be no more danger of a receivables loss than with your other accounts. When an account has been in business for years, continues to be profitable, and is known for a policy of putting some weight on its suppliers (chronically 15 to 25 or 30 days slow), this account is not involved in a budding bankruptcy; it is a way of life. This account doesn't care what the credit ratings say. It has the money to pay closer to terms, but exercises a combination of arrogance and purchasing clout to exploit a position of strength—and it persists in releasing supplier payments many days beyond terms.

Avoid any account that represents an unacceptable credit risk. Watch for companies that have been in business for two or more years, have made little or no progress, and are reported by their suppliers to pay 30 to 45 days slow—and getting slower. When current suppliers report such unsatisfactory payments experience, you should avoid the account and the inevitable collection problems that your company would soon face. Consider how the loss of a key customer would impact a firm already struggling to survive.

The loss of that key customer almost certainly would push the business into a Chapter 11 filing.

Manufacturers, distributors, and service companies can make money from a relationship with a customer who virtually ignores sales terms, if the percentage of profit for the goods or services is high enough to compensate for chronic slow-pay—for the loss of the contribution to cash flow that the receivables dollars would have made if the account paid closer to terms. Be very wary of the area into which you would be moving some of your company's receivables before you take on any of these accounts. You must be satisfied completely that the potential customer who does not pay within terms—who apparently rarely has paid any supplier within terms—offers a potential for profitable business that your credit policy can accommodate and poses no threat to your annual provision for bad debt loss.

"NSF" Checks— The End of a Relationship

It is appropriate to close this chapter with a look at the effect "bad checks" have on a credit relationship. Substitute any euphemism you choose (NSF, Insufficient Funds, Refer to Maker, etc.), but if the check doesn't clear the drawer's bank, the relationship between the two parties has been damaged. If the problem is with the bank and not your customer, a full measure of understanding is in order. When the problem is not the bank's and there is the suspicion that the customer released the check knowing there would not be enough money in the account for the bank to pay it, it is the beginning of a major break in the relationship between supplier and customer. What if you receive a second "bad check" within a short period of time? The relationship is at great risk of being strained beyond the point where a policy of credit sales—or accepting company checks for C.O.D. sales—can or should be continued.

People who make credit decisions often have minds that are compartmentalized, minds that enable them to tap into an accumulation of past experiences. This repository of credit experiences is not open to customer surveillance and enables an owner/credit manager to deal quickly and firmly with those customers who begin to slide into a pattern of multiple bad checks. The customer who commits two, or more, of these acts within a period of a few weeks is severely damaging the reputation of the company or business.

Legal implications also are attached when a person or company flirts with a formal charge of passing bad checks (offering a check in payment for merchandise when the person offering the check knows that funds are not in the bank to cover the check and probably will not be, intending to defraud, etc.). The charge has a stronger chance of prevailing if the person or company offers the check as payment (or C.O.D. payment) for goods or services to be received. The key word is "intent," and it is usually so difficult to prove, that companies have neither the time nor personnel to spend building a case that fits parameters of "intent" or "knowledge of insufficient funds" when the check was offered as payment. A firm or an individual might be sending checks of this type to most of his or her suppliers, but seldom is there a provable case if checks are eventually made good.

A first-time offender—especially an account with whom you have had a satisfactory relationship—is entitled to the benefit of the doubt. There is always the legitimate possibility that a promised check from the customer's customer failed to arrive. On the basis of that promise, your customer released your check and the checks of several other suppliers.

Look at the same premise from another direction. The check from the customer's customer was received and deposited in plenty of time to cover your check and those of the other suppliers, but it was returned by the bank. There are credit managers who might scoff at the story, but it is not an uncommon predicament for a small company or business (and sometimes a larger company). Customers can issue checks in good faith against a check they received from a third party, particularly a company whose checks have always been good. Consider your own embarrassment if your company released checks to your suppliers and the big check from your customer failed to clear the bank. In such a chain of events, it is quite possible for any company or business to be the inadvertent victim. You should always give your customer the benefit of a reasonable explanation for something that has never happened before. If it happens a second time, within a time frame relatively close to the first, accepting the credibility of anything less than a rock-solid explanation is probably not wise.

Don't hesitate to view weak explanations for incidents of NSF check problems as an indication that cash trickle has replaced cash flow. When the problem reaches this point, your knowledge of the account and the account's paying habits—and the candor with which the customer states and discusses his or her company's problems—is crucial to your future relationship with the account. You may or may not continue to sell on credit terms, but do not let yourself be blindsided! The receivables dollars that your company has invested in this account might be at serious risk, unless the customer gives full and candid disclosure of the company's problem(s), explains what is being done to correct it, and offers a reasonable time frame for correcting it. If your experience with the customer is such that you have no reason to question the explanation, the corrective measures, or the time frame, your decision probably will be to carefully monitor the customer's actions in the weeks and months ahead, while working with him or her to overcome the problem(s).

Customers whose NSF checks cause suppliers to give them the option of buying on C.O.D. terms (cash, cashier's check, bank money order, etc.) or not at all, rarely agree with that decision. As a major confidence, the customer might admit to what is described as a "minor short-term cash-flow pinch." With another account, it could be true. This account's attorney, unfortunately, could at that very moment be drawing up the papers for a Chapter 11 filing (reorganization of the business under the protection of the bankruptcy court). It is hardly necessary to add that your first notice from the Bankruptcy Court—a notice in which the Referee in Bankruptcy will advise you of the filing and state the date for the first meeting of creditors—will be your first and an after-the-fact notice. At that point, you are already on the hook.

Can all of the above occur from one or more NSF checks? It is quite possible, because when a customer begins to give your company NSF checks, it means almost certainly that other suppliers are having the same experience. Once the pattern starts, it is very difficult for a company to reverse the deep-seated cause(s) that has led to this effect. Do not prematurely abandon an account, and certainly do not abandon it if you can determine that the company has the capabilities to overcome the problem. Do not, however, try to hang on to an increasingly difficult and dangerous customer, one whose problems might have surfaced with one or more NSF checks, but have increased dramatically in the weeks since the customer's bank returned those first NSF checks unpaid. Your company can build something new and meaningful with a replacement customer, or you can, at the very least, avoid becoming one of the creditors of record when the "NSF'er" goes feet first into the murky waters of Chapter 11.

7

Other Important Management Duties

Credit management is primarily the management of credit and accounts receivable, but when a person breaks the two terms into their component parts, it confirms that what might appear to be two relatively narrow areas of responsibility are in actuality a rather diverse group of financial and administrative duties.

Few people are aware that the credit manager is one of the more important people in the implementing of any company policy that stresses putting the company's "best foot forward." Everyone knows that every department should interface effectively with other departments, but are there personality clashes too frequently that could or do work to the detriment of the company? The credit manager is involved in the writing of contracts, the implementing of contracts, and the monitoring of contracts to ensure that all terms and provisions of the contractual agreement conform to the company's desires and requirements. These and other topics are discussed and explained in the pages that follow.

Putting Your Company's "Best Foot Forward"

It is not unusual for the owner of a small company to be the president, general manager, financial officer, production officer, sales manager and credit manager. Isn't that enough? Throw in the additional burden of being the controller, quality control supervisor, and purchasing manager. Any depth of experience is rare in more than two or three of the areas of responsibility that stop at the owner's office door.

The division of responsibilities in a larger company usually involves a number of people, with one or more of them having the responsibility for one specific area. There is often a staff of several people to assist the person whose title is manager, director, etc., and the presence of staff members makes it possible for the department's manager to do a more complete job. There isn't a comparable overlapping of needs and responsibilities in the larger companies that is true in the smaller, owner-operated companies and businesses.

The administrative phase of credit management is responsible for the support activities and services that keep the company's credit customers satisfied—satisfied with the way shipments are handled, satisfied with the way invoices and payments are received and processed, and satisfied with the way in which credit memorandums are issued. It is administration's responsibility to deal with pricing errors, errors in quantities allegedly shipped and/or received, and allowed or disallowed discounts. Whether the company or business is large or small, the person who makes credit and accounts receivable decisions must spend time exchanging credit experience and general credit information with owners and managers at other companies, must interface with bankers other than his or her own, and must work to improve the tools in order to do a total job of credit management. Credit Administration is, in this context, that phase of credit management which deals with problems and areas other than specific decisions in the credit and collections process. It is the support area of credit management and, as such, serves an indispensable need (see Figure 7-1).

One of the more important support functions of credit management is the creating of internal memorandums (guidance, instructional, inquiries to other departments, etc.), form letters (to other suppliers, bankers, credit applicants, etc.), forms for reports within the department, the company, or for assisting other companies to furnish requested information. Examples of forms and letters that attempt to aid in "putting the company's best foot forward" (any form, letter, or procedure that enables the credit department to work more efficiently is a part of the "best foot forward" process) are in applicable sections of this book (see Figure 7-2). A specific example of "best foot forward" is a Credit Authority & Responsibility program that was devised to give small outside sales offices some credit clearance control in the processing of first orders (see the following presentation of that example).

Although it is a phrase that does not normally warm the heart of a credit manager, credit administration is overhead in its purest form. It is, moreover, a part of the company's total package of administrative overhead that is miniscule in the number of dollars chargeable to it and significant beyond the dollar investment in its contribution to the effectiveness of the credit management program. There is no legitimate way to escape its demand of time and, if used properly, no way exists to measure the significance of its benefits. Make credit administration—the support area of

(Your Company's Letterhead)

October 12, 199X

The Wallace Corporation
1759 Beaumont Drive
San Jose, CA 95123

Attention: Accounts Payable Department

Our company's line of products has recently been added to the merchandise carried by your branches at Los Angeles, Wichita, Chicago,
and Minneapolis. We are also about to conclude agreements with the
branches in Seattle, Phoenix, and Boise, which means that we shall be
shipping product(s) to those locations before the end of this month.

Before we inadvertently create a mess for ourselves and for your office,
it will be appreciated if you can forward a list of the "bill to" addresses
for the branches listed above. Our sales representatives have obtained
some information, but we prefer to assure ourselves of accurate information by contacting your office before invoices are mailed.

If there is ever a time or a situation when this office might be of assistance to your department, please do not hesitate to contact the undersigned.

We greatly appreciate your assistance.

Sincerely,

Credit Manager

Figure 7-1. Letter on "bill to" addresses for branches and divisions.

credit management—your full partner. The time you spend on administration, and thinking about administrative matters, should improve the efficiency of your credit operation, improve your own effectiveness as the
manager of your company's credit and collections operation, and enable
your department to make a more meaningful contribution in the area of
your company's "best foot forward."

In many small companies or businesses, the owner is the chief financial
officer, office manager, sales manager, credit manager, and wearer of many
other hats. In companies large enough to employ a credit manager, that

October 19, 199X

To Our Customers:

We have no desire to project the image of a whining, complaining, or ungrateful supplier. Our customers are much too important for us to slide into any of those unpleasant behavorial attitudes. This is meant only to be a mutual self-help, and if it works for you it will automatically work for us.

When you receive an invoice that lists a quantity of product that does not agree with the quantity you received, please do not change the invoice and pay what you calculate to be the correct amount. It may be correct, but call us with the information so we can promptly issue a credit, mail it to you, and protect your discount on the specific invoice for 10 days beyond the normal discount period. Issuing the credit simplifies our bookkeeping and should also simplify yours, if for one reason or another we calculate two different amounts for the goods billed, but not received.

Are there errors or questions regarding the price quoted to you and the price billed? Please contact this department as soon as you notice the discrepancy—and before the invoice is input for payment. We'll either promptly correct the problem with a credit for the difference or have our sales representative call you to discuss or clarify any misunderstanding that might have occurred.

We can do our best job for you when your telephone call puts the matter of correcting our mistake or problem exactly where it belongs—in our lap.

Many thanks for your cooperation.

Sincerely,

Henry Bonner
Credit Manager

HB:ac

Figure 7-2. Memo to customers: errors in invoicing, seller to issue credit.

person is often called upon to do other things, some of them more in the nature of financial rather than credit management.

The following bank presentation package was put together to accommodate a client's request for help. It was successful for that client, has been rewritten twice for other clients, and was given to a regional accounting firm to offer to their clients. The format for this familiarization package is a folder indexed to include the seven categories of major interest to the banker. It is an introductory tool that will acquaint a banker with your company's background, product lines, market area(s), financial situation, and other relevant areas of information. The package offers a solid base of information that can be expanded readily in a subsequent meeting with an interested banker.

Familiarization Package

- Section 1—Company Background
  This section is a one-page synopsis (history) of the company from beginning to current date. Stress the positive factors of ownership, growth, and success, but be straightforward in your presentation of facts.

- Section 2—Product Lines
  List and briefly describe the company's product lines: proprietary products, private label, nationally-known, or regionally recognizable nonproprietary product lines. Also list work done as a subcontractor furnishing a component part for an item assembled and marketed by another company, etc. (Do not exceed two pages.)

- Section 3—Market Area(s)
  If your company is a manufacturer, processor, distributor, or wholesaler, state the scope of your marketing area and the concentration of customers in local, intermediate, and distant areas. Illustrate the growth and acceptance of your products and/or services with a series of comparisons: sales figures now versus two years ago, five years ago, etc. If your growth has been steady in all market areas, make the point in your presentation. If growth has been more obvious in the local (or regional) market area, point out that your small company does not have the personnel (and perhaps has not had the production or distribution facility) to do more than service the company's local or regional market.

- Section 4—Financial Data
  Attach copies of the three most recent annual financial statements and a copy of the most recent quarterly or semiannual profit and loss statement. A brief letter from your accounting firm attesting to the quality of the internal controls and systems would be an appropriate and an effective companion piece to the financial data.

- Section 5—Benefits To Be Derived from Proposed Loan
  The banker will want to know how you propose to use the loan proceeds. A new and enlarged plant facility should enable the company to operate more efficiently at a lower cost. Perhaps the company will increase production and warehouse facilities, replace or modernize production or processing machinery, or add additional units to provide greater production and warehousing capacity. Emphasize the potential for increasing business and improving the profit percentages.

- Section 6—Key Personnel
  Of interest to the banker will be the quality and levels of experience that the company's key people (regardless of how few) bring to the company. If the owner makes major decisions in several areas of the business, that is important information. If there are one, two, or more experienced people in key positions (production manager, quality control, etc.), that is important. The "other employees" category should list the number of employees by major job classification only.

- Section 7—Business Projection for the Next 12 Months
  In a one-page recap, state what the company is expected to do—sales, growth, and profits—during the next 12 months. Capsulize what level of success, growth, and profits you feel is attainable during the coming 12 months. Explain your reasoning for those projections, and extend the projection to include where you feel the company will be five years from now.

(See Figure 7-3, "Business Projection—12 Months." Also see sample cover letters for the Familiarization Package in Figures 7-4 and 7-5.)

These are some examples of a credit manager or a credit administrator performing management duties that extend beyond the sometimes narrow scope of credit and receivables management. In the context of the above paragraphs, the credit manager has been active in devising and formulating report data that enhances the image of his or her business or company. As these examples indicate, the credit manager can do a great job in many areas of helping to put the company's "best foot forward."

Interfacing with Other Suppliers/Bankers/Reporting Agencies

It is especially important to maintain a good relationship with the people from whom you get account information—and who contact you for your account experience. Whether it is the banker with whom you speak daily or a banker with whom you may have a one-time conversation, there is an

---

Business Projection—12 Months

This Business Projection is being prepared in lieu of a conventional Business Plan and it covers (in general terms only) the 12-month period subsequent to ___(Date)___ .

We have used the phrase "in general terms only" because of our current move from Santa Clara to Oxnard, and what we anticipate will be a transition period of from three to six months. This transition period will see us devoting more than a normal amount of time bringing production lines to proper levels of efficiency, making appropriate adjustments in material requirements, preparing the warehouse to accommodate supplies and finished products, and doing our utmost to settle quickly and effectively into the new, 28,000 square-foot facility.

It is appropriate to note, however, that the transition period will see us actively soliciting the business of several new customers—primarily private label people who, prior to our move, had contacted us regarding the possibility of packing their product(s) for them. Negotiations that we had put on hold at Santa Clara, because we lacked the production and warehouse space to take on meaningful new business, can now go forward.

Our position at this point is both advantageous and unique. Very few packers in the area of California that is north of Los Angeles have the capacity or the capability to take on several thousand cases of new business per month. We frequently are contacted by private label distributors who are almost desperate in their search for a packer who, one, will accept their product or, two, can deliver a satisfactory product—on time and in the required volume. Even more uncertain is the plight of the private label distributor who is searching for a manufacturer willing to produce a specialty food item in relatively small batches. It is usually a very profitable business, but most manufacturers and processors are unwilling to adjust their production schedules to accommodate these smaller orders.

We have the technical skills and the production experience necessary to satisfy the needs of a broad range of customers, from the person with a product idea who retains us to develop and produce that product to, and through, the experienced distributor who brings to us his or her monthly requirement for several hundred or several thousand cases of product.

Happily, we now have the production and warehouse facility to take advantage of these opportunities.

Figure 7-3. Business projection—12 months.

(Your Company's Letterhead)

October 21, 199X

Mr. Lawrence C. Bartlett, President
North County National Bank
1462 Wayside Boulevard
Oxnard, California 93030

Dear Mr. Bartlett:

The attached familiarization package offers a brief description of our product lines and customer base, a description of our new Oxnard processing and packaging facility, a look at our more than three decades of business success, and a few words regarding our pattern and philosophy for a carefully controlled growth.

It is our intention to become both participating and contributing members of the Oxnard business community. To fulfill that expectation, we need the support and services of a community-oriented bank—one that will help us to attain our projected goals via a sound program of financial support.

Please contact me when you have had an opportunity to review the attached information.

Sincerely Yours,

(Your Name)
(Title)

Figure 7-4. Company familiarization package for bank.

ongoing need to handle these relationships in the most cordial manner possible. Your credit decisions will hinge on the quality and quantity of the information that these people furnish to your company.

Confidentiality is the one thread that runs through every relationship among suppliers, bankers, and credit reporting agencies. There must be a mutual respect for what governs the free exchange of information and account data among the various categories of credit professionals. Nothing can more effectively destroy cooperation among two or more credit grantors (or credit reporting agencies) than for a credit manager to learn

(Your Company's Letterhead)

October 30, 199X

Mr. Lawrence C. Bartlett, President
North County National Bank
1462 Wayside Boulevard
Oxnard, California 93030

Dear Mr. Bartlett:

I greatly appreciate the interest you expressed in this company during our October 28th telephone conversation.

The attached package of information has been put together to show you where we have been, where we are now, where we expect to go—and how we expect to get there.

It will be my pleasure to answer questions or provide additional data. Please contact me at your early convenience.

Sincerely Yours,

(Your Name)
(Title)

Figure 7-5. Owner/president thanks banker for response.

that another credit manager has repeated confidential information virtually verbatim to the creditor's customer. (Example: When a similar situation occurred some years ago in a credit group of which my company was a member, we suspended the offending company from all participation in credit group activities for six months, helped the company find a new credit manager, then fidgeted for an additional year until group members gradually became comfortable when the offending company's new credit manager sat in with us.)

Is this behavior unfair? Not at all. The rules of the game are very clear. The legal implications of statements directly attributable to a source, and perhaps distorted for additional effect, are too ominous for any credit group—or individual credit manager—to settle for anything less than total compliance.

Relationships with bankers can be more difficult than those with most suppliers. Suppliers may not be in your company's area of business or industry, but they understand the importance of requests for experience data from other suppliers, and are usually more forthcoming with information than most bankers. This is not to infer that bankers as a group deliberately withhold helpful information because they are unwilling to help suppliers avoid credit-account losses. Many bankers tend to be extremely conservative when called upon to furnish information regarding their experience with accounts. Their reluctance is rooted in a fear that information given in confidence might somehow become distorted and, through some inappropriate reference or application, cause damage to the business or the principals. There is protection for bankers and others who release experience data in good faith, but a litigious society tends to inhibit some of those who might otherwise be quite helpful.

Interfacing with a credit reporting agency is not difficult because membership is a criterion for using this type of service. You are expected to furnish experience data to the reporting agency when requested to do so, but the contract with the reporting agency eliminates any question regarding your company's legitimate access to report data. Relationships with credit reporting agency personnel are usually impersonal, other than the possibility that a territory representative may contact your company on an annual basis to discuss the renewal of a contract, the scope of the current service contract, and the possibility that the contract might be increased to include more and/or other services in the upcoming contract year.

A key objective of every good credit professional should be to build a solid, first-name rapport with fellow industry credit managers, and to cultivate personal relationships with those managers that will enable the credit professional to pick up the telephone and have a frank, one-on-one exchange of information and experience data.

The same objective should extend to relationships with bankers and credit reporting agencies. A reluctant banker may need to be reminded that you are being asked to supply credit to the bank's customer—and whether you do or do not supply that line of credit may impact the customer's ability to fulfill his or her payment obligation(s) to the bank. If that approach is ineffective, suggest to the prospective customer that he or she contact the bank and instruct the bank to release the experience data that your firm needs to complete a credit evaluation of the applicant business.

Interfacing effectively with every person, company, or department with whom your department comes in contact is an integral part of the credit department's function (see Figure 7-6). Strong communications skills—spoken and written—serve to enhance the effectiveness of the department's work. Be as courteous and as helpful to the people in other companies as you expect them to be to you and to other members of your company's credit department staff.

(Date)

Richard Cameron, Controller
The Chestnut Corporation
3652 Wendell Way
Blaney, Nevada 00000

Dear Mr. Cameron:

A current check of the information in our customer credit files has revealed that many of these files are incomplete. In that category is our file of information on your company.

The attached Account Information Sheet, when completed and returned with a copy of your most recent financial statement, will give us the appropriate balance of background and current business information.

Your cooperation is appreciated.

Sincerely,

Credit Manager

Figure 7-6. Incomplete credit files; request for information.

Negotiable Instruments

Although the most common form of a negotiable instrument is a check drawn on a bank account, it is by no means the only one. A negotiable instrument might be a check, a promissory note, a bill of exchange, a trade acceptance, a letter of credit, or some other "negotiable." What are the special qualities that make an instrument "negotiable?" The guidelines are that it must be in writing, must bear the signature of the maker (or drawer), must promise without condition(s) to pay a specific amount of money, and must be payable on demand or at an established (or determinable) future date. The instrument must be payable to the bearer or to order. When it is written in favor of a drawee, the person or entity addressed must be identified in such a way that the drawer's intent is reasonably clear.

Every person who endorses a negotiable instrument turns that instrument into a separate contract. Your signature, or the signature of another endorser, turns the negotiable instrument into a new contract—one apart from the maker or other endorsers. You cannot disqualify a negotiable instrument from that category because it bears no date, has no stated dollar amount or other consideration, or has no indication as to where it was drawn or where it is payable. An undated negotiable instrument is considered "dated" as of the date (or time) it was issued. Bank checks are a very familiar type of negotiable instrument, and it is good to know that the rules governing checks apply to other negotiable instruments as well. Words (written or printed) govern figures, and provisions that are in writing control printed ones.

Two general classifications of endorsements exist on negotiable instruments: general or qualified. A general endorsement is given without qualification or reservation. A qualified endorsement is one that, in addition to the endorser's name, has written words (or a written statement) which purport to limit the general liability that would be implied if it were the name alone. Limiting liability is important, and the words "without recourse" generally are used to clarify that intent.

One of the less clear-cut areas is the status of a check given to your company in payment of an account balance, marked "in full payment of account" when it does not pay the entire balance. It is not "in full payment" if there is no dispute as to the amount the customer owes. In the absence of a dispute regarding the account balance, the creditor (or supplier) is generally safe if he or she deposits the check and contacts the customer for the balance of the money. If, however, there is a dispute between your company and the customer regarding the account balance, do not endorse and deposit any check that bears the statement "in full payment of account," or any other statement of similar intent or wording. It is possible that, under the condition of a disputed account balance, you could jeopardize or forfeit your chances of collecting the difference between the "in full" check and the disputed account balance. Be very wary of any endorsement on a check or other negotiable instrument that restricts or eliminates your rights or options. Only when there is no question in your mind that the endorsement is acceptable should you add your signature.

"Part 4—International Credit Sales" explores in great detail the types of negotiable instruments that are used in this category of sales. Look to that section of the book for an explanation of how and when the following types of payments are applicable.

Irrevocable Letters of Credit (Confirmed)

Irrevocable Letters of Credit (Not Confirmed)

Revocable Letters of Credit

C.O.D. or S/D (Sight Draft)

Cash Against Shipping Documents

Bank Acceptance (Domestic or Foreign Bank)

Consigned Stock

Letter of Advice

C & F (Cost and Freight)

F.O.B. (Free on Board)

F.A.S. (Free Alongside)

FCIA (Foreign Credit Insurance Association)

Part 4 (Chapter 3) of the book provides comprehensive answers to the conventional and the unusual questions that surround these types of negotiable instruments. There are also examples of documents and how they relate to the various types of foreign sales and the payments for those sales.

Contracts (Oral and Written)

It would be very difficult to point a finger at a business transaction in today's business world that does not have its roots in a contract—written or oral. Whether two firms or two individuals do or do not come together for a formal signing of contract documents, a real or an implied contract usually has its roots in the standards of a company's products, in the claims the manufacturer makes for them, in the standards of performance for an industry, or in some other yardstick or combination of guideline levels of quality and/or service. Contracts can be written or oral, real or implied. An improperly or inadequately written contract can cost your company a tidy sum if the sleeves of your deal begin to unravel.

Basic Requirements for a Contract

A document must meet four basic requirements before it qualifies as a contract. An endless array of other material might be a part of a contract, but these are the essentials:

- Something of value must change hands.
- The contracting parties must be mentally competent.
- The subject matter must meet the legal requirements for a contract.
- There must be an offer and an acceptance.

No amount of extraneous legal jargon will give a document contract status if what is purported to be a contract does not meet the basic four-point criteria. A contract must offer a promise to do something or a promise not to do something, or agree, on the part of the promisor, to make something happen. All of these "somethings" must be between a minimum of two or more people, entities, etc., in order to raise a legal-appearing document to the level of a contract. Cosmetic appeal is fine, but if a document does not meet the criteria for a contract, it is only masquerading as one.

Oral Contracts

Oral contracts are legal. However, in all but the most simple, concise, and straightforward transaction or deal, you should not use them. Between two people of unimpeachable integrity—two people who have done business for decades and traditionally have looked each other in the eye, struck their, "I'll buy these cattle today, all 800 head of them, for 40¢ a pound," and sealed it with a handshake—a case could be made for it. But in too many other situations and circumstances, a disagreement can develop between the parties who contracted orally. Unless impartial witnesses can recall the exact language of the oral contract, it can become a courtroom slugging match with the word of one man or woman attempting to prevail against the word of the other. What happens when more than two people are involved in the oral contract? The more people that are involved in the contract, the more versions of the alleged agreement the court will hear when the matter has to be decided in a courtroom.

Written Contracts

Today's climate for lawsuits (both the capricious and the justified) does not lend itself to settling for something as charming—and probably as dangerously archaic—as an oral version of "my word is my bond." It simply does not hold up. I might give you that verbal assurance when we shake hands, and I might believe it and intend to stand by it, but if later you do not remember the deal exactly as I do, and follow through exactly to my recollection of what was said, I'll sue for what memory tells me is mine. People do not remember the wording of agreements that are not committed to paper, and especially when the remembered version of one party differs seriously with what the other (or others) is saying, doing, or delivering.

This chapter is not a course in law, contracts, or other areas. Not only am I unqualified to teach such a course, but the potential for misguiding people is not something that I care to challenge. What I tell you in this area, however, is to protect yourself and your company (or your employer's business and business assets) at all times. Do not try to do something—as in the law—for which you have no training or experience. When there is a contract to be written, do not attempt to write it yourself unless you are qualified to do so. Get your company's attorney to write any special agreement(s), legal forms, or contracts that you will use from time to time in the course of your business activity, or for any other specialized or nonroutine legal work. A mistake in the construction or terminology of a contract (or any legal document) can be a disaster. Any competent, experienced credit person should be able to handle flawlessly any routine tasks involving the law. Your company's attorney should examine any other matter, including the reading and interpreting of any contract or legal document that you do not thoroughly understand, before you sign or accept anything. Do not take chances and assume that you understand or are correctly interpreting the subtleties and combinations of legal language.

The best advice ever given to me came out of an early career association with a testy old gentleman who never bothered to look up when I asked him a question. One day I asked him a question about what I thought was a binding contract, and he seemed to bend lower to his desk than usual. "You got a problem with it?" he asked. I replied that I wasn't sure whether it was binding on both parties. Without showing me an eyeball, he impacted the subsequent decades of my professional life. "Have I done or said anything to make you think I'm an attorney?" He didn't wait for an answer. "We've got an attorney. Get on the goddamn phone and ask him!"

My advice to you—after deleting the expletive—is the same, although I ask you to accept my word that I am looking directly at you as I say it. Any person who handles credit and accounts receivable (an owner, a neophyte, or a well-schooled professional), and does not consult his or her company's attorney when a contract or a provision of a contract is unclear, is putting the company or business at unreasonable risk. It is unwise to assume that you know enough regarding applicable law(s) to make a competent judgment regarding the position of your company under the terms of a contract, unless you are an attorney or a trained paralegal. If you aren't one or the other, then call your attorney for advice and to prepare your contracts and other legal documents.

Factoring of Accounts Receivable

Whether you have ever had peripheral exposure to this method for improving cash flow may depend on your reading habits. Small advertisements frequently appear in the business and financial sections of daily newspapers in which the advertiser offers to "buy your invoices for cash." The offer might say "cash within 24 hours, no term contracts to sign, bank-to-bank transfer of funds, and invoices purchased on a nonrecourse basis." It sounds interesting, but you would not turn to these sources unless your company was at a point or in a situation where your bank—where no bank—would agree to offer the additional funds your company needs for the short or long term.

The factoring of receivables, whether through an old and large factoring firm or through one of the advertisers mentioned above, is a substitute for the more conventional use of receivables as collateral for a revolving bank loan to augment cash flow. Because of business or economic conditions, your company's banker might feel that the company's financial and business position will not support an increase in the bank's lending commitment. At that point, especially if you are confident that the need to accelerate cash flow will be temporary, factoring the company's receivables through an established, reputable factoring firm could be the answer to getting a faster turnaround of your receivables dollars. It is not, however, a form of financing you should seriously consider (certainly not in most industries) unless bank support, or additional bank support, is not available. In the scenario of a relatively short-term need, it could be worth exploring.

Invoices are factored on a recourse or a nonrecourse basis. At some point in your discussion with the factor's representative, he or she will ask for a list of your accounts and copies of recent receivables aging reports. The factor will review your experience with the accounts and, from that evaluation, will delete accounts that are unacceptable. If your discussions with the factor lean toward a relationship where accounts are factored on a recourse basis (you guarantee that you will pay the factor within a specified period of time for monies advanced on invoices charged to approved accounts), then the factor will accept more borderline accounts and advance a higher percentage of each invoice total. What is nonrecourse invoicing? The factor assumes the responsibility for collecting the full amount of invoices for goods and/or services on accounts approved for purchase. Because the factor's risk is higher, the percentage advanced to you of each invoice total will be smaller.

Factors and factoring have been a part of domestic and international commerce for decades, with special emphasis on activity in the textile industry. Some factors, known now as "commission agents," continue to make loans against merchandise and discount sales. Others are no longer involved in selling, and concentrate exclusively on credit checking and making loans against inventory and accounts receivable. This latter activity, which has been extended to industries other than textiles, is factoring as we know it today.

It should be noted that factors protect themselves in the same way that manufacturers, distributors, banks, and other credit grantors protect their interests. They do it via a filing under the Uniform Commercial Code.

The Art of Negotiation

In a great many of the nation's smaller companies and businesses, managing the company's credit accounts and accounts receivable balances is not a full-time job. The person who handles these interlocking responsibilities might also do the company's purchasing; that assignment demands some expertise in the art of negotiation.

When you temporarily close your mind to the problems of credit and collections to become the company's purchasing manager, your goal is to buy materials, supplies, or products for the best prices, on the most advantageous terms, and on a delivery schedule that coincides with your company's needs. Your supplier wants to sell his or her products or services for the best prices, on the most advantageous terms, and with only minimal warehousing of materials until the customer needs them. There is really no difference between buyer and seller. Both parties are trying to move toward the same goal, and both parties need to be satisfied that they're getting a good deal.

The questions you want to ask yourself should include:

- Am I negotiating from a position of some, little, or no strength?

- Have I succeeded in raising my company's level of credibility in the eyes of this supplier to the point where there is a willingness to make certain concessions to encourage my level of purchases?

- Am I hearing platitudes or is this supplier making a genuine effort to understand and to accommodate the needs of my company?

- If I am not hearing the level of interest that tells me we're on the same wavelength, should I try to work out a better long-term arrangement with another supplier?

Take Charles Gardner, for example. Charles needed six separate shipments of parts from his supplier in order to keep his cash flow in line and still ensure that his company has the products it needs to satisfy a possible new customer. In this instance, Charles' supplier, William Kastel, vice president of marketing of Poly Products, Inc., proved accommodating, and a deal was made that benefited all parties.

"Let me recap the key points, Bill. You're saying that you won't have any problem supplying the parts that I'm ordering today on my P.O. 6491?"

"That's right. We have more than enough in inventory to take care of the shipments on January 5th, 19th and 31st, and we have a production run scheduled for the week of January 8."

"Bill, are you sure the run will be big enough to take care of our February 9th, 21st, and March 2d shipments and still leave you with plenty of product to handle your other commitments?"

"No problem, Charles. We'll meet each of the six shipping dates that you've given me."

"I don't want to put you on the spot, Bill, but we've taken this order on a low-end profit margin to show the trade and this customer what we can do.

I need your agreement that your company will prepay the freight charges on each of the six shipments."

"You want prepaid freight on all six increments of the one order?"

"Look at it this way, Bill. Your company would prepay the freight charges if we took the entire order in one delivery. We can't do that, and you've just told me that you don't have enough product in stock to make a shipment of that size."

"That's true. The best we could do right now is to fill your order in two shipments." Kastel took a deep breath. "Oh, why not? We'll prepay the freight on all six shipments."

"Thanks, Bill. I'll send out the P.O. today with a cover letter outlining our agreement, including a breakdown of the six deliveries by shipping date and percentage(s) of the total order."

"Good enough, Charles. I appreciate the business, and good luck with your customer."

"Thanks, Bill. Talk with you soon."

Charles had been working with Bill Kassel at Poly Products for some time now, and although he thought they'd always come through for his company, now he knew for sure that he could rely on them to work with him. Suppliers like Poly Products were hard to come by, and Charles was pleased he had found them. And if business continued to improve as it had during the past year, any concessions that Bill Kastel might make on behalf of Poly Products would be returned in the form of larger and more frequent orders.

The ability to negotiate effectively is a very important tool of the credit professional. Credit professionals in companies large and small are constantly negotiating with one customer or another over account payments, the release of orders, the timing of payment and order releases, etc. The credit manager or administrator negotiates with salespeople in his or her own company over pending orders, credit worthiness, and, if the account isn't very good, what the best the credit manager will do for the account is versus what the account seems to think it needs. What about people in other departments of the company? Negotiate with data processing for more frequent accounts receivable aging reports, and for changes in the report that might require a change in the program. Professionally, life is one continuous negotiation—and the person who understands and can handle skillfully what is an art form cannot avoid being one long step ahead of the rest of the field.

To Factor or Not to Factor?

Your company could be a candidate for short-term factoring of its receivables (a minimum of one year) if one or more of the following is true:

1. The company's accounts receivable is not a part of the security agreement with the bank.

2. The bank has already granted your company credit lines for the purchase (or lease) of manufacturing and warehouse equipment, land acquisition, and development costs for a 50,000 square-foot factory and office building.

3. The bank has financed the lease of office, plant, and warehouse equipment (a fork lift, a pickup truck, a two and one-half ton delivery truck, chairs, desks, a computer, a word-processing typewriter, etc.)

4. When approached regarding a cash-flow credit line against the company's accounts receivable, the bank indicated that it had already invested heavily in the company and was not currently receptive to the thought of yet another line of credit.

5. When your company suggested to the bank that the aging of accounts receivable was well within the standards for your industry (and your company's credit plan) and should provide more than an adequate level of security, the bank again declined to offer a credit line secured by the accounts receivable.

(Two good options? Short-term factoring or another bank.)

An example of a Balance Sheet (Financial Spread Sheet) is shown in Figure 3-6. The format that is illustrated can accommodate as few as one balance sheet (the current one) or as many as five of the most recent financials. While it is not likely that most suppliers will be able to get copies for more than one or two years, it should not discourage credit managers from trying for copies of additional statements.

These are important documents—documents that present a financial picture in dollars—that detail what happened during the company's past two, three, four, or five years of business operations. The figures can speak of growth that has been consistent and of a minor or major setback that escaped the notice of suppliers or credit reporting agencies; the story that some of these figures tell may require an explanation. Have both the business trend and profits been increasing on an annual basis? Unless there is something derogatory in the company, industry, or economy that would negatively influence a continuation of growth and profits, there is good reason to assume that the trend will continue.

I should mention again that a credit manager must know whether the financial statements have been internally or externally prepared and whether they were prepared from audited or unaudited data. When this key question has been put to rest and the credit manager is looking at a side-by-side comparison of credible financial statements for two or more years, an invaluable decision-making tool will have been added to the credit manager's pool of experience data.

PART 2

Accounts Receivable

Manufacturers, distributors, wholesalers, and some businesses that deal in a service cannot aspire to a future tinted with the rosy glow of growth and success if the quality of their accounts receivable is incapable of achieving or sustaining it. The company's business plan might have included what seemed to be a very attainable role for receivables, but if the quality isn't there, the problem of liquidity becomes increasingly acute. There is no viable alternative to an accounts receivable total whose performance is exactly as represented in the financial statement—a liquid asset.

The restricting burden of too many flawed accounts on the receivables aging report of a business is more than most can bear successfully. Accounts receivable should turn over rapidly—within terms or within a very few days of terms—and if they do not, the financial burden on the company begins to become heavier and heavier. In this scenario, the basic premise of liquid receivables is to minimize bank borrowing for the purpose of augmenting internally generated cash flow. But if receivables are not liquid, or do not have enough liquidity to provide the major source of cash flow, liquidity becomes trapped in a maze of accounts that owe too much and pay too many days past terms. When that occurs, the company is forced to rely more frequently and more heavily on bank support to provide the necessary level of cash flow.

Build quality into your accounts receivable, but build it to standards that are compatible with the goals, the ambitions, and the business plan of your company. The goals of your company may differ dramatically from those of most other members of the same industry or business group. Credit decisions might have to be made that compromise the criteria for a quality accounts receivable in the interest of rapid growth— a type of growth dictated frequently by a management anxious to convey a short-term image of exceptional success. Early in Part 1 of this handbook, I outlined the virtues and the pitfalls of three credit policies (restrictive, moderate, and liberal). The quality of your company's receivables—of any company's receivables—is tied directly to the pressure for growth that falls from top management to land upon the marketing and sales department, and upon the credit department.

A sale that cannot be booked because the credit department will not authorize a credit line or release a one-time order, doesn't slow the relentless drive for sales; if a liberal credit policy has been mandated by top management, it doesn't improve the overall quality of the receivables. Accounts receivable is undoubtedly your company's largest liquid asset, and a credit professional will do his or her best to see that this asset retains the maximum percentage of liquidity. How effective that effort will be may be dictated by the rules under which the credit manager is expected to play. Is the credit manager expected to maximize the flow of cash from the company's receivables? Exercise your best professional judgment and give the job your best efforts, but the amount of cash flow that you will generate from receivables balances can only be proportionate to the quality of the receivables themselves. What about accounts that have been oversold for their companies and payment histories? Payments will be slower, aging will be a constant problem, and the payment weakness of the account will diminish the percentage of net profit on the product(s) sold to it. Money will have to be borrowed to compensate for the weakness of this and similar accounts, and bank charges will further diminish the profit margin on sales to these accounts.

The need to maximize cash flow is a goal of companies, businesses, and commercial ventures everywhere. It is the goal of manufacturers who distribute, of distributors, of wholesalers, of those in the service industries who offer their customers credit accounts, and of retailers who accept credit accounts. No business in any of the above listed categories has a realistic chance of achieving lasting success, unless the largest liquid asset of each—their accounts receivable balances—can be converted rapidly and consistently into cash flow (see Figures P2-1 and P2-2).

The Options for Manufacturers Who Distribute

Manufacturers in many industries have a distribution network that consists of company-owned sales offices and warehouses in areas of their home state, in a region (Pacific Coast states, Rocky Mountain

```
(Date)



Company Name
Street Address (or P.O. Box Number)
City, State, Zip Code

Attention: _____(name and title)_____

Dear Mr. (or Ms.) ____(name)_____:

The attached copy (copies) of invoice (invoices) _____
(and _____ ) is (are) being forwarded as you requested
during our telephone conversation on ____(date)_____.

This information should enable you to verify the accuracy of this (these)
invoice balance (balances) and expedite the processing of payment.

Sincerely,


Credit Manager
```

Figure P2-1. Copies of invoices attached.

states, etc.), in a large area (West of the Mississippi, East of the
Mississippi, etc.), or in company-owned sales offices and warehouses
throughout the United States (and perhaps also in Canada). These
companies prefer to control the manufacture and distribution of their
products from factory to the user or consumer. There is seldom a
question in the minds of management people who direct the fortunes of
these companies that total control is, for them, the most effective way
to do business.

Other manufacturers prefer a mix of the methods available to
distribute their product(s). These manufacturers may, while retaining
control of product distribution in specific areas of their home state or
specific regions or sections of the country, select distributors in other
areas of the state or country who are well established or give strong
promises of developing into aggressive and successful representatives
for the manufacturer's products.

What is credit management's role in this situation? Manufacturers
who distribute their own products exercise 100 percent control over
their customer base. The logical sequence is that no customer who asks
to buy on credit terms is shipped the manufacturer's products until and

Figure P2-2. Copy of invoice attached.

unless the company's credit department has screened the account to determine whether it is credit worthy at the requested level of purchases.

When the screening procedure has been completed and the order (or credit line) has been approved or disapproved, the manufacturer will either ship the order or explain to the customer why the order cannot be released on credit. Monitoring the account and collecting the account balance is the responsibility of the manufacturer's credit department. If the account fails to adhere to credit terms, or pays so slowly that it becomes a problem, the responsibility for accepting the account cannot be shifted to a third party.

How does the situation change when the manufacturer makes intrastate sales from company offices and warehouses scattered around the company's home state, but has a small network of distributors who handle sales in the other 10 of 11 western states? The first difference is that this manufacturer does not have the same control of the company's revenues from sales as does the company described in the preceding paragraph. Whether this manufacturer receives prompt payment for its products from the various out-of-company distributors is related directly to the credit department's thoroughness in screening the capabilities of potential distributors (financial status, business reputation, quality and experience of personnel, location and size of office and warehouse, territory serviced, years in business, etc.) before a distributor agreement is finalized and signed.

This manufacturer's distributors—any manufacturer's distributors—are only as good as the quality of the distributor's customers. There are other circumstances that might cause a distributor to begin to lose momentum, but customers who handle their accounts properly are a must. If the distributor does not receive payment on a reasonably prompt basis from sales to customers of this and other manufacturer's products, the distributor's payments to the manufacturer are going to become slower and slower.

When the manufacturer's distributor also handles other nonconflicting lines, reference data received from the prospective distributor should enable the manufacturer's credit department to promptly resolve any questions regarding the manner in which the distributor handles supplier accounts. This data is also indicative of the prospective customer's attitude and thoroughness in screening its customers. If payments to the distributor's suppliers are within or close to terms, it indicates that the distributor's customer base is strong. When fast-turning receivables are providing the company with a strong cash flow, one of the manufacturer's major concerns has been eliminated.

The Options for Businesses in Service Industries

Businesses that operate in a service industry (plant security, accounting, janitorial services, etc.) and offer credit terms to their customers have an entirely different set of problems. A product might be an integral part of the service (an example is bottled water), but it is very frequently a product that, once it has been delivered, cannot be recovered if the customer fails to pay. The service company is in the not unusual position of having a payroll to meet and the unusual situation of having little or no possibility for recovery of product(s) in the event of a business failure.

It is imperative that service industry members screen prospective credit customer accounts with care, and proceed with caution in any situation where there is an unanswered question regarding the customers ability to meet its obligation to the supplier of services. Part 3 of this book will examine the provisions of the Uniform Commercial Code and how your firm—regardless of the state in which it is located or the number of states in which it does business—can take appropriate measures to ensure the maximum amount of protection for its receivables. Any company or business that offers credit terms to its commercial customers cannot afford to avail itself of every protective action and/or device that is available to grantors of commercial credit. There may be customers who feel that a filing under the provisions of the Uniform Commercial Code is a reflection on the financial stability of its firm.

There is, in Part 1 (Chapter 5), a detailed listing of sales terms other than credit. While noncredit terms do not offer a customer the advantages that accrue when purchases are made on credit terms, the manufacturer, supplier, or service industry company will sometimes conclude that it is not in the company's best interest to offer credit terms. Whether the prospective customer chooses to accept terms other than credit and attempts to build toward a credit relationship is a decision that must be made on an individual company basis. The possibilities are many, but none are as attractive as credit. It follows that the privilege of making credit purchases hinges on whether there is a strong record of paying suppliers within acceptable parameters.

Retailers Who Do a Credit Business

Some of the larger retail merchandisers (Macy's, Sears, Wards, Mervyn's, The Emporium, etc.) offer credit terms to many of their customers via credit cards issued by the individual retailers or via other cards such as VISA, MasterCard, American Express, etc. Purchases made on cards issued by major and area retailers are, in this context, the only true credit sale made by these retailers. When the customer uses VISA or MasterCard to make a purchase, the retailer does not immediately have access to the proceeds from these sales. It is true, however, that the retailer usually has access to the proceeds from these sales in a shorter period of time than from monthly payments received on the same type of purchases and charged to the retailer's in-house credit card.

Remember, however, that the merchandiser who offers customers the store's own credit card, or who accepts credit accounts on other and sometimes longer terms (30/60/90 days or special account or special purchase terms of 12, 24, or 36 months), adds to those accounts a finance or service charge. Many retail merchandisers insist that the finance or service charge that is added each month to the unpaid balance of the credit card account should not be construed as profit; these people insist that the monthly charge on an unpaid balance does nothing more than offset the cost to the merchandiser of not receiving immediate payment. There is, they say, the necessity to augment cash flow with a higher level of bank borrowing.

I do not have expertise in the area of retail sales or retail credit sales. My discussions with representatives of major and regional merchandisers does, however, tend to give credibility to their claim that a finance (or service) charge on unpaid balances of more than 30 days is not lining their pockets with a layer of gold. In today's highly competitive retail marketplace—and given the sharply higher costs of labor, benefits programs, per square foot of retail and warehouse space, taxes, advertising, increasing cost of merchandise, etc.—a strong case might be made for the position of these merchandisers. Cash or a personal check? It puts the money in the till immediately. There is no lag time between the sale, the charge to the customer's store, VISA, MasterCard, or other card, and the store receives its money for the merchandise sold.

Your company's largest liquid asset, if you offer credit to your customers, is accounts receivable. How you handle the screening, monitoring, and collecting of those balances will go a long way toward determining the success of that company. If you are the entrepreneur, the company is small, and you do the credit work, learn everything you can about credit management to protect this most critical asset. If you are an employee of a larger company whose job it is to protect the company's assets and to maximize the amount of internally generated cash flow, do the best and most professional job that your training and experience will allow, and if your training and experience are deficient in any area, raise the level of your professionalism as quickly and as effectively as you can.

8

Receivables Management

The importance of good accounts receivables management cannot be overemphasized, but in order to have good receivables to manage, there must be strong and effective screening procedures. A company's financial statement might list an impressive receivables total (a total that is allegedly a "quick asset"), but if the individual accounts within the receivables total are so slow-turning that they fail to supply a strong percentage of the monthly cash-flow requirement, that "impressive total" soon reveals itself to be a negative force.

Inconsistency will be the hallmark of accounts that find their way onto the Accounts Receivable Aging Report of the company whose credit department does not use effective screening procedures, screening procedures that minimize the danger of adding accounts that fail to meet the company's criteria for an acceptable credit account. What are some of the benefits that a company may derive from good receivables accounts? Good receivables can be . . .

. . . the security base for bank loans

. . . the primary source of internally generated cash flow

. . . the nonliquid base that can lead to the filing of a Chapter 11 bankruptcy and/or business failure

. . . the channel of financial liquidity that is a primary force in developing and sustaining business growth and promoting business longevity

. . . the internal source of low-cost money for a variety of external uses and purposes

... the credit manager's ultimate report card; the tally sheet that addresses whether he or she did a good job from screening of the applicants through collection of the receivables

These are not the only benefits to be derived from strong accounts receivable balances, or the negatives that can accrue when a receivables base has too many weak accounts. The potential to the company for beneficial uses of good receivables balances goes well beyond the few benefits (and negatives) cited in the foregoing examples. Suffice to say that good receivables are a dimension unto themselves. There is no acceptable alternative to accounts receivable that, when called upon to do so, will deliver on their promise to pay—and pay when due.

Strong Screening Procedures

When a credit manager screens the qualifications of an applicant for credit, he or she should look at the applicant's credentials through the mental equivalent of a gauze filter, and then allow his or her eyes to add an overlay of dollar signs. This will give the credit person the proper perspective for evaluating what is often, to the credit person, a business that is an unknown entity to which he or she is being asked to commit various amounts of the company product(s) or service(s) assets.

There is no consistently effective alternative to a credit procedure that is sequential in the steps that must be taken before a credit decision can be made. The pitfalls that await when shortcuts are attempted have been mentioned in an earlier chapter. Nothing can be left to chance. If the credit manager or administrator is as conscientious about doing a good job as he or she should be, a shortcut to avoid one or more essential procedural steps is not an acceptable alternative to the thorough, sequential approach of checking and evaluating an account.

Strong screening procedures are essential if the process is to deliver accounts of acceptable quality. When credit experience data has been gathered from the sources discussed in Part 1 (Chapter 3), the credit manager's evaluation of the data is crucial to whether the account is accepted or rejected, whether the account does or does not perform as expected, and if it does not meet earlier expectations, understanding what went wrong. Were one or more clues missed, during the account evaluation, that would have been indicative of what the credit grantor should have expected in the future?

Search the data for signs of strengths and weaknesses. Do not concentrate on one or the other because both are important, and some of both may be present in most accounts. The trick is to recognize the strength of the plusses and the strength of the weaknesses, and determine from that evaluation which is the more dominant. If weaknesses overshadow strengths, or the presence of weaknesses is sufficiently disturbing enough to raise questions regarding the direction (and speed) in which the prospective customer is headed, the account may warrant a small credit line, or none at all. Strengths should be in the important areas of the business (financial, quality of the company's personnel, product line(s), strength of the customer base, competition and competitive pressures, etc.). Weaknesses should be in areas that relate to problems that are correctible (erratic pricing structure, deliveries not always on time, credits not issued properly and/or promptly, etc.). An experienced credit manager might find a preponderance of primary strengths enough to greatly diminish negative factors and warrant a credit line commensurate with the company's size, quality, annual growth and earnings, and years in business.

What are the financial benefits that can accrue from credit accounts that have been properly screened and monitored? Perhaps the primary benefit is that the turnover of receivables balances should be rapid. The average aging for receivables balances should never average more than a few days beyond terms of sale. The rapid turnover of receivables achieves the goal of maximizing the contribution of internally generated cash flow while minimizing the amount of bank borrowings needed to meet the company's cash-flow requirement.

There is a "bottom line" to the foregoing recap of accrued benefits that directly and indirectly impacts the "bottom line" of the company's financial statement. If good control over the quality of credit accounts can be translated into accounts receivables balances that are paid rapidly—and at a percentage that is on the high end of industry collection averages—then the annual total of interest dollars paid to the company's bank will be decreased substantially. Those dollars, when allowed to take their rightful place in the company's "bottom line," will be a strong incentive to continue the screening procedures that delivered such gratifying results.

Strong screening procedures strike hard at another credit management problem: the occasional account that becomes a bad-debt write-off. When bad-debt write-offs are reduced to the lowest possible number, the dollars that would have slipped into a pit with other nonrecoverable receivables losses will instead take their place in the bottom-line figure. No less important is the fact that dollars that might have been borrowed to replace lost working capital will not be needed. Working capital (cash flow) remains intact, the bank line is not reduced by the amount (if a significant loss) needed to restore working capital to an acceptable level, and the company will not be paying additional interest charges to the bank.

The offering of commercial credit terms to customers is an integral part of business life for the overwhelming majority of manufacturers, distributors, wholesalers, and members of some service and retail industries. A company cannot enjoy the benefit of good credit decisions unless there are a clearly defined credit policy and sound credit procedures. The person who is charged with managing the credit function or department must have the knowledge and experience to make effective credit decisions. It must be someone who knows the criteria for screening new credit customers, and who knows how to watch for problems in existing accounts and how to move quickly and effectively when an account begins to slip into a pattern of recurring past-due balances. The credit manager must know whom to sell, when to sell, when to work out a payment arrangement, when to hold orders, and when to put a once-acceptable credit account on C.O.D. terms.

Is It a Credit Worthy Account?

The question is one that might draw a variety of answers, answers shaded in varying degrees of caution, depending upon the parameters established by individual companies. Some companies use more liberal guidelines than others in arriving at an answer. As an example, your company might routinely extend credit terms to accounts whose traditional payment pattern is to pay several days after due date. This might not be compatible with the cash-flow requirements of companies who don't feel they can afford to carry customers for those additional days. Your credit department will screen credit applicants on the basis of a more liberal set of criteria than will companies that do not carry accounts (or as many accounts) that pay consistently several days past terms.

Selling on credit terms is not without a special set of dangers. Any company that offers credit terms must have good credit and collection procedures, procedures that ensure the strength and liquidity of accounts receivable on an ongoing basis. Good credit management has its foundation in well-conceived programs and controls, and effective credit management is locked into that strong foundation.

It is irrelevant to the subject of credit worthy accounts whether your company is a manufacturer and distributor, distributes the products of other companies, or is in a service industry. If your company sells its products or services on credit terms, the company's credit accounts should represent the most comprehensive compilation of data—and analysis of that data—that your experience and judgment can bring to bear. If you do not have much experience in evaluating accounts (or prospective accounts), guidelines are crucial in avoiding costly judgmental errors. There must be a set of procedures and guidelines for determining what is and what is not an acceptable credit risk. Nothing should be lost, not a single dollar, because there was a momentary sloughing of one or more phases of the guidelines.

The following guidelines should help you get the information and ask the questions that will enable you to recognize whether an account is or is not "credit worthy." These guidelines will help you select and refine data and information to the point where your evaluation of the account (assuming the requisite level of experience and training) is going to make reaching the right decision—a good decision—much easier.

A credit worthy account should offer the following:

1. Good supplier experience and strong bank experience data. Example: Does the company or business use a bank line for augmenting cash flow? Does it use the credit line each month? Occasionally? Seldom? Not at all?

2. Financial statements (for two or three years) that indicate good profits and steady growth.

3. A business plan that is committed to a pattern of steady rather than sporadic or accelerated growth.

4. A business history that is long enough to have established a favorable trend (or favorable indicators, if the business is less than two years old).

5. If a sole proprietorship or partnership, the reputation(s) and experience of the principal(s) is at the core of an evaluation of the business. If a partnership, is the balance of skills and experience adequate for long-term success? If a sole proprietorship, what does the proprietor bring to the business in the areas of management, sales, and other skills? Does he or she have one or two employees whose skills and/or experience compensate for gaps in the owner's experience and/or skills? And, quite important to good continuity, have these employees been with the business for months or years?

6. If a corporation, antecedent data relating to the experience and reputation of top management (CEO, COO, Finance Officer, etc.).

7. If a corporation, has it made a public offering? Is it positioning itself for one? If there has been a public offering, how has the stock been received? Is it up from the initial offer price? Down from that price?

8. If the corporation has not made a public offering, is it positioning itself for one? Is management adhering to sound principals of business or is it pushing to book sales (doubling every quarter, etc.) at the expense of receivables that will not turn rapidly enough to make the necessary contribution to cash flow?

9. No account (unless top-rated) should be approved for the release of an order or the assigning of a credit line, unless enough quality experience data has been received and evaluated.

10. Are there weak credit controls within the customer company? This can jeopardize cash flow and the customer's payment capability.

11. After evaluating the prospective customer, does it fit the guidelines of your company for an acceptable credit risk?

12. If it fits the guidelines, you have a new credit customer. If it does not fit the guidelines, try to work with the customer on terms other than straight credit. Conditions within the company may change for the better, which might then enable your company to gradually phase into a relationship of low-dollar credit sales.

The effective use of good screening procedures will save time and dollars: the time of the credit manager and his or her department, and the accounts receivable dollars of the credit manager's company.

Control New Account Exposure

Every business and company must continue to add new accounts to sustain the process of growth and to replace accounts that, for one reason or another, take their business to another supplier. Attrition in the roster of accounts is caused also by changes within a customer company, such as the de-emphasizing or the discontinuing of certain lines of merchandise, changes in styles, preferences or requirements, or the changing of the customers' focus to another segment of the marketplace. Nothing is ever static, nor should it be. If your company ever falls into the trap of failing to progressively and aggressively address the needs of its market, within a relatively short period of time the customer base will erode to a dangerously low level.

New accounts that have been properly screened present the credit grantor with an opportunity for sales growth. They also present two other possibilities, neither of which will become known until accounts receivable balances begin to come due. In the situation that the credit manager visualized when he or she offered credit terms to the account, the account should pay on time and without prompting; the reverse side of the same account situation finds the credit manager looking at an account that has, almost from the first sale, paid in an erratic and an unsatisfactory manner.

The answer is to control new account exposure. The translation? Set realistic credit lines and adhere to them. Do not be swayed by pressures and comments such as, "Our payments to suppliers have been a little slow the past six or eight months, but we're working our way out of it. I don't know what the suppliers will tell you, because we've been on this terrific roller coaster ride of very rapid growth followed by a real downer: a regional recession and an even stronger recession in our own industry." A big smile, a nod, and a wink. "Give us a good line of credit, partner, and we'll make some good money for your company."

I hope you recognize "con" when you read it or hear it. What you have just read is an attempt to con a supplier (a manufacturer/distributor) into giving a prospective customer (a wholesaler) something that the facts do not warrant. What are the suppliers saying? They're saying that payments have slowed to the point where orders are being held until part or all of past due balances have been paid. Some say they are selling on a "two dollars for every one dollar of merchandise" basis. Suppliers say they see no evidence to support the statement that the customer is "working their way out of it." What about that "great roller coaster ride of very rapid growth" that preceded the regional and industry recession? A few calls to peer credit managers bring the information that the wholesaler had, six months earlier, virtually trashed the price structure in its marketplace area, flooding the market at ridiculously low prices and selling on credit terms to everyone who would buy.

The saying "don't give away the store" is appropriate in the context of controlling your company's exposure when dealing with new customers. Does the customer have an excellent financial statement and a good record with suppliers and the bank? Sell the account to a good credit limit, but try to avoid approaching too quickly the maximum credit line that your company would allow. Your company should first become comfortable with the account—performance, paying habits, etc.—before you push the credit line too close to the account's ceiling. Do not, however, hesitate to voluntarily reward a good account by sending a letter in which you express your company's appreciation for the exemplary way in which the account has been handled. Close the letter with the icing on the cake; a credit line increase that, as you assure the customer, has indeed been earned. The customer is pleased, and your company may receive orders in dollar totals high enough to move the account onto the new and higher plateau of credit.

What about accounts that do not offer uniformly acceptable reference data? Some suppliers seem to be paid in a satisfactory manner, while others report sporadic payments that badly abuse supplier terms. There might also be a block of supplier accounts that receive payment treatment that is more erratic than sporadic—the hills and valleys of those whose payment pattern is erratic (not consistent or uniform) are not as deep as those whose payment pattern is sporadic (at irregular intervals). This is an area in which close control of your company's exposure is of the utmost importance.

Constant Monitoring
of Accounts

If there is one assumption that cannot be made with any assurance that it will be self-fulfilling, it is the assumption that, "this is a good account and does not need to be watched." Not true. "Monitoring" is the credit profession's synonym for "watching" and the importance of that activity is not to be taken lightly. Every account, regardless of how strong it might seem to be when your company offers a credit line, has the potential to become a problem. That statement does not exclude the likes of General Motors, Ford Motor Company, IBM, Apple Computer, and any other company that depends for its success on the domestic or worldwide marketplace.

The demand for product(s) changes. The technology that for several years made one company a winner must inevitably be superceded by the more advanced technology of another firm. Perhaps not "inevitably," but too frequently, the long-time leader in a particular field of business or technology becomes complacent. The R & D that made the high-tech company a leader no longer receives the emphasis it once did; therein lies the crux of a tale of lost leadership. When leaders no longer exert the effort required to be preeminent in a field or an industry, the credit manager at one of the key suppliers will eventually begin to pick up the first indicators of an emerging weakness and a growing instability. When that occurs, and unless there is a turnaround that embraces both attitude and technology, the company that was once a leader may have to struggle to retain a big enough percentage of market share to remain profitable, or to keep losses at a minimum.

Whether the credit department gets a receivables report update once a week or twice a week is not relevant to the requirement of constant monitoring of receivables accounts. Monitoring should be done on a daily basis and preferably immediately after payments have been posted to the manager's copy of the aging report. Every time a new receivables report is delivered to the credit manager, he or she should go down the listing of accounts, account by account, and page by page, to determine which accounts have failed to pay a promised past-due balance, or have failed to pay within their usual parameters of time. Minor deviations from the usual pattern of payments should be monitored carefully and on an ongoing basis to ensure that the unexpected minor deviation does not suddenly become a major account problem.

Smaller and weaker companies are even more vulnerable when there is a loss of business. The loss may be due to a change in customer buying habits or the result of a national, regional, or industry recession, but the reason is irrelevant if the impact on one or more customer companies causes them to post progressively larger losses. Companies whose financial resources are limited cannot weather indefinitely a pattern of quarterly losses—a pattern that portends serious financial consequences to the company and to those who have associated themselves with it. Suppliers are especially vulnerable, and although they might have made the appropriate protective filings under the Uniform Commercial Code, there is no guarantee that an assets value that decreases each quarter will be adequate—if there is a Chapter 11 filing—to pay more than a small percent on each dollar of secured claims. In such a scenario, substantial loss to the creditors is inevitable.

Assigning a credit limit is just the first step in what then becomes a constant state of alertness to ensure that the company's receivables asset—an asset already at one level of risk because it is controlled by another company—remains as safe as you thought it was when the credit line was assigned. The following will help you to touch the important bases:

1. Monitor the current payment habits of your customers against what they did three, six, or twelve months ago.

2. Compare how the customer is currently handling payments to other suppliers versus the experience data in your file folder for the account.

3. Take your current accounts receivable aging report and compare the account aging against a report that is three or six months old.

4. Is there a change in the pattern of payments over the past three, six, or twelve months? Should the change be categorized as minor, progressively more noticeable, or major?

5. Is there a noticeable increase in the number of past-due days in one, a few, or several accounts?

6. Have you made it a priority to find out the problems or reasons for the slowing of payments?

7. Are you working with these customers to reduce the average number of days from invoice date until past-due invoices are paid?

8. Are you comfortable with the safety of a few, some, or all of the accounts whose open balances are more than a few days past due?

9. If you are concerned regarding the safety of certain account balances, what are you doing to reduce or eliminate your company's risk?

Monitoring the company's accounts receivable on an ongoing basis is one of the most effective ways to identify problems in their earliest stages (see Figure 8-1). It is obvious that an account whose payment record with your company has, for the past 12 months, been "Prompt to Slow 10 or 15 days" is breaking new and potentially dangerous ground when the oldest open balances slip to 20 to 30 days past due. Something is impacting the company's cash flow and it is the credit manager's responsibility to get answers—and

Memorandum

Date   cc: _____

                                                          _____

To: _____

From: Credit Department   _____

Subject: _____

My telephone conversation this date with _____
_____ indicates that the listed unit/system is not operating within specifications, and payment will not be released until it is.

   Job Number_____

   Invoice Number_____

   Invoice Date_____

   Invoice Amount _____

   Customer P.O._____

   Type of Unit/System_____

   Customer's Description of Problem _____

_____

_____

_____

Please advise what corrective action has been/will be taken to help expedite payment of invoice.

                         _____

- -

To:
I have taken/I am initiating the following corrective action.

_____

_____

_____

                         _____

Figure 8-1. Memo regarding nonperforming product.

money—as rapidly as possible. An experienced credit professional will look at the most current receivables aging report and notice immediately any changes in the size and aging of account balances.

When credit managers identify and react promptly to early warning signs, there is an excellent chance that the company's receivables balance can be collected. It should also be noted that what may appear to be the start of an unfavorable trend might be a temporary situation that has a logical explanation. If the explanation is logical—and the situation does appear to be temporary—arriving at a mutually acceptable way to work through the temporary situation may pose no problems. But you, the credit manager or credit administrator, must assure yourself that the account is not sliding into a problem or a situation that may prove to be irreversible.

Monitor constantly your company's receivables accounts. Look for that first, almost imperceptible sign of a weakness or a deviation from normal aging and payment patterns. Pay close attention to the comments of peer credit managers, your company's sales representatives, and data or information that comes to you in monthly credit meetings or in reports from agencies such as NACM and Dun & Bradstreet. Pay particular attention to what you see and hear when you see the customer at the customer's place of business. You might observe something significantly different from what you observed on prior visits (unusually low levels of inventory, which might indicate that the customer is having difficulty getting suppliers to release normal quantities of product[s] on credit terms).

An ongoing program of monitoring your company's receivables accounts—and moving swiftly at the first sign of a potential problem—is the best safety net you can provide for the protection of the company's receivables.

Updating Credit Files

The credit information that you use to open an account is comparable in its shelf life to a loaf of fresh-baked bread. When information from suppliers, the banker, and credit reporting agencies is current, your credit decisions are based on a loaf of information that is fresh from these sources. To rely on that information for longer than three to six months (especially when the account is new and the supplier payment pattern has been somewhat inconsistent) is comparable to serving stale, rock-hard bread at a formal dinner. The texture of the account (as in the texture of the bread) could have changed dramatically in the three to six months since you granted the credit line, and now you need to know what is going on!

Your own experience with an account will tell you whether three or six months is a proper time frame before the credit file of an account should be updated. It is also true that not every account should be handled under one guideline; some accounts should be updated every three months and others at the end of six. There is no inflexible rule for selecting a time frame for updating customer accounts. The one, the only, inflexible is to have currently applicable information in the file folder of each account.

The Customer Credit File

One of the most important considerations when you are setting up or rebuilding your company's credit department is to establish a format for good customer files. A customer credit file should contain all of the information that was relevant to the first credit decision, plus the experience that the supplier/creditor company has had with the customer. A manila folder with the customer's name on the tab and a disorganized jungle of notes and reports on the inside does not qualify as a credit file. To qualify as a credit file, there should be a systematized sequence for filing the various forms, credit reports, letters, and other material relevant to the account. Information is the key ingredient when a supplier/customer relationship is getting its start. The emphasis shifts gradually to experience as the supplier and creditor builds a base of business experience with the customer company—a base that can become a useless mass of nonrelated, nonintegrated material if it isn't put together in manageable form.

The following practical guide for systematizing the contents of your customer credit files should be done when the account first receives a credit line. It is a Section 1 (Chapter 1) function, and I would urge you to integrate this procedure into your sequence for processing new accounts. Some account folders will expand more slowly than others after the initial input of forms, reports, and letters; others will quickly expand to the point where they become candidates for a Weight Watchers' program. Important points to remember: take the time to properly set up file folders; add papers, letters, and reports in a systematic rather than a haphazard manner; make dated, clear, and accurate notes regarding any discussion, telephone conversation, or subject that might have future relevance or importance, and never allow yourself to wonder if the time spent maintaining good and complete files is a waste. Let me assure you that it is not.

The first (or top) document is numbered "1." File folders should be set up with documents in the following order:

1. The Resale Card (Sales Tax Exemption Number)

2. Financial Statements (first and updates filed together)

3. Credit Application Form

4. Request for Experience Information (from Credit Application references)

5. Credit Investigation Form (consolidates bank/supplier data)

6. Credit File Control Sheet

7. Letter Notifying Customer of Credit Line

8. Dun & Bradstreet Reports (if any)

9. Incoming or Outgoing Letters (re: discounts, missing invoices, etc.)

10. Customer Call Sheet

Documents and correspondence not listed above (Chapter 11 filings, third-party collection assignments, etc.) may become part of a customer's file. If the file folder is set up properly, you should have no difficulty fitting a new category into the appropriate location (see Figures 8-2 and 8-3).

Customer File Folder

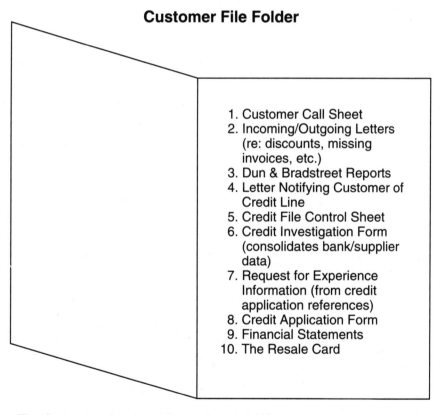

1. Customer Call Sheet
2. Incoming/Outgoing Letters (re: discounts, missing invoices, etc.)
3. Dun & Bradstreet Reports
4. Letter Notifying Customer of Credit Line
5. Credit File Control Sheet
6. Credit Investigation Form (consolidates bank/supplier data)
7. Request for Experience Information (from credit application references)
8. Credit Application Form
9. Financial Statements
10. The Resale Card

(The first or top document is numbered *1*. When you open a customer's file folder, the top document should be the Customer Call Sheet.)

Figure 8-2. Customer file folder.

```
Date:
                               CUSTOMER MASTER FILE PRINT-OUT
=============================================================================================================

-------------CUSTOMER------------  ADDRESS - 1        CITY           TELEPHONE #  TYP  SLM TAX?----TAX-----    CRD-LMT  TR BM
  NUM  NAME                         ADDRESS - 2        ST    ZIP                   P/L  DIV                              SF SC

  0.    FIRST COVENANT CHURCH       790 COE AVENUE     SAN JOSE       000-000-0000      99  N  TAX #        250.00  1 0
                                                       CA    95125                 1   99                           Y  Y

  00365 S.R. FLAKS CO.              815 S. SIERRA MADRE COLORADO SPRING303-471-0821     99  N  TAX #       5,000.00  1 0
                                                       CO    80903                 1   99                           Y  Y

  00367 FLAVORFUL DIST. CO.         1777 ANGELA ST.    SAN JOSE       408-286-8400      99  N  TAX #          0.00  4 0
                                                       CA    95125                 1  408                           1  .

  00369 FLOWER'S DIST. CO.          206 LINDEN STREET  RENO           702-826-3860      88  N  TAX #       2,500.00  1 0
                                    P.O. BOX 1543      NV    89805                 1  702                           Y  Y

  00375 FOOD BROKERS INT            1952 WILLIAMS ST.  SAN LEANDOR    415-357-0550      99  N  TAX #          0.00  1 0
                                                       CA    94577                 1    0                           Y  Y

  00387 FUN FOOD                    1524 N. 18TH AVE.  PHOENIX        602-257-0302      99  N  TAX #       2,500.00  1 0
                                                       AZ    85007                 1  602                           Y  Y

  00390 FUN WAYS CARNIVAL           2492 EL CAMINO REAL SANTA CLARA   000-000-0000      99  N  TAX #       1,000.00  1 0
                                                       CA    95051                 1   99 SY-GH-26735181-001         Y  Y

  00395 GEARY WHOLESALE CO.         4120 PERALTA       FREMONT        415-794-4498  1   99  N  TAX #          0.00  1 0
                                                       CA    94536                 1  415                           Y  Y

  00401 GELLER DIST. CO.            804 APGAR ST.      OAKLAND        415-654-4940  9   99  N  TAX #      15,000.00  1 0
                                                       CA    94608                 1  415 SRCH21-066422             Y  Y

  00402 GEM STATE DIST. INC.        350 INDUSTRIAL LN. POCATELLO      208-237-5151      99  N  TAX #      10,000.00  1 0
                                    P.O. BOX 2499      ID    83201                 1  208 00165505-03-3-1           Y  Y

  00407 G.L. ADAMS CO.              829 RISKE          W. SACRAMENTO  916-371-6370      99  N  TAX #          0.00  3 0
                                    P.O. BOX 1194      CA    95691                 1   88                           Y  N

  00408 G.L. ADAMS   #2             829 RISKE          W. SACRAMENTO  916-371-6370  9   99  N  TAX #          0.00  5 0
                                    P.O. BOX 1194      CA    95691                 1    0                           Y  .

  00410 GLOBAL ASSOCIATES           P.O. BOX 12156     OAKLAND        415-834-8242      0   N  TAX #       5,000.00  1 0
                                    OAKLAND ARMY TERMINAL CA  94604                 1    0                           Y  Y

  00414 GOLDEN EMPIRE CANDY         810 OAK ST.        CHICO          916-342-1857      88  N  TAX #       3,500.00  1 0
                                                       CA    95926                 1   88 CRMH 02-000411            Y  Y

  00415 GOLDEN PRODUCTS             3162 16TH ST.      SAN FRANCISCO  415-861-9702      99  N  TAX #         500.00  1 0
                                                       CA    94103                 1   99                           Y  Y

  00421 GOOD TIME FOODS             48839 KATO RD      FREMONT        415-490-3434  9   88  N  TAX #       3,500.00  1 0
                                                       CA    04538                 1   99 SY CHA26-696658           Y  Y

  00423 GRACE LUTHERAN CHURCH       188 E. COOPER ST.  CRESCENT CITY  707-464-4712  1   99  N  TAX #         500.00  1 0
                                    P.O. BOX 459       CA    95531                 1  707                           Y  N
```

Figure 8-3. Master file printout of customers and credit lines.

If your company belongs to a credit reporting organization such as Dun & Bradstreet or the National Association Of Credit Management, you might decide to selectively order credit reports on an interval of six months. You can arrange with either of these reporting agencies for this type of service. It should not be necessary, however, to order semiannual (or more frequent) reports on more than a small number of the company's accounts. It is a tool worth remembering, and one worth using to update credit file information and to ascertain the current status of specific accounts.

Discounts—Authorized and Unauthorized

The practice of allowing discounts for the early payment of invoices and/ or account balances is a standard practice in some businesses and industries, a matter of individual company choice in others, and not allowed at all in others. When discounts are given, there must be evenhandedness in the application and the policing of the discount policy. It must be administered in a manner that eliminates any question regarding preferential treatment and the creation of a competitive advantage for one company over another or others. Unearned discounts for whatever reasons must be carefully documented (see Figures 8-4 and 8-5). Fair Trade practice demands that discounts should not be given in a manner that creates a

---

Memorandum

(Date)

To: _____(Name)_____ , Treasurer or V.P. Finance)

From: Credit Manager

Re: Write-Off of Unearned Discount Balances

The attached list of Unearned Discounts totals $_____and covers the period from _____ to _____ . The majority of these balances are one-time occurrences and represent such a small amount of money that the department could not justify spending several times the amount of the discount balance in an effort to collect it.

The few larger uncollected balances represent one-time sales or other such nonleverage situations, an explanation for which is included on the attached list of items.

(Signature)

Figure 8-4. Cover memo: write-off of unearned discounts.

Unearned Discounts

Customer Number	Customer Name	Amount of Discount	Reason for Write-Off

(Items listed on this report should represent rare exceptions to your company's guidelines for administering the discount privilege.

Writing off large numbers [or large dollar numbers] of unearned discount balances is not an acceptable pattern for your credit department to use in handling this problem. It represents a competitive advantage that is unfair to those companies that do abide by your company's discount policy and, if allowed to continue unchecked, might be interpreted as an illegal pricing preference.)

Figure 8-5. Unearned discounts (report of customer balances).

competitive advantage for one customer over another. If a manufacturer and/or supplier can show that the extra one-half or one percent discount given for a quantity purchase reflects an actual cost savings to the seller, the criteria for avoiding a violation under the Robinson-Patman Act (which protects individual competitors against the unfair or discriminatory trade practice of competitors) has probably been met.

Promotional discounts are another form of discount—one used primarily to introduce a new product, to try to increase sales of existing products, to reduce the inventory level of a particular product or products, and to motivate customers to buy an extra order or increase the size of a regular order to a level where it will qualify for the discount. Many companies use this tactic if their product(s) has seasonal peaks and valleys. A promotional incentive is another calculated risk that must deliver a higher level of orders from customers who do not usually buy at that level. If the only result is to motivate volume buyers to put a large supply of discount product(s) in their warehouse, and to reduce the size of the next few orders until they have sold the discounted product, then the promotion has failed to deliver the desired results.

Example: A receivables problem developed at one company as the result of a promotion that went on while I was consulting for the supplier. The problem surfaced when customer payments began arriving that the credit department could not reconcile with referenced invoices. Not until someone in the office remembered seeing a letter sent out by the marketing department—one that announced an additional discount of 3 percent for a period of 90 days on a specific product—did I begin to understand the problem. Telephone calls to several accounts quickly confirmed that many customers were participating in the program, many were taking normal discounts *plus* the additional 3 percent, and many were forwarding checks for these net amounts. Good? Hardly. The promotional discount was not supposed to work that way.

The crux of the problem was the original letter to customers and prospective customers which outlined the requirements for qualifying for the promotional discount. It failed to state clearly that the promotional discount—the additional 3 percent—would be applied in the form of a customer credit to respective customer accounts based upon the total amount of promotional discounts earned during the 90 days of the promotion. Customers had no problem accepting the offer of an additional 3 percent discount. The problem took shape because the offer letter left the matter of computing the discount to the company's customers (see Figures 8-6, 8-7, and 8-8).

The marketing department's failure to clearly define the guidelines by which the company would compute promotional discounts generated a small mountain of extra paper work. The company had to send letters of

August 10, 199X

Henry Parnell
The Parnell Company
5631 Barnhart Avenue
Roanoke, VA 24018

Dear Mr. Parnell:

You will want to compare the attached application of payments against
the notations that were on The Parnell Company's checks 1261 and
1262.

A second 3 percent discount was deducted from certain of the invoices
listed on your checks. Because it was not an applicable deduction (only
one 3 percent discount is allowable), it was necessary to adjust the
amount of money applied and change the mix of invoices involved.

I hope the attached detail sheet will give you the information necessary
to adjust your records, and that it does not impose an unreasonable
burden.

Sincerely,

Cecil Bond
Credit Manager

Figure 8-6. Took a second unauthorized three percent discount.

explanation, credit memos, and/or invoices to customers, correcting the
amounts of discount taken. A letter soon followed that was both an apology
for the ambiguity of the original letter and a restatement of the promotion.
The fact that the offer should not have generated such complications
became lost in the flurry of extra letters, telephone calls, and related work
that diverted the time and attention of an already busy credit department
staff. The confusion generated because the absence of a key piece of payment information diminished some of the positive aspects of the promotion, especially for those customers who had thought they were abiding by
the guidelines, only to find themselves adjusting payment records, paying
more money, or waiting for the credit or invoice to arrive so they could
adjust their record.

August 17, 199X

Henry Parnell
The Parnell Company
5631 Barnhart Avenue
Roanoke, VA 24018

Dear Mr. Parnell:

Many thanks for your call. After our conversation this afternoon, I reviewed the problem with Ed Wilson, the company's sales manager.

Ed's May 8th letter to our dealers did indeed state that an additional promotional credit of three percent (3%) could be earned on net invoices on all purchases above stated figures during the period April 1 through July 31, 199X. The Parnell Company's base figure upon which the promotional credit could be built was $131,418.

Unfortunately, Mr. Wilson inadvertently omitted from the May 8th letter the information that our company will prepare credits for each dealer account. Sales figures for the subject period will be the basis for determining credit amounts and should pose no computation or reconciliation problem for our dealers.

The inconvenience is regrettable, but we must ask you to continue to pay invoices in the normal manner, applying the promotional credit only after the specific figure has been received from us.

Sincerely,

Cecil Bond
Credit Manager

Figure 8-7. Follow-up to call from customer about three percent discount.

Credit is squarely in the middle of any confusion that results from a mass-mailed special sales offer that invites extensive misinterpretation. Be sure that any correspondence over which you have control is well-constructed. It will save time, money, and aggravation—your company's and that of your company's customers.

August 25, 199X

Cecil Bond, Credit Manager
Ziegler & Company, Inc.
5932 College Avenue
Santa Clara, CA 95051

Dear Mr. Bond:

Thank you for your two recent letters. I have taken to heart your letter
of August 17 and will proceed to pay invoices taking only my three percent. I place my additional three percent in your capable hands. How's
that for blind faith?

Enclosed is a check for Invoice 4891, less three percent. I understand
that our most recent shipment has been found in the wilds of North
Carolina so you will have more checks in the near future.

It is very reassuring to know that Ziegler & Company has a competent
credit department working for its business success and the success of
your distributors as well.

Sincerely,

Harry Parnell
President

Figure 8-8. Letter from customer with check minus three percent attached.

Unauthorized or Disallowed Discounts

An unauthorized discount is usually taken by a customer who knows
that your company does not give a discount, but hopes you'll overlook
the arbitrary deduction. Game players will hammer you with the tactic if
you allow them to get away with it. If one customer succeeds in establishing a pattern that puts a hole in the integrity of your discount terms,
your company is discriminating against every customer who does play
by your rules.

Disallowed discounts are another branch of the same tree. The classic
example of this abuser is a customer who waits until the 13th, 14th, or 15th

(Date)

Customer Name
Street Address (or P.O. Box Number)
City, State, Zip Code

Dear Mr. (Ms.) _____

We have applied your check number _____ to the invoice (invoices) listed on the remittance section of the check. Unfortunately, the deduction (deductions) taken on invoice (invoices) numbered _____ (and _____) is (are) not allowable on the basis of information in our files.

If you can provide us with information that will substantiate the deduction (these deductions), we shall be happy to adjust our records. If that is not possible, please forward your check in the amount of _____ to cover the unauthorized deduction (deductions).

Sincerely,

Cecil Bond
Credit Manager

Figure 8-9. Check applied and discount disallowed.

of the month before mailing a check for an invoice that should have been processed early enough for the check to reach the supplier's office between the 1st and 10th of the month. Every customer who takes the discount within your terms, or does not take it at all, is paying more for your product(s) or services than the customer who takes your discount policy and tries to bend it into a mockery of fair, competitive practices and solid business integrity.

It is important that you do not allow any customer to compromise the competitive position of your other customers through the abuse of your discount policy. Protect your company's good reputation. Your company's chances for continued success hinge as much on its good reputation as on any other single factor. (Figures 8-9 and 8-10 show samples of letters covering disallowed discounts, unauthorized payment deductions, and missing invoices.)

(Date)

Customer Name
Street Address (or P.O. Box Number)
City, State, Zip Code

Ladies and Gentlemen:

We are unable to allow the discount(s) taken on your check number _____ and applicable to invoice(s) _____.

The deduction was taken after the discount period had expired, so we
must ask that you include the disallowed amount of $_____ as a part of
your next account payment.

Sincerely,

Credit Manager

Figure 8-10. Check applied and discount allowed (different format).

Accounts Receivables Reports

No single document is more important to the effective management of
your accounts receivable than a properly prepared Aged Trial Balance
Report. Special or extenuating circumstances might be applicable to certain balances on the report sheets, but an Accounts Receivable Aged Trial
Balance Report (an Aging Report) should put you on top of what is or is
not happening to your accounts receivable. Each report should give you
data in detail for each account through the date of the report. If that data
is not in a format that you can handle easily and effectively, take the necessary steps to make changes immediately.

Figure 8-11 is an example taken from a computer-prepared Accounts
Receivable Report. Variations occur between computer programs (see
Figure 8-12), but this example is a satisfactory product from an acceptable
program. A keypunch operator inputs certain information for each

account (invoice data, credit information, payments, etc.) which subsequently is brought together when a receivables printout is run. The operator who puts data into your receivables accounts must be experienced to handle the responsibility. Receivables aging reports that are loaded with errors create problems that become long-lasting headaches.

Note the column of three-digit numbers on the left side of the sample report. These digits are account numbers that are assigned to identify the various accounts—numbers that can be increased to four or five digits if the company's active accounts number is in the thousands. List all branch locations that have their own payables section below the home office location and assign them a subaccount number. A home office account number 2655 would have branch listings of 2655.1, 2655.2, etc. You can generate and post invoices for each location, thereby respecting the autonomy of the various branch and subsidiary locations.

Customer names, invoice dates, invoice numbers, and invoice amounts extend across the report to, and through, the "Total Amount" column at midsheet. "The Date" is the point from which you begin individual invoice aging, issue credit memos, identify invoices to which credit memos apply, and post the dollar amount of each invoice or credit memo. List individual open account totals, as of the report date, directly below individual invoice and credit memo totals in the "Total Amount" column.

The sample Accounts Receivable Aged Trial Balance Report reflects aging of accounts on credit terms of Net 30 Days. The comments that follow are applicable to other sales and credit terms as well.

0- to 30-Day Accounts

This account column is either the "not to worry" or the "too early to worry" column. The totals in this column represent current invoices, all still within your terms, and, at this point, probably warrant your attention only if older balances are behind them. The assigned credit line or limit is the primary thing to watch at this point. If your company has a separate order desk, you can simplify interfacing with your department for credit clearances when you key the program for storage of individual accounts receivables data to refuse any order that would push the open credit limit beyond the assigned credit line. Order desk personnel will not be able to process the order unless you or a member of your department allow the order to bypass the credit limit. This simple and automatic safeguard eliminates unpleasant surprises, testy confrontations, and bruised egos. You should watch for signs that a 0- to 30-days account is slipping—or slipping more frequently—into the 31- to 60-days column. A developing pattern of late payments can be a potentially dangerous sign.

Date: November 26, 1992

Accounts Receivable Aged Trial Balance
as of 11/26/92

Customer Number/Name	Document Date/Number	Total Amount	0–30	31–60	Aging 61–90	91 and Over
406	405-632-1098					
Gladings Co.	8/28/92 12345	1,140.00			1,140.00	
	9/24/92 12418	1,140.00			1,140.00	
	10/31/92 12522	936.00	1,488.00		936.00	
	11/04/92 12345	1,488.00				
		1,140.00–			1,140.00–	
		1,488.00	1,488.00	0.00	0.00	0.00
414	213-564-1053					
Gladstone Co.	10/30/92 12508	748.10	748.10			
	11/14/92 12508	748.10–	748.10–			
		0.00	0.00	0.00	0.00	0.00
415	916-145-3902					
Gold Star Ind.	9/30/92 12438	108.00		108.00		
	10/10/92 12463	112.00		112.00		
	11/10/92 12541	135.00	135.00			
	11/21/92 12438	108.00–		108.00–		
		247.00	135.00	112.00	0.00	0.00

Acct		Date	Invoice					
421								
Gopher's	415-173-2956							
		9/24/92	12420	180.00	0.00	0.00	180.00	0.00
		11/18/92	12420	180.00–			180.00–	
				0.00	0.00	0.00	0.00	0.00
425								
Graystone, Inc.	800-429-3618							
		10/27/92	12493	46.50	46.50			
		11/07/92	12493	46.50–	46.50–			
				0.00	0.00	0.00	0.00	0.00
427								
Gregorio's	213-196-5827							
		10/30/92	12515	292.50		292.50		
				292.50	0.00	292.50	0.00	0.00

Figure 8-11. Accounts Receivable Aged Trial Balance Report.

```
Date:                                                                              Page   6
                              ACCOUNTS RECEIVABLE AGED TRIAL BALANCE
                                            AS OF

DOCUMENT TYPES:   1 = INVOICE   2 = PAYMENT  3 = CR MEMO   4 = FINANCE CHARGE   5 = DEBIT MEMO   6 = WARRANTY    OVER CREDIT - *
===============================================================================================================================

----------CUSTOMER-----------  SMA-DOCUMENT----- APPLY    CREDIT      TOTAL      --------------------AGING--------------------
  NUM  NAME                     TYPE  DATE  NUMBER TO-DOC  LIMIT      AMOUNT     0-030 DAYS 031-060 DAYS 061-090 DAYS 091-OVER DAYS
            DEBIT MEMO           5 08/28/86 12347           3,123.70                                                 3,123.70
            DEBIT MEMO           5 09/05/86 12380           1,299.65                                                 1,299.65
            DEBIT MEMO           5 09/24/86 12423           2,572.58                                                 2,572.58
            DEBIT MEMO           5 09/24/86 12424             269.35                                                   269.35
            PAYMENT              2 10/07/86  9528 12347     3,186.20-                                               3,186.20-
            INVOICE              1 10/10/86 12465              96.80                                                   96.80
            PAYMENT              2 11/05/86 110586 12424       251.15-                                                 251.15-
            PAYMENT              2 11/05/86 110586 12380     1,190.45-                                               1,190.45-
            PAYMENT              2 11/05/66 110586 12423     1,318.08-                                               1,318.08-
            INVOICE              1 12/04/36 12595            1,439.65                            1,439.65
            INVOICE              1 12/15/86 12633            2,152.47                            2,152.47
            INVOICE              1 12/24/96 12664            1,278.56                1,278.56
            DEBIT MEMO           5 01/16/87 12684            1,541.82                1,541.82
            INVOICE              1 01/24/87 12724            2,098.33   2,098.33
            INVOICE              1 01/28/87 12738               60.00      60.00
            PAYMENT              2 02/05/87    72 12595      1,439.65-                           1,439.65-
            PAYMENT              2 02/05/87    72 12633      2,152.47-                           2,152.47-
            PAYMENT              2 02/05/87    72 12664      1,278.56-               1,278.56-
            INVOICE              1 02/10/87 12761            1,817.07   1,817.07

                                                           5,933.42   3,975.40    1,541.82        0.00    416.20 (??)

  555 KEYSTONE CO.             88  408-998-2221  10,000.00  (CK)
            INVOICE              1 10/30/86 12517             485.50                                                  485.50
            INVOICE              1 01/27/87 12730             500.75     500.75
            PAYMENT              2 02/09/87 92807 12517       485.50-                                                 485.50-
            INVOICE              1 02/12/87 12765             647.50     647.50    PP 2/20
            PAYMENT              2 02/12/87 65721 12730       500.75-    500.75-

                                                             647.50     647.50        0.00        0.00      0.00

  565 LA TORTILLA FACTORY      99  707-544-9355   5,000.00  (CK)
            INVOICE              1 01/23/87 12710            3,361.20   3,361.20
            INVOICE              1 02/06/87 12758            4,452.00   4,452.00

                                                           7,813.20   7,813.20        0.00        0.00      0.00

  587 H.H. LEDYARD             88  408-462-4400   5,000.00  (CK)
            INVOICE              1 02/06/87 12756             607.68     607.68    PP 2/20

                                                             607.68     607.68        0.00        0.00      0.00

  609 LUGO CONCESSION          88  916-922-8300   2,000.00  (CK)
            INVOICE              1 11/18/86 12569             135.00                                                  135.00
            PAYMENT              2 02/09/87  6769 12569       135.00-                                                 135.00-

                                                               0.00       0.00        0.00        0.00      0.00
```

Figure 8-12. Accounts Receivable Aged Trial Balance Report (a different format).

31- to 60-Day Accounts

Do not underestimate the potential for trouble in this aging category. It is quite possible that an account item or balance is only a few days removed from joining the black sheep in 61- to 90-days. Accounts that are only a few days past 30 days might not represent a problem, particularly if balances are frequently in that area. Balances that are stretching to and through 50 and 55 days are another matter. It is never good news when accounts begin to lean against aging of 61 to 90 days.

A telephone call to the customer who has an unpaid 40- or 50-days balance is a must. If the balance is several days beyond the usual payment pattern, push the payables person into giving a reason(s) for the delay. If something is happening, externally or internally, to impact cash flow for more than a temporary period, you want to know it *now*. When a couple of telephone calls bring no promises—or promises, but no check—and the aging has stretched to an uncomfortable 50 or 55 days, you might want to consider holding orders until the account pays all (or the oldest) past-due balances. Again, your past experience with the customer will have considerable bearing on the action you take.

61- to 90-Day Accounts

A balance in this category means that the account is between 30- and 60-days past due, and that is unacceptable. Unless you have made arrangements in advance to allow one-time aging of 61 to 90 days—perhaps because of some temporary cash flow drain, the reasons for which are very clear—you would not sell additional product on *any* terms until you have received a satisfactory lump sum payment or a C.O.D. payment of $2.00 or $3.00 for every $1.00 of product you release. If the customer needs your product(s), and you have good reason to assume that serious problems exist, insist that your company receive regularly-scheduled, lump-sum payments *plus* C.O.D. payments as described previously. When it becomes obvious that payments to all suppliers are slowing, a long-term customer relationship is no longer your primary concern. Your primary concern—once you have determined that the customer's downhill slide appears to be irreversible—is to collect your company's money as rapidly as possible.

91-Day and Over Accounts

When your company is not receiving regular payments on any balance in this aging column, do not delay. Send out your final payment demand letter, if you haven't already done so. If you do not receive payment by the deadline date specified in your letter, assign the account to your collection agency. You should not continue your own collection effort at this time. These accounts need aggressive collection attention, including the possibility of having an attorney obtain a judgment. Your work with other accounts would demand that you devote a disproportionate amount of your time to an account in this type of trouble.

Should you sell to an account that you have assigned to a collection agency? No, not a dime's worth of anything until it has paid the assigned balance, it has paid all other balances, and it has reimbursed your company for any suit and/or collection fees. Perhaps at this point there might be a strong reason to consider selling the account, but only on a C.O.D. basis. Once you have gone the collection or suit-and-collection route with an account, there should be no incentive for you to tempt fate again with open account sales. You still could be in a vulnerable position if you accept company or personal checks in payment of C.O.D. purchases. If there is any indication that suppliers are experiencing NSF check problems with this customer, tell the customer you will accept only cashier's checks and bank or postal money orders.

Minimize the number and dollar value of the accounts that slide into this column. The odds of a collection assignment or a bad-debt loss increase dramatically as accounts travel across the company's receivables aging report. By the time balances are in the 91-days and over column, the percentage of loss is very high.

If there is a high level of activity in your business, two or more Accounts Receivable Aged Trial Balance Reports each week is appropriate. Under no conditions should you try to get by with less than one new report each week.

When properly prepared and used, the "aging report" is your most important information and control tool. Each new report should include all billing and payment activity through the report date, providing the credit administrator with a complete report of all open items on each account. It's easy to forget the handwritten notes and reminders that you added to the preceding report. Although you don't want to clutter a new report with an excessive number of notations, you should transfer items that are still applicable to the new report.

If you have been concerned about the problems attached to converting to a data processing system, don't fight it. We are decades past the early IBM era when credit managers raised their voices in anguished protest, as they called the roll of benefits and information that most certainly would be lost forever in the transition from bookkeeping machines to a card-punched IBM system. Were they right? Did we lose much in the transition from old to new? A few things were lost, but in the final analysis the change has been enormously beneficial to credit people everywhere.

The accounts receivable trial balance report (your receivables aging report) is the repository for all of your receivables problems, large or small. It is also the report that enables you to know virtually to the penny (less pending credits, etc.) the amounts owed by your customers. Whether or not you personally handle the collection of receivables, the receivables report is at the core of your weekly and monthly planning for cash-flow requirements. You or whoever handles your receivables accounts must know the payment pattern of your company's customers and recognize and monitor payment patterns when payments begin to become less prompt. Stay on top of the aging of your company's accounts receivable; the effective use of the accounts receivable aged trial balance report is the single most important tool in the process of controlling and collecting receivables balances (see Figures 8-13 and 8-14).

Accounts Receivable Aging Sheet

Date_____

Account Number	Amount Owing	Current	Past-Due 1–30 Days	Past-Due 31–60 Days	Past-Due 61–90 Days	Past-Due Over 90

Figure 8-13. Accounts Receivable Aging Sheet.

Past-Due Balances

Report Date _____

Account Name	Account Number	Current 0–30	31–60	61–90	91 and Over	Total

Figure 8-14. Past-due balances (current thru 91 plus days).

Ratios and Trends

Ratios are not inflexible guidelines, although there are areas of application where any variation from generally accepted industry, business, or accounting standards should be minimal, if at all. They have varying levels of importance in measuring how well two different departments or functions might be doing as they relate to each other. Ratios have, however, considerable value when used to measure the in-house effectiveness of a company's controls, financial and other.

For example, in most companies, there are two areas that tie up the bulk of working capital: inventory and accounts receivable. The ratio of inventory to sales is relevant to the question of whether too much money is invested in inventory for the level of monthly or quarterly sales; accounts receivable must justify the number of days that sales are in the receivables total, if dollars are to be generated rapidly enough for receivable to make its expected contribution to cash flow. Fast-turning receivables should generate the major share of the company's cash-flow needs, thereby reducing the amount of borrowed money needed to maintain cash flow, and reducing interest costs because less money had to be borrowed, and perhaps for a shorter period of time. Reduce the investment in inventory when the ratio to sales is too high (too many days sales in inventory) and reduce the aging of receivables when it is higher than the median average of days sales for a firm of comparable size in your industry, or when it is higher than a level acceptable to your company. Holding these ratios at acceptable levels is directly related to whether financial control is doing a proper job for your company. If it isn't, tighten it!

In all areas of its performance, your company should compare favorably with others in your industry of similar size. It is not an easy comparison to make, however. Your sales figures might be comparable, your territory of somewhat similar size, and your approach to merchandising your product(s) not unlike, but what effect do the small differences between your company and the others have on the annual results? Is your sales philosophy the same as your competitors? What about your company's credit philosophy? Do you hold accounts to a relatively few days past terms, carry them longer, or even carry some too long? Compare your company's performance with others in your industry of similar size, but don't try to lock your company into an exact fit with others. Small differences in company attitudes and philosophies can translate into ratios that are close to your own, but are not a perfect match. Unless your ratios vary greatly from others, you probably have no reason to question your own ratios.

Key Ratios

Defining and applying ratios is a simple and a frequently used method for determining how a company or business measures up in the context of standards that are generally considered to be normal for a specific industry, a company of specific size, etc. Ratios shed some light on where a business has been, where it is now, and what its future condition may be. Basic ratios are the following:

1. Fixed Assets/Net Worth

2. Net Sales/Net Worth

3. Average Collection Period (Accounts Receivable/Daily Sales)

4. Net Sales/Inventory

5. Net Profit/Net Sales

What is the significance of these ratios? Too high a percentage of *Fixed Assets to Net Worth* causes a shortage in working capital (cash flow). Fixed assets may, however, appear to be the cause of a ratio imbalance because net worth is lower than it should be. *Net Sales to Net Worth?* When net sales is too high and net worth is low, the ratio indicates the possibility that there is a heavy amount of debt, and particularly current debt. Too high a ratio of debt also puts a company at greater risk if there is a strong competitive challenge or a severe economic downturn. *Net Sales to Inventory?* Generally speaking, the higher the ratio of sales is to inventory, the better it is for the company. Excessive quantities of inventory are indicative of an inadequate sales effort or the inability to order properly to maintain satisfactory levels of inventory. *Average Collection Period?* This figure represents a key area of the credit department's report card, the effectiveness of the new account screening procedure, the monitoring of accounts receivable, and the collection of those receivables within the lowest number of days from invoice date. *Net Profit on Net Sales?* Once again, the higher this ratio is the better. Maximizing net profit from net sales is the goal of every company.

Ratios that have a direct relationship to working capital (cash flow) have considerable impact on the day to day success of the company. Ratios can be determined by dividing the word(s) that follows the slash (/) into the word(s) that precedes the slash. These secondary ratios include:

1. Current Ratio (Current Assets/Current Liabilities)

2. Current Debt/Net Worth

3. Total Debt/Net Worth

4. Inventory/Working Capital

5. Long-term Debt/Working Capital

6. Net Profit/Net Worth

An explanation of the secondary ratios? *Current Ratio* (Current Assets/Current Liabilities) relates to the ability of the business to meet current obligations as they become due. The ratio may vary throughout the year but it has value as an indicator. *Current Debt/Net Worth?* This tells the creditor who owns the higher percentage of the business, the owners or the creditors. If it is the creditors, it doesn't mean that the business is doomed to failure. The ratio is, however, an indicator of the company's ability to pay its obligations. *Total Debt/Net Worth?* Long-term debt is added to current debt to provide a view of the company's total debt obligation. *Inventory/Working Capital?* Inventory is classified as a quick asset, but cannot always be liquidated quickly or sold for the full price. There are many factors that might distort or decrease the book value of inventory. *Long-term Debt/Working Capital?* The usual purpose of this ratio is to identify whether money has been diverted from long-term debt to cover operating expenses. It is an indicator of the financial integrity of the company. *Net Profit/Net Worth?* This ratio is used to determine the rate of return on invested capital and is used by prospective investors to evaluate the future prospects of the company.

Do not panic if you find occasional deviation in your company's ratios from what industry members consider to be standards. There are numerous reasons why certain of your company's ratios might not be in line with those of other industry members. Your company might be carrying higher than normal levels of inventory because it is about to launch a territory-wide sales promotion. There are not many good reasons, however, why your company's Average Collection Period should not be at or below the standard for your industry. The prompt collection of accounts receivables balances is a ratio over which the credit department must exercise proper control.

9

Aged Trial Balance Reports

The ability to understand, evaluate, and accurately interpret a receivables aged trial balance report is essential if management of receivables balances is to be successful. If you see a report (see Figures 8-11 and 8-12) that is filled with names, numbers, dates, and columns of figures that you do not understand, or does not appear to have appropriate relevance, then that report may not be as effective a tool as it should be.

The receivables aging report is the single most valuable control document that any person charged with accounts receivable responsibility can have at his or her disposal. It is (or should be) orderly, comprehensive, and applicable within the requirements of your company's customer base and order activity—and you should never try to administer receivables without it. If the aging report that you are using is not set up to offer the maximum level of support (including essential data such as customer name, invoice number and date, credit limit, total amount owing, and individual invoice totals aged from 0 to 30 days thru 91 plus days), then you must make whatever format adjustments are necessary to maximize the benefits to you and your department. Without good, current aging reports, your chances of staying on top of the company's receivables might be compared to being marooned on an uncharted island, whose highest elevation is 15 feet above sea level, 18 minutes before the arrival of a 40-foot tidal wave. You must have a good receivables aging report, and you must have the knowledge and confidence to use it effectively.

Figures 8-11 and 8-12 were taken from a computer-prepared accounts receivable report and reflect receivables aging based upon credit terms of Net 30 days. Computer programs can be written or purchased that offer variations from this example, but the format shown here is both practical and acceptable. Columns of information include (from left to right) the customer account number, name of the customer, and type of entry (credit memo, invoice, payment, etc.). The next column includes the customer's telephone number, invoice dates, and invoice numbers. Other columns include the customer's credit limit, total open balance, and aging of that balance: current balances 0 to 30 days, balances 31 to 60 days, balances 61 to 90 days, and balances 91 days and over. Use your receivables aging reports constantly and wisely.

Maintaining a Fast-Turning Receivables Base

The proper management of accounts receivable is vital to the survival and growth of a company, and keeping an accurate accounts receivable aging report is essential to good management of the receivables accounts. The credit manager's goal should be an aging report that's loaded with fast-turning, close to terms accounts. When receivables have that level of liquidity, the task of internally generating enough money each month to service a high percentage of the company's cash-flow needs should not be a problem. If sales are good, the quality of the receivables must be equally good to avoid an increasing shortfall in the amount of money generated each month from receivables' balances. A situation of this type would put your company in the position of borrowing increasingly larger amounts each month to meet its cash-flow requirement.

A conscientious professional will not settle for a receivables aging report that is heavily populated with accounts whose balances range from current to 30, 60, and 90 days past due. The more heavily laced the receivables report is with accounts that pay slow and slower, the more the company will have to rely on the banker. And what if too many of the receivables do not have an appropriate level of liquidity? The monthly shortfall of internally generated cash will inevitably increase, and the company's ratios (quick cash to current debt, etc.) will display a decreasing amount of elasticity. There might be hundreds of thousands (or millions) of dollars on the company's receivables aging report, but if you, the credit manager or administrator, cannot collect those dollars in a timely fashion, your company is on a direct course for trouble.

Accounting gathers and puts together the data that the credit manager or the person charged with the credit responsibility uses to determine the actions to be taken to collect past-due balances. But by the time account balances are on an aging report, it is too late to do anything about the screening and account monitoring process that put them there. It is not, however, too late to take appropriate action to ensure, one, that past due balances are held within acceptable parameters and, two, that no new credit charges find their way into the receivables balances of accounts that are already abusing the credit privilege.

When customers allow their credit balances to become more than 10 or 15 days past due, the account is no longer a contributor to a fast-turning receivables base. What about customers who allow (or are allowed to let) their account aging to become 30, 45, 60, or more days past due? These accounts could be costing the supplier money if the profit margin on the products or services that created the receivable is narrow. When receivables do not turn rapidly, your company is, one, denied the full benefit of the profit on the product(s) sold, two, unable to promptly put the proceeds back into cash flow, and, three, must pay interest on borrowed money to supplement the inadequate level of internally generated cash.

A fast-turning receivables base can make a major contribution to your company's financial stability and to the "bottom line." Over the period of 12 months, the prompt payment of receivables and the availability of those dollars, for investment in more materials, labor, services, and other expenses, will reach a very meaningful total.

Quality Receivables— An Attainable Goal

Before any company can have fast-turning receivables, there must be quality receivables: accounts that have been screened properly, were assigned credit lines that are appropriate for the needs and financial strength of the customer, and balances that have been monitored since the first credit sale appeared on the company's accounts receivable aging report.

Whether your own efforts to put the highest percentage possible of quality receivables on the company's aging report have been or will be successful involves a combination of factors, primary of which are the information gathering techniques and the evaluation and screening procedures discussed at length in Part 1, Chapters 3 thru 6. If the fundamentals are not assigned their legitimate role and recognized for their importance, the account, the credit lines, and the credit balances that find their way onto the receivables aging report will not deliver dollars when they should or in the quantities expected.

As the custodian of the company's credit policy and the decision-making guardian of its investment in accounts receivable, the credit manager is responsible for the decisions that determine whether the "attainable goal" of quality receivables is achieved. The credit manager is responsible for the quality of the dollars in receivables accounts and whether those dollars deliver a constant, swift-flowing river of cash or a sporadic, undependable flow that consistently falls short of needs and expectations.

Accounts that qualify as "quality receivables" at your company might be over- or under-qualified at another. A company's credit policy is the guideline that determines what is an acceptable level of risk for that company's credit accounts, but there is a minimum level of qualification for credit that should not be flaunted by the most generous of credit grantors. Taking on high-risk credit accounts is not the way to provide a dependable flow of cash or to avoid an excessively high ratio of bad-debt accounts.

Quality receivables is an attainable goal and one that should be the objective for every company. If your company's receivables are not meeting that criteria, review your procedures for screening and evaluating new accounts, and for monitoring accounts already on your receivables aging report. You may find that a little fine tuning here and there will enable you to meet the major portion of your company's cash-flow requirements from that best of all worlds—internally generated cash flow.

Changes in Payment Patterns

The reasons for changes in payment patterns are many and diverse. In addition to cash-flow or other business problems, they can range from a missing invoice to a difference in goods received versus quantity billed, a pricing problem, unauthorized quantity and price deductions, and discounts taken after the maximum allowable date. These problems are the easy ones, or the ones that should be the easiest to correct.

A missing invoice can become a problem because you do not know that the customer doesn't have a copy—not until the invoice begins to move across the receivables aging report and you make the first call regarding payment. It isn't a problem if the account pays within terms. You'll pick it up almost as soon as the balance slips into the past-due column. But what are you looking at if the account frequently has balances that extend from 30 to 60 days past due? Until you receive a check for other invoices issued during the same time period, or unless you verify with the customer which invoices the customer lists as unpaid, you won't know whether the customer's list of open invoices agrees with those listed on your aging report.

Customers sometimes will pay an invoice that differs in the quantity received from the quantity billed, computing the value of the goods not received, deducting that amount from the invoice, and sending a check for the quantity received. Prompt payment is never out of season, but handling it in this manner could be the first horror in an escalating chain of horrors. What you want your customer to do is to call your office when there is a difference—in the unit price or in the quantity received—so you can issue a credit memo. Not only does this solve the problem of an incorrect payment from the customer, but also it enables your company and the customer to clear up any difference in a conventional manner. Customers are not looking to create extra work for you or for themselves. A mailing to your credit customers of the form letter shown in Figure 7-2 should be a giant step in your effort to eliminate dangling balances when a customer computes his or her own credit allowance.

Other changes in payment patterns have roots that are deeper, more serious, and more potentially damaging. When the change in the payments pattern of an account can be traced to an increasingly obvious cash-flow problem, the credit manager must determine the reason for the problem and the probability that it can be reversed. One or more of the following reasons and situations could be applicable:

1. Has the customer's business been adversely impacted by a regional or national economic downturn?

2. Has a new and aggressive competitor entered the customer's marketplace area?

3. Has there been change in the industry itself (in customer preferences, technology, etc.) that put the long-term survival of the industry at risk?

4. Is there ongoing company and/or industry R & D to re-establish the marketplace presence of the company and its product(s)?

5. Has there been a change in the ownership or in the percentage of ownership of a closely held company?

6. Has there been a change in the policy-making agreement (because of illness, retirement, etc.) among members of the partnership?

7. If the company is not publicly owned, is there evidence to support the thought that the founders are moving to position the company for a public offering?

8. Has the company recently been acquired by a large, diversified company with a reputation for plundering the assets of its acquisitions while slowing payments to the newly acquired company's suppliers?

9. If none of the above reasons seems to offer a valid explanation for the customer's deteriorating condition, perhaps the entrepreneur or founders (if a partnership or a sole proprietorship) are devoting a decreasing amount of time to the business and more to other activities.

The following is an additional set of reasons for changes in the payments pattern of a company. These are often entwined with one or more of the possibilities on the preceding list.

1. Internal problems caused by the death of a partner or a dissolution of the partnership with the resulting loss of expertise in one or more key management, production, or sales areas.

2. The use of bank borrowings or other funds to buy out the interest of a partner.

3. Expansion of the business too rapid for the available financial resources, and often without an appropriate level of management experience to direct it.

4. Liquidity of the accounts receivable. Has there been a change in the customer company's credit policy, the screening and evaluation procedures, the diligent monitoring of existing accounts, or a new credit manager who is not doing as aggressive a job of collecting receivables?

When owners or partners become too detached from the day to day management of the business, the business may slide onto a plateau of "no growth." At this point, the owners have a serious, but probably unrecognized problem. A plateau of "no growth" inevitably leads to the failure to replace customers who leave as part of the normal process of customer loss. Given such an unfavorable environment for continued business success, the outcome is a gradual to rapid decline.

These are some of the more obvious reasons for a firm whose payment pattern has been satisfactory for months or years to slide into a mode of increasingly slow payments. To turn such a situation around demands the earliest possible action by a strong and competent management. What is your response to signs of a problem(s) in one of your customers? No blanket answer will cover all problems and conditions. Monitor the account's actions closely. Deal with the account from a position of caution, and continue to sell the account only when, and as, your judgment and the available information indicate that you can do it safely. You will want to hold past-due balances to a minimum number of days, applying payment pressure to the account as you feel the necessity to protect your company's receivables interest. Your criteria for what you must do in any situation is always the same. You are sympathetic to the legitimate problems of a customer, but you must ultimately do what is in your company's best interest.

Improvement in Payment Patterns

At the opposite end of the payments pattern is the account that gradually (or suddenly) improves the way it handles payments to supplier companies. There can be any number of reasons for the improvement, or a combination of the following reasons:

1. An infusion of cash as a result of the company attracting new investors.

2. A first or second public offering of the company's stock.

3. A new product that has been in R & D (and a long-term drain on cash flow) has been brought successfully to the marketplace.

4. The customer has expanded successfully into a new market area and/or has expanded its activity in the original area.

5. The company's previous CEO has been replaced with a person who has succeeded in turning the company into a dynamic and successful force in its industry.

6. New financial controls have been put in place, which have given management much more effective control of expenses and the use of cash flow.

7. The customer company has revised its credit policy, tightening its qualifications for granting credit to new and existing accounts.

8. The customer company has been purchased by a much larger company and is now operated as a division of the parent company. Suppliers have been notified that the parent company intends to provide the financial support necessary for the newly acquired company to meet its supplier obligations on a "within terms" basis.

9. The customer has expanded its product base and is enjoying strong market and financial success with new products that are contributing a higher percentage of profit than the original product line(s).

Past-Due Balances

Unless your credit responsibility never exceeds a very few accounts, it is difficult to visualize a time when you will not have past-due accounts on your receivables aging report. The form shown (see Figure 8-13) should enable you to consolidate problem accounts into an effective recap of what is taking place on the aged trial balance report. Whether the report is just for your information or goes to a managing owner, a partner, or the financial officer of a larger corporation, the form is an effective weekly, semimonthly, or monthly tool for relating the number and status of accounts in the various past-due categories. A bracketed line or two under each listed account will remind you (or indicate to the person to whom you give a copy) of the status of the action you are taking to collect these balances.

Certain accounts will regularly appear on a past-due list, because their cash flow is not strong enough for them to do better. Careful monitoring on your part should pick off most serious problems, but whether the account is a regular or a first-timer on the past-due list, move quickly when you see signs of trouble.

Remember that your company can put an end to one of the customer's chief sources of frustration and anger by promptly issuing credit memorandums. Payment for invoices will no longer be delayed because the supplier has not properly addressed errors in pricing, size, color, quantity, etc. There may be financial reasons why payments are not made within a more favorable time frame, but your company will have taken the appropriate steps to eliminate problem areas that are within your control.

DSO—Days Sales Outstanding

The key to determining whether the aging of your accounts receivable balances is within parameters that best serve the company's needs is a simple mathematical procedure. It is used by credit management people to measure the aging of their accounts receivable balances as a group to ensure that the average aging of unpaid balances is at an acceptable number of days' sales. The mathematical procedure is also an excellent yardstick for measuring the effectiveness of your company's account screening, monitoring, and collection programs versus the company's target for satisfactory aging of accounts receivable. It is helpful to compare your figure for daily sales outstanding versus the average for your industry. This is usually compiled from figures supplied by yourself and by industry peers. If your company's sales terms are Net 30 days, the average aging of receivables balances could be 38 days (good), 43 days (not bad), or 51 days (Don't just sit there! Collect your money!).

The following is a simple calculation that can put the overall aging of your receivables into meaningful focus by calculating the number of days' credit sales that are outstanding. The company's annual credit sales are divided by 360; the accounts receivable are then divided by your average credit sales per day:

Annual credit sales	$5 million
$5,000,000—360 days	$14,000 (rounded)
Average daily sales	$14,000
Accounts receivable	$616,000
$616,000—$14,000	44
Total DSO	44

These calculations pinpoint what it will take for the company to reduce its DSO to the target figure of 40 days. Every $14,000 represents one day of sales. When the Accounts Receivable total has been reduced by $56,000 (down to a total of $532,000), the company will have reduced its DSO to 40 days, plus adding $56,000 to cash flow. Internally generated cash is a much less costly source of funds than a visit to the company's banker. When accounts receivable aging of 40 days is compatible with the company's cash-flow needs, maintaining that level of receivables liquidity will enable your company to limit the use of bank borrowings for cash-flow purposes.

Do not, however, allow yourself to become too complacent when your company's DSO seems to have settled at 40 days. Unless your receivables accounts are an uncommonly uniform group (always pay within 10 or 12 days after due date), there is no reason why you should not continue to nudge certain slow pay accounts into a DSO time frame that is compatible with your standard of 40 days. If your product(s) is priced fairly, and it must be if your company is to be successful, then you cannot afford the luxury or the risk that attaches to accounts receivable that do not turn over in a timely manner. Each of your company's products should deliver a predetermined percentage of profit based on properly developed cost standards and procedures. If slow paying credit accounts are allowed to diminish the projected level of profit from each sale, your control over the vital financial area of accounts receivable is not as strong as it should be.

Expecting customers to pay for their purchases within a reasonable period of time, and never more than a few days past your credit terms, is the proper way to administer the company's receivables. To let customers use your company as a secondary source of financing is not good credit management, not good financial control, and not an acceptable business practice. What do you do if the customer wants additional time beyond the "few days past terms of sale" just mentioned? Unless the problem or circumstance that prompted the request is something that could not be foreseen when the order was placed, arrangements for extended terms should be made at that time, and not after the account balance is about to become past due.

What are the differences between a receivable of good quality and one of poor quality? The following offers a comparison of the differences between the two.

Good Quality

1. Pays within the terms of sale or no more than 10 days past the due date.

2. Never attempts to take a discount when one has not been earned.

3. Has a good reputation for prompt payment among all current and past suppliers.

4. Has access to a high-dollar level of bank support, but has used it sparingly and in amounts that have been well below the credit line. The bank reports that repayment of loan funds has been as agreed.

5. Does not use ploys, such as a missing invoice, an overdue credit memo, or a discrepancy in the quantity shipped versus the quantity ordered, to delay a payment.

6. Is a consistently dependable contributor to the monthly cash-flow figure. Balances can be included in cash-flow projections with the assurance that the check will arrive within the projected time frame.

Poor Quality
1. Never pays unless or until the credit department has made one or more reminder calls.

2. Has suppliers report that the customers receivables base has too many slow-pay accounts, which causes a cash-flow problem of constant and significant proportions.

3. Has bank reports that loan repayments are not always handled as agreed. This has resulted in the bank reducing the customer's credit line.

4. Has frequent reports of missing invoices, errors in the product count shown on invoices versus quantity received, etc.

5. Is an account that has been in business for three to five years, has not succeeded in establishing a growth trend, and is the victim of a management team that is ill-equipped to do a good, well-balanced job.

6. Suffers from consistently inadequate cash flow for the volume of the customer's business.

7. Operates under weak budget and financial controls. The annual budget is not the well-crafted criteria for controlling the company's expenditures that makes a major contribution to a year of good profits—or one of minimal bottom-line achievement.

8. Produces a good product (or product line), but is not an effective merchandiser. The company does not effectively evaluate marketplace potential before committing itself to an unproductive and financially unrewarding new territory or a financially costly sales promotion.

It is never possible to be comfortable with the condition of your company's receivables balances when it has been determined that too many receivables dollars are invested in accounts that are below the company's standard for accounts of good quality. And if an analysis of the accounts receivable report reveals several accounts of poor quality, a change in the processes of screening, evaluating, and/or monitoring is obviously necessary.

10
Spreading
Receivables Risk

A major danger in any program of credit account sales is concentrating the major share of the company's receivables dollars in a very few accounts. They impose the additional hazard of putting the major share of receivables dollars in companies that are located in the same industry and the same marketplace area.

There are successful companies that sell the major share of their product(s) to one or two national distributors, to a major soft-goods manufacturer and/or retailer, or to a specialized hard-goods industry, such as automobiles, major appliances for home and industry, etc. These are companies that choose to accept the marketplace risk that accrues when a company confines its sales to one, two, or a half-dozen customers. The loss of one major customer from a very short list of majors can prove to be a crippling blow for all but the most financially solid company.

The majority of companies follow the generally accepted admonition to broaden their customer base to the point where the loss of a major account would not have a devastating effect on the company. A broad base of credit risks (monetary, industry, and geographic) has the effect of cushioning the loss of a key account and should enable the company to continue to move forward with no noticeable loss of momentum. Shock waves might ripple through the company, but the disrupting effect of having to shut down a production line, furlough good people, and otherwise attempt to maneuver the company through a very traumatic experience is unlikely to occur.

A good credit customer—one whose receivables balance is never a problem—can be found in almost any area of the country and in almost every industry or business. Whether an area is or is not economically depressed has bearing on the condition of virtually every type of business in the area.

What the term "economically depressed" does not address, however, is the quality of the management at the companies and businesses in the area of economic depression. The receivables risk may be greater with a higher percentage of companies than in more economically stable areas, but careful screening should enable the credit manager to find well-managed, successful companies in what is basically an unattractive area in which to invest receivables dollars. An unattractive area does not preclude the possibility that one or more companies, who are doing a good job, might be interested in the products sold by your company.

How to Analyze Your Company's Risk

The parameters for analyzing your company's receivables risk have been set (or should have been set) in the company's credit policy. Part 1 (Chapter 1) of this book illustrates and examines at some length the three types of credit policies, and what payment pattern generally develops as the result of each type. What are the three types? They are restrictive (a company growth rate that is minimal, and faces minor credit risks), moderate or middle-of-the-road (mixes good accounts, average accounts, and some accounts that are consistently slow to 30 days), and liberal (a credit policy that is generally based on a desire to grow rapidly, and a policy that can become a high-risk adventure).

The business plan is also relevant to what is an appropriate level of risk for your company. Do the company's goals place an unreasonable financial demand on the accounts receivable? If they do, the company's receivables risk will be higher than in companies whose goals are more conservative. Has the company's top management changed the immediate or long-term goals of the company without making the appropriate adjustments in the business plan or in the company's credit policy? If such changes occur, it is essential that the people who administer the various income-producing programs (accounts receivable, etc.) are promptly advised of any change in their guidelines and/or parameters for dealing with *risk*.

There is a point beyond which the element of risk is excessive for any company. No company—regardless of its financial strength, credit policy, or desire to grow rapidly—should accept a credit customer whose payment record with suppliers is spotted with episodes of third-party collection assignments, frequent and/or consistent C.O.D. sales by one or more suppliers, and negative experience reports from one or more banks (especially when there is evidence that the reason for a short-term experience with one or two banks is because the banks terminated what was, for them, an unsatisfactory relationship).

These negatives are the trademarks of an account whose ability to survive is always at a high cost to those with whom the company has a credit account relationship. There is rarely a point in the life span of the business (whether one, two, or five years) when the account isn't scratching and clawing to survive—and generally losing a bit of ground with each new or recurring crisis. This is not the type of account that offers stability or longevity to its suppliers; it offers, instead, the chance to be sucked into a downward spiral that must inevitably end in a Chapter 11 filing, or the even more depressing situation of simply closing its doors and making no pretext of attempting to work out a continuation agreement with the creditors. The total of receivables dollars lost by the failed customer's suppliers will, in itself, be a hard lesson, a lesson that must inevitably leave its mark in the bottom line of financial statements of supplier companies.

Other customers may offer less obvious roads to the loss of receivables dollars. Example: Does your company accept a disproportionate number of accounts that are too new to have established a business trend, yet the credit line and the number of dollars on the aging report is as high as the credit lines for many well-established accounts? There is something to be said for befriending an account whose business trend has yet to be established, but it is foolish to be unrealistically generous. If your company thinks that a credit applicant has growth potential—and the credit evaluation gives high marks to management's experience, integrity, business location, quality of personnel, territory, product line, etc.—then the credit line should be scaled to move from a relatively low level of exposure to and through progressively higher levels of exposure as the customer's growth and payment records warrant such action.

Increasing the credit line of a customer is not automatic; it is earned because the customer has handled the account in a manner that, if not totally in conformity with terms, is on an acceptable line with them. No one should expect a new or a fairly new company to pay its suppliers within terms—not every time and not every invoice. Unless the young company is uncommonly fortunate, money is not going to be in generous supply. It is more probable that generating money will be one of the company's major priorities, and, if there is a gap of five or ten days between the due date of an invoice and the date payment is received (and the customer is still within your assigned credit limit), there should be no reason for alarm. Monitor closely all such accounts, but give these customers a little room to catch their breath before they commit to climbing toward the next plateau in their pattern of growth.

How does your company handle the older customer companies, the ones that for one reason or another have peaked and seem to be attempting to hold at a specific plateau or are in a gradual decline? Would a review of your receivables aging report indicate that the company has a surprisingly high percentage of accounts in this category? Are you gradually reducing the credit line of these companies as they seem to pay more slowly? In many such instances, it is not necessary to notify the customer that the credit line has been reduced, because the customer is not buying as much or buying as frequently as in past years.

The reason for a decline? The business has been sold; a founder or partners have retired; the new management isn't as effective or as efficient; the business or marketing philosophy has changed; the product(s) is not keeping pace with changes in technology, or changes in customer needs and preferences. There are more reasons for the decline of a once-prosperous company or business, but your company's primary interest centers in whether the company can pay for what is being purchased, and, if in decline, how long the customer will be able to continue to pay within acceptable terms and within acceptable parameters of receivables safety. Also, at what point might the decline begin to accelerate so rapidly that suppliers have no chance to reduce their stake in the impending Chapter 11 filing?

Your company signifies its willingness to accept risk every time an order of merchandise is sold on credit terms. There is no way to avoid normal factors of risk if the company is going to be competitive—is going to survive—in an area of industry or business where credit is used as a primary tool of sales. The buzz phrase here is "too narrow:" avoid concentrating receivables dollars in too narrow a base of credit accounts; avoid too narrow a marketplace area; avoid too narrow a segment or section of any industry; avoid selling to accounts whose cash flow is too narrow to pay within parameters that are acceptable to your company; avoid too narrow a management perspective when you evaluate prospective accounts or monitor existing accounts. You should not accept high-risk accounts, nor should you attempt to concentrate the company's receivables in areas of minimal risk. Unless the company's credit policy is geared to a very conservative approach to credit, there should be a broad base of risks (exclusive of high-risk accounts) with the major share of receivables dollars in accounts that turn rapidly enough to make a major monthly contribution to cash flow.

The Categories of Risk

When I think of the categories of *risk,* my first inclination is to compress it into its two lowest denominators: acceptable risk and unacceptable risk. Although this might be an over-simplification of the categories of risk, it states precisely what a credit manager or credit administrator is attempting to determine when he or she screens credit applicants, monitors the ongoing status of credit accounts, or attempts to eliminate certain accounts from the receivables aging report before they slide into the mire of a Chapter 11.

"Acceptable" and "unacceptable" have validity as the two basic, down-to-earth categories of risk. There are those who might argue that there is a grey area between these two categories that should be assigned a life of its own; there is a point, but it is not strong enough to prevail. It is quite true that some accounts do not fit into either of the two definitive categories. They are in every sense "grey area" accounts, but "grey area" is not, in the context of this subsection, a separate category. There are borderline areas within each of these two categories, areas that call for a certain amount of calculated risk if the account is at the low end of "acceptable," or bordering on the grey area that is on the outer fringe of "unacceptable." There must ultimately, however, in every instance of a borderline account, be a decision that lifts the account out of the grey area and puts it in the category of the "acceptable" or the category of the "unacceptable."

No credit manager or credit administrator can evaluate an account and say to him or herself, "I don't know about this account. It has been in business for more than three years, but has made very little progress—certainly no definite upward trend. We need a good customer in the applicant's area, but this one has cash-flow problems that cause it to abuse supplier terms by as many as 30 and 40 days. If there was ever a 'grey area' account, this one fits that category." Unfortunately for this credit manager, there is no category for grey area accounts. The credit manager must decide whether the account is acceptable (and qualifies for credit under the most liberal interpretation of the credit policy set by the company) or is unacceptable, under the most liberal interpretation of that same credit policy.

An account that has been evaluated and found to be an unacceptable credit risk is just that—*unacceptable*. There are, however, subcategories of risk within the category of "acceptable." Acceptable credit accounts are blanketed under that one heading, but the decision-making and monitoring processes have identified accounts on the receivables aging report as belonging to one of the following types of accounts:

1. High risk

2. Median (or average) risk

3. Low risk

4. No risk (?)

High Risk

It is difficult to find a good reason for one of these accounts making it onto your receivables aging report. When high-risk accounts were discussed earlier in this chapter, it was noted that the top management of a company might have some reason for allowing a one-time release on open-account terms, or a low-level credit line to accommodate a contractor who might act as guarantor for essential job-related products or materials. If a credit sale(s) is made to a high-risk account, that account has, for the moment (and hopefully on a limited basis), been brought into the category of the acceptable.

Median (Average) Risk

This is where the major share of a company's receivables dollars are invested. There is risk, but it is risk that is calculated to prove beneficial to the company in the context of the total pool of average risks. It is the type of risk that might occasionally spin out of control and result in a business failure or in a customer who seeks the protection of a Chapter 11 filing. There should be ongoing monitoring of these accounts, but except for the occasional one that goes astray, concern regarding the safety of this subcategory of accounts should not be high. Your best defense against the loss of these receivables dollars is vigilance—monitoring payment patterns, reviewing up-dated reports from credit reporting services, conversing with peer credit managers, and taking account of information passed along by members of your company's sales and marketing force.

Low Risk

These accounts are exactly what the subcategory implies: established accounts that operate with little or no bank support, have a strong financial picture, and generate internally all of the cash needed to service short- and long-term obligations. Annual financial statements report net profits that are consistently in the upper median for industry accounts of their size. Management is experienced, has remained the same for several years, and the company enjoys an excellent reputation among its customers.

This is a subcategory of the category "acceptable accounts" that rarely experiences the loss of a receivables balance. These customers operate within parameters of conservatism that virtually ensure the safety and liquidity of their receivables balances, which minimizes the chance that a problem might occur which could threaten the customer's financial capability. What is the biggest danger? Probably in the extreme conservatism of the customers' approach to credit sales. In the long term, a more aggressive company might succeed in stifling the conservative customers' small percentage of annual growth. If lost customers (normal attrition) are not replaced, there will be a gradual eroding of the customer base, the sales base will shrink, profits will decrease, staff and facilities will have to be reduced, borrowed money will be needed to sustain a faltering business, and the gradual downward spiral will pick up speed.

No Risk (?)

Any experienced credit person will tell you that there is no such thing as a "no risk" credit account. There is, however, a subsection of ultraconservative accounts that are so financially secure, whose account lists are so solid gold, and who are so well entrenched in their industry and marketplace area as to pose virtually no risk to their creditors. Notice that I did not say "no risk." What I did say is "virtually no risk." The difference is that the word "virtually" could mean the difference between never having to do a bad debt write-off of an account balance from this sub-category or, at some point in your credit management experience, losing a "no risk" account, because it should never have been allowed to settle into your receivables account without bringing with it the smoke alarm word "virtually."

The account may be so strong that the question of risk is virtually nonexistent, but there is always a tiny chance that risk will grow to become an account-threatening presence.

Minimizing Risk Factors

If someone tells you that *risk* is not a built-in part of credit decisions, you should not believe them. People like yourself, who spend the better part of their working day in the imprecise world of judgments, must make credit decisions, and *Risk*—hopefully reasonable and manageable, but still spelled with a capital *R*—is the ever-present challenge to the success of those credit judgments and decisions. Even in a work environment where the full scope of decision-making tools is available—data such as supplier references, the banker's reference, commercial credit agency reports, financial statements, peer information within a trade credit group, and an experienced professional to analyze and evaluate the data—the resulting decisions will be imprecise judgments that include varying elements of *risk*.

Too many unknowns and intangibles exist for the credit manager or owner/credit manager to expect to make only infallible judgments, regardless of his or her experience level. How can you know that an applicant or a current customer is not concealing personal, health, or business problems? How can you be sure that an apparently successful business partnership is not being bent and twisted from within to the point where it is no longer very stable? Do you like what you've seen of the small company that is asking you for a sizeable credit line? Is the founder going to tell you that he is about to retire, or that he is quietly reducing his interest and activity in the company, and that future management control and decisions will be in the relatively inexperienced hands of his son-in-law? No. You probably will not hear a word of warning about any of the above in any of the given situations. Is there *risk?* You'd better believe it!

What does the owner of a small company or the credit manager of a larger company do to be sure that his or her company has the strongest level of protection from bad-debt losses? One of the best things to do is to load the evaluation and decision-making processes of the credit function with procedural uniformity. It has a nice ring, but the truth is, nobody cares how it sounds if it doesn't contribute something. Fortunately, it does. It can help to minimize the number and potential effects of the risk-prompting variables, while improving the effectiveness of the credit management process. It can be one of the strongest and most effective allies in helping the credit manager or administrator to make a higher percentage of good credit decisions. Do everything in sequence. Make the sequential approach your guideline for dealing with applicants from the first contact through the years of your association with companies that become customers. You will take your accounts through other sequences in the credit management process, but nothing will make your work easier, your hours of credit management more productive, or your credit department more effective than adopting, as your everyday guideline, one phrase—procedural uniformity.

Follow the lead of experienced credit managers and look constantly for the hedge against the unknowns, the intangibles, and the imprecise. Experienced credit managers look also for evidence of stability in a company's financial depth and the quality of its personnel. They look also for well-planned growth and the potential for trouble-free longevity. Their hedge against *risk* should be a combination of the depth and experience of a company's management, the high-profile recognition factors of the product line(s), the company's financial stability, and the unique geographic nature of the market area (a semiprotected market with little or no competition). You must follow their lead and try to hedge your *risks*—those unknowns, intangibles, and the imprecise. You will try to assemble the greatest number of plusses and the smallest number of minuses before making a judgment that puts your company's money at *risk*.

You can live with your credit decisions—even the occasional one that turns sour—if you never allow yourself to forget that all decisions are sprinkled liberally with ingredients and factors about which you have no knowledge and over which you have no control. This fact does not mean that, when you sit down to make credit decisions, you are putting your hand on the throttle of a runaway train. You must always be in control of your decisions and of the decision-making process. You are the one who controls the approval of orders and credit lines. The hand on the throttle is yours, but absolutely no reason exists for a runaway train. When your decisions are the result of a good input of information, sound evaluation and judgment, and procedural uniformity, your hand, that is on the always-in-motion affairs of your credit department, will ensure a steady and a professional ride.

A professional credit manager—or an owner who doubles as his or her company's credit manager—always will regret the loss of a receivables balance, but you will not waste time dwelling on the loss. If you did a solid job with the account, save the self-chastisement for a situation where you really should have seen the emerging problem before it was too late.

Avoiding the losers has always been the name of the credit management process, but no person who manages credit for any length of time succeeds in avoiding every loser. Rid yourself of any preconceived notions regarding the infallibility of a professional. Every professional will lose one now and again, just as the less-experienced person does. The difference between the professional and the inexperienced or less-experienced manager is that, if a professional is good, he or she will seldom, if ever, make the same mistake in judgment a second time. You must do the same thing. Take each negative experience and turn it into a learning one, one that you can use successfully in your future efforts to reduce the toll taken by the intangibles and by *risk*. Pride in a job well done isn't the only thing that should motivate you. You should be interested in what happens to the company's "bottom line," and if you happen also to be an owner or a partner, how much additional incentive does a man or woman need?

How can you maximize your chances of picking a high percentage of winners for your company? In addition to what has already been mentioned, let me suggest that you do not give away the store. Who would do such a foolish thing? When an owner or a credit manager develops a friendship with a customer, you must never allow that relationship to influence your business judgment as it relates to the amount of credit or the credit terms that you offer the company or business. The personal relationship must never intrude or interfere with the business relationship. Never let the personal relationship inhibit you from insisting that the customer make his or her account payments within the parameters of good credit management and of your company's credit policy. Avoid letting your customer maneuver you into an involvement that is not a good credit risk—not just a borderline account, but one that is clearly not a good risk. The only acceptable credit philosophy is the one that attempts to sell only to accounts that can, and will, pay—and pay in a manner compatible with your credit terms and credit policy. An account that becomes a bad-debt loss because of an error in judgment is as damaging to your company's financial statement as the common theft of money or merchandise. You must face the fact that the customer is not always right and not always honest. The customer's abuse of the credit privilege is the same as that customer having a hand in your till. You don't need that kind of help or that kind of business.

Some credit administrators will shy away from an account or an order that cannot be handled within regular credit terms. If the account meets your company's criteria for an acceptable credit risk, it would be foolish not to try to work out terms that satisfy the customer and can be accommodated by your company.

Example: A customer is stretching to break into a new market and needs more of your company's product(s) to meet the requirements of several new customers. After hearing the customer's plans, your best judgment confirms that the new area should deliver a good volume of business. Let the customer know that you want to help, but tell the customer that carrying several hundred (or several thousand) dollars of new credit on extended terms would unfavorably impact your company's cash flow.

Guided by the nature of the order and the quality of the customer, ask for a payment of 25 percent or 50 percent of the dollar total when you accept the order. With the major portion of your manufacturing or production costs covered, you then will be in a position to offer mutually acceptable terms on the balance. Another extended-terms option is a one-third payment with the order (when the order is delivered or 30 days after delivery), a second one-third payment 60 days after delivery, and the final one-third payment 90 days after delivery. Credit on extended terms is not for everyday use, or you will be looking at a receivable aging report that has too many special, slow-pay deals. Relate "extended" to "special," but do not overwork either term by too frequently linking them with another word in common credit management usage; that word is "terms." With special dating, extended terms to help the customer put more of your product(s) into the new sales area, the additional business should more than offset the costs to you of longer terms on an occasional special order.

The Broad Base of Accounts— And Account Dollars

There has been some earlier examination of the advantages that accrue from a broad base of receivables risk. To review some of those advantages: there is less likelihood of a major credit loss; one credit loss in a broad base of accounts will not turn the flow of internally generated cash from a flow to a trickle; a broad base of accounts tends to ensure that a product is getting equally broad marketplace exposure; a broad base infers that all accounts are not concentrated in one relatively small (or compressed) marketplace area; a broad base also offers the probability that all of the company's marketplace areas will not be impacted unfavorably and simultaneously if there is an area, regional, or industry downturn in the economy.

The broad base of accounts means also that receivables dollars are somewhat insulated against the type of catastrophic loss that can occur when one of a company's major customers fails. If a major customer fails and the customer's receivables account is carrying 25, 50, or 75 percent of the supplier company's receivables total, the impact will be devastating. It will still be a major blow to the company's receivables base and to cash flow if the percentage of loss is no more than 10 or 15 percent. Did I say *only* 10 or 15 percent? If the industry in which the company operates is highly competitive and the net profits from a well-managed business are 3 to 5 percent, the company could find itself looking at an operating loss for the fiscal year in which the major account failed. Unless the company comes up with a volume replacement account, or several smaller accounts whose cumulative total of purchases equals that of the failed major account, the supplier will be forced to make appropriate across-the-board reductions to bring expenditures into alignment with income.

The suggestion that your company should strive for a broad base of credit accounts does not mean that it should be unwilling to accept a few major accounts, perhaps a few majors whose total receivables balances would represent 20 to 30 percent of the receivables total. Very few companies have so much good business that they can arbitrarily legislate against the possibility of acquiring more good business. Whether good business comes from a strong small firm or from a strong larger account, each should be embraced for what it can do for the supplier company.

If a prospective major customer has all of the requisites to become a contributor to the growth and success of a company, it will be difficult to find valid reasons for declining the account. One of the few possibilities is production capacity. When production facilities are limited or are operating at near-capacity, and the projection for company growth does not include the type of plant expansion that would accommodate more than one new major account, the company obviously must decline many opportunities for new business. What if there are unused production, distribution, and warehouse facilities? One or two strong major accounts could be what the company needs to maximize the use of the company's facility and to lift profits to the next higher plateau.

A company whose receivables base is broad is automatically in the position of having a broad base of receivables dollars. Whether the receivables accounts are of a quality that virtually assures a rapid conversion to dollars hinges on whether the accounts have been properly screened and monitored. If accounts are broad based and all facets of the criteria for selecting quality receivables have been applied, the potential for generating strong cash flow from the broad base of receivables dollars should be excellent.

Unacceptable Risks

The potential for becoming involved with an unacceptable risk is constant. An unacceptable risk is as easy to come by as the credit manager's mistake of relaxing his or her vigilance during a screening procedure, of failing to stay with the sequential processing of an application for credit, or of being swayed by what is alleged to be "potential," rather than what experience and facts say is "reality." No credit person is immune from the possibility of being drawn into an account situation that is saturated with risk.

Example: The Kyrman Company has recently gone through a voluntary Chapter 11 proceeding that was lengthy, and was filled with recriminations regarding mismanagement of the company and slipshod, if not blatantly dishonest, handling of the company's funds. The creditor's committee found that thousands of dollars—dollars that were owing to creditors— were diverted into personal channels such as expensive nonbusiness related trips, two expensive cars purchased allegedly for business use by each of the partners, and an occasional gambling junket to Las Vegas.

The two partners are charismatic individuals who, although they filed a Chapter 11 petition owing creditors something in excess of a million dollars, have succeeded in getting creditors to accept a debt forgiveness and payment plan. The plan calls for an 80 percent write-off of unsecured obligations (no UCC filing, etc.), 10 percent tied to profits and to be paid over a period of six years and 10 percent in three cash payments over the next 12 months. The bankruptcy court has returned the business to the partners, the partners are endeavoring to entice suppliers into new credit arrangements, and your company has been approached to sell on credit at a credit line of medium five figures.

It should not be necessary for me to ask whether your company is going to agree to extend a credit line of $50 or $60 thousand to this unacceptable risk. One of your first thoughts should be to verify that nothing has changed. The two partners, who caused their creditors to lose substantial sums of money, are still in control of the company, and there is no reason to assume that their personal and managerial styles have changed. Why should they? Although they have agreed to a plan that holds past debts to suppliers and creditors at arms length, there is no provision for punitive action if the partners fail to fulfill their obligation to creditors, as worked out in Chapter 11. The worst that can happen is that payments will not be made as agreed, the creditors will force the customer back into bankruptcy court, and the Chapter 11 will be changed to a dissolution of the business.

The partners? They won't lose a thing. They will, in fact, gain the months or years from the date the plan of arrangement is approved by the court and when the control of the business is reverted to the partners. If your company is foolish enough to sell this customer on credit terms, any action by creditors who are signators to the continuation plan to force liquidation of the customer's business will drag your company's receivables balance down with it. If your company should sell the account, the hope is that it is able to protect itself with a Uniform Commercial Code filing. In such a case, your company's status as a secured creditor will improve its chances of recovering most or all of what is owed to it.

The by-product of a credit administrator's search for good accounts is those accounts that are identified as unacceptable risks. Your goal is to recognize major problems in prospective customers before these accounts can transfer some of their problems to your accounts receivable aged trial balance report. Stop them at the screening and evaluation stage. Do not allow these accounts to make a place for themselves on your company's annual report of bad-debt items.

When you find that a prospective account is unacceptable, or that an account to whom you are selling has become unacceptable, take the appropriate steps to stop credit sales to the customer and to collect money that is owing before the account can slip into a Chapter 11 filing. Collections is covered in Section 2 (Chapter 5), but the following steps will introduce you to collection procedures:

1. Call the customer. Tell him or her that you are holding orders effective immediately and that you are sending a payment schedule that same day.

2. The payment schedule will require a specific payment every week, every ten days, or every two weeks. Product may be purchased on a "$2 cash for $1 of product" basis.

3. Set up the payment schedule to reduce the open balance as rapidly as possible.

4. Make frequent telephone calls to ensure compliance.

5. Send a "final demand" letter if payment requirement is not met.

6. Assign the account to a third-party collection agency.

Your company should have little difficulty avoiding unacceptable credit risks if the credit administrator is experienced, the company's credit guidelines are good, and there is ongoing monitoring of receivables accounts.

Cash Flow Requirement— And Product Profit Margins

The cash-flow requirement can vary enormously from one company to the next. A young company will normally require a higher percentage of cash to service debt than the company whose customer base and business growth is more firmly established. The established company's requirements for property, production space and equipment, distribution and warehouse facilities, office space, personnel, and equipment of all types has, in general, already been met. The debt for many of these items has already been partially or totally discharged. The established company might be at a point in its growth where major borrowing has already provided for current and short-to-long term growth. Many of the bank loans for equipment and vehicles have been repaid. A bank loan to expand plant and office facilities could have been negotiated three or four years ago, used two or three years ago, and might currently be in the final months of repayment, or already have been repaid. The purchase of bare land or land with buildings is a long-term investment; such a loan might require a monthly payment for several years.

Of the various loans in the company's package with the bank, the most active is probably the revolving loan that supplements internally generated cash flow. Good receivables should provide a high percentage of the company's monthly cash-flow requirement, and high-profit-margin products will help to provide the cushion of funds that will determine how frequently the company must supplement internally generated cash flow with bank borrowings.

Many companies have no choice; they must use their cash-flow credit line on a monthly basis. In addition, however, to the problem of repayment, there is the more damaging loss of interest dollars, dollars that will never find their way into the company's "bottom line." What can and should be done to cut down on this loss of profit dollars? Accounts receivable must be held to the lowest number of DSO (Days Sales Outstanding) consistent with a credit policy that does not want to restrict unduly its credit sales. The credit policy and sales goals of the company will have a great deal to do with the shaping of the quality of the receivables' base, but collection of outstanding receivables in the shortest period of time consistent with credit policy and sales goals is the province of the credit manager or administrator. He or she can do a great deal to increase the speed with which receivables—receivables of any quality—can be collected.

The more rapidly receivables balances can be turned over, the better the flow of internally generated cash to meet the company's monthly obligations. Add to this the speed with which receivables are converted into cash, plus a lower level of bank borrowings to support cash flow, and a higher percentage of the company's profit on its products will find its way into the "net profit" line on the financial statement.

Concentrating Credit Risks in One Geographic Area

It is understood that if your company or business manufactures, distributes, wholesales, or retails products locally or within a narrow surrounding geographic area, there is very little that it might do to change the pattern regarding the concentration of risks in the one narrow surrounding area. Your company or business is, by choice or by necessity, both a prisoner and beneficiary of the options available to it to market its products or services. Limited facilities for manufacturing and/or distributing product(s), no desire to expand the marketplace area, and a profitable business that is virtually debt free are only a few of the reasons why a company that operates within a relatively narrow geographic base would not be interested in changing the focus of its operation.

Companies that are more regional in scope have the option to sell their product(s) or service(s) in a larger geographic area. The sales base of these larger companies may be in one or more communities, a county, several counties, one or more states, the entire nation, and/or other countries. There is, in any of the foregoing sales and credit bases, a distribution of risk over a larger area—a distribution of risk that transcends, depending heavily on the economy of one type of commerce or industry, whether it be farming, mining, a high-tech industry, river- or ocean-related traffic, tourism, or some other form of income-producing activity.

The ideal format for credit risks is to spread them over a broad industry and geographic base. How the term "broad base" should be related to a specific company or business depends largely on its size, type, product(s), and goals. What if your company does not aspire to be more than a local or an area player? Then the goal of your company also dictates that the base for distributing credit risks will be narrow, narrow by necessity and by choice. Safety of the receivables in this scenario should still be good if the credit manager or administrator follows appropriate guidelines.

Examples: A company or business that sells seeds, fertilizer, machinery, and other products to farmers is limited to that marketplace area. It might be the sales area that is its own base or, if a larger company, a national and regional sales area, where farming is the principal occupation and the principal form of commerce. A company that sells products and services which are used by farmers must do business in one or more farming communities or regions, regions where farming is the primary activity.

Another company might manufacture and distribute a product that is used in a broad cross section of homes or industries, resulting in a geographic base that, because of the nature of the product, almost automatically spreads receivables risk over many or all regions of the country. Some products are concentrated in a limited number of national manufacturers and distributors (household appliances, autos, production machinery, etc.), again assuring a broad base of credit risks.

As noted above, there are a variety of circumstances that might push a company into a concentration of credit risks in one relatively narrow geographic area, just as there are other circumstances that would make a broad geographic base of credit risks virtually inevitable. What should be remembered and applied in all areas of industry and commerce is the fact that the risk(s) to receivables—the receivables total of every company—is greatly diminished when it is possible and feasible to broaden customer, industry, and geographic bases.

11

How to Forecast Cash Flow

Of primary importance to the financial well-being of a company is a dependable flow of cash; other elements that contribute to the company's well-being may be equally important, but no single piece of financial information stands above it. The ability to accurately forecast the amount of cash available from receivables over a period of four or five weeks is indispensable to the company's financial officer. If there is to be a shortfall of internally generated cash during one or more of the next four or five weeks, the financial officer must have that information. Unless forecasting is accurate within a variable of five or six percent, the financial officer has no way to determine how much money he or she must borrow, or for which week or weeks it must be borrowed.

There is no mystique surrounding the forecasting of cash receipts. To do a good job, the credit manager or credit administrator must know the paying habits of the company's major accounts. When that information has been committed to memory, the process of forecasting becomes a matter of practice and fine-tuning. In a large company, it is the credit manager's responsibility to deliver an accurate forecast to the financial officer. When the company or business is small and there is no multitier of experience, the responsibility for turning receivables balances into a cash-flow forecast that has a high degree of accuracy might be the owner's or a designated employee's.

Forecasting Cash Flow

What must a credit manager, a credit administrator, or an owner and manager do to become a skilled forecaster of receivables collections? First, he or

263

she must become an authority on the paying habits of the company's credit accounts: who pays within terms, within five to ten days past due date, between 10 and 30 days past due date, etc. A successful forecaster must know the payment's pattern of the company's major credit accounts. No forecast is meaningful unless the forecast is within five percent of the receivables payments and has a decreasing, but meaningful level of accuracy for weeks three, four, and five. Anything below the five percent accuracy level would not serve the intended purpose. Using the Cash Forecast (see Figure 2-3) and the Cash Forecast Summary Sheet (see Figure 2-4) should help you bring the accuracy of your forecasts into acceptable parameters within a few weeks. Effective financial control demands that the forecasting of accounts receivable payments attain a high level of accuracy to ensure that more money than is necessary is not borrowed to sustain the requirements of cash flow. The accurate forecasting of internally generated cash during one fiscal year will save the company an impressive number of interest dollars.

These forms impose only one requirement—that you are thoroughly familiar with the payment pattern of the company's volume accounts. If you can produce that information from your aged trial balance report, you should have no trouble developing accurate cash forecasts.

To use the work sheet for weekly cash forecast, list alphabetically from the company's aged trial balance report those major accounts whose open balances you project will be paid during each of the weeks from one through five. If payment of one or more invoices will be delayed because of a problem with price, quantity invoiced versus quantity received, etc., back those totals out of your projection for week one, and probably out of week two unless there is a strong ongoing effort to resolve the matter.

List some of the small accounts and projected payment totals below the list of major accounts. Add a heading for miscellaneous small/smallest accounts and under that heading, forecast a figure for each of the five columns. Add each of the five columns and enter totals at the foot of each column.

Fill in the requested information through Collectible A/R Total on the Cash Forecast Summary Sheet. Bring the work sheet totals forward and enter in weeks one through five under "Collections by Week."

The other headings—"Projected," "Actual," and "Difference"—will be your (the credit manager's) personal report card. At the end of each week you should enter your projected totals against the total accounts receivable dollars collected during that week.

Forecasting your internally generated cash flow is not difficult. The key to making successful projections is how well you know the payment patterns of your accounts and how accurately you break receivables balances down into your weekly forecast figures. If forecasting cash flow has always seemed an intimidating experience or an experience that you have somehow managed to avoid, now is the time to start. Do it as an exercise for the first three or four weeks, comparing your payments projection for each week against payments received. When accuracy is at the five or six percent level, let the financial officer know that you are ready to deliver dependable figures on a weekly basis. If you are the financial officer and double also as the credit manager, you will quickly wonder how you got along without an accurate cash-flow projection. The prospect of having the benefit of reliable receivables forecasting on a weekly basis should be incentive enough for you to refine the input until it becomes an invaluable tool.

The Importance of Accurate Projections

An inaccurate cash-flow projection brings with it the potential for substantially distorting the difference between internally generated cash flow and the number of dollars that must be borrowed from the bank to supplement the shortfall between requirement and customer payments. The amount of borrowed money needed to close the shortfall between accounts receivable payments and cash-flow requirements will vary from one week to the next, but it can be a disaster if the cash-flow projection—short- and long-term— is not within the previously mentioned error rate of 5 percent. What about a weekly projection that fluctuates between an error rate of 5 and 10 or 12 percent? It has the potential for being much more harmful than none at all.

Can you imagine the frustration of a financial officer who projects the company's cash-flow needs for the next one or two weeks on the basis of a receivables forecast so inaccurate that borrowings for the two-week period are $40,000 to $50,000 more than the amount needed? Reversing the same situation, the financial officer suddenly finds himself or herself scrambling to get another $40,000 or $50,000 into the company's cash-flow pipeline when the projection for receivables payments is off target—way off target!

Inaccurate cash-flow projections can lead to a variety of financial problems that might have a daily impact on the business life of the company. When a credit manager is so out of touch with the payment realities of his or her receivables accounts that projections within acceptable parameters are not being delivered, it is followed by a valid question: "How many others things are out of synch?" If you were the company's financial officer and your credit manager supplied you with projections of inconsistent accuracy and quality, you would be well advised to take a hard look at his or her performance in other areas of credit responsibility. It is understandable that the first three, four, or five weekly projections made by a credit manager who is new to the process or is new to the receivables accounts are probably not going to be accurate within standards acceptable for plotting cash-flow requirements. The quality of these projections should, however, become increasingly more accurate until they settle into an area where they become a useful financial tool.

Example: When a credit manager's projections for receivables payments is consistently inaccurate over the period of three, four, or five weeks—and inaccurate to 10, 12, or 15 percent—there can be multiple problems. A key problem might be with the company's revolving line of bank credit. Payments might have been promised to certain suppliers on the basis of a projected level of internally generated cash flow. If payment of receivables balances falls below the projection by a substantial percentage, and the revolving bank line has been drawn down to the maximum allowable under the loan agreement, suppliers who have been promised payment will not be paid the first week, more will be unpaid the second week, and there will be a snowballing of unpaid suppliers and other creditors over the weeks that follow. Expect this situation to continue until the financial officer, or the person who has been relying on the projections, realizes that the projections are inaccurate to the point of being dangerously misleading.

Accurate forecasting and projecting of receivables payments for the first and second weeks of the forecast should be extremely accurate. The original projection for weeks three, four, and five will be decreasingly accurate, but this is corrected by adjusting and/or fine-tuning the figures that were projected the preceding week. The forecast for your company covers a period of five weeks. Each week the most immediate forecast is put to the test, the results are recorded, adjustments are made in forecast figures for the other four, and a new "fifth week" forecast is added. The procedure of dropping one week and adding another is endless and should provide one of the most beneficial financial tools available to your company's financial officer, or, in the situation of a small company, the owner and manager.

The day-to-day operation of any company is tied directly to its monthly cash flow. Internally generated cash is augmented by cash borrowed from the bank. If the forecast is inaccurate, too much might be borrowed, which would result in paying too many interest dollars. If the forecast is inaccurate and there is a shortfall of cash, the financial officer must react promptly to cover it; as noted in the first half of this example, the solution is not always a simple one.

Bank Borrowing to Augment Cash Flow

As I have noted in two earlier books, the old fashioned banker is, in most areas of the country, a vanished breed. Competition among banks in an industry where the shadow of huge intrastate and interstate banks looms increasingly large has changed the face of competition among banks from intense to fierce. Today's bankers are merchants, purveyors of services who push a broad variety of products from which the bank generates its revenues. Look at the lobby of almost any bank. It is indicative of how the scope of lending and services activities have changed in recent years, frequently resembling a magazine store with racks of booklets and pamphlets that recite the virtues of the bank's own version of a public offering. Many of these services are helpful, but be careful that your company doesn't become a "bank services junkie."

Good financial control, and good control of your company's receivables accounts, should enable your company to reduce the amount and frequency of money borrowed to supplement monthly cash flow. Any new or added sense of financial awareness or any financial control that puts a rein on the amount of money your company must borrow to supplement internally generated cash flow is money saved (interest and loan charges) for another purpose. The key to successfully managing bank borrowings is to anticipate the company's current, upcoming, and long-term financial needs—and plan for them! Anticipate and plan; there is no more effective combination for dealing with any management problem, but it is an especially effective combination when the subject is money.

For the many entrepreneurs and managers who function as their company's CEO, financial officer, credit and sales manager, and any other area that isn't covered by one of a very few employees, let me urge you not to forget the money-saving potential in the bank's practice of requiring compensating balances—or the money-saving potential in negotiating your company's interest rates.

Compensating Balances

Most banks ask, or require, that a percentage of the customer's credit line be left on deposit, a practice referred to as the "compensating balance." The compensating balance is often 10 percent of the line of credit with an additional 10 percent of the money borrowed. This is, however, a negotiable with most banks, so *do not* accept 10 percent and 10 percent as a compensating balance situation over which you have no control.

If your company is a start-up or in the very early stages of growth with a business plan, a budget, and projections for generating sales and cash flow that are realistic and healthy, there should be no reason to be diffident or hat-in-hand when presenting the company's proposal. Is there a good financial statement or two? So much the better. You are offering the bank something attractive, something that should prove mutually profitable and carries with it a low-end package of risk factors. If the bank says it wants compensating balances of 10 percent of the line of credit and 10 percent of the money borrowed, negotiate for an agreement that includes just one of the two. If the bank is adamant in stating that it must have both, and after talking with other banks, this one is the bank of your choice, then negotiate for compensating balances of 10 percent of the line of credit and 5 percent (or if you must give ground, 6 percent, 7 percent or 7.5 percent) of the money borrowed.

If you do have the option of going to another bank on terms that are somewhat more favorable, let the bank of your choice know you want to do business with it, but that you want to see some concrete reciprocal evidence of its interest in your company. This is not arrogance on your part. This is honestly exercising the relatively small amount of leverage that you bring to the meeting. There is no reason for your company, whether a start-up or one that is small, but growing, to pay the bank a top rate of interest for borrowed money and still be deprived of a meaningful percentage of the credit line. For the bank, this is having it both ways. You should see more commitment than you're getting when the bank is withholding compensating balances of 10 percent and 10 percent, or even 10 percent and 5 percent.

Although you should never make unreasonable requests of your banker, you will never know just how much give there is in the bank's approach to your company's credit line unless you make an articulate, well-prepared, and well-documented effort to gain reasonable concessions. The money you save in bank fees and charges is indicative of your strong commitment to effective financial control, which translates into getting the most for your company's dollars.

Negotiating Interest Rates

This is not a function of the credit manager in larger companies that have hundreds or thousands of employees in many well-structured departments. It relates, as does the subject of "Compensating Balances," to smaller and small companies, where an entrepreneur and manager, or a very small group of managerial types, perform more than one managerial or administrative function.

When a business is young, when a business is slow, when the economy in the country, in a region, or in an industry is slow, or when the problems of growth are weighing heavily on a small cadre of overworked owner(s) and managers, things that normally would be remembered might be in danger of slipping through a crack. With some things, there may be no real damage. If it is a financial thing and not doing it can cost the company money, those types of cracks should be avoided.

The interest rate(s) that your company pays for borrowed money can be crucial to the question of whether it will or will not be profitable, and, in the worst of all possible scenarios, whether it will survive. In addition to the factors mentioned above, a low-profit product in a highly competitive marketplace allows no latitude for loose or casual financial controls.

Example: The prime interest rate, the interest rate banks charge their strongest commercial customers, is at 12 percent. With the possible addition of some minor loan preparation charges, the customer, who is, in the bank's judgment, a totally secure credit risk, pays 12 percent—and no added percentage or points. Your company is younger, smaller, in a growth mode, and its trend is not firmly established. Very few of the company's assets are unencumbered, although there is equity in the land, in production equipment and machinery, and in raw materials, finished goods, and receivables.

The bank offers your company (Warburton-Schwartz, Inc.) the prime rate of 12 percent plus an additional 1, 1½, or 2 percent. Are you not happy with this package? You should be. The bank is recognizing and assigning an extra risk factor to your company that is neither necessary or warranted with a stronger, established customer.

You must recognize that the bank's position is correct and realistic. What you can and should do is present your best possible case for getting the bank to trim ½ percent or more from the add-on percentage above the prime rate of 12 percent. You must push for what should be recognized mutually as a reasonable concession, based upon the security already held by the bank in other lending areas (land, equipment, etc.), a consistently upward trend in sales and marketplace acceptance, an increase in the amount and percentage of net profit from one financial statement to the next, the obvious effectiveness of your company's financial controls as evidenced throughout the company, especially in the area of accounts receivable quality and collection, and clearly-defined prospects for successful future growth with an increased level of business and profits for the bank.

Although you should be fair to the bank, you are entitled to expect and to receive the benefits of a reciprocal business relationship. When you have a business that is successful or is becoming successful, and it is growing at a pace parallel to what was projected in a well-conceived business plan, you are not without a reasonable amount of leverage with your bank. It is quite possible that the bank would not have given your start-up firm an opening credit line if the banker(s) had not been impressed with the business plan, with the background and experience of the partners or principals, and with what they believed these owners and managers could do with the company. You might have a strong relationship with your bank, but you must still deal from whatever positions of strength the growth and success of your company enable you to bring to the negotiating table. These factors, plus the company's solid projections for continuing growth and success, increase the number and value of your company's bargaining chips.

The amount of money that your company is forced to borrow to meet its monthly cash-flow requirement will cost more, less, or what it should, depending on how effectively the interest rate was negotiated on the revolving loan for supplementing cash flow. If the rate is good and the loan is used effectively, the cost will have minimal impact on profits.

Seasonal Product Lines/ Fluctuating Cash Flow

If your company is in a business that involves seasonal highs and lows, highs and lows that cause comparable fluctuations in the company's requirements for cash, an extra measure of pressure is transferred to the credit manager to deliver the maximum amount of cash from receivables balances. Other players in your company's recurring pattern of highs and lows who would feel additional pressure are the production or manufacturing manager, the personnel manager, the purchasing manager, the company's controller, etc. None of these people or departments can escape the roller coaster effect that goes with seasonal highs and lows.

Packers, canners, and frozen products processors of fruits and vegetables must be ready to handle crops that build rapidly to a peak, sustain that peak for a relatively short period of time, then subside into varying periods and degrees of production and processing inactivity. A product that has been warehoused during the flurry of processing activity—or, if fresh fruit or produce, has been packaged and sent to national or international marketplaces—has gone from production and/or processing to the warehouse, to the customer, and to accounts receivable.

At the point where product—large quantities of it—has become a major addition to accounts receivable, the credit manager moves out of the shadows surrounding the frenzy of a seasonal high and onto the center of the company's stage. There are always receivables balances to be collected, but when, over a short period of time, large sums have been invested in product, there is always a sense of urgency until the flow of cash has been regenerated. Because of dramatically elevated costs for labor, raw materials, and other packing and/or production costs, the revolving bank line for supplementing cash flow will probably be at a point of near-zero availability.

Where does the pressure settle when there is a cash crunch? It settles on the credit manager—the man or woman who is expected to turn big receivables balances generated from the sale of fresh or newly processed products into a crunch-relieving flow of cash. The credit manager is expected to stimulate the flow of payments, orchestrating an increasing flow of cash with the skill and control of a symphony conductor. He must liberate receivables dollars that have escalated rapidly in number—escalated so rapidly that anything less than a knowledgeable and diligent effort will not return the company to the point of liquidity where it must be before the next costly surge of seasonal activity.

Some companies experience one seasonal high, operate briefly at a reduced level of activity, then build quickly into another high. This is the pattern of many packers, canners, and processors of fruits and vegetables. It is also true of seasonal or cyclical industries, industries that point to one or two specific seasons as their time in the marketplace sun, such as specialty manufacturers and distributors whose products are designed for use in the summer season, like outdoor furniture, barbecue equipment, beach umbrellas, and surfboards, and auto manufacturers. Why do so many of these companies put unnecessary pressure on their personnel and their financial resources by failing to integrate the production of items for the summer season into a wider time frame? Why not use production time as it becomes available throughout the year to produce and stockpile the merchandise for sale in summer?

The company's credit manager might hardly notice the change. If the company elects to manufacture a seasonal product throughout the year, it must contend with the added factor of producing goods so far in advance of the marketing season that large sums of money become frozen in inventory that cannot be liquidated for several months. If product is manufactured early and stored for several months, there is a substantial investment in labor, materials, manufacturing costs exclusive of labor, accounting, and warehouse space—all items that must be charged against the product. This takes a substantial sum of money out of available cash flow, forces the company to borrow from the bank, and further decreases the profit margin on product that has been stored for months.

What role does the credit manager have in what I have just outlined? If merchandise is unsold in a warehouse, the credit manager must feel no pressure, right? Wrong! The added pressure of labor, material, and overhead costs for merchandise that won't be sold for months will have the credit manager mining receivables accounts for every dime that can be extracted. The cash crunch that may result when inventories are well above normal, whether inadvertently or on purpose, must be offset with a major effort to reduce the company's receivables average of days sales outstanding (DSO). The collection effort must deal effectively with balances that were on the aging report when the accelerated seasonal activity began to peak and with balances added subsequent to the seasonal production effort.

The role of the credit manager is never a passive one, but in this particular scenario there is an urgency attached to the receivables responsibility that elevates normal standards for acceptable results. When the seasonal processing of the company's product or the seasonal availability of the raw material(s) or ingredient(s) that are an integral part of the product require prompt processing and the stockpiling of inventory at very high levels, these circumstances do not create an environment in which the credit manager plays a secondary role. When "money" is not just at the center of the problem, but is itself the problem, the company whose credit manager has demonstrated that he or she is capable of responding effectively to the challenge is of enormous value.

Level the Peaks and Valleys

Modifying periods of peaks and valleys into a pattern whereby they become minor dips and rises is a goal over which the credit manager has no control. If it is the nature of the company's type of business to experience extremes of peaks and valleys, the credit manager is locked into doing the best he or she can do to turn receivables as rapidly as possible without exerting unreasonable pressure on good customers. In some seasonal industries it should be possible to adapt to a more flexible and/or well-rounded production effort. When possible, the company should produce products of high seasonal demand during various times of the year when there is available production-line time. This should help to bring the peaks and valleys into a more livable business terrain, one in which the need to produce large quantities of product for a peak season of sales is integrated into a longer time frame of production.

There is another facet to the problem of leveling peaks and valleys that is the other side of the problem of seasonal product lines and seasonal highs. Your company's customers may be the ones who must face the problem of building to a high level of product to accommodate seasonal demand. This puts a strain on the customers' ability to pay within normal terms, so a customer might ask your company for an additional 30 days beyond normal credit terms—or perhaps a combination of a consignment of product above the customer's normal requirement, which would be paid for as sold.

Is it a reasonable request? It could be if your customer's customer base and seasonal demand are consistent with the request. If there is no real question regarding the customer's stability, the reasonableness of the request, or the seasonal demands of the market, your company will probably go along with the request. Agreeing to "additional invoice dating" puts a bit more pressure on your own cash flow, but agreeing to the reasonable request(s) of a good customer(s) is one of the best ways to assure the growth of your own company. There are times in the business life of your customers when, if asked, you are expected to be there. What if the customer has an unusual or a seasonal request? The criterion is the quality of the customer and whether the request can be justified. When a request is rooted solidly in the strength of a good business decision, your company cannot fail to support its good customer(s) when called upon to do so.

This is also a situation where your company has not been in the position of revving up for its own "peaks and valleys" production problem. Your company should be able to handle the legitimate request of this customer from inventory, especially if this customer and other customers experience the same types of needs on an occasional or seasonal basis. There is no reason why inventory levels that have been found to be adequate over a period of several years should not have brought these types of situations into the determination of what is and what is not an effective level of inventory.

Your company must have enough flexibility in its approach to the needs of its customers to respond favorably when the customer has good reason to ask a favor. The favor will turn a profit for your company, perhaps not quite as much when the terms are extended as when terms are standard, but there will be a profit. Looking on down the road, the dependability of your company and the understanding of the credit department will usually pay extra dividends in the months and years ahead.

Overcoming Cash Trickle

Cash flow and cash trickle have, at several points in the preceding pages, managed to assume their rightful role of prominence. It would, however, be almost foolhardy not to note that when the subject is cash flow and cash trickle, a bit of redundancy is one of an author's more forgivable shortcomings.

A company either runs on cash flow—an adequate flow of internally generated cash frequently supplemented with bank borrowings—or it struggles to try to survive on cash trickle in what may ultimately become an increasingly swift downward spiral. Cash trickle can be the result of several things, but it will not be "credit manager failure" if he or she has properly screened the company's credit accounts, does a professional job of monitoring and collecting accounts receivables balances, promptly refers nonresponsive customers to a third-party collection agency (or an attorney), and generally administers accounts receivable in a manner that is effective and efficient.

Cash trickle can be the result of an excessive investment in a product or products that sell reasonably well, but not well enough to justify an exceptionally high level of inventory. Cash trickle might also be the unhappy result of stockpiling large quantities of a product that was projected to sell very well, but has failed to generate more than a minimal level of buyer interest. Slow-turning receivables is another key reason—perhaps the most important one—for cash flow becoming cash trickle. When more than one of these ingredients is present, a corporation, a partnership, or a sole proprietorship is not going to have the volume of cash flow that is necessary for it to survive.

The cumulative effects of an advanced state of cash trickle are reviewed far too frequently by members of a creditor's committee in a Chapter 11 bankruptcy. Unless there is an infusion of new cash, a turnaround in the way credit accounts are processed, a more aggressive approach to the way receivables balances are collected, or a recognition by key management personnel that cash trickle is the business life comparable to hardening of the arterial walls in a human being, then the prognosis for the business patient is that it will slide gradually into a condition as dangerous as that of the person who goes about his or her daily business on an increasingly restricted flow of blood. Are no corrective measures taken in either situation? Expect then that both the business and the human patient are destined to become—certainly prematurely—vital statistics.

There is no more effective way to overcome cash trickle than to ensure that it does not happen. The aspirations for growth that move most companies along a successful path can be the undoing of a company that is not patient or has not planned well. Expanding a business too rapidly is an enormous drain on cash flow that might continue to be adequate under less demanding circumstances. Before any major change is contemplated, the change in cash flow requirements should be projected to determine whether the business can tolerate the additional drain imposed on cash flow.

Excessive Bank Borrowing?
Additional Interest Burden

When internally generated cash is not doing its share to support cash-flow requirements, the shortfall must be closed with borrowings from the bank, a practice that takes its toll directly from potential profits.

Example: A small company finds it necessary to borrow an annual average of an additional $5000 per month to sustain an adequate monthly cash flow. Assuming an average annual interest rate of 14 percent, the small company is paying $700 in interest charges on money that should have been generated from accounts receivable. A larger company might borrow an average of $25,000 per month at a somewhat lower interest rate, perhaps 12 percent. The annual total of interest paid to the bank would be $3000, an unnecessary expense to the company that probably was necessitated because receivables balances were not collected within a time frame consistent with the company's credit terms. Higher levels of borrowing might also be the result of inadequate or ineffective planning for the types of volatile business growth or planned business expansion discussed in earlier sections of this chapter.

Credit managers should determine the reason for unusually high levels of borrowing and/or interest charges on financial statements, from bank reports, from conversations with peer suppliers, and from other sources. They should examine this information in the context of whether the company is generally well managed and this is an isolated weakness, or it is quite consistent with management's weaknesses in other areas. Is the entrepreneur or the company's management known for a flamboyant, seat-of-the-pants management style? If so, it is a style that might be successful for a period of time, but as the company becomes larger and issues and decisions become more complex, there is every reason to assume that the company will slide into serious financial trouble.

The spending habits—personal and business—of an entrepreneur can work to ensure adequate cash flow for the business or they can remove so much cash from the business that what remains is a destructive cash trickle. Larger companies have more complex reasons for putting and/or finding themselves in the position of trying to survive with a business that demands a high monthly cash flow and a receivables base geared to deliver an inadequate percentage of the monthly requirement.

Something has to give and it must inevitably be the company seeking refuge in a Chapter 11 filing. The company's chief hope in this and many other scenarios is that management will decide to make the necessary hard decisions in time for the company to have a chance for a turnaround, either before or after a filing under Chapter 11.

12
Collection Techniques

The credit decisions that you made yesterday and the yesterdays before that ultimately will settle into one of these three categories: the good, the fair, and the ugly. Unless you change the guidelines for a particular account, your experience with the account probably will continue to reflect no measurable change. From that earliest point when you relied solely upon the experience of others, your experience with the account gradually becomes the experience of primary importance. What peer credit managers are doing and experiencing will always be relevant to your own decisions, but secondary to your own experience. Your evaluation will become the determining factor in any decision to continue selling on the terms and dollar level you first assigned, or, if your company's account experience indicates you should, to make an upward or a downward adjustment.

Watch for signs. Any account that requires two or three collection calls each month, particularly after a long period of an acceptable payments pattern, warrants careful monitoring. When such a customer begins to slip, dig for answers. You don't need a medical degree to know when the vital signs are faltering. Are changes occurring in the way an account makes its payments? Get some answers!

Occasionally you will have an account whose response to your strongest in-house collection effort is verbal abuse. Hold your temper, but take that response as your cue not to drag out your in-house collection effort. Assign the account to a collection agency—one that specializes in commercial accounts. For a variety of reasons (especially to avoid having a formal collection assignment picked up by a credit reporting service, or having a suit become a matter of public record), the first notice from a collection agency can sometimes jar the delinquent account into sending all or part of the money that you have been trying to collect. When that happens and your collection service agreement specifies "10 days free demand," the usual collection fee of 20 to 35 percent (percentages vary from one agency to another and according to the dollar amount of the assignment) is not applicable. What happens if the demand letter sent to your customer by the collection agency draws a "payment in full" response within 10 days of the collection agency's letter? With the "10 days free demand" provision, there is no collection charge. Remember, however, that when one of your customers is sliding, whatever the collection service gets for you is that much more than your own efforts generated. If it collects your money, it earns its fee.

Any account that slips into the category of the ugly, which is 90 days and over past due, dulls the luster of what might be an otherwise well-managed receivables aging report. The in-house collection guides and procedures that follow should be helpful in stopping most potential candidates for the "ugly" category from marching nonstop from "current" to "90 days and over."

Keep It Legal

Some collection tactics are unethical and illegal regardless of the circumstances. It is illegal to threaten or harass a debtor. You must be very careful that what you consider to be nothing more than a good, aggressive collection effort does not stray from that corridor into the sometimes grey areas of harassment or threats. Ambiguity is in any area where you cannot clearly draw lines, but it is particularly frustrating to walk a tightrope of ethical collection conduct when you know that the person or company with whom you are dealing is addicted to devious thinking and behavior. When the situation is extreme, the benefits of the law definitely tip in favor of the unscrupulous. The law is meant to be equitable for all parties, and it is legally and morally correct to protect against threats and harassment, but the law sometimes loses sight of where justice begins and ends. The following is an example of what you *should not* say or threaten to do when attempting to collect an unpaid balance.

Wilburn Spindler, credit manager for the Mold-Tight Rubber Company, is about to contact a delinquent account. Spindler is not a happy man. Account balances are 30, 60, and 75 days past due, and three promises within the past 20 days to pay the two oldest balances have not been honored.

Spindler identifies himself to the switchboard operator at the customer company and asks to speak with the company's controller, Clarence Burnside. There is a pause while the operator makes the connection.

"This is Clarence Burnside."

"Burnside, this is Wilburn Spindler, credit manager at Mold-Tight Rubber Company."

"Yes, Mr. Spindler. What can I do for you?"

"For openers, you can inject some integrity into that organization of yours by making good on the three promises of immediate payment you've given me in the past 20 days." Before Burnside can respond, Spindler erupts. "If I don't get payment satisfaction within the next 10 days, I'm going to let the industry know what a deadbeat company Warmsby Rubber Products really is!"

Burnside is momentarily taken aback by the ferocity of Spindler's attack. When he does begin to speak, he is in full control.

"Whether I did or did not make good on these alleged promises, Mr. Spindler, I would advise you not to infer or to state to any person or any company or firm that Warmsby Products is 'a deadbeat company.'"

Spindler is unrepentant.

"What would you call it if the spokesman for a company gave you three payment promises that were lies? Any company that would allow a spokesperson to deliver a constant stream of lies to suppliers regarding the payment of past-due balances doesn't deserve to stay in business!"

Wilburn Spindler did not know that Clarence Burnside had recently returned to work after undergoing open heart surgery. Burnside did not need the aggravation imposed by Spindler's attitude and remarks.

"Mr. Spindler, you haven't talked to me three times—in fact, you haven't talked to me at all. I returned to work four days ago after being away from the company for almost eight weeks. In my absence various people have been trying to cover, and there has been confusion—a lot of confusion—but we here at Warmsby Products are never deliberately misleading or dishonest."

Wilburn Spindler began to tread water.

"What do you know! Now that I reread the notes from the three recent telephone conversations, I see the calls were taken by people who identified themselves as members of your staff." Belligerence had gone over the side, leaving Spindler to squirm alone. "It's an obvious misunderstanding that should have been corrected . . ."

"What should have been corrected, Mr. Spindler, is the name on the purchase orders that Warmsby Products has given to your company over the past four years." Despite the doctor's admonition against allowing himself to become involved in stressful situations, Burnside's voice began to rise. "If you had taken the time to check our payment record, you would have seen that, until the past two months—months during which, due to my absence, there was a breakdown in the processing and releasing of supplier payments—Warmsby Products has never had an unpaid balance that was older than 30-days past due." He snorted. "That, Mr. Spindler, is hardly the record of a deadbeat company!"

"I understand, Mr. Burnside, and I apologize for . . ."

"A check for the balances that are 60- and 75-days past due will be mailed tomorrow. A second check—one for the balance that is 30-days past due—will be mailed this coming Friday." As Spindler attempted to interject a continuation of his apology, Burnside's voice rolled over it. "Any balance that is currently due or is about to become due will be paid by the end of this month. Mr. Spindler," disgust permeated his voice, "I'm sure that when I make the facts known to our purchasing people, the switch to another supplier will be automatic and will take place immediately."

The click on Burnside's end of the line left Spindler sputtering. He had overreacted. He had not bothered to thoroughly familiarize himself with the record of telephone calls made by a member of his staff, and relied on assumptions and a perfunctory look at what was written on the call sheet. Spindler had made the unprofessional mistake of making an unjustified accusation and an illegal threat against the reputation of Warmsby Products with the intent to damage that company's reputation with trade and supplier members. His unprofessional conduct had also cost the Mold-Tight Rubber Company a customer whose payment record and level of purchases qualified it to be considered "good."

It should be obvious to any person who handles credit accounts that there is a level beyond which you cannot escalate your company's collection effort without incurring the probability of a legal response. The people who own or manage a company or business may have treated your company quite badly, but you must be sure that your collection effort remains within the boundaries of ethical conduct. In that same context, never use the services of a commercial collection agency whose reputation for ethical practices is not well known. Your company could incur liability because of the questionable or blatantly illegal practices of an authorized representative. Problems of this nature can get very complicated and quite expensive if a suit becomes a trial and the judge or jury is persuaded that the actions of your company—or the company's representative—were illegal. Such a verdict can only result in a substantial monetary award in favor of the plaintiff company.

How can a credit manager ensure that his or her collection effort is legal within the most rigid interpretation of the laws governing illegal collection practices? The primary canon of conduct is that you do not threaten an individual or a company; do not make threatening or intimidating telephone calls to the residence of the owner, manager, or any other employee; say nothing that is not factual when asked by another company for your experience with an account. Never offer derogatory opinions or remarks regarding the management, personnel, or conduct of the business, and never put yourself or your company in the position of facing a suit for damages resulting from remarks and/or efforts allegedly made by you or a member of your staff while harassing one or more key company members or while attempting to discredit the customer company with other members of the trade, bankers, credit report companies, industry groups, etc.

Many legal options are available for attempting to collect your company's money: your own efforts, the efforts of a commercial collection agency, or the use of an attorney who is a collection specialist. Never let an obligation become a bad-debt item because you failed to use every legitimate tool to collect the receivables balance, but *do not* fall into the trap of allowing your zeal to cross into the area of illegal collection practices.

If you have used every conventional collection procedure that has been discussed in this section of the book, including obtaining a judgment against assets that cannot be found or may no longer exist, then you have confirmed that this is a bad-debt account. Put it in the category of a learning experience. Charge the account balance against the "Bad Debt Reserve" and get on with managing your other accounts.

(During the four years I was corporate credit manager for Dysan Corporation, that high-tech company went from annual sales of $5 million a year to sales in excess of $100 million a year. "Procedures and Goals" and "A Sequential Collection Effort" were adapted from guidelines I had used at Applied Materials and Burke Industries, and during three days of a seminar session in Las Vegas for the Western Floor Covering Association in the early 1970s. If used in conjunction with other guideline material in this book on the collection of past-due balances, I believe you will find it to be an excellent format for resolving past-due balances more rapidly and more frequently [see Figure 12-1].)

Collections— Procedures and Goals

1. The Aged Trial Balance Report of customer accounts should be split into sections of approximately equal size; not equal in the number of accounts assigned to each account section supervisor, but approximately equal in the work load assigned to each supervisor. As growth warrants, accounts on the receivables report can be realigned between section supervisors to accommodate new sections.

2. Certain major accounts (to be designated by the credit manager) will be handled by the credit manager or the assistant credit manager. The assistant credit manager will monitor the accounts that are assigned to him or her and make the necessary telephone or letter contacts.

3. The assistant credit manager will monitor the work of the section supervisors, answer questions that are within the range of his or her experience and authority, and refer other questions to the credit manager. Section supervisors will have access to the credit manager, but to avoid any appearance of undercutting the assistant manager's authority, such contacts must be through the assistant manager.

Figure 12-1. Collection guidelines.

Memorandum

To: Credit Department Personnel

From: The Credit Manager

Subject: Collection Guidelines

1) *Past-Due Balances of $500 or Less*
When there has been no response to three consecutive month-end statements—the third of which is to carry the statement "payment by ___(date)___ or collection"—account will be forwarded to third-party collection.

2) *Past-Due Balances of $500 to $2500*
When there has been no response to two month-end statements, the customer will be contacted for payment at the time the third statement is mailed. If a payment of acceptable size is not received within 10 days of the phone call, the account will be assigned to collection.

3) *Past-Due Balances of $2500 to $10,000*
When there has been no response to two month-end statements, a call will be placed to the customer as the third statement is about to be mailed. The customer will be notified that the company is on "Hold Order" status until past-due balances have been paid, with payment of all invoices past-due more than 30 days to be paid within 10 days. (Example: The customer is called on March 10th. Payment of all invoices more than 30 days past-due must be in our hands by March 20th.) If payment has not been received by March 20th, the account will be assigned to collection.

4) *Past-Due Balances between $10,000 and $25,000*
Statements will be forwarded to these accounts as they are received from Data Processing. At this exposure level, any past-due situation will be handled with telephone calls. The statement is perceived to be a document which the customer may or may not use in reconciling his or her figures with ours, or to provide us with information to enable us to correct our records.

All of the collection tools will be available for use in this category of accounts—holding orders, C.O.D., payment programs, collection assignments, etc. We make every effort to work with the customer, regardless of his or her level of purchases, but it is not possible to assign the same amount of time to accounts in the "$500 and below" category that is assigned to accounts with higher receivables balances. Accounts in this dollar bracket will be assigned for third-party collection action *only* after every reasonable collection effort has been made by our own department.

Figure 12-1. (*Continued*) Collection guidelines.

5) *Past-Due Balances above $25,000*

Statements will be forwarded to these accounts as they are received from Data Processing with the exception of situations where it might be mutually beneficial to note certain information—or to ask certain questions about times or balances that do not seem to be clearing in a normal time frame.

All of the collection tools mentioned in number (4) are available in this category, but we are not dogmatic or precipitous in our use of collection tools that could prove damaging to an account relationship that should be saved—if saving the relationship is in our best interest. When an account is moderate-to-high volume, has performed well for a reasonable period of time, then begins to stretch our sales terms into borderline or unacceptable areas of aging, we make every reasonable effort to get to the bottom of the problem and, if possible, help the customer to work out of the problem.

It does not work well for us if the account has substantial balances consistently in the "Over 60" and "Over 90" columns. If the account seems to be slowing with each of its major suppliers, we must monitor carefully the number and past-due aging of those balances. The credit manager will provide the guidelines for action appropriate to individual situations and will either monitor personally these major accounts or work closely with the person who has been given responsibility for the account.

6) *Past-Due Balances in Excess of $100,000*

Statements will be forwarded to these accounts, but it is especially important (as in *all* of the categories of accounts) that *invoices* are mailed promptly and faithfully. Accounts Payable Departments pay from invoices and purchase order numbers so it is imperative that invoices are prepared accurately (all data correct, including purchase order number) and mailed promptly. If a check for payment of several invoices fails to include an invoice from the same block of numbers as those paid, call the Payable Department to determine whether they received the unpaid invoice. If they have no record of it, mail a copy immediately.

When the payment pattern of a high-volume account becomes slower, the credit person who handles the account should ask for an explanation from his or her contact at the account. If the explanation is too ambiguous or superficial to be at the root of the problem, the credit manager should follow up with other credit managers and credit reporting agencies. In situations where the credit manager has a good rapport with the Controller or VP Finance, a straightforward answer is possible.

4. Aged Trial Balance Reports (whether on a once a week, twice a week, or more frequent schedule) will be delivered to the credit manager's office. He or she will make appropriate notations on the assistant manager's copy, then pass that copy and copies for the section supervisors on to the assistant manager.

5. The assistant manager will see that appropriate notations are included on the copy received by each section supervisor. These comments will address the sequence of collection priority—the type, timing, and progressive strength of the collection actions to be taken—and the point in a given collection situation where the credit manager has indicated he or she will review the effort to that point and authorize a written "final demand." Other notations regarding special actions or special effort will also be made on section supervisors' copies by the assistant manager.

6. Section supervisors will use call sheets in each account file folder to briefly recap collection and other conversations with the customer or the customer's employees. Customer folders, with recaps of these conversations, will be put on the assistant credit manager's desk at the close of each business day. Payment commitment data will be transferred from individual file folders by the assistant manager to a list that will be put on the credit manager's desk by 10:00 the following morning. The credit manager will then enter payment commitment data on the Receivables Projection Form which will be attached to the master (currently applicable) copy of the accounts receivable aging report.

7. Customer folders that require review will be put on the credit manager's desk at the end of each business day. If special action is indicated, it will be detailed in a note which will be attached to the folder or discussed with the assistant manager. Folders will be returned to section supervisors for the indicated action. (If standard action has been or seems about to be productive, the assistant manager will initial the account "calls recap sheet" and return it to the section supervisor without additional comment.)

8. If a collection call or letter triggers any form of unreasonable or abusive customer response, the conversation or letter will be brought to the attention of the credit manager as soon thereafter as is practicable.

9. Every Monday morning in a 30-minute session the credit manager will discuss with the assistant manager and account sections supervisors both the positive and negative results of the previous week's work, where the emphasis is to be placed during the current week, and what is expected from these and other collection actions. (If a procedure or an approach does not seem to be working or is less effective than it was in the past, the Monday morning meeting is the time for fine-tuning, cor-

recting, or changing a procedure with the goal of improving the effectiveness of each call.

10. Credit clearances will continue to be the overview responsibility of the credit manager, but the assistant manager has the authority to authorize the open-account release of goods to a maximum of 10 percent above established credit limits. When a credit request is not in line with prior order clearances, or when there is any question regarding open balances or payment history, the credit decision will be deferred until the credit manager is available. (If, in one of the above described situations, the credit manager is not available to make the decision, it will be referred to the financial officer or the controller, in that order.)

11. In every collection and/or past-due situation, the initial goal is to collect the balance(s) and to retain enough customer goodwill so the customer can continue to be serviced on terms somewhere between C.O.D. and Open Account. In some situations, it will be obvious that the emphasis of the effort is to collect the past-due balance(s); the customer has reached a point in the downward slide where there is no thought of future business; the objective is to collect what is owed to the creditor and walk rapidly away from the customer. (The credit manager will indicate at the outset of the collection effort, or at some point during that effort, whether there is a customer to be saved or whether the only objective is to save the creditor's dollars.)

Sequence of the Collection Effort

Supervisors of account sections will make collection calls to all accounts with past-due balances of $200 or more. Calls will be in an approved sequence, or, if there is variation from that sequence, will be as directed by the credit manager (see Figure 12-2).

The following is the basic procedure for the collection effort, unless section supervisors are given other instructions for individual accounts.

1. A telephone call is to be made to the customer when the account balance is 10 to 15 days past due. If the customer says the payment has been mailed and the customer has a good reputation for telling the truth, there should be no problem.

2. If payment has not been mailed, remind the customer of your sales terms and mention that, although you do not expect all invoices to be paid within terms, you do expect payment to be made within a very few days of those terms. (Put a reminder note on your calendar 10 days from

Figure 12-2. Accounts receivable collection procedure.

Memorandum

To: Credit Department Personnel

From: The Credit Manager

Subject: Accounts Receivable Collection Procedure

1. Statements mailed each month to all accounts.
2. When customer balances reach the "Over 30" column on the Aged Trial Balance Report, a first collection call will be made.
3. When customer balances reach the "Over 45" point on the Aged Trial Balance Report, a second collection call will be made.
4. When customer balances reach the "Over 60" column on the Aged Trial Balance Report, a collection letter will be sent to the customer. Five days after the collection letter has been mailed, the credit department person who has account responsibility will make a collection telephone call.
5. There may be some variation from the above (the spacing of letters and telephone calls) based upon the following criteria of priority and/or urgency:
   a. When balances are in two or more columns, the urgency is based upon the combination of dollars and aging. (All balances are past-due or open balances or are a combination of current and past-due.)
   b. Our past experience with the account plus the past and current experience of other suppliers. If our report data isn't current (D & B and NACM), those reports should be updated.
   c. The quality of the customer's response to the first letter or telephone call—key person not available, no return telephone call, etc.
   d. Whether there appears to be a trend downward in the customer's business.
   e. Whether cash flow seems to have been impacted by any single factor or a combination of extremely rapid growth, management that has not kept pace with growth, the loss of a key person or key personnel, or the loss of what may have been a long-standing advantage in the marketplace.
   f. Any product-related litigation that might involve the potential for a damaging financing settlement or that might incorporate the possibility of a negative impact on the customer's marketplace image.
   These are some of the factors that influence the timing and the amount of effort that we put into collecting past-due balances. They are some of the factors that dictate how much time and effort com-

Figure 12-2. (*Continued*) Accounts receivable collection procedure.

pany credit department personnel will expend on an account before the account is assigned to an outside collection agency.

6. When a customer's balance or a part of that balance reaches the "Over 90 Days" column on the Aged Trial Balance Report, the credit manager will have taken one or more of the following steps:

   a. Orders would have been held when the account became 45- or 60-days past due. The quality of our experience with the account in the past and what we are able to ascertain regarding the account's present condition will determine the exact timing of a hold on orders.

   b. If a satisfactory payment arrangement is worked out with the customer (payments every week or every two weeks which reduce the total open balance while allowing for the release of some goods; a payment arrangement of two dollars for every one dollar of goods released, etc.), then the "hold" on the release of orders can be eased.

   c. If an account falls increasingly deeper into the category of slow-pay accounts and the problem is not just a temporary cash-flow problem, but is the result of some new, adverse business problems, then the credit manager will monitor the account's trend with the person who has responsibility for the account.

7. When an account has a past-due balance that has reached the "Over 120 Days" column, it may already have been a third-party (outside collection service) collection assignment for 30 or more days. The credit manager will review each week all accounts on the past-due lists of department personnel with responsibility for accounts. As some accounts begin to slide deeper into the past-due columns, action appropriate to the specific account will be authorized by the credit manager.

8. When an account has been assigned to a collection agency, the company's products will not be available to the assigned account until the account has been paid in full. Unless there are unusual extenuating circumstances that would justify a change in our credit policy, the account may buy products on C.O.D. terms, but will not be allowed to buy our products on credit terms.

There are no inflexible criteria for handling most credit and collection problems. The primary criterion is the company's credit policy which sets parameters of some latitude and flexibility, not the least of which is the department's need and mandate to deal fairly and honestly with the company's credit customers—and the phrase "company's credit customers" includes virtually every customer who buys on a regular basis.

(*Continued*)

Figure 12-2. (*Continued*) Accounts receivable collection procedure.

> Department staff with account responsibility is to monitor all accounts on an ongoing basis, prorating time and energy to focus on major customers with an account or a payment problem, accounts with a lower dollar volume and some new or recurring payment problems, and an increasingly diminishing amount of time on the lower-to-lowest dollar volume accounts.
>
> We do not expect to lose a single dollar in bad-debt write-offs that could have been avoided with solid, diligent monitoring and collection procedures. The customer is king—but his or her crown diminishes in size and importance as it relates to the quality (payment performance) of the account.

the date of the first call. This note will refer you to the customer file folder and your customer call sheet, which should give details of the conversation: date of the call, person with whom you spoke, payment commitment date (if any), and date payment was mailed or will be mailed.

3. If the customer has not paid within 10 days of your first call, call again. The customer may say that a check has been mailed (get the check number, date, amount, and date mailed), in which event the problem may be resolved. If the customer has not by this time paid a balance that is now 30 to 40 days past due, tell the customer that orders will be held effective immediately until past-due balances have been cleared. (At this point, the customer should also be advised that failure to clear past-due balances before they become 45 days past due may result in the account being assigned C.O.D. terms.)

4. If there is no telephone call or payment response within the 10 to 12 days allowed by the "final demand," the account will be assigned to a third-party collection service, as stated in the final demand. All such accounts will be brought to the attention of the credit manager for collection assignment if the final demand has not triggered the required payment.

5. When an account has been assigned to a third-party collection service, any telephone or letter contact from the customer will be referred to the credit manager. The customer will have been advised in the final demand letter that a third-party collection assignment reduces any future supplier-customer relationship to a C.O.D. basis, and even that limited relationship will be available to the customer only after all open balances have been paid. If it can be determined that a check was mailed at some point in the sequence of calls, but it did not reach the creditor, have the customer stop payment on the first check and forward immediately a second check. This should be noted in the customer file folder.)

Summary: In any collection procedure it is important to establish and maintain the promised sequential continuity of collection steps as outlined in telephone calls and letters to the customer.

If the integrity of the creditors' intentions is established with the first written reminder or telephone call, there is a good chance that the account of an honest customer will not deteriorate to the point where it requires the collection assistance of a third party. Third-party collections will certainly be reduced to situations where there is an inability to pay, an inability or an unwillingness to work out a payment plan, or a disregard for the customer's responsibility to the suppliers.

The customer should be given every reasonable opportunity to clear his or her account with the credit grantor. Only when collection efforts have been thwarted via the filing of a petition in bankruptcy—either the protection and continuation provisions of Chapter 11 or a formal filing for liquidation of the business and relief from creditor obligations—should a creditor company move the account balance into the category of a bad-debt item.

(The size of your company's credit department will govern the number of receivables section supervisors and whether there is an assistant credit manager. In a smaller company, the credit manager will handle all supervisory duties and will work directly with the people who handle sections of receivable accounts. A small company? A small staff. A larger company? A correspondingly larger staff.)

A Credit Manager's Nightmare

A major problem shared by companies who experience unregulated growth is the quality of their accounts receivable. If the procedure for screening new accounts or for monitoring existing accounts is not adequate to ensure a high quality of fast-turning receivables, the company's growth will be inhibited. A high percentage of any company's monthly cash-flow requirement must be generated internally. If the quality of accounts receivable is not strong enough to provide this level of financial support, the cost to the company of relying on bank borrowings to supplement monthly cash-flow requirements becomes an unacceptable financial burden.

No business should be expected to have long-term success if financial planning is not sound, financial controls are ineffective, and internally generated cash is disproportionate to the dollar total of accounts receivable. Manufacturing, marketing, purchasing, research and development, accounting, and other components may be in synch with what it takes to build a successful business, but the failure of management to provide strong financial guidance must, in the long-term, doom the company or business to failure.

This book emphasizes credit and credit management topics, but it follows that because credit and credit management are an integral part of the financial management of a company or business, I shall periodically relate credit and credit management to other elements of the enterprise—good or bad.

This brings to mind the problems that can arise when a company's rapid growth is the result of pressure from either the founder(s) or venture capitalists to move rapidly toward a first public offering of the company's stock. If the timing is right—market trend, investor interest in the company's products, state of the economy, etc.—the first public offering can be a bonanza for the founders and the venture capitalists. And what about members of the general public who might be swayed into investing in the company's stock because of its record of "doubling sales every quarter?" Does the public know that the highly praised doubling of quarterly sales has been accomplished at the expense of sound credit and receivables management? Does the public, or the Securities and Exchange Commission, know that the $2, $5, or $10 million in receivables is of very poor quality? Do prospective investors and the SEC know that the majority of receivables balances are 45- to 90-days past sales terms? Does the investing public know that the media hype surrounding the company's exceptional growth has been fueled primarily on the doubling of sales each of the last three quarters, and nothing else? What happened to good credit selection and management practices? They were waived at the insistence of a top management totally immersed in ensuring that those media-dazzling quarterly sales goals were achieved.

Why, you may ask, doesn't the credit manager in one of these artificially inseminated growth situations go public with what he or she knows and does each day? As an employee, the credit manager has virtually no leverage to influence top management to step away from the policy of "short-term growth at any cost" and develop a growth program that offers the business or company some chance for survival. In the face of a top management whose unalterable goal is a public offering at the earliest possible moment, the credit management person has no chance to persuade the company's policy makers to allow the principles of good credit management to guide the evaluation, acceptance, and management of receivables accounts.

Doubling a company's sales each quarter (or showing a 20 percent or 25 percent sales growth every quarter) is not in itself a criterion for disaster. It becomes the short path to disaster only when short-sighted entrepreneurs, managers, management teams, and venture capitalists force a company into a position where financial gridlock and a subsequent slide into oblivion is the usual result. The "quick buck" philosophy has, in recent past years, been most visible if not most prevalent in the electronics, semiconductor, and computer industries. It has frequently been a disaster for investors large and small who bought the first public offering of stock in companies whose management was motivated by the desire to produce short-term rather than long-term results.

Aggressive management is a legitimate and an often successful management style, but to be successful it must be fueled by motivational components that are not overshadowed by callous greed. An early and a well-based offering of stock in a company that has been positioned for long-term success, rather than the glitz and color of a Fourth of July fireworks display, is something credit managers can live with, and so can corporate and private investors.

Customer Payment Patterns

People who have limited credit management experience learn very quickly that some customers do not have the cash flow necessary to pay invoices within sales terms. This is not usually a problem if everything else is within acceptable parameters. Depending upon your company's credit plan, you usually can sell such accounts on credit terms, knowing that your company will wait an additional 10, 15, or 20 days for its money. It is the other category of credit customers—the ones who rarely fail to pay within terms—whose failure to pay on time causes concern. There is rarely a past-due item on this category of accounts, so the first reaction is to wonder what is going wrong. This reaction is tempered promptly by the more reasonable realization that one past-due invoice does not indicate a disaster in the making.

The credit manager, or the person who makes the credit decisions, should be thoroughly familiar with the payment patterns of his or her accounts. He or she should know which accounts traditionally pay within terms, which accounts will occasionally pay 10-days slow, which accounts might pay at any point between 10- or 15-days slow and a occasional 40- to 50-days, and which accounts seem to enjoy an ongoing struggle to keep their payment pattern within 50- to 60-days past due. When a credit manager has been on the job for a minimum of three to six months, he or she should be getting a good feel for the payment patterns of the company's customers. Experience with the accounts is the only way a credit manager or administrator can begin to determine the reason(s) for a deviation from past payment experiences.

Why Doesn't
the Customer Pay?

Money isn't the only reason a customer doesn't pay an invoice. Would you be in a hurry to pay an invoice if you were shipped defective or out-of-spec products? Would you hurry to pay if you received goods that had been damaged in transit? How quickly would you authorize payment for a shipment that had one or more of the wrong quantity, size, color, or formula? If that sampler of bad news is not enough to hold up a check, how thrilled would you be to find that the invoiced price is substantially more than the price quoted when you placed the order? When there is more than one of the previous items on the same invoice, the customer will not pay that flawed document until you have corrected it. You would not rush to clear such an invoice, and your customer will not rush to clear yours.

The items just listed are a few of the legitimate reasons for a customer who always pays within, or near, terms to withhold payment for an invoice or statement items. The trick is for you, the credit manager, to take the initiative. Don't wait for the customer to do something about it. When you see that an item has become past due, call the customer's payables person or department and ask the question not covered in the previous paragraph: does payables have a copy of the invoice? If not, revive the payment process by putting a copy in the mail. If the problem isn't one of a missing invoice, the information you receive from payables regarding the reason(s) for holding up payment should put you in a position to move toward doing whatever is necessary to eliminate the problem.

The credit manager's experience with an account is the best source of information for determining the reasoning behind a customer's request. A quick way to determine whether a customer likes to use "buy time" ploys is to check the file folder. Does the customer wait until you call to ask about a past-due invoice before requesting an invoice copy? Has the customer recently requested one or more invoice copies? Have those requests all come within a short period of time? Have you been experiencing unauthorized deductions from payments, which then required calls and/or letters before you resolved each incident? Is the customer attempting to take discounts, when it is obvious that the discount was taken days past what would have been a more than generous one-time extension of the discount period?

The purpose of these questions is to help you find an explanation for deviations from a normal industry or customer processing and payments pattern. Under normal circumstances there is nothing unreasonable about a request for an invoice copy. Your company might not have mailed the customer a copy. It might have slipped into the limbo of lost mail, or it could have disappeared after it reached the customer. Unauthorized payment deductions usually are isolated incidents caused by specific, nonrecurring facts or assumptions. When you find that a customer has developed a fondness for taking payment deductions to which the company is not entitled, stop it before the customer can claim that a string of unchallenged deductions is precedent for continuing the practice. How do you handle disallowed discounts?

When you know the payment patterns of your customers, it will be much easier to get to the bottom of any deviation from an established payment pattern. Can you be sure that invoice charges are correct? Were products shipped as the customer ordered them (type, quality, color, size, number, arrival time, etc.)? Is the customer waiting for a credit memo that was promised some time ago, but has not been prepared and forwarded? If unearned discounts are the problem, notify the customer in writing that the practice will not be allowed to continue. Tell the customer that you will not be able to ship in-house orders for product until unearned discounts (enclose a list of them) have been paid.

It's *Your* Money!

When an account begins to show you one or more of the following symptoms, move quickly to update your information. Review your recent payments experience with that of other suppliers, add any additional relevant pieces of information you might have culled from conversations with other owners—at an industry meeting, from a commercial credit report, or from some other source—and prepare to take a firmer hold on the credit reins. It might be only a momentary problem before the account settles back into a normal pattern, but you don't want or need any surprises that could become costly.

What is the "much less than worst" scenario? Your customer files for protection under Chapter 11 of The Bankruptcy Act within two, three, or four months after you have collected your money. Other creditor companies will be unhappy when they learn that you are no longer involved. Some unpaid creditors will voice the opinion that your company received "preferential treatment." The burden of proof is theirs. Never voluntarily surrender your money to a trustee who has been elected by the creditors so he or she can take it and throw it back into the "general assets" pot. The court might order you later to do just that, but if it is the trustee who wants you to return the money, he or she might have very little leverage to force it. Most bankruptcy cases have few assets, and there is usually not enough money available—or money involved in your alleged "preference"—to justify spending some of it on a possible extended in-court effort to prove that you knew the debtor's precarious situation when you got the alleged "preferential payment(s)." If the amount is large, the trustee might consider making the effort to take it from you. If the amount is not large, there probably will be nothing more threatening than bluster.

Remember that *you* were the one who saw the problem developing and had the good judgment to get all, or most, of your company's money before there was a bankruptcy filing. You did your job. Unless you arranged something with the debtor that was truly preferential, there should be no successful claim against your money. The problem with many who complain of a preference is that they did not do as good a job as you did. It's always pos-

sible for one creditor to get a piece of information through legitimate channels and, on the basis of that information, decide to accelerate the collection of an account balance. What will probably happen the next time there
is a similar Chapter 11 filing? Another creditor might get information that
will enable his or her company to get out of an account before you and
other creditors. Of course you won't be pleased, but if your information
indicates that the one creditor got out of the account as the result of information he or she obtained legitimately, you should have no problem with it.

You always should investigate rumors—particularly persistent ones.
When you hear that an owner or partner is spending too much time away
from the business, is driving a new and expensive car, and is getting into a
lifestyle that is not reconcilable with the size and quality of the business, do
some investigating. Any significant change in lifestyle or a change in a long-
term pattern of responsible, effective management is an indicator of some
potentially serious problems for the business. Any serious business problem
is a threat to the safety of your receivables dollars.

The following line is redundant because it has been said in so many different ways, but it is so important to the success of any company or business:
never, *never* lose sight of the fact that customers are important people, but
never forget that it is *your* company's money.

Customer Call Sheet

The Customer Call Sheet is an important part of the ongoing record keeping for each account. It is particularly important because you will use it to
record the facts of calls regarding payments. If the Call Sheet is properly
maintained, you won't have to go back over six months of receivables aging
reports to know how a certain account has been handling its obligations.
Your Call Sheet record will show no collection calls, an occasional call, or a
number of calls. It might not tell you whether the account pays on a discount or prompt basis, but it will tell you at a glance whether the account
has been a problem.

The Call Sheet is a key record in the systematic accumulation of verbal
and written customer contacts. When an account is doing well, you might
have almost nothing on your Call Sheet, and only an occasional letter relating not to a payment problem, but to a missing invoice or a pricing error.
When an account consistently requires telephone calls to get your money
released, it is a problem that eventually might lead to a bankruptcy filing. If
that occurs and your company eventually must qualify the failed account as
an allowable bad-debt deduction (for IRS purposes), a record of good continuity between collection calls and collection letters should ensure that a
write-off of the balance will not be challenged successfully. Your records will

substantiate the quality and the consistency of your in-house collection effort, an effort which might or might not have included assignment to a third party. Whether you did or did not assign the account will depend upon the circumstances of the business failure and would be relevant to qualifying the write-off, if your records of telephone calls and letters indicates a consistent and an appropriately aggressive approach to the account.

Make your comments on the Call Sheet (see Figures 12-3, 12-4, and 12-5) brief, but complete as to what you said, what the customer said, and what was promised as a result of the call. In the "Follow" column you should note the date for the next call, if what was promised during the conversation—and by a specific date—is not done. You consistently might contact one person, but be sure to note any change from the name shown at the top of the sheet. In some of the larger companies, it is not unusual for the "contact name" to change once or twice a year. Names are important. You might remember the person's name if you had to call again, but in your absence your assistant might not know who in payables had made the payment commitment.

Collection Calls

The purpose of these examples is to give you some guidelines for how various types of collection calls might be structured. These are not scripts for collection calls, only some guideline material. Unless collection calls have the flavor and style of the caller, they will not be effective. Deliver your company's message in a way that is comfortable for you, being careful to control the content and flow of the conversations from the moment you place the call. You want the customer to know what your company expects, and it wouldn't be necessary for you to make a collection call if the customer's payment performance met those expectations.

You might feel a certain amount of hostility toward a customer who has evidenced a callous disregard for honesty and integrity in his or her relationship with your company. If you have such feelings, don't let them surface in conversations with the principal or other people at the account. When you call the firm, tell them what you expect them to do, the time frame within which you expect them to do it, and what you can and cannot do for them during the period of time it takes to resolve the problem.

A telephone call to an occasionally troublesome account is another matter. The call should address directly the problem of a past-due balance. You know that the account is past due (perhaps 25 to 40 days), the customer knows that the account is past due, and both of you know the reason for the call. This is a customer whose problems might be becoming increasingly less manageable. Therefore, it is your responsibility to hold the aging of these receivables balances within parameters that are acceptable to your

Customer Call Sheet

Owner _____ Company Name _____

Contact _____ Phone _____

Date	Contact	Subject/Comments	Follow-Up

Figure 12-3. Customer call sheet (individual account).

Customer: _____   Phone: _____

_____   Time Difference: _____

Date Called   *Call Details*

_____   _____

_____   _____

_____   _____

_____   _____

_____   _____

_____   _____

_____   _____

_____   _____

_____   _____

_____   _____

_____   _____

_____   _____

_____   _____

_____   _____

_____   _____

_____   _____

_____   _____

_____   _____

_____   _____

_____   _____

_____   _____

_____   _____

_____   _____

_____   _____

Figure 12-4. Call sheet (individual account with details of calls).

Account Number	Customer Name/Location	Date Called	Payment Promised		Date Promised	Date and Amount Received
			Invoices	Amount		

Past-Due Balances—Calls as Listed

Figure 12-5. Call sheet (various customers).

company. Is the account at a point where past-due balances must be reduced? Insist that the customer make regularly scheduled weekly or biweekly payments until the receivables aging is acceptable, then hold the balance of shipments and orders at your target level for the account. What if the customer subsequently fails to make a scheduled payment? Hold shipments of product (which should be no more than 50 percent of each payment to ensure an acceptable decrease in past-due balances) until the payment program is in step with scheduled payments.

Example: Suppose a customer has past-due balances and you have arranged for biweekly payments of $400 until those balances have been cleared. It is February 9th, a product shipment of $225 has been scheduled to be released today, but the biweekly payment of $400, due on February 7th, has not arrived. Do you release the $225 worth of product and hope the payment arrives within the next couple of days? You do not! You place a call to the customer's accounts payable section.

"This is Donna in payables."

"Lawrence Gerber at Pinnacle Products, Donna."

"Yes, Mr. Gerber."

"We have a problem, Donna. A shipment for $225 worth of product should go out today, but I haven't received the $400 payment that was due the day before yesterday."

"Oh, yes." There is a short pause. "We weren't able to mail the check last Friday, Mr. Gerber, but I know we need the product."

"I'm afraid that isn't good enough. The aging of your company's receivables balance requires payments on schedule or we can't release product on any basis."

"Not even on C.O.D.?"

"Not unless the C.O.D. is on a payment basis of $2 for every $1 of product. But I'll tell you what we'll do this one time. We'll ship the $225 worth of product today, but the C.O.D. total will be $450. The additional $225 will be applied to past-due balances. Incidentally Donna, the freight company has been instructed to accept only postal money orders or a cashier's check."

"Well, if that's the only way we can get product . . ."

"I'm afraid that it is, Donna. I also want to be sure that you'll get back on schedule with the $400 biweekly payments. I'm looking at $2085 that's between 30- and 65-days past due, so I expect our account to receive priority payment attention until the old balances have been cleared. Can you do that?"

"Yes. I'll move some payments around to be sure we stay on the biweekly schedule."

"I appreciate your help, Donna. The shipment will go out today so you'll have a $450 C.O.D. arriving either tomorrow afternoon or Friday morning."

"The check will be ready."

"Thanks, Donna. Goodbye."

"Goodbye, Mr. Gerber."

The following is an example of a collection call to a customer who owes $3488 for products covered by an invoice that is now 20-days past due. This customer has done business with your company for years, usually pays within 10 days of Net 30 terms, and is rarely past due more than 10 or 15 days. You want to generate payment, but your primary concern with this account is the possibility that the customer did not receive a copy of the invoice.

Your call goes through to accounts payable.

"This is Marcie in payables."

"Marcie, this is Frank Martin (*you*) at the Turnkey Company in Seattle, Washington."

"I'm sorry. I didn't hear the company name."

"Turnkey, Marcie—the Turnkey Company."

"Oh, yes. We don't have a very good connection."

"Marcie, our records don't indicate that we've received your payment for an invoice that's 20-days past due. I'm wondering if you received it, and, if you did, when you expect to release payment."

"Let me check it for you. What's the invoice date and number?"

"The number is 592, dated 5/15, amount of $3488."

"Number 592 dated 5/15. Just a minute, please."

"Thank you."

(A minute or two of silence, then Marcie returns.)

"I'm glad you called, Mr. Martin. Someone had filed the invoice in the paid folder."

"I thought it must be something unusual because you almost always pay closer to terms. When should you have the payment processed and released?"

"It's early enough so I can input the data today. The check will go out this Friday."

"Great! Thanks for your help, Marcie."

"You're welcome. Good-bye."

"Good-bye, Marcie."

Now let's change the scenario to reflect less cooperation on the part of your customer or your customer's payables person. Remember that when you're dealing with a person in accounts payable, or dealing with a person who is in accounts payable, if that person isn't the owner or a management person, he or she might not be authorized to process or to release your check unless instructed to do so by the owner, financial officer, controller, or another designated financial person. Accounts Payable employees get as fed up with the hassles that result from stall tactics and broken promises as you do. When there's a payment problem that obviously is beyond the control of the payables person to whom your account is assigned (as in a several-person department), go right on up the line to the payables supervisor, the controller, or the financial officer. If your product(s) is one the customer must have and the account is more frequently allowing balances to become borderline unacceptable before paying, use any personal relationship you may have developed to expedite payment. You might call the customer's purchasing manager to tell him or her that you are going to hold shipments of product if account balances are not paid closer to terms. The customer's purchasing manager will involve the manufacturing manager and the company's financial people to ensure that there is no interruption in the flow of product from your company, and that the flow of payment checks is more timely.

You place a call to the controller of this firm, a firm whose payment record and promises of payment have been inconsistent. The firm has made payment promises, but has rarely kept them. It frequently takes two or three collection calls before you receive the promised check, and then it may be two weeks or more after the first call and payment promise before you receive it.

Your call is taken by the controller.

"Frank, how are you?"

"My health is fine, Carter. It's your account that's my problem. What happened to the $1862 check you agreed to mail not later than last Friday?"

"The money just didn't come in, Frank. I would have called you, but right up until Friday afternoon I thought we could release your check."

"You did get some money? Were you able to release some checks?"

"Oh, sure. A few that I simply had to let go."

"Good. Now as of this moment, Carter, I want you to consider that my check for $1862 is among those that you must release on Friday of this week."

"I'll try, Frank, but when the money doesn't come in, I can only do so much."

"I understand, but I've waited longer than a reasonable length of time. Do what you have to do, but we're at a point where the check arrives in my office by next Tuesday or I don't release any more product until it does."

"Hey! We need those shipments! Our manufacturing people will be all over me if you hold orders!"

"That isn't my problem, Carter. If you want an uninterrupted flow of product(s), I want an uninterrupted flow of payments. Don't tell me you'll send a check by a specific date and then fail to do it."

"You don't believe in making things easy for a person, do you?"

"I can't make it easy for you when we're dealing with a past-due balance the size and age of this one. We sell to customers who pay within terms or close to terms, and I expect your company to do the same. You'll get the check out by this Friday?"

"I'll see that it's released."

"I appreciate it, Carter. Good-bye."

"Good-bye."

The following example is the only one that I shall personalize. I developed this relationship while I was a corporate credit manager in the floor coverings industry, and it spanned the 14 years I was in that industry. It is an excellent example of rapport at its finest between a corporate credit manager (myself) and an owner whose integrity was as sustaining for me as my willingness to work with him was for his company—and for him. Remember that strong customer relationships are at least as important for the small company as they are for credit management people in the bigger companies. Develop good relationships with key people in your major customer companies. Many relationships will be confined to telephone conversations or an occasional meeting at an industry function. Others will involve a lunch now and then, not only because you have business to discuss, but also because there is genuine pleasure in getting together. It couldn't be better for your company!

I receive a telephone call from the president and owner of a 26-year-old firm (floor covering contractor and retailer) with whom my company has done an ever-increasing level of business. At this point in the relationship, our annual sales to this company exceed $400,000. The conversation is as follows:

"This is Cecil Bond."

"Cec, this is Charlie Webster. How are you?"

The call came in on my direct outside line. Charlie usually did not use that line.

"I'm fine, Charlie. This call is a surprise. What's doing?"

"I've got a problem, Cec, and it could be a big one."

"Oh? What is it?"

"One of my major customers has filed a Chapter 11, and I don't think they can come up with a reorganization plan that the creditors will buy."

"Are you secured, Charlie?" (referring to accounts receivable balances protected by a Uniform Commercial Code filing).

"Probably 40 percent of our account is in with the general creditors. I've done business with these people for 16 years. I never thought their account would be a problem."

"If you think that highly of them, probably most of their other creditors do too. It's possible you can work out a plan that's acceptable to the creditors and the bankruptcy court."

"I suppose there's a chance. Meanwhile, we won't be getting the $82,000 check that they were going to mail this week. Not getting that check puts our cash flow in a real vise."

"What about scaling back your payments to suppliers? Tell the others what you've just told me. Tell them you'll prorate payments on a percentage basis for two or three months, then you'll increase the payment amounts until you're back on a normal payment schedule."

"That schedule would give us some breathing room."

"What do you think about the cash-flow problem, Charlie? Can you work your way out of it in four to six months?"

"Oh, sure. The account is a major one, but we're in good long-term shape. We can close the gap within six months and move forward."

"Good. Charlie, use my name and our conversation if it'll help you with some of your other suppliers. If anybody hesitates, have them give me a call."

"I appreciate it, Cec. Are you going to be in the area later this month?"

"Yes, I think I'll be down there—here it is—on the 24th, 25th, and 26th."

"Pick a day and let me buy lunch."

"You're on. What about the 26th? I'll confirm with your office when I get in on the 24th?"

"Great! See you on the 26th—and thanks again, Cec."

"My pleasure, Charlie."

There is one priceless ingredient in a genuinely strong customer relationship, a relationship in which the years of your association with an owner or partner give you total confidence in the personal and the business integrity of that person. Do your best to generate those same feelings of confidence and integrity in others by your actions and deeds. A relationship of that quality can return business and personal dividends beyond any expectations.

Not every collection call will fulfill your expectation of a resolution to the past-due payments problem. Customers exist whose credibility and use of time-buying ploys will test your patience to the maximum. Following a particularly unsatisfactory string of collection calls, you might lean toward the thought that your customer list has too many people who seem to want to trash the supplier-customer relationship. You will move that thought quickly out of your mind because the overwhelming majority of your customers, if you have selected them wisely, are people of integrity who will give your company the kind of treatment they expect for themselves. It is unpleasant, however, when you start to recap a conversation on your call sheet and find that the customer cast his or her commitment not in stone but in Silly Putty.

You do not want your collection calls to become adversarial. When a customer whose account is totally out of phase with payment terms persists in trying to turn payment problems back onto your prices (too high, not competitive), your products (inconsistent quality, etc.), or your delivery time ("You don't deliver on time and that costs me money!"), do not say what you are justified in thinking. You must convince problem accounts, such as the ones just described, that credit sales are unacceptable until account balances are close to payment terms, or you should put some constraints on the when and how of product releases. Is the account past due? Is it *really* past due? Then don't release any product or perform any services until aging and balances are in line with your company's credit policy. Is the customer unhappy? You have been unhappy with the account's payment performance much longer than the customer has been unhappy. The only thing that should change this relationship is the customer's money—in the amount requested.

Collection Letters
(Including Final Demand)

The nine collection letters that follow (Figures 12-6 to 12-14) are examples of collection letters that you might use in conjunction with telephone calls or as a follow-up when your calls have been ineffective. The attitudes of customers will determine the timing for going from telephone calls to the more formal approach of a collection letter.

The first letter should state the date(s) of telephone calls, the promises of payment made to you, the balance that is past due, and the need for a prompt payment response. Do not mention in this letter any collection effort other than an in-house effort if payment is not received by the date specified. This is the first collection letter of a series that should not exceed three before you assign the account to an outside collection service. Accelerate the urgency if the first letter doesn't generate a check. Go with a second letter that leaves no question in the customer's mind regarding the seriousness of the past-due problem, but do not mention a third-party collection assignment. If you still do not receive a check, send a final demand

---

(Date)

Company Name
Street Address (or P.O. Box Number)
City, State, Zip Code

Attention of _____ (Name and Title) _____

Dear Mr. (or Ms.) _____ :

There has been no response to our telephone and letter requests for payment of your account balance, currently _____ days past-due.

We can devote no more in-house time to the collection effort. I must now tell you that the account will be referred to our collection agency on _____(date)_____ if we have not received payment in the amount of $ _____.

Sincerely,

Credit Manager

Figure 12-6. Collection letter (referral to collection if . . .).

letter via certified or registered mail to ensure that the intended recipient gets it, knows exactly what you are about to do, and is aware of the time frame available to him or to her before you take the collection action stated in the final demand letter. No longer does any latitude or inclination to negotiate a payment program with your customer exist—not if you have done a thorough job of communicating your company's payment requirements in the telephone calls and letters that preceded the final demand.

At this point in the relationship, you probably have been given three or four payment promises (all broken), a few lies or distortions of truth when you pressed for an explanation of the customer's problems, and a rather well-documented feeling that you cannot believe anything these people tell you. You have spent more time and effort trying to salvage the account than the customer's attitude deserved, so let it go. Let the people who spend their work days trying to collect money from these types of accounts handle it now. You have many other accounts whose problems have been getting less than a reasonable share of your time. Get back to doing a total credit job with all of your company's accounts.

(Date)

Customer Name
Street Address (or P.O. Box Number)
City, State, Zip Code

Dear Mr. (or Ms.) _____ :

Our payment records do not show that we have received your check for _(month and year)_ invoices in the amount of_____.

If our records do not agree, please contact the undersigned so we can go over our respective records, locate the problem, and make whatever adjustment(s) may be necessary. If our records to agree, prompt payment of the above-listed balance will appreciated.

Sincerely,

Credit Manager

Figure 12-7. Collection letter (if records do not agree . . .).

(Date)

Company Name
Street Address (or P.O. Box Number)
City, State, Zip Code

Attention of ___ _____ (name and title) _____

Dear Mr. (or Ms.) _____ :

Our company takes great pride in developing good customer relationships. Most of our customers have been with us for a number of years,
which I guess is one of the positive results from what we try to do to support our customers.

Not every customer can discount invoices, pay within terms, or even pay
a few days past terms. We accept that fact when account data is evaluated
and a credit line assigned to a customer. From that point forward it
becomes a matter of developing a rapport with the customer—a rapport
that will enable both of us to address any problem that may arise before
it can become a contentious issue.

We have slid to a point with your account where there is an unanticipated problem—and no rapport. Your account is ____ days past-due, we
needed $_____ yesterday, and the promises made during telephone
conversations have brought no money.

I must now hold orders until we have your check for $____ which must
arrive prior to ___ (date) ___. The hold also includes any C.O.D. orders
that have not been released.

Sincerely,

Credit Manager

Figure 12-8. Collection letter (hold all orders . . .).

(Date)

Company Name
Street Address
City, State, Zip Code

Attention of _____ (name and title) _____

Dear Mr. (or Ms.) _____ :

The call sheet for your account indicates that telephone calls to your office on _____(date)_____ and _____(date)_____ were not successful in obtaining a payment commitment for past-due balances. Copies of the subject invoices were mailed almost two weeks ago, and there has been no indication that the merchandise failed to arrive on time or in good condition.

Customers are very important people, but the continuing success of our company demands a solid reciprocal with our customers: we give you good merchandise and good service at a fair price and we expect payment within (or near) sales terms. Anything less—on your part or ours—erodes the relationship to the point where there no longer is mutual confidence.

Your check for $_____ (Invoices _____ and _____) in our offices by _____(date)_____ is the confidence builder we need to consider future open-account sales.

Sincerely,

Credit Manager

Figure 12-9. Collection letter (customers are important *but* . . .).

Third-Party Collection Assignment

The "final demand" letter should bring a telephone call or a payment response unless the customer's financial health has reached the point where there is virtually no cash flow with which to address payables balances. Your final demand letter should state that payment of a specific sum is to be in your office before a stated date to avoid having the account

(Date)

Name of Company
Street Address (or P.O. Box Number)
City, State, Zip Code

Attention of Mr./Ms._____ , Controller

Dear Mr./Ms._____ :

Our auditors tell me thay have not received a response to their request for confirmation of the balance owed to this company on September 30, 199X.

The figure they are asking you to confirm is _____ . If that figure does not agree with your records, please note in the space provided at the bottom of this letter. Your prompt "yes" or "no" will enable the auditors to complete their year-end work for us.

Many thanks for your cooperation.

Sincerely,

(Company Name)

Credit Manager

____ The above figure is correct.

Our records show a 9/30/9X balance due of $_____ .

Date _____   _____
                                                      (Signature and Title)

Figure 12-10. No response to auditor's verification request.

Applied Materials, Inc.
2999 San Ysidro Way
Santa Clara, California 95051
(408) 555-0600

Attention Accounts Payable

Ladies and Gentlemen:

Our auditors have asked that we verify the present status of various In Source 1500 Systems; also the status and location of faulty original system components and various replacement components furnished as warranty replacements.

Warranty replacement components (Power Source, Source, Control) are billed to our customers at the list price for each replacement unit. When the replaced defective unit is returned to us, we issue a credit to eliminate the original charge from the customer account.

Please let us know whether the listed unit(s) has (have) been returned for credit. A copy of the bill of lading, freight bill, or other appropriate documentation is all we need to eliminate the charge.

Purchase Order	Invoice No.	Invoice Date	Invoice Amt.

If the unit(s) has (have) not been returned, we assume payment is scheduled for current release. Please give us a payment release date on the unit(s) you intend to keep.

Sincerely yours,

Applied Materials, Inc.

Cecil Bond

Cecil Bond

Figure 12-11. Verification request for specific high-tech product.

(Date)

Company Name
Street Address (or P.O. Box Number)
City, State, Zip Code

Attention: _____ (name and title) _____

Dear Mr. (or Ms.)_____ :

Attached is a copy of invoice _____ date _____ in the amount
of _____ . This invoice is __ days past-due and is unfavorably impacting
the aging of your account.

Please contact me if there is a problem with the merchandise. If there
is no problem, your payment response by _____ will be greatly
appreciated.

Sincerely,

Credit Manager

Figure 12-12. Collection letter with invoice copy attached.

referred to third-party collection on that date (see Figure 12-6). If the
account is referred for collection, there is usually a "free demand" period
of 10 days, during which time the collection agency makes a written
demand on the debtor for the total amount of the collection assignment.
If within that 10 days the assigned balance is paid in full, your company
should not owe a collection fee. Check the contracts of individual collection agencies for this "no fee" provision. What if the agency is unable to get
the debtor to pay, but there is evidence to support the thought that an
attorney could attach certain of the debtor's assets? In a case of this type,
you might want to authorize this additional step in the collection process
(see Figures 12-15, 12-16, and 12-17).

Still No Money?

When a collection agency or an attorney is unable to locate the debtor
(now no longer dignified by the term "customer"), locates the debtor, but

finds no assets or attachable assets, or the debtor feels the hot breath of collection pressure and opts for a filing under Chapter 11 of The Bankruptcy Act, prepare to induct the account into your "Bad Debt Hall of Infamy." If you're a secured creditor under the Uniform Commercial Code in your state, there might be some hope for a percentage recovery if assets are liquidated, but there is also the possibility that a continuation agreement will enable the company to restructure its debts and move forward. It is also quite probable that the debtor will not be able to come up with an acceptable plan for handling old obligations, generate new bank funding for the purpose of cash flow, or convince already scarred suppliers to accept the idea that there is still hope for the company or business and to release new merchandise on open account terms. No continuation plan has a strong chance for success if the majority of suppliers want cash for product sold after the Chapter 11 filing. There is natural and justifiable apprehension when a company asks for more product, but offers little to convince suppliers that mistakes of the past were unfortunate, but are not indicative of the future course. Unless there is a complete restructuring of

---

(Date)

Name of Account
Street Address (or P.O. Box Number)
City, State, Zip Code

Attention of Accounts Payable

Dear Mr./Ms. _____ :

Our receivables records indicate that payment(s) has (have) not been received for ____(month or months)____ invoicing in the amount of $_____.

Please verify promptly and clear this/these balance(s) which is/are several days past our Net 30 terms.

Sincerely,

(Company Name)

Credit Manager

Figure 12-13. Collection letter (payment for two or more months).

(Date)

Customer Name
Street Address (or P.O. Box Number)
City, State, Zip Code

Our payment records do not show that we have received your check
for ____ and ____ invoices in the amounts of ____ and ____ .

If our records do not agree, please contact the undersigned so we may
go over our respective records, locate the problem, and make whatever
adjustment(s) may be necessary. If you find that our records do agree,
prompt payment of the items listed above will be appreciated.

Sincerely,

Credit Manager

Figure 12-14. Collection letter (payment for two invoices).

the company or business, such as new management or a complete shift
from destructive business practices of the past, your company should be
very wary of a new open account relationship. Some of these reorganizations do succeed in turning a company onto the right track, but too many
of them do not.

Daily Follow-Up Schedule

The form shown in Figure 12-18 fills the need of every credit person who
has collection responsibility, serving as an effective reminder system to
ensure that follow-up collection calls or letters receive attention when, and
as, necessary. You can file the "Daily Follow-Up Schedule," which covers a
two-week work period, in a reference binder. It offers an alternative answer
to the problem of failing to do a follow-up on the proper day or at the
proper time. The columns are purposely narrow. They are not intended to
be a substitute area for notes on yellow-ruled paper or for the recapping of
telephone conversations on individual customer call sheets.

	Collection Assignments				
Account Number	**Account Name**	**Date Assigned**	**Amount Assigned**	**Collection Agency**	**Status of Collection**

Figure 12-15. Collection assignment (what, when, and to whom).

Memorandum

To: Branch Offices

From: Corporate Credit Manager

Re: Suits Filed against Nonpaying Out-of-State Customers

In any account situation where this company is doing business in a state other than one in which it is qualified (or licensed) to do business and we have a collection problem with an account that ultimately requires the services of a local or an area attorney, corporate legal counsel has advised that we proceed in the folowing manner:

We do not initiate a suit as The Brighton Corporation representing itself in the matter. Prior to the filing of suit against the customer, the account will have been assigned to any one of several collection agencies for a conventional run at collecting the company's money. If that approach fails, the collection agency will then refer the account to an area attorney. The attorney will notify our company via the collection agency of his or her requirements—suit fee (refundable court costs) and contingency fee. The licensed and bonded collection agency with whom we do business in California will send an assignment form (similar to the attached) which transfers ownership of the account to the collection agency. the form empowers the collection agency to assign the account to the licensed in-state agency (customer's state) for whom the attorney works. He or she will then proceed to file the suit.

The attorney will deal directly with the collection service. In the event a settlement offer evolves from pretrial or trial, that offer will be transmitted to this company via the non-California agency to the California agency with whom we have direct contact. The California agency will then contact this company with the settlement offer, this company will respond favorably or with a counter-offer, and the information will be sent back through the chain to the attorney.

Whether this company's status in the customer's state is classified as qualified or nonqualified, this company's position in these matters—when handled as outlined—is alleged to give us maximum protection under procedural law.

Fenton Lancaster
Corporate Credit Manager

Figure 12-16. Suits filed against nonpaying out-of-state customers.

ASSIGNMENT

For Value Received (I/We) hereby sell, assign, and transfer unto
_____ all (My/Our) right, title,
and interest in and to (My/Our) claim and demand against _____
_____ standing in the amount of
$_____, with full power to sue and collect the same. We hereby cer-
tify that this is a valid and subsisting claim and no defenses, counter-
claims, cross-complaints, or offsets exist as of this date on this account.
Assignee shall not be liable for any claim so made. Assignor shall furnish
such witnesses and such testimony of such of its officers, employees, or
agents as may be reasonably required.

(Seal)   _____

                                   _____

                                   _____

Dated: _____

When returning this assignment, it is essential that we are advised on
the following:

   1. Are you a corporation?   ( ) Yes ( ) No
       If a corporation, advise State in which incorporated:

       _____

   2. Are you a copartnership?   ( ) Yes ( ) No
       If a copartnership, give names of partners:

       _____

       _____

   3. Are you an individual transacting business under a fictitious
       name?   ( ) Yes ( ) No

   4. Has trade style been filed?   ( ) Yes ( ) No
       If yes, under what name: _____

Figure 12-17. Assignment of account (power to sue, etc.).

Daily Follow-Up Schedule

Monday	Tuesday	Wednesday	Thursday	Friday	Monday	Tuesday	Wednesday	Thursday	Friday

Figure 12-18. Daily follow-up schedule (two weeks).

If you currently use a large calendar pad or an appointment book to keep track of this information, and it works well for you, then you might not need this form. Use the form or method that gives you an appropriate level of day-to-day control over these follow-up obligations. Be consistent. When you say you are going to do something, be sure that the commitment does not get lost. A consistent and a persistent pattern of calls and letters is imperative if you are to achieve maximum success with your collection efforts.

Suing in Small Claims Court

One of the few remaining areas of collection that is not routine (as opposed to telephone calls, letters, etc.) is the participation of creditors in the filing and participating in suits filed in Small Claims Court. It is the court where, in California, creditors who have claims of up to $5000 may file suit against debtors, appear for their company, present the company's case, and within a few days receive from the court a judgment in their favor or in favor of the debtor (the defendant).

The Small Claims Court statute for California was changed effective January 1991 to reflect higher levels of credit activity and to remove hundred of cases in smaller dollar amounts from increasingly cluttered court calendars. The California legislature raised the limit for small claims actions to $2500 and revised the statute to place a limit on suits filed by individuals to two per year for amounts that do not total more than $5000; no limit was placed on the number of suits that can be filed when the amount is less than $2500. It will be some time before figures are available to reflect the effectiveness of the legislation in reducing the number of cases that would have moved into the pipeline of high courts—or what impact the increase on the case load of Small Claims Courts may have on the speed with which hearings can be scheduled and verdicts rendered (see Figures 12-19 thru 12-27).

Nothing in California's revised legislation will help the plaintiff who has had a judgment entered in his or her company's favor to collect the amount awarded. Getting a judgment, having it entered against the defendant, and collecting on that judgment is a chain of events that has not been improved. The creditor who receives a judgment must continue to struggle to find something that can be seized or attached to satisfy the judgment—debtors traditionally do nothing to simplify that process.

Small Claims Court is "do it yourself" law, the place where a business person takes the suit cycle from forms to filing and on through the court's decision. The forms used to illustrate this section are from the Municipal Court of California, Santa Clara County Judicial District, Small Claims Division, and plaintiffs filing in that judicial jurisdiction should be the only people to use them or be guided by them. You must sue in the right court and in the

INFORMATION FOR THE SMALL CLAIMS PLAINTIFF

This information sheet is written for the person who sues in the small claims court. It explains some of the rules and some general information about the small claims court. It may also be helpful for the person who is sued.

WHAT IS SMALL CLAIMS COURT?

Small claims court is a special court where disputes are resolved quickly and inexpensively. The rules are simple and informal. The person who sues is the **plaintiff**. The person who is sued is the **defendant**. In small claims court, you may ask a lawyer for advice before you go to court, but you cannot have a lawyer in court. Your claim cannot be for more than $5,000 (*see below). If you have a claim for more than this amount, you may sue in the civil division of the municipal court or you may sue in the small claims court and give up your right to the amount over $5,000. You cannot, however, file more than two cases in small claims court for more than $2,500 each during a calendar year.

WHO CAN FILE A CLAIM?

1. You must be at least *18 years old* to file a claim. If you are not yet 18, you may ask the court to appoint a **guardian ad litem**. This is a person who will act for you in the case. The guardian ad litem is usually a parent, relative, or adult friend.

2. A person who sues in small claims court must first make a **demand** where possible. This means that you have asked the defendant to pay, and the defendant has refused. If your claim is for possession of rental property, you must ask the defendant to pay the rent or move out by serving the defendant with a **Three-Day Notice to Pay Rent or Quit**.

3. Unless you fall within two technical exceptions, you must be the **original owner** of the claim. This means that if the

claim is assigned, the buyer cannot sue in the small claims court. **You must also appear at the small claims hearing yourself unless you filed the claim for a corporation or other entity that is not a natural person.**

4. If a corporation files a claim, an employee, officer, or director must act on its behalf. If the claim is filed on behalf of an association or other entity that is not a natural person, a regularly employed person of the entity must act on its behalf. A person who appears on behalf of a corporation or other entity must not be employed or associated solely for the purpose of representing the corporation or other entity in the small claims court.

WHERE CAN YOU FILE YOUR CLAIM?

You must sue in the right court and **judicial district**. This rule is called **venue**.

If you file your claim in the wrong court, the court will dismiss the claim unless all defendants personally appear at the hearing and agree that the claim may be heard.

The right district may be any of these:

1. Where the defendant lives or where the business involved is located;
2. Where the damage or accident happened;
3. Where the contract was signed or carried out;

4. If the defendant is a corporation, where the contract was broken;
5. For a retail installment account or sales contract or a motor vehicle finance sale:
   a. Where the buyer lives;
   b. Where the buyer lived when the contract was entered into;
   c. Where the buyer signed the contract;
   d. Where the goods or vehicle are permanently kept.

SOME RULES ABOUT THE DEFENDANT

1. You must sue using the defendant's *exact legal name*. If the defendant is a business or a corporation and you do not know the exact legal name, check with: the state or local licensing agency; the county clerk's office; or the Office of the Secretary of State, corporate status unit. Ask the clerk for help if you do not know how to find this information. If you do not use the defendant's exact legal name,

the court may be able to correct the name on your claim at the hearing or after the judgment.

2. If you want to sue a government agency, you must first file a claim with the agency before you can file a lawsuit in court. Generally, you must do this no later than *six months* after the act or event you are suing about.

HOW DOES THE DEFENDANT FIND OUT ABOUT THE CLAIM?

You must make sure the defendant finds out about your lawsuit. This has to be done according to the rules or your case may be dismissed or delayed. The correct way of telling the defendant about the lawsuit is called *service of process*. This means giving the defendant a copy of the claim. **YOU CANNOT DO THIS YOURSELF.** Here are four ways to serve the defendant:

1. **Service by a law officer**
   You may ask the marshal or sheriff to serve the defendant. A fee will be charged.

2. **Process server**
   You may ask anyone who is *not a party* in your case and who is at least *18 years old* to serve the defendant. The person is called a *process server* and must personally give a copy of your claim to the defendant. The person must also sign a proof of service form showing when the defen-

dant was served. Registered process servers will do this for you for a fee. You may also ask a friend or relative to do it.

3. **Certified mail**
   You may ask the clerk of the court to serve the defendant by certified mail. The clerk will charge a fee. You should check back with the court prior to the hearing to see if the receipt for certified mail was returned to the court. **Service by certified mail must be done by the clerk's office. You cannot serve the defendant this way yourself.**

4. **Substituted service**
   This method lets you serve another person instead of the defendant. You must follow the procedures carefully. You may also wish to use the marshal or sheriff or a registered process server.

* The $5,000 limit does not apply, and a $1,500 limit applies, if a "defendant guarantor . . . is required to respond based upon the default, actions, or omissions of another."

(Continued on reverse)

Form Adopted by the
Judicial Council of California
SC-150 (Rev. January 1, 1992)

**INFORMATION FOR THE PLAINTIFF
(Small Claims)**

Rule 982.7

Figure 12-19. Small claims form (information for plaintiff—page one).

4. Substituted service *(continued)*
A copy of your claim must be left:
— at the defendant's business with the person in charge;
— or, at the defendant's home with a competent person who is at least 18 years old. The person who receives the claim must be told about its contents. Another copy must be mailed, first class, postage prepaid, to the defendant at the address where the paper was left. The service is not complete until *10 days* after the copy is mailed.

No matter which method of service you choose, the defendant must be served by a certain date or the trial will be postponed. If the defendant lives in the county, service must be completed at least *10 days* before the trial date. This period is *15 days* if defendant lives outside the county.

The person who serves the defendant must sign a court paper showing when the defendant was served. This paper is called a **Proof of Service**. It must be signed and returned to the court clerk as soon as the defendant has been served.

WHAT IF THE DEFENDANT ALSO HAS A CLAIM?

Sometimes the person who was sued (the **defendant**) will also have a claim against the person who filed the lawsuit (the **plaintiff**). This claim is called the **Defendant's Claim**. The defendant may file this claim in the same lawsuit. This helps to resolve all of the disagreements between the parties at the same time.

If the defendant decides to file the claim in the small claims court, the claim may not be for more than $5,000 (**see reverse*). If the value of the claim is more than this amount,

the defendant may either give up the amount over $5,000 and sue in the small claims court or file a motion to transfer the case to the appropriate court for the full value of the claim.

The defendant's claim must be served on the plaintiff at least *5 days* before the trial. If the defendant received the plaintiff's claim *10 days* or less before the trial, then the claim must be served at least *1 day* before the trial.

Both claims will be heard by the court at the same time.

WHAT HAPPENS AT THE TRIAL?

Be sure you are on time for the trial. The small claims trial is informal. You must bring with you all witnesses, books, receipts, and other papers or things to prove your case. You may ask the witnesses to come to court voluntarily. You may also ask the clerk of the court to issue a **subpena**. A subpena is a court order that *requires* the witness to go to trial. The witness has a right to charge a fee for going to the trial. If you do not have the records or papers to prove your case, you may also get a court order prior to the trial date requiring the papers

to be brought to the trial. This order is called a **Subpena Duces Tecum**.

If you settle the case before the trial, you must file a **dismissal** form with the clerk.

The court's decision is usually mailed to you after the trial. It may also be hand delivered to you in court when the trial is over and after the judge has made a decision. The decision appears on a form called the **Notice of Entry of Judgment**.

WHAT HAPPENS AFTER JUDGMENT?

The court may have ordered one party to pay money to the other party. The party who wins the case and collects the money is called the **judgment creditor**. The party who loses the case and owes the money is called the **judgment debtor**.

Enforcement of the judgment is **postponed** until after the time for appeal ends or until after the appeal is decided. This

means that the judgment creditor cannot collect any money or take any action until after this period is over. Generally, both parties may be represented by lawyers after judgment.

More information about your rights after judgment is available on the back of the **Notice of Entry of Judgment** form. The clerk may also have this information on a separate sheet.

HOW TO GET HELP WITH YOUR CASE

1. **Lawyers**
   Both parties may ask a lawyer about the case, but a lawyer may not represent either party in court at the small claims trial. Generally, after judgment and on appeal, both parties may be represented by a lawyer.
2. **Interpreters**
   If you do not speak English, you may take a family member or friend to court with you. The court should also keep a list of interpreters who will interpret for you. You may choose an interpreter from the court's list. Some interpreters may be free, and some may charge a fee.
3. **Waiver of Fees**
   The court charges fees for some of its procedures. Fees are also charged for serving the defendant with the claim. The court may excuse you from paying these fees if you cannot afford them. Ask the clerk for the **Information Sheet on Waiver of Court Fees and Costs** to find out if you meet the requirements so that you do not have to pay the fees.

4. **Night and Saturday Court**
   If you cannot go to court during working hours, ask the clerk if the court has trials at **night** or on **Saturdays**.
5. **Parties Who Are in Jail**
   If you are in jail, the court may excuse you from going to the trial. Instead, you may ask another person who is not an attorney to go to the trial for you. You may mail written declarations to the court to support your case.
6. **Advisors**
   The law requires each county to provide assistance in small claims cases free of charge. Here is some important information about the small claims advisor program in this county:

   DEPT. OF CONSUMER AFFAIRS
   SMALL CLAIMS ADVISOR
   408/299-4216

SC-150 (Rev. January 1, 1992)

INFORMATION FOR THE PLAINTIFF
(Small Claims)

Page two

Figure 12-20. Small claims form (information for plaintiff—page two).

MUNICIPAL COURT OF CALIFORNIA
SANTA CLARA COUNTY JUDICIAL DISTRICT
SMALL CLAIMS DIVISION

☐ Santa Clara Annex   ☐ Los Gatos Facility   ☐ Gilroy Facility
    1675 Lincoln St., SC 95050   14205 Capri Dr., LG 95030   7350 Rosanna St., GI 95020
    (408) 246-0510   (408) 866-8331   (408) 842-6299

☐ Palo Alto Facility ·   ☐ Sunnyvale Facility
    270 Grant Ave., PA 94306   605 W. El Camino, SV 94087
    (415) 324-0391   (408) 739-1502

CASE NO. S. C. _____

PLAINTIFF HAS DEMANDED THAT DEFENDANT PAY THE SUM AND IT HAS NOT BEEN PAID.

1. My Name (plaintiff) _____

2. My Address _____ ZIP _____

3. My Telephone Number _____ 4. Amount of Claim _____

5. Nature of Claim _____

6. Date and place where damages or injury occured, or where obligation was to be performed _____

    Claim for Automobile Damages: I am _____ the registered owner of the vehicle.

7. THIS COURT IS THE PROPER COURT FOR HEARING YOUR CLAIM. SEE INFORMATION FOR PLANTIFF FORM FOR ASSISTANCE AND INDICATE PROPER LETTER IN BOX ☐. FOR F OR G ENTER PROPER NUMBER IN BOX ☐.

8. (a) If you are suing individual, give his full name. (b) If you are suing a business firm, give the firm name and the name of the owner. (c) If you are suing a partnership, you must name the partners. (d) If you are suing a corporation, give its full name, and the name of a director of said corporation. (e) If your suit arises out of an automobile accident, you must name the driver and registered owner.

9. I UNDERSTAND I HAVE NO RIGHT OF APPEAL FROM A JUDGMENT ON MY CLAIM.

10. I have not filed more than one other Small Claims action in California during this calendar year in which the amount demanded is more than $2,500.

11. My claim is against (defendant)

NAME	ADDRESS	CITY	ZIP

DECLARATION OF NON-MILITARY STATUS

The declarant is the Plaintiff in the annexed and foregoing action, and/or he takes this declaration for said Plaintiff and declares the Defendant, and each of them, of more than one, is not now a person in the Military Service of the United States as defined in Sec. 101 of the Soldiers' and Sailors' Relief Act of 1940, and amendments thereto.
I declare under penalty of perjury that the foregoing is true and correct.

Executed on _____ Signature _____

The declaration under penalty of perjury must be signed in California, or in a state that authorizes use of a declaration in place of an affidavit, otherwise an affidavit is required.

ORDER TO PLAINTIFF TO APPEAR

Your case will be tried on _____ at _____ M., in Dept. _____ of said court.

YOU ARE HEREBY DIRECTED TO APPEAR on said date and to bring with you all books, papers and witnesses needed to prove your claim.

> **IMPORTANT:** Please check the Court Calendar in the lobby of the building for the Department of this Court that will hear this matter.

REQUEST FOR DISMISSAL

If case is paid or settled before trial, sign below and mail this form to the above entitled court. THIS CASE MAY BE DISMISSED.

Signature _____

Figure 12-21. Small claims form (plaintiff's demand on defendant).

PARTY ☐ PLAINTIFF ☐ DEFENDANT *(Name and Address)*:   TELEPHONE NO.:   FOR COURT USE ONLY

NAME AND ADDRESS OF COURT:

PLAINTIFF(S):

DEFENDANT(S):

| **PROOF OF SERVICE** (Small Claims) | HEARING DATE: | DAY: | TIME: | DEPT./DIVISION: | CASE NUMBER: |

1. At the time of service I was at least 18 years of age and not a party to this action, and **I served copies** of the following:

   ☐ Plaintiff's Claim   ☐ Order of Examination   ☐ Other *(specify)*:
   ☐ Defendant's Claim   ☐ Subpena Duces Tecum

2. a. Party served *(specify name of party as shown on the documents served)*:

   b. Person served: ☐ party in item 2.a.   ☐ other *(specify name and title or relationship to the party named in item 2.a.)*:

3. By delivery   ☐ at home   ☐ at business
   a. date:
   b. time:
   c. address:

4. **Manner of service** *(check proper box)*:
   a. ☐ **Personal service.** I personally delivered to and left copies with the party served. **(C.C.P. 415.10)**
   b. ☐ **Substituted service on corporation, unincorporated association (including partnership), or public entity.** By leaving, during usual office hours, copies in the office of the person served with the person who apparently was in charge and thereafter mailing (by first-class mail, postage prepaid) copies to the person to be served at the place where the copies were left. **(C.C.P. 415.20(a))**
   c. ☐ **Substituted service on natural person, minor, incompetent, or candidate.** By leaving copies at the dwelling house, usual place of abode, usual place of business, or usual mailing address other than a U. S. Postal Service post office box of the person served in the presence of a competent member of the household or a person apparently in charge of the office or place of business, at least 18 years of age, who was informed of the general nature of the papers, and thereafter mailing (by first-class mail, postage prepaid) copies to the person to be served at the place where the copies were left. **(C.C.P. 415.20(b))**
   d. ☐ **Date of mailing:**   From *(city)*:

   Information regarding date and place of mailing is required for services effected in manner *4.b.* and *4.c.* above.
   Certified mail service may be performed only by the Clerk of the Court in small claims matters.

5. **Person serving** *(name, address, and telephone number)*:   a. **Fee** for service: $
   b. ☐ Not a registered California process server
   c. ☐ Exempt from registration under B&P Section 22350(b)
   d. ☐ **Registered** California process server
      1. ☐ Employee or independent contractor
      2. **Registration Number:**
      3. **County:**

6. ☐ I declare under penalty of perjury under the laws of the State of California that the foregoing is true and correct.
7. ☐ I am a California sheriff, marshal, or constable and I certify that the foregoing is true and correct.

Date: ▶

(SIGNATURE OF SERVER)

Form Approved by the
Judicial Council of California
SC-104 [New January 1, 1992]

PROOF OF SERVICE
(Small Claims)

Code of Civil Procedure
§§ 415.10, 415.20

Figure 12-22. Small claims form (proof of service).

MUNICIPAL COURT OF CALIFORNIA, SANTA CLARA COUNTY JUDICIAL DISTRICT, SMALL CLAIMS DIVISION

SMALL CLAIMS CASE NO.

— NOTICE TO DEFENDANT — YOU ARE BEING SUED BY PLAINTIFF	— *AVISO AL DEMANDADO* — *A USTED LO ESTAN DEMANDANDO*
To protect your rights, you must appear in this court on the trial date shown in the table below. You may lose the case if you do not appear. The court may award the plaintiff the amount of the claim and the costs. Your wages, money, and property may be taken without further warning from the court.	*Para proteger sus derechos, usted debe presentarse ante esta corte en la fecha del juicio indicada en el cuadro que aparece a continuación. Si no se presenta, puede perder el caso. La corte puede decidir en favor del demandante por la cantidad del reclamo y los costos. A usted le pueden quitar su salario, su dinero, y otras cosas de su propiedad, sin aviso adicional por parte de esta corte.*

PLAINTIFF/DEMANDANTE *(Name and address of each)*:

DEFENDANT/DEMANDADO *(Name and address of each)*:

See attached sheet for additional plaintiffs and defendants.

PLAINTIFF'S CLAIM

1. Defendant owes me the sum of $ _____ , not including court costs, because *(describe claim and date)*:

2. I have asked defendant to pay this money, but it has not been paid.

3. This court is the proper court for the trial because ☐ *(In the box at the left, insert one of the letters from the list marked "Venue Table" on the back of this sheet. If you select D, E, or F, specify additional facts in this space.)*

4. I have not filed more than one other small claims action anywhere in California during this calendar year in which the amount demanded is more than $2,500.

5. ☐ I have filed more than 12 claims in this court, including this claim, during the previous 12 calendar months. I understand that

6. a. I may talk to an attorney about this claim, but I cannot be represented by an attorney at the trial in the small claims court.
   b. I must appear at the time and place of trial and bring all witnesses, books, receipts, and other papers or things to prove my case.
   c. I have no right of appeal on my claim, but I may appeal a claim filed by the defendant in this case.
   d. If I cannot afford to pay the fees for filing or service by a sheriff, marshal, or constable, I may ask that the fees be waived.

7. I have received and read the information sheet explaining some important rights of plaintiffs in the small claims court.

I declare under penalty of perjury under the laws of the State of California that the foregoing is true and correct.

Date:

▶

....
(TYPE OR PRINT NAME)   *(SIGNATURE OF PLAINTIFF)*

ORDER TO DEFENDANT

You must appear in this court on the trial date and at the time LAST SHOWN IN THE BOX BELOW if you do not agree with the plaintiff's claim. Bring all witnesses, books, receipts, and other papers or things with you to support your case.

TRIAL DATE FECHA DEL JUICIO		DATE	TIME	PLACE	COURT USE
	1.				
	2.				
	3.				
	4.				

Filed on *(date)*:   Clerk, by_____, Deputy

— **You have a right to a small claims advisor free of charge. Read the information sheet on the reverse.** —

Form Adopted by the
 Judicial Council of California
 SC-100 (Rev. January 1, 1991)   **PLAINTIFF'S CLAIM AND ORDER TO DEFENDANT**
                              (Small Claims)   Rule 982.7

Figure 12-23. Small claims form (plaintiff's claim).

MUNICIPAL COURT OF CALIFORNIA, SANTA CLARA COUNTY JUDICIAL DISTRICT, SMALL CLAIMS DIVISION

Case No

NOTICE TO ALL PLAINTIFFS AND DEFENDANTS:	AVISO A TODOS LOS DEMANDANTES Y DEMANDADOS:
Your small claims case has been decided. If you lost the case, and the court ordered you to pay money, your wages, money, and property may be taken without further warning from the court. Read the back of this sheet for important information about your rights.	Su caso ha sido resuelto por la corte para reclamos judiciales menores. Si la corte ha decidido en su contra y ha ordenado que usted pague dinero, le pueden quitar su salario, su dinero, y otras cosas de su propiedad, sin aviso adicional por parte de esta corte. Lea el reverso de este formulario para obtener información de importancia acerca de sus derechos.

PLAINTIFF/DEMANDANTE *(Name and address of each):*

DEFENDANT/DEMANDADO *(Name and address of each):*

☐ See attached sheet for additional plaintiffs and defendants.

NOTICE OF ENTRY OF JUDGMENT

Judgment was entered as checked below on *(date):*

1. ☐ Defendant *(name, if more than one):*
   shall pay plaintiff *(name, if more than one):*
   $ principal and $ costs on plaintiff's claim.
2. ☐ Defendant does not owe plaintiff any money on plaintiff's claim.
3. ☐ Plaintiff *(name, if more than one):*
   shall pay defendant *(name, if more than one):*
   $ principal and $ costs on defendant's claim.
4. ☐ Plaintiff does not owe defendant any money on defendant's claim.
5. ☐ Possession of the following property is awarded to plaintiff *(address of property):*

6. ☐ Payments are to be made at the rate of $ per month, beginning on *(date):*   and on
   the   day of each month thereafter until paid in full. If any payment is missed, the entire balance becomes due
   immediately.
7. ☐ Other *(specify):*

8. ☐ This judgment results from a motor vehicle accident on a California highway and was caused by the judgment debtor's operation
   of a motor vehicle. If the judgment is not paid, you may apply to have the judgment debtor's driver's license suspended.
9. ☐ Enforcement of the judgment is automatically postponed until the time for filing an appeal expires, and if filed, until the appeal is decided.
10. ☐ This notice was personally delivered to *(insert name and date):*
11. CLERK'S CERTIFICATE OF MAILING – I certify that I am not a party to this action. This Notice of Entry of Judgment was mailed first
    class, postage prepaid, in a sealed envelope to the parties at the addresses shown above. The mailing and this certification occurred at
    the place and on the date shown below.
    Place of mailing: , California
    Date of mailing:
        Clerk, by _____ , Deputy

—You have a right to a small claims advisor free of charge. Read the information sheet on the reverse.—

Form Adopted by the
Judicial Council of California
SC-130 (January 1, 1990)

NOTICE OF ENTRY OF JUDGMENT
(Small Claims)

Rule 982.7

Figure 12-24. Small claims form (notice of entry of judgment).

INFORMATION AFTER JUDGMENT

HOW DO YOU FIND OUT ABOUT THE COURT'S DECISION?

When your small claims case has been decided, the court clerk will mail or deliver to you a form called the **Notice of Entry of Judgment**. The **judgment** or decision of the court appears on the front of the form. The court may have ordered one party to pay money to the other party. The winner of the case and the person who can collect the money is called the **judgment creditor**. The loser of the case and the person who owes the money is called the **judgment debtor**.

Enforcement of the judgment is **postponed** until after the time for appeal ends or until after the appeal is decided. This means that the judgment creditor cannot collect any money or take any action until after this period is over. Generally, both sides may be represented by lawyers after judgment.

WHAT HAPPENS IF YOU LOSE THE CASE?

1. If you lose the case on your own claim and the court does not award you any money, the court's decision on your claim is FINAL. You may not appeal your own claim.

2. If you lose the case and the court orders you to pay money, your money and property may be taken to pay the claim unless you do one of the following things:

   a. PAY THE JUDGMENT
   The law requires you to pay the amount of the judgment. You may pay the judgment creditor directly, or **pay the judgment to the court for an additional fee.** You may also ask the court to order monthly payments you can afford. Ask the clerk for information about these procedures.

   b. APPEAL
   If you disagree with the court's decision, you may appeal the decison *on the other party's claim.* You may not appeal the decision on your own claim. However, if any party appeals, there will be a new trial on **all** the claims. If you appeared at the trial, you *must* begin your appeal by filing a form called a **Notice of Appeal** within *20 days* after the date this Notice of Entry of Judgment was mailed or handed to you at the time of the small claims hearing. Your appeal will be in the superior court. You will have a **new trial.** You may be represented by a lawyer.

   c. VACATE (OR CANCEL) THE JUDGMENT
   If you did not go to the trial, you may ask the court to vacate (or cancel) the judgment. To make this request, you must file a **Motion to Vacate the Judgment** *within 30 days* after the date this Notice of Entry of Judgment was mailed to you. If your request is denied, then you have *10 days* from the date the motion was denied to appeal the denial.

   The period to file the **Motion to Vacate the Judgment** is *180 days* if you were *not properly served* with the claim. The 180-day period begins on the date you found out or should have found out about the judgment against you.

WHAT HAPPENS IF YOU WIN THE CASE?

1. If you were sued by the other party and you win the case, then the other party may not appeal the court's decision.

2. If you win the case and the court awards you money, here are some steps you may take to collect your money or get possession of your property:

   a. COLLECTING FEES
   Sometimes fees are charged for filing court papers or for serving the judgment debtor. These extra costs can become part of your original judgment. To claim these fees, ask the clerk for a **Memorandum of Costs.**

   b. VOLUNTARY PAYMENT
   Ask the judgment debtor to pay the money. If your claim was for possession of rental property, ask the judgment debtor to move out. THE COURT WILL NOT COLLECT THE MONEY OR ENFORCE THE JUDGMENT FOR YOU.

   c. STATEMENT OF ASSETS
   If the judgment debtor does not pay the money, the law requires the debtor to fill out a form called the **Judgment Debtor's Statement of Assets.** This form will tell you what property the judgment debtor has that may be available to pay your claim. If the judgment debtor willfully fails to send you the completed form, you may ask the court to impose penalties.

   d. ORDER OF EXAMINATION
   You may also make the debtor come to court to answer questions about income and property. To do this, ask the clerk for an **Order of Examination.** There is no fee for this order, but there is a fee if a law officer serves the order on the judgment debtor.

   e. WRIT OF EXECUTION
   After you find out about the judgment debtor's property, you may ask the court for a **Writ of Execution.** A writ of execution is a court paper which tells a law officer to take property of the judgment debtor to pay your claim. Here are some examples of the kinds of property the officer may be able to take: **wages, bank account, automobile, business property, or rented property.** For some kinds of property, you may need to file other forms. See the law officer for information.

   f. ABSTRACT OF JUDGMENT
   The judgment debtor may own land or a house or other buildings. You may want to put a lien on the property so that you will be paid if the property is sold. You can get a lien by filing an **Abstract of Judgment** with the County Recorder in the county where the property is located. The recorder will charge a fee for the Abstract of Judgment.

   g. AFTER PAYMENT
   If you are paid in full, you must fill out a form called an **Acknowledgment of Satisfaction of Judgment.** The form is located on the back of the Notice of Entry of Judgment. When you have filled out the form, you must mail it to the court *immediately* or you may be fined. If an Abstract of Judgment has been recorded, you must use another form. See the clerk for the proper form.

Form Adopted by the Judicial Council of California SC-131 [Rev. January 1, 1990]	**INFORMATION AFTER JUDGMENT** **(Small Claims)**	Rule 982.7

Figure 12-25. Small claims form (information after judgment).

Figure 12-26. Small claims (judgment debtor's statement of assets).

MAIL TO THE JUDGMENT CREDITOR
DO NOT FILE WITH THE COURT

TO JUDGMENT CREDITOR *(fill in name of judgment creditor)*:

FROM JUDGMENT DEBTOR *(fill in your name)*:

SMALL CLAIMS CASE NO.

JUDGMENT DEBTOR'S STATEMENT OF ASSETS

The **judgment debtor** in this small claims case is the person (or business) who lost the case and owes the money. The person who won the case is the **judgment creditor**.

TO THE JUDGMENT DEBTOR:

The small claims court has ruled that you owe money to the judgment creditor.

1. You may appeal a judgment against you only on the other party's claim. You may **not** appeal a judgment against you on your claim.

   a. If you appeared at the trial and you want to appeal, you must file a Notice of Appeal within 30 days after the date of mailing on the Notice of Entry of Judgment or the date you received it in court.

   b. If you did not appear at the trial, before you can appeal, you must first file a **Motion to Vacate the Judgment** within 30 days from the date the Notice of Entry of Judgment was mailed or delivered to you, and the judgment cannot be collected until the motion is decided. If your motion is denied, you then have 10 days from the date the notice of denial was mailed to file your appeal.

2. Unless you pay, appeal, or move to vacate, you must fill out this form and send it to the person who won the case within **30 days** after the Notice of Entry of Judgment is mailed to you by the clerk.

3. If you file an appeal or a Motion to Vacate, you do not need to fill out this form unless you lose your appeal or motion to vacate. Then you will have **30 days** to pay or complete this form and deliver it to the judgment creditor.

If you fail to follow these instructions you may have to go to court to answer questions or the court can impose penalties on you.	Si usted no sigue estas instrucciones es posible que tenga que presentarse ante la corte para contestar preguntas, o la corte puede imponerle multas.

If you were sued as an individual skip this box and begin with no. 1 below. Otherwise, check the applicable box, attach the documents indicated, and complete no. 12 on the reverse.

   a. ☐ (Corporation or partnership) Attached to this form is a statement describing the nature, value and exact location of all assets of the corporation or the partners, and a statement showing that the person signing this form is authorized to submit this form on behalf of the corporation or partnership.

   b. ☐ (Governmental agency) Attached to this form is the statement of an authorized representative of the agency as to when the agency will pay the judgment and any reasons for its failure to do so.

EMPLOYMENT

1. What is your occupation? *(Please provide job title and name of division or office in which you work.)*

2. Name and address of your business or employer *(include address of your payroll or human resources department, if different)*:

3. How often are you paid?
   a. ☐ daily ☐ every two weeks ☐ monthly
      ☐ weekly ☐ twice a month ☐ other *(explain)*:

4. What is your gross pay each pay period?
   $

5. What is your take home pay each pay period?
   $

6. If your wife or husband earns any income give the name and address of the business or employer, job title, and division or office:

(Continued on reverse)

Form Approved by the Judicial Council of California SC-133 (Rev. January 1, 1992)	JUDGMENT DEBTOR'S STATEMENT OF ASSETS (Small Claims)	Rule 982.7

(Continued)

Figure 12-26. (*Continued*) Small claims (judgment debtor's statement of assets).

CASH, BANK DEPOSITS

7. How much money do you have in cash? . . . . $

8. How much other money do you have in banks, savings and loans, credit unions, and other financial institutions either in your own name or jointly *(list)*:

Name and address of financial institution	Account number	Individual or joint?	Balance
a.			$
b.			$
c.			$

PROPERTY

9. List all automobiles, other vehicles, and boats owned in your name or jointly:

Make and year	Value	Legal owner if different from registered owner	Amount owed
a.	$		$
b.	$		$
c.	$		$
d.	$		$

10. List all real estate owned in your name or jointly:

Address of real estate	Fair market value	Amount owed
a.	$	$
b.	$	$

OTHER PERSONAL PROPERTY *[Do not list household furniture and furnishings, appliances, or clothing.]*

11. List anything of value not listed above owned in your name or jointly:

Description	Value	Address where property is located
a.	$	
b.	$	
c.	$	
d.	$	
e.	$	
f.	$	
g.	$	
h.	$	
i.	$	
j.	$	

12. I declare under penalty of perjury under the laws of the State of California that the foregoing is true and correct.

Date:

. . . .
(TYPE OR PRINT NAME)   (SIGNATURE)

Mail or deliver this completed form to the judgment creditor at the address shown on the Notice of Entry of Judgment form.

SC-133 [Rev. January 1, 1992]   **JUDGMENT DEBTOR'S STATEMENT OF ASSETS**   Page two
                                                      (Small Claims)

MUNICIPAL COURT OF CALIFORNIA, SANTA CLARA COUNTY JUDICIAL DISTRICT, SMALL CLAIMS DIVISION

☐ **Palo Alto Facility**
270 Grant Ave., PA 94306
(415) 324-0391

☐ **Los Gatos Facility**
14205 Capri Dr., LG 95030
(408) 866-8331

☐ **Gilroy Facility**
7350 Rosanna St., GI 95020
(408) 842-3111

☐ **San Jose Facility**
200 W. Hedding, SJ 95110
(408) 299-2271

☐ **Sunnyvale Facility**
605 W. El Camino, SV 94087
(408) 738-1502

SMALL CLAIMS CASE NO.:

— INSTRUCTIONS —

A. If you regularly do business in California for profit under a fictitious business name, you must execute, file, and publish a fictitious business name statement. This is sometimes called a "dba" which stands for "doing business as." This requirement applies if you are doing business as an individual, a partnership, a corporation, or an association. The requirement does not apply to nonprofit corporations and associations or certain real estate investment trusts. You must file the fictitious business name statement with the clerk of the county where you have your principal place of business, or in Sacramento County if you have no place of business within the state.

B. If you do business under a fictitious business name and you also wish to file an action in the small claims court, you must declare under penalty of perjury that you have complied with the fictitious business name laws by filling out the form below.

C. If you have not complied with the fictitious business name laws, the court may dismiss your claim. You may be able to refile your claim when you have fulfilled these requirements.

FICTITIOUS BUSINESS NAME DECLARATION

1. I wish to file a claim in the small claims court for a business doing business under the fictitious name of *(specify name and address of business)*:

2. The business is doing business as
   ☐ an individual
   ☐ a partnership
   ☐ a corporation
   ☐ an association
   ☐ other *(specify)*:

3. The business has complied with the fictitious business name laws by executing, filing, and publishing a fictitious business name statement in the county of *(specify)*:

4. The number of the statement is *(specify)*:   and the statement expires on *(date)*:

I declare under penalty of perjury under the laws of the State of California that the foregoing is true and correct.

Date:

▶

. . . .
(TYPE OR PRINT NAME)   (SIGNATURE OF DECLARANT)

Form Approved by the
Judicial Council of California
SC-103 [Rev. January 1, 1992]

FICTITIOUS BUSINESS NAME DECLARATION
(Small Claims)

Rule 982.7(b)
Code of Civil Procedure, § 116.430

Figure 12-27. Fictitious business name declaration.

right judicial district—a rule called venue. Contact the Small Claims Division (or Court) of the judicial district in which you will file your claim. You will be told where to obtain the necessary forms and instructions.

You might encounter few, or many, variations in the filing procedure from one major jurisdiction to another, but what is included here should be typical of the basic process of filing through judgment (and through appeal, if that option is exercised by the defendant). In the subject jurisdiction (Santa Clara County Judicial District), the number of forms is seven. If the defendant appeals to the Superior Court from a Small Claims Court ruling in favor of the plaintiff, the defendant would activate the eighth form: Notice of Filing Notice of Appeal.

Copies in sequential order follow a brief description of each form. Also included is a copy of the Fictitious Business Name Declaration and an explanation of its importance and relevance in California, and also in many other states.

- *Suit Form*—Plaintiff's name, defendant's name, nature of the claim, etc.

- *Proof of Service*—States how, where, and by whom relevant papers were served on the defendant.

- *Plaintiff's Claim*—Describes the amount of the debt, effort to collect, and rules of the court.

- *Defendant's Claim*—Counter-suit stating amount owed defendant, effort to collect, etc.

- *Order to Appear for Examination*—Issued against Judgment Debtor and/or Third Person because the Judgment Debtor claims the Third Person has possession or control of property which belongs to the Judgment Debtor, or concerning a debt owed the Judgment Debtor by a Third Person.

- *Abstract of Judgment*—Judgment Creditor or Assignee of Record applies to the court clerk for a certified copy of the Small Claims Court judgment.

- *Memorandum of Credits, Accrued Interest, and Costs After Judgment*— Self-explanatory. All payments and charges pertaining to the case through the date executed.

- *Notice of Filing Notice of Appeal*—Judgment Debtor appeals to the Superior Court from the Small Claims Court judgment or denial of motion to vacate the judgment.

You will use an additional form in conjunction with a filing in Small Claims Court in California and many other states. It is the Fictitious Name Declaration. Failure to comply with California Law (and the law in other states) could cause the court to dismiss your claim. To use the example of California, you file the Fictitious Name Declaration with the clerk of the county in which the principal place of business is located or in Sacramento County if the filing firm has no place of business within the state. Whether your state does or does not require the filing of a "fictitious name" or "dba" statement is information you will want to obtain when you inquire regarding the "how and where" of filing your claim in Small Claims Court.

The thought that you will be acting as your own attorney should not be inhibiting. This court is not a court where silver-tongued oratory is a requisite. Presenting your case does not demand the skills of a Clarence Darrow. The trial itself is informal and the rules simple:

- Be in court on time.

- Bring with you all witnesses, books, receipts, and other papers or things to prove your case.

- Ask the clerk of the court to issue a subpoena if a witness is reluctant or unwilling to come to court. A subpoena requires the witness to appear.

- Be prepared to pay a fee to the witness for his or her court appearance.

- Get a court order requiring that the necessary records or papers be brought to the trial to prove your case, if you do not have them, but know where they are.

- File a dismissal form with the court clerk if the case is settled before the trial date or time.

- You might receive the court's decision in the mail or someone might hand-deliver it to you in court when the trial is over. The form used for the decision is called The Notice of Entry of Judgment.

- The person who wins the case is called the judgment creditor; the loser, and the one who owes the money, is called the judgment debtor.

- You cannot enforce judgment until after the period for filing an appeal has ended. After judgment has been rendered, and if the judgment is appealed in Superior Court by the judgment debtor, both parties may be represented by attorneys.

Other requirements are necessary before the Clerk of the Small Claims Court can accept a filing (making a final demand on the debtor, etc.). Every jurisdiction should offer some advice and assistance in the preparation of claims cases. In California, it is the Department of Consumer Affairs, Small Claims Advisor, Sacramento. In your city or state there is probably a similar source for information and assistance. If the court in which you would file a claim does not provide such assistance or advice—and I question whether any court that does not permit attorneys to appear would be so insensitive to the needs of litigants—then you should be directed to the appropriate source for such information.

Statute of Limitations

Collection procedures never should be so poorly organized that an account which you carry as active—a receivables balance on your aged trial balance report—is lost because the statute of limitations has run out. You must be aware of the statute in any state or jurisdiction in which you might want to use Small Claims Court or a conventional civil suit to press for a judgment against the debtor-customer. Take appropriate collection action, but initiate it within the period of years prescribed by the appropriate jurisdiction. Virtually no set of circumstances could provide justification for such a level of inattention to the aging of a receivables balance.

If your best in-house collection efforts have not been effective—telephone calls, letters, and a "final demand" letter—then assign the account to your collection service. If the collection service is unable to locate the debtor or determines that there are no assets against which you could hope to levy a judgment, charge the account balance against your company's bad-debt reserve. At that point you will have made every reasonable effort to collect your company's money.

Under certain circumstances, a debtor might surface after the statute of limitations has seemingly pushed your old account balance—now a bad-debt item—beyond your reach. Unless you are notified that the individual, partnership, or company filed for bankruptcy, and your debt was among those listed and discharged by the bankruptcy court, there is the possibility of life after the statute of limitations. Other pieces also must fit the criteria for reviving the account balance, and it is imperative that you have your company's attorney make that decision. Let him or her tell you whether there is hope, what must be done to make reviving the account a possibility and, if there is a possibility that you can return the debt to the category of a legally collectible item, are there now any assets against which you could obtain a judgment and collect?

Your time is split in too many directions to waste it attempting to revive accounts that are as dead as your bad-debt assignment indicates, or as dead as a judgment, with no assets against which to levy it. Unless it is a rare situation, you are well advised to move on past accounts such as the above and focus your time and attention on your active accounts.

The Remedy of Replevin

Replevin is much too broad a subject to discuss in any detail in these pages. It is important to mention it, however, because it is the remedy used to recover a chattel by one who has a general or a special property in what has been taken or detained. The rules regarding replevin vary from one state to another, so it is not possible to do a neat "one statement covers all" package on the subject. However, to recover in replevin is not that much different from certain types of litigation where recovery of a chattel is the goal. To recover in replevin, a plaintiff is required to show a possessory right or a title superior to that of the defendant.

The problem of replevin occurs most commonly in conditional sales and chattel mortgage contracts. Credit people have a real problem when both title and possession of a chattel have passed to the buyer; the seller company is suddenly faced with the fact that it has no right to maintain a replevin action. It is, in that circumstance, a done deal. When does the seller maintain the right of a replevin action? Only when the sale is made on conditions which are performed by the buyer—the buyer's failure to perform prevents a title from passing to it—does replevin remain an option.

If your company encounters a situation where it seems possible that the "remedy of replevin" might be used, or if you have any questions regarding the rules governing replevin in your state or the states in which you do business, let me urge you to consult your company's attorney. Any attempt to apply generalities to a specific situation could have the effect of damaging or diminishing your company's options to the point where it must deal from weakness rather than strength.

A collection technique that worked well with one account may not work with the next one, or it might not be as effective as the circumstance requires. Try a different verbal approach, or if the focus of the collection effort has involved a series of collection letters, make any adjustments in the format that your experience with the account indicates might be helpful in resolving the past-due problem. Be flexible in your approach to specific accounts. After a certain period of time, you should begin to read accounts well enough that you will be able to adjust your collection effort to fit the attitudes and individual business patterns of specific problem accounts.

13
Bad-Debt Accounts

One of the more frustrating experiences for a credit manager is the loss of an account via a Chapter 11 filing, and the strong probability of an eventual write-off of the balance against the Bad-Debt Reserve. When there is a bad-debt loss, it is difficult to accept any correlation between profits realized during the years your company sold the account and the balance that was owing when the account filed the Chapter 11 petition. It is a definite negative, but it should not be a negative to which the credit manager devotes a disproportionate amount of time. Whether the account relationship was short or long term, examine it for whatever might be learned—then write it off.

There are no guarantees to ensure against the probability that certain accounts—accounts that have performed well for several or many years—might not go into a slow or a swift decline. When you have done everything to protect the interest of your firm that could reasonably be expected of you, there is no justification for placing an unreasonable load of blame on your shoulders. The next time, and there will be a next time, do exactly what you did in the current situation. Move quickly to do the very best that your experience and judgment will allow.

Setting Up a Reserve

Standard accounting practice calls for firms that offer credit terms to trade accounts to provide annually for bad-debt losses anticipated during the company's upcoming fiscal year. The basis for the provision is a fractional percentage of annual sales, a figure which varies from one firm to another and among the various types of businesses and services. A quarter percent to one-third of one percent of gross sales is an acceptable annual bad-debt loss figure for many industries. The credit policy of a firm can be the primary culprit in whether the bad-debt figure is inverted or inflated. Bad-debt losses that are consistently out of phase with industry standards indicate an excessive number of judgmental errors or a credit (and sales) policy that is not providing realistic guidelines to the company's goals or well being.

At the end of each fiscal year, you should review your aging sheet (Aged Trial Balance Report) for accounts that you have assigned to third-party collection within the past 12 months where there has been little or no collection progress, for accounts that have filed under Chapter 11 and offer little hope for any appreciable recovery, for accounts that have gone out of business (failed and/or skipped town) with no success in tracing the owner, and for accounts that have a balance(s) in the maximum past-due columns of your aging sheet and do not respond positively to your in-house collection effort. Any account on your aging report, including the occasional one that never pushed your terms more than 10- or 20-days past terms, but went out of business in what seemed midstride, is eligible for your list of current and projected bad-debt write-off items for the current or upcoming fiscal year. You must project by name the accounts you expect will become bad-debt items during the next fiscal year, and thereby ensure that the Bad-Debt Reserve is funded properly to start the new year. You also must add the monthly accrual percentage (or figure) to provide for the unanticipated losses. This figure will sustain the level of your requirement for bad-debt funds throughout the year.

Some fiscal officers like to see a Bad-Debt Reserve account that is so lean it isn't realistic. Others take a more practical approach, especially when the credit manager has been dealing effectively with the company's accounts for two, three, or more years. Never set a figure that is more than a reasonable one. The money in your bad-debt account is held hostage from the bottom line of your business and should never be more than a prudent figure based upon past and anticipated experience. Remember also that the unexpected failure of a major account can make a shambles of your bad-debt reserve. Pay close attention to your major accounts at all times, not just when you are evaluating them as a part of your bad-debt projection for the next fiscal year.

If the business is new, you will have no track record for setting an appropriate percentage of sales as the guideline criteria for your company's experience. Your own experience with another company in the same industry could be helpful, as could an industry association or national credit group which publishes annual figures for percentages of loss experienced by respondent members. How the industry leaders prepare the industry guideline(s) is relevant to what your company might experience. If the guideline breaks bad-debt loss experience into the various categories of regional location and/or annual credit sales, it will be far more helpful in relating to your experience than a national figure would be that is prepared from firms of all sizes and regional locations.

The formula for determining the bad-debt percentages of sales for a fiscal year is to divide the adjusted gross annual sales (after returns and credits) into the dollar total of bad-debt losses. Example: Assume that a company has adjusted gross annual sales of $1,326,000. Divide that figure into a bad-debt loss figure for the same year of $33,400, which equals a percentage figure of 0.252. At just over one-quarter of one percent of sales, this figure is well within acceptable parameters for many businesses and industries. When you have a bad-debt percentage figure for the past two or three years, combine those figures with your current figure, divide by the number of figures used, and come up with one that represents your company's average annual bad-debt experience for those years.

Bad-Debt Write-Offs

To adequately fund the reserve for the upcoming fiscal year, you should prepare your monthly accrual on the basis of the dollar totals of accounts currently on the aging report, accounts that you expect to charge off during the coming fiscal year (Chapter 11s that have not worked out, third-party collection assignments, certain in-house collections, and any accounts that your analysis of the aging report for accounts receivable indicates might be weakening rapidly). Use the projected sales figure for the upcoming fiscal year versus the total of your list of potential bad-debt accounts to arrive at a dollar figure and percentage of sales. You should review and adjust the monthly accrual figure on a monthly or quarterly basis to ensure that the figure reflects current needs and current analysis. Remember also to include in your calculations for a monthly accrual figure the amount that will be in your reserve for bad debts *after* you write off bad-debt charges for the current year. If, for the upcoming year, you project a bad-debt percentage of 0.30 against annual sales of $1.5 million, you can decrease the $45,000 that you project as a bad-debt write-off to an accrual of $40,000—if $5000 is still in the Bad-Debt Reserve after current write-offs. So the monthly accrual figure, with $5000 in the reserve, will begin at $1200 a month rather than the $1350 that would be required if there were zero funds in the reserve. You might occasionally pull most of what would be a carry-over reserve, in this instance $5000, out of the Bad-Debt Reserve and add it to the "bottom line," into Net Profits, if management feels a need to add more meat to the financials. Whatever the decision regarding carry-over money, be sure to provide adequately for your projected write-off of next year's bad debts with an appropriate monthly accrual to your Bad-Debt Reserve account.

There is a cardinal rule in the matter of bad-debt accounts and it goes something like this: no company wants, at any time, to see a receivables balance become a bad-debt item, but when a balance is lost, it should not be lost in the first few months of the supplier-customer relationship. Virtually every account that fails within a time frame of the first few months is going to take some of your company's money with it. On the other hand, if the account has done business with you for years, the failure will not be a joy, but you should recognize that the account was profitable over the many years of your association. Be especially watchful of new accounts. Do not let them come in too strong or too fast unless their credentials are impeccable. Should the less-than-impeccable customer try to pressure you into increasing the credit line beyond what you consider to be an acceptable figure, do not be coerced into going along with something that you know is not right, or is not right for your company.

In a chapter dealing with bad-debt accounts and bad-debt reserves, it is appropriate to repeat an earlier question: is the customer always right? The customer is very, very important and you must approach the relationship with the attitude that the customer is usually right, but *never* is the customer right when he or she is flagrantly abusing the customer-supplier relationship. It is an unacceptable attitude, an attitude that your company does not need and should not tolerate. If your intolerant attitude costs the company a relationship with an account that is constantly abusing the customer-supplier relationship in ways that are or could be financially costly, your company will be better off not doing a credit business with the abuser (see Figures 13-1 thru 13-3).

How to Minimize Write-Offs

The obvious answer to minimizing bad-debt write-offs is with good account selection and good monitoring procedures. Unfortunately, it is not possible to avoid an occasional bad-debt loss, unless your company has such a restrictive credit policy that the loss of a credit account would be unthinkable. In the real world of credit management, the credit manager's goal is to minimize the number, the dollar amounts, and the frequency of these profits-debilitating experiences.

Careful screening of credit applicants before they can become accounts receivable is a primary way to avoid the type of account that takes your company down the rocky road to a bad-debt loss. Once the order has been shipped, it is no longer possible for your company to exercise the degree of control that it had while evaluating the account and making a decision whether to grant the credit request.

You must change from passive to aggressive monitoring of accounts receivable when there is a change in the payment pattern, when aging begins to become a problem, or when there is information in a credit report or from a peer credit manager that indicates a downward trend in the firm's marketplace acceptance, a change in management's approach to fiscal responsibility, or the purchase of the company by another company with a resulting negative impact on the autonomy of a company

---

March 15, 199X

To: My readers
From: Cecil Bond
Re: Attached **Recap of Bad-Debt Charges—1978**

The letterhead copy is a photocopy of the letter that I prepared for the auditors, state and federal tax reports, and the company's records.

The cover letter total of $48,023.43 was supported by three pages of itemized Bad-Debt Charges, the first page of which I have attached to the cover letter. Pages two and three were a continuation of the same format and involved listing a total of 31 accounts. The total of the three supporting pages—the 31 accounts—equalled the cover letter total of $48,023.43.

Each write-off was supported by the weight of our effort to collect from these 31 accounts—an effort that was documented in the file folders of these accounts with copies of collection letters, a call sheet which detailed all collection calls (date called, person with whom the credit department member talked, the questions asked, and the responses and promises given in return), a record of the collection agency's efforts to collect (or copies of Chapter 11 proceedings, a conclusion of bankruptcy, etc.).

By the time the account had reached the point of becoming a Bad-Debt Item, all steps possible had been taken to collect the balance.

Cecil Bond

Figure 13-1. Cover letter (annual write-off of bad debts).

that was formerly a good and a dependable customer. Appropriate monitoring followed closely by an appropriate level of collection activity are the crucial elements in the pattern of whether your company does or does not have a relatively high stake in a customer's bankruptcy proceedings.

Dysan   *CORPORATION*   2388 Walsh Avenue/Santa Clara, California 95050/(408) 555-4109

November 6, 1978

This recap of Bad-Debt Charges for the year 1978 includes all items that qualify for the category, plus an adjustment for old credit balances.

Bad-Debt Charges (Total includes major balances plus various very old, small balances.)	$47,874.39
Additional Bad-Debt Charges (Numerous small sales tax, freight, and quantity discrepancy charges not documented by customer. Average individual balance is less than $5.00.)	516.70
Credit Balances (Various small credit balances such as overpayments of invoices, sales tax added to payments, etc.)	−367.66
Total	$48,023.43

DATE: November 6, 1978   Prepared by: *Cecil Bond*
                                              Credit Manager/DYSAN CORP.
                                Approved by: *J.R. Jarrets*
                                              Treasurer/DYSAN CORP.

Figure 13-2. Bad-debt charges (names and categories). (*Form courtesy of Dysan Corp.*)

Figure 13-3. Breakdown of bad-debt items.

Bad-Debt Charges—1978		
Account Name and Location	*Amount*	*Remarks*
Acctg. Equip., Inc. 1896 Rock County Rd. Casper, Wyoming (#1184)	$ 734.97	March and April 1977 invoices. Assigned third-party collection on 10/4/77. Many broken payment promises. Debtor has no money.
Action Planning Inc. P.O. Box 439 Paoli, California	$ 212.62	April 1977 invoicing. Collection assignment on 10/14/77. Paid $350.00 of $562.62. Collection Association is working on the balance. Collection doubtful.
American Systems 1314 Piedmont Blvd. Bushnell, Montana	$ 507.04	November and December invoices. Company reorganized in January 1977. New problems in late 1977 and early 1978.
Carmichael Corp. 1791 Carter Way Roanoke, Virginia	$14,953.38	April and June 1977 invoicing. Repeated efforts to get debtor to pay. Balance of $16,195.28 reduced to current total when $1241.90 received 4/5/78. Sent another letter 11/2/78. Payment not expected at this late date.
Business Applications 949 Acorn Drive San Francisco, California	$ 912.53	October and November invoices. Could not locate this business when I was in the San Francisco area in February 1978. Out of business.
Computer Research, Inc. Dunham Drive Phoenix, Arizona	$ 228.19	October 1977 invoice. Out of business via bankruptcy. Nothing left for unsecured creditors.

Figure 13-3. (*Continued*) Breakdown of bad-debt items.

Bad-Debt Charges—1978		
Account Name and Location	*Amount*	*Remarks*
Computer Space 1599 Temple Drive Ogden, Utah	$ 1,515.07	December 1977 and February 1978 invoices. All assets were assigned as collateral for an SBA loan. The corporation failed in the early part of 1978 with no assets available for distribution to the unsecured creditors.

Too many credit managers are short-sighted in their approach to third-party collection assignments. They are reluctant to assign accounts to a collection agency or to a collection attorney until their own nonproductive efforts have continued too long. If you have tried every approach in your company's bag of collection tools and there has been no acceptable payment response, what are you waiting for? Assign the account to a collection agency or a collection attorney. So the collection assignee collects the money and you must pay a collection fee based upon the amount of the assignment. It certainly makes better sense to give your company the chance to receive 50 percent, 75 percent, or 80 percent of an account balance that you have been unable to collect than it does to take additional amounts of your time and energy away from other credit department duties and other accounts receivables balances. If your company can benefit as the result of a third-party collection assignment while separating itself from an account that identifies itself increasingly as a potential business failure, there is no reason to begrudge the payment of a collection fee to the company or individual who managed to accomplish what you could not.

An accounts receivable balance that becomes a bad-debt item because your company has been victimized by an unscrupulous customer is unfortunate—and it may raise your anger level to a point where retribution or vengeance looks very attractive. Forget it. Learn as much from the experience as you possibly can, and do everything that is legally possible to collect some or all of the debt, but do not wander from a totally legal collection effort. When legitimate collection efforts have failed and the account has slid into a Chapter 11, wait for the Chapter 11 proceeding to run its course. You may recover some or none of the money owed by the account, but you do not want to push a collection effort that puts your company in the high risk area of a suit for damages. Bad-debt items are at the top of any credit manager's list of unattractive items, but if legitimate collection procedures cannot get the job done, there is no incentive to pursue a course that is clearly illegal, unprofessional, and potentially costly.

Inadequate Bad-Debt Reserves

A reserve for bad debts that is not properly funded must eventually impact the bottom line of a company's financial statement with memorable severity. It is not helpful to the company for a credit manager to project account names, the number of accounts, and the total dollars of bad-debt losses for the next fiscal year if the financial officer does not use those figures to provide a monthly accrual to the reserve for bad debts that, at year-end, will be adequate to offset them. No financial officer should consider that he or she has done a complete job for his or her company if, at the end of a fiscal year, a large sum of money must be deducted from what should have been the net profit figure to fund the year's total of bad-debt items. Providing for an annual write-off of bad-debt items is much less painful if it is done as a monthly accrual.

Credit managers should evaluate carefully all prospective bad-debt accounts, especially when the company's cash flow is tight. It is not good business for a company to borrow money to fund monthly cash flow, if a portion of what is being borrowed is used to offset an unrealistically high monthly accrual for bad-debt write-offs. Trim the accrual to a realistic figure, one that can be justified on the basis of the list of account balances that you project will be written off at the end of the fiscal year. Every legitimate candidate for the category of bad-debt write-off should be on the credit manager's list, and it is the responsibility of the financial officer to make a monthly accrual adequate to fund the fiscal year-end write-offs of those accounts.

Surprises? Of course there will be one from time to time, and occasionally the amount of the surprise will be more in the nature of a shock. When an unprojected receivables loss occurs, there may not be enough money in the reserve for bad debts to accommodate the write-off of anticipated losses plus the addition of one or two large, unexpected ones. In such a situation, there is no alternative, but to transfer additional funds into the reserve account, enough to raise the reserve total to the level required to write off accounts that can no longer be classified as collectible.

No Losses? Too Restrictive
a Credit Policy

In an earlier chapter of this book it was noted that the various types of credit policies impact a business in a variety of ways. A restrictive credit policy has the obvious advantage of minimizing and/or virtually eliminating bad-debt losses. It is a concept that offers the creditor an aged trial balance report of accounts receivable that can be expected to pay their bills virtually without fail, certainly no worse than 99 percent of the time. Is the prospect of never losing a receivables balance because an account filed a Chapter 11, and never came out, or simply closed its doors and disappeared into the night not utopian in its appeal? Wouldn't your company or business be better off with accounts of inflexible integrity?

Your company would not be better off because to never experience a bad-debt loss is indicative of a credit policy that is incredibly restrictive. If your company's credit policy were that restrictive, the company might never have a bad-debt loss, but the cost in sales and business growth would be so prohibitive as to be unacceptable. Sales volume would not be adequate to pay expenses; generating a profit from such a tight-fisted approach would not be possible. The best hope for the company would be that, for a period of time, it might remain static before gradually slipping into a decline that could ultimately spiral it into a Chapter 11.

The bad-debt ratio of your company should be in line with the average for your industry *or* it should be in line with the credit-policy and the cash-flow requirements of your company. If the bad-debt ratio of your company is below that of others in your industry, but the company is enjoying an acceptable level of growth, good profits, satisfactory R & D, and is generally moving forward in its industry, the credit policy obviously is not too restrictive. If the bad-debt ratio is well above the industry average, growth is sporadic, profits are thin or not at all, and the company isn't making the mark in its industry that was projected for it, credit policy may not be the major culprit, but it could be a contributor.

You don't want to lose receivables dollars to the bad-debt account because your company's credit policy incorporates an invitation for this type of disaster. At the same time, you do not want to minimize receivables losses because the company's account standards are unrealistically restrictive.

Documenting Your
Collection Efforts

When your company loses a receivables balance to the bad-debt account, the credit department must be able to substantiate its claim that every effort was made to collect the money before it was written off. There must be no question regarding the diligence and the continuity of your company's effort to collect. Your company will use these legitimate write-offs to reduce the annual tax obligation, but the IRS will not accept the validity of these write-offs unless there is indisputable documentation to support the statement that there was a total, aggressive collection effort before the balance or balances were charged to the bad-debt account.

The credit department should have a special section in its file cabinet for accounts that have been written off. In each of these account folders there should be copies of all correspondence pertaining to payment of the obligation that was sent by your company; any letters or notes that were received from the debtor should also be in this folder. There should be a copy of the form for recording telephone calls that were made to the debtor, a recap of each conversation, and a statement regarding any promises of payment that were made by the debtor to a member of your credit department.

It is imperative that the record of telephone calls and letters should reveal a consistent pattern of increasingly insistent and/or urgent messages and statements from your company to the debtor. There should be clear evidence that your company made every reasonable effort to get the debtor to pay his or her obligation to your company. A copy of the letter or form that was used to refer the account to third-party collection, including your instructions to the agency or the collection attorney, should also be a part of the file; also include a record of your conversations with the third-party collection agency or attorney, plus copies of any notes or memorandums received by your department or initiated by it. And finally, if the agency or attorney returned the account with an explanation of what it had done to try to collect (or if the business had closed and there had been an unsuccessful attempt to skip trace the owner, owners, or partners) a memo covering that phase of the collection effort should also be a part of the file.

The IRS could challenge one or each of the items that your company claims as a bad-debt loss as the company attempts to reduce its obligation for a specific tax year. If the information received by the IRS is not complete, the IRS might demand more data pertaining to the effort made by your company to collect from the debtor. If the debtor filed a Chapter 11, then failed to produce a plan for continuing the business that was acceptable to the creditors and the court, the subsequent transferring of the Chapter 11 to a straight bankruptcy and subsequent liquidation of assets should provide all of the documentation necessary to verify final disposition of the case.

This situation does not, however, ensure that your company will be allowed to deduct an account balance as a bad-debt loss, unless there is sufficient documentation (letters, records of telephone calls, third-party collection assignment, etc.) to prove that your company's collection effort prior to the filing by the debtor of a Chapter 11 meets the criteria of the IRS for diligent and aggressive collection effort. You must do your job, and be able to provide the back-up data to prove that you did it as effectively as circumstances would permit.

When a list of potential bad-debt customers and balances is prepared from the company's accounts receivable aging report, it is often difficult to project the time frame within which certain of the company's problem customers will complete their demise. It is also difficult to project whether the percentage of loss to your company will be 10 percent, 25 percent, 50 percent, 75 percent, or more of what is owed when the account is declared to be uncollectible—a certified bad-debt balance. The provision for bad-debt items should be as accurate as possible, but to project whether an uncollectible balance will become a bad-debt item this year or the next is, in the instance of some accounts, a very difficult situation.

The following are examples of what should be considered when the credit manager sets out to provide a bad-debt provision against which write-offs can be charged on a quarterly or annual basis. Will your company be able to collect a part of the account balance, or will it be a full or partial write-off?

1. Has the account been in Chapter 11 for several months?

2. Have the company's creditors been unwilling to accept any of the proposed continuation plans?

3. If a continuation plan has been offered and accepted by the creditors, how does the plan deal with prior debts?

4. Have prior debts been deferred for one or two years with payments of 5 percent per year scheduled to be paid from third- and subsequent-year profits—if any?

5. Has there been a change in management personnel or in the business philosophy of the company that would seem to give the continuation plan a reasonable chance to succeed?

6. Will the company be issuing stock for a major part of the debt owed to creditors?

7. If stock is a part of the restructuring of old debt, what is the time frame and the criteria for selling the stock?

8. If a continuation plan has been accepted, has it been accepted because the alternative would be to liquidate the company, pay some of the secured creditors as much as the liquidated assets would cover, with nothing left for some of the allegedly secured creditors and all of the unsecured creditors?

9. If your own evaluation of the company's chances for pulling out of the Chapter 11 is not optimistic, review your monthly bad-debt provision to ensure that funds will be available to accommodate the write-off.

10. Do not be intimidated by the wishes of credit committee members who may have their own personal and/or company agenda for wanting creditor companies to accept a specific plan or recommendation. Do remember, however, that what has been worked out by a creditor's committee and approved by the bankruptcy court is probably the best solution for the majority of the creditors and should be viewed from that perspective. Almost no plan that a creditor's committee might devise would please every creditor, so a plan that is acceptable to a majority of the creditors is generally a plan that represents the best interests of creditors. What about your own company? If you're a smaller creditor, you might prefer another plan—something that might be more favorable to the smaller creditors—but the rule of the majority (in number, dollars owed, etc.) is virtually certain to prevail.

14
Factoring

Your peripheral exposure to this form of improving cash flow might have been one that you did not recognize as part of the "factoring" concept, such as small advertisements in the financial sections of daily newspapers in which the advertiser offers to "buy your invoices for immediate cash." The offer might say "cash within 24 hours, no term contracts to sign, bank-to-bank transfer of funds, and invoices purchased on a nonrecourse basis." Interesting, but in most instances and in most industries, your company would not turn to these sources unless your company is at a point or in a position where your bank—where no bank—will agree to offer the additional funds you need to sustain or expand cash flow for the short or long term. There are companies whose integrity in this field is unquestioned, but for most companies in most industries, this is a "supplier of last resort."

An Alternative Source to Improve Cash Flow?

This is an alternative method for converting accounts receivable into cash before the customer pays the invoice. It is one of the more expensive ways to obtain cash to sustain or to increase cash flow, and it should not be used as a substitute for the more conventional types of financial support (bank loans, venture capitalists, stock issues, etc.), when those options are still available to a company or business. But in certain situations, and in certain industries where factoring has, for decades, been an integral part of the financial picture, it is an alternative that might enable a company to generate the additional cash flow that cannot be obtained from bank credit lines.

If your company is having difficulty handling its financial commitments within the constraints of its present bank-loan agreements, a short-term factoring arrangement to generate an additional contribution to monthly cash flow might be worth considering. For the long term, however, and in most businesses or industries, there is very little to commend this type of financing as a permanent part of a company's financial picture. A company should evaluate and restructure its expenses and financial commitments before it turns toward a source whose costs might more than offset the additional or more rapid flow of cash. (The foregoing assumes that your company's accounts receivable are not already tied to the bank as security for a revolving cash-flow loan, or part of the total loan package. If it appears that receivables have not been pledged as collateral, then you should be free to use them. Be sure, however, to examine your agreements with the bank to ensure that selling receivables accounts to a factor does not violate any section or specific restriction in your loan agreement[s] with the bank.)

There are various reasons why your banker might not want to exceed certain loan-limit parameters. Because of business or economic conditions, he or she might feel that your company's financial and business position will not support an increase in the bank's lending commitment. At that point, particularly if you are confident that the need to accelerate cash will be temporary, factoring your receivables through an established, reputable factoring firm could be the answer to getting a faster turnaround of your receivables dollars. It is not a form of financing that you should consider seriously (certainly not in most industries) unless bank support—or additional bank support—is not available. In the scenario of a relatively short-term need, it is worth exploring.

Qualifying Your Company's Receivables

Factors do not want to become involved with your problem accounts. They are interested in accounts that have a good payment record with your company (within or near terms) or a payment record that rarely includes balances that are more than a few days past due. Factors are not sitting on mounds of in-house cash. They must borrow large sums of cash which they then loan at considerably higher rates of interest to generate a profit and to compensate for the factors of risk that are characteristic of the industry.

Your company will be asked to submit a list of accounts, including their payment history for a period of time that might vary from one industry to the next, for example, three or six months to one year or more. Factors are not philanthropists; they are in business to make a profit. Accounts that do not meet the criteria for an acceptable account will be promptly rejected. Other accounts might be accepted immediately or there might be a request for additional payment and/or historical data. Within a short period of time the factor will tell your company what is, for his or her firm, an acceptable account—and whether it is acceptable to the factor on a recourse or a nonrecourse basis.

Recourse Accounts

A "recourse account" is one that is acceptable to the factor on the condition that your company guarantees, as part of the factoring agreement, to pay the factor within a specified period of time for monies advanced on invoices charged to approved accounts *if* the factored account fails to pay the factor. When such an arrangement is in place, it is customary for a factor to accept more accounts that do not pay promptly and to advance a higher percentage of each invoice total. Because there is a recourse agreement, the company (your company) has the same responsibility for ensuring that the account pays within an acceptable time period as would be true if the accounts had not been factored. You want that customer to pay within the time frame of your recourse agreement with the factor; if the account does not pay within that time frame, you not only must repay the factor the amount advanced against the account balance, but also lose the financing charges, which are definitely not waived by the factor.

The factoring agreement may state that your company is to be advanced 70, 75, or 80 cents against each one dollar of the individual (or cumulative) total of invoices. The agreement normally covers all accounts with the exception of those that have been reviewed by the factor and found to be unacceptable. Even in a recourse agreement, it is the factor's prerogative to decline certain accounts. Remember that the factor does not want problem accounts; problem accounts inevitably lead to a payment pattern that increases the administrative work between your two companies.

Asking your company to return funds that were advanced and spent 30 or 40 days before is not a favorite request of the factor. The factor knows that your company has certain strengths, but it also knows that the company has an ongoing cash-flow problem. If the factor is advancing 70 cents from each one dollar of invoiced product(s), money to repay invoice balances that do not clear within the contract-specified time frame will decrease the number of dollars available to service your company's cash-flow requirements.

What if the factor advances 70 cents on every dollar of accepted invoices? Not only do you have an obligation to see that the customer pays within the time frame stated in your contract with the factor, but there is also the other 30 percent, the 30 percent for which you receive no money from the factor. If you are not as aggressive in your collection effort as you were before the factor became involved, then the advantages of receiving 70 cents promptly from each invoiced dollar might be offset—or more than offset—by the fact that the factor's charges, plus a slow-turning 30 percent of too many invoices, could undermine a program that was designed to improve cash flow.

Nonrecourse Accounts

The advantage of this form of financing receivables invoices is that the factor assumes responsibility for collecting the full amount of goods and/or services invoiced to accounts that the factor has accepted. These accounts —the ones that are accepted on a nonrecourse basis—are listed by name, and that list becomes an integral part of the contract between your company and the factor. Because the factor's risk is higher, the amount advanced from each invoice to your company will be smaller than when accounts are being serviced on a "recourse" basis.

It is imperative that you thoroughly investigate the reputation of the factoring firm before you settle into any serious negotiations. If a contract is set up for the factor's services on a "nonrecourse" basis, you must remember that your company assigns all collection rights to the factor. If the factor approaches your customers with payment demands that are eyebrow-lifting at best, there is literally nothing your company can do about it. You might protest, of course, but it is not reasonable to assume that the factor will change the collection procedure to accommodate your company. These are nonrecourse accounts, and the factor's money is on the line. Your company is, by contractual agreement, eliminated from having any say in the collection procedure. Any question(s) that your company might have regarding the effort the factor will expend to collect from your customers should be put to rest; suffice to say that the factor will use any collection technique that is legal to force payment from your customer(s) and, unlike your company, the factor has no interest in preserving a long-term relationship with the account.

This is not to say that factors ride roughshod over every past-due account, but to make money the factor must get his or her money within a specific number of days. To go beyond that period decreases the return on the receivables investment and puts the account executive (the factor's representative who is handling your account) in an unfavorable light with the people who monitor his or her performance. Does your company have a problem with the thought that its customers, when put in a factoring situation that involves a nonrecourse contract, could be subjected to a much stronger collection effort from the factoring company than they have seen from yours? If that is true, you may want to weigh the possible short-term advantage of a factoring agreement versus a continuation of the current level of bank borrowings, and attempt to restructure some payments and expenses over a longer period of time.

Factoring accounts receivable is not inexpensive and, in almost every industry or situation, it should not be the financial arrangement of preference. It is, for most companies, something to be explored only after less costly forms of financing have been found to be unobtainable. If there are reasons why additional funds cannot be obtained from the bank, from private investors, from a stock issue, or from a venture capitalist, then your company might want to take a look at some factored money.

PART 3

The Uniform Commercial Code

The UCC has been in effect for a varying number of years in each of the 50 states, the District of Columbia, and the Virgin Islands. State legislatures have put a personal imprint on the resulting legislation, diluting to some degree the original concept of a "uniform code," but what has been passed by the various state legislative bodies is still much more effective than were prior controls. Suppliers are now able to protect their intrastate and interstate interests in goods via a Purchase Money Security Agreement with a subsequent UCC filing. This procedure not only gives companies or individuals a security interest in their goods until payment has been received and the filing cancelled, but also gives protection for an appropriate dollar interest in proceeds from the sale of those goods.

UCC Filings
and Your Company

If your company sells to a variety of customers and those customers are located in your immediate service area or scattered throughout one or more states, it is probably unwise if you are not availing yourself of the

UCC's protection. It can provide some of the protection you need to sell businesses and companies that have potential, but are not fully established; enable your company to stock new distributors or dealers at levels you could not consider were it not for the UCC; protect the interests of your company with appropriate filings to cover consumer goods, crops, business equipment, etc.

UCC filings enable companies to sell goods or services to customers whose credit records (payments to suppliers, etc.) might, under conditions of an unsecured sale, be too uncertain for the supplier(s) to take the risk. Not that a UCC filing automatically ensures payment or payment in full—not so. There are still elements of risk that can be minimized, but not totally eliminated, and there is credit management work that must be ongoing after a perfected filing has been made. A credit manager should ask questions such as the following:

1. Are there UCC filings on record ahead of the one I would file to protect my company? Contact the appropriate authority to obtain a list of the prior filings. You may also want to obtain copies of individual filings to determine whether they have been prepared and filed properly.
2. If the bank was the first to file, what is included in that filing?
3. Have other suppliers established a priority with their filing? And again, what exactly do these filings cover?
4. If there are prior filings, have the companies that filed established a valid priority claim? You might want to order copies of these filings to be sure that they are proper—or perfected—filings.
5. In the event of a Chapter 11 filing by the customer, would your company's UCC filing put it in a priority position in the line-up of secured customers?

There are other questions that should be asked, but the above are typical of what a credit manager must look at before he or she makes a protective filing under UCC, or ships any product or performs any service that should be covered by a filing. If your company is not making the first filing, you must know who stands ahead of your company and what asset or assets is covered by the one or more filings that are ahead of yours. Do not file just for the sake of filing. If a filing is not going to give your company the protection it needs, then the priority position of other suppliers and creditors could put your company too far down the line. If that is the situation, you should reevaluate the order for goods or services before deciding whether it is an acceptable risk.

How Uniform Is the Code?

A quick and a somewhat accurate answer to the foregoing question is to note that each of the 50 states, the District of Columbia, and the Virgin

Islands has its own UCC forms. There is, however, basic uniformity within UCC legislation passed by the 52 government entities. There is not, however, the total commitment to uniformity that was visualized when the National Conference of Commissioners on Uniform State Laws first met in 1940. That meeting, which was to consider amendments to the Uniform Sales Act to avoid conflict with a proposed Federal Sales Act, then evolved into a proposal to devise a single comprehensive statute. The concept of the UCC was created in 1940, the official text was approved and became available in 1952, and Pennsylvania enacted Code legislation in 1953.

The New York legislature, however, found the Code to be unsatisfactory, referred it to the New York Law Revision Commission, and that Commission in 1956 reported that the UCC was not satisfactory. This led to additional revisions by the National Conference of Commissioner's editorial board, and was subsequently followed by "official drafts" in 1957, 1958, and 1962. The 1962 version is the one that has been accepted in the 50 states, the District of Columbia, and the Virgin Islands.

A permanent editorial board was appointed in an attempt to minimize the tendency of the various states to amend sections of the Code out of what is self-interest. The board aggressively sponsored its 1966 official recommendations and its 1966 amended version. This was followed in 1972 by a revised code that included major changes in Article 9 (Secured Transactions). Other modifications have been made in the years since 1972 to ensure that the code remains in tune with the needs of those who look to it for protection.

In keeping with what was mentioned earlier regarding the differences between states in the forms and procedures for filing under the UCC of a specific state, request a set of the appropriate filing forms from the secretary of state (or other designated jurisdiction) in which the filing is to be made. Some examples of forms that have been used by the various states are included (Figures 21-1 thru 21-12) and indicate how each state has set about to modify the definition of "uniform" to something that is uniform in a rather broad interpretation of the word.

There is some validity for changes that have been made by the various state legislatures. Some changes have been influenced by the commerce of a state, whether its chief source of economic strength is manufacturing (and what types), farming, forestry and/or forest products, fishing, etc., could have a nuance that might not fit one-hundred percent if every state had to accept the exact same UCC format. What if no changes were allowed at all, and no state had the right to alter the specifics of the UCC in any manner, shape, or form? That would not be realistic, and if it were true, we would still be struggling to get legislation through the first few states. Had that been the case, it would have taken many more years than it did for the 50 states, the District of Columbia, and the Virgin Islands to pass UCC legislation.

Differences in the Code between States and Jurisdictions

One of the primary differences is the procedure that must be followed to make a UCC filing. The place for filing varies from state to state. In one state it may be the office of the County Recorder; in another it might be the office of the Secretary of State. Other states require filings to be made at the office of the Clerk of the Superior Court in the county where the debtor resides, or with the Clerk of the Circuit Court or the Clerk of the Town of the debtor's residence, etc.

It is obvious that the credit manager or the person who handles UCC filings must have a current reference source such as the National Association of Credit Management's Credit Manual of Commercial Laws, 1991 or 1992, to know where to file, the filing fee, and other data pertinent to a proper filing. The Credit Manual of Commercial Laws is indispensable if your company is into UCC filings, should be into them, or is about to look into the process. What if your company manufactures, distributes and/or wholesales Consumer Goods (used or bought primarily for personal, family, or household purposes), Equipment (used primarily in business, etc.), Farm Products (crops, livestock, or supplies used or produced in a farming operation), Inventory (goods held for sale, lease, furnished or to be furnished under contract[s], etc.), or Fixtures (goods that are fixed to a building or to real estate so as to become part of it)? If your company or business is in any of the foregoing categories, you need to know enough about the Uniform Commercial Code to make some intelligent decisions regarding it and the filings you could and should be making.

For a small service fee, your company may request and receive from the filing officer of a jurisdiction a certificate that will show whether a secured transaction document is on file, the date and the hour the document was filed (recorded), any currently effective financing statement naming a particular debtor, any statement assigning interest in the recorded transaction, and, if there is such an assignment, a record listing the date and hour each statement or assignment was filed, plus the name and address of secured parties named in the recorded documents.

The Uniform Commercial Code can only be effective if you learn how to use it. Do not trust your judgment regarding what does or does not appear to be correct until you have enough experience dealing with certain sections of the Code to be comfortable with it. Do not, however, make the mistake of assuming that you know how to file in a specific jurisdiction unless you understand the form(s) and the procedure. Do you have a question? Your company's attorney should be an automatic call.

15

When and How to Use UCC Filings

A person whose job it is to manage credit accounts must have a working understanding of the "when and how" of UCC filings, and to do that requires some recognition of the Code's component parts. The credit manager or administrator should be able to identify and locate which of the Divisions (or Articles) is applicable to a specific problem or need. It is not necessary for a credit manager to be able to recite sections and subsections of a Division of the UCC, but it is appropriate for a credit manager to know where to look to locate the applicable part of the Code (see Figure 15-1).

The pages that follow identify the Divisions of the UCC and identify the sections and subsections in considerable detail. It is sufficiently comprehensive for a person to be able to locate the specific area of interest in the statute itself.

Uniform Commercial Code—The Divisions

The UCC is a key tool of the credit administrator and is used to protect goods, property, and accounts receivables assets. In each of the 52 jurisdictions, it is the legal structure which governs such secured transactions as bailments (the delivery of property by one, known to the bailor, or to another, know to the bailee, or to be held in custody for certain purposes), consignments, leases, trust receipts, chattel mortgages, conditional sales, assignment of accounts receivable, and factor's liens. Under the current requirements of the Uniform Commercial Code, these types of transactions qualify as Secured Transactions.

357

			Acknowledgment		Date Financing
Name and Location	Filing Date	City, State Where Filed	Copy in File	Renewal Date	Statement Terminated

Uniform Commercial Code Filings—Current Closed

Figure 15-1. Uniform Commercial Code filings (current/closed).

The Uniform Commercial Code consists of 11 Divisions (or Articles), each of which is composed of numerous parts and subsections. Because I am not an attorney and because UCC statutes vary somewhat from one jurisdiction to another, I do not attempt to give legal advice or interpretation to these statutes. When in doubt regarding the interpretation of the UCC or any other area of the law, *consult your attorney for guidance.* You cannot conduct the business of the credit department—or if you are an entrepreneur, the business of your company—by assuming that you understand areas of the law that, if misinterpreted or misunderstood, could cost your company large sums of money.

The following several pages have been excerpted from California's Uniform Commercial Code.

The Uniform Commercial Code—An Analysis of Its Provisions

The UCC is applicable generally to all types of commercial transactions. It consists of the following Divisions/Articles and a varying number of Chapters within each of the Divisions.

Division 1—General Provisions

    Chapter 1—Short Title, Construction, Application, and Subject Matter of the Code

    Chapter 2—General Definitions and Principles of Interpretation

Division 2—Sales

    Chapter 1—Short Title, General Construction, and Subject Matter

    Chapter 2—Form, Formation, and Readjustment of Contract

    Chapter 3—General Obligation and Construction of Contract

    Chapter 4—Title, Creditors, and Good Faith Purchasers

    Chapter 5—Performance

    Chapter 6—Breach, Repudiation, and Excuse

    Chapter 7—Remedies

Division 3—Commercial Paper

    Chapter 1—Short Title, Form, and Interpretation

    Chapter 2—Transfer and Negotiation

    Chapter 3—Rights of a Holder

    Chapter 4—Liability of Parties

    Chapter 5—Presentment, Notice of Dishonor, and Protest

    Chapter 6—Discharge

    Chapter 7—Advice of International Sight Draft

    Chapter 8—Miscellaneous

Division 4—Bank Deposits and Collections

    Chapter 1—General Provisions and Definitions

    Chapter 2—Collection of Items: Depositary and Collecting Banks

    Chapter 3—Collection of Items: Payor Banks

9505. Acceptance of the Collateral as Discharge of Obligation

9506. Debtor's Right to Redeem Collateral

9507. Secured Party's Liability for Failure to Comply with This Part

Division 10—Effective Date and Repealer

10101. Effective Date

10102. Provision for Transition

10103. General Repealer

10104. Laws Not Repealed

The preceding presents a comprehensive look at the Divisions and major sections of the Uniform Commercial Code. I did mention, however, that the Code is loaded with sections and subsections which break each of the Divisions and major sections into categories that define the statute.

The reader who has an interest in a subsection or subsections that have not been detailed should refer to the Uniform Commercial Code for his or her state. If you have any problem understanding the legal language or interpreting the meaning of certain phrases, subsections, or sections, contact your attorney for whatever assistance or clarification seems appropriate. Do not assume that you understand areas of the Code if they are not crystal clear. The consequences of an erroneous interpretation can be too costly to proceed on the basis of assumptions or guesswork.

Fraudulent Conveyance

When the economy is good, the consequences of this problem causes creditors to annually lose million of dollars; when the economy is in a period of recession, the losses to creditors increase with the depth and scope of the economy's problems. Fraudulently conveying the assets of a debtor to a third party is a ploy utilized by unscrupulous debtors in an attempt to avoid their legal obligations and to make it virtually impossible for a creditor to find an asset upon which to get and levy a judgment.

The Uniform Fraudulent Transfer Act was approved in 1984 by the National Conference of Commissioners on Uniform State Laws. It is an attempt to provide creditors with a comprehensive tool to use against these dishonest debtors. It has been adopted by approximately 30 percent of the states and is widely regarded as providing an effective approach for dealing with problems that have their roots in fraud and fraudulent conveyance.

The Uniform Commercial Code contains regulatory statutes to protect the rights of creditors who transfer and sell in bulk various types of goods, merchandise, and fixtures. Merchants, who in the past might have quietly worked out a deal with another merchant to buy merchandise and fixtures, must now give creditors enough advance notice of the impending sale for them to protect their interest against the possibility of a fraudulent transfer.

Notice is required to be given in the form of a registered letter or a notice given personally to the creditor. In the few states where the foregoing procedures for notification do not apply, notice of the intended transfer must be recorded. This imposes a much higher level of risk to the creditor than is present when the method of notification is hand delivery or registered mail.

Remedies of Creditors

Creditors whose claims did not exist at the time of the transfer of goods or property are not protected under Article 6. When a creditor receives a notice of sale, the remedies available under state law—attachment, injunction, etc.—are the creditor's recourse. If the sale takes place in a jurisdiction where the buyer is required to see that the purchase price is applied to the payment of creditors' claims, there is protection for creditors to the amount of the money that changed hands when the goods were transferred, if creditors follow statutory guidelines as they apply to filing their claims.

The transferee has a clear cut obligation under Section 6—106 to have safeguards to ensure that any payment(s) made when there is a transfer of title is applied to the debts of the transferor; a list of debts must be furnished by the transferor or filed in the space stated in the notice within 30 days after the notice has been mailed. A pro rata payment is made to creditors when the amount received is not enough to cover in full all obligations of the transferor.

The responsibility of the purchaser is considerable. In any bulk transfer, all persons must be notified who are named on the list furnished by the transferor. The Code, as written in some states, requires that notice be sent to persons, known to the transferee, to have an assertable claim against the transferor. Does the transferor omit a name from the list of creditors? The transferee is fully protected if the transferee had no knowledge, information, or belief regarding the creditor's claim.

Three other provisions which pertain to Bulk Transfers have special significance for creditors:

1. Creditors of the transferor cannot make a claim against the transferee, unless the transferor's creditors can prove or have proof that there was collusion between a transferee in bulk and subsequent purchasers.

2. If within six months after the transferee takes possession of the goods, there is evidence to support the belief that there was collusion between the transferor and the transferee, the Uniform Commercial Code provides that a proceeding may be brought to set aside the transfer. Bulk Transfer Laws, however, do not always provide a time limitation, so the

applicable limitation depends upon the type of action that prompted the request for relief.

3. The transferor must, as stated previously, provide the transferee with a list of creditors and a schedule of property to be transferred; this is so the transferee can monitor payments to creditors as prescribed under Article 6 of the UCC. The Code requires also that the transferee reserve these lists (creditors and property) for a period of six months following the transfer and hold it available for inspection by any of the transferor's creditors.

Security Rights

It is well to remember that security rights which were created prior to the enactment of the Uniform Commercial Code are still governed by superceded statutes. The UCC did not wipe out on a retroactive basis those security agreements and interests that had been set up to conform with pre-existing statutes and regulations. Security rights and agreements that were set up on a long-term basis may or may not have been modified in the post-UCC era. If a basic change has taken place in the pre-UCC agreement, it should probably have been modified or rewritten to conform with currently applicable UCC requirements.

There are certain forms of secured transactions which existed prior to the UCC, but still meet requirements of the Code; these are items such as bailments, consignments, leases, trust receipts, chattel mortgages, conditional sales, assignment of accounts receivable, and factor's liens. Each of these has made the transition from pre-UCC secured transactions to transactions that meet generally the requirements for the UCC of the 50 states, the District of Columbia, and the Virgin Islands. Explanations of some of them follow:

Bailment. Examples are the delivery of securities for an agent to transfer, a vehicle which is in possession of a mechanic and is to be repaired, and the rental of equipment or the storing of an automobile. Bailment is defined as an agreement whereby there is the delivery of personal property to another for some special or particular purpose with the agreement between the parties that it will be returned to the person who delivered it, held for instructions regarding disposal, or held until it is reclaimed by the person who delivered it. Remember that the person who delivers property is the bailor; the person who receives it is the bailee.

Consignments. A consignment is the category that describes goods delivered to a merchant, an agent, or a commission merchant to be sold by that person as the agent of the consignor. When goods or merchandise is transferred in this manner, title continues in the consignor. This type of transfer is not to be confused with a conditional sale or contract of sale, because the unique relationship between consignor and consignee incorporates no intention that a title will pass from one to the other. The consignee is the agent for selling the goods of the consignor, whereas in a conditional sale, the purchaser obligates himself or herself to buy the goods, merchandise, or property. The title to the goods transfers directly from consignor to buyer, with the consignee (the sales agent) receiving compensation on a basis established at the time the consignor-consignee relationship was established.

Trust Receipts.   An example of trust receipts as the control for collateral is when a bank makes a seasonal loan to the canner of fruits and vegetables. The bank and the cannery start with an inventory, add the various types of products as they are canned, and subtract from the type of products as they are sold. The bank starts with an inventory record of the warehouse totals (perhaps a bonded warehouse) of the various products, receives a copy of each shipper as product is withdrawn from the warehouse, deducts those withdrawals from the inventory, and receives payment for goods sold against the total amount of the seasonal loan. If goods have remained in the warehouse of the canner, an inventory will be taken at specified intervals. If goods have been put in a bonded warehouse, the warehouse will make appropriate reports regarding sales of goods to the lender.

The origin of trust receipts was tied to the importing of merchandise and is still used in that area of commerce. In recent years, however, the primary use of trust receipts has been between automobile and household equipment manufacturers and their dealers. A bank or other financing institution pays the dealer's price of each unit, receives the bill of lading or other documents of title, pays the manufacturer/seller, and that company is out of the transaction. The dealer has received the goods and the bank has the documents of title; when a unit is sold, the dealer delivers the unit to the customer and pays the financing institution the factory cost plus carrying charges (interest charges).

The Uniform Commercial Code has replaced the Uniform Trust Receipts Act and the UCC has classified trust receipts as a type of secured transaction under Article 9 of the Code.

Conditional Sales Contracts.   They are defined as any contract for the sale of goods where possession is with the buyer and the ownership of the goods, when all or part of the price has been paid, is to vest in the buyer. Conditional sales may also be any contract that covers the bailment or leasing of goods and under whose terms the bailee (or lessee) contracts to pay a price approximately equivalent to the value of the goods. The terms must also make it clear that when terms of the contract have been fulfilled, the bailee (or lessee) will become the owner of the goods.

The basic concepts and philosophy of conditional sales agreements were, for years, under the jurisdiction of the Uniform Conditional Sales Act, and continue to be used in arranging security agreements under the superceding jurisdiction of the Uniform Commercial Code.

Chattel Mortgages. The UCC makes no distinction between a chattel mortgage and a conditional sales contract and supercedes in all states the laws which previously governed this category of contract. Jurisdiction over these contracts now rests in Article 9 of the UCC. Some states continue to use chattel mortgages as a form of security agreement, a form of agreement that is subject to the requirements of the Code.

Although the UCC makes no distinction between chattel mortgages and conditional sales contracts, there are important differences when a chattel mortgage is the contract that is used to retain title. The voice of common law (or title theory) says that a transfer of title to the mortgagee is effected through the use of a chattel mortgage. It states that title reverts to the mortgagor when payment, performance, and conditions have been met as stated in the mortgage. The title theory gives a mortgagee title to a property when the mortgagor defaults on his or her contract. The lien theory allows a chattel mortgage to give to the mortgagee a lien upon the property to which the mortgagor retains title. Default on conditions of the chattel mortgage by the mortgagor gives the mortgagee the right to initiate and enforce forclosure proceedings against property covered by the mortgage.

General Usage of a Contract of Conditional Sale

It is used in conjunction with the purchase and sale of goods.

Title is originally in the mortgagor or passes from seller to buyer.

Buyer may prepare a document to transfer title back to the seller or secure the purchase price with a lien on the property.

General Usage of a Chattel Mortgage

It is used to cover property that belongs to the mortgagor and is used to secure the repayment of loans.

Title remains with the seller and does not pass to the buyer until terms of the contract have been fulfilled.

Chattel mortgage is the more formal document. It usually includes the signature of the mortgagor and the signatures of witnesses who attest to the authenticity of the mortgagor's signature, the date the document was signed, etc. Some states have other requirements such as an affidavit of good faith, which must be filed with the mortgage. The basic requirement for most mortgages, however, is that they must be acknowledged, witnessed, or proved. "Proving" a document involves having a witness sign the document, and then appear before a notary public, a judge, or other authorized officer and testify to the validity of the signature(s) thereon. "Acknowledging" an instrument (document) requires a signator to the document to appear before a notary and swear under oath that he or she signed the document.

Factor's Lien Laws. Most factors in this late-twentieth-century economy are in the business of making loans against inventory and accounts receivable. This is the basic function of what is known as "factoring" or the business of being a "factor." The Uniform Commercial Code enables a factor to obtain a lien on goods pledged as security without taking possession of the goods, which normally remain in the warehouse(s) of the factor's client(s). In addition to the goods covered by the factor's lien, proceeds from the sale of those goods are also included. A notice of lien is filed with the filing officer of the appropriate jurisdiction of the Uniform Commercial Code.

(As noted in discussing the categories of trust receipts, conditional sales contracts, and chattel mortgages, factor's lien laws are now covered in all states—plus the District of Columbia and the Virgin Islands—by the Uniform Commercial Code.)

The control section of the Uniform Commercial Code is UCC5-114. Credit managers may check the jurisdictions in which they do business to determine whether jurisdiction(s) of interest have adopted what is referred to as the broad or narrow (liberal or conservative) view of UCC5-114.

The narrow or conservative view puts the letter of credit in danger unless language is incorporated into the letter, which requires the beneficiary to complete performance of the underlying contract before payment is made. The danger in this procedure is of claims that cannot be substantiated and disputes pertaining to the underlying contract, which would delay the payment process and add to the total costs.

One school of thought contends that a creditor should not be able to attach a beneficiary's interest in a letter of credit because it is not property. As comforting as this might seem, potential beneficiaries of letters of credit should remember a landmark decision in New York, which stated that the innocent third party—a bank—should not be expected or required to experience a loss because of an attachment. Would the court have handed down the same ruling if no innocent parties were involved? Perhaps, perhaps not. No one will know for certain until such a case reaches the courts and the decision becomes a landmark for similar situations.

It is an area that credit people should approach with caution and concern until guidelines are more definitive.

Good credit managers are looking constantly for an "edge." They look for something they can use that will help them to minimize the possibility of financial loss to the company. The Uniform Commercial Code, when used frequently and properly, can be a major factor in the protection of receivables balances. The phrase "good credit management" implies that the individual who has the management responsibility is utilizing every tool at his or her command to make that expression a reality. Don't fail to provide your company with the same level of competence.

What is an example? Your company does not have the distribution network it needs in various sections of the company's home state and in surrounding states to do a proper job of getting customer exposure for its products, and finding financially strong companies whose existing product lines fit well with what your company manufactures is difficult. If your company has prescreened prospective distributors to the point where it is known that there is mutual interest, but the prospective distributors have cash-flow and some other financial problems, your company might look into the possibility of covering inventory with an Article 9 (Secured Transactions) filing for goods sold or consigned to a stated dollar figure. Your company would be able to do a monthly or quarterly inventory of its products, resupply the distributor's stock of merchandise, and know exactly how much has been sold and the dollar amount owed to your company.

What if the distributor's business increases to the point where the dollar figure used in your company's original filing is no longer adequate? You can amend the original filing to increase the dollar amount to a higher figure, one that your company and the distributor feel is high enough to cover future increases in the distributor's sales of your products. There is appropriate protection—properly prepared and filed UCC protection—every step of the way.

UCC Filings and Shipments of Goods

Allow me to reiterate an earlier warning: unless you have had experience in the preparation and perfecting of filings under the Uniform Commercial Code, have your attorney go over the completed forms before you forward the package to the appropriate filing authority. Do not assume that you have met the criteria for a perfected UCC filing in a specific state if you are not qualified to properly interpret the statutes (UCC and other) of that state. How bad can the penalty be for your company if the UCC filing is flawed? For openers, a creditor who secures his or her company's position after yours can challenge your imperfect filing. The bottom drops out of your company's position if the referee in bankruptcy rules that yours is not a perfect filing. From what should have been a perfect filing (all required information correctly stated and placed, and a provable Security interest), your company could suddenly find itself joining the unsecured creditors— the absolute depths of the pit as it relates to your chances for salvaging meaningful receivables dollars.

Services are available whose business it is to prepare UCC filings for clients who do not have the time or prefer to have their filings handled by specialists. Before you hire one of these service companies to do a first filing, get references—and check them! Have the company advise you in writing, on the company's letterhead and over the signature of a company officer, what the amount is of the performance bond carried by the company. Have the company attach a photocopy of the bonding agreement to the just-mentioned letter, which should also include a minimum of three current customer references. If the customer references indicate a high level of satisfaction with the service, and the bonding company verifies the agreement, you might want to give the service a try.

Unless the credit department is so understaffed that there are too many responsibilities for too few people, I do not accept the premise that a credit manager should not handle the UCC filings for his or her company or instruct someone in the department to handle the preparation and filing of these documents. If you are the instructor, be sure that your own level of competence is such that you can take a guideline volume, such as the NACM's Credit Manual Of Commercial Laws, go to the section or sections pertaining to the UCC, pick up the differences in the filing requirements between the 50 states, the District of Columbia, and the Virgin Islands, translate those differences onto the proper form(s) for the specific state in which your company intends to file, and pick up on any quirks or nuances that might escape the attention of one who does not understand how to read and/or interpret the guidelines for filing. It is a responsibility that might often involve significant dollar amounts, so see that the responsibility is approached with the respect it deserves.

Shipment of goods—and when title passes from seller to buyer—has always been a somewhat controversial area. There have been presumptions prior to the Uniform Commercial Code that attempted to deal with the question of when the parties (buyer and seller) intended title to the goods to pass. Nothing was ever clearly stated and stated in the context of law. That was corrected when the UCC became the law in all areas of our country. When goods are to be shipped from seller to buyer, what is the guideline for determining when title has been or will be passed? Possession passes to the buyer, and with it the risk of loss, when the goods are delivered to the carrier. Exception: When goods are to be shipped on a destination contract (F.O.B., San Francisco, CA, where goods are to be shipped to the buyer in San Francisco), possession and risk of loss, do not pass to the buyer until the freight carrier delivers the goods at their destination. Is this not particularly important? The transfer of title is particularly relevant when a tax liability must be determined or some public regulation imposes itself upon the shipment of goods. In these latter instances, Section 2-401 is the source for determining when a title passes. Title generally passes, however, when the seller delivers, ships, or mails documents of title for the goods. Title may also pass when a contract is signed, but goods that are shipped subsequent to the signing of a contract must be so identified and/or designated by the seller.

Erroneous Filing

It is pertinent to note that a filing, made in good faith in an improper place or not in all of the places required by Article 9, is considered to be effective as it pertains to any collateral for which the filing complies with the requirements of Article 9. Translation: it means that certain honest mistakes or errors of omission do not in themselves brand the filing "imperfect" or cause it to lose its position as a "perfected" filing. An erroneous filing, which may also be a "good faith" filing, is also considered effective as it relates to collateral covered by the financing statement against any person who has knowledge of the financing statement. In some states a filing made in the proper place continues to be effective even after the debtor's residence, place of business, location, and use of collateral has changed.

Consignments

The question of whether a transaction is a conditional sale, a contract of sale, or a consignment of goods has to be dealt with very carefully to ensure that one is not presented in such a manner as to risk being interpreted under the governing statutes as a category different than what was intended.

Merchandise is commonly sold on consignment, a method of selling merchandise that involves delivering it to an agent, a distributor, or a commission agent who represents the manufacturer. The manufacturer, who is known as the consignor, retains title to the merchandise until the consignee sells the merchandise, at which time title passes to the buyer. The consignee's obligation to the consignor is to represent the consignor company as prescribed in a contract between the two parties, businesses, or companies, and to pay the consignor company its share of the proceeds from the sale of merchandise or products.

There could be a problem, however, if the contract is not clearly written, that is, if the intent of the relationship between the two parties is not spelled out clearly. If the contract creates the impression that there is an intention to pass title to the merchandise to the consignee, it could tip what was meant to be a consignor-consignee relationship into the area of it being construed as a contract of conditional sale. When that is the situation, unless there is compliance with the statutory requirements for filing or recording the contract, the attempt to reserve title will be void.

There are elements that determine whether a contract covering goods will be interpreted as a consignment, as a sale, or as a conditional sale. The following are important in such a consideration and should be represented appropriately to determine which of these areas (consignment, sale, or conditional sale) is covered by a specific contract.

1. Is there an obligation to pay for the goods?
2. Is title tied directly to the proceeds of sale?
3. Does the contract include the right to fix the selling price of the goods?
4. Does the contract include the right to return the goods?
5. Can the consignor compel the consignee to return the goods?

These are all important elements in determining the type or the nature of a transaction. The presence or the absence of one or more of these elements is important in helping to determine the nature of the transaction, but the absence of one of the elements is not conclusive as to the intent of the people or companies who are party to the transaction. The courts will, in any legal test, judge the document and be guided in making a decision by the total concept of facts and intentions as they appear to be stated. A discernible intent is obviously crucial to a determination of whether the document pertains to a consignment, a sale, or a conditional sale. If the intent of the parties is unclear, any judicial interpretation of the agreement could have ramifications that are unfortunate and costly. Do the terms of the contract state that the receiver of goods for resale is obligated to pay for goods that are not sold? This is not a standard obligation in a contract covering goods that have been consigned for resale; such a stipulation will probably result in the court ruling that the contract covers a sale or a conditional sale and does not meet the criteria for an agreement covering the consignment of goods.

Whether a contract covers liability for the payment of unsold goods is important in the determination of the nature of the contract. Courts have held that a contract obviously violated the rules for the consignment of goods because it imposed upon the receiver the obligation to pay for goods that were not sold. A straight consignment would obligate the receiver to pay for goods sold, but would include some equitable arrangement for unsold goods (in original condition, cartons, etc.) to be returned without the obligation of payment. A contract of sale (or return) differs from a consignment contract in that the purchaser buys the goods and receives title to them, but, if they are not sold within a contract-stipulated period of time, the purchaser can return the goods without payment obligation.

Another provision that distinguishes a consignment contract from contracts of conditional sale is the consignor's right to require that the receiver return any goods that have not been sold. Other provisions of a consignment contract should make it clear that the consignor is entitled to a return of his or her company's goods on demand or when the contract is terminated. If, however, there is a provision in the contract whereby the buyer, at the termination of the contract, is to buy the unsold merchandise at the market price, the agreement may meet the criteria for a sale rather than a consignment.

It is obvious that all such agreements—consignments, contracts of sale, conditional sales agreements, etc.—should be drawn by an attorney who specializes in this area of the law. Of equal importance is the absolute obligation of all parties to such a contract or agreement to comply with its provisions and obligations. In a true consignment, the consignor does not reserve any security interest because title to the goods does not pass until the consignee sells some or all of it. There is, in this situation, no requirement that the consignor must comply with the provisions of UCC, but to protect the company's interest against other of the assignee's creditors, it is wise to follow the filing and notice requirements of the Code.

Conditional Sales Contracts

A conditional sales contract is defined under the Uniform Commercial Code as "any contract for the sale of goods under which possession is delivered to the buyer and the property in the goods is to vest in the buyer at a subsequent time upon the payment of part or all of the price; or any contract for the bailment (the delivery of property by one known as the bailor to another known as the bailee to be held in custody for certain purposes) or leasing of goods for which the bailee or lessee contracts to pay as compensation a sum substantially equivalent to the value of the goods, and by which it is agreed that the bailee or lessee is bound to become the owner of such goods upon full compliance with the terms of the contract."

The above quote has all the trappings of legal mumbo jumbo, but it really shouldn't be confusing. The first part of the statement describes a straightforward sale of goods: the seller delivers the goods to the buyer and property (or title) in the goods goes to the buyer upon payment of part or all of the price. The second half of the statement says that, if there is a contract that covers the transfer of property or goods, the seller promises that when there is full compliance with the provisions of the contract (payment, etc.), the buyer shall have title to the goods.

Conditional sales contracts are usually in writing and are filed or recorded by the seller to protect the seller's interests against the rights of third parties. Some jurisdictions recognize a contract as being valid against the claims of third parties—although it may not have been filed or recorded—if the third party or parties know that title to the goods remains with the seller. This can become a high-risk adventure. It is unwise not to give your company the benefits of a protective filing or recording. The time it takes to check with the appropriate filing or recording authority to determine if there are prior filings, and then to prepare and make a filing for your company, is a "common sense" business practice.

Protecting an interest in fixtures can be a problem as it relates to the law governing conditional sales. If fixtures have been attached to real property and they have taken on the character of that property, there is a question regarding the seller's right to retain title to them against purchasers or others who acquire an interest (or title) in the property to which the fixtures have been attached. Does the seller have no rights or only a slim chance of recovering these fixtures? The law has generally ruled that the seller is protected if the fixture(s) are attached to the property in such a way that they can be removed without material damage to the property. The seller's position is usually valid against the buyer, but it becomes more complex (may be disputed and/or contested) by subsequent purchasers of the property. Can fixtures be removed from the property without diminishing or impairing its usefulness? Most courts have upheld the seller's right to retain title.

Example: You are the manufacturer of seats—upholstered, chair-type seats—and you have sold 4600 of them to the owner and builder of a new center for the performing arts. This is to be a first class center, but because it was underfinanced and there were construction delays, artists and shows that had been booked (tickets printed, advertising dollars spent, etc.) had to be cancelled because the building was not ready. Meanwhile, your seats have been attached to the floor of the building; if you attempt to have them removed, what will it do to the integrity of the property? Removing the seats could do great damage to the floor of the building (concrete, carpeting, etc.) and would make it impossible for the owner(s) or a subsequent owner to rehabilitate the building as a concert hall and/or a center for the performing arts.

What does this do to your company's position as the owner of the 4600 seats? The seats (fixtures) are firmly attached to the floor of the performing arts center; if there are no seats, the building cannot function as an enter-tainment center. Whether your position as the seller will be upheld by the court might depend on whether the seats can be removed without material damage to the building, whether you are still dealing with the person or corporation to whom you sold the seats, or whether the building has been sold and you are dealing with a purchaser who is contesting your claim to the "fixtures."

I cannot tell you what the decision of the court would be. My best advice is that you would file and record your interest in those fixtures at the desig-nated place, but prior to the filing, you would have arranged for payment of one-third of the total purchase price when the seats were shipped, another one-third when the seats were delivered, and the final one-third when installation was completed. A UCC filing would be appropriate, because your company's interest in the fixtures would be ongoing through installation and until payment of the final one-third had been received. Attaching fixtures of such a high-dollar value to the type of real property that has been described in this example would be a high risk, unless there were substantial payments prior to installation of the seats (fixtures), or construction funding for the building had been guaranteed by a perfor-mance bond, a bond issue, underwritten by a city, county, or federal agency, or there was a special building fund set up and guaranteed by a group of civic-minded people of unquestioned resources and integrity. What I'm suggesting is that anything involving "fixtures" should be reviewed very carefully before there is acceptance of risk.

Sales

The sale of commercial goods between a manufacturer and distributor or a distributor and a customer is done much more frequently with a pur-chase order than with a written contract. The purchase order is usually the only physical evidence of a contract between the two parties—seller and purchaser—but acceptance of the purchase order by the distributor or manufacturer elevates the purchase order to the level of a contract offered and accepted.

To be an effective instrument, the purchase order should include the number of units to be purchased (one, a dozen, a gross, etc.), the unit price which would have been quoted verbally, in a memorandum, or in a letter, the delivery date(s), whether freight is to be paid by the seller or the pur-chaser, and any other data pertinent to the transaction. If the manufacturer or distributor (the seller) is unable to meet the delivery requirements or if the unit price is misquoted on the purchase order, the seller must promptly notify the buyer of the problem. There must be agreement between the parties or there is no purchase agreement.

Conditionally Sold Goods
(Goods Sold for Resale)

It is difficult for a seller to retain title to goods that are sold to a buyer who will then sell the goods (conditionally sold) to third parties. Sellers have had success, however, in selling to a buyer under a contract which requires the buyer to pay the seller from the proceeds of the resale of the goods. Where the conditional buyer is not required to provide the seller with an accounting of the proceeds, such transactions have been considered generally to be an absolute sale rather than a conditional one.

The majority of states have ruled that either party may assign his or her rights under a conditional sales contract. The exception would be if a contract between the parties specifically prohibits either party from taking such action on a unilateral basis. If there is any thought when the agreement is being drawn that one party or the other might want to exercise an option to assign rights under a conditional sales contract to a third party, a clause should be inserted that, with the permission of the other party, would allow such an assignment of contract rights.

There is always the possibility that goods will be lost or destroyed (a fire, earthquake, or some other form of natural disaster) and there will be no insurance to cover the loss. In the event of an uninsured loss, who must absorb it? Will it be the seller or the buyer? The rule in the majority of states has been that, unless the contract between the parties states otherwise, the risk of loss is the buyer's.

The "First to Protect" Rule

A good example of the rule of "first to protect" relates to priority tax liens. Any supplier or creditor who perfects a properly prepared Uniform Commercial Code interest in goods or merchandise will collect his or her company's money ahead of government agencies *if* the company's security interest was perfected before the government filed its tax lien. The person or company who perfects a security interest (UCC, Mechanic's Lien, Judgment Creditor or Purchaser) has priority over the federal tax lien. The exception to the statement regarding priority over the federal tax lien does not apply to monies owing to the Internal Revenue Service. This obligation (and monies owed to the Social Security Administration, etc.) have a priority that is not diminished by the filings of other creditors.

The basic reason for filing under the UCC is to protect your company's assets in the event of the customer's business failure. Your goal, although not always attainable, is to be the "first to protect" your company's accounts receivable, its consignment inventories, fixtures, farm products, or any other types of products that can be insulated against loss. You do not want

your company to be an unsecured creditor or a secured creditor whose company stands behind one or more other secured creditors for proceeds from the same type of collateral or goods. To be a secured creditor is a giant step above the pool of unsecured creditors, but whether being included among secured creditors is truly meaningful in a liquidation process depends largely on where your company's "secured position" is in relation to being first.

"First to protect" should be the goal of any business or company that finds itself in a situation where a UCC filing offers a level of security not attainable under any other form of protection. Has your customer company gone voluntarily into a Chapter 11 and, after numerous attempts to put together an acceptable continuation plan, the case is ultimately transferred to straight bankruptcy and liquidation? What your company will realize from the liquidation depends on the liquidation value of the assets, and the company's position in the line-up of secured creditors. In most bankruptcies, even with a UCC filing, there is no such thing as a recovery of 100 cents on the dollar. A liquidation proceeding is frequently a disappointing experience for creditors who filed under the UCC, only to see a final recovery total that may range from 10 to 50 cents on the dollar. What about the unsecured creditors? There is seldom more than 5 or 10 cents on the dollar—or they may receive nothing at all.

The credit manager who does not try to make an early UCC filing is not doing a complete job for his or her company. It is important to use every tool and every opportunity to protect the company's assets, regardless of whether the assets are accounts receivable, goods, fixtures, or another category of asset. Those who make few or no filings, or filings that are not timely, should realize that the UCC and "first to protect" must be used effectively and whenever applicable to achieve maximum results.

Filing Procedures

There was comment earlier in this chapter regarding the differences between the states in forms and filing procedures. It is imperative that an individual who handles the preparation and filing of UCC forms (and support documents) for a company whose customer base covers many states be aware at all times of the differences among states. Obtain the appropriate forms for each of the states in which you make a filing; double check to ensure that you know where the filing is to be made, and complete the forms exactly as the instructions state.

Typographical errors are not generally considered to be adequate cause to declare a recorded filing to be "imperfect," unless the error(s) changes the meaning of the filing or causes the meaning to be unclear. The stakes are much too high not to do a complete and thorough job of preparing UCC documents for filing and recording. A recorded filing should be in compliance with all of the requirements for filing and recording. There should be no sustainable reason to question the accuracy of the document(s), but if a question is raised by another creditor, the integrity of the document(s) should be affirmed promptly.

The Forms

To illustrate the differences among forms used by the various states, copies of several are used here. Any reference to specific time frames pertains only to California's UCC statutes.

- *Information Request (Figure 21-1):* A form sent to the filing officer of the state or intrastate jurisdiction requesting copies of any currently effective financing statements which name your customer as the debtor. (It is very important for you to know how many suppliers have an earlier or a prior claim). The form requests names and addresses of the secured parties, the file number, and date and hour of the filing.

- *Security Interest (not a form):* The secured party can protect his or her Security Interest by taking possession of the collateral or filing notice with the appropriate filing officer that he or she has a Security Interest in the property covered by the Security Agreement. This protection is secured by filing a Financing Statement.

- *Financing Statement (Figure 21-6):* A Security Interest is protected against the claims of third parties when the secured party takes possession of the collateral or files notice with the appropriate filing officer that he or she has a Security Interest in the property or goods covered by the Financing Statement. A Financing Statement might or might not state a maturity date. If the maturity date of the secured transaction is less than five years, the filing will remain effective for 60 days after the maturity date. If the filing has no maturity date, it is good for five years from the date and time of the filing.

- *Financing Statement Change (Figure 21-8):* The Financing Statement Change is a multipurpose form covering any one of the following: the continuation of the original Financing Statement between a debtor and secured party (file number and date); the release by secured party of the collateral covered by an earlier filing and described in another section of the form; the assignment of the secured party's rights to an assignee named in an earlier section of this form and including the original Financing Statement file number and a description on this form of the collateral; the termination of the security interest in a named Financing Statement, including the file number; the amendment to a Financing Statement bearing a stated file number and setting forth the terms of the amended Financing Statement.

How to Use the Forms

It is important to recognize and to understand the forms, but unless you know how to use them, there is no benefit to your company. The following should help.

The Information Request Form.   Your company receives an order from a firm whose credit rating and standing among the suppliers is not very good; it is certainly not good enough for your company to sell it on an unsecured basis at the dollar level stated in the order. The order could be very profitable and your company would like to have the business, but there is concern regarding the safety of the receivable.

The credit manager should promptly send a completed Information Request form to the filing officer of the state or intrastate jurisdiction in which the filing would have been made. When a report is returned by the filing officer and it lists one or more prior filings against the same collateral as yours, your company might have second thoughts regarding the order. There is no way that your position as a potential secured creditor can be improved. Is second, third, or fourth in the line of secured creditors the best you can do? That much distance between your company and a proper level of protection might not be acceptable. Almost any other approach to the sale would involve a higher level of risk. Regardless of the type of contract you might work out with the customer, prior UCC filings would benefit ahead of your company in any liquidation of the debtor firm.

Security Interest.   A Security Interest is created when there is an agreement—a Security Agreement—between the debtor and the secured party. The guideline statement in such an agreement is, "Debtor hereby creates a security interest in favor of the secured party in the follow party," which is then described in the agreement. When such an agreement has been properly filed and recorded, the secured party gains the additional protective advantage of having the right to take possession of personal property identified in the agreement in the event the debtor fails to pay.

Remember that there can be no Security Agreement if there is no Security Interest. The Security Interest must be indisputable to validate the filing of a Security Agreement.

Financing Statement.   The guideline for Financing Statements is met when the following information is included:

1. The financing statement is signed by the debtor and the secured party.

2. There is an address for the secured party at which place information may be obtained regarding the security interest.

3. The document includes the debtor's mailing address.

4. The items or the types of collateral are described in enough detail so they are recognizable.

5. The financing statement can be filed before a security agreement is made or there is a security interest. It is understood that the financing statement will not be valid against the claims of third parties if it develops that there is no security interest and no security agreement.

6. A copy of the security agreement may be used as a financing statement if it includes the above information, and if it has been signed by both parties.

7. In some circumstances, a financing statement is acceptable though it may carry only the signature of the secured party. If the financial statement otherwise conforms with the requirements for financing statements, it is an acceptable document.

If there is a valid security interest, the key to a perfected filing is the Financing Statement. When it is properly prepared, is first in line, and is filed to conform with the appropriate jurisdictional guidelines, it can be a fortress.

Financing Statement Change.   The earlier description of this form confirmed that it is the workhorse of the set—a multipurpose form that fills virtually every need not covered by the others. The multiple purposes and possibilities for using this form are expressed quite accurately in the name: Financing Statement Change.

What if your company no longer has a security interest in collateral covered by an earlier filing? Complete a copy of the Financing Statement Change, forward it to the filing and recording office where the Financing Statement was filed, and your company's interest in specific collateral will be cancelled. Remember to include a description of the filing (file number, etc.) that you want cancelled, or, if you are cancelling only a part of that filing, identify which part is to be cancelled and which is to be continued as covered in the original filing.

Has there been a change in the ownership of the debtor company and you want the original filing to be changed to reflect the assumption of presale debt responsibility by the new owner(s)? Prepare a Financing Statement Change and include in the body of the form all data relevant to the ownership change (names, addresses, etc.), a statement in detail regarding the type and dollar amount of collateral under the amended filing, and a copy of the agreement whereby the new owners assume payment responsibility for what is included in the amended filing. Send the Financing Statement Change, with a copy of the debt-assumption agreement, to the appropriate filing and recording authority. When a copy is returned with the date and time of recording stamped on it, your company should have the same quality of protection it had with the original filing. (It is assumed that you have not perpetuated an error that was present in the first filing. If there was no disqualifying error in the first filing, you should have a filing that is perfected against the claims of creditors who filed after your original filing.)

Duration of Filing

It is timely to mention again that a filed financing statement, which states a maturity date of five years or less, is effective until the maturity date, and for 60 days thereafter. Any other filed financing statement is effective for a period of five years from the date of filing. If the five years of protection is drawing to a close and the secured party's security interest will continue beyond that point, a continuation statement should be filed before the lapse of the financing statement.

(Please remember that there are differences in filing and other procedures among the various states. The Uniform Commercial Code is not, as discussed earlier, totally uniform throughout the 50 states, the Virgin Islands, and the District of Columbia. You must check the requirements in the state where your company will be making a UCC filing—or amending or cancelling a filing—before you can feel comfortable that what you have filed is a perfected filing. If you have a question regarding any phase of what is a complex Code, consult your attorney!)

Five Types of UCC Filings

The five classifications into which goods are placed for filing under the Uniform Commercial Code provide an umbrella that is all-inclusive. Whether it is a commercial product, a farm product (in an unmanufactured state), equipment, fixtures, or inventory, there is a category into which it will fit comfortably. There are variations in requirements, however, which must be observed when filings are to be made in the various categories.

Consumer Goods

This category covers goods that are bought and used for personal, family, or household purposes. Manufacturers and/or distributors of grocery items, hardware items, building supplies, clothing, household items, etc., are all candidates to make a UCC filing under this category. A manufacturer or distributor should have no problem establishing a security interest in products covered by this category, and making an appropriate filing.

Equipment

This category covers goods that have been purchased for use in a business, farm, profession, or government agency, subdivision, or nonprofit organization, and do not qualify in the definition of consumer goods, fixtures, or inventory farm products. Business machines (computers, printers, etc.), farm machinery (tractors, generators, etc.), and similar products are included in this category. Others belong in the other categories.

Farm Products

This category is comprised of crops, livestock, or supplies which are used or produced in farming operations. They may be any of the above in their unmanufactured state if possession is held by a debtor engaged in farming operations.

It is important to note that the Rights of a Buyer of Goods, who, in the ordinary course of business, takes possession and title to goods free of any security interest created by the seller, does not have that same protection when buying farm products from a person who is engaged in farming operations. In the case of a piece of farming equipment whose original purchase price does not exceed $2500, a buyer takes ownership and title free of any security interest; and that occurs whether the security interest is perfected or not.

When there is a security interest in crops, the financing statement must describe the crops (whether they are growing, planted, or about to be planted); it must also include a general description and location of the property on which they will be grown or are being grown, and include the name of the land owner of record. A perfected security interest may also be given for "new value." This enables the debtor to produce crops during the growth-production season if it is given not more than three months before the planted crops begin to grow. (If you are in farming operations, these remarks are generalities only. Be sure you understand the UCC statutes and the filing requirements in the state or the jurisdiction in which you intend to file, and be sure to adhere to those requirements.)

Inventory

The elements in this category include goods held for sale or lease or goods that are to be furnished under service contracts or raw materials, work in process, or materials or supplies used or consumed in the production of goods or in some other area of the business operation.

A security interest in inventory collateral may be formalized with a UCC filing that describes the items of inventory, the quantity and/or dollar amounts of inventory to be replenished on a revolving basis (as sold), and the anticipated duration (if known) of the security interest. It may of course be amended at any time to reflect a change in the type of level of the security interest.

Fixtures

These are goods that are attached to real property in such a way that they become a part of that to which they are attached.

The definition of Fixtures does not include building materials such as bricks, metal work, glass, lumber, etc. As mentioned earlier in this chapter, the statutes covering security interests in fixtures can become very difficult to sort out, depending upon the type of the fixture, to what it has been attached, and what permanent harm or damage might be done if it were to be removed. The UCC statutes of the various states determine whether a security interest that attaches to goods before they become fixtures takes priority over the claims of others, or whether a specific security interest stands in the sequence of priorities.

There are other categories of UCC filings that address different types of security interests. Some of these are as follows:

1. Purchasers of chattel paper (an indebtedness secured by chattels, title and possession of which may be in the debtor, but which could pass to the purchaser if the debtor defaults).
2. Purchasers of nonnegotiable instruments (cannot be transferred by endorsement or by endorsement and delivery).
3. Rights of a holder in due course of a negotiable instrument.
4. A holder in due course to whom a negotiable document of title has been negotiated.
5. The priority of certain liens.
6. The priorities among conflicting security interests in the same collateral. Looking at the Rules of Priority as they apply to:
   a. A perfected security interest in crops for new value, etc.
   b. A purchase money security interest in inventory collateral.
   c. A purchase money security interest in collateral other than inventory.
   d. The order of filing when two or more filings are perfected.
   e. The order of perfection unless both are perfected by filing.
   f. The order in which a security interest attaches between two or more security interests that are not perfected.

Mechanic's Lien Laws

Just as the Uniform Commercial Code is not uniform in what the 50 states, the District of Columbia, and the Virgin Islands require to have a perfected filing, so Mechanic's and Materialmen's Lien Laws vary from one state to another.

The majority of states accept the premise that any person who furnishes material or does work on a property can file a lien. An individual, a partnership, or a corporation can file a lien, and no regulation states that a person or entity must be a resident of the state in which they wish to file the lien. Labor or material is the basis for a Mechanic's or Materialmen's Lien. To qualify, both must have become part of the property or added value to it.

The filing of liens by subcontractors and materialmen is governed by two different concepts. A filing is made not because one concept or the other is the choice of the person or company filing, but because it is based on whether the state in which you are filing the lien follows the New York or Pennsylvania requirements to qualify a given situation as eligible for exercising lien rights. The New York concept sets the allowable lien limit at the amount owed by the owner to the general contractor. If the amount owed to the general contractor doesn't cover the subcontractor's claim, the burden of proving that the owner owes the greater amount rests with the subcontractor. Pennsylvania and the states that follow its concept do not limit the amount of the subcontractor's allowable lien to the amount owed by the owner to the general contractor. Pennsylvania and its followers give the subcontractor a direct lien regardless of whether there is proof that the owner has made payments to the general contractor.

The same warning applies here as with a UCC filing. Do not try to file a Mechanic's or Materialmen's Lien unless you are familiar with the procedural requirements in the jurisdiction where you are filing. Filing requirements do differ from state to state; the schedules of filing fees are not consistent; the duration of liens may vary; the requirements for what must be included in the lien notice itself are often complex. Until you have gone through the filing process enough times and in enough jurisdictions to know how and where to look for the guidelines, let your company's attorney guide you through the process. And as you listen to him or her, also become familiar with NACM's Credit Manual of Commercial Laws.

Why Should Your Company File?

The protection offered by the Uniform Commercial Code combines the two best reasons for making a UCC filing: one is self-interest and the other is self-protection. These benefits are worth the relatively small amount of time necessary to check for prior filings that cover the same goods or type of goods as your filing would cover. If there is one or more prior filings in the same type of goods—your company's type of goods—your company is then in a position to decide whether its level of protection would be reduced to an unacceptable point by these prior filings.

Remember also that a decision to proceed with a filing, although it might put your company second or third in the line of companies with allegedly perfected filings, is still much better than not filing at all. What if your company doesn't file? In a Chapter 11 filing, it automatically joins a floundering mass of unfortunate creditors—unsecured creditors—who stand little or no chance in a liquidation of assets of recovering anything more than a token sum.

File under the Uniform Commercial Code whenever it is a fit; you'll be surprised to learn how frequently it is the only sensible thing to do.

16

Secured Transactions (Division 9)

The importance to a credit management person of the UCC's Division 9 cannot be overstated. Every division deals with an important element of the commercial process, but Division 9 governs all transactions in which a security interest in personal property is created. It is the Division that covers, among other subjects, the sale of accounts receivable.

Very few of the people who will buy this book are engaged in farming operations. The majority of readers will be people who, either as employees or part of the owner/manager process, manage credit and collections for their company. They are the people who bear the responsibility for maintaining receivables accounts of good quality; they maintain accounts that have a rapid rate of turnover and a minimum per account investment of time and energy.

The Scope and Importance of Division 9

The umbrella of protection that is available under Division 9 is far more extensive than is understood by a large majority of credit managers. It is a complex statute—not easy to understand—and to understand thoroughly all areas of the Uniform Commercial Code and to feel comfortable working with the Code a person either must be an attorney or must have taken numerous courses and seminars on the UCC.

It must be said, however, that if your company is not utilizing the potential of filing under Division 9 of the UCC, the single most important opportunity to minimize your company's vulnerability to unsecured credit losses is being overlooked or disregarded. The benefits will, over a period of one or two years, make an impact that cannot do less than improve the company's annual-profits performance. When accounts are protected with a perfected filing under Division 9 of the Uniform Commercial Code, it represents a major step by your company toward total professionalism in the protection of a wide range of assets.

Division 9 is generally considered to be the most important Article of the Uniform Commercial Code because it deals with personal property and the protection of security interests in that property. It has introduced a broad range of new ideas and concepts to assist in accomplishing its primary objective of providing uniform rules to govern the security of chattels and to ensure that they meet the needs of modern commerce.

Under the UCC, Division 9 has been separated from real property mortgages to concentrate on covering the financing of chattels. Division 9 has been carefully drawn so that it does not interfere with certain state and other statutes that govern items such as the regulation of interest rates (usury) and various legislation covering small loans. It does not conflict with state and local statutes as those statutes may apply to the creating of liens in favor of materialmen, landlords, or other "preferred creditors." There has also been no attempt to impeach the integrity of existing federal legislation dealing with the recording of a security interest in collateral such as airplanes or ships, or state laws governing the licensing and operating of automobiles, trucks, or other such vehicles. Each category of existing laws has been accommodated in such a manner that it fits without change into the concepts of Division 9. The creation, attachment, and perfection of a security interest has, for the first time, been treated, by Division 9, in a way that is integrated, comprehensive, and uniform.

The fiber of Division 9 is that secured transactions represent a conveyance of a security interest in a single unit, package, or entity of personal property to secure the payment of a debt. There is in Division 9 a rejection of any distinction that might be based upon the form or designation of the device employed, whether it be a chattel mortgage, a conditional sales contract, a trust receipt, or another form of documentary security. In the context of the nature or use of the collateral, results may be different based upon whether the grounds are deemed to be functional.

For purposes of covering collateral with a Security Agreement, and the subsequent filing of a Financing Statement, the classifications of goods that may be covered by this Division are as follows:

Consumer Goods—bought for use primarily for personal, family, or household purposes.

Equipment—bought for use primarily in business (including farming or a profession), or a nonprofit organization government subdivision or agency; goods which are not included in the categories of inventory farm products, consumer goods, or fixtures.

Farm Products—crops or livestock used or produced in farming operations, or the same in their unmanufactured state if in the possession of a debtor engaged in farming operations.

Inventory—held for sale or lease; to be furnished under contracts; work in process or materials used in the business or in manufacturing, building, or creating a product.

Fixtures—so attached to a property as to become a part of it.

In the context of what has been outlined in the paragraphs directly preceding the listing of five categories of goods, collateral is divided into four classifications. The fifth classification in the above list—Fixtures—is not included in the four classifications of collateral that a business holds for sale, materials used, manufactured, or consumed.

The Division also addresses the important question of whether the secured party acquires title to the collateral or a lien. This question is addressed further in a subsection of Division 9 which gives a consignor or a lessor of goods the right and/or the authority to protect his or her security interest against the creditors of the consignee or lessee by filing a financing statement.

The scope of Division 9 is, as just noted, quite comprehensive as it relates to personal property (goods) and the protection of a security interest in that property. Very few credit managers would be so foolish as to sell a customer whose credit rating and payment record with other suppliers is so questionable that, without some security or secured position, there is reason to wonder whether the account will be paid before the customer files for protection under Chapter 11 of the Bankruptcy Act.

Under the conditions just described, there is no acceptable rationale for selling this customer a large order of goods on an open account. If the customer files a Chapter 11 before your company has been paid, and your company has not protected its security interest by filing a financing statement under Division 9, your company's unsecured claim will join the claims of other unsecured creditors in what becomes frequently a hopeless vigil, a vigil that seldom returns more than a few pennies on each dollar of receivables balance.

A person or a company with a security interest in a specific type or types of goods is best served if their UCC filing is the first to be recorded for that type of goods. To be first in the line of creditors while holding a perfected security interest in inventory, accounts receivable, or goods of one type or another is the best way to maximize the percentage of recovery on your receivables dollars. When a business is declared a bankrupt and the assets are sold for the benefit of creditors, a perfected UCC filing is far superior to an unsecured claim, regardless of where it stands in the priority order. A security interest that has been perfected via a properly prepared and filed financing statement under Division 9 of the Uniform Commercial Code is the best chance for any company to experience a meaningful recovery of its dollars.

What is covered or answered under the Code's Division 9? Many of the topics are complex in their explanations, discussions, procedures, and in the recitation of circumstances or sequences of events that must occur or prevail to obtain specific results. If you are unfamiliar with the Code and its provisions or if you have difficulty reducing "legalese" into the more conventional language used by those who do not have a mind oriented to legal form and terminology, call on your attorney. Your company's attorney should interpret for you the meaning and/or requirements of the Code's various Articles, sections, and subsections. Failure to understand the Code's provisions or guidelines is no defense against a challenge by a secured creditor whose filing is dated after yours, but who has challenged your claim and has proven to the bankruptcy court that yours is an imperfect filing.

The following are examples of the topics and the answers to be found in this Division:

- What is a security interest? How is it created?

- What is a financing statement? What is the procedure for filing it?

- What constitutes a perfected security interest? Do the requirements vary from one state or jurisdiction to another?

- What documents or instruments are required to perfect a security interest?

- Is there such a thing as "perfection without filing" to perfect a security interest?

- What are the differences among the various jurisdictions as they relate to the place of filing and the filing fees?

- Is it legally acceptable to file a financing statement before a security interest is made or has attached?

- What is the effective duration of a filing? Does this vary from one jurisdiction to another?

- If a filing lapses inadvertently, is their a period of protection subsequent to the lapse?

- What is the purpose and the form of a continuation statement? How is one prepared and filed?

- Is it possible to assign a security interest; if so, under what conditions?

- Are filing fees consistent from one jurisdiction to another?

- What are the guidelines for releasing collateral from a filing under this Division?

- How does one determine whether the laws in one state or jurisdiction prevail over those in another or others?

- What is the governing criteria for property that is brought into one state and is already subject to a security interest in another? Does the law of the jurisdiction where the property was located when the security interest attached determine the validity of the security interest in the latter state?

- When there are unperfected security interests versus the rights of third parties, what are the rights of the third parties?

- Do the purchasers of chattel paper and nonnegotiable instruments take their chances when they make these purchases? Do they have specific rights as purchasers?

- Is the priority of certain liens over others a valid concern or not? Should a lien holder be aware of his or her rights as they relate to the type of lien that is held?

- How does Division 9 deal with priorities among conflicting security interests in the same collateral? Are there specific guidelines for sorting out these priority situations?

- Are the guidelines dim, clear, or do they tend to merge when the issue is establishing priority when goods are attached to or become a part of other goods?

- Under what conditions might a priority be subject to subordination? Would it be voluntary, involuntary, or are both valid options under appropriate circumstances?

- Is it true that a secured party is not obligated on the contract of a debtor as that contract pertains to the claims of third parties?

Answers to the above questions and thousands of others can be found in the Uniform Commercial Code statutes for your state and for state(s) in which you might have a security interest in goods, chattels, collateral, etc. I again recommend to you the National Association of Credit Management's Credit Manual of Commercial Laws (printed each year) for a summation of the Divisions of the UCC for changes that have taken place within the preceding year, for decisions and interpretations of the various courts and jurisdictions that might have bearing on past and future filings within these jurisdictions, for the rights and responsibilities of secured creditors, for how, when, and where to file in the various jurisdictions, and for a wealth of other information pertaining to the UCC.

During the many years when I was active as a corporate credit manager, and subsequently during the years when I have consulted for various companies, the National Association of Credit Management's Credit Manual of Commercial Laws (printed every year) has been an invaluable source of information. It continues to do the same outstanding job and continues to be a reference source for me when I must verify the accuracy of a statement, a meaning, or a procedure against the Code itself or the statute of a specific state as interpreted by the Credit Manual of Commercial Laws. I have used it and continue to use it to jump-start my thinking regarding areas such as the sequence of certain procedures or the priorities that might attach in various situations, activities, or programs. It *is not* a substitute for your attorney if you are unclear as to a meaning, a procedure, or any facet of the UCC that might, if improperly handled, unfavorably impact the interest(s) of your company. It is, however, an indispensable tool for the credit person whose knowledge of the UCC is considerable or who has the experience and capacity to begin to learn from exposure to it.

How to Live Successfully with Division 9

To live successfully with something as complex as the UCC—specifically with Division 9—requires you, as the credit manager, focus your attention to determine how Division 9 can work best for your company. Analyze the type and quality of account that your company currently sells on open terms. Are there accounts that you should not have accepted, or should not have allowed to reach their current level of credit sales without securing your company's position—as with a UCC filing? Is your security interest in a few of the larger accounts almost a textbook situation for why the UCC is such an important protective device for credit managers everywhere? And what is your reaction when a firm, that has not been in business long enough to have established an industry payment pattern, wants to buy a large first-time order of your floor-covering products? If your company sells the account and the products are installed on the floor of an office building, on the floor of offices in a warehouse, or in some other area where the goods attach to a permanent structure, they may become a part of the building. If the customer cannot pay, will your company be put in the position of losing the proceeds from the sale? Will your company attempt to remove the tile from the floor (although this is not practical and it is impossible to salvage the product for resale), or will your company be in the position of having protected its security interest in these goods with a filed security agreement and financing statement?

Protecting the security interests of your company under the UCC statutes as adopted in the various states should be one of the first things to be considered when the credit department evaluates the credit worthiness of a customer. Is this customer's credit history satisfactory for the current level of activity? If there is growth and the customer looks to the company for higher levels of credit, will your company be able to accommodate the customer if you do not have the protection of a UCC filing to cover current and subsequent deliveries of goods to a specific dollar limit? Should the probability that a UCC filing might be required within the first year be formalized with a security interest filing at the outset of the relationship? How would you handle the possibility that because your company and the customer are new to each other, the customer might be reluctant to accept a UCC filing at this time? If there is reluctance, remind the customer that the filing not only protects your company's current security interest, but also will protect the customer's need for a higher level of credit as the security interest increases. The two companies, businesses, or individuals should formalize in advance of need the type of financing statement and security agreement that provides for higher dollar amounts of credit. This type of advance planning ensures that there will be no delay or question (assuming that payments and the rest of the relationship has gone well) when the time arrives for the preapproved increase in the level of open, but secured, credit.

It is reasonable to think that the title for this section should not be "How To Live Successfully With Division 9," but rather "How Can You Not Use Division 9 And Still Live Successfully?" If your company is not a believer in the selective use of UCC filings, it follows that too many key transactions whose security interest has not been protected have been assigned by default to a swirling grey mass of unsecured transactions; this is the absolute worst fate to which any company might subject one or more of its chattels, shipments of goods, etc.

There can be no justification for the failure of a business to avail itself of every reasonable and legitimate protective device in every reasonable and applicable situation. The Uniform Commercial Code has, after a lengthy and torturous process, been added to the statutes of all 50 states, the District of Columbia, and the Virgin Islands. People of good faith wrangled and fought for years to produce the type of Code that would ultimately gain the level of acceptance that it now has. Thousands of hours of work by many people went into shaping and reworking what eventually evolved into the Uniform Commercial Code. How much money has it saved for credit grantors—people with a security interest in goods and chattels—whose security interest in various types of collateral would have been unprotected had they not availed themselves of the Code's provisions? It is impossible to put a cap on the millions or perhaps the billions of dollars that have not been lost to parties whose security interests and financing statements were properly filed and recorded. The UCC is waiting to do its good job for any person or company whose security interest in goods, chattel, etc. falls within the broad scope of its protective coverage.

If your company's annual sales is in the tens of millions of dollars, or if it has sales of half a million dollars or less, there is a point at each company's levels of risk when someone in authority has to say, "We could use this piece of business, but unless there's some way to protect ourselves, the dollars are too high and the risk is too great." It does not have to end at that point with the order going to another company—one better prepared to deal with business situations that do not slip conveniently into one of the company's standard credit patterns. Hopefully someone will speak up and explain that the company's security interest in the goods that has been ordered is a fit for a filing under the UCC.

Transactions That Can Be Secured

The Uniform Commercial Code has impacted many areas of commerce, offering new, revised, or updated statutes to supercede previous controls over the various types of transactions. Before UCC became a part of the statutes of every state, the District of Columbia, and the Virgin Islands, many of the laws that regulated the various types of transactions (Law of Chattel Mortgages, Retail Installment Sales Laws, Uniform Conditional Sales Act, etc.) had not kept pace with the changes in commerce. The Uniform Commercial Code changed all of that, bringing to security interests and secured transactions a vast number of changes and improvements.

Examples of some of these changes and improvements relate to the handling of chattel mortgages and conditional bills of sale; the UCC put both of these instruments under its protective umbrella. In the years prior to the states adopting UCC, there had always been a distinction between chattel mortgages and conditional sales. Both now are classified as secured transactions under the provisions of Division 9. It is also pertinent to note that under the UCC statutes of some states, chattel mortgages are still used as a form of security agreement.

What are some of the other types of transactions that can be secured under UCC? The following is a partial listing:

Consignments—Consignors can protect their security interest against the claims of other creditors of the consignee. If the consignor is to have that protection, he or she must follow the filing and notice requirements of the UCC for the state in which the filing is to be made. In the context of dealing with consignments, the word "consignor" is a valid substitute for "secured party" on the financing statement.

Leases—If a lessor negotiates with a lessee a conventional lease of personal property, that conventional lease is protected although it may not be filed under the UCC. But if it is a lease that includes the ingredients of a security interest, it can and should be filed under Division 9 of the UCC. Good and strong advice is that to avoid the possibility of a problem regarding the status of a lease—the question of whether it is a true lease or a security interest—a filing under Division 9 is advisable to protect the lessor's interest.

Trust Receipts—They are no longer used exclusively in the importing of goods; their use in recent decades has been expanded to include domestic trade. Examples of both domestic and import use would include automobiles (foreign and domestic), appliances, or other large hard goods items from manufacturers. Example: A buyer places an order with the seller and the goods are shipped to the buyer. A lending agency (bank or other) pays for the goods and receives a document (bill of lading, etc.) that conveys title to the goods. Result? The seller has been paid and is out of the transaction; the buyer owes the bank or other financial institution, but is in possession of the goods; and the documents of title are in the possession of the bank or other financial institution. At some more distant point in the transaction, the buyer will issue a trust receipt to the bank or other financial institution. As trustee for the bank, this enables the buyer to retain possession of the goods.

This is an area that, prior to UCC, was covered by the Uniform Trust Receipts Act. Since the legislative bodies of the 50 states added the Uniform Commercial Code to their statutes, it has greatly facilitated the handling of these transactions.

Conditional Sales Contract—The UCC's definition of a conditional sales contract is "a contract for the sale of goods which directs that possession of the goods is delivered to the buyer." Possession of the goods does not include an immediate transfer of ownership; that goes to the buyer at a later date when payment has been made of whatever part of the purchase price is still owing.

Under the UCC, oral contracts are not valid and/or effective against the claims of third parties. If the seller's interests are to be protected against the rights of third parties, the contract must be in writing and filed and recorded by the seller.

Sales of Fixtures—This is often the most troublesome of problem areas because fixtures, when they are attached to real property, often take on the characteristics of that property. Conditional sellers have in some jurisdictions used a title retention contract to cover the sale of their fixtures but the removal of those fixtures because of nonpayment has been an unclear area for the seller.

There is a general rule that says a fixture does not lose its identity or characteristics as personal property if it has been attached to real property and can be removed from that property without major damage to the property. What constitutes "major damage" is often not easily resolved between a conditional seller and the buyer. Whether the fixture can or cannot be removed without damage to the property, the seller's title to the fixture(s) is generally held to be valid against the interest(s) of the buyer. The only ones who have a right to dispute claims of title by the seller are subsequent purchasers.

Question: What does the UCC say about a chattel that is attached to realty in such a way that removing it will not injure the value of the realty, but it will adversely affect the use of the building or the types of uses for which it might be used? In this example, the claim that title to the fixture continues to belong to the seller has not been upheld by the courts. So what is a secured party to do? The option is that he or she can remove collateral that has been attached as fixtures, but the person or company removing the fixture(s) must reimburse the owner of the property for any damage caused by removing it. What is the moral? Be *very* careful to whom you sell fixtures that will be attached to property and may take on the characteristics of that property!

Chattel Mortgages—One of the innovations of the UCC is that it offers no distinction between chattel mortgages and conditional sales. Under Division 9 of the UCC, both of these categories qualify as secured transactions. If it is a contract that is payable in installments, the governing statute is the state law governing retail installment sales. These installment transactions must comply with the provisions of the Retail Instrument Sales Law plus be in compliance with the applicable law governing chattel mortgages (Chapter 8 of the UCC covers Retail Installment Sales Laws).

The purpose of a chattel mortgage is to secure the repayment of a loan; a contract of sale is used when goods are purchased or sold. It is, however, not uncommon for the seller to take back a purchase money chattel mortgage from the buyer. It has the same status as a conditional bill of sale and whether the parties to the transaction describe it as a chattel mortgage or a conditional bill of sale is immaterial to the transaction itself. The more formal instrument is the chattel mortgage, but that does not diminish the quality or the legal strength of the conditional contract of sale.

The usual rules of contract assign themselves to a mortgage. There may be the requirement that it be signed, witnessed, or proved. Witnessed contracts require one or two persons to sign after watching the parties to the contract sign. A contract or instrument is "proved" when a witness signs the instrument, then goes before a notary public or other authorized officer and swears (takes an oath) to the validity of the signatures and the document.

Assignment of Accounts Receivable—Division 9 governs in that it sets the rules for all transactions in which a security interest in personal property is created. If most of your company's business is intrastate, it is imperative that you have a copy of the official UCC statute as it has been accepted by the state in which you are or will be doing business. It might also be helpful if you find a book written by an attorney or other person who specializes in the UCC, but can break down the legalese into a basic, understandable picture of what you must do to conform with the chapters, divisions, and subsections of the Code.

If your company's business or your business interests cross the borders of two or more states, it is not mandatory that you have a copy of the Code for each state in which you do business or in which you might make a UCC filing. What would be helpful, however, is a copy of NACM's Credit Manual of Commercial Laws. The filing information that it provides for each of the 50 states, the District of Columbia, and The Virgin Islands is sufficiently comprehensive so that a person who has some experience in the UCC process should find the guideline material helpful to the process of filing security agreements and financing statements.

Remember, however, that nothing in this publication or any other (Credit Manual of Commercial Laws, etc.) should be used as a substitute for the services of your personal or your company's attorney in any situation where the appropriate process, procedure, or answer to a question or a problem is not absolutely clear in your mind. There are too many variations and nuances between security interests, no security interest, perfected filings, imperfect filings, priority in the order of filing, the preparation of forms, and the filing procedure from one jurisdiction to another to make procedural and other statements that have no exceptions. Learn from each UCC experience, but do not make each a costly one. The stakes are too high for any person—even an experienced credit professional—to avoid seeking the advice of the company's legal counsel.

Chattel Financing

Division 9 is the part of the UCC that deals with the financing of chattels, a procedure which is described as "the financing of any type of personal property as distinguished from real property." The Code separates the financing of chattels from what was the predecessor of chattel financing, the real property mortgage.

In the context of Division 9, chattel financing pertains to the financing of inventory, consumer goods of all types, equipment, and farm products. It reiterates that there must be a valid security interest in goods for the seller or the person who has a security interest to make a filing under the UCC that will prevail against the claims of third parties. The term "floating lien" is often used to describe the protection of a security interest in inventory that is frequently enroute between the manufacturer and the debtor. A strong "floating lien" fulfills the need for something that will keep the security agreement responsive to the ongoing acquisition of inventory and the sale of other inventory.

When the chattel is not in the possession of the person who has a security interest, the Code permits a notice to be filed in lieu of the security interest itself. The procedure consists of the filing of a notice or a statement in which a general description of the collateral is given. The document also contains the signature(s) and address(es) of the secured party and the debtor. A notice of this type is used to facilitate the perfecting of a security interest where the collateral and the amount of the indebtedness change constantly.

It is appropriate to remember that the word "chattel" in a description of a type or category does not mean that all "chattels" are the same. A chattel, or chattels, may be linked with one or two other words to give the name or title an entirely different meaning.

Chattel financing? It pertains to the financing of inventory, consumer goods, equipment, and farm products.

Chattel paper is not to be confused with a chattel or chattels. It is just what the name describes; a specific paper or instrument in which the person who owns it or the person who has purchased it has security interest which has been or may be perfected under the UCC.

Chattel mortgage is another type of paper; an indebtedness, that has been secured by chattels, title, and possession of which may be in the debtor, but upon the debtor's default, may pass to the creditor. The default of a debtor may result in the creditor taking physical possession of the chattel; it may result in regaining title to the chattel, selling it to a third party, transferring the rights of title and possession to that buyer, and filing or recording the mortgage as required by the UCC, unless the mortgage property is in the possession of the mortgagee.

Why a Perfected Security Interest?

The Uniform Commercial Code provides for security interests to be perfected against third parties by either pledge or record notice. Only creditors who have obtained a lien without being aware of a security interest and before it has been perfected are in a position to prevail over the security interest. A perfected security interest and the priority of that secured interest can be the difference between a major recovery of inventory, receivables dollars, or other collateral versus a minimal return if there is a bankruptcy that culminates in liquidation. Priority, generally speaking, belongs to the one who perfects first, regardless of notice and regardless of the order of attachment.

Although the "first to perfect" rule is the basic criteria for determining the priority of filings, there is an exception to the order of priority when one of the claimants has a purchase money security interest to secure the purchase price of newly acquired goods and the other claimant claims the purchased collateral under an after-acquired property clause. If inventory is the collateral that is the object of dispute between the two claimants, the claimant who has the purchase money security claim has priority over the conflicting security interest. Is that it? No. The claimant has priority only if he or she perfects his or her claim before the debtor gains possession of the collateral (excluding a 10-day grace period for filing). The purchase money security claimant must also give notice of his or her claim to the individual, company, or agency that financed the inventory.

Acquiring Title to Collateral

An earlier examination of what is meant by the term "collateral" made it clear that there are several categories, some of which are listed here:

1. Goods
   - Consumer Goods
   - Equipment
   - Farm Products
   - Inventory
   - Fixtures

2. Chattel Paper/Nonnegotiable Instruments

3. Instruments and Documents

4. After-Acquired Property and Future Advances

Title to collateral that has been protected by a UCC filing must be transferred to the debtor upon written demand when there is no longer any outstanding obligation. When there is no longer a commitment to make advances, incur obligations, or otherwise retain a security interest, title to the goods must be relinquished by the secured party. When the debtor's relationship with the secured party meets these requirements, the debtor may make a written demand on the secured party for a statement in which the secured party acknowledges that he, she, or "the company" no longer has any security interest claim on goods that have been identified by a numbered, recorded financing statement.

If the secured party fails to furnish the debtor with the termination statement within a period of 10 days (in most jurisdictions), a penalty of $100 (more in some jurisdictions) is due the debtor plus damages for any loss that the debtor may have incurred because the secured party did not respond within the legally specified time frame.

When a third party signs the termination statement, it must be accompanied by a statement from the secured party of record stating that he or she has assigned the security interest to the third party—the person or entity whose name appears on the termination statement. This combination of releases enables the debtor to take title to the goods and sell or transfer them without further obligation to the secured party of record or the person or company to whom the security interest was assigned.

Consignor's and Consignee's Interests

The UCC states that in a true consignment, no security interest is reserved by the consignor. It also urges a consignor to protect his or her interest in goods against the claims of other creditors of the consignee by filing under the guidelines of the Code in the state or jurisdiction where filing is to be made.

Consignors usually include in their consignment contracts a clause that gives them the right to demand the return of all unsold goods. Contracts of conditional sale do not have such a clause for the simple reason that the "return of goods" clause is what separates contracts of conditional sale from consignment contracts. It is not necessary, however, for the "return of goods" clause to be included in a consignment contract when it is obvious from the terms of the contract that it is a consignment—one that gives the consignor the right, on demand or on termination of the contract, to demand return of the goods. The clear-cut nature of a consignment contract is jeopardized, however, when there is language that addresses specifically the right of a buyer at termination of the contract to purchase unsold goods at market value. This interjects an obvious challenge to the contention that the contract between the parties is a consignment contract and not a contract of conditional sale.

The role of the consignee is that of the consignor's agent and, as such, the consignee is required to manage the consignor's property with an acceptable degree of skill and care. Negligence on the part of the consignee is not acceptable and introduces the distinct possibility that the consignee will incur liability for damages. The rules of the relationship are spelled out in the consignment contract with consignees perhaps incurring the heavier obligation in that they must follow the consignor's instructions as they relate to the selling of goods consigned, or in dealing with any problem that might occur as a result of the consignee's failure to follow instructions in the agreement.

Consignees have an interest in the goods consigned to them that includes the cost of properly maintaining and caring for the goods plus any commissions earned by the consignee as the result of selling the goods. The consignee's interest in goods is defined under the UCC as a lien, a lien good only during that period of time when the goods are in the consignee's possession. The lien continues as long as there is an ongoing consignment contract between the parties, until goods are no longer in the consignee's possession, or until the consignee has been paid commissions due from the sale of the consignor's goods.

There is another possibility that is outside the parameters for a consignor-consignee relationship—just far enough outside to put the relationship in a category that is close, but different. The point has been made that a consignment contract puts the consignee under no obligation to pay for goods that have not been sold. These goods must be returned, but if it is a true consignment contract, no burden is placed upon the consignee to buy the unsold goods.

The "other possibility"—a contract of sale (or return)—offers an entirely different concept. In a contract of sale there is a seller and a purchaser rather than a consignor and a consignee. The purchaser buys the goods, acquires title to them, and has the option of returning them within a contract-specified time period. Contracts of sale will also deal with such specifics as how the value of returned goods will be determined, whether at purchase price or market value.

Whether a seller finds it more advantageous to have a consignor-consignee relationship rather than a contract of sale (or return) depends entirely on the philosophy and needs of the seller company versus the attitude and cash-flow position of the consignee and/or purchaser. A contract of sale might be written to offer the seller's standard sales terms, or perhaps special terms that are linked to a time frame compatible with giving the purchaser an opportunity to sell substantial percentage increments of the amount covered by the contract of sale before the contract's mandatory payment plan is activated. This gives the purchaser an opportunity to avoid taking money out of current cash flow to pay for goods that should sell rapidly enough to keep pace with the payment plan contained in the contract of sale. The seller's viewpoint? If the seller's cash position is tight, it would be preferable to generate cash from the sale as rapidly as possible. There are mutually acceptable ways to handle payment for goods.

Example: The contract of sale states that payment for goods covered by the contract will be paid in five increments of 20 percent each, the first

20 percent to be paid 60 days from shipping date of the goods. Payments two thru five (90 days, 120 days, 150 days, and 180 days) will be due at intervals of 30 days after the first payment due date. This payment arrangement doubles (60 days) the normal interval between shipping date and due date of the first payment. It gives the purchaser an important additional 30 days in which to generate income from the sales of goods before the first 20 percent payment is due.

When the interests of consignor and consignee slip inadvertently into the area of seller and purchaser, the language of the contract may not be clear enough to eliminate all doubt as to the intentions of the contracting parties. It is preferable to avoid unclear contractual waters because no one can safely say that a court's decision will unfailingly reflect the original intent—the true wishes—of the contracting parties. The court must reach its decision based upon the contract, the testimony, and any other evidence that may come before it. If one party fails to be truthful, an injustice could be done to one of the contracting parties.

The Rights of Creditors of a Consignee

In any analysis of the rights of a creditor of a consignee, the first priority is to establish the position of the consignor. If the transaction has as its foundation agreement a consignment contract, title to the goods remains at all times with the consignor.

The simple transfer of goods is not a valid consignment, nor does it give an alleged consignment contract legal credibility, unless proceeds from the sale of the consignor's goods is kept separate from the consignee's other monies. Proceeds from consignment sales are the property of the consignor and must be remitted to the consignor in a time and a manner consistent with the consignment contract. A consignment creditor must assure himself or herself that the contract meets the criteria for that category of transaction, and that the following conditions are present in the contract:

1. An obligation to pay for goods received (proceeds to be kept separate from consignee's other monies and remitted promptly [or as stated in the contract] to the consignor).

2. Title to proceeds of sale is reserved in the seller. (If there has been a UCC filing based upon the security interest of the consignor, proceeds from the sale of goods by the assignee will be protected from the claims of third-party creditors.)

3. Does the seller retain the right to set the selling price? (If the consignee has that right, it raises the question of whether what exists between the two parties is more a contract of sale than a consignment contract.)

4. Does the contract as written compel the consignee to, at the end of the contract period, return unsold goods or does it give the consignee the nonmandatory right to return those goods? (The difference between a contract-mandated return of unsold goods and the "right" to return those goods impacts the question of whether the consignor and consignee are really a seller and a purchaser.)

When all of the four conditions listed above have been identified in the contract, it has met that phase of the criteria for a consignment contract. If one or more of the conditions is absent from the agreement or contract, and if other loose ends tend to cast a shadow on the intent of the principals, it may so distort "intent" as to move it into the area of a contract of sale, or of no valid contract at all.

The overview of Secured Transactions Division 9 of the Uniform Commercial Code is that it applies to any transaction, regardless of its form, which is intended to create a security interest in personal property or fixtures, including goods, documents, instruments, general intangibles, chattel paper, and accounts or contract rights pertaining to any financing sale of accounts.

Division 9 does not apply to the following security interests:

1. To U.S. statutes that regulate the rights of parties who have a security interest or third parties who may be affected by transactions in specific types of property

2. To the lien of a landlord

3. To a lien given for services or material (except when there are priority rights

4. To an assignment of wages

5. To an equipment trust that covers railroad stock

6. To the transfer of accounts as part of a sale of the business out of which they arose

7. To a transfer of a contract to an assignee who is to perform the contract

8. To a transfer of an interest or claim on a policy of insurance

9. To a right represented by a judgment

10. To any right of set-off

11. To a transfer of a tort claim or bank account

12. To fixtures as they relate to the creation or transfer of an interest in a lien upon real estate, including a lease or rents resulting from that lease

Although Division 9 does not apply strictly to true leases of personal property, Division 9 suggests that a financing statement should be filed to eliminate any question regarding whether there was retention of a security interest by the lessor. Perfection of security interests under Division 9 is a primary form of protection that should not be disregarded as unnecessary or inappropriate for the best interests of your business or that of your company.

17

Creating the Security Interest

The preceding chapter has referred frequently to a "security interest" and the fact that a person, business, or company must have one in goods or in some other collateral before any steps can be taken to protect that interest under the Uniform Commercial Code. Under Division 9 of the Code, the guideline for creating a security interest or for determining if one exists is quite clear. There must be a security agreement—a legal document—between the secured party and the debtor. When it is combined with a financing statement, it becomes a package that is filed in the appropriate jurisdiction to perfect the security interest of the secured party.

The key phrase in a security agreement is, "Debtor hereby creates a security interest in favor of the secured party in the following property: (a description of the property is inserted here)." When the security agreement has been prepared and signed by both the secured party and the debtor, the secured party has taken a giant step toward protecting himself or herself and/or his or her company if the debtor should default.

How to Do It

A form for the security agreement must incorporate all of the necessary ingredients or it might be challenged successfully by a creditor who, although his or her filing was made at a later date, might succeed in having the earlier "perfected" filing changed to an imperfect filing. An imperfect filing is, as was mentioned in Chapter 2, a sudden awakening to the fact that there is no filing at all. What was thought to be a perfected filing has been downgraded through an imperfect filing to become an unsecured claim.

The following is an example of what must be included to have a comprehensive Security Agreement for Accounts Receivable:

1. Date of the agreement; names of the parties to the agreement; principal places of business of the "secured party" and the "debtor."

2. Creation of the Security Interest (Personal security interest in collateral is granted by the debtor and is assigned to secured party.)

3. Collateral (all of the debtor's current and future accounts receivable, all current and future personal property, and all proceeds from described collateral).

4. The Debtor's Obligations (to pay or turn over to the secured party all proceeds from sale of goods, etc., as agreed in the security agreement; to pay all indebtedness to the secured party if the debtor defaults under terms of the security agreement; to pay on demand all legal and other expenses incurred by the secured party to protect its interests or to exercise its rights and remedies under the security agreement; to pay secured party on demand any balance due to secured creditor when account debtors fail to pay in a manner that enables the debtor to satisfy its obligation to the secured party; collateral shall not be subjected by debtor to interests from third persons, or bring suit to enforce payment, without advance notice in writing and written consent from the secured party; debtor shall furnish to the secured party, at any time that it is required, writings, acts, and assurances as needed by the secured party to assure and enforce its interests, rights, and remedies as stated in the security agreement; proceeds and collateral of the security agreement are to be held separate from the debtor's other funds or property until they can be deposited or paid as specified in the security agreement).

5. A statement in which the debtor states the location of its principal place of business, addresses the types of accounts that are covered by the security agreement, and warrants that the account is not subject to prior or subsequent assignment, claim, lien, or security interest other than the one held by the secured party. Debtor also represents and warrants that the secured party's claim is not subject to any counter-claim, offset, defense, allowance, etc.

6. Debtor's Default (This security agreement for accounts receivable shall be in default if any of the following occurs: any misstatement or false statement that the debtor may make in connection with noncompliance or nonperformance of any of the debtor's obligations under the security agreement; death, insolvency, business failure, appointment of a receiver, or other similar acts that diminish the rights and protection of the secured party's interest.)

7. Rights and Remedies of Secured Party (Exclusive of default, the secured party or its agent may do the following: give written notice to the debtor requiring debtor to notify account debtors to remit payment(s) directly to the secured party, and also to take the proceeds of these accounts that may be in the debtor's possession; take whatever steps may be necessary to collect these accounts, reclaim collateral, and apply it to debtor's indebtedness to secured party under terms of the security agreement; make periodic calls and/or inspections of records at debtor's place of business as they relate to transactions or collateral between secured party and debtor; take the debtor's place as regards rights, interests, and remedies as they relate to account debtors who have goods covered by the security agreement; insert a short paragraph covering the rights of the secured party under the UCC in the event of the debtor's default and as those rights relate to the date of the security agreement.)

8. Rights and Remedies of a Debtor (A debtor is empowered to exercise whatever rights are necessary to function as the secured party's agent for all accounts until the secured party notifies the debtor that it will collect any and/or all accounts as set forth in the security agreement.)

9. Debtor's Additional Agreements and Affirmations (The debtor affirms that his or her only places of business are those listed in this agreement and that the secured party will be promptly notified if there is a change of location or the addition of a new location; the debtor is the lawful owner at the time the secured party's security interest attaches, has the legal right to transfer any interest in the subject goods, and will defend against the lawful claims and demands of all persons the collateral and its proceeds.)

10. Mutual Agreements (As used in this agreement, the terms "secured party" and "debtor" include the following: heirs, administrators, executors, successors, representatives, receivers, trustees, and assigns of those parties; it is agreed that the laws of (name of state) govern both parties to this agreement; the security agreement is all-inclusive and includes all writings that are pertinent and excludes from this agreement anything that is not in writing; any provisions of the security agreement that are not valid under the laws of the applicable jurisdiction shall be construed as not to exist and as such will not be enforceable against either party.)

The agreement is then dated and signed by both the debtor and the secured party.

The above outline for a Security Agreement for Accounts Receivable is a version of one that I first saw more than 15 years ago in the pages of an annual edition of Credit Manual of Commercial Laws. I subsequently had my company's attorney adapt that agreement to our specific requirements and found it to be a very comprehensive and effective document. Let me caution you, however, not to use the foregoing or any other such legal document unless you first run it by *your* company's attorney; also let him or her decide whether it is applicable in the situation for which you intend to use it. It may be a perfect fit or that call to your company's attorney might save you from making a costly mistake.

There are similar security agreements to cover equipment and other chattels. The format should be similar to the foregoing example for accounts receivable with the obvious difference of an itemized listing of collateral (year, type, and description of each piece of equipment). Other headings and subheadings are similar with perhaps more specifics in certain of the subheadings as they relate to the assembling, availability, disposal, liability, inspection, and general care of the collateral. There are waivers and other such variations from the Security Agreement for Accounts Receivable, but, as stated before, the format is essentially the same.

Why Your Company Should Do It

I believe it is obvious from what has been presented to this point in the chapters and subsections of Part 3 that no well-managed company, whether small or large, should fail to add the protection potential of the Uniform Commercial Code to its other good business practices. How could a credit manager or the person who has credit management authority justify his or her failure to use aggressively the major tool in the credit manager's arsenal of receivables defenses? How could that individual risk a major loss because the company's inventory, receivables balance, or other collateral had been left unprotected—left, in fact, with the status of an unsecured receivable?

There are rarely enough assets in a business failure (bankruptcy and liquidation) for all of the priority and/or the secured creditors to receive 100 cents on each dollar of their claim. The filing of a security agreement and a financing statement does not guarantee that there may not be some percentage of loss. The priority of those UCC filings has great bearing on which creditors receive the highest percentages of recovery.

After the matter of priority of the UCC filings, a major factor in any recovery is the liquidation value, not the book value, of the assets. Many liquidations are a disaster for the creditors in that the sale of assets may generate as little as 10 or 20 percent of book or purchase value. Whether a creditor has a perfected security interest that is high on the priority filing list will influence the percentage of recovery that his or her company receives. It is worth mentioning again that a properly constructed inventory agreement should preserve the integrity of that asset and keep it from being comingled with goods—yours and others that were sold to the debtor for resale.

It is unacceptable for a person who has been given the responsibility to protect the company's assets to fail to put Uniform Commercial Code filings at the top of the list of protections available to the company. Not every account is protected; filings are made selectively and generally on the criteria of risk exposure: dollars, quality of the company, impact on the creditor if the debtor's business failed, and whether a filing could be made that would put the creditor's company at the top, or high on the list, of protected security interests.

There is the additional dividend of the more favorable impression that a company creates among bankers, individual investors, and venture capitalists when they become aware that the applicant for financial support is an active believer in UCC filings. People who are asked to put personal, depositor, or investor funds at risk via credit lines, property mortgages, equipment financing, etc., invariably use the UCC to protect their security interest in goods, receivables, or chattels. It would be unthinkable for a banker or a venture capitalist to commit a sum of money to an existing company or a new venture without the maximum levels of protection; those levels of protection do not exist if there is no filing of the security interest and the financing statement. Credit grantors who maximize the safety of their company's dollars realize that there is more to ensuring the safety of those dollars than dealing with companies who have a good product, personable people, a good location, and goals that seem realistic and attainable.

The key questions beyond the positives that have just been stated can be narrowed to two: does the customer company have satisfactory standards for granting credit, and does the customer company protect itself and its suppliers via the use of UCC filings to shelter major exposure in key accounts? It is obvious that the accounts receivable or other goods or collateral of the creditor company is at a much higher level of risk if the debtor company is not diligently protecting its own receivables assets and the interests of its creditors with appropriate UCC filings.

There can be no question regarding the wisdom of creating a security interest—a formal security agreement—that may then be combined with a financing statement to complete the filing package. A creditor will seldom hear more reassuring words than, "Debtor hereby creates a security interest in favor of the secured party" in property that is subsequently described in sufficient detail to satisfy the requirements of a filing under the Code. The overwhelming majority of knowledgable credit administrators endorse enthusiastically the principal of "when in doubt create a security interest," then take that security interest to its logical conclusion—a perfected filing under the Uniform Commercial Code of the appropriate jurisdiction.

Recognizing the
Security Interest

It might be unfair to suggest that every security interest is easy to recognize and, because recognition should not be a problem, to suggest that protecting the security interests of your company or business in every transaction is something that cannot be done routinely. It might be unfair to make that suggestion, but actually it is not. Why shouldn't you or the person who handles credit matters for your company be sufficiently aware of what constitutes a "security interest" to recognize immediately when one has been created?

A manufacturer or distributor has a security interest in goods that he or she sells on credit terms to a customer; that customer is generally in the business of selling the goods to third parties who may or may not be the ultimate user or consumer. All goods in this context have monetary value and if the creditor (supplier) is selling to the debtor (customer) on credit terms, the creditor has a valid security interest in the goods until the debtor has paid for them. And is the debtor's responsibility to the creditor altered if, through no fault of the creditor, the debtor is unable to meet the terms of his or her arrangement with the creditor? Not at all. The debtor's responsibility to the creditor is unchanged by circumstances that have no bearing on the creditor's fulfillment of his or her obligation to the debtor.

It is imperative that a commercial creditor recognizes when and how a security interest is created and takes the appropriate steps to protect that interest within the time frame allotted by the UCC jurisdiction in which the filing should be made. Remember that recognition of the existence of a security interest is not an end in itself. If the creditor does not follow through to take the steps required by the Code to protect the security interest of his or her company's goods, the creditor may get high marks for "recognition," but could eventually be in deep trouble if the debtor fails or opts to seek the protection of the Bankruptcy Court.

You may recognize that your company has a valid security interest in certain accounts, but you do not choose to combine a formal security agreement with a financing statement to protect the receivables balance under the UCC. Is there any reasonable rationale for not making a filing? If "reasonable rationale" means evaluating receivables accounts for size, liquidity, and potential impact on your company if the business should fail, and from that analysis you select a small percentage of accounts that are not protected by UCC filings and promptly cover them with a filing, then the criteria of "reasonable rationale" has been served.

There are accounts that do not warrant the time and expense of a UCC filing, although the expenditure of time and money might be small. The balances are relatively small, the companies or businesses are well established, payments to the trade are strong, and there is nothing in the financial or marketing picture of these customers that is not well managed. This is the category of account whose modest to moderate balances pose no threat to the bad-debt reserve of your company. There is no justification for perfecting your security interest via a UCC filing when balances are non-threatening and the debtor companies in this category of accounts display none of the characteristics of problem accounts.

Never dismiss the possibility that your company might not benefit enormously—either short- or long-term—from a priority filing. As your professionalism increases and as the scope of your responsibilities matches your professional growth, you will not only "recognize the security interest," but you will also develop the ability to perceive from a compact group of facts which accounts should or should not be protected. Don't allow yourself to be caught in a situation that in retrospect should clearly have been translated into a protected position—where recognition of the security interest should have been translated into a perfected UCC filing. Recognition of the security interest should never become a lost opportunity for a creditor to protect his or her company's interests against the default of a debtor.

Do not join the ranks of those who have, from time to time, found themselves in the company of creditors who "failed to do so," which is a synonym for "welcome to the ranks of the unsecured creditors." There has been mention earlier of the sorry percentages of recovery that accrue to creditors who are in the category of the unsecured. Your company deserves better than that! Do not let it wander unprotected into a situation that represents for your company a meaningful number of dollars. Take "recognition" through the additional steps of the UCC to protect your company's interests against the insolvency of a debtor.

Nonpossessory Security Interest

The key criteria in almost everything that is covered in Division 9 of the Code is whether there is a Security Interest. Does the person who wants to make a filing have a security interest in the collateral? No security interest? Then there cannot be a security agreement, financing statement, and UCC filing.

What is the situation when the debtor has possession of the collateral? Does that automatically shunt the person or company whose claim to having a security interest in the collateral is fortified by the fact that the person or company with the security interest(?) has received no money—or some money? Has the right to be known officially as a "secured creditor" been lost for the seller? Not at all.

Any Secured Party with a Security Interest can protect that interest against the claims of third parties either by taking possession of the collateral or by filing an appropriate notice with the filing officer. The notice will state that he, she, or the company has a security interest in the collateral covered by the Security Agreement. The secured party nails down his or her interest in the collateral by filing a Financing Statement. If, however, a financing statement is not filed, the security agreement will remain valid, but the failure to file gives another secured creditor who files earlier the opportunity to gain a priority.

The term "nonpossessory" is applicable to almost every commercial transaction where there is the sale of goods by a manufacturer or distributor and the transfer of those goods to the warehouse, storeroom, or sales facility of the customer. It is the ongoing hope of every manufacturer or distributor that collecting for goods transferred to the customer for resale will not be a problem, and if the seller has made a protective filing under the UCC, there should be no question regarding the presence of "security interest" when the goods were shipped and the filing recorded.

A nonpossessory filing does not give the secured party the same level of security that he or she would have if the goods were still in possession, but that isn't commerce and it isn't the way business is conducted. Commerce is a meaningless word unless goods are shipped, received, and sold, and money is transmitted to the secured party to clear his or her interest in those goods. There never was a credit transaction that was totally without risk—that applies to individuals, companies, or businesses whose UCC filings are as strong as Gibraltar.

After-Acquired Property

This provision is one of the most beneficial for creditors in that it enables them to enter into a commercial or other relationship with a debtor before any collateral or goods has changed hands. Example: A banker might grant a revolving credit line of $500,000 to augment cash flow, taking as security the company's accounts receivable—current and future accounts. It is not necessary for the banker to name individual accounts in the bank's security agreement, nor is it necessary for the bank to periodically update the UCC filing with a list of current receivables accounts. One filing, one time should be adequate to perfect current and future receivables accounts.

Division 9 of the Code provides that all current and future obligations which are covered by a security agreement shall be secured by after-acquired collateral. This provision locks in the secured position of the person or business which has a security interest and ensures that collateral acquired after the security agreement has been filed shall become a part of the collateral.

How many manufacturers or distributors would take a chance with a new business or a borderline credit risk if the creditors could not protect current and future inventory or accounts receivable advances with the one filing? It would be impossible for a credit department to initiate changes and updates rapidly enough to keep up with the flow of goods if a security agreement covering current and future advances of product and/or collateral could not be filed the one time, thereby covering all changes in the mix of collateral.

The security agreement can cover current obligations and provide for the protection of collateral to be furnished in the future. The commitment to enter into a security agreement enables the debtor and secured party to have the agreement on file before there have been any advances or collateral and before anything of value has been exchanged. The maximum amount of protection with a minimum amount of follow-up is the goal of every person who files a security agreement under Division 9 of the Code; a proper filing will protect you and your company's interest in after-acquired property.

18

Perfecting Your Company's Security Interest

It is not enough to have a security interest in goods, instruments, documents, chattel paper, negotiable instruments, or goods in possession of a bailee; you must take the necessary steps to ensure that a perfected filing is on record in the appropriate jurisdiction. The Uniform Commercial Code is fifty-two separate pieces of legislation—basically the same from one major jurisdiction to another, but with nuances and more obvious differences that have only limited areas of forgiveness. If you do not make a textbook filing in one state, but your intentions are quite clear as to what is being covered, where the goods are located, etc., the state in which you are making the UCC filing may accept your financing statement as prepared. If a challenge to your filing occurs at some point down the road, your filing may very well withstand the challenge of a third party, but do you really want to put yourself and your company through the trauma of a filing that has not been prepared to conform with the requirements of the jurisdiction in which it was filed?

Remember that a security interest is perfected under the UCC when it has attached to one of the following and has attached in the manner and form prescribed by that jurisdiction. Examples follow:

1. *Chattel Paper or Negotiable Instruments*—Security interest in either is perfected by filing.
2. *Instruments (other than those that are a part of chattel paper)*—To have a perfected filing, the secured party must take possession of the instrument(s).

415

3. *Goods in Possession of Bailee*—A security interest is perfected when a document is issued in the secured party's name, by the bailee's receipt of notification, or by a filing that details the nature and quantity of the goods.
4. *Instruments or Negotiable Instruments*—A security interest is perfected for 21 days without filing if it is for some new item of value and is given under a written security agreement.
5. *A Twenty-One Day Security Interest*—Subject to the following conditions, the security interest is perfected without filing during this period of time:
   a. When the debtor has goods or documents representing goods that have been made available to him or her for eventual sale, exchange, or other commercial transfer.
   b. When an instrument is received by a debtor for eventual sale or exchange, presentation, collection, renewal, registration, or transfer.
   c. When the twenty-one-day period is at an end, perfection does not occur unless there has been compliance with applicable provisions of Division 9.

There will be reference in this chapter and in the chapter that follows to "accessions," which is almost the same as "accession." I say it is almost the same because *The American Heritage Dictionary* defines "accession" as "the attainment of rank and dignity; an increase by means of something added; an addition." The attainment of rank and dignity has no part in the use of "accessions" in conjunction with filings under the Uniform Commercial Code. NACM's Credit Manual of Commercial Laws defines "accessions" as "a security interest in goods before they are installed in or affixed to other goods," which meets the dictionary's second definition of "an increase by means of something added" or "an addition."

Many manufacturers and distributors of building products, components for the automobile, tractor, truck, and other industries have products that become a part of other goods. They are installed in or attached to other products, to various types of facilities, and often become an integral part of a piece of machinery, a piece of machinery that cannot function properly without what may be a small, but essential component. It is imperative that creditors who have a security interest in products or goods that by their nature become an essential part of other goods (products, collateral, etc.) should protect their interest with an appropriate filing.

Its Potential Dollar Importance

A security interest that is not protected with an early filing of the security agreement is an invitation to, one, the subsequent loss of collateral, goods, accounts receivable, or the proceeds from the sale of those goods; two, the loss of what might have been a preferred creditor position if a timely filing had been made when the security interest first attached; three, the probability that an unprotected security interest, which dramatically diminishes to the status of an unsecured debt any security interest in collateral, will, in the event of the debtor's business failure or Chapter 11 bankruptcy, put the creditor below all secured creditors in the event there is a liquidation of assets.

Unsecured creditors must wait until priority creditors have received the benefits from their secured positions before they receive a penny; if the liquidation of assets does not deliver a high percentage of return per dollar (assets are usually bid at a fraction of their book value in an auction or other liquidation of assets), the probability that unsecured creditors will share in the dividend is remote. If they do share? A reasonable return for unsecured creditors in the liquidation of a debtor's assets is 5 to 10 percent; a return of 15 or 20 percent on the dollar might be tantamount to a windfall.

It makes no sense that a person or a company which has available to it the protection of the Uniform Commercial Code would not use it frequently and wisely. The protective devices available to creditors are never enough to deflate *risk* to the point where it is not an omnipresent shadow, a shadow that threatens the potential profits of a company or business with the loss of receivables balances and goods via the route of a bad-debt write-off. A Uniform Commercial Code filing? It should be one of the first considerations—new or old—whose average balance or level of individual purchases involves a dollar total high enough that, in the event of loss, would unfavorably impact the company's performance figures.

It is not possible to say that a company should make UCC filings for a specific percentage of its accounts. Circumstances will determine the number of filings and the dollar minimum at which those filings should be made. It is a decision that should have as its basic criteria the realization that filings under the Uniform Commercial Code make good business sense. Protecting the security interest of your company in goods and collateral is uncomplicated, the fees are nominal, and a perfected security interest is the sensible way to protect the appropriate categories of the company's assets against loss.

The dollar importance of a perfected security interest under the UCC cannot be overemphasized. Over the decades an enormous amount of work has gone into the drafts—from the original to the most recent updates—that provide individuals and companies with a tool for protecting their security interest against the failure of a debtor to perform as agreed in the security agreement. The secured party's position is clear if there has been a proper filing. When there has been a proper filing, the chances for a recovery of collateral (of dollars from the sale of collateral) at a level approximating the value of collateral and/or proceeds covered by the filing should be very high.

It is important that whenever possible your company's UCC filings should be first in line or in a near-top position to ensure the highest level of protection and the maximum potential for a high percentage of return in the event the debtor is unable to fulfill the terms of the security agreement. An inquiry to the filing officer of the jurisdiction of interest will bring information regarding filings that may still be effective and would have priority over any you might make for your company. You will want to determine the number, the nature, and the probable value of these filings before your company releases goods or other collateral to your customer (the debtor).

If it is established that your filing will not be in a priority position (first or second in line) and your company has reservations or questions regarding the level of protection offered by a filing that is lower than first or second, it would be prudent to make a prefiling arrangement for a partial payment before goods or collateral are released to the debtor. You do not want to allow a debtor to exercise control over goods or collateral that is beyond what your investigation has indicated is a reasonable amount. Regardless of your decision regarding a dollar limit, a UCC filing to protect the security interest of your company is a must.

Perfecting by Record Notice

The term "record notice" refers to the filing by a secured party of a notice that he, she, or the company filing the notice has a security interest in goods or collateral that has been covered by the security agreement. When a financing statement has been filed, it protects the secured party against the claims of a third party and enables the secured party to take possession of the goods or collateral. It has been stated earlier in this section that filing a financing statement is not a mandatory step; a security agreement is not invalidated because no financing statement was filed. What the filing of a financing statement does, however, is enable another secured creditor to obtain a priority position over the company or person who does not file immediately after receiving information from the filing officer that there are no prior active filings. To delay beyond that time frame is to risk squandering the prime priority position of a first filing.

Chapter 5 of Part 3 lists the basic filing requirements for the various jurisdictions. The listed filing data should be viewed as a helpful, reasonably current indicator of the procedures for filing in each of the jurisdictions, but it should not be used as the current definitive guide. Before you attempt to file in any jurisdiction, check with the Central Filing Office of the state or district in which the filing is to be made. Changes continue to be made in procedural requirements (forms, fees, where to file for specific categories of collateral, etc.) from one year to another so it is imperative that you validate the filing guidelines included in this text before you use them. A minor change might have no bearing on whether your filing is or is not perfected, but you should not take that chance.

When the filing officer answers your inquiry regarding active filings for a particular business or company, it will include a list of currently applicable filings, or a statement which says that as of a specific time and date, there were no active filings. This opens the door for your company to make an immediate filing of its security interest before another company acquires a priority filing. If, however, the filing officer's report lists several active filings against an account about which you already have some reservations, then it is not a situation calculated to ease your mind.

Duration of a Filing

A Uniform Commercial Code Filing—generally a package that includes a Security Agreement and a Financing Statement—is effective for a period of five years from the hour and date it was recorded. Filings do not renew automatically at the end of the five-year period. They must be extended prior to the lapse of the original filing through the filing of a continuation statement or terminated at some point during the five years with the filing of a termination statement. The termination statement must be filed within 10 days of the termination of a security interest in the collateral covered by the original filing of the financing statement, or the financing statement as amended one or more times over the effective period (five years) of the filing.

When a debtor becomes insolvent while a perfected filing is in force, and during the time when insolvency proceedings have been initiated by or against the debtor, a perfected security interest continues to be perfected until the insolvency proceedings have ended and for a period of 60 days after that point. It should be understood that the foregoing applies to the five-year effective period of the filing only as it relates to the possible termination of the filing during the course of insolvency proceedings. It relieves the secured party of the probability of loss due to the lapse of the effective filing period, at a time when the secured party's attention might be focused upon problems created by the debtor's insolvency and the potential for loss by the secured party.

The lapse of a security interest can be a costly mistake. It can open the gates for a person or company which became a lien creditor or a purchaser before the lapse of the security interest to prevail against the claim of the person or company whose "secured position" has been invalidated by the lapse of the financing statement. Contracts such as real estate mortgages are of course not thrown into a pit filled with unsecured debts. These contracts remain effective as "fixture filings" until terms of the contract have been satisfied.

The Security Agreement as a Financing Statement

In any discussion of security agreements as a financing statement, the question invariably arises as to the reason for completing and filing a financing statement. If a security agreement is, according to its terms, an effective document between the parties to the agreement, why does it need to be supported by the crutch of a financing statement? If a security agreement is effective against purchasers of the collateral and against creditors of the debtor, why can't it stand alone? Why must it be supported or under what circumstances must it be supported by a financing statement?

Some of the reasons are hidden in the statutes of the various states, but a financing statement must be filed to perfect all security interests except the following:

- When a secured party assigns a perfected security interest
- When there is a security interest in collateral that is in possession of the secured party
- When a security interest in instruments or documents has been temporarily perfected without delivery or in proceeds for a 10-day period
- When a security interest that appears as a beneficial interest is being transferred during the trust proceedures of a decedent's estate
- When there is a purchase money security interest in consumer goods
- When a fixture filing is required to establish priority over conflicting interests in fixtures
- When there is an assignment for the benefit of the transferor's creditors, and subsequent transfers by the immediate assignee

Every security agreement is important, but the one that may have the most relevance for a majority of credit managers is the Security Agreement for Accounts Receivable. Because the accounts receivable of a company or business is the primary source of internally generated cash flow, it is imperative that all actions relating to the safety and control of this asset should be handled properly. Agreements—especially as they might favorably or unfavorably impact the safety of an asset such as accounts receivable—must be written properly and executed in the manner prescribed by the Uniform Commercial Code of the jurisdiction where the filing is to be made. (Allow me to caution that *all* agreements and contracts, whether they do or do not relate to UCC statutes and filings, should be written and executed in the manner prescribed by the statutes of the appropriate jurisdiction—local, state, or federal. Content is important. Be sure that the contracts you initiate and the contracts you sign promise, offer, or say what you think they say or what you intended for them to say.)

What follows is a general listing of the information that is relevant and necessary for a Security Agreement for Accounts Receivable to be an effective document. This information is not offered in lieu of a properly written Security Agreement for Accounts Receivable, nor is it intended to be a substitute for the professional services of your attorney. It is also possible to obtain approved forms from the state central filing offices of the UCC, from firms whose business it is to publish and sell legal forms that conform to the requirements of all jurisdictions, and from some stationery or office and legal supply firms.

1. *Creation of the Security Interest*—Debtor grants a personal security interest and assigns collateral, described in the following, to the Secured Party.

2. *Collateral*—Refers to Accounts Receivable existing currently and in the future, in which the debtor has an interest now, but hereafter will be in the control of the secured party, as will proceeds from the collateral.

3. *Obligations of the Debtor*—Includes payment of all proceeds from sale of collateral, all indebtedness applicable to collateral, and obligation upon default.

4. *Default of the Debtor*—Includes the numerous conditions that would constitute Default under the terms of the Security Agreement.

5. *The Secured Party's Rights and Remedies*—Lists the Rights and Remedies available to the Secured Party in situations other than the Default of the Debtor.

6. *The Debtor's Rights and Remedies*—Collecting and enforcing payment of accounts as agent for the Secured Party, termination of agent relationship upon default of Debtor, or Secured Party notifies Debtor that Accounts created under Security Agreement will be collected by the Secured Party.

7. *Additional Agreements and Affirmations*—These are Agreements and Affirmations made by the Debtor to the Secured Party regarding places of business, notification of Secured Party by Debtor in the event one or

more business locations are changed or a new location added, Debtor's right to transfer Secured Party's or other interest, restrictions regarding collateral and proceeds, and Debtor's pledge to defend collateral and its proceeds against persons making lawful demands or claims.

8. *Mutual Agreements*—"Second Party" and "Debtor" are terms which include all heirs, successors, executors, receivers, trustees, and assigns of the parties to the agreement. This section names the state whose laws are to govern all parties and sections of the agreement, confirms that the Security Agreement contains all of the amendments, supplements, assignments, documents, instruments, Accounts, and writings submitted by the Debtor to the Secured Party before the Security Agreement was signed. It also states that nothing is binding on either party that is not in the written Security Agreement.

9. The Agreement, which is quite lengthy, is then dated and is followed by signatures of the Secured Party and the Debtor.

When a Security Agreement is the complete legal document that the foregoing data indicates it should be, there should be no question regarding the quality of the document as a potential financing statement.

When a Secured Debt Is in Default

A secured party does not enter into an agreement with a debtor expecting that it will end in default. Security agreements are made with the feeling that there is something worthwhile in the agreement for both parties. If that isn't the situation, then at least one of the parties is making a mistake. A security agreement is a contract and unless the agreement meets the criteria for a contract, it cannot be a mutually beneficial document. And if your uneasy security agreement finds the debtor failing to make payments per your agreement? As the secured party, do you immediately notify the debtor that you are invoking a provision in the security agreement that allows you to take control of the collateral in the event of a default? You should. Before the defaulting debtor slides beyond the brink of a Chapter 11 filing, it is in your best interest to take possession of the collateral.

Division 9 of the UCC allows a secured party to proceed to reclaim collateral without taking court action if it can be done with a peaceful confrontation. If tension between the parties would not lend itself to a peaceful transfer of collateral, or such a transfer has been met with resistance, the secured party should invoke the weight of the court. If there is a provision in the security agreement that requires the debtor to gather the collateral and make it available to the secured party at a convenient time and place, a recalcitrant debtor runs the risk of having the court impose an order much more severe than would be the case if the debtor had made the collateral available as stated in the security agreement.

The secured party is free to dispose of the collateral in any manner he or she sees fit, remembering, however, that any such sale must be made or conducted in what the Code refers to as a "commercially reasonable manner." This means that the secured party must attempt to sell the collateral in a manner and under conditions that will bring a reasonable price. A debtor has rights in the collateral unless after default he or she signed a document renouncing those rights. It is especially important for the secured party to remember that when the debtor's interest in the collateral is 60 percent or more of the cash price or loan amount of the purchase money security interest in consumer goods, the secured party in possession of collateral has 90 days after taking possession in which to dispose of it under conditions stated by the Code. If it is not disposed of within that period of time, the debtor may recover the collateral under conversion. In other cases where consumer goods or other collateral is involved, the secured party in possession has the option of retaining collateral as an offset to part or all of the obligation. If the secured party selects the latter course, he or she must notify the debtor of that decision.

When collateral is consumer goods, the secured party is not required to give another notice. If collateral is not consumer goods, the secured party is required to notify any other secured creditor from whom he received written notice of a claim of his intentions to retain the collateral. There is a 21-day period during which those who were notified must reply. If there is no reply within the 21 days, the collateral may be retained by the secured party as a partial or full offset of the debtor's defaulted obligation.

Liquidating Collateral

When a debtor is in default to the secured party and the secured party has, under terms included in the security agreement, taken possession of the collateral, there is a decision to be made regarding its disposition. Although the decision is simplified if the debtor's interest in the collateral is very small, the secured party must still follow prescribed UCC procedures for protecting both his or her and the debtor's interests. If, however, the debtor has a 60 percent interest in the collateral, the rules of the game (as noted in preceding pages) offer a much more limited set of options for the secured party.

Collateral that a secured party takes from a debtor who has defaulted is subject to certain custodial guidelines:

- It must be stored properly (protected against weather, deterioration, fire, flood, acts of vandalism, or any other acts or conditions that would reduce or destroy its value.

- When there is a sale of collateral in which a debtor has a substantial interest (60 percent or more), the secured party must proceed with caution and with integrity.

- When a sale of debtor collateral is scheduled, it must be advertised in a manner appropriate to the type of collateral being offered and must be presented to reach the greatest number of potential buyers.

- The location must be readily accessible to prospective buyers, prices must be set (if a general sale) to get the highest level of return, minimums must be set (if an auction) to allow auctioneers to withdraw items that are bid at an unrealistically low figure.

If a sale of collateral in which the debtor has a substantial interest is conducted in a haphazard or slipshod manner, the person who has set up the sale may be setting himself or herself up for legal action from the debtor. Regardless of whether the debtor did or did not do everything within his or her power to avoid defaulting on the security agreement, the debtor's interests in the collateral are fully protected under the Uniform Commercial Code.

A mental memo should be entered into the memory bank of secured parties and debtors against the day when a debtor has to default on a security agreement. What will the memo say that might be so important and helpful at a time when disappointment is riding high? It will remind secured parties that "vengeance is not theirs," and it will remind debtors that "humility in the face of disaster" is not the worst way to confront the problem of defaulting on a security agreement.

A Debtor's "Fair Value" Interest

There is a close relationship among this subject, the taking possession of collateral by the secured party, and the liquidating of the collateral by the secured party. A debtor may default on a security agreement and the default may cause any number of problems for the secured party, but it does not mean that the debtor loses automatically whatever "fair value" interest he or she might have in the collateral.

If the debtor has very little interest in the collateral, but has accumulated certain monetary obligations to the secured party that are not offset by the debtor's interest in collateral (and the debtor is about to file for Chapter 11 bankruptcy relief), then the secured party has little or no obligation to the debtor other than any applicable guidelines in the UCC. Does the debtor have a "fair value" interest that may be a combination of goods and accounts receivable (from the sale of collateral under the security agreement), and is the debtor's "fair value" interest 60 percent or more of the collateral? No debtor's interests can be brushed aside, but this is a debtor who must be dealt with fairly and carefully.

"Fair value" might be classified as the book value of items of collateral or it might be the fair market value of items carried at a book value that does not reflect the current market value of these items. In some areas of commerce, goods may stay on the warehouse shelves for a matter of several months. During that period of time, there can be upward or downward fluctuations in the market or sale price of items, and the book value of these items may be understated as it relates to the marketplace value. The debtor? The debtor is entitled by law to have collateral priced at "fair value," especially when an attempt is being made to establish the amount of the deficiency between figures that were stated in the security agreement, less monies paid to the secured party prior to the debtor's default, plus any additional collateral shipped under the umbrella of the security agreement, plus monies owed but not remitted to the secured party from the sale of collateral, minus the amount of collateral that was still in the debtor's hands when the secured party took possession. In this and other situations, "fair value" is certainly relevant to a fair and amicable decision.

Having gone through some of the debit and credit steps that must be resolved before a secured party and a debtor can reduce the security agreement to an adjusted figure owed by the debtor, there are obvious reasons for a secured party to tread carefully when establishing fair value of collateral taken from a defaulting debtor. And if the secured party moves on to the final phase—the sale of collateral to generate cash and finalize the amount still owed by the debtor under the security agreement—there is reason for concern. It is generally true that a sale conducted under what is perceived to be "distress conditions" will generate only a small percentage of the book value of the collateral.

Why such a low return for good merchandise? Buyers know that under conditions of distress, they can down-price items to a fraction of their value. If the items are being offered under auction conditions, minimum bids can be set for major items, but when the need for cash is strong, a motivated seller (and that includes secured parties whose own cash flow may have been impacted because of a failed security agreement with a debtor) is often forced to settle for the best bids or negotiated prices that he or she can get. In a scenario of this type, the debtor's "fair value" interest might be undercut by the need to convert collateral into cash at a price buyers are willing to pay.

The UCC Filing—
Differences among the States

The following example illustrates the differences among some of the states when filing to protect a security interest in collateral. It focuses on the differences among five states which were selected because there are differences of varying significance in their requirements for filing to protect a security interest.

A manufacturer and distributor of floor-covering products (floor tile, cove base, carpet base, and commercial weight carpeting) decided 12 months ago to expand the company's marketplace exposure into four adjoining states. The vehicle for this expansion was a chain of floor-covering stores with commercial and retail floor covering outlets in each of the four states. Because the chain of stores—22 of them in various sections of the four states—had only been in business for three years, the floor coverings manufacturer had the company's attorney prepare an appropriate security agreement. The debtor signed the agreement, copies of the agreement were made, financing statements were prepared on forms obtained from the central filing offices of each of the four states, and the four packages were sent to the filing officers of the four jurisdictions (note that I did not say the four packages were sent to the filing officer at the central filing office of each state).

For purposes of this hypothetical case, the manufacturing plant and general offices of the floor covering manufacturer and distributor have been located in Southern California. The four states to which the manufacturer decided to expand are Hawaii, Nevada, Oregon, and Washington. The floor covering chain is about to open three stores in Arizona, so that state is being included in the comparison of location requirements for making the UCC filings for consumer goods.

It is understood that the manufacturer has complied with the requirements of each state as regards the approved forms for financing statements, security agreement, and filing fees. Where must the filing be made for the respective states? Note the variety of locations listed below:

Arizona
Consumer Goods—Local Filing (Office of County Recorder)

Hawaii
Consumer Goods—Central Filing (Registrar of Conveyances, Bureau of Conveyances, Honolulu, Hawaii) (for purchase money security interest, no filing except for fixtures)

Nevada
Consumer Goods—Local Filing (County Recorder)

Oregon

Consumer Goods—Central Filing (Secretary of State, Salem, Oregon) (for purchase money security interest, no filing except for fixtures)

Washington

Consumer Goods—Central Filing (The Department of Licensing, Olympia, Washington)

Five states in the same region, and among them enough variations in filing requirements to keep our manufacturer and distributor wide-eyed to the potential for errors. What if one or more errors are or were made? Perhaps they were or will be errors of good faith and at some future date they will be challenged and reviewed, but not determined to be imperfect—nonetheless, would you care to inadvertently put your company at risk because you "assumed" that the content of the security agreement and of the financing statement contained everything necessary to make it a perfected document? Or perhaps you put the company at risk by failing to know exactly where, how, and when to make your filings?

I sincerely hope we aren't talking about you.

19

The Financing Statement

The provisions of Division 9 apply to any transaction in which there is an intention to create and protect a security interest in personal property, goods, documents, instruments, general intangibles, accounts receivable, or chattel paper. It is without question the most important section of the Code as to the protection of security interests in collateral.

A security agreement provides protection as it applies to the terms of the agreement between the parties, and extends that protection against creditors and purchasers of the collateral. The debtor must, however, sign a financing statement which is then filed to perfect the security interest. The security agreement may also be used as a financing statement if it is signed by the debtor and includes all pertinent transaction data.

Filing Requirements for Financing Statements

It is the goal of people and companies who protect security interests with Uniform Commercial Code filings that the filing should be a perfected filing—one that cannot be successfully challenged or ruled to be imperfect because it did not follow the requirements of the jurisdiction in which it was made. It is a reasonable goal, this goal of perfected filings, despite the fact that credit executives in California make filings in Colorado, Oklahoma, Ohio, Vermont, or any of the other Code states. How can the California credit executive know that he or she has used the appropriate forms for the state in which he or she intends to file, or abided by the rules for preparing and filing a financing state in that jurisdiction? A copy of the Uniform

Commercial Code for your state should contain information regarding the filing requirements in the other 49 states plus the District of Columbia and the Virgin Islands. The definition of the terms that are used in the filing requirements of the various states is vital to an understanding of these requirements:

Consumer Goods—Purchased primarily for home, personal, or family uses

Equipment—Bought for use in a business or in a nonprofit or government department or agency; goods that are not within the categories of inventory, consumer goods, or farm products

Farm Products—Crops, livestock, or supplies used or produced in farming operations; goods which are products of crops in their unmanufactured state, etc.

Inventory—Goods held for sale or lease, furnished or to be furnished, etc.

Fixtures—Goods that are so much a part of real estate as to have become a part of them

To make a proper filing, you must contact the jurisdiction of the state in which you will be making a filing to get instructions and copies of the forms approved by that state. You will also need information regarding fees for filing, which should be forwarded at the time the appropriate forms and documents are mailed to the filing address. A letter or phone call to the central filing office of the state where a filing is to be made will enable the credit administrator to obtain the proper forms and instructions for completing and filing them.

No attempt has been made to make the following information a complete and definitive guideline; that would involve more pages than can be allotted to the one area. It would also involve delving into filing-related costs (filing fees in the various states, filing nonstandard forms, etc.) that are subject to frequent change. (Example: over the past several years, the cost of making a UCC filing in California with an approved form has gone from $3 to $5, a nonstandard form has gone from $4 to $6. The cost in New Jersey has gone from $10 for a financing statement to a UCC filing fee of $25. State agencies, anxious to increase revenues, have found UCC filings and other service fees a fertile area for these increases.)

The following compilation of the basic requirements in the 50 states, District of Columbia and the Virgin Islands is important as a source for obtaining the forms and instructions necessary to make a proper filing in the applicable jurisdiction of a state. Central address information for each of the jurisdictions has remained constant for some years, but the rest of the material is furnished as general information only and not as guideline material to be used in the preparation and forwarding of agreements and forms for filing under UCC. First contact Central Filing in each of the states to determine the currently applicable how, what and where of your proposed filing. Much of the attached information has, however, been constant for the past ten to fifteen years and because of this continuity remains helpful in acquainting the credit person with the major share of the filing locations for the various types of goods.

Before moving on to a listing of the states and the guideline criteria for filing in each of them, I am going to use the data for the state of **Alabama** (precedes this material) for an explanation of the relationship between the various topics and/or categories.

Central Filing—Indicates where the majority of filings are to be made. Any questions regarding procedures, forms, a copy of the UCC for Alabama, or any questions regarding a filing in any jurisdiction within the state should be addressed to the Secretary of State, UCC Division, etc.

Local Filing—When you have determined that the filing is to be a Local rather than a Central one, you must then file with the Judge of the Probate Court for the appropriate jurisdiction. It is important to the perfection of your filing that it conforms with the requirements of the state (Alabama) and is filed with the Judge of the Probate Court in the appropriate jurisdiction.

Central Filing—This repeat of the heading lists the various types of goods and collateral that are designated by the Code to be filed with the Secretary of State, UCC Division, etc. The guideline data for some of the categories of goods, equipment, and chattels is much more comprehensive than the one- or two-word descriptions that are included under the category "Central Filing." It is imperative that you are aware of the nuances that are a part of certain of these categories. Example: the category General Intangibles is listed under Central Filing, except if intangibles are from the sale of farm products by a farmer, in which case it becomes a local filing.

Local Filing—This repeat of the heading refers to the categories of goods, equipment, and collateral that are designated by the Code to be filed with the Judge of the Probate Court for the appropriate jurisdiction. Be aware of the filing requirements for the various categories of goods, etc., to ensure that a category which appears to require a central filing does not have attached to it a description of an alternate circumstance(s) that would require a local filing.

When the subject is something as important as the dollars that should receive the protective benefits of a UCC filing, be absolutely sure that the filing guideline you use is *currently applicable.* It is almost invariably the responsibility of the credit executive to ensure that filings in the various Code jurisdictions are in compliance with current requirements. When there is a breakdown in the way this responsibility is handled, the cost in dollars to the creditor company can be substantial.

Alabama

Central Filing—Secretary of State, UCC Division, State Office Building, Room 536, Montgomery, Alabama 36130 (205) 261-7200

Local Filing—Judge of Probate Court

Central Filing—Accessions (varies according to goods), Accounts Receivable, Chattel Paper, Documents, Equipment, General Intangibles, Inventory, Timber

Local Filing—Timber (to be cut), Consumer Goods, Farm Equipment, Accessions, Farm Products, Accounts from Sale of Farm Products, Fixtures (where land is located)

Instruments Do Not Require a Filing—Possession Perfects

Alaska

Central Filing—UCC Central File system, 3601 "C" Street, Suite 1132, Anchorage, Alaska 99503 (907) 762-2104

Local Filing—Recorder of Recording District

Central Filing—Accessions (various according to goods), Accounts Receivable, Chattel Paper, Documents, Equipment, General Intangibles, Inventory, Timber (uncut)

Local Filing—Accessions (varies according to goods), Consumer Goods, Farm Equipment, Farm Products, Fixtures, Minerals

Instruments—No Filing

Arizona

Central Filing—Secretary of State, 1700 W. Washington, 7th Floor, Phoenix, Arizona 85007 (602) 255-4285

Local Filing—County Recorder

Central Filing—Accessions, Accounts Receivable, Chattel Paper, Documents, Equipment, General Intangibles, Inventory, Timber

Local Filing—Accessions, Consumer Goods, Farm Equipment, Farm Products, Fixtures, Minerals, Timber (to be cut)

Instruments—No Filing

Arkansas

Central Filing—Secretary of State, State Capitol Bldg., Room 256, Little Rock, Arkansas 72201 Attn: UCC (501) 682-5078

Local Filing—Clerk of Circuit Court and Ex-officio Recorder

Central Filing—Accessions, Accounts Receivable, Chattel Paper, Documents, Equipment, General Intangibles, Inventory, Timber

Local Filing—Accessions, Consumer Goods, Farm Equipment, Farm Products, Fixtures, Minerals, Timber (to be cut)

Instruments—No Filing

California

Central Filing—Secretary of State, UCC Division, P.O. Box 1738, Sacramento, California 95808 (916) 445-8061

Local Filing—County Clerk and Recorder

Central Filing—Accessions, Accounts Receivable, Chattel Paper, Documents, Equipment, Farm Equipment, Farm Products, General Intangibles, Inventory, Timber

Local Filing—Accessions, Consumer Goods, Fixtures, Minerals, Timber (to be cut)

Instruments: No Filing

Colorado

Central Filing—Secretary of State, Uniform Commercial Code, 1560 Broadway, Suite 200, Denver, Colorado 80202 (303) 894-2000

Local Filing—County Clerk and Recorder

Central Filing—Accessions, Accounts Receivable, Chattel Paper, Documents, Equipment, Inventory, Timber

Local Filing—Accessions, Consumer Goods, Farm Equipment, Farm Products, Fixtures, Minerals, Timber (to be cut)

Instruments: No Filing

Connecticut

Central Filing—Secretary of State, UCC Division, 30 Trinity Street, P.O. Box 846, Hartford, Connecticut 06115 (203) 566-4020

Local Filing—Town Clerk

Central Filing—Accessions, Accounts Receivable, Chattel Paper, Consumer Goods, Documents, Equipment, Farm Equipment, Farm Products, General Intangibles, Inventory

Local Filing—Fixtures, Accounts Receivable (minerals, etc.)

Instruments—No Filing

Delaware

Central Filing—Department of State, Uniform Commercial Code, P.O. Box 793, Dover, Delaware 19901 (302) 736-4279

Local Filing—Recorder of Deeds

Central Filing—Accessions, Accounts Receivable, Chattel Paper, Consumer Goods, Contract Rights, Documents, Equipment, Farm Equipment, Farm Products, General Intangibles, Inventory

Local Filing—Fixture

Instruments—No Filing

District of Columbia

Central Filing—Recorder of Deeds, 6th and D Streets NW, Washington, D.C. 20001 (202) 727-5374

Local Filing—None

Central Filing—Accessions, Accounts Receivable, Chattel Paper, Consumer Goods, Contract Rights, Documents, Equipment, Inventory

No Special Provisions—Farm Equipment, Farm Products, Fixtures, General Intangibles, Minerals, Timber

Instruments: No Filing

Florida

Central Filing—Department of State, Bureau of Uniform Commercial Code, P.O. Box 5588, Tallahassee, Florida 32314 (904) 487-6055

Local Filing—Clerk of the Circuit Court

Central Filing—Accessions, Accounts Receivable, Chattel Paper, Consumer Goods, Documents, Equipment, General Intangibles, Inventory, Timber

Local Filing—Accessions, Farm Equipment, Farm Products, Fixtures, Minerals

Instruments—No Filing

Georgia

Central Filing—None

Local Filing—Clerk of the Superior Court in county of debtor's residence; if a nonresident or business, in county of debtor's principal place of business; if no principal place of business, county where property is used or kept

Central Filing—None

Local Filing—Accounts Receivable, Chattel Paper, Consumer Goods, Documents and Goods, Equipment, Fixtures, Inventory.

No Special Provisions—Accessions, Farm Equipment, Farm Products, General Intangibles

Instruments—No Filing

Hawaii

Central Filing—Registrar of Conveyances, Bureau of Conveyances, P.O. Box 2867, Honolulu, Hawaii 96803 (808) 548-3108

Local Filing—None

Central Filing—Accounts Receivable, Chattel Paper, Consumer Goods, Equipment, Inventory

No Special Provisions—Accessions, Farm Equipment, Farm Products, Fixtures, General Intangibles, Minerals, Timber

No Filing Necessary—Documents, Instruments

Idaho

Central Filing—Secretary of State, Statehouse, Room 205, Boise, Idaho 83720 (208) 334-2300

Local Filing—County Recorder

Central Filing—Accessions, Accounts Receivable, Chattel Paper, Consumer Goods, Documents, Equipment, Farm Equipment, Farm Products, General Intangibles, Inventory, Timber

Local Filing—Accessions, Fixtures, Minerals, Timber (to be cut)

Illinois

Central Filing—Secretary of State, UCC Division, Centennial Bldg., Springfield, Illinois 62756 (217) 782-7518

Local Filing—Recorder of Deeds

Central Filing—Accessions, Accounts Receivable, Chattel Paper, Documents, Equipment, Inventory, Timber

Local Filing—Consumer Goods, Accessions, Farm Equipment, Farm Products, Fixtures, Minerals, Timber (if to be cut)

Indiana

Central Filing—Secretary of State, 201 State House, Indianapolis, Indiana 46204 (317) 232-6531

Local Filing—County Recorder

Central Filing—Accessions, Accounts Receivable, Chattel Paper, Contract Rights, Documents, Equipment, General Intangibles, Inventory

Local Filing—Accessions, Consumer Goods, Farm Equipment, Farm Products, Fixtures

Instruments: No Filing

Iowa

Central Filing—UCC Division, Secretary of State, Hoover Building, Des Moines, Iowa 50319 (515) 281-3326

Local Filing—County Recorder

Central Filing—Accessions, Accounts Receivable, Chattel Paper, Consumer Goods, Documents, Equipment, Farm Equipment, Farm Products, General Intangibles, Inventory, Timber

Local Filing—Accessions, Fixtures, Minerals, Timber (if to be cut)

Kansas

Central Filing—Secretary of State, Attention: UCC, 2d Floor, Capitol Bldg., Topeka, Kansas 66612 (913) 296-2236

Local Filing—Register of Deeds

Central Filing—Accessions, Accounts Receivable, Chattel Paper, Documents, Equipment, Farm Equipment, Farm Products, Inventory, Timber

Local Filing—Accessions, Consumer Goods, Fixtures, Minerals, Timber (if to be cut)

Kentucky

Central Filing—Secretary of State, UCC Section, Capitol Building, Frankfort, Kentucky 40601-3493 (502) 564-3490

Local Filing—County Clerk

Central Filing—Accessions, Accounts Receivable, Chattel Paper, Documents, Equipment, Inventory

Local Filing—Accessions, Accounts Receivable, Chattel Paper, Documents, Consumer Goods, Equipment, Farm Equipment, Farm Products, Fixtures, Inventory

Instruments—No Filing
   (Kentucky provides for local *and* central filing in several of the categories listed above. Check the UCC for Kentucky to determine guidelines for which jurisdiction prevails in what situation or circumstance.)

Louisiana

(Louisiana has adopted other Articles of the UCC, but has not adopted Division 9.)

Maine

Central Filing—Secretary of State, UCC Bureau, State House Station 101, Augusta, Maine 04333 (207) 289-3676

Local Filing—Clerk of Municipality

Central Filing—Accessions, Accounts Receivable, Chattel Paper, Consumer Goods, Documents and Goods, Equipment, Farm Equipment, Farm Products, Inventory, Timber

Local Filing—Accessions, Fixtures, Minerals, Timber (to be cut)

Maryland

Central Filing—Department of Assessments and Taxation, 301 West Preston Street, Baltimore, Maryland 21201 (301) 974-3421

Local Filing—Clerk of Circuit Court

Central Filing—Accessions, Accounts Receivable, Chattel Paper, Documents, Equipment, General Intangibles, Inventory, Timber

Local Filing—Accessions, Consumer Goods, Farm Equipment, Farm Products, Fixtures, Minerals, Timber (to be cut)

Instruments—No Filing

Massachusetts

Central Filing—Office of the Secretary of State, Uniform Commercial Code Section, 1 Ashburton Place, Room 1711, Boston, Massachusetts 02108 (617) 727-2860

Local Filing—Clerk of the Town

Central Filing—Accessions, Accounts Receivable, Chattel Paper, Documents, Equipment, Inventory, Timber

Local Filing—Accessions, Accounts Receivable (see Code), Consumer Goods, Farm Equipment, Farm Products, Fixtures, Minerals, Timber (if to be cut)

Instruments—No Filing

Michigan

Central Filing—Department of State, UCC Unit, Lansing, Michigan 48918 (517) 322-1144

Local Filing—Register of Deeds

Central Filing—Accessions, Accounts Receivable, Chattel Paper, Documents, Equipment, Inventory, Timber

Local Filing—Accessions, Consumer Goods, Farm Equipment, Farm Products, Fixtures, Minerals, Timber (to be cut)

Instruments—No Filing

Minnesota

Central Filing—Secretary of State, UCC Division, 180 State Office Bldg., St. Paul, Minnesota 55155 (612) 296-2434

Local Filing—County Recorder

Central Filing—Accessions, Chattel Paper, Accounts Receivable, Documents, Equipment, General Intangibles, Inventory, Timber (except when to be cut)

Local Filing—Accessions (specific types), Consumer Goods, Farm Equipment, Fixtures, Minerals, Timber (to be cut)

Instruments—No Filing

Mississippi

Central Filing—Secretary of State, UCC Division, P.O. Box 136, Jackson, Mississippi 39205-0136 (601) 359-1350

Local Filing—Clerk of the Chancery Court

Central Filing—Accessions, Accounts Receivable, Chattel Paper, Documents, Equipment, Farm Products, General Intangibles, Inventory, Timber

Local Filing—Accessions, Consumer Goods, Farm Equipment, Fixtures, Minerals, Timber (if not cut)

Instruments—No Filing

Missouri

Central Filing—Secretary of State, Uniform Commercial Code, P.O. Box 1159, Jefferson City, Missouri 65102 (314) 751-4179

Local Filing—Recorder of Deeds

Central Filing—Accessions, Accounts Receivable, Chattel Paper, Documents, Equipment, General Intangibles, Inventory

Local Filing—Accessions, Consumer Goods, Farm Equipment, Farm Products, Fixtures

Instruments: No Filing

Montana

Central Filing—Secretary of State, UCC Bureau, State Capitol Room 225, Helena, Montana 59620 (406) 444-2034

Local Filing—County Clerk and Recorder

Central Filing—Accessions, Accounts Receivable, Chattel Paper, Documents, Equipment, Farm Equipment, Farm Products, General Intangibles, Inventory

Local Filing—Accessions, Consumer Goods, Fixtures,

Instruments—No Filing

Nebraska

Central Filing—Secretary of State, UCC Division, Lower Level, State Office Building, Lincoln, Nebraska 68509 (402) 471-2554

Local Filing—County Clerk

Central Filing—Accessions, Accounts Receivable, Chattel Paper, Documents and Goods, Equipment, General Intangibles, Inventory, Timber

Local Filing—Accessions, Consumer Goods, Farm Equipment, Farm Products, Fixtures, Minerals, Timber (to be cut)

Instruments: No Filing

Nevada

Central Filing—Secretary of State, UCC Division, Capitol Complex, Secretary of State's Office, Carson City, Nevada 89710 (702) 885-5298

Local Filing—County Recorder

Central Filing—Accessions, Accounts Receivable, Chattel Papers, Documents, Equipment, Farm Equipment, Farm Products, General Intangibles, Inventory, Timber

Local Filing—Consumer Goods, Fixtures, Minerals, Timber (to be cut)

Instruments—No Filing

New Hampshire

Central Filing—Secretary of State, UCC—Records, 71 South Fruit Street, Concord, New Hampshire 03301 (603) 271-3242

Local Filing—Clerk of the Town

Central Filing—Accessions, Documents, Equipment, Inventory, Timber, Chattel Paper, Accounts Receivable

Local Filing—Accessions, Consumer Goods, Farm Equipment, Farm Products, Fixtures, Minerals, Timber (to be cut)

Instruments—No Filing

New Jersey

Central Filing—Secretary of State, UCC Division, State House, Trenton, New Jersey 08625 (609) 984-1900

Local Filing—Register of Deeds and Mortgages (Counties of Camden, Essex, Hudson, Passaic and Union) or County Clerk

Central Filing—Accessions, Accounts Receivable, Chattel Paper, Documents, Equipment, General Intangibles, Inventory, Timber

Local Filing—Accessions, Consumer Goods, Farm Equipment, Farm Products, Fixtures, Minerals

Instruments—No Filing

New Mexico

Central Filing—Secretary of State, UCC Division, Legislative Executive Building, Santa Fe, New Mexico 87503 (505) 827-3600

Local Filing—County Clerk

Central Filing—Accessions, Accounts Receivable, Chattel Paper, Contract Rights, Documents, Equipment, General Intangibles, Inventory

Local Filing—Accessions, Chattel Paper, Consumer Goods, Contract Rights, Documents, Equipment, Inventory

Instruments—No Filing

New York

Central Filing—Department of State, UCC Division, 162 Washington Avenue, Albany, New York 12231 (518) 474-4763

Local Filing—Clerk of County (City Register in Bronx, Kings, Queens, and New York Counties)

Central Filing—Accessions, Accounts Receivable, Chattel Paper, Consumer Goods, Documents, Equipment, General Intangibles, Inventory, Timber

Local Filing—Accessions, Consumer Goods, Farm Equipment, Farm Products, Fixtures, Minerals, Timber (to be cut)

Instruments—No Filing

North Carolina

Central Filing—Secretary of State, UCC Division, Raleigh, North Carolina 27611 (919) 733-3924

Local Filing—Register of Deeds

Central Filing—Accessions, Chattel Paper, Accounts Receivable, Documents, Equipment, Farm Products, General Intangibles, Inventory, Timber

Local Filing—Accessions, Consumer Goods, Farm Equipment, Farm Products, Fixtures, Minerals, Timber (to be cut)

Instruments—No Filing

North Dakota

Central Filing—Secretary of State, Capitol Building, Bismark, North Dakota 58505 (701) 224-2900

Local Filing—Register of Deeds

Central Filing—Accessions, Accounts Receivable, Chattel Paper, Documents, Equipment, Inventory, Timber, General Intangibles

Local Filing—Accessions, Consumer Goods, Farm Equipment, Farm Products, Fixtures, Minerals, Timber (to be cut)

Instruments—No Filing

Ohio

Central Filing—Secretary of State, UCC Division, State Tower Office, Columbus, Ohio 43216 (614) 466-3126

Local Filing—County Recorder

Central Filing—Accessions, Accounts Receivable, Chattel Paper, Documents, Equipment, Inventory, Timber

Local Filing—Accessions, Consumer Goods, Farm Equipment, Farm Products, Fixtures, Minerals, Timber (to be cut)

Instruments—No Filing

Oklahoma

Central Division—County Clerk of Oklahoma County, 320 Robert S. Kerr, Oklahoma City, Oklahoma 73102 (405) 236-2727

Local Filing—County Clerk

Central Division—Accessions, Accounts Receivable, Chattel Paper, Documents, Equipment, Inventory, Timber

Local Division—Accessions, Consumer Goods, Farm Equipment, Farm Products, Fixtures, Minerals, Timber (to be cut)

Instruments—No Filing

Oregon

Central Filing—Secretary of State, UCC Division, Room 122, State Capitol, Salem, Oregon 97310 (503) 389-4139

Local Filing—County Clerk if a Recorder of Conveyances, otherwise County Recorder (Linn, Marion, and Umatilla counties)

Central Filing—Accessions, Accounts Receivable, Chattel Paper, Consumer Goods, Documents, Equipment, Farm Equipment, Farm Products, General Intangibles, Timber, Inventory

Local Filing—Fixtures, Minerals, Timber (to be cut)

Pennsylvania

Central Filing—Secretary of Commonwealth, UCC Division, Harrisburg, Pennsylvania 17120 (717) 787-7630

Local Filing—County Prothonotary

Central Filing—Accessions, Accounts Receivable, Chattel Paper, Documents, Equipment, General Intangibles, Inventory, Timber

Local Filing—Accessions, Consumer Goods, Farm Equipment, Farm Products, Fixtures, Minerals,

Instruments—No Filing

Rhode Island

Central Filing—Division of Uniform Commercial Code, Office of the Secretary of State, State House, Room 18, Providence, Rhode Island 02903 (401) 277-2357

Local Filing—Recorder of Deeds

Central Filing—Accessions, Accounts Receivable, Chattel Paper, Consumer Goods, Documents, Equipment, General Intangibles, Inventory, Timber

Local Filing—Accessions, Farm Equipment, Farm Products, Fixtures, Minerals, Timber (to be cut)

Instruments—No Filing

South Carolina

Central Filing—Secretary of State, UCC Section, P.O. Box 11350, Columbia, South Carolina 29211 (803) 734-2158

Local Filing—Register of Mesne Conveyances (Aiken, Charleston, Greenville, Lexington, Richland, Spartanburg, and Sumter Counties) or Clerk of Court

Central Filing—Accessions, Accounts Receivable, Chattel Paper, Documents, Equipment, Inventory, General Intangibles

Local Filing—Accessions, Consumer Goods, Farm Equipment, Farm Products, Fixtures

Instruments—No Filing

Inventory—Central Filing

South Dakota

Central Filing—Secretary of State, 500 East Capitol, Pierre, South Dakota 57501-5077 (605) 773-3537

Local Filing—Register of Deeds

Central Filing—Accessions, Accounts Receivable, Chattel Paper, Documents, Equipment, Farm Equipment, Farm Products, Inventory, Timber

Local Filing—Consumer Goods, Fixtures, Minerals

Instruments—No Filing

Tennessee

Central Filing—Secretary of State, Commercial Code Division, C1-100 Central Services Building, Nashville, Tennessee 37219 (615) 741-2286

Local Filing—County Register

Central Filing—Accessions, Accounts Receivable, Chattel Paper, Documents, Equipment, Inventory, General Intangibles

Local Filing—Accessions, Consumer Goods, Farm Equipment, Farm Products, Fixtures

Instruments—No Filing

Texas

Central Filing—Secretary of State, UCC Division, P.O. Box 13193, Austin, Texas 78711-3193 (512) 463-5701

Local Filing—County Clerk

Central Filing—Accessions, Accounts Receivable, Chattel Paper, Documents, Equipment, Farm Equipment, Farm Products, General Intangibles, Inventory, Timber

Local Filing—Accessions, Consumer Goods, Fixtures, Minerals, Timber (to be cut)

Instruments—No Filing

Utah

Central Filing—Division of Corporations and Commercial Code, UCC Division, P.O. Box 45801, Salt Lake City, Utah 84145-0801 (801) 530-6700

Local Filing—County Recorder

Central Filing—Accessions, Accounts Receivable, Chattel Paper, Consumer Goods, Documents and Goods, Equipment, Farm Equipment, Farm Products, General Intangibles, Inventory, Timber

Local Filing—Accessions, Fixtures, Minerals, Timber (to be cut)

Instruments—No Filing

Vermont

Central Filing—Secretary of State, UCC Division, Montpelier, Vermont 05602 (802) 828-2363

Local Filing—Town Clerk

Central Filing—Accessions, Accounts Receivable, Chattel Paper, Contract Rights, Documents, Equipment, General Intangibles, Inventory

Local Filing—Accessions, Consumer Goods, Farm Equipment, Farm Products, Fixtures

Instruments—No Filing

Virginia

Central Filing—UCC Division, State Corporation Commission, P.O. Box 1197, Richmond, Virginia 23209 (804) 786-3689

Local Filing—Clerk of the Court of the County or Corporation

Central Filing—Accessions, Accounts Receivable, Chattel Paper, Documents, Equipment, General Intangibles, Inventory, Timber

Local Filing—Accessions, Consumer Goods, Farm Equipment, Farm Products, Fixtures, Minerals, Timber (to be cut)

Instruments—No Filing

Washington

Central Filing—The Department of Licensing, UCC Division, P.O. Box 9660, Olympia, Washington 98504 (206) 753-2523

Local Filing—County Recording Officer

Central Filing—Accessions, Accounts Receivable, Chattel Paper, Consumer Goods, Documents, Equipment, Farm Equipment, Farm Products, Inventory, Timber

Local Filing—Fixtures, Minerals

Instruments—No Filing

West Virginia

Central Filing—Office of Secretary of State, Capitol Building, Charleston, West Virginia 25305 (304) 345-4000

Local Filing—County Clerk

Central Filing—Accessions, Accounts Receivable, Chattel Paper, Documents, Equipment, General Intangibles, Inventory, Timber

Local Filing—Accessions, Consumer Goods, Farm Equipment, Farm Products, Fixtures, Minerals, Timber (to be cut)

Instruments—No Filing

Wisconsin

Central Filing—Secretary of State, UCC Division, P.O. Box 7847, Madison, Wisconsin 53707 (608) 266-5801

Local Filing—Register of Deeds

Central Filing—Accessions, Accounts Receivable, Chattel Paper, Documents, Equipment, General Intangibles, Inventory, Timber

Local Filing—Accessions, Consumer Goods, Farm Equipment, Farm Products, Fixtures, Minerals, Timber (to be cut)

Instruments—No Filing

Wyoming

Central Filing—Secretary of State, State Capitol Cheyenne, Wyoming 82002 (307) 777-7378

Local Filing—County Clerk

Central Filing—Accessions, Accounts Receivable, Chattel Paper, Consumer Goods, Documents, Equipment, Farm Equipment, Farm Products, General Intangibles, Inventory

Local Filing—Accessions, Accounts Receivable, Chattel Paper, Consumer Goods, Documents, Equipment, Farm Equipment, Farm Products, Fixtures, Inventory

Instruments—No Filing

There is no uniformity among the states as it relates to where a central filing should be made. The office of the secretary of state is the department that is designated most frequently, but other divisions and departments have their representation. It would be a mistake not to verify the requirements of each state before there is an attempt to prepare a filing package that meets the test of correct forms and correct content. The previous recap of major filing requirements of the various states confirms that there is a high level of uniformity in the types of items that are processed at the central filing center of a state. Local filings are not that uniform. They run a gamut of filing locations including County Clerk, Register of Deeds, County Recording Officer, Clerk of the Court of the County, etc.

What Must Be Included

The format of financing statements varies from one state to another, but the information required by the various forms is substantially the same. Here are some examples of the differences in these requirements:

1. Some states require a financing statement signed by the debtor to perfect a security interest. (California is among those states that do not require the debtor's signature to perfect a security interest.)

2. The name of the debtor (or assignor) is an important part of the financing statement. (California also asks for trade styles to be included, although the failure to provide that information does not diminish the effectiveness of the financing statement.)

3. The debtor's Social Security number is not a requested piece of information on many financing statements. (A small number of states request the debtor's Social Security number to simplify the indexing of these documents.)

4. When collateral is crops, most financing statement forms require a complete description of the crops that are growing or are to be grown; also they require the location of the property. (A few states require a legal description of the property on which crops are growing or are to be grown. Not every state requires a description of the real estate.)

5. Timber or minerals can be substituted for a description of the type and location of crops growing or to be grown. (When goods become fixtures on real estate, financing statements may in some states be filed in the real estate records.)

The Financing Statement is comprehensive in the amount and the quality of information that is required. The Financing Statement that is used by states which have adopted the 1972 revision of the Code is lengthy. It asks for a substantial amount of information, is careful to get all information pertinent to the secured party/debtor relationship (collateral, products of the collateral, items of property, names of all debtors, names of all secured parties—a totally comprehensive document that leaves nothing to chance.)

The Financing Statement that is used by states which have not adopted the 1972 amendments to the UCC (Indiana, Kentucky, Louisiana, Missouri, New Mexico, South Carolina, Tennessee, and Vermont) is a much shorter form than the one described in the preceding paragraph. It asks for the following information in the listed chronological order:

Name and address of debtor (or assignor)

Name and address of secured party (or assignee)

1. This financing statement covers the following types (or items) of property: (Description)

2. (If collateral is crops) The crops just described are growing or are to be grown on: (Description of the real estate)

3. (If collateral is goods which are or are to become fixtures) The goods just described are affixed or are to be affixed to: (Description of real estate)

4. (If proceeds or products of collateral are claimed):

5. Proceed—Products of the collateral are also covered

Signature of Debtor (or Assignor)

Signature of Secured Party (or Assignee)

This form is less comprehensive than the one previously described, but it has all of the essential ingredients to ensure that a properly completed form will deliver a perfected UCC filing. It is also an example of the differences that persist in the approach of the respective states to the Uniform Commercial Code. It is unclear why the 1972 amendments have not been adopted by every state, but they have not been.

Filing Fees

Each state sets the schedule of fees that it will charge for UCC services, and from the UCC's earliest days there has been a broad variation in the fees charged for similar services by the various states. Perhaps more surprising than the variation in the schedules of fees is the fact that the fees charged in 1991 are frequently the same or only moderately higher than they were in 1976. Fifteen years of escalating prices in almost every other commercial and service area does not seem to have crossed over to send UCC fees on an upward spiral. The UCC structure of most states has managed to avoid rushing to put new layers of costs on those who do business within those states—and that is commendable.

In this book and the two that have preceded it—*Credit and Collections for Your Small Business* (Tab Books, McGraw-Hill, 1989) and *Hands-On Financial Controls for Your Small Business* (Liberty Hall Press, McGraw-Hill, 1991)—I have made it a goal to avoid topics or material that might be candidates for revision or become inapplicable within a relatively short period of time after publication date. People should not buy books with the expectation of a long-term benefit only to discover that much of the material is transitional in nature or is subject to major annual or biannual changes.

It is interesting, however, to compare a few of the fees charged by some states in 1976 versus their fees for the same services in 1991. There is an occasional state that has an upward surge in every category of fees, but the preponderance of states have held increases in these fees to a very modest percentage. A look at what has happened within and among a few of the states follows:

	Statements							
State	Termination		Financing		Assignment		Release	
Florida	$5.00	$5.00	$5.00	$ 5.25	$5.00	$ 5.00	$ 5.00	$ 5.00
Georgia	$1.00	?	$2.00	?	$2.00	?	$ 2.50	$ 5.00
Illinois	$4.00	$4.00	$4.00	$ 4.00	$4.00	$ 4.00	$ 4.00	$ 4.00
Massachusetts	$2.00	$5.00	$5.00	$10.00	$5.00	$10.00	$ 5.00	$10.00
Nebraska	$1.00	$6.00	$1.00	$ 6.00	$0.50	$ 6.00	$ 1.50	$ 6.00
New Jersey	$5.00	?	$5.00	?	$5.00	?	$10.00	$25.00
New York	$1.00	$1.50	?	?	?	?	$ 2.00	$ 7.00
Washington	none	none	$1.00	?	$1.00	?	$ 3.00	?

(1976 figures are to the left of each vertical line; 1991 figures are to the right of each vertical line.)

It is important that a check for the filing fee should accompany the security agreement and financing statement (this also applies to other filings such as the termination statement, the release of a security interest, the assignment of an account, etc.) to avoid a delay in getting them recorded. You want the releases, assignments, and terminations to be handled in a timely manner, but your primary concern—your overriding concern—is the prompt filing of the papers that protect your security interest. A delay of one or two days might never be a problem for your company, but there is always the chance that another filing—a filing of which you are not aware—will be made during the delay.

Amending the Financing Statement

Nothing in the Uniform Commercial Code statutes of the various states is so inflexible that it cannot be released, assigned, continued, or amended. There is a procedure to cover each of these actions and a service fee for each. There is also, in the situation of a release or a termination of a security interest, a specific number of days in which to file a release or a termination of the security interest. Just as the UCC encourages a person or company to protect its security interest, so it is equally protective of the debtor's rights when the secured party no longer has a security interest in the collateral that was the basis for the filing.

Financing statements may be filed before a security interest is made or a security interest attaches. If you are a farmer and have planted or are about to plant crops, there is nothing to which a security interest might attach until the crops have reached the point where they have value. The format of the financing statement will remain relatively consistent from one type of collateral to the next, but the descriptive material will not be consistent. The financing statement for some types of collateral includes, in addition to the standard data regarding the debtor and secured party, a brief description of the collateral and the address where it is stored. Descriptive material in the body of the financing statement is not consistent from crops to minerals to trees to consumer goods, etc. Filings are to be made in different jurisdictions depending upon the type of goods or collateral that is to be protected.

Amending a financial statement must be done carefully, but it is no more complex than filing a paper (an amendment) which has been signed by both the debtor and the secured party, in which the amendment addresses itself to the specific area of the financing statement that is to be amended. It must state clearly what change(s) is being made in the original filing, whether the change is for the duration of the filing or for a shorter period of time, and whether additional collateral is being added to the original financing statement. It will be necessary to describe the collateral that is being added, where it will be warehoused, etc. Both parties to the amendment should understand that the addition of new collateral does not give protection that is retroactive to the filing date of the financing statement. Protection for any new collateral is effective from the filing date of the amendment.

How Effective Is an Erroneous Filing?

The phrase "erroneous filing" has an implication of impending disaster comparable to the driver who goes up an off-ramp onto a freeway, facing an onrushing wall of automobiles. An erroneous filing, fortunately for the person who makes it, does not have the same implication of a crunching blow to the assets of the company that the wrong-way freeway driver faces.

The definition of an "erroneous filing" is one that is made in good faith, but in the wrong place or not in all of the places required in Division 9. It is still effective as it relates to goods or collateral covered by the filing as the filing complies with the rest of the requirements of the Code. The filing is also effective as it pertains to collateral covered by the financing statement against any person or persons who have knowledge of the contents of the financing statement.

The key phrase in determining whether an erroneous filing provides the protection for which it was intended is "good faith." Did the person or company that made the filing believe that it was being made in the proper manner and at the proper place? Did the person who made the error(s) realize at some point before the filing was made that an error(s) had been made? And if there was a realization prior to or after the filing that an error or errors had been made, what was done to amend the filing to correct the errors, including filing in the wrong jurisdiction?

Of great importance to the credibility of the "good faith" concept is an answer to the question of whether an effort was made to correct (amend) the filing before the debtor's deteriorating financial condition manifested itself in an inability to make payments as required under the security agreement. Was an effort made to correct the filing well in advance of the debtor's financial crisis? If not, then the credibility of "good faith" as the defense for an erroneous filing might not be sustainable. If, however, the filing error is not discovered until the debtor is in serious trouble, the erroneous filing might prevail if "good faith" can be proven as a continuing condition.

Release of Collateral— All or Part

When a security interest in collateral has been formalized with the filing of a financing statement under the appropriate UCC jurisdiction, that filing will generally have a life span of five years (a continuation statement may be filed to extend it another five). If at any time during that five-year period the debtor fully or partially satisfies the obligation that he, she, or a company has to the secured party, the secured party must, within one month of the full or partial termination of the security interest, file a termination statement. This must be done in every jurisdiction where a financing statement was filed and must state that the secured party no longer has an interest in the collateral covered by the financing statement. If it is a partial release of collateral, the collateral being released must be identified clearly and the financing statement must be identified by file number.

The debtor may also make a written demand on the secured party for the release of that portion of the collateral for which the debtor has satisfied his or her company's obligation under the terms of the financing statement. Within 10 days following receipt of the demand letter, the secured party must file a termination statement with each of the filing offices in which the financing statement is filed, and also forward a copy to the debtor. The termination statement must confirm that the secured party no longer claims a security interest in all or specific parts/areas of collateral covered by the earlier filing of a financing statement.

The failure of a secured party to file a termination statement or to forward a copy to the debtor within 10 days after receiving the debtor's demand for such notice incurs a liability to the debtor of $100, plus the more inhibiting potential for legal action resulting from any additional loss that might be attributable to the secured party's failure to make timely filings or to notify the debtor as required by the Code. No person or company should take the provisions of the Code lightly. It was created for the protection of persons and companies who have a security interest in collateral, but it is not without appropriate regard for the rights of the debtor.

As I have mentioned before, there is a fee for these filing services in every one of the UCC jurisdictions. The cost of these filings, as well as the responsibility for seeing that they are prepared and filed in accordance with the respective UCC jurisdictions, is the responsibility of the secured party. Although some portion of risk is shared by the debtor, the main burden of risk and of protecting against loss rests with the secured party. It is in his or her company's best interest to ensure that the Code's provisions for protection are used promptly and effectively.

Assignment of Security Interest

The reasons for assigning a security interest are numerous and the Uniform Commercial Code recognizes and provides for the assigning of those interests. Such an assignment might be a part of the original financing statement and should indicate the assigning to an assignee named in the financing statement of a security interest in the collateral. The security interest might also be assigned by a separate assignment at the time of the filing of the financing statement, at a later date, or as a copy on the face or on the reverse side of the financing statement.

The secured party may assign all or part of his or her rights in the collateral. Assignment can be made by filing a separate statement of assignment in which the secured party transfers all or part of his or her rights in the collateral to an assignee who is identified as such (name, address, description of the collateral being assigned, etc.) in the body of the assignment. It must also contain the name and address of the debtor, and the file number and date the financing statement was filed. When the filing officer has filed the assignment, it then becomes "an assignment of record" under the Code of the jurisdiction in which it was filed, and the assignee becomes the "secured party of record."

If a UCC filing is to continue to be effective, it is vital that procedures, such as an assignment of security interest, follow the guidelines prescribed for such changes. Whether it is the assignment of a security interest, the release of collateral to the debtor, the continuation of a security agreement, or any other of the procedures and options provided under the UCC, there is no room for carelessness in the handling of any security interest or financing statement.

The small company whose individual UCC filings cover collateral to a level of several hundred to one or two thousand dollars and the big company whose individual UCC filings cover collateral from hundreds of thousands of dollars to several million share the need for protection. In the context of the size of each company, the filings of hundreds to a few thousand dollars are as important to the welfare of the small company as the big company's hundreds of thousands or multimillion dollar filings are to it. Each must protect effectively a security interest in collateral that is vital to the welfare of the respective companies. The big company is, generally speaking, in no better position to lose millions of dollars than the little company is able to lose hundreds; the losses, should they occur, would be important money to both, and comparable in effect on the financial health of each.

Termination Statement

The termination statement is used by the various states to indicate when the secured party no longer has a security interest in the collateral. It can be filed at the end of the five-year-effective period of a financing statement or it can be filed at any time during those five years. The key phrase in determining when the financing statement is to be cancelled is "when the secured party no longer has a security interest in the collateral."

When the secured party forwards a termination statement to the filing officer, an extra copy of the statement should be sent with the original. The filing officer will write the pertinent filing information (file number, date and hour of the filing) on the copy and return it to the person or company that sent the material to be filed.

The file number for the financing statement should be forwarded with the termination statement and the filing fee to ensure that there is no delay in processing the filing. When requested to do so, the filing officer will issue a certificate upon which he or she will list prior filings (date and hour), any financing statement that names a specific debtor, and any statement of assignment pertaining to the filing (date and hour of filing each statement plus names and addresses of secured parties).

A Lien Creditor

A lien creditor is one who has the right to satisfy a debt from certain property owned by the debtor, against property in which the lien creditor has a valid security interest, or in property against which the creditor has a lien.

When a supplier and/or a person in the ordinary course of his or her business furnishes services or materials for use on or with goods that are subject to a security interest, a lien upon the goods in the possession of such person and given by statute or rule of law regarding these materials or services assumes a priority position over a perfected security interest, *unless* the lien is statutory and the statute expressly provides for some other procedure or remedy. It is a position of somewhat more than nominal risk, but one that leaves no question or doubt regarding the standing of the lien creditor.

Example: A plumbing contractor who furnishes fixtures, pipes, and labor to the general contractor or owner who is constructing or remodeling a building in which the plumbing contractor's services and materials are being used is allowed to protect himself or herself under the Mechanic's Lien Laws. This is a special statutory lien on buildings or other improvements—a lien which is not a part of the provisions of the Uniform Commercial Code—which is granted in favor of designated classes of people to ensure that they receive compensation for labor and materials which are related to the construction, repair, or renovation of subject buildings and improvements.

Floor covering contractors, electrical contractors, and dry wall contractors are all people who might not be willing to extend credit for a specific project if they were unable to obtain the type of protective lien that is available to them under Mechanic's Lien Laws.

20
Establishing Priority

The question of priority—who needs it, who has it, and who wants to establish it—is at the heart of every filing under the UCC. It is the key phrase that determines the pecking order in the event of a business failure or the filing of a petition in bankruptcy under Chapter 11 of the Bankruptcy Act. "Priority" is the word that determines which creditor shall be first, second, or third in the line of priority for whatever dividends might result from the liquidation of a failed business or company. It determines which secured creditor will recover collateral sold to the debtor or what collateral of a non-priority or unsecured creditor will find its way into the pockets of creditors who filed security agreements and financing statements in a timely manner.

Priority is especially important when the secured party's commitment of collateral is higher than the company or business would normally offer to a firm whose growth might be somewhat overextended for the available operating capital. A security agreement that offers priority protection for the secured party against third parties and against the misdeeds of a debtor is vitally important to both parties to the security agreement. If there is no agreement, the secured party would not be willing to supply goods (collateral) at the level requested; without that strong supplier support, the business would be unable to obtain the volume of merchandise and/or supplies needed to properly stock the shelves of the company's one or several distribution centers or retail outlets.

Manufacturers of hard goods for sale to consumers need component parts from many suppliers to be able to complete and ship their products. If the manufacturer's major supplier(s) is reluctant to supply the manufacturer at the required level because cash flow is too tight to properly service the growth cycle, then it is imperative that the party with the security interest (the supplier) instructs the company's attorney to draw up a security agreement that protects the supplier, but is not unresponsive to the rights of the customer (the debtor). If such a security agreement is offered to the

453

debtor company, it should be signed promptly by that company's authorized representative.

Priority determines who gets paid first in the event of a business failure, and, of those who do get paid, which of them gets the most (or an amount closest to 100 percent of the total covered by the UCC filing) from whatever assets may be available to creditors who secured their accounts. Creditors who are not locked into a priority position—all the way down the payment line to an unsecured position—are not going to be happy when confronted with priority filings that greatly diminish the assets pool available for distribution among their group.

Are you concerned that some of your less diligent peers tend to scowl and mumble when they see you? Frankly, Scarlet, you don't give a damn! You made the right and the diligent move for your company when you checked with the filing officer of the state in which you intended to file, and determined from the filing officer's report that your filing would be first, second, or third in the filing order, which assured your company of a top or near-top position on the list of priority creditors in the event that the debtor became unable to meet the terms and conditions of the security agreement.

It is in your best interest and the best interest of your company that you maintain a good working relationship with peer credit professionals. What is not in the best interest of you or your company is concern regarding acts or actions by peer credit managers that do not reflect the type of diligent, competent professionalism that separates the winners from the losers. Are you and your company winners? Then don't apologize!

Who Has Priority?

Priority is established most frequently by an experienced credit administrator who knows the short- and long-term value of a perfected security interest filing. Such an administrator will avail himself or herself of every opportunity to use the Uniform Commercial Code when the involvement of collateral (goods, dollars, etc.) is a big enough number so that, if lost, it would be a meaningful amount. What are the specific priorities and who has them? The following is a list of priorities, when and how they attach, and the benefits to those who have the priority positions.

■ The priority of liens accrue when services and material are furnished by a person in the ordinary course of his or her business when those services and materials are subject to a security interest. Priority is given to a lien upon goods in the possession of such a person over a perfected security interest unless there are provisions in the statutes that mandate other procedures or actions.

- The question of who has priority among conflicting security interests in the same collateral is complex and should be determined by the company's attorney or by a credit administrator who has enough experience to properly interpret the appropriate section of the Code. The Code's many sections are applicable to different types of collateral (consignments, documents, proceeds, bank collections, accounts receivable, crops, etc.) and unless the person preparing a filing is thoroughly familiar with the Code, costly mistakes can be made.

- The priority order of those who have a security interest in fixtures (goods which have become attached or related to a piece of real estate in such a way that the interest is judged under the statutes of real estate law) is another complex area of the Code's Division 9. It states the conditions and circumstances under which goods are or can become fixtures, how it affects the jurisdiction where filings for fixtures must be made (office where the mortgage on a piece of real estate is filed or recorded), and conditions by which a mortgage may become a construction mortage when an improvement on land is secured. (Building materials are excluded from the context of this security interest. They are covered by Mechanic's Lien Laws (see brief synopsis on pages 554 and 555.)

- The priority when goods are attached to other goods can become a problem for manufacturers of components whose products become an internal, attached, and integral part of another part of the whole or a direct internal or external attachment to the end product. The Code states that a security interest in goods that exists before they are attached to or integrated into other goods has priority over the claims of all persons except for subsequent purchasers of the end product (see Section 9), creditors with a lien obtained by a judicial proceeding, or a prior perfected security interest in the whole. (There is much more to this and other sections than I am recapping in these paragraphs. Do not attempt to unravel these complex and often intertwined laws pertaining to priority, or any other phase of UCC, unless your academic training and business experience qualify you to interpret and understand the legal language in which these laws are wrapped. To misunderstand or to misinterpret and to proceed on the basis of such an error can be a costly experience for you and for your company.)

- The basic rule for a security interest that was perfected before goods were comingled or processed into other goods (a larger component or a product) is that the security interest remains effective after the goods have become a part of the product or other entity. An example is a product that becomes part of a more complex product and loses its own identity in the process. The financing statement should, in this instance, not only

cover the collateral, but also state the type or nature of the manufactured, processed, or assembled product into which it will be merged,
immersed, or attached.

- Does a person who has priority have the right to subordinate that right by
  agreement? The person or company does indeed. An example would be
  the request of a debtor's banker for a subordination agreement from the
  debtor's supplier which would enable the banker to restructure loan
  agreements and advance the debtor enough money to clear certain of the
  debtor's pressing obligations, including that of the supplier being asked
  to subordinate. The supplier might agree to subordinate if the debtor and
  banker agree in writing that the bank will pay the supplier a stated amount
  from the loan proceeds before or as the proceeds are released to the
  debtor. Why this route? The supplier cannot lose the advantage of a priority filing, the waiver will enable the bank to have the priority filing it
  requires to secure its loan, and the debtor receives the loan proceeds less
  the amount of the payment made by the bank to the debtor's supplier.

How Is Priority Established?

Priority is established by the simple process of doing your UCC work in a
prompt and timely fashion. Decide first if any existing account or an
account representing a new order poses a risk to collateral that requires the
protection of a UCC filing. Discuss your decision that a filing is needed with
the customer. If there is no objection, and there should be none, proceed
to the next step in the process.

To establish whether others have filings that would be a priority over your
own, contact the filing officer in the appropriate filing jurisdiction (usually
the Central Filing area for a state). The filing officer will send a list of any
currently effective filings and from that list you can determine whether the
filing that is being contemplated will provide the level of protection
required. The number and dollar value of the filing that would be priority
to yours is important to whether you will want to restructure your security
agreement, opt for partial payment in advance of shipment, or in various
other ways reduce the elements of risk in a one-time transaction.

When the filing involves an account with whom you have had a satisfactory
relationship at an exposure level somewhat less than the figure you are being
asked to approve, you should not downgrade the worth or the necessity for a
UCC filing. Accounts that have been winners at one level may encounter
problems relating to growth that will only magnify their financial problems.
A business or company may be getting in over its head and going beyond its
capability to structure itself for a growth move to the next plateau. If that
occurs, or when it does occur, your company should have a perfected UCC
filing to give it the priority position and the security necessary to recover most

or all of its secured interest in the event of a business failure and liquidation or a bankruptcy filing under Chapter 11 of the Bankruptcy Act.

Do not squander the opportunity to have UCC protection, and do not commit an unrealistic amount of collateral (goods, etc.) to any one customer if you do not or your company does not have the protection of a priority perfected filing. To paraphrase American Express: "Don't let the collateral leave your warehouse without it!"

The Rights of Buyers of Goods

Buyers of goods have been well protected under Division 9 of the UCC. The guideline statute says that a buyer in the ordinary course of business (day to day business transactions) takes free and clear of a security interest the goods that he or she purchases from the seller. This guideline includes security interests that have been perfected and is not affected by whether the buyer did or did not know about the existence of a perfected security interest. The exception to taking this category of goods free of a perfected interest is when the goods are farm products bought from a person who operates a farm.

Consumers who buy goods (automobiles, appliances, floor coverings, clothing, furniture, etc.) for their own or family use take those goods from the seller free of any security interest if they are purchased without knowledge of the existing security interest. A business-wise consumer might assume that a manufacturer, distributor, bank, finance company, or factor is financing the merchant's inventory and that many of the suppliers must have a perfected security interest in some or all of the seller's stock. This could be true, but you and the seller's other customers are not expected to know whether it is or is not. Any assumption you may make is not knowledge of a specific protective filing, so you and most other customers should have no problem fitting into the category of "no knowledge of an existing security interest."

Consumers who buy in the marketplace for their own or family use have no problem with the title to purchases. When money (cash, credit card, check) changes hands at the cash register and a receipt is dropped into the bag with the merchandise, the consumer has taken possession "free of any security interest." Any other statutory consideration would be inconceivable. The following is a hypothetical situation based upon laws that *do not exist.* Imagine the chaos if secured creditors operated under an umbrella of law that somehow allowed them to reach beyond the retailer and maintain an "after the sale" security interest in a consumer's house full of new carpet. That knock on the consumer's door? It might not be a friend stopping by for small talk and a cup of coffee. It could be a representative of the floor-covering manufacturer/distributor with a bill for $3956.41—the value of the carpet installed recently in the consumer's home. If our UCC laws were not well written, a floor-covering manufacturer/distributor could hold the retailer's customer responsible for money owing as the result of the retailer's default on the terms of the security agreement. Fortunately, this is not true, and we avoid what would be an even more litigious society than the monster we have now.

Who Has Priority When Goods Are Commingled?

A perfected security interest in goods does not become ineffective because all or part of the goods becomes a part of a product or other entity. A security interest continues when goods are manufactured, processed, or commingled in such a manner that the identity of the goods in which there is a perfected interest becomes lost in the product or other entity. It is also important that the financing statement covering the original goods also covers the product into which the goods have been absorbed or integrated.

Has more than one security interest attached to the product? Each secured party is entitled to equal consideration in regards to the ratio of the original cost of the various filings represented versus the percentage each represents of the cost of the finished product or entity. Whenever goods are commingled or processed, there is ongoing protection for the respective goods of those suppliers who perfected their security interest when the financing statement identified the product. Loss of identity in the product does not invalidate a perfected filing.

Example: A manufacturer of electric motors is a major supplier for a company that manufactures washers and dryers. The manufacturer has a perfected security interest in its motors with a filed financing statement that covers the motors and describes the products in which the motors will be installed. These motors lose their identity when they become part of a washer or dryer, but they do not lose the protection of the UCC filing. If the manufacturer were to slip into a default of the security agreement or slide into a Chapter 11 bankruptcy filing, the electric motors in the manufacturer's warehouse stock, on the assembly line, and in finished products would continue to be under the protection—hopefully the priority protection—of the Code filing.

Conflicting Security Interests in Collateral

The topic of conflicting security interests in the same collateral was discussed briefly in the "Who Has Priority?" subsection of this chapter. It is not possible to explore each of the many areas of this topic, but I shall touch briefly on some of the more important and common situations where the problem is involved.

The rules of priority as they focus on banks and their security interests in items being collected is Section 4-208; how security interests are perceived in jurisdictions other than the one in which a filing has been made is covered in Section 9-103; the exploration of the multiple facets of consignments is detailed in Division 9-114. Does this mean that a person can skim through the Code, sorting out what seems appropriate to a particular situation, whether there is or is not an adequate understanding of what and how the Code delivers its messages? Absolutely not. The Code is complex, the code is couched in legal language that frequently seems so convoluted that the reader despairs of understanding what it is saying, and the Code can turn on the unwary as quickly as it can be a friend to those who use it properly.

Example: The Code states that a perfected purchase money security interest in inventory has priority over a conflicting security interest in the same inventory. It also states that the same purchase money security interest has priority when the target is cash proceeds that can be identified and are received on or before the delivery of inventory to the buyer. No problem with those statements? The problem is that the rather uncomplicated statements made above have a suffix after the word "buyer"—that word is "if". The target is cash proceeds that can be identified and are received on or before the delivery of inventory to the buyer "if . . ."

- a purchase money security interest is perfected at the time the debtor receives possession of the inventory.

- the holder of the conflicting security interest is notified in writing by the party who has the purchase money security interest of the conflicting interests, and if the holder of the conflicting security interest had covered the same inventory by filing a financing statement before the start of the 21-day period, which allows for temporary perfection of a security interest before the secured party has made a filing or has taken possession of the collateral.

- notice is received by the holder of the conflicting security interest from the purchase money secured party within five years before the inventory passed into the debtor's possession.

- the person giving the notification states therein that he or she expects to acquire a purchase money security interest in the debtor's inventory, and includes in the notification a complete and detailed listing of the inventory items.

There is much more to this subsection, just as there is much more in most of the guideline material that has been taken from Division 9. A sampling of information such as that given above will not enable the reader to make complex decisions or resolve more complicated problems based upon the Code's sections and subsections. As I have said before, the Code was written basically by attorneys to be interpreted by attorneys. Of course, there is much that a credit manager or secured party can do for himself or herself, but unless a person who reads the Code for the purpose of dealing with it or operating within it has a better than average grasp of statutes that all too frequently may seem convoluted or created to confuse, that person is in over his or her head.

Much of the UCC material that is covered in this book is intended to familiarize the reader with examples of content rather than to attempt to define uncomplicated paths down which the credit person, secured party, debtor, or other persons of interest can chart a safe course. I must again repeat the admonition that you *do not* attempt to deal with the complexities of the Uniform Commercial Code unless guided by an attorney who is thoroughly familiar with it. There are too many ways for any but the most experienced to be blind-sided by something that might have seemed minor, but becomes major subsequent to a flawed decision-making process that included overlooking key points while misinterpreting others.

The UCC is a special area of law and in matters and areas other than the routine, it requires the attention of an attorney whose specialty is avoiding problems or solving problems dealing with the Code. Does that mean that I do or do not make my own decisions as they relate to the UCC? I make most of them. Do I ever use the services of a specialist in UCC law to interpret the ramifications of a particularly large and worrisome interstate transaction? I do indeed, and so should you!

Lien Creditors

These are creditors who acquire liens on a property involved by attachment, levy, or a similar procedure. They include the following:

1. An assignee for the benefit of creditors from the time of assignment

2. A trustee in bankruptcy from the date of the filing of the petition

3. A receiver in equity from the time of appointment

A person who becomes a lien creditor while a security interest is perfected takes subject to the security interest only to the extent that it . . .

1. Secures advances made before the person becomes a lien creditor.

2. Is made within 45 days thereafter.

3. Is made without knowledge of the lien.

4. Is pursuant to a commitment entered into without knowledge of the lien.

The priority of certain liens was covered in earlier paragraphs, but it is appropriate to mention that certain liens take priority over a perfected security interest. This is not an across-the-board statement, but pertains primarily to the priority of a perfected security interest as it relates to a statute or rule of law for the described materials or services.

Before moving to another topic, this is the point in the book where I should insert a brief recap of *Mechanic's Lien Laws.* Just as the Uniform Commercial Code is not uniform in what has been enacted by the legislatures of the 50 states, the District of Columbia, and the Virgin Islands, so Mechanic's and Materialmen's Lien Laws vary from one state to another.

Most states accept the premise that any person who furnishes material or does work on a property is entitled to file a lien. An individual, partnership, or corporation can file a lien, and no regulation states that a person or entity must be a resident of the state in which they wish to file the lien. Labor or material is the basis for a Mechanic's or Materialmen's Lien. To qualify, both must have become part of the property or have added value to it.

Two different concepts govern the filing of liens by subcontractors and materialmen. A filing is made not because one concept or the other is the choice of the person or company filing. It is based on whether the state in which you are filing the lien follows the New York or Pennsylvania requirements for a given situation qualifying as eligible for exercising lien rights. The New York concept sets the allowable lien limit at the amount owed by the owner to the general contractor. If the amount owed to the general contractor doesn't cover the subcontractor's claim, the burden of proving that the owner owes the greater amount rests with the subcontractor. Pennsylvania and the states that follow its concept do not limit the amount of the subcontractor's allowable lien to the amount owed by the owner to the general contractor. Pennsylvania and its followers give the subcontractor a direct lien regardless of whether there is proof that the owner has made payments to the general contractor.

The same warning applies here as with a UCC filing. Do not try to file a Mechanic's or Materialmen's Lien unless you are familiar with the procedural requirements in the jurisdiction where you are filing. Filing requirements differ from state to state; the schedules of filing fees are not consistent; the duration of liens may vary; the requirements for what must be included in the lien notice itself are often complex. Until you have gone through the filing process enough times and in enough jurisdictions to know how and where to look for the guidelines, let your company's attorney guide you through the process. And as you listen to him or her, it would also be helpful if you became familiar with NACM's Credit Manual of Commercial Laws.

Installed Property

It is interesting to note that a security interest may be created in goods which are fixtures or it may continue in goods which become fixtures, but no security interest exists under Division 9 in ordinary building materials incorporated into an improvement on land.

When goods become attached to real estate in a manner that makes it difficult to recognize or remove them without damaging the appearance or value of the whole, they become "fixtures." As "fixtures," they then become candidates for what is called a "fixture filing" in the office (county recorder, etc.) where the mortgage on the real estate is filed. A financing statement which covers goods that are to become fixtures will be recorded in the same office as that in which the real estate mortage is filed.

As stated in other paragraphs, a security interest may be created in goods which are fixtures or which become fixtures. Division 9 does not, however, prohibit putting a mortgage on fixtures, as may be allowed in real estate law. It should also be noted that a person or company holding a mortgage on real estate or owning said real estate stands behind a perfected security interest in fixtures *if* . . .

- the security interest is a purchase money interest.
- the interest of the mortgage holder or property owner arises before the goods become fixtures.
- a fixture filing protects the security interest before the goods become fixtures or within 10 days thereafter.
- the debtor is in possession of the real estate or has an interest of record in the real estate.
- the fixtures are office or factory machines, or consumer goods which are replacements of household appliances, and the security interest is perfected before the goods become fixtures.

Questions of priority can become very complex when they relate to property that has been installed. Under certain conditions, a secured party has priority over owners and encumbrancers of real estate. Under other conditions, a security interest in fixtures is subordinate to the conflicting interest of an encumbrancer or owner of the real estate who is not the debtor. If the above is not challenging enough, consider that a security interest in fixtures is subordinate to a construction mortgage recorded before the goods become fixtures, if the goods become fixtures before the construction is completed.

The overriding question regarding the secured party and property is, whether in a default situation, the secured party has the priority right to remove his or her collateral over claims against the real estate by owners, mortgage holders, and others. It is understood that the secured party must reimburse the owner of the property or any person or company who is not the debtor, and who has not agreed to an amount to cover the cost of repairs after removal of the goods (now fixtures), and to ensure that there is no decrease in the value of the property which might be attributed to removal of goods that became fixtures.

Imperfect Security Interests

One of the more costly and devastating things that can occur to a secured party is to sit helplessly as a bankruptcy or a civil court judge reduces what was thought to be a perfected filing down to the status of an imperfect filing—the equivalent of an unsecured creditor.

Those who file security agreements and financing statements should know that acceptance by a filing officer does not mean that the filing is perfected against the challenge of a third party—usually a secured creditor with a filing which is assumed to have a lower priority—to have it disallowed. The filing officer accepts a filing package based on format rather than content. If the financing statement is on the proper form and there are no errors or omissions that would disqualify it as a qualified document, it will be filed. If the security agreement is improperly prepared (does not contain the necessary facts regarding the agreement) and the financing statement fails to properly cover, describe, or include collateral which should have been a part of it, the filing officer has no responsibility in this area.

A security interest assumed to have been perfected with a UCC filing might be ruled imperfect for one or a combination of reasons. The following list is not complete and in some situations might not lead to a ruling of an imperfect filing. If the secured party makes an error, but can prove that his or her intentions were within the guidelines of the statutes, it is possible that the filing would be allowed.

1. The name of the debtor is incorrect.

2. The name of the secured party or parties is incorrect or incomplete. (One of two names may have been inadvertently omitted from the document.)

3. There is a failure to adequately identify the type and/or nature of the collateral.

4. When the collateral is crops, an incorrect description of the real estate on which the crops are being or will be grown could create an identification problem.

5. The proceeds of collateral is an important area. If it is not included or checked (there is a "proceeds of collateral are also covered" line on the financing statement forms of many states), it eliminates from UCC protection an important section of the filing. (Whether it is goods or proceeds from the sale of those goods, collateral must be given the full protection of applicable UCC statutes.)

6. If the collateral is goods which will be attached to real estate in such a manner as to become a fixture (an unidentifiable and/or an integral part of the whole), it should be stated in the financing statement. The loss of identity when such goods become fixtures does not terminate the protection given the collateral when the filing is made, but it does add complexities to the question of determining priority security interests in the collateral (now fixtures), should the debtor be unable to comply with the terms of the security agreement.

An example of a security interest at serious risk is a manufacturer who has shipped product to a customer for a period of several weeks, then decides belatedly to protect the company's security interest with a UCC filing. There are two questions that draw immediate attention to this hypothetical occurance. Has the secured party waited too long to make a UCC filing that will retroactively protect goods shipped over the period of several weeks? While the manufacturer was shipping product to the customer, how many filings that now have priority were made during those weeks by other suppliers? The manufacturer who did not file promptly may be well down the list of priority creditors.

The Uniform Commercial Code does not specifically forbid filings that seek to retroactively protect goods shipped weeks before, as well as current and future shipments. It does, however, urge people and companies with a security interest to file early. Quote: "A financing statement may be filed before a security agreement is made or a security agreement otherwise attaches." It is also well to remember again the window of forgiveness which states that a financing statement that is in substantial compliance with the requirements of the section on financing statements is still effective, despite containing minor errors that do not mislead in a manner that would seriously jeopardize the rights or actions taken by others who might have a security interest that would be seriously influenced by the prior filing.

Example of an Imperfect Filing: The Avery B. Wallace Company, a manufacturer of ski equipment, has been asked by a prospective customer to ship the first of what is thought will be a series of large orders of men's and women's ski equipment. The Wallace Company runs a credit check on the prospective customer and determines that the nine-store chain of retail stores has been in business less than two years, has had cash-flow problems from day one, and has not improved. New stores have been opened before earlier ones had an opportunity to establish themselves, thereby increasing the drain on cash. There is a well-founded feeling in The Wallace Company that the prospective customer's drive to grow rapidly has many of the elements of self-destruction.

The Wallace Company finally agrees to ship the first order if the customer will agree to sign a security agreement and financing statement. The customer agrees, a security agreement is drawn up, a financing statement is prepared, and a filing is made under the appropriate jurisdiction of the Uniform Commercial Code. End of story? Not quite.

Less than six months after The Wallace Company shipped the ski equipment and filed a financing statement to protect its security interest, the customer filed a Chapter 11 to get the protection of the bankruptcy court. The bank had triggered the customer's action by cutting off its lines of credit and, although the situation for continuation of the business appeared to be grim, The Wallace Company had no qualms regarding its priority claim on funds in a liquidation of the business. Concern for the company's position was minimal.

The Wallace Company was jarred out of its feeling of complacency when a creditor lower on the priority list than Wallace dramatically improved its chances for a higher percentage of return when it challenged The Wallace Company's filing. To the dismay of those at Wallace whose job it was to make effective UCC filings—filings that could not be overturned via a simple challenge—the bankruptcy court confirmed what the third party alleged in its petition regarding the filing. The financing statement covered collateral in great detail, but not a word pertaining to "proceeds of collateral" had been included. And because the customer had sold much of its inventory and remitted only a small percentage of it to The Wallace Company, using the balance to delay the collapse of the business, there was very little warehouse inventory that could be converted into cash.

What happened to The Wallace Company's UCC filing? The court ruled that it was a perfected filing only as it covered collateral described in the financing statement. The company was entitled to share in the liquidation of inventory, but, because it had failed to include "proceeds of inventory" in its financing statement, The Wallace Company was barred by the bankruptcy court from participating in any cash generated by collecting receivables balances. And because receivables balances represented the major share of the customer's assets, The Wallace Company recovered a very small percentage of its investment in the customer account.

21

The Forms (and How to Use Them)

The person who is responsible for using the various forms that are a part of the filing and follow-up procedures under the Uniform Commercial Code should have a working knowledge of what is required in each of the jurisdictions. It is not necessary for the person who handles these matters to know every form, but the person should know enough about the purpose of each form to adjust to differences in the information requested.

Each of the following forms has relevance beyond formalizing a security interest, a security agreement, a financing statement, and a filing. It is not possible to say how many of the forms will be used during the lifetime of a single filing, because it will depend upon conditions as they pertain to an individual filing: short-term, long-term, changes in the financing statement, assignment of the security interest, release of the collateral, and termination of the financing statement prior to the end of the five-year term of a filing. But whether your company has one, two, or several of the forms that are associated with UCC filings, there must be enough knowledge of what is required to enable the designated person to use effectively each one of the prescribed forms.

The form or the format for a security agreement might vary from one state or jurisdiction to another or from one attorney to another. A portion of a suggested format is shown below, but the emphasis in this chapter is on forms that are tied into Division 9 of the Code; these forms are available from each of the UCC jurisdictions, although there is some variation among the forms used by the various states.

The forms are listed here with a brief description of each. Subsequent subsections are built around in-depth examinations of the purpose and the preparation of each.

1. The "security interest" is created by an agreement called the "security agreement," which is between the secured party and the debtor. The secured party, after entering into a security agreement, may take possession of the collateral if the debtor defaults.

2. The financing statement (filing is required to perfect the security interest of the secured party).

3. Amendments (filed when there is a change in the financing statement).

4. Continuation statement (used to extend the protection of a filing that is about to run its five-year course).

5. Termination (a termination statement filed by the secured party with the filing officer of each jurisdiction where there is a security interest that is no longer effective under the filed financing statement).

6. Assignment of Security Interest (filed by a secured party in the jurisdiction where the original filing was made to indicate that the secured party's interest in the filing is being assigned to a third party, etc.).

7. Release of collateral (when the secured party signs a statement releasing collateral covered by a filed financing statement).

Chapter 18 of this section contains examples of what must be included in a Security Agreement for Accounts Receivable and a Security Agreement for Equipment. Neither is shown as a complete agreement, but rather as a guideline to indicate the various areas that must be covered to have an acceptable security agreement. If any of the essential material is not included (a complete description of the collateral, obligations of the debtor, secured parties rights and remedies, debtor's rights and remedies, etc.), the filing may be "perfected" as it applies to appropriate descriptions of a majority of the collateral items, but it may fail to include some other collateral items. That failure could mean the loss of a substantial number of dollars if the debtor's ability to meet the terms of the security agreement and the financing statement led to the debtor's default.

There are samples of forms throughout this chapter that illustrate the differences in format among some of the states. Many forms contain similar information, but present it in a different alignment or format; others differ slightly in the information that is requested of the secured party and of the debtor. To ensure that you meet the requirement of an acceptable form for the jurisdiction in which the filing is to be made, use forms that are standard for that jurisdiction or state. Of course, no filing can be considered a perfected filing if all essential information is not accurate and complete.

The central filing location of most states is where copies of forms can be obtained. It is appropriate to note, however, that Louisiana is the only state that has not adopted Division 9 of the UCC. Other sections of the UCC have been adopted, but there is no provision for filings of the type discussed in the last several chapters. Whether Louisiana will eventually adopt Division 9 becomes increasingly questionable as the gap between 1992 and the Code revisions of 1972 becomes wider. But with the exception of Louisiana, a letter or a telephone call to the filing officer at the central filing office of the jurisdiction of interest will bring copies of the requested forms and information pertaining to current filing fees. (Caution: Be sure to forward the correct filing fee for each UCC filing. If the amount forwarded does not meet the required fee, the filing could be returned or held by the filing officer until you respond to a note advising you of the deficiency.)

It is wise to call someone in the central filing office to determine the charge for the forms you will be requesting. There was a time when many states did not charge for them, but growth demands on state treasuries has caused an increasing number to charge for everything that relates to the Uniform Commercial Code. If the amount sent for forms is less than the required amount, some states will send the forms and bill your company for the balance. This should, however, be considered the exception rather than the rule, so avoid delays by sending a check for the correct amount of money.

Request for Information

When the fee for requesting or requested information is not known, filing officers suggest that the individual or company attach a blank check, made payable to the appropriate filing jurisdiction, and the filing officer will fill in the correct amount. This procedure eliminates any delay in receiving requested information and offers no risk as it relates to the number of dollars entered on the check.

This solves your primary agenda in contacting the central filing office of a state with which you have not previously had contact. You will be able to get the information you need, to get copies of currently active filings that would have priority over your filing, and be able to familiarize yourself with the filing requirements for the jurisdiction in which you have an interest (see Figures 21-1, 21-2, 21-3).

Most states have a form with the same or similar designation: Form UCC-11—*Uniform Commercial Code—Request for Information or Copies.* If your company has had no prior contact with the UCC in a specific state, an inquiry submitted in letter form and incorporating the information requested on the sample Form UCC-11 should suffice for the first time. It will be expected, however, that future requests will be made on the approved form and will be accompanied by the prescribed fee for information or copies.

It should be noted that one of the nonstandards among the UCC of the various states, the District of Columbia, and the Virgin Islands are the form names and numbering systems used to identify them. There are not many major differences, but enough subtle variations among jurisdictions to cre-

Figure 21-1. Request for copies or information—Massachusetts (short form).

ate a few problems for the unwary. The following examples are typical of the differences:

Alabama

Financing Statement	UCC1	(5 parts)
Financing Statement	UCC2	(3 parts)
Financing Statement	UCCE	(Extension Sheet)
Continuation Statement	UCC3	
Termination Statement	UCC3	
Assignment	UCC3	
Release	UCC3	
Request for Information	UCC11	

California

Financing Statement	UCC1
Continuation Statement	UCC2
Termination Statement	UCC2
Release	UCC2
Assignment	UCC2
Amendment	UCC2
Information	UCC3

ARIZONA UNIFORM COMMERCIAL CODE
REQUEST FOR INFORMATION OR COPIES — Form UCC-2

REQUEST FOR INFORMATION OR COPIES — Present in duplicate to filing (recording) officer.

1. Debtor(s) (last name first, and address(es):	2. Party requesting information or copies (name and address):

☐ List below any presently effective financing statement(s) naming the above named debtor(s) and any statement(s) of assignment thereof.
☐ Furnish exact copies of each page of financing statements and statements of assignment listed below.

FILE NUMBER OR DOCKET REF.	DATE AND HOUR OF FILING (RECORDING)	NAME AND ADDRESS OF SECURED PARTIES AND ASSIGNEES

CERTIFICATE: The undersigned officer hereby certifies that:

☐ the above list is a record of all presently effective financing statements and statements of assignment which name the above debtor(s) and which are filed (recorded) in this office as of_____, 19____at_____.M.

☐ the attached_____pages are true and exact copies of all available financing statements or statements of assignment listed in above request.

Dated:_____

Secretary of State/County Recorder.

STANDARD FORM UCC-2 APPROVED BY THE SECRETARY OF STATE OF ARIZONA 7-67   By_____

Figure 21-2. Request for information or copies—Arizona (long form).

REQUEST FOR INFORMATION OR COPIES. Present in Duplicate to Filing Officer

1. ☐ INFORMATION REQUEST. Filing officer please furnish certificate showing whether there is on file any presently effective financing statement naming the Debtor listed below and any statement of assignment thereof, and if there is, giving the date and hour of filing of each such statement and the names and addresses of each secured party named therein.

1A.	DEBTOR (LAST NAME FIRST)		1B. SOC. SEC. OR FED. TAX NO.
1C.	MAILING ADDRESS	1D. CITY, STATE	1E. ZIP CODE
1F.			

Date_____19____ Signature of Requesting Party_____

2. CERTIFICATE:

FILE NUMBER	DATE AND HOUR OF FILING	NAME(S) AND ADDRESS(ES) OF SECURED PARTY(IES) AND ASSIGNEE(S), IF ANY

The undersigned filing officer hereby certifies that the above listing is a record of all presently effective financing statements and statements of assignment which name the above debtor and which are on file in my office of_____19____at_____ __M.

_____19____
(DATE)

_____
(FILING OFFICER)

By:_____

3. ☐ COPY REQUEST. Filing officer please furnish_____copy(ies) of each page of the following statements concerning the debtors listed below ☐ Financing Statement ☐ Amendments ☐ Statements of Assignment ☐ Continuation Statements ☐ Statement of Release ☐ Termination Statement ☐ All Statements on file.

FILE NUMBER	DATE OF FILING	NAME(S) AND MAILING ADDRESS(ES) OF DEBTOR(S)	DEBTORS SOC. SEC. OR FED. TAX NO.

Date_____19____ Signature of Requesting Party_____

4. CERTIFICATE:

The undersigned filing officer hereby certifies that the attached copies are true and exact copies of all statements requested above.

_____19____
(DATE)

_____
(FILING OFFICER)

By:_____

5. **Mail Information or Copies to**

NAME
MAILING
ADDRESS
CITY, STATE
AND ZIP

UNIFORM COMMERCIAL CODE-FORM UCC-3

Rediform 5S803

Figure 21-3. Request for information or copies (long form/generic).

Colorado

Financing Statement	UCC1
Financing Statement	UCC1
(where assignment is indicated)	
Continuation Statement	UCC3
Assignment Statement	UCC3
Amendment Statement	UCC3
Release Statement	UCC3
Termination Statement	UCC3

Delaware

Financing Statement	UCC1
Continuation Statement	UCC3
Termination	UCCT
Amendment	UCC2
Search	UCC11

Most of the states code their forms with the designations UCC1, UCC2, UCC3, and UCC11. Where they may differ is in the use of a lower case letter (UCC2a) to indicate a second page or UCCT to indicate a Termination. Nebraska uses double digits with UCC letters to identify its forms: UCC30 (Financing Statement), UCC50 (Assignment, Amendment, Continuation, and Termination), and UCC50 (Release of Collateral).

Financing Statement

A Security Interest can be protected by taking possession of the collateral or by filing a Financing Statement with the appropriate state, region, district, or county authority. The Financing Statement is notification to any third party who may have an interest that the person or company that filed the financing statement has a security interest in the collateral described and specified in the filed notice. As mentioned in an early chapter, failure to file a financing statement does not mean that the security agreement is not valid, but it does offer an opportunity for a creditor who files more promptly to establish a priority over the person or company that did not act promptly.

Financing Statements are not different from other UCC forms in that there are variations in the form from one state to another. Many states will accept a filing submitted on the form of another state (a nonstandard form for the state in which the filing is to be made), but the acceptance of a non-standard form usually involves a higher filing fee plus the possibility that some piece of information vital to the perfection of the security interest might not be included in the nonstandard form, thereby diminishing the effectiveness or the perfection of the filing (see Figures 21-4, 21-5, and 21-6).

Nonstandard forms should be used to avoid a filing delay or if other forms (standard for the state in which the filing is to be made) are not available. Use a nonstandard form when nothing else is available and when the form is acceptable, but try to anticipate a first-time filing and order the appropriate forms. The quality of your secured position and the priority of your filing may both be improved.

The content of a financing statement is vital to the security that it will or will not give to your filing. If it is incomplete, fails to adequately describe the collateral in which you or your company claims to have a security interest, does not name the debtor or the debtor's address or place of business, does not include a location to which the collateral was shipped and is stored, and is generally not a document that fulfills the obligation of describing and locating goods that are to become fixtures (including a description of the host product, area, etc.), the question of whether the security interest has been perfected becomes very real.

Figure 21-4. Financing statement—New York (short form).

This FINANCING STATEMENT is presented to a Filing Officer for filing pursuant to the Uniform Commercial Code | Maturity date (if any):

1. Debtor (s) Name (Last Name First) | 2. Debtor (s) Complete Address | This space for use of Filing Officer. (Date, Time, File Number and Filing Office)

THE SPACES TO THE RIGHT HAVE BEEN DESIGNED FOR USE IN A WINDOW ENVELOPE WHEN RETURNING THE SECOND COPY TO THE PERSON FILING.

3. & 4. Secured Party (ies) and Complete Address

5. & 6. Assignee (s) of Secured Party and Complete Address

7. This financing statement covers the following types (or items) of property:

8. When collateral is crops or fixtures complete this portion of form.

( ) (If collateral is crops). The above described crops are growing or are to be grown on:

a. Description of real estate (Sufficient to identify the property).

b. Name and complete address of record owner.

CHECK (X) THE ITEMS WHICH APPLY.

( ) (If collateral is goods which are or are to become fixtures). The above described goods are affixed or are to be affixed to:

9 a. ( ) Proceeds of Collateral are also covered.   9 b. ( ) Products of Collateral are also covered. | No. of additional sheets presented. ( )

( ) Filed with Register of Deeds and Mortgages of _____ County.   ( ) Secretary of State.
( ) Filed with the County Clerk of _____ County.

Signature (s) of Debtor (s) | Signature (s) of Secured Party (ies) or Assignee (s)

FILING OFFICER COPY — This form of financing statement is approved by the Secretary of State of New Jersey.
STANDARD FORM—UNIFORM COMMERCIAL CODE—FORM UCC–1

Figure 21-5. Financing statement—New Jersey (long form).

This **FINANCING STATEMENT** is presented for filing pursuant to the California Uniform Commercial Code

1. DEBTOR (LAST NAME FIRST)			1A. SOCIAL SECURITY OR FEDERAL TAX NO.
1B. MAILING ADDRESS	1C. CITY, STATE		1D. ZIP CODE
1E. RESIDENCE ADDRESS (IF AN INDIVIDUAL AND DIFFERENT THAN 1B)	1F. CITY, STATE		1G. ZIP CODE
2. ADDITIONAL DEBTOR (IF ANY) (LAST NAME FIRST)			2A. SOCIAL SECURITY OR FEDERAL TAX NO.
2B. MAILING ADDRESS	2C. CITY, STATE		2D. ZIP CODE
2E. RESIDENCE ADDRESS (IF AN INDIVIDUAL AND DIFFERENT THAN 2B)	2F. CITY, STATE		2G. ZIP CODE
3. DEBTOR(S) TRADE NAME OR STYLE (IF ANY)			3A. FEDERAL TAX NO.
4. ADDRESS OF DEBTOR(S) CHIEF PLACE OF BUSINESS (IF ANY)	4A. CITY, STATE		4B. ZIP CODE

5. SECURED PARTY
   NAME
   MAILING ADDRESS
   CITY   STATE   ZIP CODE

5A. SOCIAL SECURITY NO., FED. TAX NO. OR BANK TRANSIT AND A.B.A. NO.

6. ASSIGNEE OF SECURED PARTY (IF ANY)
   NAME
   MAILING ADDRESS
   CITY   STATE   ZIP CODE

6A. SOCIAL SECURITY NO., FED. TAX NO. OR BANK TRANSIT AND A.B.A. NO.

7. This FINANCING STATEMENT covers the following types or items of property (if crops or timber, include description of real property on which growing or to be grown):

7A. Maximum amount of indebtedness to be secured at any one time (OPTIONAL).

$ _____

8. Check [X] If Applicable	A ☐	Proceeds of collateral are also covered	B ☐	Products of collateral are also covered	C ☐	Proceeds of above described original collateral in which a security interest was perfected	D ☐	Collateral was brought into this state subject to security interest in another jurisdiction

9.

                   (Date)_____ 19____

By:_____
    SIGNATURE(S) OF DEBTOR(S)   (TITLE)

By:_____
    SIGNATURE(S) OF SECURED PARTY(IES)   (TITLE)

CODE
1
2
3
4
5
6
7
8
9

10. This Space for Use of Filing Officer
(Date, Time, File Number and Filing Officer)

11.   **Return Copy to**

                        NAME
                        ADDRESS
                        CITY, STATE
                        AND ZIP
                        CODE

(1) FILING OFFICER COPY

STANDARD FORM — FILING FEE $2.00   UNIFORM COMMERCIAL CODE — FORM UCC-1
    Approved by the Secretary of State

Figure 21-6. Financing statement—California (long form).

Before you send a security agreement and a financing statement to the filing officer of the jurisdiction in which you want the security interest recorded, take a few minutes to check the financing statement for the data covered in the preceding paragraph. When you have satisfied yourself that the financing statement has been properly prepared, send the filing package to the filing officer. If the work you have done is thorough, your security interest or that of your company should be perfected.

Amendments to Financing Statements

Remember that financing statements, though recorded, are not set in stone. Conditions may change as they relate to the recorded security interest, and the UCC provides the form and the procedure to make the necessary amendment(s) to the original filing.

An amendment to a financing statement is used to correct (or to amend) an error or errors in the original filing that might cause it to be challenged and subsequently ruled an imperfect filing; an amendment also reflects changes of importance between the date of the filing of the financing statement and the current date (change in name and/or trade style of the debtor, a change in the type, size, quantity, and location of the collateral, etc.) which could be of interest to third-party creditors. Any unamended change that might adversely impact the security interest or the potential security interest of a third-party creditor could be a threat to the assumption of perfection held by the person or company whose filing is about to be challenged.

In addition to the pitfalls cited in the preceding paragraph, a well-written amendment can save an enormous amount of clerical labor and paper work. Were you aware that if a debtor changes his or her name, trade style, or business or corporate structure to the point where a filed financing statement becomes seriously misleading, the filing will not protect collateral acquired more than four months after major changes in the original filing were made if they were not covered subsequently by an amended filing? An amended filing can continue the level of protection that the secured party had on the date the original financing statement was filed.

Remember that any major change(s) from what is contained in the original filing should be covered immediately with an amended filing. What about a financing statement that has minor errors only and cannot be construed to mislead or distort? Such a filing should continue to be effective, but be careful that your interpretation of "minor errors" is well within the parameters of that term as it might be interpreted by others. Nothing that would mislead or distort can ever be considered a minor error or an error of no consequence (see Figures 21-7, 21-8, and 21-9).

STATE OF ARIZONA, County of_____ss.

I do hereby certify that the within instrument was filed (recorded) at the request of_____

on_____A.D., 19____at_____o'clock_____M.   Docket_____

Page_____,File Number_____, Records of this office.

WITNESS my hand and official seal the day and year first above written. _____

Secretary of State/County Recorder.

Return copy or recorded original to:

By_____

ARIZONA UNIFORM COMMERCIAL CODE
FINANCING STATEMENT CHANGE — Form UCC-3

This Statement is presented for filing (recording) pursuant to the Arizona Uniform Commercial Code. | 1. No. of additional sheets presented:

2. Debtor(s) (last name first, and address(es):

3. Secured Party(ies) and address(es):

4. This Statement refers to original Financing Statement FILE NO._____DOCKET_____PAGE_____

Filed (recorded) with_____Date filed (recorded)_____19_____

5. ☐ CONTINUATION. The financing statement described above is continued.

☐ TERMINATION STATEMENT — The financing statement described above is terminated.

☐ ASSIGNMENT. The interest of the secured parties under the financing statement described above has been assigned to the Assignees whose names and addresses appear below.

☐ AMENDMENT. The financing statement described above is amended as set forth below.

☐ RELEASE. The secured party releases the collateral described below from the financing statement described above.

6.

_____   Dated:_____

_____   _____

_____   _____

SIGNATURE(S) OF DEBTOR(S)   **SIGNATURE OF SECURED PARTY**
(Required only on Amendments)

STANDARD FORM UCC-3 APPROVED BY THE SECRETARY OF STATE OF ARIZONA AS REVISED 9-67

Figure 21-7. Financing statement change—Arizona (long form).

This **STATEMENT** is presented for filing pursuant to the California Uniform Commercial Code

1. FILE NO. OF ORIG. FINANCING STATEMENT	1A. DATE OF FILING OF ORIG. FINANCING STATEMENT	1B. DATE OF ORIG. FINANCING STATEMENT	1C. PLACE OF FILING ORIG. FINANCING STATEMENT

2. DEBTOR (LAST NAME FIRST)		2A. SOCIAL SECURITY OR FEDERAL TAX NO.

2B. MAILING ADDRESS	2C. CITY, STATE	2D. ZIP CODE

3. ADDITIONAL DEBTOR (IF ANY) (LAST NAME FIRST)		3A. SOCIAL SECURITY OR FEDERAL TAX NO.

3B. MAILING ADDRESS	3C. CITY, STATE	3D. ZIP CODE

4. SECURED PARTY

4A. SOCIAL SECURITY NO., FEDERAL TAX NO. OR BANK TRANSIT AND A.B.A. NO.

NAME

MAILING ADDRESS

CITY   STATE   ZIP CODE

5. ASSIGNEE OF SECURED PARTY (IF ANY)

5A. SOCIAL SECURITY NO., FEDERAL TAX NO. OR BANK TRANSIT AND A.B.A. NO.

NAME

MAILING ADDRESS

CITY   STATE   ZIP CODE

6.

A ☐ CONTINUATION—The original Financing Statement between the foregoing Debtor and Secured Party bearing the file number and date shown above is continued. If collateral is crops or timber, check here ☐ and insert description of real property on which growing or to be grown in Item 7 below.

B ☐ RELEASE—From the collateral described in the Financing Statement bearing the file number shown above, the Secured Party releases the collateral described in Item 7 below.

C ☐ ASSIGNMENT—The Secured Party certifies that the Secured Party has assigned to the Assignee above named, all the Secured Party's rights under the Financing Statement bearing the file number shown above in the collateral described in Item 7 below.

D ☐ TERMINATION—The Secured Party certifies that the Secured Party no longer claims a security interest under the Financing Statement bearing the file number shown above.

E ☐ AMENDMENT—The Financing Statement bearing the file number shown above is amended as set forth in Item 7 below. (Signature of Debtor required on all amendments.)

F ☐ OTHER

7.

8.

(Date) _____ 19____

By: _____
SIGNATURE(S) OF DEBTOR(S)   (TITLE)

By: _____
SIGNATURE(S) OF SECURED PARTY(IES)   (TITLE)

C O D E

1
2
3
4
5
6
7
8
9

9. This Space for Use of Filing Officer (Date, Time, Filing Office)

10.   **Return Copy to**

NAME
ADDRESS
CITY
STATE
AND ZIP

(1) FILING OFFICER COPY

STANDARD FORM—FILING FEE $2.00   UNIFORM COMMERCIAL CODE—FORM UCC-2
Approved by the Secretary of State

Figure 21-8. Financing statement change—California (long form).

This STATEMENT is presented to a Filing Officer for filing pursuant to the Uniform Commercial Code:		No. of Additional Sheets Presented:	Maturity Date 3. (Optional):
1. Debtor(s) (Last Name First) and Address(es):	2. Secured Party(ies) (Name(s) and Address(es):		4. For Filing Officer: Date, Time, No., Filing Office

5. This Statement Refers to Original

Financing Statement No._____ Filed (date)_____ with_____

6. ☐ A. Continuation — The original Financing Statement bearing the above file number is still effective.

☐ B. Termination — The Secured Party of record no longer claims a security interest under the Financing Statement bearing the above file number.

☐ C. Release — From the Collateral described in the Financing Statement bearing the above file number, the Secured Party of record releases the following:

☐ D. Assignment — The Secured Party of record has assigned the Secured Party's rights in the property described below under the Financing Statement bearing the above file number to the Assignee whose name and address are shown below:

☐ E. Amendment — The Financing Statement bearing the above file number is amended as set forth below: (Signature of Debtor is required if Collateral is added.)

7. Description of Collateral:

8. Name(s) of Record Owner(s):

By_____
Signature(s) of Debtor(s) (Only on Amendment)

By_____
Signature(s) of Secured Party(ies)

(1) FILING OFFICER COPY—ALPHABETICAL
FORM UCC-3—MISSOURI UNIFORM COMMERCIAL CODE

Approved By: _James Kirkpatrick_
Secretary of State

Figure 21-9. Financing statement change—Missouri (short form).

Continuation Statement

Although the name of this document is self-explanatory as it relates to its function, its usage is not nearly so simplistic. There are several simple, but important rules which must be followed if the filing of the continuation statement is to accomplish what is expected of it. The failure to observe simple, but important guidelines could diminish or negate the effectiveness of the filing.

1. A continuation statement must be signed by the secured party.
2. It must identify the original financing statement by file number and must state that the filing is still effective.
3. Continuation statements must be filed within six months prior to the expiration of the five-year effective duration of the filing.
4. A written letter of assignment, which has been signed by a person other than the secured party of record, must accompany a continuation statement.
5. A continuation statement that has been filed within the prescribed time frame extends the original filing for a period of five years from the date of the filing of the continuation statement.
6. There is no limit on the number of continuation statements that can be filed to extend the effectiveness of a financing statement.

7. Lapsed filings are removed and destroyed after one year, or they may be destroyed immediately after they have lapsed if a photographic copy of the filing is retained.

8. Original filings over five years old which have been continued by the filing of a continuation statement shall be retained by the filing officer.

Many security interest filings are known to be long-term when the initial filing is made; others eventually reflect a change in circumstances from what was thought to be a short-term filing to one that becomes long-term, going from years to decades. To continue a filing that has been properly prepared and recorded should pose no problem for the person who prepares the continuation statement.

Release of Collateral

The release of collateral by the person who has held the security interest in it is the last act in what may have been a series of filings. The person with the security interest in collateral might at some point have amended the original filing, might later have amended the filing a second time, then might either have released the collateral, assigned the security interest to a third party, or filed a continuation statement to renew the filing. What happens when there is a termination of interest in collateral or goods (not the same as a release of collateral) will be discussed later in this chapter.

To release collateral from a UCC filing, a secured party simply prepares and signs a statement in which he or she relinquishes all interest and all claims to a security interest in the collateral. If the release of security interest involves less than 100 percent of the collateral, a signed statement covering the parameters of the release is all that is necessary. The statement must contain a description of the collateral being released, the names and addresses of the debtor(s) and secured party, and the file number that was issued by the filing officer when the financing statement was recorded.

The sequence in the release of collateral involves a request by the debtor to the secured party: the secured party then forwards the required statement to the filing officer releasing the security interest: the filing officer(s) of the jurisdiction(s) marks the date and time of filing on the statement of release, then he or she adds that information to the filed copy of the financing statement.

Fees must accompany the documents requesting release of the security interest or they could be returned, held at the filing office while a form letter is sent advising the secured party of the deficiency, or they might be recorded as an accommodation by a filing officer who is willing to take on the extra work of billing the person or company for the required fee.

Assignment of Secured Party's Interest

An assignment might be made by a secured party either at the time the financing statement is filed or as a separate filing made at some future date. If the assignment is made when the financing statement is filed and is included as a part of that financing statement, it will be handled by the filing officer in the same manner as any other filing of a security interest.

Some security interests in collateral are of relatively short duration; others may extend the full five years of the original filing, be renewed for a second five years via the filing of a continuation statement, and then subsequently experience one or more additional extensions. Other categories may involve more people in the body of those with a security interest—people who might find it questionable business practice to continue to offer changes in the security interest and the people involved for a relatively long period of time.

Assignments are given for reasons that stem from a single category or a combination of categories. An assignment on a percent or a section of the collateral might be given to a lender as collateral for a new or special piece of financing, or as collateral for the financing with the manufacturer of a new line of goods. It is assumed that the rapid turnover of the goods that are being purchased through the use of a partial assignment against other collateral will be liquidated rapidly. This will enable the party who gave the assignment on a part of the secured collateral to repay the debt from the sale of goods, file an amendment to the financing statement and assignments, and return the financing statement to its original level(s) of security.

A secured party may find it necessary or advantageous to assign his or her rights under a financing statement. To be an effective assignment, it must be made in the place or at the places where the original financing statement(s) was made, must be written on a separate statement of assignment by the secured person, must include the file number(s), names, and addresses of the secured party and of the debtor, and must describe the collateral in such detail as to make it readily identifiable to a third party or to any other party of interest (see Figures 21-10, 21-11, and 21-12).

When the filing officer receives the assignment, he or she follows the same procedure that is used for other filings: when the filing is for consumer goods, the document is marked with the date and hour of the filing and the assignment is noted on the index of the financing statement. Assignments covering fixture filings, timber to be cut, or all types of minerals are handled with variations on the just described procedures.

■ Assignments of mortgages are indexed under the name of the assignee.

This FINANCING STATEMENT is presented to a Filing Officer for filing pursuant to the Uniform Commercial Code | Maturity date (if any):

1. Debtor(s) Name (Last Name First) and Complete Address	2. Secured Party(ies) and Complete Address	This space for use of Filing Officer. (Date, Time and Filing Office.)

This statement refers to original Financing Statement bearing File No. _____ Dated _____ 19 _____

A. Continuation ( )	B. Partial Release ( )	C. Assignment ( )	D. Termination Statement ( )	E. Other (
The original financing statement between the foregoing Debtor and Secured Party, bearing the file number shown above, is still effective.	From the collateral described in the financing statement bearing the file number shown above, the Secured Party releases the following:	The Secured Party certifies that the Secured Party has assigned to the Assignee whose name and address is shown below, Secured Party's rights under the financing statement bearing the file number shown above in the following property:	This statement of termination of financing is presented to a Filing Officer for filing pursuant to the Uniform Commerical Code. The Secured Party certifies that the Secured Party no longer claims a security interest under the financing statement bearing the file number shown above.	
(FEE $3.00)	(FEE $3.00)	(FEE $3.00)	(FEE $1.00)	(FEE $3.00)

3. When collateral is crops or fixtures complete this portion of form.
   a. Description of real estate (Sufficient to identify the property).

   b. Name and complete address of record owner.

4a. ( ) Proceeds of Collateral are also covered. 4b. ( ) Products of Collateral are also covered. | No. of additional sheets presented. ( )

( ) Filed with Register of Deeds and Mortgages of _____ County. ( ) Secretary of State

( ) Filed with the County Clerk of _____ County.

Signature(s) of Secured Party(ies) or Assignee(s)

Dated: _____ 19 _____

_____
Not Valid unless signed.

FILING OFFICER COPY — This form of financing statement is approved by the Secretary of State of New Jersey.
STANDARD FORM — UNIFORM COMMERCIAL CODE — FORM UCC-3.

Figure 21-10. Statements of continuation, partial release, assignment, etc.—New Jersey (long form).

PIONEER BUSINESS FORMS, INC., TACOMA

A complete Source of Supply with Standard Forms for all Internal and External Processing necessary to be used with the Uniform Code System.

STATE OF WASHINGTON

UNIFORM COMMERCIAL CODE—STATEMENTS OF CONTINUATION, RELEASE, ASSIGNMENT, TERMINATION, ETC. — FORM UCC-3

INSTRUCTIONS:
1. PLEASE TYPE THIS FORM IN BLACK. DO NOT FOLD FOR MAILING.
2. Remove Secured Party and Debtor copies and send the other three pages with interleaved carbon paper intact to the filing officer.
3. Use the following Fee Schedule:

	Std.	Non-Std.		Std.	Non-Std.
(There is no fee for CONTINUATION FEE	3.00	5.00	AMENDMENT FEE	3.00	5.00
a Termination Statement.) ASSIGNMENT FEE	1.00	2.00	RELEASE FEE	1.00	2.00

4. If the space provided for any item(s) on the form is inadequate, the item(s) should be continued on additional sheets preferably 5"x 8" or 8"x 10". Only one copy of such additional sheets need be presented to the filing officer with a set of three copies of this statement. Indicate the number of sheets attached in the space provided.
5. At the time of filing, filing officer will return the third copy as an acknowledgement to the secured party(ies).
6. One or more transactions may be accomplished by a single filing of UCC-3. If multiple filings are intended, check the appropriate boxes and enclose the proper fee for each transaction.
7. DO NOT WRITE IN BOX 4.

This STATEMENT is presented to filing officer for filing pursuant to the Uniform Commercial Code.	No. of additional sheets presented:	3. Maturity date (if any)
1. Debtor(s): (last name first, and mailing address(es)	2. Secured Party(ies) and address(es)	4. FOR FILING OFFICER ONLY (Date, time, number and filing office)

5. This Statement refers to original Financing Statement No. ....

Filed with .... Date filed .... 19 ....

☐ CONTINUATION. The original financing statement between the foregoing Debtor and Secured party, bearing file number shown above, is still effective.

☐ TERMINATION. Secured party no longer claims a security interest under the financing statement bearing file number shown above.

☐ ASSIGNMENT. The secured party's right under the financing statement bearing file number shown above to the property described below has been assigned to the assignee whose name and address appears below.

☐ AMENDMENT. Financing Statement bearing file number shown above is amended as set forth below.

☐ RELEASE. Secured Party releases the collateral described below from the financing statement bearing file number shown above.

Assignee(s) of secured party(ies) and address(es):

BY: _____
SIGNATURE(S) OF DEBTOR(S)
(Required only on some amendments)

BY: _____
SIGNATURE(S) OF SECURED PARTY(IES)

1—FILING OFFICER—ALPHABETICAL

WASHINGTON STATE UCC-3   FORM APPROVED BY A. LUDLOW KRAMER, SECRETARY OF STATE (4-67)

Figure 21-11. Statements of continuation, partial release, assignment, etc.—Washington (short form).

- Fixture filings, timber to be cut, or minerals (a category that includes gas and oil) are indexed under the name of the assignor as grantor.

- Has the debtor no recorded interest in the real estate? The financing statement and any amendments to it must show the name of the owner of record. (A party with a security interest in crops, timber, or minerals in or on land not owned by the debtor would, prior to advancing any funds or filing a financing agreement and statement, satisfy himself or herself regarding the debtor's written agreement and/or arrangement with the record owner of the land. The potential for complications could be many and expensive if the party with the security interest failed to do his or her homework before advancing any form of collateral [funds, machinery, etc.] or filing a security agreement and a financing statement.)

Amendment to Original Financing Statement

Financing statements are subject to amendment. It is the nature of commerce for a person or a company to have a security interest in collateral which, due to business changes, market changes, or financial necessity, does not have the same position in the secured party's financial or commercial scheme as it did when the UCC filing was first made. Conditions change and, fortunately for both the debtor and the secured party, financing statements can be amended to reflect those changes.

Example: A food processor might advance money to a grower against the value of a crop that has been contracted for delivery at maturity to the food processor. The food processor advances money to the grower to cover labor and other costs. The farmer (now the debtor) has already

Figure 21-12. Statements of continuation, partial release, assignment, etc.—Oklahoma (short form).

signed a security agreement and a financing statement which has been forwarded to the filing officer of the jurisdiction in which the farm (and crops) is located. The food processor, being an old hand at securing its position, has had the security agreement and financing statement signed and filed before it becomes necessary to begin to fulfill the terms of the agreement, which are essentially that the food processor will advance specific sums of money at each of several stages in the growth and harvesting of the crop(s).

The farmer obtains his seed and his planting money from the local bank; the costs of tending the growing crop (cultivating, watering, etc.) are also covered primarily by his commitment from the bank. Where the food processor's security interest enters the scenario is during the stage immediately preceding the picking of the crop through delivery of the crop to the processor's plant.

If, in the course of the food processor's arrangement with the farmer, it becomes necessary for the processor to advance more money than is covered in the original financing statement, the food processor will amend the financing statement by filing a written statement which is signed by the debtor and the secured party. Because the amendment adds collateral to the original financing statement, the amendment is effective only as it pertains to the collateral (money) being added to the original financing statement and only from the filing date of the amendment.

An amended financing statement should be filed if the contents of the original financing statement become so clouded by change that they distort or mislead. There is no protection in a financing statement that has not kept pace with major changes. The only way to ensure that a financing statement remains effective is to amend it as often and as completely as circumstances may require. What about minor changes? It is not necessary to amend a financing statement that has one or two such errors, errors that do not convey a false picture or give information that might prove to be damaging to a third party.

Protect the integrity of your original financing statement. Update it by filing appropriate amendments as changes occur that would have a meaningful impact on the original document.

Termination of Interest in Goods

This occurs when the security interest no longer exists that was the basis for filing the financing statement. When the debtor has satisfied his or her obligation to the secured creditor and there will be no further advances or commitments of collateral, the secured party is obligated to file termination notices with each of the filing officers with whom the financing statement was filed. These notices must state that the secured party no longer has an interest in the collateral, must identify each of the filings by their location and file number, and must see that the debtor receives copies of the termination notice or a termination statement within 10 days after the debtor has made proper demand. Failure to meet this criteria exposes the secured party to a liability to the debtor of $100 plus any additional monetary loss suffered by the debtor because of the delay.

It is obvious that a secured party should respond to the debtor's demand for a termination statement within the 10 days specified in the Code. The possibility that a debtor might claim the loss of thousands of dollars because the filing officer's records led a third party to believe that the financing statement (a lien) against the goods (collateral) was currently applicable is a real and a potentially actionable cause. Has a debtor's obligation to a secured party been satisfied, but not removed from the record of filings because of the secured party's failure to follow through with the appropriate termination statement? This is not good enough to prevail in a suit involving loss or losses sustained by a third party who could not know that a termination statement should have been filed to end the effectiveness of the financing statement. And let us not forget the potential for a suit by the debtor or former debtor when he or she becomes aware that the continuing presence of an invalid financing statement is causing potential customers to back away from the collateral.

A termination statement must be signed by the person(s) who signed the financing statement. If the termination statement is signed by another person, a separate statement signed by the secured party of record must be included for the termination statement to be accepted by the filing officer(s) of the jurisdiction(s) in which the original filing(s) was made. The appropriate fee must accompany the termination statement or it probably will not be accepted for recording. (Some jurisdictions have been known to record a financing statement, a termination statement, or other document in a situation where the fee was not enclosed. Filing officers have then returned copies of the filed document(s) to the individual or company with a statement of the amount owing for filing services.)

I would not, however, advise any person or company to forward a document for filing without the appropriate fee being included and expect the filing officer to handle the transaction in the manner described. Filing officers have no obligation to incur additional work for their respective departments by giving a level of service that complicates the normal flow of paper work and is not mandated in any of the statutes.

PART 4

The Bankruptcy Act

The "Bankruptcy Code," which is the everyday terminology for the Bankruptcy Reform Act of 1978, was amended in 1984 by the Bankruptcy Amendments and Federal Judgment Act as a means to establish bankruptcy law in the United States and to ensure that all states would adopt the standard procedures represented by such legislation. Bankruptcy is a jurisdiction of the federal government and is governed by laws enacted by the federal government. The states are prohibited from enacting any laws that infringe upon or conflict with federal prerogatives in this area.

It was appropriate in past years to refer to a person, a sole proprietor, a partnership, or a corporation against whom a case had been filed under bankruptcy law as a "bankrupt." It was, for decades, an accepted terminology; it is, however, one that has been replaced with the term "debtor." You will not find reference to a "debtor" as a "bankrupt" in any proceeding that has been filed in recent years. In retrospect, the wonder is that it took such a long time to correct what was a major inaccuracy.

A sole proprietor, partnership, business, or company filing for protection under The Bankruptcy Act is not necessarily a bankrupt, and certainly is not so by definition until there has been due process under The Bankruptcy Act. There are often substantial differences among debtors; perhaps a partnership or company is as close to a breathing spell and a gradual reversal of business fortunes as a few concessions from creditors, while another company's position is so bleak as to be hopeless. One example would seem to offer a strong possibility for a return to the main stream of business life, while the other offers a slim chance for a turnaround. But until there is no flicker of life in the sole proprietorship, partnership, business, or company, none of them will quite have reached the point where there is neither life nor hope.

Creditors would be in deeper trouble than they are now if there was no federal bankruptcy statute. The Bankruptcy Act enables creditors to administer, via a creditor's committee and under the guidance and supervision of the bankruptcy court, the gathering of a debtor's assets under one umbrella for the protection and satisfaction of the creditors. It is obvious that some creditors are going to be much more satisfied than others (priority UCC filings, etc.), but the formal structure and procedures of a bankruptcy case impose the maximum amount of control in an area where, prior to the filing of a bankruptcy petition (voluntary or involuntary), there might have been a state of business and financial chaos. Whether the conclusion of a bankruptcy case results in the liquidation of the debtor's assets or acceptance by the creditors of a plan for continuing the business, the structured process offers the best chance for creditors and debtor alike to salvage the maximum result.

Commercial debtors benefit from a filing under Chapter 11 of The Bankruptcy Act because it gives them an opportunity to evaluate their situation without being subjected to collection calls from creditors asking payment of their past-due account. A filing under Chapter 11 gives the commercial debtor immunity from the collection efforts of creditors, collection agencies to whom they have assigned the accounts, or suits filed by attorneys retained by collection agencies or individual creditors. To earn the continued protection of the bankruptcy court, debtors are expected to adhere to a conduct of honesty in their relations with the bankruptcy court and with their creditors. The bankruptcy court is indeed the "court of last resort," and all too often the debtor has put the business or the company into a decline that is irreversible, but salvaging the business for the benefit of creditors, employees, and customers is often worthwhile and seldom without some reward.

In a "worst case" scenario, the debtor's business is not salvagable, assets are liquidated, creditors are paid their appropriate shares, and the debtor is discharged by the court. When this occurs it can be much more than a personal tragedy for those whose entrepreneurial vision went awry so badly and so completely that it was eventually forced into a bankruptcy situation. There are no winners in this situation. A few secured creditors (UCC filings) might step away from the bankruptcy with most or all of their money, but the majority of creditors will not fare so well. There will not only be the loss of receivables dollars, but, if the account has been a customer for several years, there will be the very real loss of a customer whose business was very profitable until the final few months of the relationship.

Who and what is a bankrupt? A bankrupt is any business or company which for one or many reasons fails to develop market share, loses market share, has a product that cannot compete successfully (price, quality, style, technology, need, etc.), is underfinanced for its level of rapid growth, or is underfinanced for the long-term task of carrying the young company until it can develop enough business to reach the break-even point, and then move on into profitability. It is any business or company whose management is not equal to the challenges of growth, of changing technology, of the constantly changing face of the marketplace, and of the priorities for effectively maximizing the use of cash flow. A bankrupt is a debtor carried to the ultimate power; if the effort to succeed has been genuine, it is a tragedy that transcends the regrettable loss of jobs and loss of an entrepreneurial vision.

Your Business, Your Customers, and the Bankruptcy Code

How should you approach The Bankruptcy Code as an entrepreneur, a corporate financial management person, or the credit manager for a company or business? The primary and obvious admonition is to avoid becoming a part of it, either as a creditor whose receivables dollars or other collateral is involved, or as an entrepreneur who is struggling to turn a fledgling company into a survivor, and eventually into a winner. Be wary of the bankruptcy process as it relates to your company's chances for recovering a substantial amount of a debtor's obligation to your company. Unless your company goes into a bankruptcy procedure as a creditor with a perfected UCC filing—a filing that has a top priority—the ratio of assets to liabilities will probably tilt heavily in favor of the liabilities.

When a bankruptcy situation finds your company in the position of an unsecured creditor, hope for an unexpected, but meaningful conversion of receivables (collateral) to cash. Unless the debtor company does exceptionally well in a liquidation of assets, the odds are strong that your company will not receive a settlement that represents a high percentage of the amount owed. Your company and others will do well to receive a cash dividend of 5 to 10 percent of each one dollar of receivables; the possibility of a 5 or 10 percent cash payment could be further diminished if there is an inability to convert assets into strong amounts of cash.

Throughout this and my two other books, I have consistently and aggressively advised readers to establish, to maintain, and to use high standards when screening the applications of prospective credit accounts. I have reminded readers that today's borderline credit account is either tomorrow's runaway success story or a candidate to become a part of tomorrow's bankruptcy statistics. And what are the chances that an account whose performance record is barely good enough to keep it in business will suddenly and miraculously step from the shadows into the bright light of success? Do I really need to ask? Of course they are not favorable—certainly not favorable enough for your company to accept more than a minimal amount of risk.

Terminology

In any discussion regarding bankruptcy or a bankruptcy procedure, words or terms that have special application in the context of bankruptcy will find their way into writings or discussions pertaining to individual cases. These are terms that are germane to proceedings of this type (terms which appear in writings or are used in discussions). To facilitate your ability to understand and to apply these terms, I am listing a few and giving an explanation of their meaning or application. These are not dictionary explanations, but are couched in the manner of self-helps.

Debtor: A sole proprietorship, partnership, business, or corporation against whom a case has been initiated under bankruptcy law.

Voluntary Petition: A petition filed by a debtor with the bankruptcy court to seek protection from creditors under the bankruptcy act.

Involuntary Petition: A petition filed by creditors of a debtor to force the debtor to seek relief under the Act and to bring about the appointment of a trustee to conserve the debtor's assets.

Bankruptcy Judge: The presiding judge in bankruptcy proceedings.

United States Trustee: The person who has administrative responsibility for the bankruptcy judge and who, among other duties, is charged with monitoring all Chapter 11 proceedings.

Interim Trustee: A disinterested person who is appointed by the court to act as trustee immediately after there has been a filing for debtor relief.

Trustee: This is the court's permanent officer who is elected by the creditors to liquidate the debtor's assets. Certain guidelines such as competence, experience, and residence enter into the selection of a permanent liquidating officer.

Insolvent: A debtor is judged to be insolvent when the total of debts, exclusive of exempt or fraudulently transferred property, is greater than the total of assets.

Examiner: A person appointed to handle a reorganization in a situation where the court has not appointed a trustee.

Creditor: A person, business, or company whose interest in the debtor's estate can be substantiated by sales, invoices, receivers, accounts receivable, and other transaction records.

There are other terms relating to bankruptcy and the bankruptcy process that surface throughout the lifetime of a case, but the majority of them are more easily identifiable than many of those just defined.

The Chapter Most Important to Commercial Creditors

The usual procedure in any filing of a voluntary or an involuntary petition in bankruptcy is for the debtor (or the debtor's creditors) to file for relief under Chapter 11 of The Bankruptcy Act. If the process of examination by the debtor's creditors and subsequent debtor efforts to come up with a continuation plan do not bring creditor acceptance, the bankruptcy court will dissolve the Chapter 11 and order a liquidation of the debtor's assets. Until that happens, the Chapter 11 process is the best hope for most creditors.

It should be noted that Chapter 11 is not universally popular with creditors. A creditor who has a priority claim under the UCC might not be pleased with the possibility of a continuation plan involving annual payments of 5 or 10 percent of individual debt obligations over a period of the first five years, with shares of stock to be issued for the remainder of individual creditor balances. If the priority creditor has no intention of resuming a credit relationship with the struggling survivor company, the creditor might prefer to see the assets liquidated and proceeds distributed to the creditors. In that scenario, the creditor would have all or almost all of its money available for use in other areas of the business.

Chapter 11 of The Bankruptcy Act offers creditors the opportunity to sit down with a debtor, question the debtor regarding the circumstances leading to the company's present position, question the debtor regarding the continuation plan that must be submitted within a court-specified number of weeks, and ultimately to determine whether the continuation measures that have been proposed can be implemented with the present personnel (or changes as indicated) by a company in its current state of business and financial disarray.

There is a strong element of risk when creditors accept the proposal(s) of a debtor who has come before them and has sold this once-stung group of creditors on the idea that a repeat of the present situation is highly unlikely. What, you must ask yourself, is the debtor proposing to do that offers such an improved level of maturity in the areas of business and financial management? If there is, at this point, a major negative as it pertains to the born-again zeal of incumbent management, address it in this manner: if the ideas being proposed are so good, so fresh, and so likely to succeed, what was occupying these same minds during the months when the business was sliding into the toilet? If there has been a track record of lax business controls, a pattern of excessive expenditures and ill-conceived business decisions, and a generally inadequate approach to building a business that can survive, what do you now see or hear to make you believe that this is one that can be made to rise from the depths? And if you grant the possibility that it can be made to rise, can it be done with the same management team at the controls?

There are some businesses which have been so poorly managed that it is better to liquidate them, pay the creditors their rightful percentages of the liquidated assets, and get on to other business. Frequently, however, Chapter 11 is the instrument that allows a desperately troubled business a second chance—an opportunity to cast aside the mistakes that brought the business to the brink of destruction, turn it around, and help it to move slowly toward the goals of break even and eventual profitability. An intelligent, conscientious, and hard-working entrepreneur should be given every reasonable chance to salvage his or her business or company; it's good business for everyone in the long haul. But what about an entrepreneur or a company whose work ethic is weak and whose effort to succeed is secondary to perks and salaries inconsistent with the debt structure of the business or company? That entrepreneur deserves what he or she usually gets from the creditors and the bankruptcy court: an enthusiastic thumbs down!

Secured Creditor Status

This is a brief reprise of the time we spent examining the wisdom and the value of taking full advantage of the provisions of the Uniform Commercial Code. Nothing is quite so satisfying as the knowledge that in a bad bankruptcy situation—one that promises to slide quickly into a liquidation of a very limited number of assets—your priority UCC filing is quite probably going to get your company 100 cents on the claim for receivables dollars that you have filed with the bankruptcy court. Are there charges of an imperfect filing by disgruntled peer creditors hoping to overturn your filing? Let them go ahead and try. If you have had your attorney guide you through the process of preparing the documents, or if you are knowledgable in the process, your careful preparation of the security agreement and financing statement should leave no room for doubt regarding the perfected status of your filing.

Secured creditor status is, as has been detailed in Part 3 of this book, the epitome of protection. It is light years ahead of creditors who must take their chances with the unsecured. There are priority levels in secured positions and it is to your advantage to have a top or near-top priority in any situation where a large dollar total of collateral (by the standards of your company or business) has been put at risk. What if, you might ask, the customer's credit rating is good and there appears to be adequate cash flow for the volume of business it transacts? Do not hesitate to protect your company's large receivables investment in the customer company with a security agreement and a financing statement. The majority of customer companies will applaud your attention to what is one of the best and most prudent of good business practices.

An Unsecured Creditor? Swim for Your Life!

An unsecured creditor who has been cast into a pool filled with the other unsecured creditors of a bankrupt debtor is in the most unenviable of positions. The unsecured creditors are forced to watch with envy as priority creditors (federal income tax, social security taxes, etc.) and creditors who have established priority claims among those who have perfected UCC filings prepare to absorb most or all of the money generated from a liquidation of the debtor's assets. Once it becomes a bankruptcy case, there is nothing an unsecured creditor (or any other) can do to improve his or her position. When a creditor chooses not to invoke the protection of a UCC filing, thereby accepting the role of an unsecured creditor, it is difficult to generate sympathy for that creditor when the debtor's business comes apart.

Is there any acceptable reason why a creditor whose investment in a debtor is substantial by the standards of his or her company should choose to be an unsecured creditor? None whatsoever. Although it is a question that may never be weighed in the sense of "should we or shouldn't we," the option is available in every situation where there is more than minimal risk or more than minimal exposure. Why should you choose to "swim for your life" in a pool where there are no UCC life preservers, where there are far too many other unsecured swimmers for the size of the pool and the amount of the water, and where the suspense does not end until the secured creditors have siphoned off all of the liquidated assets and the unsecured are left standing on the bottom of an empty pool? You should not allow yourself or your company to be in the position of receiving no share from the liquidation of a debtor's assets. Do not allow hundreds or thousands of your company's dollars to be buried with others in the "no dividend" land of the unsecured. Would you put $50,000 in a bank that offers no deposit insurance when you have a choice of banks that offer FDIC protection on an individual account to $100,000? You would make the obvious decision. You would go with a bank that offers protection for your funds over the one that offers a lobby snack of free coffee and slices of stale fruit cake, but no deposit protection.

Do not allow your company's receivables or its other collateral assets to face the world of commerce without the protection of a UCC filing. If you have good screening and monitoring procedures, it is conceivable that your company might avoid a major receivables loss for quite a period of time. But when one of those unprotected accounts suddenly files for relief under Chapter 11 of the Bankruptcy Code, it is too late for your company to experience the relief it could have felt if the receivables balance (or other collateral) had been given the protection of a UCC filing.

A single experience where the loss to the unsecured creditor is more than minimal is one loss more than any creditor should experience. The occasional small loss is a part of doing a credit business, and if you don't have one occasionally, your credit policy is probably too restrictive, but there should *never* be a Chapter 11 filing in which your company's debtor takes your money (receivables, goods, etc.) into the pool of unsecured creditors because someone in your company failed to do their job. Now, if the responsibility for these decisions is yours, shouldn't you be giving your company's assets the level of protection they deserve?

22

When a Debtor Files for Protection

It is seldom possible for a creditor to have a precise fix on the problems of a debtor or to successfully judge the day or the week in which those problems will slip from manageable to out of control. There might be a gradual slowing of receivables payments over a period of months or there might be a sudden and precipitous crisis—something that occurs without warning—caused by the failure of a major customer of your debtor. There is little difference in the end result, whether a problem escalates to a crisis slowly or suddenly; the impact upon creditors whose investment in the debtor company is substantial can send shudders through the cash flow of a creditor company.

Shock therapy may have its place in certain areas of the medical profession, but it is unwelcome in the field of credit management. Good news in this profession is rarely something of such magnitude that the person who receives it has a reaction that exceeds surprise. Bad news, however, can come in assorted sizes and flavors, including the shock therapy of a development so catastrophic that it can cause the failure of a major customer. It follows that surprises, if we must have them, should be held at a minimum and their magnitude held always at a level well below that of shock.

The Filing

There are general and specific guidelines to determine when a debtor may file a voluntary petition for relief from creditors under Chapter 11 of The Bankruptcy Act, or when the debtor's creditors may file an involuntary petition. If the petition is involuntary and the debtor does not challenge the filing, the bankruptcy court will issue an order for relief. If the debtor challenges the petition, the bankruptcy court will grant an order for relief if the following conditions exist:

1. The debtor (company, partnership, or sole proprietorship) has not been paying its debts on a "when-due" basis.

2. The debtor's problems are so many and complex that a custodian was appointed and/or took possession of the debtor's property during the 120 days preceding the filing of the bankruptcy petition.

3. An involuntary petition is filed by three creditors who have undisputed claims that total $500 more than the value of any lien on the property securing the claim.

4. The total number of creditors is less than 12, and any one of the creditors files an involuntary petition.

5. Petitioners file an improper or a frivolous petition against a debtor; such petitioners are subject to severe penalties. The debtor's business could be severely damaged, which could also result in a civil action and substantial damages.

6. Involuntary petitions, dismissed as a finding of the bankruptcy court, result in the court awarding to the debtor costs, attorney's fees, and damages arising from a creditor taking possession of the debtor's property.

Forms for filing a petition may be obtained at any of the United States District Courts for the district in which the filing is to be made. If there is a U.S. District Court, there is a U.S. Bankruptcy Court attached to it in a subordinate position.

When a debtor files a petition, it automatically activates a stay of any legal proceedings that might be working against the debtor. The stay protects the debtor against the collection efforts of creditors, third-party collection agencies, and attorneys. It puts the actions of all creditors on hold and eliminates any possibility that one or more creditors might move to gain an advantage over the others. If a creditor does not have an established advantage—a legal advantage—by the time a debtor files for protection, the time for obtaining such an advantage has passed. And if a creditor attempts by fraudulent or other means to gain an after-the-filing advantage, the penalties can be severe.

There are some things that can and cannot be enforced after the bankruptcy court has issued a stay. Among the areas in which the bankruptcy court does not have jurisdiction are criminal matters. The following are not effected when a stay is issued by the bankruptcy court:

1. The issuance of a tax deficiency. (Creditors may be absorbing the beating of their lives, but various entities of the government will be doing whatever is necessary and legal to get 100 cents on each dollar of debt obligation.)

2. Criminal proceeding that have been filed or are about to be filed against the debtor. (The bankruptcy court has no jurisdiction in staying these matters.)

3. Civil court mandated obligations of alimony, child support and/or maintenance, or support received from property that are exempt from being included in the debtor's estate.

4. Police actions or regulatory actions by units of the government.

What cannot be enforced against a debtor after the petition has been filed? Any judgment that has been obtained against the debtor cannot be enforced. During the time frame when the lien is in effect, no new lien can be created or enforced against the debtor's estate. The stay remains in force until the case is closed, dismissed, a discharge is granted or denied, or property that has been protected against the actions of creditors no longer belongs to the debtor's estate. And during the time frame when the stay is in effect, no new lien can be created or enforced against the estate.

I do not want to create a false impression regarding the debtor's duties and responsibilities. The debtor does not move into the sanctuary of the bankrupt's protection without incurring a court-imposed timetable for information and reports. One of the first reports required by the court is a list of creditors to whom the debtor owes money from the sale of product or owes for goods or collateral still unsold and in the debtor's warehouse. It is the debtor's obligation to prepare a list of balances owing, including those that are disputed. When the bankruptcy court furnishes creditors with a copy of the list, it is the responsibility of each creditor to check the accuracy of account balances on this published list. If the creditor's records indicate a higher balance than the one listed by the debtor, the creditor should take steps immediately to forward copies of records (invoices, receivers signed by the debtor or the debtor's representative) that will substantiate the dollar total claimed by the creditor.

In addition to a list of creditor obligations, the debtor is required to furnish to the bankruptcy court a schedule of all assets and liabilities. The schedule must be clear as to the description and location of the assets, their age, condition, and life expectancy. Within the same time frame the debtor must furnish the court with two reports of an overlapping nature: the first statement details the condition of the company's financial affairs, and the second is a schedule or a projection of the company's income and expenses for the next week and month.

Income and expenses should both drop after the filing of a Chapter 11 petition. Many who owe money to the debtor will attempt to take advantage of the debtor's precarious financial situation by delaying account payments. Expenses for certain service and supplies will drop because the business, if still operating, will be doing so on a very controlled basis. Suppliers and vendors who have leased trucks, automobiles, production machinery, buildings, and real estate to the debtor will be in the same position as the other creditors.

Debtors must cooperate with the trustee (this includes surrendering to the trustee any records or property important to the trustee's work: documents, papers, ledgers, data processed reports, etc.); debtors must attend the meeting of creditors and be examined by them or by their representatives; debtors must cooperate fully with the bankruptcy court and with the creditors' committee in meeting timetables set for submitting a plan for continuation of the business (if that is thought by the court and the creditors' committee to be a viable option); if the first proposal is rejected, debtors must meet the timetable for a second version of the plan.

Notification to Creditors of the Filing

The first official word that most creditors receive when one of their customers files for protection under Chapter 11 is when the notice arrives from the bankruptcy court. There may have been rumors—perhaps something even more substantive than rumors—but the notice to creditors of the filing for Chapter 11 protection says it all. The notice for a first meeting of the debtor's committee follows quickly; creditors are requested to attend the first meeting to participate in questioning the debtor and to select the creditors' committee, which will work with the judge of the bankruptcy court. The sequence of events from filing through the first meeting of creditors is as follows:

1. The debtor files a petition in Chapter 11.
2. The court appoints a receiver of the debtor's property or a trustee in bankruptcy who continues in possession of the debtor's property.
3. The court may appoint an appraiser.
4. The court mails notices of the first meeting of creditors from a list of creditors given to the court by the debtor (see Figure 22-1). (If available, a copy of the debtor's proposed "arrangement"—how the debtor proposes to handle creditor balances and how the business would be continued—is included with the notice.)

Figure 22-1. United States bankruptcy court order (meeting of creditors).

UNITED STATES BANKRUPTCY COURT
CENTRAL DISTRICT OF CALIFORNIA—LOS ANGELES
CHAPTER 11
IN RE:_____ CASE NUMBER:_____

95103   8723987
U.S. BANKRUPTCY COURT
ROOM 906, U.S. COURTHOUSE
312 NO. SPRING ST.
LOS ANGELES, CA 90012-4701

CHAPTER 11
ORDER FOR MEETING OF CREDITORS, COMBINED WITH
NOTICE OF AUTOMATIC STAY

To the debtor, his or her creditors, and other parties in interest:
An order for relief under 11 U.S.C. Chapter 11, having been entered
on a petition filed by (or against) the above named debtor on
December 27, 199X
IT IS ORDERED, AND NOTICE IS HEREBY GIVEN THAT:
1. A meeting of creditors pursuant to 11 U.S.C., 341(a) shall be held at:
U.S. TRUSTEE HEARING ROOM   DATE
U.S. FEDERAL BUILDING   JAN. 6, 199X
300 N. LOS ANGELES ST., RM 3114 HOUR
LOS ANGELES, CA   3:15 P.M.

2. The debtor shall appear in person (or, if the debtor is a partnership,
by a general partner, or, if the debtor is a corporation, by its president
or other executive officer) at that time and place for the purpose of
being examined.
YOU ARE FURTHER NOTIFIED THAT:
The meeting may be continued or adjourned from time to time by
notice at the meeting without further written notice to creditors.
At the meeting the creditors may file their claims, examine the
debtor, and transact such other business as may properly come before
the meeting.

As a result of the filing of the petition, certain acts and proceedings
against the debtor and his property are stayed as provided in 11
U.S.C. 362(a).

The debtor (or trustee) has filed or will file a list of creditors and
equity security holders pursuant to Rule 1007. Any creditor holding a

(Continued)

Figure 22-1. (*Continued*) United States bankruptcy court order (meeting of creditors).

listed claim which is not listed as disputed, contingent, or unliquidated as to amount, may, but need not file a proof of claim in this case. Creditors whose claims are not listed or whose claims are listed as disputed, contingent, or unliquidated as to amount and who desire to participate in the case or share in any distribution must file their proofs of claim on or before the last day fixed for filing a proof of claim. Any creditor who desires to rely on the list has the responsibility for determining that his or hers is accurately listed.

LOCAL RULE 3001 (B) PROVIDES THAT A PROOF OF CLAIM, INCLUDING AMENDMENTS THEREOF, MAY BE FILED AT ANY TIME PRIOR TO CONFIRMATION OF THE PLAN UNLESS A DIFFERENT TIME IS FIXED BY THE COURT ON NOTICE AS PROVIDED BY BANKRUPTCY RULE 3003 (C) (3).

FILE CLAIM FORM ON THE REVERSE SIDE IN DUPLICATE WITH:
  U.S. BANKRUPTCY COURT
  ROOM 906, U.S. COURTHOUSE
  312 NO. SPRING ST.
  LOS ANGELES, CA 90012-4701

Dated: DECEMBER 2, 199X   By The Court
AT LOS ANGELES, CA
CHARLES A. MILLER, CLERK OF COURT

[*Author's Note:* The reverse side of the original copy of this Order, and Notice, is the Claim Form. Complete it in duplicate, make a copy for your file, and forward the original and a duplicate as instructed.]

5. The judge presides at meeting(s) and examines the debtor (along with creditors and attorneys for the creditors) as to reasons for the insolvency or inability to meet obligations, to hear witnesses, and to receive written acceptances (or rejections) from creditors on the proposed "arrangement."

6. Debtors seldom have an "arrangement" to present at the first meeting of creditors. The bankruptcy judge will set a time frame within which the debtor must file the plan of arrangement. The judge then adjourns the first meeting of creditors until a minimum of 15 days after the date when the debtor must deliver the plan of arrangement to the court. The 15-day time lag between delivery of the plan and the next meeting of creditors provides enough time for the judge and the creditors' com-

mittee to examine the proposed arrangement, to have copies prepared, to include the recommendations of the creditors' committee (acceptance or rejection of the proposal), and to mail with a copy of the notice for the next creditors' meeting.

These steps take the Chapter 11 proceeding to the point where creditors have been notified of the filing, have had a first meeting at which time they examined the debtor, were given reasons—as seen by the debtor—for the present sorry state of the debtor's business or company, and have been sent a copy of the debtor's proposal for dealing with creditor obligations as set forth in the Chapter 11 filing, while concurrently trying to turn what is currently a loser into, at minimum, a survivor.

At this point in the procedure, there are many unanswered questions. Will the creditors accept the plan as submitted? Will they send it back for anything from a fine tuning to a major overhaul? Is there a lingering suspicion that the debtor has been less than candid in his or her assessment of the reasons for seeking the protection of the bankruptcy court? Are assets unaccounted for or are there flagrantly high expenditures which raise the question of whether the debtor has been systematically syphoning sums of money from the business at what appears to be creditor expense? Candidly, is this debtor an honest person who simply lost control of the business or a scoundrel who can hardly wait for the proceedings to end so he or she can disappear to another part of the country, live high for a period of time on the proceeds from this bankruptcy, then do it all over again? Stay tuned in!

Before moving on to the next topic, a word regarding the notice for a first meeting of creditors and the debtor's obligation to furnish the bankruptcy court with a list of creditors.

The notice for a first meeting of creditors should have, on the reverse side, a claim form and instructions for completing and returning it to the bankruptcy court. In some jurisdictions the claim form might be on a separate sheet of paper, but the point is to be sure that you complete and return it promptly.

Instances occur where a debtor will fail to list a creditor, either because the debtor disputes the balance allegedly owed or simply overlooks the creditor's account when preparing the list that must accompany the forms for a Chapter 11 filing. Why was your firm notified of the first meeting of creditors if your firm's name wasn't on the list of creditors given to the court? It could have been on the original list and been inadvertently deleted when the court prepared lists for mailing to creditors. If your firm is listed, but the firm's name is followed or preceded by an asterisk, it indicates that the debtor has questioned the validity of the obligation or the amount of it. If the amount is not listed correctly, you should attach data to substantiate the amount of your claim when the claim form is returned to the court.

Jurisdiction of the Bankruptcy Court

The bankruptcy court has jurisdiction in all areas of the bankruptcy process in the specific district of its authority (see Figure 22-2). Those areas include:

1. The filing of a bankruptcy petition.

2. The granting of a stay against the collection efforts of collectors or their agents (see Figure 22-3).

3. The notifying of creditors who appear on the debtor's list.

4. The appointing of a trustee or conservator.

5. The scheduling of a first meeting of the creditors.

6. The examining of the debtor by the creditors or the creditor's representatives.

7. The appointing of a creditors' committee.

8. An evaluation of the validity of secured claims alleged to have a priority versus the claims of other secured or unsecured creditors.

9. A ruling on the merit of challenges to the preferred or secured status of UCC filings.

10. The placement of government claims of tax priority in their proper context and sequence.

11. The presidium over the examination of debtor(s) by creditors or representatives of creditors.

12. The ensurance that no creditor gains an unlawful preference over one or all of the other creditors who file claims against the debtor's estate.

13. The work done with the creditor's committee and the debtor in what should be a joint effort to determine whether the debtor can offer an acceptable plan of arrangement (see Figures 22-4 and 22-5).

14. An order for either a dissolution and sale of assets for the benefit of creditors or an approval of the plan of arrangement proposed by the debtor and accepted by the creditors.

In addition to the above, the bankruptcy court is responsible for the trustee's reports, notices to creditors regarding creditors' meetings, notices and recommendations from the creditors' committee, and the dissemination of all pertinent information pertaining to the activities of that committee. Progress reports prepared by the creditors' committee are reviewed and approved by the court, then printed and mailed to creditors of record. Creditors' committee meetings may be few or numerous, depending upon

Figure 22-2. Use of collateral (protection secured by lien on property).

FRAZER, CARTER, WALSH, BENSON & HARRIS
A Professional Corporation Franklin Carter
529 California Street
Suite 1350
San Francisco, CA 94120

Attorneys for North Bay National Bank

UNITED STATES BANKRUPTCY COURT
FOR THE NORTHERN DISTRICT OF CALIFORNIA

In Re:	)	Bankruptcy No. 5-89-16524-M
	)	
XYZ CORPORATION, INC.,	)	Chapter 11
A California Corporation	)	
	)	
Debtor	)	
	)	

STIPULATION PERTAINING TO USE OF COLLATERAL PROVIDING FOR ADEQUATE PROTECTION SECURED BY LIEN ON PROPERTY OF THE ESTATE UNDER s364(c), MODIFICATION OF STAY AND ORDER THEREON

TO: THE HONORABLE WILBUR A. HANSEN, BANKRUPTCY JUDGE:

XYZ Corporation, Inc., the Debtor and Debtor-in-Possession herein, and North Bay National Bank, the Secured Party, apply to this Court for an Order authorizing use of collateral, providing for adequate protection and the pledging of collateral in connection therewith, and to borrow funds pursuant to 11 U.S.C. s364(c) and pledge collateral in connection therewith.

1. On September 14, 199X, the Debtor filed its Petition under Chapter 11 herein, and is Debtor-in-Possession.

2. The Debtor's business consists of a health spa and athletic club. Debtor is the owner of certain real property, as more particularly described on the deed of trust attached as part of Exhibit "A" hereto ("Real Property"), rents, issues and profits, equipment, and pro-

---

(Continued)

Figure 22-2. (*Continued*) Use of collateral (protection secured by lien on property).

ceeds thereof as set forth in Exhibit "A" (collectively the "Collateral"), used in the operation of the business.

(Page Two)

3. The Debtor requires funds to operate said business and to preserve the Collateral.

4. The Debtor is presently without funds necessary to operate, other than funds generated from the operation of the club, restaurant, other facilities and member fees.

5. Other than certain ongoing services and supplies provided by trade vendors, the Debtor is unable to obtain credit on a basis other than under s364(c) of the Bankruptcy Code.

6. The Secured Party and Debtor acknowledges that the unpaid balance of the loan by Secured Party to Debtor (the "Loan") as of August 7, 1988, including principal and interest only, is $6,945,286. The Secured Party has agreed to consent to use of its Collateral as provided for hereinafter, on a basis that will provide adequate protection and security. In that connection, Debtor and Secured Party have agreed that adequate protection and the necessary security can be provided through use of Collateral secured pursuant to the Loan and the loan documents ("Loan Documents") previously entered into between the Secured Party and the Debtor (copies of which are attached hereto and incorporated by reference herein and are attached as Exhibit "A"), as modified pursuant to the terms of paragraph 7 hereof and this paragraph. Except as expressly modified herein, the Loan Documents shall remain in full force and effect.

7. The Secured Party and the Debtor hereby agree as follows:

(a) Secured Party consents to the continued use of Collateral by the Debtor, for use by the Debtor as hereinafter set forth, provided that the Court has approved this Stipulation and the

(Skipped Pages 3 Through 14)

(Page Fifteen)

20. Nothing herein is intended to create any right on the part of any third party to assume the terms and conditions of this Stipulation and

Figure 22-2. (*Continued*) Use of collateral (protection secured by lien on property).

agreement, and Secured Party retains its right to declare all principal, accrued interest, associated fees and charges, immediately due and payable upon the sale or transfer by the Debtor of the Real Property, or any interest therein, or upon any change in the ownership of the shares of stock of Debtor in excess of 25% of the outstanding shares, or effective change in control of the Debtor.

WHEREFORE, the parties hereto pray that this Court enter its Order authorizing the Debtor to use cash collateral, to borrow funds under s364(c) of the Code from the Secured Party pursuant to the terms of this Stipulation, and each of the terms of this Stipulation be authorized, and declaring that the notice and opportunity for hearing which has been given in respect to this Stipulation are appropriate in the particular circumstances.

DATED: November 22, 199X.
              NORTH BAY NATIONAL BANK
              (Secured Party)
              By:_____
              Its:_____
DATED: November 22, 199X.
              XYZ CORPORATION, INC.
              (Debtor)
              By:_____
              Its:_____

the debtor's level of cooperation. If there is good cooperation, it is often possible to minimize the number of meetings while maximizing the results. There is, however, an ongoing effort on the part of the bankruptcy court to move all parties toward a speedy and an equitable solution to the filing.

Appointing a Trustee (or Conservator)

It is mandatory in any filing of a voluntary petition in bankruptcy that immediately after the judge issues his or her order for relief, an interim trustee must be appointed by the United States Trustee. If the district is a part of that system, the United States Trustee will appoint an interim trustee from a panel of prequalified names. If no member of the United States Trustee's panel is able or willing to serve, the United States Trustee

Figure 22-3. Notice of hearing (debtor-in-possession).

UNITED STATES BANKRUPTCY COURT
FOR THE NORTHERN DISTRICT OF CALIFORNIA

IN RE:)BANKRUPTCY NO. 8-42-16341-Z
XYZ CORPORATION, INC.   ) CHAPTER 11
A CALIFORNIA CORPORATION   )
)
)
                    DEBTOR.   )
_____   )

NOTICE OF HEARING
ON APPLICATION OF DEBTOR-IN-POSSESSION
REQUESTING APPROVAL OF STIPULATION
PERTAINING TO USE OF COLLATERAL
PROVIDING FOR ADEQUATE PROTECTION SECURED BY LIEN
ON PROPERTY OF THE ESTATE
UNDER SECTION 364(c), MODIFICATION OF STAY

TO: THE CREDITORS OF THE ABOVE-NAMED DEBTOR AND
       OTHER PARTIES IN INTEREST:

NOTICE IS HEREBY GIVEN THAT XYZ CORPORATION, INC.,
Debtor-In-Possession herein, has filed an Application with the Court
seeking approval of a Stipulation and Agreement between the Debtor
and Urban Bank, and that said Application will be heard, considered,
and passed upon at the coutroom of the HONORABLE CHARLES C.
MONROEL, UNITED STATES BANKRUPTCY JUDGE, ROOM 396,
U.S. POST OFFICE BUILDING, NORTH FIRST & ST. JOHN STREETS,
SAN JOSE, CALIFORNIA, on: WEDNESDAY, OCTOBER ___23___, 199X,
AT___2:00 PM.___.

The Stipulation and Agreement negotiated between the Debtor and
Urban Bank contains a number of provisions, terms and conditions,
under which the Debtor will continue to operate its business known as
the Centurian Club. Because of the complexity and comprehensive
nature of the Stipulation and Agreement between the parties, a copy of
the complete Stipulation and Agreement is attached to this notice to
provide creditors and parties-in-interest with complete information and
details regarding the transaction. Exhibits to the Stipulation are on file
with the Court.

Figure 22-3. *(Continued)* Notice of hearing (debtor-in-possession).

Reference is hereby made to all pleadings and documentation on file with the Court with respect to this Chapter 11 case, which information is available for inspection. Creditors or other parties-in-interest having any questions, or wishing additional information regarding the matter, may contact the Debtor's Counsel, CARL M. GREEN, GREEN & GREEN, 19 NORTH MARKET STREET, SUITE 168, SAN JOSE, CALIFORNIA 95123, 408 555-9999.

Dated: September 16, 199X

GREEN & GREEN
Attorneys for Debtor and
Debtor-in-Possession

(ANY CORRESPONDENCE REQUIRING AN ANSWER FROM THE COURT SHOULD BE ACCOMPANIED BY A STAMPED, SELF-ADDRESSED ENVELOPE.)

is obligated by law to serve. When a trustee who is not a member of that panel has, prior to the order for relief, been serving in that capacity, the United States Trustee may appoint that person to continue. Interim trustees have all the powers of trustees, receive the same pay, must be disinterest parties, and serve only until a permanent trustee has been appointed or elected. In districts where there is no United States Trustee, the bankruptcy court appoints the interim trustee.

Involuntary bankruptcies present a different timetable for appointing an interim trustee. Because the filing of an involuntary petition in bankruptcy is an expression of extreme concern by one or more creditors regarding the debtor's business or company, an interim trustee may be appointed before an order for relief has been issued. An interim trustee, appointed by the court after notice and a hearing, becomes trustee of the debtor's estate with the goal of preserving that property. Whether the interim trustee takes possession of the property or attempts to operate the debtor's business is something that is decided by the circumstances of each case. In a situation where the trustee does take possession of the estate and begins to operate the debtor's business, the debtor cannot reclaim the business unless a bond of sufficient size is posed to meet the court's requirement.

Electing a Trustee

A trustee may be elected if creditors who have 20 percent of the allowed, unsecured, liquidated claims request it. Each creditor has a vote who holds an allowed, liquidated, or unsecured claim that is not entitled to priority, has no interests materially adverse to the interest of the general unsecured creditors, and is not an insider. A candidate for the position of trustee is elected if creditors who hold 20 percent in amount of claims just described actually vote and the candidate receives a majority in the amount of the

---

(Date)

To: Unsecured Claimants
From: Creditor's Committee
Re: Plan of Arrangement/Continuation (Dated _____)
  Case Number 14969-92—Bertram Manufacturing Company

It is the judgment of your creditor's committee that the attached Plan of Arrangement/Continuation represents the best and most equitable arrangement that the debtor company's position will allow.

Please read it carefully. If you agree that the provisions of the plan are acceptable as presented, indicate your acceptance by marking the box that precedes YES. If you do not agree that the plan is acceptable in its present form, indicate that decision by marking the box that precedes NO. Add your reason(s) for rejecting the plan and what changes would, for your company, make it acceptable.

The creditor's committee urges claimants to approve the plan by the percentages necessary for the court to certify the plan (two-thirds of the total claims dollars of claimants who vote and over 50 percent of the number of claimants who vote).

_____ *Yes,* we accept the plan as presented.
_____ *No,* we do not accept the plan in its present form.

It is our feeling that the following change(s) should be made:_____

_____

_____

_____

For the Committee,

_____   (Date) _____
     (Chair)

Figure 22-4. Cover letter (creditors' committee to creditors about debtor's plan of arrangement/continuation plan).

votes cast. If for any reason a trustee is not elected, the interim trustee will continue to serve.

The duties and powers of a trustee are considerable and very important to the success of the Chapter 11 process. Examples of the trustee's duties and responsibilities are as follows:

(Date)

To: Unsecured Claimants
From: Creditor's Committee
Re: Modification(s) to Plan of Arrangement/Continuation
    (Dated _____)
    Case Number 14969-92—Bertram Manufacturing Company

The attached modification of the Plan of Arrangement/Continuation incorporates changes requested by a majority of creditors who responded to the Committee's cover letter and original version of the Plan of Arrangement/Continuation which was dated _____ . It includes the two major changes that were requested by the creditors and brings the plan within parameters defined by a majority of the respondents.

The Creditor's Committee requests that claimants approve the modified plan and return the ballot portion of this cover letter by _____ (date) _____ .

Your cooperation is appreciated.

_____
       Chair

To: Creditor's Committee
From: (Name of Creditor Company)

____ *Yes,* we accept the plan as modified on _____ (date) _____ .
____ *No,* we cannot accept the plan as modified _____ (date) _____ .

Signed,

_____
      (Title)

Figure 22-5. Cover letter (modification[s] to plan of arrangement).

1. Collect money and convert property of the estate to money.

2. Close the estate (if a liquidation) as rapidly as is compatible with the bankruptcy process and the interests of creditors.

3. Keep accurate records. Be accountable for property received from the debtor.

4. Examine proofs of claims. If necessary, object to the allowance of any claim that seems to be improper.

5. When the examination warrants, oppose the discharge of the debtor.

6. Furnish information concerning the state when requested by a party in interest.

7. If the trustee is continuing the debtor's business, file periodic reports with government tax collecting agencies.

8. Make and file a final report with the bankruptcy court that has jurisdiction/administration of the estate.

9. File a bond with the court in favor of the United States predicated on the faithful performance of the trustee's duties.

10. Ensure that the debtor makes payments for administrative expenses and percentage fees for a private Chapter 13 trustee.

11. Take the necessary steps to see that the debtor makes appropriate payments to creditors.

The trustee has other powers, some of which are known as Avoidance Powers. One of these powers is the status of a Lien Creditor, which attaches to the trustee on the date of the filing of the petition. Another of these powers is the avoidance of statutory liens on the property of the debtor, which are subject to a series of disclaimers and conditions (when a bankruptcy case begins, when a custodian is appointed, when a debtor becomes insolvent, etc.). Subject to the court's approval, the trustee may also assume or reject any unexpired lease of the debtor's or any executory contract (contracts on which some performance is still due). Under the old Bankruptcy Act, leases containing bankruptcy clauses were permitted. When a bankruptcy was filed, these leases were automatically terminated. This clause was found to hinder efforts to reorganize a business or company and is no longer allowed.

When a trustee is by order of the bankruptcy court about to liquidate a company or business, that bankrupt should forget about "book value" or "fair price" as the criteria for judging what might be realized from the court ordered sale. Bargain hunters will have a field day which does not add up to prices approximating the legitimate value at which the bankrupt company has been carrying assets items. The unfortunate bankrupt doesn't need the additional burden of pennies on the dollar for the company's assets, but it is unlikely that the revenue from mandated or forced sales will ever change.

The Creditor's Committee

In any Chapter 11 proceeding, the conduit for the majority of the creditors, the debtor, and the bankruptcy court is the creditors' committee. It is composed usually of three to eleven members; the number is based frequently on the willingness of creditors to serve, which is often dependent upon considerations of the extra time and travel necessary in the performance of the committee's duties. It should also be noted that the committee is not closed to smaller creditors (based upon amounts owed by the debtor) if their presence is deemed appropriate for a good balance of large and small creditors.

The creditors' committee is appointed (or elected) at the first meeting of creditors, which normally occurs within a short period of time after the bankruptcy court has issued the order for relief. It is never held earlier than a minimum of 10 days after creditors have been notified of the meeting date. The debtor is required to be present with certain of the company's financial records (if not offered voluntarily, the creditors will request that the court subpoena them). If it is a corporation, key financial and management officers—usually accompanied by legal counsel—will appear for the company. Creditors whose claims involve a substantial sum of money are also likely to be accompied by counsel, which can lead to some spirited exchanges as anxious and frustrated creditors demand acceptable answers. The first meeting, incidentally, is not one at which the bankruptcy judge presides. Because he or she is not allowed to be present, the presiding officer is either the interim trustee or the United States Trustee.

The creditors' committee is empowered to consult with the trustee regarding the administration of the estate and it may offer suggestions relative to the performance of his or her duties.

Summary of Duties and Responsibilities

If the seven largest shareholders have agreed to serve on the committee, and have perhaps been joined by one or two smaller creditors, the work of the committee can begin.

1. The committee's first official act immediately after it has been appointed will be to meet with the trustee. It is a familiarization meeting at which some business will be transacted and a discussion of an agenda for future meetings will take place.

2. At the committee's request, and at the discretion of the court, the committee may select professional assistance such as an attorney or an accountant. This is done at one of its first scheduled meetings.

3. Committee members and the trustee or debtor in possession must work together to ensure that the case is properly administered.

4. The committee will investigate in depth the way the debtor has been operating the business, whether it thinks the business can be returned to profitability, and other matters relevant to the preparation of a plan or arrangement.

5. It is a responsibility of the committee to help with the preparation of a plan and, before presenting the plan to the creditors for approval or rejection, to assure itself and the court that it does represent the best interests of all parties.

6. When one has not already been selected, the committee will request the appointment of a trustee or an examiner.

7. The committee's duties also include performing and/or supervising the performance of other services which are necessary to protect the interest of creditors.

A creditors' committee may present a plan to the membership with the recommendation that it be accepted or rejected, or it may make no recommendation at all. It is required, however, to push the creditors to make a judgment (written ballot) for or against a plan and its subsequent revisions. When the plan as submitted is rejected by the creditors, committee members and the debtor, working under the direction of the court, must attempt to make changes that will make it acceptable to creditors and the debtor. The alternative to a plan that is not acceptable to creditors, and after various revisions and modifications is still not acceptable, is the liquidation of assets and the discharge of a debtor who has become a discharged bankrupt.

If you should ever find yourself in a situation where your company is a creditor in a Chapter 11 case, do not shy away from membership on the creditors' committee. If you can arrange to take the time necessary to attend meetings and to work with other committee members, do it. Examining the conduct of a debtor's affairs, seeing and hearing the reasons for the company's slide or plunge into insolvency, examining and considering documents and arrangements with peer credit managers, and negotiating with the debtor hopefully will bring the entire process together into an acceptable arrangement for continuing the business under conditions that are beneficial to creditors and debtors alike. This can be an enormously satisfying and a truly beneficial learning experience.

Key Phrases

There are a few phrases that recur frequently when the subject is bankruptcy. Here are a few definitions that may make it easier to interpret what has been written or is being said.

- *Creditor:* One who holds any kind of claim against the debtor.
- *Debtor:* The person or entity in any straight bankruptcy or liquidation of assets.
- *Debtor in Possession:* A debtor who has been allowed by the court to retain possession of the property. It may also be a trustee appointed by the court to serve during the term of the case.
- *Claim:* This category includes all rights to payments whether from judgment, liquidation of assets, secured or unsecured, etc. It alsoincludes the right to a cash settlement in a breach of performance (contract, personal or company services, product failure, etc.).
- *Corporation:* Any company or association that has the rights of a corporation, excluding a partnership or an individual.
- *Party in Interest:* A person or entity who has an interest in the proceedings (debtors, creditors, members of the creditors' committee, and equity security holders).
- *Petition:* This term includes all voluntary, involuntary, and joint petitions filed in a case commenced under The Bankruptcy Act.

Secured Claims Versus Unsecured Claims

The familiarity that comes with having used certain terms for many years occasionally causes me to use the terms "secured creditors" and "unsecured creditors," terms that have been replaced in the Code by "secured claims" and "unsecured claims." What has not changed is the simple fact that secured claimholders are entitled to receive payment prior to general claimholders (including priority claimants) to the full amount of their secured interest. If the secured interest exceeds the value of the property securing the claim, the claim will be broken down into two parts: a secured claim, to the extent that the value of the collateral covers the claim (value to be determined by creditor, trustee, debtor in possession, or, if there is no agreement among them, by the court), and an unsecured claim for the balance. It is not uncommon for a debtor's balance to occasionally exceed the creditor's secured claim, but the hope is that any amount in excess of the filing is small—preferably *very* small!

What is the difference between a secured claim and an unsecured claim? Without reverting to more than one cliche, perhaps the most appropriate phrase for describing what is an enormous difference between secured and unsecured claimants is to say they are like "night and day." A secured claim has so many things going for its company, that comparisons between the two extremes are ludicrous. If you are a secured creditor, your company has a perfected Uniform Commercial Code filing. Your company may also have a priority secured position and the knowledge that the debtor's Chapter 11 filing cannot impact your company because of the priority filing; the fact that, in the event of a liquidation of the business, the creditor company is virtually assured of receiving the full amount of its claim gives the peace of mind that goes with having prepared well for just such an occurrence.

Secured creditors are business people who know what can happen to a creditor who does not protect the assets of his or her company. If the creditor has not protected the company's security interest with a financing statement and a UCC filing, the person charged with protecting the company's assets is shooting craps with the company's money. When a creditor company does not secure its major accounts, the odds strongly favor one or more of those accounts sliding eventually into the limbo of a Chapter 11 filing. And what hope for recovery does the unsecured creditor have if the debtor goes from the traumatizing effects of a Chapter 11 filing into the depths of a liquidation of assets for the benefit of creditors? Something in the limited frame of "little to none."

The unsecured creditor who is looking at the liquidation of the debtor's assets is looking at a disaster for the unsecured creditors. Unless there is a major miracle, it is unlikely there will be enough money to pay in full each of the priority creditors, which means that the scramble for a few dollars among unsecured creditors can become acrimonious and bitter.

Priority Claims

The term "priority claim" gives the impression that the creditors in this category are in a privileged position—that their claims are ahead of those in other categories. That is not true. The claims that follow have priority, in the order listed, but only over other unsecured claims:

1. The costs of administration, including expenses of preserving the estate (wages, salaries, taxes incurred by the estate, expenses of creditors recovering property for the benefit of the estate, compensation for an attorney or accountant).

2. When the filing was involuntary, any unsecured claims arising from the debtor's business after the start of the case and before a trustee was

appointed (expenses incurred after the trustee was appointed are priority costs of administration).

3. Wage claims up to $2000 for each employee (includes vacation, severance, and sick leave pay) earned 90 days before the earlier filing of the petition or the end of the debtor's business.

4. Contribution to employee benefit plans within 180 days of the filing of the petition to the earnings limit of $2000 per employee (substract from that contribution the total amount paid in priority wage claims and payments to other employee benefit plans).

5. Deposits of up to $900 per individual for unsecured consumer claims (deposits made on family or household goods that were not delivered).

6. Income taxes for which a return is due within three years of the commencement of the case, property taxes for one year, unemployment, withholding and excise taxes, custom duties, and tax penalties.

The failure of creditors to protect their security interests with prompt and proper UCC filings can be a costly learning experience. The failure of creditors to check with the filing officer for prior active filings before they release any product or collateral to a potential debtor is the freeway route to a credit disaster. Could your company afford to suffer a major loss—a major loss that could have been avoided if the most basic protective structure had been utilized? No creditor should fail to secure accounts whose dollar totals are big enough to cause financial worry if they aren't given an appropriate level of protection. For a creditor to lose a large sum of money because the debtor's account has not been protected with a UCC filing—the most basic of protective devices—indicates that there is an inappropriate level of professionalism, one that needs some immediate attention. And when there is an inappropriate level of professionalism in one area, there is an assumption that other areas are not being administered as effectively as they should be. Don't put yourself in the position of having to defend against these types of assumptions.

Challenges to UCC Filings

Creditors who find themselves unsecured or who are secured for less than the amount of their claim frequently do what they feel is necessary to improve their position. Desperate for a way to recoup as much of a large claim as they can, these creditors comb the filings of creditors who allegedly have perfected filings and may be secured for all or most of their company's claim. Creditors whose flawed filing has been overturned as the result of these efforts refer to it as the "jackal mentality"; when they have been the one who found the major flaw in the filing of a creditor whose claim was filed prior to theirs, the buzz phrase changes from "jackal mentality" to "a piece of perceptive credit work."

A challenge to a filing from an unsecured creditor may be the last and/or best hope in a Chapter 11 or liquidation situation where it has become obvious that the debtor's assets will not be enough to satisfy priority and secured creditors without getting into the claims of unsecured creditors. If your claim is unsecured, why wouldn't you exhaust every possibility of receiving some dividend—small though it might be—from a liquidation of the debtor's estate? Unless it has been examined carefully, there is always the possibility that a perfected filing is flawed, not in an inconsequential way such as a misspelled street name or a typographical error, but in a flagrant way that obviously does not represent the intent of the person or company whose filing is being examined such as the description of goods or collateral (the amount or type) or other data that might distort or confuse a third party who has legitimate interests in the goods or collateral.

A secured claimant who alleges a preference over another due to the fact that his or her filing was recorded prior to the filings of other secured claimants is assured of close scrutiny by secured, priority unsecured, and unsecured claimants. Claimants who hope to improve their position do not wait until a Chapter 11 gives way to a liquidation before challenging the filings of other claimants.

Introduction to Plan of Arrangement

If the Plan of Arrangement developed by a debtor is to have a reasonable chance for acceptance, it must contain settlement terms calculated to deal fairly with all claimants within a framework that offers a reasonable chance for success. Secured claimants are of course already on a plateau safely above that of the priority unsecured and unsecured claimants. They have a level of security unequalled by other categories of claimants, but it is not a situation wherein anything is taken for granted. If a debtor has few or no assets, a claimant's secured position is worthless, which translates into secured claimants having the same interest level in a Chapter 11 filing as the pool of unsecured claimants.

The Plan of Arrangement will be discussed in more detail in Chapter 26 of this section (Part 4), but there are some points that should be mentioned now:

1. Claims against the debtor must be filed within 90 days after the date set for the first meeting of claimants.

2. A claim that appears on the trustee's or debtor's schedule of liabilities is considered to be filed unless it is preceded or followed by a special mark or designation, thereby indicating a disputed or contested claim.

3. Although the creditor's name may appear on the trustee's or debtor's schedule before the claimant has filed a proof of claim (the form is usually on the reverse side of the notice advising creditors/claimants that the debtor has filed under Chapter 11), it is wise for claimants to submit claims to which they should attach photocopies of invoices, etc.

4. When a secured creditor files a claim for an amount in excess of the secured total, the difference between the secured total and the claim submitted is categorized as unsecured debt and goes into the pool of general unsecured creditor claims. The Uniform Commercial Code filing protects the claimant—if the claim has been prepared properly—for the full amount of the filing, but it does not protect the amount that is in excess of the UCC filing.

5. It is mandatory that a "debtor in possession" must file a plan for reorganization within 120 days following the filing of the petition.

6. "Parties in interest" may also file a plan, but only if a trustee has been appointed, the debtor has failed to file a plan within the 120 days alloted, or the debtor's plan has been presented to the various classes of creditors, but has failed to win their acceptance within 180 days of the filing.

23

The Bankrupt's Obligations to Creditors

There is the frequently held belief among those who extend credit—whether it is a manufacturer/distributor who sells to wholesale and retail accounts or a retailer who sells to consumers—that the bankruptcy process is too easy; it is believed that the process of filing for bankruptcy, being examined, filing continuation or restructuring plans that offer no reasonable expectation for success, and ultimately being declared a bankrupt and receiving a discharge from debts is done too frequently and too frivolously by individuals and businesses who find it a convenient way to cancel their legitimate obligations.

Not many decades ago, any company, business, or individual who took bankruptcy as the route to escape legitimate obligations was generally categorized as a "deadbeat" if, within a reasonable period of time after the bankruptcy, the bankrupt did not begin to repay creditors the amount of their losses. The discharged bankrupt had no obligation to do this (as there now is no obligation for discharged bankrupts to repay their debts) but it was a matter of honesty, integrity, and honor. The principals of a company, a partnership, or a sole proprietorship wanted to remove a stigma from the names of those who had opted for bankruptcy as their route of escape from obligations to creditors.

Some bankruptcies are the result of misfortunes over which the owner(s) of a business had little or no control; other bankruptcies are the result of a management that was ill-equipped to cope with the problems of growth beyond the first stages of start-up, growth that was allowed to accelerate too rapidly; other companies lacked the management skills necessary to cope with a company, an industry, or an economic downturn. Companies and businesses whose management has the experience and the ability to meet these kinds of challenges with the requisite levels of management skills will usually guide their company or business through almost any maze of problems and take it successfully to the next plateau. There will be no filing of a bankruptcy petition for a company that has planned well, has no self-delusory plans for growth beyond the safety net of its financial and business capabilities, and has the management know-how necessary to walk a narrow line when there is an industry or an economic downturn.

Are bankruptcies ever justified? Of course. There are circumstances where bankruptcy is the only solution. But is the bankruptcy process used too frequently as a convenient method for a person, a business, or a company to trash the legitimate claims of those who have supported the business or the individual with money, raw materials, services, or goods, often at credit limits which stretched their own resources? Yes indeed! The bankruptcy process is used too frequently, too casually, and too callously by people whose integrity, values, and moral fiber have the strength of wet noodles.

There are abusers who make bankruptcy an integral part of their business plan. It may not be written into the plan, but it is a key element in the thinking of people whose modus operandi is to set up a business, get the maximum amount of merchandise and credit from as many suppliers as possible over a relatively short period of time, sell the product(s) at prices that undercut those of other area businesses, pay a portion of the account, but order much more new merchandise than the value of the merchandise sold, live high or stash the money for a later binge of high living, and eventually put the business into a position where all payables accounts are in default. At that point the bankruptcy court will be the recipient of another filing and the creditors can prepare themselves for little or no return on their claims.

Research the background of every applicant before you extend more than a token amount of credit. If you find anything that is suspicious—anything that is indicative of questionable business practice or integrity—get *all* the facts before your company commits any part of its resources to a relationship.

First Meeting of Creditors

This meeting is important to all creditors (claimants) in that it gives them the opportunity to examine the debtor. The debtor must attend the meeting and be prepared to answer the questions of creditors or their representatives (these could be attorneys, accountants, or management consultants who are known for their expertise in the bankrupt's area of business). Is the debtor an individual? He or she might bring an attorney, an accountant, and certain of the records of the business. A partnership? The procedure is the same, exclusive of silent or limited partners. Attorney(s), accountants, and key business records would be appropriate. When the debtor is an incorporated business or company, key board members and officers of the company must represent the debtor company. They will, of course, be represented by attorneys, accountants with appropriate records, and any other key person who might have information or data helpful to the company's position.

The court, upon the request of any interested person, may order any person to appear and be examined who might have knowledge of the debtor's business, the whereabouts of any missing assets, or anything relevant to the business for which the creditors have a right to demand an answer. If the business gave no real advance warning that insolvency was imminent, the creditors will want to know if the major cause was the absence of effective financial controls, poor timing for an expansion of the business, expensive R & D that did not have a payoff in an improved or a new product, etc. The debtor, the debtor's spouse, or any other person who might have information relevant to the insolvent state of the business can be ordered to appear, and if it takes a subpoena to bring the individual, business records, etc., to court, the court has that power and will use it.

Because the bankruptcy judge cannot attend the first meeting of creditors, the interim trustee or the United States Trustee will preside. Examination of a debtor (for purposes of this example, a partnership) might go something like this:

> *(The trustee addresses the partners, who are flanked by their attorney and accountant.)*
>
> TRUSTEE: Are you prepared to answer questions from the creditors regarding the bankruptcy petition that has brought us to this first meeting?
>
> FIRST PARTNER: We are, your honor.
>
> TRUSTEE: And you are?
>
> FIRST PARTNER: Harry Gilmore, President and General Manager.
>
> TRUSTEE: I'll recognize creditors on a show of hands. (*He points to the first to raise his hand.*) State the name of your company, your position and title, the amount of your claim, then proceed with your question.
>
> FIRST CREDITOR: My company is Handleman, Incorporated. I'm the Owner and our claim is an accounts receivable balance of $4892.27. (*He points a finger at the partner who spoke.*) What happened to the $38,500 payment you received from Walburg and Morris five days before you filed the petition?
>
> FIRST PARTNER: (*Glances quickly at second partner and attorney.*) I think we disbursed that to several suppliers.
>
> FIRST CREDITOR: You think you disbursed it? My company hasn't seen any money from your company for the past 34 days. Why didn't we receive

some of the $38,500? (*Before the first partner can respond, the first creditor leans forward.*) Did you prorate the payments among the creditors and, if not, why not?

TRUSTEE: Let's hold the questions down to a maximum of two at a time.

SECOND PARTNER: I probably have more information regarding the $38,500 than Mr. Gilmore.

TRUSTEE: Your name and position?

SECOND PARTNER: Frank Lansdorf, Partner, V.P. of Finance and Controller.

TRUSTEE: Thank you. Please continue.

SECOND PARTNER: I didn't prorate payments because we were being threatened with an involuntary filing by three of our major creditors.

FIRST CREDITOR: What do you consider a major creditor?

SECOND PARTNER: Two 30/60/75-days past-due balances of $39,438 and $23,579. There's also a third 30/60/90-days past due balance of $36,914.

FIRST CREDITOR: You paid the entire $38,500 to these three creditors?

SECOND CREDITOR: That's correct.

FIRST CREDITOR: I may be thick, but what in the hell did you expect to gain by handling the $38,500 in that way? Did you think that the rest of us would sit on our hands and do nothing in gratitude for receiving nothing from you?

SECOND PARTNER: (*Shrugs*) There wasn't enough to do any good if I had prorated it among all of the creditors, so I tried to buy some time by handing it the way I did.

(The second creditor is recognized by the trustee.)

SECOND CREDITOR: I'm Sam Balstrom, Owner and President of Balstom & Company. Our claim is for $10,462.19. (*He points to the first partner.*) When I drove past your office about two weeks ago, I saw you getting into a new and very expensive automobile—a hell of a lot more expensive than I can afford to drive. (*He begins to lose control.*) Apparently you bastards were living high on the hog on our money (*a sweeping gesture takes in the 23 creditors represented in the room*) and now you want this court to pat you on the head, screw these creditors by giving you a discharge from your debts, and send you back out to try the same scam a year from now on another group of creditors!

TRUSTEE: That will do, Mr. Balstrom. Statements of that nature don't contribute anything helpful to this hearing. (*The trustee points to a third creditor.*) Go ahead.

THIRD CREDITOR: I'm the credit manager for Arnholder Incorporated and our claim is for $46,592. (*He points to the second partner.*) You handle all financial matters for your company?

SECOND PARTNER: I do.

THIRD CREDITOR: When did you receive the check for $38,500? What was the date?

SECOND PARTNER: *(He refers to a printout of payments received from customers.)* We received it on the 14th of May.

THIRD CREDITOR: *(Nods.)* The 14th of May. *(He glances at some notes.)* Do you recall our conversations on April 30th, May 8th, and May 16th regarding the $46,592 account balance—all of it past due from 20 to 85 days—and how I stressed the necessity for an immediate payment?

SECOND PARTNER: I recall one or two of those calls, yes.

THIRD CREDITOR: Do you recall telling me on May 16th that you had no money, but you were expecting a check for several thousand dollars later in the week and we would be receiving a minimum of $5000 from it?

SECOND PARTNER: I might have said something to that effect.

THIRD CREDITOR: No, that is exactly what you said. What I want you to explain is why my company received no payment from the check for $38,500 which was already in your hands when I talked with you on May 16th.

(The second partner looks from the first partner to the attorney. The attorney speaks.)

ATTORNEY: Mr. Mercer has already explained his rationale for disbursing the $38,500. *(He shrugs.)* He was under a great deal of pressure at the time you talked with him and . . .

THIRD CREDITOR: *(Interrupts attorney by addressing the trustee.)* May we have the debtor read the exact amounts of the payments made to the three creditors from the $38,500 check, and incidentally *(he points to the debtors)* I believe those payments constitute preferential treatment under the Act.

TRUSTEE: It has been noted. *(He turns to the second partner.)* Do you have the amounts, names of payees, and check dates and numbers?

SECOND PARTNER: Well, yes, but I don't know if I have that data here.

TRUSTEE: This is important, Mr. Mercer. If you don't have the data here, the court will place a call to your office. *(The second partner is looking at a printout.)* Have you found it?

SECOND PARTNER: Yes, I have. Uh . . . one check for $7500 was mailed to Slocum Products; a second check for $10,000 was mailed to The Trimble Company; the third check—it was for $6000—was mailed to Hannibal-Schuckle Incorporated.

TRUSTEE: *(Waits a few seconds.)* That's it?

SECOND PARTNER: Yes. Three checks to three suppliers.

TRUSTEE: *(Hands are up all over the room. He waves them down.)* I'm not a math major, Mr. Mercer, but the three figures you just read to this meeting of creditors totals $23,500. The check you received, and you stated earlier, and paid out to these three creditors totalled $38,500. That's a difference of $15,000, a difference, Mr. Mercer, that was not paid to the three creditors as you stated earlier (*the trustee leans forward*) and I remind you, sir, that these statements are being made under oath.

ATTORNEY FOR PARTNERS: I believe, your honor, that Mr. Mercer can explain the $15,000 and the error he made in the earlier statement.

TRUSTEE: Good, counsel. But before your client responds, let me suggest that you advise him to make a full and complete disclosure of what has happened to the $15,000 (*leans forward again*), and why he felt it was necessary to perjure himself regarding the disposition of that money.

We leave the meeting at this point. Did the second partner commit perjury or was it a momentary lapse of memory? If you believe it was a momentary lapse of memory, perhaps I could interest you in some truly junky junk bonds. How many of the other creditors will involve themselves and their companies with questions that could extend the meeting from early morning into the midafternoon hours? At least 75 percent of those present will ask one or more questions. Will the partners be revealed to have willfully squandered money that should have gone to their creditors? The question isn't "did they?", but "how much?"! How will the creditors' committee, the judge, and the individual creditors look upon any plan of arrangement that would leave the partners in charge of the business? Oh, please! No indecision on this one! If there is approval of a plan of reorganization, the partner will be out and the trustee will run the business until the court can find an experienced manager. In this area, the recommendations of creditors within the debtor's industry will be very helpful.

The dialogue illustrates the early phase of the first meeting of creditors and is quite typical of what can and does occur. These meetings can become extremely hostile and acrimonious as creditors, who are understandably upset at the prospect of losing thousand of dollars, gouge and pry for answers that might provide some level of satisfaction. Satisfaction, unfortunately, is an elusive commodity when the debtor is sitting in a meeting of creditors whose claims seem to total much, much more than the book value of the company's assets. It is not a time for humor, for understanding, or for satisfaction.

Offenses of Bankrupts, Court Officers, Etc.

The bankruptcy court has total control over the bankruptcy proceedings as it relates to bankruptcy matters. It does not have jurisdiction over the prosecuting of a debtor for fraud, grand theft, or any of the charges that are handled as criminal cases. It also does not have jurisdiction over the trial and/or sentencing of trustees, marshals, custodians, or other court officers who have appropriated, knowingly and fraudulently, any part of the assets of a bankrupt estate. If convicted on one or a combination of offenses listed under Title 18 of the U.S. Bankruptcy Code, the guilty person may be imprisoned for a maximum of five years and/or fined not more than $5000.

Some of the offenses punishable by a prison term, fine, or both are, one, concealing assets from a trustee, marshal, or custodian; two, making a false oath (swearing to something that is known to be untrue); three, presenting a claim under oath that is known to be false; four, receiving property from a debtor after the filing of a petition with the intent to gain a preference and/or to defeat the purpose of the Code; five, changing, destroying, or mutilating a document in such a way that it will affect or relate to the affairs of the debtor after or during the contemplating of a filing under the Code; six, believing, as judge, trustee, or receiver, that one has evidence that an offense under the Bankruptcy Code has been committed and failing to report it to the U.S. Attorney for the district in which the offense was committed, or is alleged to have been committed; and seven, failing to reveal evidence that the mails have been used to defraud, in which case an indictment should be sought at the place where the mailing was made or at the place where the letter was received. A debtor cannot be put in the position of being forced to give testimony that can be used against him or her in a criminal proceeding. If the debtor requests and receives immunity, the debtor must testify. If the debtor is denied immunity, the debtor may then decline to testify, claiming the privilege against self-incrimination. A debtor who refuses to answer questions after being granted immunity will not receive a discharge.

Jurisdiction, Function, and Compliance

As I mentioned in a prior subsection, the bankruptcy court has jurisdiction—subject to specific controls of the district court—in all areas relating to the bankruptcy process. All participants in the process—debtor, creditors, trustee, examiner (in lieu of trustee), committee of unsecured debtors, etc.—must comply with the lawful order of the bankruptcy court.

What are some examples of the jurisdiction, function, and lawful orders of the court? The following are a few of the more important examples:

1. The court orders the debtor to appear on a specific date for a first meeting of the creditors, at which time the creditors will examine the debtor.

2. When a debtor files a petition, it creates an automatic stay of all judicial proceedings; the stay must be honored as it relates to the collection of debts.

3. Acting upon the request of a party in interest, the court will determine whether a trustee should be appointed to take control of the debtor's business and property.

4. Acting upon the request of a party in interest, the court may terminate the trustee's appointment and return possession of the property and management of the business to the debtor.

5. The court is empowered to change a reorganization case to a liquidation, or dismiss the case. This is a "best interest of creditors" decision and is usually the result of unreasonable delay by the debtor in submitting a plan of reorganization, an inability to produce an acceptable plan, or some similar reason.

6. When there is a good reason or reasons, the court may increase or decrease the 120 days in which a debtor is allowed to file a plan of reorganization and the 180 days after the court issues an order of relief for creditors to accept a plan submitted by the debtor.

7. Approve the written disclosure statement which outlines and explains the plan of reorganization. The court confirms that it contains enough information for the creditors to reach an informed judgment regarding its merits.

8. The court will confirm the reorganization plan if it meets requirements established in the Code and if the required number (and amount) of unsecured creditors has voted to accept it.

9. The debtor will be directed to take actions necessary for the plan to be consummated. If this includes the transfer or delivery of property, the debtor will be instructed to execute and deliver any documents necessary to effect the transfer.

The function of a bankruptcy court is to establish the ground rules for all participants, to protect the assets of an insolvent debtor for the benefit of the debtor's creditors, to protect the debtor against unfair or illegal seizure of the debtor's assets, and to guide all participants through a prescribed process in as efficient, speedy, and painless a manner as is possible. Not all bankruptcy cases run their course as textbook examples of what those who framed the Bankruptcy Code, and those who have subsequently revised it, had in mind.

People who file a petition range in stripe from honest, hard-working types whose major crime is having made errors in judgment which have proven costly to themselves and their suppliers, people who have done everything within their power to avoid admitting and formalizing the insolvency of their business, to the charlatans and rogues who work the opposite end of the human spectrum. The latter types file their petitions, go through the motions of being interested in a reorganization of the business, pretend to agonize when reorganization becomes liquidation, then ultimately take their discharge and live well for 12 or more months on proceeds stashed methodically for some time prior to the filing. What do the charlatans and rogues do after 12 or more months? They set up a business in another section of the same state or in another area of the country.

It is important to remember that these types do come back, and they'll be as deceitful and ruthless in building toward the second, third, or fourth bankruptcies as they were the first time. My best advice? Beware of any prospective customer who cannot or will not give you full access to his or her background. It is a warning that should not be dismissed casually, or the eventual cost to your company could be something that is remembered for a very long time.

Property of a Debtor

After a filing, only one person other than a custodian is entitled to hold property of a debtor—that person is the trustee. Property of negligible value may continue to be held by a custodian, subject to the court's approval, but any property of value to the estate must be recognized by the holder as a part of the debtor's estate that must be turned over to the trustee. Anyone who owes money to the debtor is required to pay the trustee, although in actual practice it is not uncommon for individuals and businesses who owe money to an insolvent debtor to delay paying any part of the obligation short of legal action by the trustee. Why do they delay? Because the estate of many debtors does not have the funds for a trustee to pursue costly and/or lengthy collection proceedings, and the person or company who delays paying an obligation until a suit is about to be filed has the use of that money for an additional period of time.

Custodians who were appointed prior to the filing are required to turn over to the trustee any assets (money, property, etc.) that have come into the custodian's possession during the period of his or her tenure as "custodian"—defined in the Bankruptcy Code as a receiver or a trustee in a non-bankruptcy case or proceeding (an assignee for the benefit of creditors, etc.). Although custodians have many of the same powers as trustees, they are not empowered to make disbursements from the assets of the debtor's estate unless such a disbursement(s) is necessary to preserve the property of the estate.

The court's umbrella of authority protects the work of a custodian, including the court's protection for obligations incurred by the custodian in the performance of his or her duties. The court is authorized to provide reasonable compensation and expenses for the custodian while also keeping a watchful eye on the amounts expended and authorized for expenditure by the custodian. If the custodian authorizes disbursements that are excessive in number or amount or are improper in any way, those amounts will be charged back to the custodian by the court.

The doctrine of fair play is as applicable to the debtor as it is to the debtor's creditors. It is the duty of the court and the duty of all court-appointed custodians or trustees to perform their duties with that thought uppermost in their minds and in their actions. Fortunately for creditors and debtors, the doctrine of fair play is the core material upon which the Bankruptcy Code has been built. It is virtually impossible for a debtor or the debtor's creditors to receive less than equal treatment under the Code.

Challenging Proofs of Claim

It is common practice for secured and unsecured claims to be challenged by the trustee or by other parties in interest. The objective of a challenge from the trustee is to remove what appears to be a claim of uncertain merit from the list of creditor claims. Any claimant whose claim is challenged by the trustee is given the opportunity to submit documents or other evidence to the court to substantiate the claim. If the evidence is sufficiently conclusive, the court will allow the claim to remain as submitted. Any problem with the amount of the claim will diminish it by an amount set by the court or cause it to be eliminated from the list of approved claims.

Challenges put forth by "other parties in interest" (other claimants, etc.) are usually aimed at bringing down the secured claims of creditors, the claims of those creditors who filed security agreements and financing statements with the filing officer of the Uniform Commercial Code jurisdiction that allegedly is applicable to the security interest. Self-interest is the motivating factor—a self-interest that, for unsecured creditors, needs all the help it can get because the chances of the insolvent debtor's estate having enough assets to satisfy more than a fraction of the amount owing to unsecured creditors is a faint hope at best.

As stated in an earlier paragraph, the court has the power to allow or to disallow a challenge, or to determine the percentage of a claim that will stand. Be sure that any claim you file on behalf of your company has the appropriate substantiating documentation attached to it, or, if it is not attached, that the appropriate documentation is available when and as required. To decrease the chances that a hopeful fellow creditor will attempt to challenge your secured claim, make it a standard practice to authenticate claims by attaching documentation. An experienced professional will continue down the list of claimants until he or she finds one that has a much better chance of not holding up under close scrutiny.

A debtor may challenge the claim of a creditor which does not agree with the debtor's records. Any such challenges should not be frivolous because the bankruptcy court will tire quickly of any repeated or obvious attempts to delay the forward progress of proceedings with tactics of this type. If, however, a balance was in dispute prior to the filing of a petition by the debtor, the debtor has every right to challenge a debtor's claim which includes the disputed balance. When the difference between the debtor's figure and the total claimed by the creditor cannot be reconciled between the two of them, the court is empowered to review the conflicting claims and determine a settlement figure.

When a secured claim is found to be flawed (imperfect), the court may either disallow the secured status of the entire UCC filing or, if a part of it was properly perfected, reduce the part that was filed improperly to the status of an unsecured claim. A creditor should never be put in the position of having a secured claim disallowed because of a major error in either the security agreement or the financing statement. It represents less than a professional effort on the part of the person who prepared the package for filing and, of even greater importance, it represents a change from secured to unsecured status and the potential loss of a substantial amount of the creditor company's money.

A Preferential Transfer?

A creditor who has received from the debtor what is challenged by the trustee as a "preferential transfer of assets" must be prepared to defend the circumstances of the transfer (payment, etc.) or risk having the court order the creditor to return or repay it to the trustee; at that point it would become a part of the debtor's undistributed assets. One or more creditors might charge that a payment received by the creditor whose claim is being challenged was made for the benefit of the creditor and within the 90 days prior to the filing of the petition—a time when the debtor is presumed to be insolvent. This is a fertile area for creditors to furnish information to the trustee in the hope that he or she will be able to force a recovery of the payment or property that was transferred.

The possibility that one or more creditors have received preferential transfers during the period—90 days prior to the filing—when the debtor is presumed to have been bankrupt is an act that incites those who have not been the recipients of a preference. The creditor who received what is alleged to be a preferential transfer will defend it as the result (or the reward) for a good job of collecting a part of the past-due balance owed to the company. Creditors who have failed to collect any recent payment from the debtor will want to examine carefully the circumstances on the grounds that his or her collection effort was no less diligent or forceful than that of the company which received what might have been a substantial payment. The inference, if it is not verbalized, is that there must have been additional leverage or some type of "deal" between the parties. If it can be proved to be a preferential transfer, then the other creditors will expect the trustee to force the one creditor to turn the money (property, other asset, etc.) over to the trustee.

If the accused creditor company considers its position to be strong, the company will not panic and it will not be coerced into returning the payment(s) because some peer creditors have convinced the trustee to try to recover the money. If the creditor worked hard to get the debtor to make the payment and offered or received no special treatment or consideration, it will take more than the threats of the trustee to get the creditor to hand over the money or the property.

Creditors who are in this position should remember that debtor's estates traditionally have very little money for such expenses as legal fees to take legal actions which involve a payment or payments that, if returned, might not significantly impact the debtor's assets total. Trustees are reluctant to do anything that might put the proceedings in a position which would delay progress while the question of a legal payment or an illegal preference is being litigated. The trustee must be quite certain that the position he or she takes in any legal action in an area such as preferential transfers or preferential treatment will not further diminish the debtor's estate. The trustee must be reasonably certain that his or her position will prevail and that there will be no added expense of attorney and court costs which cannot be recovered because the trustee's position does not prevail.

And what if the creditor's position is questionable? What if there is a legitimate question as to whether the challenged payment(s) escapes being a preferential one? The creditor can afford to gamble (if the money is not significant in the context of the debtor's estate) that the trustee will not push the issue to a legal showdown. If, however, it becomes obvious that it is about to reach that point, the creditor can always abort the possibility of legal action by agreeing suddenly to hand over the asset(s).

The trustee in any bankruptcy is authorized to void any preferential transfer. Whether the trustee can get the creditor to agree without legal pressure that his or her company has been the beneficiary of an illegal preference is another matter—one we have already explored. The following are examples of voidable or illegal preferences that are within the authority of the trustee:

1. Any transfer that is made for the benefit of the creditor.

2. Any transfer made by the debtor to lower an antecedent debt owed prior to the transfer.

3. Any transfer that is made within 90 days of the filing of the petition.

4. As it is with "insider trading," the term "insider" is in the context of a preferential transfer defined as one made by a person whose close relationship with the debtor might give him or her (relatives, partners, relatives of partners, directors, corporate officers, their relatives, etc.) access to information not available to others in interest. Because there is in such a relationship a potential for insider knowledge, any transfer between 90 days and one year is subject to review as a possible preferential transfer (one that would serve to benefit one creditor more than other creditors of a similar class). As an example, the bankruptcy court (and the trustee) must uphold the principle of equal treatment for all creditors who are unsecured. If one creditor's treatment by the debtor is found to be preferential, it would be an unacceptable injustice to other creditors of the same class if it were allowed to remain unchallenged.

Not all payments or transfers of assets can be lumped into the category of a voidable or an illegal preference. A trustee might be encouraged by other creditors to investigate a transfer that appears to be preferential, but when the trustee takes a close look, it may be one of the following types of legal transfers:

1. An exchange between debtor and creditor for new goods or other value given as a contemporary exchange with no application or relevance to antecedent debt.

2. A payment made for a debt incurred by the debtor in the ordinary course of business and in accordance with customary business terms.

3. A transfer to a creditor after the creditor gave new unsecured credit or value to the debtor.

4. A creditor's perfected security interest in inventory or receivables, unless the creditor's position was improved during the 90 days prior to the filing of the petition.

5. A security interest for new value when that security interest was perfected within 10 days after receipt of the goods or property by the debtor.

6. A transfer of real property is said to be perfected when it is valid against a bona fide purchaser.

7. A perfected transfer takes effect when it is made within 10 days. The UCC also states that if a transfer is not perfected within 10 days of the transfer, it does not take effect until it is perfected.

Fraudulent Transfers

It is a duty of the trustee to act promptly and decisively when evidence to support the charge of a fraudulent transfer is brought to his or her attention. The time frame for acting on such a transfer is one year prior to the filing of a petition by the debtor.

What constitutes fraud in the context of a transfer? A transfer is said to be fraudulent when there is an attempt by the debtor to hinder, delay, or defraud a creditor, or to attempt to mislead a trustee by concealing facts relative to the location, value, transfer, or existence of properties of the estate. Any transfer alleged to be for a current consideration must meet the test of value of approximately equivalent worth; as an example, there is nothing allowable about a transfer to the creditor of $2500 in exchange for goods worth no more than $500. This is not "equivalent worth" and would be disallowed by the trustee if the debtor became insolvent because of this and similar transactions or knowingly incurred debts which exceeded his or her ability to pay. Transfers of partnership property are also a concern of creditors and the trustee. The one-year time frame for reversing these transfers is available to the trustee.

Transfer to Trustee of Foreign Properties

Properties that are held by debtors in foreign countries are subject to the same rules of transfer as those applicable to properties in this country. All such assets, whether domestic or foreign, fall within the jurisdiction and the mandate of the trustee. The bankruptcy court has put the trustee in the position of conservator/manager for the purpose of preserving the debtor's assets, and that conservatorship is not limited to domestic properties. It includes the debtor's assets in every corner of the world and for a debtor to knowingly withhold the transfer of properties (assets) to the trustee is to risk having the court summarily terminate the debtor's petition.

Any property that has value to the estate must be turned over to the trustee, with the exception of property that has no value or property for which the debtor (or a debtor of the insolvent petitioner) obtained a court order which allows it to be kept separate from properties controlled by the trustee.

A company or a person owing money to the debtor is required to pay it to the trustee, but if the amount is small in the context of the total value of the debtor's estate, many who owe the debtor will be very slow to pay. Their rationale will be the one discussed in the foregoing paragraphs: the trustee will not spend money on legal fees or take valuable time away from other estate duties to try to pry relatively small sums of money from people who are determined to hold onto it. The trustee will get everything that he or she can within the constraints of time and money—both being only moderately flexible guidelines that must be considered before the trustee takes any action that might consume excessive or unrealistic amounts of one or both.

The term "foreign properties" includes property owned by the debtor company in a foreign country, office machines, production equipment and machinery, trucks, fork lifts, automobiles, inventories of raw materials and finished goods, and any accounts receivable balances that have been billed and collected from the foreign branch or factory. Cash or securities? A priority transfer to the trustee. Anything and everything of value, regardless of its location, is within the trustee's area of responsibility. The trustee must not only know the book value of items, goods, and properties in the debtor's estate, but a trustee must do everything possible when estate items are offered for sale to get the best prices for them. The trustee's value to the court, to the creditors, and to the estate depends upon a variety of abilities and how those abilities are focused to obtain the maximum benefits for all parties of interest.

Debts Not Affected by a Discharge from Bankruptcy

People who have had very little experience with bankruptcies have misconceptions regarding what a "discharge of debts" does and does not do for a bankrupt. One of the major misconceptions pertains to a continuing liability for certain local, state, and federal taxes. Other debts may disappear when the bankruptcy judge decrees that the insolvent debtor is entitled, under the provisions of The Bankruptcy Act, to a discharge of debts. This is not true when the debt(s) is taxes—property, state sales, social security, income, withholding, etc.—owed to various levels of government. Here are some examples:

1. Tax returns not filed or filed late within two years before the filing date of the petition for relief

2. Taxes on gross sales for the tax year ending on or before the filing date of the petition

3. Taxes owed on income or gross receipts within 240 days before the filing date or commencement of the case

4. Taxes not assessed prior to commencement of the case, but that were assessable under law or by agreement after the case began

5. Property taxes assessed before commencement of the case

6. Any taxes that the debtor was required to withhold or collect

7. Any excise taxes on transactions that occurred before the filing of the petition and for which a return is due three years before the filing date of the petition

8. Certain federal, state, or local tax claims which were created between the time the petition was filed and the entry of an order of relief

9. The use of fraud, false pretenses, or a false financial statement to obtain money, property, or services

10. The debtor's failure to list debts in time for a creditor to take the action(s) necessary to protect his or her rights

11. Any debts incurred by the debtor as the result of fraud or embezzlement while acting in a fiduciary capacity

12. Alimony, child support, maintenance, or any special or separate agreement that is related to an order of a court

These are some examples of the various types of debts from which the granting of a discharge in bankruptcy court does not release the debtor; the obligation to make an appropriate payment arrangement remains.

When a debtor receives a discharge, there is no longer any obligation on the debtor's part to repay debts covered by the discharge. There was a time when a debtor, in advance of the discharge, could put certain debts outside the scope and jurisdiction of the discharge. The debtor was saying, "I need relief from my debts and I want the court to discharge me from those debts, but there are certain ones that I am going to pay. It may take six months, a year, or even longer but I intend to pay my debt to . . . ," at which point the debtor would give the court the names of two, three, or more companies or individuals who were to be excluded from the discharge.

Reaffirming a discharged debt (the debtor agrees to repay a creditor after the discharge has been granted) is not something which is encouraged by the Bankruptcy Code. It does allow a discharged debtor to make a reaffirmation agreement with a creditor whose obligation was discharged, but it gives the discharged debtor a window of 30 days from the date of the reaffirmation agreement to rescind it, without penalty, liability, or jeopardy to its status as a discharged debt. Reaffirmations of consumer debt must be approved by the court after it has concluded that the reaffirmation is in the debtor's best interests. Reaffirmations involving consumer debts are made before the discharge is granted and allow the debtor to rescind the agreement within a period of 60 days.

It quickly becomes obvious that by the time a bankruptcy proceeding has reached the point where a debtor is to be discharged, The Bankruptcy Act

(Code) allows almost no latitude for creditors to attempt to gain "life after discharge" for their claim. The purpose of the bankruptcy process is to free debtors from what the debtor alleges has become an oppressive burden of debt. The Act/Code does not encourage debtors to reaffirm obligations, offers windows of escape for debtors who reaffirm an obligation, but subsequently have second thoughts, and attempts generally to create barriers which will discourage any continuing obligation to pay a legally discharged debt.

The bankruptcy court does, however, demand ethical conduct on the part of the debtor if the debtor is to be granted a discharge, or if a discharge that has been granted is not to be revoked for cause. What might cause the court to revoke a discharge? If subsequent to the granting of a discharge it is determined that the debtor obtained the discharge through fraud or other similar acts or behavior which was intended to mislead the trustee, the creditors, or the court (and these acts were unknown to the court) the discharge will be revoked. The statute of limitation is one year if the court is to revoke a discharge on the basis of fraud. When a debtor has acquired property and not reported it to the trustee, or has refused the court's lawful order to testify, the request to revoke the discharge must be made within one year from the later of the date of the discharge or the closing date of the case.

(*Warning:* These pages include only a relatively small sampling of what is in the Uniform Commercial Code and in The Bankruptcy Act/Code. *Do not* obligate yourself or your company or make decisions—decisions that should be rooted in law(s)—which are based on what you read in these pages unless you understand fully the intricacies of the UCC and The Bankruptcy Act. The material in this book is written to acquaint and to familiarize. It is not to be used as a substitute for a text on the law, nor is it to be substituted for the services of your personal or company attorney.)

24

The Many Costs of Bankruptcy

The costs of bankruptcy cannot be dismissed as a one-time experience which, once concluded, will slip quietly into the past. Bankruptcy is several dimensions of unpleasant thoughts, actions, and behavior by many parties of interest. They may be verbalized at times, may be relegated at other times to a pattern of icy stares, and may often give way to attitudes of such heavy unpleasantness as not to lend themselves to being lightly shrugged aside.

Creditors do not like to lose money; they become especially testy when they lose money to debtors with whom they have had a very short business relationship. These types of relationships seldom result in a profitable experience for a creditor who finds himself or herself having to file an unsecured claim for the accounts receivable generated by sales to the debtor. While it cannot be denied that the monetary cost to creditors has probably the greatest impact initially, it certainly is not the only cost. It may not, in fact, be the cost that lasts the longest.

When a bankruptcy proceeding has reached the point where the court enters a discharge of the debtor's obligations, how does an observer measure the long-term damage to the reputation of the discharged debtor? How severe is the damage to the reputation and credibility of the company or individual? Has that reputation been damaged beyond the point where those with whom the former bankrupt does business (suppliers, bankers, service people, customers, etc.) can view the discharged bankrupt in the same light as before the filing, or perhaps feel as comfortable with a warranty, a guarantee, or any form of oral pledge or commitment? Has the credibility of the discharged debtor been damaged so severely that time—a long period of time—may be the only healer?

A creditor who loses a receivables balance as a result of selling to a discharged debtor might decide to resume credit sales if the former debtor opens another business or starts another company. In most situations of this type, it is unlikely that the second relationship will be as strong as the first. Although the creditor may eventually sell to the second company—and the line of credit may be as high as it was to the first company—the relationship will not be the same.

This poses a situation that would appear to be a contradiction. Why would a once-burned creditor be willing to extend a relatively high level of credit to the company or the people who in the first bankruptcy had cost his or her company several thousand dollars? How could a good owner or manager find justification for putting a fresh batch of dollars at the same risk as the accounts receivable balance that disappeared into the debtor company's discharge of debts? The rationale is not so strange when I give you another piece of information. The creditor might build the new company to a fairly high credit limit—if cash flow and management seems to have its act together—because the creditor company made a substantial amount of money over the period of its relationship with the first company. It is true that several thousand dollars were past due and subsequently lost, but the creditor's total profit from the first relationship was $105,000, a long-term profit that is the motivating factor in building the second relationship. Losing several thousand dollars is bad: turning a long-term profit several times the amount of the final loss is good— very good!

A person whose business or company failed because he or she lacked the experience necessary to take a potentially successful enterprise to the next plateau should be expected to have learned some valuable lessons. If there is to be a "next time" for this entrepreneur, there must be some strong indications that this person knows his or her limitations and that the mistakes that caused the first venture to become a bankruptcy statistic will not be repeated in this one. An intelligent person will manage a business only as far as his or her experience can safely take it before a manager with a stronger level of experience is brought in to move the company to higher plateaus of success.

No creditor should extend a significant credit line to the new business of a discharged bankrupt whose business acumen, intelligence, and capacity for growth is suspect. If there is no new, experienced leadership in the company and the person or people managing it are faces familiar to creditors from the failure of enterprise number one, there can be no acceptable incentive for a supplier to hitch a ride on what is an inevitable run to a second bankruptcy.

It is a questionable judgment call for a nucleus of people who were the owners or managers of a failed company to return to the area or region of an earlier business failure, unless the circumstances surrounding that failure were so extenuating as to greatly diminish the responsibility of the people who have formed a second company.

Was the debtor as much a victim as the creditors? Were circumstances of the company's failure so far beyond the company's control that it became impossible for the company to succeed? If these two questions represent a fair statement of why the company failed, there will be creditors who have no problem justifying a decision to give a credit line to the new company. A good credit administrator will make every reasonable effort to provide the company's customers (including one-time losers) with appropriate levels of credit support. Anything less than that level of effort is a disservice to your own company's potential for success.

Costs/Expenses of Administrating Bankruptcy Proceedings

There is a very broad spectrum of administrative and other expenses allowable and chargeable to the estate of a debtor. These expenses will be allowed whether the debtor's plan of reorganization is accepted by creditors or whether the court orders a liquidation of assets and subsequently discharges the debtor. Categories of allowable expense are set forth in the Code. It is the responsibility of the judge who has jurisdiction in a bankruptcy proceeding to ensure that the Code's guidelines are followed.

Costs and/or expenses can be broken down into two categories: expenses incurred by the court as those expenses relate to specific areas of the court's jurisdiction and expenses incurred by the trustee as he or she works under the mandate of the court and guidelines as set forth in the Code.

Some of the allowable expenses are segregated into the major category (the bankruptcy court) and the subsidiary category of responsibility (the trustee).

The Bankruptcy Court.   The costs include administering the bankruptcy proceedings, which include the court's time, a charge for clerical services, and professional assistance (legal, accounting, etc.) as required by the creditors' committee in the performance of its duties. There is also the costs of hiring an interim trustee or an examiner (appointed by the court in lieu of a trustee and used to investigate the affairs of a debtor including fraud and mismanagement, and to see that assets are conserved). All charges incurred by the trustee are reviewed by the court to ensure that they are within parameters allowed by the Code.

The Trustee.   Costs incurred by the trustee in the course of performing his or her duties include personnel such as an appraiser (to place a value on various items in the debtor's estate), an attorney (to clarify and/or transfer title to properties and perform other legal services as the trustee may require), an accountant (to examine certain records for accuracy and relevance to the value of the estate and to represent the trustee in situations where there has been an illegal transfer of property, etc.), security personnel (to provide security if there is the possibility that certain of the debtor's properties might be removed), and a management person (to run the debtor's business during the period of the proceedings if control is removed from the debtor's hands and the trustee is not experienced in managing a business such as the debtor's).

There are also the filing and court costs of attempting to recover assets transferred under conditions of a voidable preference; the cost of reducing the estate to money (ads in newspapers, trade journals, etc.) to advertise the site and time of a sale—either auction or conventional; the cost of enough people to do an on-site display of the properties to be auctioned; the cost of an auctioneer or a firm of auctioneers to conduct the sale; clerical and other help as the trustee may need it; disbursements of funds made for the preservation of estate property.

Compensation for the trustee (also an interim trustee and/or an examiner) is set within guidelines provided by the Code. Compensation in a liquidation is based upon the value of the liquidation: compensation not to exceed 15 percent of the first $1000, 6 percent when the value is between $1000 and $3000, and 3 percent on a liquidation that exceeds $3000.

It should be noted that an attorney, whether hired by the court or by the trustee, is hired for a specific fee. It may be an hourly fee or a fee for a specific body of work, but payment for the attorney's work is handled in a manner prescribed by the code. To receive payment, an attorney must file a petition with the court, a petition that states the extent of services rendered, the value of those services, and any prior compensation that might have been applicable in whole or in part to this work. An affidavit which states whether others will share in the compensation, who and what they are, and what they did to warrant earning a share of the compensation must accompany the affidavit. If the court agrees with the contents of the attorney's affidavit, it will be approved for payment.

The term "cash collateral" is used commonly when the quick assets (readily negotiable to cash) of a debtor are being discussed. It is defined in the Code as being either cash, negotiable instruments, documents of title, securities, deposit accounts, or "other cash equivalents" in which the estate and another have an interest. Mortgages, promissory notes, and instruments of that type which might be held by the debtor do not qualify as "cash collateral" because it takes time to convert them to cash.

Customers of a petitioner may already be a primary source of the company's problem, but when it becomes known that there has been a filing for protection, the problem can become magnified. Many customers who had been paying something on their accounts will stop making any payments. Customers who had not been making account payments will continue to withhold payments.

In some industries, genuine concern for the welfare of their own businesses can trigger the kinds of payment delays outlined above. An honest retailer is suddenly faced with questions from customers, who having bought or buying, must rely on a guarantee or a warranty from a manufacturer who has just filed a petition for protection under Chapter 11 of The Bankruptcy Act! Whether the majority of these customers are sophisticated business or professional people who understand the nuances and ramifications of bankruptcy is irrelevant; what is relevant is that the majority of these people know enough about "bankruptcy" to generate a major wave of concern throughout the customer base of the debtor company. Distributors, retailers, and consumers understand enough about the meaning of "bankruptcy" to know that whatever the product(s) of the Chapter 11 company—washing machines, kitchen appliances, television sets, computers, etc.—any guarantee or warranty that is offered in support of the product is only as good as the stability and reputation of the company offering it. There can be very little confidence in the worth of a guarantee offered by a company whose production lines have stopped, whose cash flow has become a dry creek bed, and whose future is questionable at best.

The Cost to Employees

When a company's business and financial affairs reach a point where it becomes necessary for management to file for relief under Chapter 11, the people who are overlooked, as shock waves go through the industry, the creditors, and the customer base, are the company's employees. If the company has been in business for several years, employees at the middle and lower echelon levels may realize that less product is coming off production and assembly lines than in years past. Employees of distributors or wholesalers may notice that the volume of incoming product has been decreasing at a steady rate; perceptive employees will begin to substitute "alarming rate" for "steady rate." In contrast to the months and years when they found satisfaction in their jobs, many may begin to listen more attentively to grapevine talk of possible opportunities or openings in other companies, if there are such companies in the area.

There are no winners when a business or a company is forced to close or to seek relief in bankruptcy court because it is insolvent. Employees lose jobs, health benefits, pension plans, and the real, if tenuous, security of a steady paycheck (tenuous in that no company, regardless of how many years it has been an industry giant, is immune from technological change, major depression, or the potentially fatal arrogance of feeling that no company or technology could successfully challenge or replace this long-time leader). There is also the self-esteem that comes with being able to provide one's family with a reasonable standard of living. Unemployment benefits do not do that. If a failing or failed company is the key employer in an area where there are almost no comparable employment opportunities, the company's employees, their families, and the merchants and services who depend upon business generated from the payroll of this company for their own survival are caught in this classic example of "trickle down."

The man or woman who has a family, has enjoyed long-term employment at a satisfactory wage or salary, and then is told suddenly that his or her job—the jobs of many people—will be lost permanently if a reorganization cannot be worked out becomes the victim of psychological and financial shock. There is the realization that the individual's current and future destiny has slipped beyond his or her control. The company is declared a bankrupt, the assets are liquidated, and the company ceases to exist. Unemployment benefits will last for a relatively short period of time, and then what? If there is no other employment in the area does the employee (now a former employee) sit around and wait for a miracle? Does the employee try to sell a house that has become unmarketable because a major employer—the area's major employer—has closed and employment opportunities have sunk to zero? What does the former employee do when the bank says it cannot continue to carry a mortgage that becomes more delinquent with each passing month? Is foreclosure imminent? Perhaps the former employee (many of them, actually, because the company employed a significant number of people) can sell his or her equity for pennies or nickels on the dollar—and what then?

The impact of an insolvent or bankrupt company—one that is unable to reorganize and hire many of its former employees—can be difficult financially for some creditors whose claims represent a high percentage of their accounts receivable totals. These suppliers may have a financial problem for a period of time, but if their loss has not been catastrophic, they should work their way back to a more solid footing.

Not so for the employees of a failed company, especially the employees of a company in an area where other employment opportunities are minimal. They are the major victims in the bankruptcy process, the one set of victims whose chances of regaining their previous standard of living does not exist in their present locality. So they move to another area and they try again. They start at a lower point on the economic scale and hope that this time there is no major disruption in their lives and the lives of their families.

Employee Wage Claims

The Code is written to give priority to the wage claims of employees over other categories of unsecured claims. There are two major areas of protection for these employees:

1. Employees have a priority claim for wages or salary up to $2000 per employee. The $2000 includes vacation, severance, and sick leave pay and must have been earned in the 90 days prior to the filing of the petition or the end of the debtor's business, whichever came first.

2. Employees have a claim for contributions of $2000 per employee to employee benefit plans from work performed within 180 days of the filing of the petition or the closing of the debtor's business, whichever came first. Deduct from the figure of $2000 per employee any wages or payments paid to other employee benefit plans before termination of the debtor's business.

How rapidly the wage and related claims of employees will be paid is dependent largely upon the amount of cash that becomes available from receivables payments and/or from the sale of certain nonessential assets of the debtor, and how rapidly these sources of cash can be made to deliver meaningful amounts. There are no other major revenue sources from which the court can authorize payment of these priority unsecured claims, so it is imperative that the trustee is successful in his or her efforts to generate cash.

It should be noted that state and federal taxes which have been withheld by an employer, but not forwarded to the respective government agencies, are not forgiven when a bankrupt is discharged or when a plan of reorganization has been approved and implemented. Any government-mandated tax program—Social Security, City, State, and Federal Income Taxes, etc.—which involves the withholding of tax dollars from the paycheck of an employee must be remitted to the appropriate agency of government. These obligations must be satisfied from funds generated by the trustee and administered by the court.

Tax obligations incurred by the debtor's business in the day to day operation of that business must also be satisfied. The debtor business is obligated to pay some or all of the following: state sales taxes, inventory taxes, income taxes (state and federal), and the employer's contributions to the

Social Security and Unemployment Insurance accounts of its employees. These and other government mandated obligations must be dealt with in a manner that conforms with statutory guidelines.

The Code attempts to cast a protective cover over the interests of all who have valid claims against the debtor's estate. Not every reorganization or liquidation has as good a result for claimants as the Code or the bankruptcy court sets out to achieve, but wage claims are processed as successfully as each situation allows.

The following is an example of what would happen to the wage claims of 48 employees in a bankruptcy where no plan of reorganization could be worked out and the trustee was instructed by the court to sell assets of the debtor's estate for the benefit of creditors.

Westerman Packaging Company employed 48 people prior to filing a petition for relief under Chapter 11. Cash flow had plunged dramatically because the company's major customer—one representing 40 percent of the company's annual sales—had unexpectedly closed its doors and filed for bankruptcy. No reorganization, just a straight bankruptcy. The trade had been commenting about payments becoming slower, and then quite rapidly, this old and apparently well-established business was on a collision course with failure.

With the overnight loss of 40 percent of its cash flow, Western Packaging went into a rapid decline. There was no way to make up the lost revenue, to meet monthly and long-term obligations, and to accommodate the needs of a company that had been doing $12 million a year and was suddenly reduced to a gross sales figure of $7 to $7.5 million a year. Within three months after its major account went out of business, Westerman Packaging Company was in Chapter 11.

The company's 48 employees entered individual claims for wages/salaries plus accrued vacation and sick leave: 17 salaried employees entered claims ranging from $2740 to $3918; 31 weekly-wage and part-time employees entered claims ranging from $628 to $3120. Under the Code, the claims of these employees were categorized as claims by unsecured creditors; however, as stated earlier, the Code gives priority status to wage and salary claims over other categories of unsecured claims. So what was the disposition of the 17 salaried claims that ranged between $2740 and $3918? The first $2000 of each claim was classed as a priority claim (wages, accrued vacation, and sick leave) with everything over the individual total of $2000 rolled over into the pool of nonpriority unsecured creditors. The 31 weekly and part-time employees, whose claims for wages and accrued vacation and sick leave ranged from $628 to $3120, were in the same position as the 17 salaried employees: each had a priority claim of $2000 with anything above that amount added to the pool of nonpriority unsecured claims.

There is a major problem when any part of a claim for wages and accrued vacation and sick leave exceeds $2000 and the excess becomes an unsecured nonpriority claim: the return on unsecured claims in a liquidation is traditionally very poor. It is not a reflection on the diligence of trustees who are conscientious in their efforts to collect the debtor's accounts receivable and get the best prices possible when assets are offered at a special, open, or an auction sale. Dividends to claimants will depend, of course, upon the willingness of buyers to pay prices that approximate true or book value. Such an experience is, unfortunately, not common. The purchase price of items offered at a liquidation sale can be expected to bring, with the possible exception of certain in-demand or scarce items, much less than the company's book value.

So what should an employee hope to get from the amount of wages, vacation, and sick leave in excess of the $2000 priority allowance? It could range from 0 to 5 or 10 percent of the excess, or if the liquidation is unusually successful and the claims of secured creditors do not soak up most of the proceeds, there is a slim possibility that a dividend could be for as much as 25 or 30 percent. Any dividend that attains or exceeds 25 or 30 percent would be, for the unsecured creditors, a miracle of astonishing proportions. Substantial percentages of recovery on unsecured claims is not the traditional fate of claimants whose misfortune it is to be in that position.

Tax Claims

The following is a listing by payment priority of unsecured claims and how tax claims of all types fit into the sequence of unsecured claims. The sequence is especially interesting as it relates to the relatively low priority position of several unsecured claims that might be expected to stand higher on the list.

1. Cost of administration (these costs relate to the bankruptcy proceedings and include the trustee's expenses of preserving the estate, including wages, salaries of support personnel, etc.).
2. Any tax incurred by the estate.
3. Expenses of creditors in recovering property for the benefit of the estate and compensation for the services of an accountant or attorney.
4. Wage claims up to $2000 for each employee (see the description of these claims in preceding paragraphs).
5. Contributions to employee benefit plans from services rendered to the debtor company within 180 days of filing of the petition or closing of the debtor's business.

6. Unsecured consumer claims to an individual claim total of $900 (for deposits or services not received).

7. Income taxes due within three years of commencement of the case. Property taxes for one year, unemployment taxes, withholding and excise taxes, custom duties, and any tax penalties.

The court may rule on any questions regarding the tax effects of a plan of reorganization after the earlier of (*a*) the taxing authority's response or (*b*) 270 days after the request by the proponent(s) of the plan.

The Code states that the judgment of the court becomes final and binding upon the taxing authority, unless there is an appeal in any case where the proponent requested the court to determine the tax effects of the proposed (or accepted) plan of reorganization.

Tax Liens on Estate Property

The Code offers an interesting sequence of steps that a trustee must use when estate property that is to be distributed is subject to a tax lien. There is a priority system for a distribution under these circumstances, a system that has the following sequence:

1. The holder of a claim that has been secured by a lien on a property that is senior to the tax lien shall receive that property over the claims of other unsecured claimants.

2. An allowed tax claim that has been secured by a lien may be paid after claims for administrative expenses, wage claims, and priority consumer creditors have been paid.

3. If payments to priority claimants did not use up the entire amount of the tax claim, the remainder shall be distributed to the tax claimant.

4. Junior lien holders are next in the order of claimants to receive payments.

5. The tax claimant may be paid any money that remains after claimants with a higher priority have been paid.

Other Priority Claims

Priority claims have been discussed in an earlier subsection of this chapter, but because their relevance is important in the distribution of the proceeds from the debtor's estate, here is a capsulized look at a variety of those claims: costs of administration; taxes incurred by the estate; expense to creditors of recovering property for the benefit of the debtor's estate; individual employee wage claims of up to $2000; contributions to employee benefit plans up to $2000 per employee, less priority wage and employee benefits claims paid earlier; unsecured consumer claims of $900 per individual claimant; income taxes from return due within three years of the filing for protection; one year of property taxes; all other tax liabilities such as unemployment, withholding and excise, custom duties, and tax penalties assessed from prior years.

Mechanic's liens, which are filed to cover labor and materials, are valid as a claim against the debtor's estate even when the notice of lien is filed after the petition in bankruptcy and if the lien was filed within the limits prescribed by the statutes of the state in which it was filed.

Certainly the one factor in a liquidation that is critical to all unsecured claimants is the size of the debtor's estate. Equally relevant to the claimants is whether the value of the debtor's assets does or does not consist of individual assets/properties whose liquidity is such that they can be converted quickly and at minimum expense to *cash*. Short of a return of 100 cents on each one dollar of claim, a large pool of relatively unencumbered debtor assets that can be quickly and inexpensively converted to cash—and a short list of secured creditors, each of whom has a very, very low security interest in the debtor's estate—is the optimum scenario for lifting the spirits of claimants who are mired in the depths of the unsecure; for those unsecured claimants who have no priority standing, there is very little hope that anything positive will come out of this hog wallow.

The Landlord

The debtor's leasing or renting of premises to house or service a company or business becomes, with the filing of a bankruptcy petition, a matter for the trustee to decide. What is there to decide if the business has come to a halt and a trustee has been appointed to take over and administer the debtor's estate? There are decisions to be made and, with input from the creditors (specifically the creditor's committee), a decision must be made regarding the continuity of the company while the possibility of a plan of reorganization is explored with creditors/claimants and the debtor. If the company was still operating when the petition was filed, and the concept of the business is fundamentally sound, there is a probability that the company can be reorganized in such a manner as to encourage a continuation under conditions that should be conducive to success.

Example: The trustee finds that the debtor's lease with the landlord runs for three more years with an option to renew for five more. The trustee is faced, under the Code, with the need to advise the landlord of his or her intentions within the period of 60 days of the granting of the order for relief. If the trustee neither assumes nor rejects the contract or lease, it is said to have been rejected.

If the trustee finds that the best interests of the debtor company will be served if he or she assumes the contract or lease, the trustee will contact the landlord prior to the expiration of the 60 days specified by the Code, agree to a continuation of the contract or lease, and provide the landlord with assurances appropriate to the value of the contract and the length of time remaining on it. The decision is made on the basis of the authority assigned to the trustee under the provisions of the Code, the trustee's investigation of the business, and the recommendation of the creditor's committee, which is not binding on the trustee. When analysis confirms the probability that the debtor business can and should be saved, and that the owner/manager is an honorable and conscientious person who is unlikely to make the same mistake(s) again, the trustee can proceed to work with the court, the creditor's committee, and the debtor to expedite the presentation and acceptance of a plan of arrangement acceptable to the creditors/claimants and the debtor.

As the court's administrative representative, the trustee conducts the business of the court in a businesslike manner. The court would not expect its representative to disregard the interests of a landlord—one whose unsecured claim for one, two, or three months rent is undoubtedly on the list of claims—by failing to contact the landlord at some point during the 60 days regarding his or her intentions toward the lease. The landlord's interest and claim is entitled to equal treatment with the claims of other unsecured creditors. The landlord's loss, should the trustee fail to assume the lease, cannot fail to exceed the amount of the claim filed: a period of vacancy plus structural and cosmetic changes to accommodate the requirements of another tenant could leave the landlord with a disproportionate financial burden.

25

Your Customer Faces Liquidation

A bankruptcy action is filled with discouraging words for creditors, but some of the most discouraging may come from the creditors' committee reports. When the committee is forced to tell the unsecured creditors that the debtor has been unable to come up with a plan of reorganization, or that the plan of reorganization submitted to the committee and passed along to the unsecured creditors for acceptance or rejection has been rejected overwhelmingly, there is very little hope that the business can be saved. When a plan is rejected by a narrow margin there is a good chance that additional fine-tuning will bring it within parameters acceptable to the unsecured creditors; when the rejection is overwhelming, there is little reason to hope that such a wide gap between acceptance and rejection can be bridged with something acceptable.

Creditors Reject the Continuation Plan

Too many debtors do not understand that a plan of reorganization does not have a chance of acceptance if it does not address the legitimate concerns of all levels of claimants. It must address the various levels of the claimant's dollar exposure with an awareness and integrity that can readily be seen as fair and equal treatment. The secured creditors are on a plateau of their own, but it is the unsecured creditors whose legitimate concerns must be addressed to their satisfaction if the company is to have any chance to escape the process of liquidation.

Continuation plans (or plans of arrangement) are accepted or rejected for a variety of reasons. Some rejections may have their roots in a long-standing belief that a self-indulgent owner put too little into the business while taking out too much. Others may feel that although the business was the victim of weak management decisions, it would ultimately have been in trouble because the company failed to stay a step ahead of the technological requirements of its customers. Other reasons for rejecting a continuation plan or plan of arrangement follow:

1. The management of the debtor company does not have a good reputation in the industry or trade.

2. The owner(s) closed a similar business five years before in another section of the state. In that situation, a voluntary petition had been filed, no plan of arrangement had been submitted that met the requirements of creditors, and there had been a substantial loss to the creditors.

3. Unsecured creditors whose claims are thousands of dollars above the average are not satisfied with the schedule for paying claims.

4. Major claimants (who are also major creditors) want a 15 percent cash payment within two weeks after a plan of arrangement is accepted, plus additional payments at six-month intervals of 15 percent, 20 percent, 25 percent, and 25 percent. A provision that would require unsecured creditors with claims over $1500 to accept 40 percent of their claim in preferred stock, which would be nontransferable for two years, is not acceptable to the debtor's major creditors.

5. The debtor and members of the creditors' committee disagree on the amount of cash that the debtor company should be allowed to retain to pay suppliers who will be unwilling to sell on terms other than cash.

6. The bank's position is secured with a Uniform Commercial Code filing, but when members of the creditors' committee asked if the bank would be willing to advance some additional funds to the debtor to support cash flow, the bank indicated that it would have to evaluate a plan of arrangement before it made a decision.

7. Members of the creditors' committee have questioned the sincerity of the debtor company's owner/managers. The court has had to admonish the debtors for failing to provide drafts of a plan of arrangement within the time limit set by the court.

8. Products that were in the company's production or distribution pipelines have been halted because of the petition.

9. Orders have been cancelled by customers who were using the debtor company as a primary or secondary source of products. These customers do not feel comfortable relying upon a company whose future is in doubt.

10. Creditors/claimants feel that the business has not prospered because there is too much well-entrenched competition in an area where there never was enough business to support another of the debtor's type.

11. There would be no incentive for claimants to approve a plan of reorganization for the debtor business when many of the claimants would not be interested in selling the debtor the needed quantities of product(s) on credit terms.

12. The owners, perceived by the creditors to be the primary cause for the problems of their business, are unwilling to accept the creditors' committee recommendation that they step aside, appoint a new manager or CEO who has the approval of the creditors' committee, and agree to detach themselves from day to day (or advisory) involvement in the business.

There are other reasons why a satisfactory plan of reorganization is never submitted by the creditors' committee to the unsecured claimants of record. One of the overshadowing questions focuses on whether a reorganized debtor company would avoid the mistakes that led it to become an insolvent debtor, one in such dire business and financial straits that it had to petition the bankruptcy court for relief from the collection efforts of its creditors. Claimants who are being asked to favorably consider a plan of reorganization want to be assured and reassured that the odds of a repeat situation are slim to none. Claimants especially do not want it to happen a second time because they (the claimants) were not tough-minded enough to recognize that the business—even with the guideline of a strong plan of reorganization—had become too fragmented and had lost too much momentum to bring about the turnaround necessary in the time frame that would be allotted.

The principal(s) in a debtor company or the entrepreneur who owns and manages a debtor business or company has more than a small influence on what happens during the course of the proceedings. Demeanor—the person's manner or attitude—often tells the court and the creditors' committee a great deal about the individual(s) who asked for protection, how they have handled the responsibility of that protection, and whether there has been a serious effort to present a plan of reorganization based upon solid business principles—and all of this with goals that are difficult, but not impossible to attain. If principals convey by statements and actions that they are fighters, whatever they present to the court, the creditors' committee, and the body of claimants will receive a full measure of consideration.

When a plan or reorganization is sent by the creditors' committee (under the watchful umbrella of the court) to the creditor/claimants, the committee covers copies of the plan with a letter which (*a*) details their reasons for urging the claimants to accept the plan or (*b*) refers to the plan as being borderline, but because it represents the best received from the debtor to date, they felt obligated to give the claimants an opportunity to say "yes" or "no." If the plan is rejected, the weight of the rejection would indicate to the committee just how much more work is needed before the plan could become acceptable to the body of unsecured claimants.

Many of the claimants will have had personal contact with the petitioner(s) during the short or long term of their creditor/customer relationship. Impressions created over a period of months or years will add shadings, either favorable or negative, to proposals that the debtor may make as he or she attempts to salvage the business or company. Creditors who were turned off because they perceived the debtor to be arrogant or less than an ethical business person will require a stronger plan of reorganization and a stronger level of persuasion than claimants whose perception of the debtor is less harsh. It is unlikely, however, that attitudes rather than substance (the quality of the plan, the intelligence of the debtor or debtor company's management, their experience, their desire to rebuild, etc.) would cause an otherwise acceptable plan of reorganization to be rejected by claimants, but it is true that deep-seated impressions of people and enterprises have considerable impact on the final decision.

The court has overview authority regarding a plan of reorganization, an authority which under the Code requires that the interests of the debtor receive equal protection with those of the estate's claimants. Because the court would never allow the vindictiveness of one or more of the claimants to determine the course of the proceeding, it is in the best interests of a conscientious debtor to work closely with the creditors' committee, the trustee, and the court. This is true even when it has become obvious that what is salvageable in the debtor business is not enough, even if it were given a second chance, to give it a reasonable chance to revive and to stabilize itself.

A creditors' committee might offer a plan of arrangement (synonymous with "plan of reorganization") as "being in the best interests of creditors" and still have the plan fail to be accepted by claimants of record. This is not uncommon. Self-interest is the guideline of primary concern in the majority of these situations. Claimants are often unreceptive to reorganizations that would defer a partial payment of past-due obligations to conserve cash and assets so the debtor business can move forward with the plan. There may, however, be pressure from the creditors' committee and other creditors (telephone calls, etc.) to induce the one or two votes needed to carry the plan to accept the will of the majority.

Claimants rely on the judgment of their creditors' committee to offer suggestions to the debtor, to monitor the progress of drafts of the plan of reorganization, and to make suggestions for appropriate changes. The committee also forwards to claimants of record any information relative to the proceeding that addresses their interests, including the forwarding for approval or rejection of any plan that they feel warrants a "yes" or a "no" judgment from each claimant. It is important that the creditors' committee performs its duties in a conscientious manner, one that bolsters the confidence of creditor/claimants whose faith in their ability to make sound credit judgments may have been shaken when the debtor filed a petition for protection.

Committee members will not, however, recommend a plan that is not in the best interests of all levels of unsecured creditors. The debtor may offer a plan that is so close to meeting what the collective judgment of committee members tells them is acceptable and workable that they will forward it, with a cover letter detailing any reservations, and attach a questionnaire with a series of guideline questions to assist the committee in its effort to develop the present plan into an acceptable one. When claimants return the questionnaire with their comments and recommendations, the committee will meet with the debtor, go over the consensus of the responses of claimants, and work with the debtor to shape the plan into its final form.

After all of the effort that the committee has put into the attempt to develop with the debtor an acceptable plan of reorganization, is it possible that the effort will ultimately end in failure and a liquidation of the debtor's company or business? It's quite possible. While the plan is being developed and fine-tuned—this usually takes a period of several weeks—there could be changes. What kinds of changes? Changes in the upper echelons of management at certain key companies which might reflect in an attitude change toward what is and what is not a satisfactory plan of reorganization; sudden changes in the industry or in the economy of the nation which would adversely impact the cash flow and the cash requirements of many companies, cash requirements that might cause a previously flexible company to insist on higher and more frequent cash payments, or they will vote to reject the plan. It should be readily apparent that any vote to reject the plan is a vote to liquidate the assets of the company. The changing requirements—cash and other—of these claimant companies can undermine the effort to devise a satisfactory plan and alter dramatically the manner in which a plan of reorganization is perceived.

The distance between an accepted plan of reorganization and a liquidation is never wider than a poorly expressed thought, a misinterpreted statement, or the insidious idea that one or a group of claimants might get more from the arrangement and reorganization than another group. Once this type of distrust begins to infect the process of developing an acceptable plan, the swing toward rejection of the debtor's plan and liquidation of the assets becomes almost inevitable.

Are There Salable Assets?

When a debtor's plight reaches the point where all efforts to come up with a plan of reorganization have failed, the only alternative is for the court to order the trustee to liquidate the debtor's assets and to distribute them on the basis of (*a*) secured debts, (*b*) unsecured priority debts, and (*c*) unsecured nonpriority debts. At the conclusion of the liquidation process, the court will discharge the debtor from responsibility for specific listed debts, declare the business or company a bankrupt, and close the case.

Before such a sequence of events can reach the point where a trustee begins to liquidate the debtor's assets, he or she must have an inventory of everything of value. The trustee must know where every item on the inventory is located, the condition of each item, whether items are marketable or must be repaired and/or refurbished before they can be marketed, what "book value" the company had placed on each item, and what price the trustee will try to get for each of them. The trustee's experience in liquidation matters is usually extensive enough for the trustee to know that pricing assets of the debtor, especially those that have been used in the day to day conduct of the business, is not an easy task. Getting a fair price for the debtor's assets can be a very daunting challenge.

Any sale of a debtor's assets that is conducted at the debtor's place of business includes an inventory hand-out sheet with all items listed and priced. What the trustee and any interested buyers know is that "asking prices" are subject to offer and/or negotiation. Nobody pays the prices assigned to items (machinery, office equipment, automobiles, trucks, fork lifts, production equipment, etc.). Every price is or should be subject to negotiation, because to undervalue items to the point where buyers are not questioning or haggling over prices is a sure sign that prices are not as high as they should be.

Unfortunately, that is seldom the problem. Prospective buyers will walk through a factory or an office, inventory list in hand, examine items of interest, pencil in their own prices, and make their offers based upon their own expectations regarding the lowest figure at which they can realistically expect to buy an item. Buyers feel they can always meet the trustee's prices somewhere in the middle, frequently much closer to their own figure.

Will the trustee not negotiate the prices of certain items? Holding the price line on certain items can mean that the trustee is calling upon recent experience in selling items of a similar type; it could mean that the trustee is using the experience of someone who has confirmed that certain of the debtor's asset items, all of them in excellent condition, are seldom available as used items. In such a situation, a good, but fair price could find a willing buyer.

Office Equipment

If the company or business has been using computers, word processors, word processing typewriters, laser printers, or photocopy machines that are fairly new, fast, clean, and can reproduce documents in color, and has desks, chairs, and filing cabinets that have not been mistreated, there is a strong probability that those items will be sold, but at a per-unit figure that is well below the company's book value.

The marketplace is already loaded with used equipment, much of it offered by dealers who have taken it in trade or by dealers who buy up large quantities from companies and sell it through a warehouse-type retail outlet. Trustees are faced with the prospect of discounting good office equipment to a figure far below the value carried on the company's list of assets. "Book value" is valid only as it relates to the original value of an item which has subsequently been discounted over the years as prescribed by law and good accounting practices. It is, however, not generally a criterion for what a trustee can expect to get for items when called upon to liquidate the debtor's estate.

Automobiles, Trucks, and Fork Lifts

This is one of the few areas where the book value of assets should be in line with their marketplace value. Vehicles that are one, two, or three years old, have been serviced and maintained in accordance with warranty and factory recommendations, and whose exterior and interior appearance is good should bring a price comparable to what dealers and individuals are getting for theirs.

Whether the trustee elects to wholesale the units in this category of assets (probably the lowest return per unit), sell them through a licensed, advertised public auction (one where the debtor's units will be brought together with many other vehicles), include them on an inventory list and display them on the debtor's premises, or include them in a newspaper and/or a televised ad for a public sale at the debtor's place of business is the discretionary choice of the trustee. His or her only mandate is to get the highest price possible for each of the debtor's assets. If the trustee elects to liquidate the major portion of the debtor company's assets at a public auction to be held at the debtor's place of business, the trustee might or might not include the vehicles in that auction.

Production Machinery

Major items of used capital equipment may be difficult to sell at book price; they might also be unexpectedly easy to sell. A number of factors will contribute to the ease or the difficulty. Among the major factors will be the type of equipment, the condition and age of the equipment, whether the equipment can be used in one or more industries, whether the industry in which it is used is subject to technological changes that accelerate the obsolescence of production and other equipment, whether the equipment is being offered in a high-tech industry, and where the equipment stands on the scale of accelerated obsolescence.

Trustees know that capital equipment represents the major investment of the debtor company; they also know that it is often expensive to move such equipment, especially if it must be transported a considerable distance. Equipment (production machinery, processing equipment, unique pieces designed for a special purpose) that is in good condition and is not in danger of near-term obsolescence should be considered salable, but being "salable" isn't the same thing as having a buyer. Pieces of capital equipment have resale value, but unless a company has a specific need for the piece of equipment that is being offered, it might not generate an offer from an area other than a dealer in used equipment, a situation that could result in a much lower sale price than the trustee had anticipated.

There is also the possibility that the manufacturer(s) of specific items of equipment might be interested in buying the unit to resell it to a customer who needs a part-time or an "occasional use" unit. Such a unit would fit the needs of the manufacturer's customer and would keep the customer thinking in terms of the manufacturer's product when it is time to upgrade to a new unit.

Patents and Trademarks

The value of patents and trademarks is often overlooked or undervalued when the assets of a company are being listed. A patent is often the base upon which a company is founded, or the base that provided the basic product line from which the company gained early momentum and recognition, and, in some instances of later failure, what seemed to be the promise of an ever-increasing success. So what happens when the early promise turns to latter day fizzle and the bankruptcy court's trustee liquidates the assets of this once-promising "never was"? The trustee is driven by court and claimant pressure to find anything and everything of value, and to get the highest price possible for it. There are physical assets such as those listed in earlier paragraphs, and then there are assets whose value must be measured by the yardstick of past and current contributions to the business plus the potential for a more impressive performance in the future.

Patents and trademarks offer an opportunity to generate cash for the debtor's estate. They can be sold to another company with the assurance that there will be no loss in the marketplace acceptance of products or services. These items represent two of the very few categories in the process of liquidation in which the trustee can negotiate from a position of some strength. Good patents and good trademarks represent strong commercial value. Whether they have been properly exploited in the past is of little consequence if the potential for success is still there and it is recognized by both the seller and the prospective buyer.

Once the court has ruled that the debtor's assets are to be liquidated, the process should move rapidly, but not so rapidly that the trustee does not have time to contact firms who might be interested in acquiring the patents or trademark(s) of the debtor company. Negotiations with prospective buyers could extend the liquidation process, but they have the potential to add a substantial number of dollars to the total available for distribution to claimants. In the final analysis, there is no reason why the trustee should not be able to sell the debtor company's patents and trademarks for a price at or near worth.

Good Will (?)

The value of "good will" is frequently an eye-opening excessive when viewed through the eyes of a seller; conversely, it is just as frequently downgraded by a prospective buyer to the level of a minor or an insignificant "add on," something that should not be dignified by attempting to give it monetary value. It is an intangible whose value, when offered for sale, can seldom be measured with any degree of accuracy.

Think of it. Can a seller—in this situation the trustee for a bankrupt debtor—assure a buyer that customers who bought the products of the seller's company will transfer their allegiance (?) to the company whose purchase of "good will" allegedly has as its base the purchase of transferable customer loyalty? Can the "good will" that the bankrupt debtor might have accumulated during the months or years of its existence be expected to prevail over new feelings of frustration and anger born in the latter weeks of the debtor company's business life? What has the fact that orders were not shipped on time or were shipped as partial orders with the back ordered portion to follow within several days done? How does the "good will" phase of the relationship figure to survive under those circumstances? Is it relevant that the customer knew or cared that the debtor company's suppliers were holding or delaying orders with increasing frequency, thereby creating the situation of partial shipments and back orders?

The problems of a supplier should never be allowed to become the customer's problems. When they do, the impact on good will is swift. A relationship that might have taken several years to build can erode within days or weeks. And when the level of erosion equals what has just been described, the trustee has a real problem. Is there or isn't there enough good will to give this intangible asset a current value: if it has some value, is it a value that is marketable? The trustee must decide whether good will was damaged only somewhat or irreparably by the debtor company's problems with its suppliers, and whether the abrupt filing of a petition by the debtor removed a customer's only source for one or more products, while also removing any lingering trace of good will.

Good will? An important intangible with value only if it wasn't too badly damaged during the debtor's period of decline. The trustee will make some exploratory inquiries and, if in his or her judgment, there appears to be any possibility of marketable value, prospective buyers will be contacted.

Forced Sale

There was mention earlier of the problems a trustee faces when he or she is instructed by the court to liquidate the assets of a bankrupt debtor. It may be a problem for the trustee, but it's certainly no problem for prospective buyers. In their eyes a forced sale is a fire sale to end all fire sales. I can think of no other situation that has less leverage for getting buyers to pay prices that come within light years of "book value" or "fair price" than a liquidation sale.

With the possible exception of a few items, it is a scavenger hunt with prices set by the trustee bearing little resemblance to prices offered by prospective buyers. The people who attend these sales know that the trustee has a limited period of time in which to conclude the sale of assets. They know that there is no tomorrow, that a trustee will not hold back certain items against the possibility that they might bring a higher price one or two weeks after the advertised sale. Only if an offer is ludicrous in comparison to the value of an item will the trustee withdraw it and try to dispose of it through another channel.

In order for the trustee to fulfill the court's mandate and generate the maximum amount of cash possible from the estate, the trustee must sell estate items, because reserving them for possible sale at a future date does not generate cash or reduce assets to the zero point where the case can be closed. Although a trustee will state on any sale literature or at an auction of estate items that any item may be withdrawn if bidding does not reach or exceed the value established and listed by the trustee, that option is exercised rarely.

Secured Claims

In Part 3, "The Uniform Commercial Code," there was extensive analysis of the two positions available to credit grantors: the option of choosing to become secured creditors with secured claims or the option of remaining unsecured creditors with unsecured claims. Although the option was examined in Part 3 of this book, there can be no justification for a creditor who has put at risk more than a few hundred dollars of the company's receivables assets not to protect the company's interest with a filing under the Uniform Commercial Code.

There are creditors who do not learn the true value of the enormous difference between a secured and an unsecured position until one of their customers has gone through a liquidation and bankruptcy. They remain unconvinced until they are in the position of watching secured creditors take their money—all of it—and walk away from a liquidation/bankruptcy that offers to unsecured creditors a dividend of pennies on the dollar.

The pecking order for settling the claims of creditors in a liquidation and bankruptcy is very specific. Secured creditors/claimants are entitled to payment before those who have general/unsecured claims, including the priority claims of unsecured claim holders. Priority unsecured claims are next—claims that include costs of administration, taxes generated by the estate, costs of recovering property for the benefit of the debtor's estate, claims for wages, and additional claims that were previously listed. And when the laundry list of priority claims has been satisfied, what is left for the great pool of general unsecured claimants? A total of the dollar amount of the claims of the general unsecured claimants versus the dollars available for distribution among this category of claimants should look something like this:

1. Thirty-one general unsecured claimants have filed claims which total $187,540.

2. The total amount of the claims filed by secured and priority unsecured claimants is $151,244.

3. After the secured and priority unsecured claimants have been paid, the amount of money available for distribution to the general unsecured claimants is $36,296.

4. The formula for determining the amount of payment to the general unsecured claimants for each one dollar of their claims is the following: $36,296 divided by $187,540 equals $0.19.

5. Individual unsecured claimants will receive a settlement of $0.19 for each one dollar of their claim, which makes it a fairly generous dividend when it is compared with the many zero to five to ten cent dividends that I have seen in comparable situations.

You have now had a few seconds to digest the impact of these figures. Can there be any doubt that the creditor who had the good sense to secure the account of his or her company with a Uniform Commercial Code filing is better off by $0.81 per $1.00 of secured debt than the unsecured claimant who is fortunate to be receiving $0.19 for each $1.00 of his or her company's claim? And if the amount of the dollars is large and the financial stability of the creditor/claimant is not strong? The difference of $0.81 per dollar of claim between a secured and an unsecured creditor could be the difference between survival or failure.

It would be wrong to suggest that secured creditors always get 100 cents for each dollar of their claims. There are situations where the debtor's assets have been depleted (poor management, loss of a major account, changes in industry preferences, regional or national recession, etc.) to the point where unsecured creditors will receive only a low-percentage dividend from the liquidation of the debtor's assets. But even under a worst case scenario such as the above, secured creditors are going to get whatever is available for distribution after the debtor's assets have been liquidated. And how do the priority unsecured and general unsecured claimants fare in this scenario? Their categories will receive nothing if the liquidated assets of the debtor do not satisfy the claims of those who are secured.

The possibility of one day being in the position of receiving nothing in a liquidation of debtor assets because the account was not secured should be incentive enough for any conscientious credit administrator to establish a figure—one based upon the size of the credit administrator's company and one that will serve as the line between a small (acceptable) loss and a larger (unacceptable) loss—and secure every account that exceeds or could exceed the figure for securing the risk or going unsecured. Consider it a financial line that your company should not cross unless the customer account is protected by a UCC filing or unless the customer is so large, so financially strong, and so well established that to secure the account would spill over into the ludicrous. But the account had better be a crown jewel in its particular area of industry or business to receive the "no protective filing" treatment. The security interest of your company makes every customer company a legitimate candidate for a protective filing under the UCC; any exceptions from the concept of an amount above a guideline figure triggering a protective filing should be considered carefully before you waive that protection.

The Unsecured Creditor

The unenviable plight of unsecured creditors in a dissolution and liquidation has been used in some earlier subsections to compare the "worlds apart" differences between a claimant whose claim is secured and one whose claim is not. When a supplier prepares to take on a new account, there is always a complete credit check—one motivated by the thought that your company does not need a credit account that is going to become a problem. So, after applying the weight of your judgment to that premise, you accept or reject the account. But months later when the account you accepted as being worthy of your company's trust suddenly files for protection in bankruptcy court, your company's investment in receivables dollars or other property or assets had better be secured or the loss may far exceed what it might have been.

The term "unsecured creditors" should be reserved for creditors whose unsecured individual accounts do not exceed a very low level of risk; in a Chapter 11 filing, it should be a level at which each creditor who has an unsecured claim does not find it a worrisome number of dollars. As outlined in the preceding paragraphs, the element of additional risk imposed by the unsecured status of an account should be limited to account totals that do not exceed a guideline sum of money—one figure applicable to every one of the company's accounts. There is no justification, not even the desire to exploit what appears to be an excellent opportunity for new business, for a supplier of money, goods, or services to increase the chances of a loss by compounding risk.

Every owner, manager, or credit administrator should do whatever is within his or her power to cut the risk of a credit loss—any type of credit loss. Reducing factors and areas of risk should be the result of credit management techniques that protect the assets of the seller (receivables, goods, property, etc.), while minimizing restrictions on the customer's access to the seller's line(s) of merchandise. Unsecured credit granted at levels above what a creditor can afford to lose—whether in one account or several—is an invitation to an early and an unhappy exit from the world of business.

Do not allow your business or company to gradually surround itself with a minefield of unsecured accounts whose balances vary from quite low to dollar totals that are much higher than any of the company's unsecured accounts should be allowed to carry. There will come a time when the absence of appropriate control over this increasingly dangerous mine field will haunt the company's bad-debt account and its bottom line with greater and more painful frequency. No company can take potentially dangerous major credit risks on an ongoing basis without eventually paying a price that is either crippling or deadly.

An Unacceptable Continuation/Reorganization Plan

Creditors/claimants are unlikely to be receptive to a continuation plan or a plan of reorganization (the two are synonymous) if the plan does not address certain major concerns of the creditor/claimants. There are several things that the format requires of a plan, things that it must agree to do and provide, and what it proposes to do in certain areas.

A reorganization plan must agree to do the following:

1. Designate the classes of claims and interests with the exception of administrative claims, unsecured claims presented between the filing date of an involuntary petition, certain tax claims, and the appointment of a trustee.

2. State the classes of claims which under the plan are not reduced or diminished in value.

3. State the classes of claims that under the plan are to be reduced or diminished in value.

4. Ensure that all claims within a class of creditors receive equal treatment.

5. Ensure the plan's confirmation by the court and its successful implementation, via a series of actions such as a merger or consolidation of the debtor's business with another, the transfer of estate property to another business or company, the correction or waiver of any default(s), the issuance of securities as part of the package to deal with claims filed by the creditors, etc.

The plan may provide for one or more of the following:

1. The benefits of retirees may be modified if the proposed changes meet the requirements as stated in The Bankruptcy Code.

2. How debtor claims against other companies or individuals should be treated which were not settled before the plan of reorganization was approved.

3. The settlement of debtor claims against others or the arrangement by which the debtor or an agent retains claims and the power to enforce collection.

If a continuation plan is not structured to, one, meet the requirements of The Bankruptcy Code and, two, address the legitimate concerns of all approved claimants, the court will reject the plan for failing to meet Code requirements or the claimants will reject it for not addressing to their satisfaction areas such as management (who will be managing the business), a disposition of approved claims (will it be a combination of preferred stock, will cash payments be based upon percentages of individual claims, what will the timetable of the payment schedule be, etc.), a revised business plan (how does the business propose to regenerate itself), financial management and controls (what will be done to generate and manage effectively a stronger and more consistent cash flow), and other areas of concern to the court and the claimants.

26

Your Customer's Acceptable Plan of Arrangement

Acceptance of the debtor's plan of arrangement offers the potential for results that are either positive or negative. If the continuation plan works, the company or business should be stronger than it had been since well before the decline that led to the filing of a petition under Chapter 11. Claimants would receive the additional benefit of receiving most or all of the money that was owing to them when the petition was filed. When a debtor company has been the victim of circumstances which were beyond its control, there is widespread satisfaction among claimants when the company is able to develop a continuation plan that is acceptable to claimants and to the court.

An acceptable plan of arrangement is not a magic wand which, when waved, will automatically return the debtor company to a position of health and industry respect. It does, however, give the company the chance to achieve those goals under conditions that may or may not include the continuing supervision of the bankruptcy court. If the court has any doubts regarding the ability of the debtor to operate successfully outside the court's supervision, the court will retain control of the company's assets until it is sure that the debtor company is being operated properly and successfully. Claimants might also petition the court to accept their endorsement of the plan of reorganization, but might suggest delaying the return of assets and control to the debtor company until the debtor has demonstrated the ability to run the company without the court's supervision.

An Arrangement or a Continuation Plan?

It was stated in the preceding chapter that the two—a Continuation Plan or a Plan of Arrangement—are different labels for the same thing. The debtor may come up with something that was written under the working title of a Continuation Plan; the creditor's committee might receive it from the debtor, forward it to the court, receive the court's approval to forward it to the claimants for their approval or rejection, then send it out to the claimants under the title "Plan of Reorganization."

The bottom line is that if the claimants accept what the debtor proposes in "the plan," they are saying that the business or company should have the chance to try to make the plan work; by voting to accept the plan, claimants are saying they believe it can work. Whether the court does or does not return all areas of the business (control of all assets, etc.) to the unsupervised control of the debtor(s) when the plan is confirmed by the court is the court's decision. It could be a year or more before the court and creditor/claimants are satisfied that the debtor company is capable of administering every facet of the company's affairs without the court's overview. What is clear, however, is that if the plan of reorganization is to have long-term success, the court must eventually step away from involvement with the business. What if the court becomes dissatisfied with the level of progress or finds that management is ignoring the plan of reorganization? Any further deterioration of the business would add additional risk to the position of the debtor company's creditor/claimants and could cause the court to terminate the continuation plan and order the dissolution of the business or company.

Debtors who are fortunate enough to have the court and creditors support their honest effort to create an acceptable plan of reorganization must also accept the fact that the vote of confidence is a very precarious one, one that can be destroyed quickly and irreparably if the debtor fails to perform in the manner expected by those who have provided him or her with a second chance. Creditors who voted to give the debtor a second chance will be quick to reverse the earlier "thumbs up" when there is evidence that the debtor has been less than straightforward in his or her representation of plans for the debtor company.

The Ingredients of a Plan of Reorganization

A plan of reorganization combines what is required by the Code, what the creditor/claimants want to get from the debtor, and what the debtor can give, is willing to give up, or is willing to do to save the business. The following are some of the ingredients of a plan that meets requirements of the Code.

1. Classes of claims and interests must be designated; exceptions to this designation are administrative claims, unsecured claims that were created between the filing of an involuntary petition and the appointment of a trustee, and various tax claims.

2. The plan shall specify which classes of claims are not impaired.

3. The plan shall explain how the interests of classes of claims that are not impaired will be handled.

4. It will provide equal treatment for all claims of the same class.

5. The plan shall be assisted toward a successful consummation by providing from within itself the following means to achieve that goal:

   - The debtor shall retain any estate property.
   - All liens are to be satisfied or modified.
   - The debtor may be merged or consolidated with another.
   - Existing defaults shall be cured or waived.
   - Securities shall be issued to facilitate the settlement of creditor claims and to promote acceptance of the plan.

6. The addition of a provision in the debtor's charter must state that no nonvoting stock may be issued by the debtor.

7. The addition of another provision must require an appropriate distribution of voting power among the classes of stock.

8. Certain secured or unsecured claims must be declared to be impaired or unimpaired.

9. Certain contracts and leases not previously rejected by the trustee may be assumed or rejected.

10. Certain agreements (collective bargaining, etc.) and retiree benefits may be modified if provisions of the Code are not violated.

11. What about claims held by the debtor against other businesses or companies which were not settled before the plan was confirmed? The settlement of these claims must be addressed in the plan or provision made for the debtor or an agent to retain claims and collect their balances.

The judge of the bankruptcy court must be satisfied that the plan of reorganization conforms with the Code's requirements and represents a "good faith" effort by the debtor. The court should see also in the plan of arrangement the recommendations of the creditors' committee as they tried to help the debtor to shape a plan acceptable to the classes of creditors. If the plan fails to meet the criteria for an acceptable document under the Code, the court's decision to return it to the debtor is mandatory.

What are the prospects for the future success of a debtor who comes out of a Chapter 11 proceeding via a plan approved by the court and the debtor's creditors? Credit management professionals have always held mixed feelings regarding the prospects of most debtor companies for long-term success, because the record tips more frequently toward failure. The odds are against the debtor doing a successful turnaround, despite the fact that creditors have voted to give the debtor a second chance.

What are some of the problems that contribute to failure? Money (cash flow) is going to be the major continuing problem; getting key suppliers to extend new credit is another major problem (many want part or all cash, and although credit extended by suppliers after a plan has been confirmed by the court is debt that has priority over old debt, many suppliers choose not to participate); rebuilding a customer base and restoring the damaged confidence of old customers are yet other major tasks; working to convince the banker to advance new funds to augment cash flow (supplement stagnant receivables payments) when the safety of what had previously been advanced remains in question; not the least of the debtor company's problems is attracting old and/or new employees (quality people who can make a contribution) to a company that has one failure chalked up against it and a very shaky mandate for the future. After reading the foregoing, it should be obvious that a turnaround after a Chapter 11 is not easy.

Too many debtors do not understand that for a plan of reorganization to have a chance for acceptance, it must address equally the concerns of all creditors of the same category. Continuation plans are accepted or rejected for a variety of reasons, some of which have been mentioned in sections that have preceded this one. For a continuation plan to be accepted, both the tangibles and the intangibles must present a solid front to creditor/claimants. The following are some examples of what must be addressed successfully to have an arrangement that has a reasonable chance for acceptance.

1. When the owner of the debtor company does not have a good reputation in the trade or industry, the chances of getting creditors to approve a continuation plan with the owner still in active control of the business is minimal. Insist that the owner step away from any active role in the company's management, propose bringing in a respected person to manage the business, and move on to resolving other problems.

2. Unsecured creditors whose claims are in the low to medium five or six figures are dissatisfied with the schedule for retiring old debt.

3. Unsecured small claimants ($1000 to $1500) do not want their claims made a part of an extended or a partial payment plan. They want a cash settlement shortly after the plan is confirmed.

   (These complaints must be resolved for the plan to have any chance to win the approval of the claimants.)

Unimpaired Claims

Whether a plan of reorganization is or is not going to impair a class of claims or interests (diminish their value) is of enormous importance to claimants who are involved. There are three ways or conditions under which this might occur, so claimants will scrutinize carefully a plan that has been submitted for comment or approval to ensure that any such impairment of claims is an acceptable part of the plan.

1. Claims are considered not to be impaired if the holder's interest or claim is not altered by the plan.

2. The plan may cure a default by reinstating the maturity rights of a holder of a claim or interest to the status it held before the default. (This could be a very acceptable point for claimants whose default would be cured, but it could prove less popular with those who have no involvement, because they might see it as reserving money that otherwise would be available for other payments.) There may also be compensation to the holder of a claim for damages resulting from the debtor's failure to abide by the contractual provision for an accelerated payment or payments.

3. Claims are considered to be unimpaired if the plan provides for a cash payment equal to the allowed amount of the claim.

When there is a security interest, unimpaired status attaches to the greater of the fixed liquidation preference assigned to the holder of interest and the fixed price at which the debtor may redeem the security from the holder. (Reference to "the security" could be shares of preferred stock issued to a specific percentage of a claim which is, by agreement, not transferable for a stated period of years, usually between two and five. Preferred stock is the vehicle most debtors try to use to deal on a deferred basis with a strong percentage of the debt repayment scheduled in the plan or reorganization/continuation.)

Claimants are very wary of any provision in the plan that will impair their claims. The fact that the creditor's customer filed for protection under Chapter 11 is, in many cases, about as much shock therapy as creditors can absorb. There are, if the filing was totally unexpected, usually initial feelings of surprise followed by feelings that bounce back and forth between anger and betrayal. Reactions such as "How dare they do this to us after all we've done for them!" and "Isn't there an ounce of integrity in that sleazy company?!" are not untypical of early reactions to the filing. As the proceeding progresses, those feelings may take on a harder edge, especially if there is evidence to support the thought that a careless or self-indulgent attitude was a major factor in the company's demise.

The hard-nosed attitudes of claimants whose assets (goods, property, etc.) have been absorbed into a pattern of what is perceived as reckless and uncaring behavior is not conducive to new negative proposals. Impairing the claims of creditors whose feelings toward the debtor have been crystallized during the proceeding range from ambivalence to "let's liquidate the debtor's assets, swallow our losses, and get on to something with positive potential." Any plan of arrangement that attempts to impair a class of claims or interests is looking at a hard, uphill sell.

The Guidelines
for Accepting a Plan

Acceptance or rejection of a debtor's plan of arrangement is the result of a series of steps which, for a debtor who has a conscientious interest in salvaging the company or business, may be only slightly less hazardous than trying to pick a course through a minefield for which there is no map to pinpoint locations. It is a complex challenge for a debtor who must approach the problem of convincing claimants that although mistakes were made (a debtor is wise to readily acknowledge them while expressing appropriate regret for losses and inconvenience to the claimants) there is buried beneath the surface layer of rubble a business or a company that deserves a second chance. The debtor's most challenging task is to prepare a plan for reorganization and continuation that addresses clearly and equitably the concerns and requirements of each class of claimants plus meets the requirements of The Bankruptcy Code.

When the debtor's work with the creditors' committee has produced a plan that committee members feel will satisfy the concerns and requirements of claimants, and that plan has been found by the court to meet the Code's requirements, the committee will send it to claimants of record with a cover letter which will detail why the committee thinks it is acceptable and why it is the best that can be expected from the debtor; the letter will also determine the criteria for determining whether claimants, after they have marked and returned ballots to the court, have accepted or rejected the plan.

The Code offers an effective balance between the interests of what are usually a very few major unsecured creditors and the much larger number of small unsecured creditors. If it were not for the two guidelines, each of which has equal weight under the Code, major creditors would probably control the acceptance or rejection of the continuation plan. The combined dollar exposure of the few major creditors would control almost invariably the guideline for acceptance of "two-thirds in total dollars of the allowed claims who cast their ballots." But the Code's salvation for the small creditors is the other guideline—of equal importance and weight—which ensures that the large number of small creditors will not be ploughed under by the wishes of the majors.

Small creditors can make their wishes decisive in the second half of the process, the half that requires a favorable vote of a minimum of one vote over 50 percent of the total number of approved claims which cast a ballot (21 out of 40, 51 out of 100 votes cast, etc.) for the plan to be certified by the court. If the plan fails to get the minimum percentages required by the Code from both guidelines (over 50 percent of the claimants that vote and two-thirds of the total dollars of allowed claims that vote), then the plan will not be certified by the court. When a vote is close to qualifying a plan for acceptance, the court may give the debtor and members of the creditors' committee additional time to see if the differences can be resolved.

Modifying the Plan

The debtor and members of the creditors' committee may initially be some distance apart in their thinking regarding what must or should be a part of the plan; differences must be resolved, however, if the plan as presented to the claimants is to have a reasonable chance for acceptance. If the creditors' committee does not feel that the plan as offered by the debtor is not in the best interests of the claimants, the creditors' committee will not endorse the plan or ask claimants to approve it. The court may direct that a plan be submitted to claimants for their approval or rejection, but the creditors' committee may abstain from requesting a favorable vote.

A plan that has been approved by claimants is not cast in stone before or after it has been confirmed by the court. If there is good reason why a section or an area of the plan should be modified, the debtor and members of the creditors' committee may present the requested modification(s) to the court. If approved by the court, information pertinent to the proposed change(s) will be mailed to claimants a minimum of 10 days before the time fixed by the court for filing objections. When the time for filing objections has passed, the court will enter an order stating that the modified plan is considered accepted by all claimants who previously voted in favor of the plan and have failed to file in writing an objection to acceptance of the modification(s) within the court-specified period of time.

When a plan that has been accepted by claimants is to be modified, any such modification of the plan must be done before there has been substantial implementation of the specific section(s) or area(s). If the time lag from approval, implementation of the plan, and the suggested modification(s) is too great, the court will probably not grant the request. If, however, a belated request for change is the result of one or more flaws that were not recognized when the plan was approved and must be corrected if it is to continue or have a chance to succeed, the chances for the court's approval are excellent.

Confirming the Plan

When claimants have voted to approve a plan, the next step is for the court to hold a hearing to determine whether the plan should be confirmed. Any party or parties who have an interest in the debtor's estate may voice objections to confirmation. In addition to the objections of parties of interest, the court must determine whether the plan meets a list of requirements as set forth in the Code. Some of those requirements are as follows:

1. All requirements of the Code concerning content and classification have been met.

2. The provisions of the Code are in compliance, including disclosure of information pertaining to the plan when it was originally submitted to the creditors, if there is a valid and/or significant reason to modify the plan, etc.

3. There was good faith when the debtor was preparing and submitting the plan. Any indication to the contrary would destroy the integrity of the proceeding.

4. The plan must include and disclose all payments made or to be made for expenses incurred during the term of the case and during the lifetime of the plan. Payments made before the plan was confirmed must be within the guideline of reasonable charges; payments made after confirmation will be subject to review by the court.

5. The plan must include full disclosure of the company or business affiliation of any person selected to serve the debtor company/business as a director, officer, or voting trustee. No individual can be appointed to these positions whose interests are not consistent with those of the creditors.

6. The plan must disclose the identity and compensation of any insider who has been retained by the reorganized debtor. (The term "insider"

refers to a partner, salaried executive, or other key upper-echelon employee who has access to or is involved in the company's planning and decision making processes and was with the company before the filing was made.

7. Holders of claims within each of the classes will receive value under the plan exceeding the value each claimant would have received in a liquidation. The plan must improve the position of unsecured claimants and must offer secured creditors property of a value not less than the secured creditor's interest in the type and value of property that secures the claim.

8. Each class has accepted the plan and each class has not been impaired because of terms the plan may offer to another class. (The plan should not be confirmed by the court if there is unequal treatment between classes of creditors that is not addressed by The Bankruptcy Code or is not the result of an allowable secured filing under the Uniform Commercial Code.)

9. The plan should provide for cash payment of all administrative expenses, or certain claims filed in an involuntary case between the date the petition was filed, the appointment of the trustee, or the entering of the order for relief—whichever of these events was the earlier—on the effective date of the plan.

10. If the plan has been accepted by the class of creditors, holders of priority claims (wages, consumer claims, contributions to employee benefit claims, etc.) will receive deferred cash payments equal in value to the amount allowed for each claim. Have classes of creditors not accepted the plan? They will receive the same treatment as those who accepted the plan; cash equal to the allowed amount of the claim on the effective date of the plan.

11. Priority tax claims will receive deferred cash payments of a value equal to the amount allowed over a period not exceeding six years from the date the claim was assessed.

12. If there is more than one impaired class—exclusive of insider claims of interest—at least one class of the impaired creditors must accept the plan if it is to be confirmed.

13. The court must be satisfied that the confirmed plan will provide all the support, guidelines, and tools necessary to prevent the debtor from subsequently starting to slide into liquidation or a second financial reorganization.

It is not the function of the bankruptcy court or the objective of The Bankruptcy Code to allow debtor businesses to pick up the pieces and use the moratorium of a plan of reorganization to take hesitant strides toward the next crisis. When a company or a business has a plan confirmed and is given the green light to resume doing business, usually under the court's supervision, it is done with mixed feelings. The court and the creditors know the variety and magnitude of the problems that the debtor must overcome to let the plan become the successful guideline that was envisioned when creditors approved and the court confirmed.

There is no panacea to ensure that every company whose plan of reorganization/continuation has been confirmed will become a comeback success story; in fact, the odds are worse than even that fewer than 50 percent of the businesses trying for a turnaround from a filing under Chapter 11 will avoid becoming part of the statistics of failure. But if the plan of reorganization is structured realistically and the right people are in place, the debtor should in many cases be given the chance to try to get the business on track and attain ultimately some measure of success.

Remember that the following things occur when a plan has been confirmed:

1. It becomes binding on the debtor, businesses, or companies that issue securities or acquire property under the plan.

2. The confirmed plan is binding on any creditor, equity security holder, or any person who is a general partner in the debtor company or business.

3. It discharges the debtor from debts created prior to the date of confirmation. It is effective against claims whether proof of the claim was filed or whether the claim was or was not allowed.

4. The discharge of debt is effective whether a proof of claim was or was not filed or allowed.

Only one plan should be submitted to the court for confirmation. If that plan is confirmed, but later is revoked, the court may then consider a second plan. When more than one plan meets the Code's requirements, the preferences of creditors and equity security holders (stockholders) will be considered when the court decides which plan should be confirmed.

Confirmation Versus Dissent

When one class of creditors who have been impaired vote to reject the plan, the court may still proceed to confirm it if all the Code's requirements have been met. This is done generally when a plan is equitable—does not discriminate unfairly—in that it applies to all classes of creditors, including the class that has rejected the plan. There is a doctrine of "fair and equal treatment" which is applicable to the dissenting class only and provides that no class higher than the dissenting class creditors (priority, etc.) shall receive more than 100 percent of its claim. Senior creditors (secured, etc.) are anxious to have the plan accepted and may voluntarily give up the right to some of their claim to ensure that a dissenting class does not receive less than its full dividend. This is not a questionable act of generosity: it is done only to facilitate acceptance of the plan.

The court may not be swayed from confirming a plan because a class of unsecured creditors, including some with priority claims, has dissented. Criteria for the court's approval impose only the admonition that the dissenting class must receive property of value equal to the allowed amount of the unsecured claim. Nothing more, just the allowed amount. The result is that no impaired class of unsecured creditors can be paid less than the full amount of the claim, or if not paid in full, no class junior (lower in the order of payment priority) to the dissenting class of claimants can receive any payment under the plan.

All equity security holders, general or limited partners, and other classes of creditors may see the court confirm the plan over majority dissent in one or more classes. Confirmation could occur if no class junior to the dissenting class shares with them or if the dissenters are not denied their liquidation preference or redemption rights under the plan. It is true that claimants within a class of creditors must be treated as equals, although the court may say that "equal treatment" has been achieved if there is "equal value" (goods or property of equal value), rather than one type or category of value that will be shared equally by all members of a class.

Example: The plan may provide for creditors of one class whose claims do not exceed $1500 to receive $500 within 60 days after confirmation of the plan, another $500 payment 150 days after confirmation, and the final $500 payment 240 days after confirmation. The plan might also provide for creditors of the same class whose claims exceed $1500 to receive a combination of cash—paid over a longer period of time—and shares of the company's preferred stock that cannot be sold or transferred for a specific period of time. If the creditors whose claims exceed $1500 are able to get claimants of their class to reject the plan, the court may override their dissent on the basis that the tests of equal treatment and equal value have been met with a three-payment cash settlement for the small creditors and a more extended cash-payment plan (possibly over two or three years) plus an issue of preferred stock which must be held for a minimum of two or three years.

If the court holds that the interests of all creditors in the one class have not been impaired or will receive treatment that is not less than equal, then the best interests of claimants and the debtor will be served if the court confirms the plan. It is unlikely that any plan would ever receive the unqualified endorsement of 100 percent of the debtor's claimants; the best that can be expected is a plan that addresses equitably the claims of claimants of a class. When the court is satisfied that a plan meets the criteria of the Code plus meeting the criteria of equal treatment within a class of creditor/claimants, the court will confirm the plan over the dissent of the majority in one or more classes.

The Results of Confirmation

When a plan has been confirmed, it assumes the stature of a contract between the debtor and the creditor/claimants. All terms and provisions are binding on the debtor, on equity security holders (holders of stock, bonds, etc.), on general partners of the debtor, and on the debtor's creditors. The court's confirmation of the plan relieves the debtor from any obligation to pay debts incurred prior to the confirmation date.

The debtor's creditors are generally regarded as the class that suffers the greatest loss in a Chapter 11 proceeding; confirmation of the plan of arrangement changes that perception. When a plan has been confirmed, the major losers are the holders of equity in the business or company (holders of stock or bonds, general partners, etc.). These people lose their rights and interest in the company when a plan of reorganization is confirmed by the court. It can be a painful experience for holders of equity when a business that prospered for a period of time loses momentum—slowly or precipitously—and becomes a part of the process of Chapter 11. Other losers include the holders of unexpired leases or executory contracts whose claims may be rejected upon approval by the court of the debtor's written waiver of discharge, a procedure initiated after the court has entered the order for relief.

The court requires that the debtor do whatever is necessary to make the plan work effectively. This includes all forms of cooperation that may be suggested or ordered by the court or included in the plan: the delivery of documents to effect the transfer of a property, perhaps to a secured creditor or other entity of interest; the surrender of one type or certain types of securities, a part of the settlement package for the debtor's major creditors as outlined in the plan; whatever act may be required of the debtor to help consummate the plan as a condition for being allowed to participate in any distribution. The penalty for failing to abide by these requirements within five years after the plan has been confirmed effectively bars a debtor from being allowed to participate.

It is important to remember that a confirmation order is not set in stone. Any plan of reorganization that has been accepted and confirmed in good faith by the bankruptcy court—if found to have been fraudulently presented within 180 days from the date of confirmation—may be revoked by the court. An order revoking the plan and containing provisions essential to the protection of an entity whose acquisition of rights was based upon good faith reliance on the confirmation will be entered by the court. If the debtor's fraudulent attempt should be dealt with in a criminal court proceeding, the bankruptcy court will make the appropriate recommendations.

Securities in a Reorganization Plan

Securities issued as part of the settlement section of a reorganization plan are specifically exempt from the usual requirements of federal, state, or local laws as they pertain to the registration and/or sale of such securities. Any offering of securities, which may be linked to an exchange arising from a creditor's claim against the debtor, a claim for administrative expenses, etc., is also exempt from regulatory controls. Add to the list of exempt transactions any stock issued under a plan which brings with it a right to convert.

There are a number of other regulatory guidelines which are applicable to securities issued as a part of the plan of reorganization or applicable to stock issued prior to the filing of the petition, but brought into the plan as part of the settlement package. Regulatory guidelines for plans in which company securities play a key role in the settlement section of a plan are covered by the Securities and Exchange Act of 1933.

As I approach the concluding paragraphs of this section on The Bankruptcy Act/Code, the problems of retail giant R. H. Macy & Company are moving it rapidly toward a filing for protection under Chapter 11 of the Code.

Burdened with debts that are reported to range between $3 and $4 billion, banks that have cut off its access to money, and suppliers who have not been shipping more than a token amount of goods to Macy's and other members of the company (I. Magnin, Bullock's, and a number of smaller specialty groups), there is enormous pressure on R. H. Macy & Company to delay no longer a filing for Chapter 11 protection. With no cash reserves, cash flow at a trickle, and cash demand at a disproportionate high, the primary concern of the unprotected retail giant should be that it will miss its payroll commitments and be forced into an involuntary bankruptcy.

Suppliers and bankers are urging the company to stop trying to put together a deal to bring in a third party to bail out the company and to file *now* for the protection that will enable bankers to advance money for operating expenses and allow suppliers to ship goods. The reason bankers and suppliers are holding until R. H. Macy & Company has filed for protection and it has been entered by the bankruptcy court, is the key that was discussed earlier in this section. When the court accepts and "so orders" the petition of R. H. Macy & Company, or the petition of any other insolvent debtor (unable to meet its commitments), bankers and suppliers who advance money, goods, or services *after* the date of the court's order move to the front of the repayment line. When the debtor officially comes under the protection of the bankruptcy court, any debts incurred subsequent to the effective date of the court's jurisdiction over the petitioner become debts that have priority over those incurred prior to the filing.

The Code recognizes that insolvent debtors, whether a large, sprawling retail giant such as R. H. Macy & Company, or a small store or manufacturing company, cannot continue to operate and preserve their customer bases if bankers and suppliers have no assurances that they will be repaid ahead of the mountain of debts that were incurred prior to filings. If a debtor is unable to operate the business until an acceptable plan of reorganization has been developed, offered to the creditors, approved or rejected, confirmed by the court, and finally put into operation, it is unlikely that anything worth salvaging would still be intact. To remain a viable prospect for reorganization and survival, an insolvent debtor must receive promptly the security given to bankers and suppliers by the umbrella of the court's protection and supervision.

In a case of the magnitude of R. H. Macy & Company, the surviving company unquestionably must be leaner, more compact, and more competitive. Some stores in the present Macy's chain will be closed or sold; other chains, such as Bullock's, I. Magnin, and the other specialty groups, will probably be sold to generate cash, decrease size, and decrease overhead. A major criterion for what should be sold and what might be retained will be the current profitability and the assessment of future profitability that attaches to individual stores within all areas of the R. H. Macy empire. Bankers and creditors will not be receptive to a plan of reorganization that does not offer an image that is lean, competitive, and tailored to success rather than size.

The filing for bankruptcy by R. H. Macy & Company will have an impact on retailers in many other lines of business. Macy's and Bullock's are centerpiece stores around which many shopping malls have been built. The continuing success of many of these malls or the increase in the decline of shopping malls impacted with increasing severity by the apparent decline of Macy's hold on shoppers will be held hostage to whether Macy's or Bullock's can survive, and whether key stores in various malls will remain open and attractive to customers. Time, the creditors, and the court will determine not only the fate of R. H. Macy & Company, but also the future of hundreds (perhaps thousands) of retailers, wholesalers, manufacturers, shopping mall developers, banks, ad agencies, etc. It becomes a loss of enormous economic proportions, one that goes far beyond the up-front image of a fallen R. H. Macy & Company.

(The interpretation and application of the provisions of The Bankruptcy Act/Code, or any problem or matter that involves legal knowledge or expertise beyond the experience, training, or capability of the decision maker, *demands* the advice and/or appropriate assistance of an attorney who is qualified in handling such problems or matters. As the publisher and I have stated at the beginning of this book, it is *not* a substitute for the advice and assistance of a qualified attorney. Do not attempt to use it for that purpose.)

PART 5

International Credit Sales

There are more opportunities in export sales today than in any period since the United States emerged as an industrial power. Countries all over the world are emerging from years, decades, or generations of being oppressed by one political system or another. They dare to stand up and look around, and they dare to hope that what seemed for so long to be unattainable is now within the realm of possibility.

So what are we waiting for? Why aren't credit people hip-deep in credit applications for the full smorgasbord of products from companies and countries in every hemisphere? With such a pent-up demand for products, supplies, and technology of all types, cargo transport on land, sea, and in the air should be taxed to capacity—or am I distorting the immediate potential of the international marketplace?

There are many countries whose economic and financial instability is so great that most companies based in the United States cannot do business with them. If they are recently free from a regime that was dominated by the USSR, there is freedom to do business with whomever they want. The problem is that there is no money—no acceptable foreign currency—with which to pay for their multiple needs. Until this group of countries can get some international monetary help, there is little any exporter can do to exploit what, under other circumstances and conditions, would be many enormously attractive opportunities.

There are many countries and areas of the world in which money— dollars or another acceptable international currency—is unavailable to pay for goods and services. The embargo on shipments of products to a limited number of countries should not be a deterrent to the company whose desire it is to take the company into international sales.

The credit manager plays a key role whether there is or is not a department or individual whose duty it is to prepare or supervise the preparation of the documents package. If the credit manager's involvement with international sales is limited to monitoring the payment arrangement, from the decision as to the mode of payment to and through the payment itself, he or she will play a key role in determining whether the transaction is a success.

Responsibility for ensuring that the payment arrangements for an export sale provide a maximum level of safety for the exporting company is an extension of what the credit manager does in the domestic marketplace. But manufacturers who want to become involved in export sales must be sure that they are ready, have the products, the personnel, and the financial capability, and have targeted the appropriate marketplace area before they make the move. In some areas and with some products, timing can be the key to a venture that fails or succeeds.

The potential rewards for a company or an industry, whose approach to the international marketplace is focused on providing goods and services that are designed to fill the needs and requirements of customers in a specific target area of the world, can be limited only by the size of the potential market. To succeed, the manufacturer must have done the appropriate market research to know that there is a market for a product similar to the one the company sells in the United States and must know also that conditions in the target market area— climate, income level, buyer need, etc.—call for certain modifications in the product to meet those special requirements.

Some companies have made what can only be categorized as half-hearted attempts to sell their products in the international marketplace. They were unwilling to make the commitment of time, money, and effort necessary for a company to begin to gain recognition in the target market area(s). In too many of these situations, international trade has been thought of as a good, painless area in which to pick up some easy money while experiencing little or no competition, especially if the product is unique to the target market area. It is possible to find a niche market so totally virgin for a specific product or type of products that the domestic company might have an unchallenged run of short-term success, but competition will come, and it will come in the form of a product that is just as good and costs less, and, if the domestic company is not marketing effectively, will be marketed more aggressively and successfully.

A company whose intention it is to sell in one or more areas of the world marketplace has more to consider than how a product is going to be received. Does the specific country or area of the world have a stable government or governments? Does the country or countries in which potential customers are located have a stable monetary system(s)? Are there United States funds in domestic (United States) banks against which international letters of credit can be drawn? Are there reliable freight forwarders in the customer's country or countries who can be expected to deliver products as directed, process paperwork relating to the delivery in a correct and timely manner, and forward the appropriate documents to the bank within the time frame required to submit a letter of credit for payment at the domestic/correspondent bank? What are the chances that the movement of freight within the customer's country is so erratic that the delivery of goods and the processing and return of the paperwork cannot be completed within the time frame of the letter of credit? If it is not completed within that time frame, will the customer authorize his or her bank to allow the correspondent domestic (United States) bank to extend the letter of credit's expiration date the additional days necessary to allow the seller to receive payment for the goods?

The questions that a company must ask and questions to which it must have answers before allowing itself to become involved in international trade is how much information should it have about a customer, the country, and the monetary system before it agrees to ship product? The seller must know in advance that conditions for the sale are right: the country is stable; the country's banks have domestic correspondents; the customer has the potential for becoming a good outlet for the seller's product(s); there is the potential with the first customer for using a successful sales program as a springboard for doing business with prospective customers in adjacent regions of the same or other countries.

The customer must be willing and able to pay for goods or services in United States dollars, and that spirit of cooperation must include the government of the country in which the customer is located. There can be no government imposed monetary restriction prohibiting payments in "foreign exchange" (United States dollars, German marks, English pounds, etc.) for the type of product(s) offered by the seller. Is the seller's product(s) on a list of goods classified as "essential" by the buyer's government? Will the customer's government authorize the release of precious foreign exchange for items such as computers, laser printers, and other high-tech products, while denying the release of money to pay for automatic washers and dryers, kitchen utensils, garden tools, etc.? A company whose hope is to sell products in a country which buys from a list of goods classified as essential by the government must do its homework to know whether the customer and the country offer a viable marketplace atmosphere. If they do not, move on to another country or area, but do not lose sight of what is happening with the country that did not classify your goods or products as essential. There will come a day when "the list" no longer controls which goods and services can come into the country. If your company remains alert to the changes within, keeps trying, and is among the first to cross the border when the list disappears, the result could be some long-term business.

It is prudent for the new player in the international marketplace to target markets in countries whose statuses are established or whose statuses as emerging nations are on ground solid enough to warrant the investment of time, effort, and money that is required of a newcomer. Countries whose development is barely beyond threshold might be less difficult to sell, but you must know whether there is the ability to pay, and to pay in United States dollars. Emerging nations need almost everything, but the problem is whether they can pay for it. There is a limit as to how innovative a seller can be when the customer is unable to come up with any acceptable international currency.

Many countries have been and continue to be the beneficiaries of loans made by the World Bank, our government, Japan, Germany, and others—loans intended to improve conditions within the country, to stimulate economic growth and development, and to aid the democratic process. These loans have the effect of jump-starting growth, accelerating the need for products and services, and making money available to buy technology and expertise (high-tech goods, consultants, support services, engineers and technicians to improve water quality, develop sources of electric power, etc.). Any manufacturer or supplier who has a desire to take his or her product(s) or service(s) into the international marketplace should be aware of what marketplace countries need, what they are buying, and what their next-step area of purchases should be. Those who would be players in the international marketplace should know which countries are getting how much money from what sources and for what purposes. Companies with products to fit the basic growth needs of threshold countries should find any number of opportunities.

In closing the introductory portion of Part 5, let me cite Colorado's experience in selling $600 million worth of products [beef, feed for cattle, and other products] to Japan in 1991. The trade representatives of Colorado and Japan enthusiastically endorse their relationship, which suggests that Colorado is being a very mature player in international trade.

Manufacturers who want to enter the international marketplace should target their market area, and assure themselves that the products they hope to sell are what prospective customers need, should like, should want to buy, should want to use, or should want to enjoy. Manufacturers should not try to force products designed primarily for the American lifestyle or marketplace on buyers whose lives, standards, and requirements are not compatible with the product.

Do what the folks in Colorado have done. Do your market research to establish the probability of a match for your product(s) with a prospective buyer in a foreign country and to try to ensure that the potential for sales is high enough to be developed within a relatively short period of time into a profitable venture.

27

Is Your Company Ready for Export Sales?

The desire of a domestic company to sell its product(s) in the international marketplace is a commendable one, but whether it is an ambition whose time has come can only be determined with honest answers to probing questions.

There can be no more basic question than the international appeal or potential of the product itself. Is it a product that has had broad appeal in the domestic marketplace, or has it been successful as a "niche market" item? What qualities does it have that should or could give it appeal as an item for export? Is it a product that would have little or no competition in the target marketplace area? If it is a manufactured product, would your company have to modify its production line(s) to run the product for export sales; if so, how much would that add to your manufacturing costs?

Going forward with the assumption that the product has established itself in a regional, national, or a niche domestic marketplace area, how do you translate that level of success into an answer to the question of potential as an export item? If your company's research determined that the product's potential is not limited to a narrow and economically unattractive market area, then the prospect for success is encouraging. Is your company's product an all-purpose one that has a solid chance to make bigger and stronger ripples as it gets international exposure? Perhaps it's that niche market product whose sales appeal may be narrow, but is channelled into economically attractive corridors of the international marketplace.

Some of the factors that could inhibit chances for success are production space, a fairly costly modification of the product to fit the requirements of for-

585

eign customers, money to finance the increase in personnel and production activity, and the time lag between shipment of product and payment of letters of credit or other instruments of payment. Is production time available and would any manufacturing downtime to prepare production lines to run a modified product for export add very little to the unit cost? If so, congratulations. Your company has moved a step closer to doing an export business.

But before there is any marketing effort, and before the first piece of machinery is adjusted to accommodate the run of product for export, examine how your company is fixed for money and personnel experienced in the business of export. Can your company afford to wait the extra days to receive payment for letters of credit, bills of exchange, or other forms of payment slower than payments from domestic accounts? Does the company's credit manager or credit administrator have the broad base of experience necessary to screen foreign accounts whose interest in your products may be flattering, but whose geographic location and financial condition might make payment for your company's products questionable at best? And if your company is fairly small, will the credit department be expected to do more than arrange for payment (letter of credit, bill of exchange, etc.)? If the credit department will not be putting together the package of export documents, does the company have on board a person with broad experience in export, or will it be necessary for the company to hire a person who knows export regulations and procedures, and how to avoid errors and delays in handling this type of shipment?

The foregoing might seem an endless stream of questions, but they are questions that must be addressed—and addressed satisfactorily—before formal steps can be taken to enter the export trade. In all but the larger companies, the credit manager will be expected to play a key role in export business. The credit manager will be expected to know enough about the requirements of export sales to ensure that the documents package is accurate and complete. If it is not in order, there may be delays at United States Customs and at the customs office of the receiving country, and any discrepancy of significance can be expected to pose a problem with the bank to whom the documents package (with a letter of credit) must be presented for payment. If the documents are not in order, there is the possibility that a letter of credit might expire before corrections can be made, which leaves the exporter in the position of scrambling to get the buyer to extend the expiration date on the letter of credit. A reputable buyer? An extension is probably not a problem. A buyer who is not so reputable? An extension can be a major problem, one that is not easily leveraged when the customer is in a distant country and perhaps in a country whose willingness to part with dollars is subject to sudden changes.

Not the least of the considerations that must be addressed prior to a "go or no" decision regarding Export is the type and category of the product manufactured by your company. If it is a high-tech product with the possibility for dual applications (conventional industrial or business usage versus the potential for being adapted for use in biological or chemical research, military research, warfare, etc.), Department of Commerce regulations may severely limit the companies, countries, and areas to which your company can ship its product(s).

If your company goes forward to the point where it has a first customer possibility, it should be a customer whose history is neither obscure, questionable, nor located in a country not on an approved list for the type of product(s) manufactured by your company. The credit manager and/or the person hired to manage export sales will have access to Department of Commerce bulletins which list countries and areas not open to certain categories of high-tech sales. Hope that your customer possibility has demonstrated that it is not in the business of receiving restricted products and then trans-shipping or diverting those goods to a country or a customer not eligible to receive them under United States Department of Commerce Regulations. Hope that your customer possibility is not one whose intention it is to use or channel the product(s) for a purpose that is banned, dangerous, or detrimental to ethnic groups with the receiving country, to countries in the geographic region of the receiving country, or to countries on a global scale.

Any company or country whose interest is in high-tech products, especially those products whose applications might be multiple, will get a long, close look from the Department of Commerce's Bureau of Export Administration before a license to export is issued. What are the types of licenses and the spectrum of other data relating to the business of export? You'll find it all in Chapters 2 thru 5 of this section.

First—A Solid Domestic Market Base

There are areas of commerce wherein a company, whose interest is to make export its major marketing thrust, would find little or no advantage in establishing first what is referred to as "a solid domestic base of product acceptance." A high-tech manufacturing firm in a small country must develop major foreign customers to promote growth. The same is true of manufacturers whose home country offers a limited marketplace for the sale of items such as automobiles, building materials, chemicals, etc.; they have no alternative but to make export sales an integral part of their long-term business plan. These are companies that cannot grow and prosper unless the thinking of top management is in synch with a recognition of the importance of export in the future of their company.

For many companies, however, the option to sell products to a foreign buyer comes only after the company has established itself in a regional or national domestic marketplace. The thought that there may be a wide world of opportunity for the company is very heady, but it isn't generally one of the thoughts that a company's top management will embrace early in the company's existence. An almost inevitable limit on the number of dollars available for day to day expenses and the needs of a business struggling to survive inhibits too much heady thinking. Only when "prosper" has joined "grow" to form the synonym "grow and prosper," which describes what is happening or has happened to your company, does the prospect of export sales become increasingly more attractive and begin to look much more attainable.

Every company determines the parameters of its market area by the size of the company, the type, style, or quality of its products, and the narrow or broad base of customer interest in those products. When a company's products have been taken to the limits of their domestic parameters (parameters defined first in the business plan then in the subsequent decisions of the founders, the board of directors, and top management), and the products have generated strong interest at one or more international trade shows or fairs, then it is very close to decision time. It is time to do an evaluation in which all factors are weighed and a decision is reached on whether export is or is not a reasonable option for this company.

Is There Surplus Manufacturing Capacity?

Before there can be an enlightened decision regarding the feasibility of the company taking on some level of international sales presence, factors such as manufacturing capacity/capability and cash flow must be added to the mix that is to be evaluated.

Successful companies almost invariably go through cycles of growth that alternately test the capabilities of the production facilities or provide a surplus of those facilities. The down side to these growth cycles is when a new production line has been added, new orders fail to materialize as rapidly as had been anticipated, and company management begins to wonder whether the additional production capability was an expensive exercise in wishful thinking. Is an increase in the company's production capability made with the goal of providing a cushion of unused capacity to accommodate reasonable growth? If this is viewed as an extension of growth in domestic sales, there should be no qualms regarding the long-term wisdom of the decision.

Company size will usually determine who evaluates the manufacturing facility to determine how much additional business the present equipment and personnel can be expected to handle. When a company is somewhere in the size categories of medium to large, the manufacturing manager is the most qualified person to do the evaluation for top management. A smaller company with less depth in the management structure? The person who does the evaluation could be a founder, a partner, or a manager who has multiple responsibilities. In either situation, it is unlikely that the company's domestic sales will have reduced the unused percentage of production capacity to so narrow a margin that the company cannot test the waters of Export Trade.

The hope of every company whose ambition it is to get into export sales is that the specs for the domestic product can be used without change or modification to produce the product that will be offered to foreign buyers. Modifications in the product, production line downtime to make adjustments or changes, and any realigning or adjusting that might result in some units of product that are rejected are changes that could escalate production costs into an area of concern. Any new production costs that might impact the per unit cost to a point where it is well above the cost of the domestic product could be unacceptable to prospective foreign buyers.

No company can expect to attract good export accounts if product(s) of similar type and quality can be obtained from another supplier for less money. When a price difference between two products of similar design and purpose can be demonstrated successfully to be a difference in quality, then a buyer will make his or her choice based upon the conventional choices—price or quality. A company whose product is recognized as "quality," and for which there is a need in the marketplace, is justified to charge a price compatible with the costs of producing "quality."

There are always customers—domestic and foreign—whose credit is so questionable that they solicit manufacturers to sell them product. They volunteer to pay more than the list price for product(s) and are generally willing to talk in numbers that would look very attractive on a purchase order. The problem is that these companies, countries, or other entities are not able to pay for the goods. If the prospective purchaser is a country, the country may be so short of dollars that it is unwilling to release any of them unless it is to purchase approved items of critical need to the welfare of the country. When the prospective purchaser is a struggling company in the country described in the preceding sentence, there is no possibility of arranging for payment in dollars.

Is production capacity available and will the company's product require no modification to meet the requirements of foreign buyers? When those two positives have been recognized, the most important of the unanswered questions is the financial capability of the company to engage in more than a token amount of export business. And if export is to be limited to an occasional order, is there someone in-house (credit department or other) who is capable of handling the package of paperwork (application for export license, an acceptable payment arrangement, shipping and export documents, etc.)? Your company should not take on new and specialized overhead if the venture into international sales is not going to have as its goal a growth-oriented, profit-making addition to the company. Is there a commitment to more than a token experience in export? Then specialized overhead can be justified when the dominant criteria for adding it is *need*.

Company Presence or Contract Sales Rep?

Unless your company is so well established that it has foreign sales offices or employee sales representatives in various countries and areas of the world, you might want to consider taking on a foreign-based sales representative (or firm of representatives) whose business it is to represent companies in nonconflicting product areas, someone whose business it is to function as a business or manufacturer's representative. Compensation for a rep (not a company employee) will be a combination of a monthly fee plus a commission on sales, which is based upon a schedule incorporated into the contract between your company and the person or organization whose services are being employed.

I have had experience with both types of representation and the results—the degree of success or the degree of failure—were more a matter of the quality of the contracted individual rather than one system being preferable over the other. Is there more control over a company employee? There is more control in most areas of the relationship, but many companies allow a company employee to perform at a lower level of achievement than would be permitted of a contract or noncompany employee. The company employee is on full salary, has a large package of benefits, and may produce at a minimal achievement level, for which he or she may offer a multitude of semireasonable excuses for failing to produce at the level of expectation. The company employee should have monthly or quarterly sales quotas, but a charismatic person who interfaces well with management and other employees can frequently buy forgiveness over a longer period of time before termination is addressed.

What about a noncompany representative who must be motivated from day one of the relationship in order to attain specific requirements of quarterly performance? Most companies are more watchful and less tolerant of a nonemployee whose contribution is below the prescribed level of expectations than they are of a company employee.

When a company has some level of international presence—one customer or several in a city, an area, a continent, or the globe—the cost of

adding a sales representative to an existing office is less than the cost of setting up a sales office (one or more sales representatives plus a secretary)
and generally more costly than contracting for representation by a noncompany sales rep. The amount of time that a noncompany rep will devote
to the business of your company will be less than what is expected of a company employee, but if the contract sales rep meets the requirements for
quarterly sales as set forth in the contract, he or she might be the better bargain, especially during the early days of your company's venture into the
business of export.

Know the Laws— Domestic and Foreign

The success of your company's move into the international marketplace
will depend primarily on your product(s), how it is marketed, and whether
the company is prepared financially, technologically, and in other areas discussed previously to meet the requirements and the competitive challenge
of something new and unfamiliar.

What your company does not want to do is to go forward with plans for
an export program before investigating thoroughly what the law requires of
an exporter. What laws and what agency control exports from the United
States? Is United States Law uniform as it applies to the exporting of high-
technology items that have one application versus those items that have the
potential for dual applications? And if a high-tech item has the potential for
dual applications, and one of those applications is not designed for a peaceful purpose, are there special constraints on the "to whom and where" of
the potential sale?

Any company whose goal it is to dip its feet into the waters of international trade, with the expectation of enjoying a successful experience,
should first contact the United States Department of Commerce's Bureau
of Export Administration for what may be identified correctly as "the rules
of the game." The fact is that to be a player in export, which is to know what
you are supposed to do and how you are supposed to go about doing it,
your company must familiarize itself with the rules administered by the
Commerce Department's Bureau of Export Administration.

The laws governing export sales are so strict that there is no life in export
sales for the company whose corporate mindset is such that it cannot play
the game, and play it by the United States Government's rules. Foreign governments have rules and regulations too, and some of them (restrictions
that prohibit the use of United States dollars to purchase all but a short list
of priority items, etc.) make it difficult or impossible for importers to buy
certain types of products. Has your company come up with a customer

whose history in the international marketplace is not clear to your firm or would perhaps have you ship your product(s) (high-tech or other) to a country whose status to receive the type of products made by your company is unclear? Submit the application for an export license to the Bureau of Export Administration's Office of Export Licensing. The OEL will pass judgment on whether an export license can be issued, and if so, which of the various types of licenses should be issued.

The Department of Commerce offers regulatory guidelines and bulletins, a World Traders Data Report, and frequent updates regarding changes in the export rules and regulations as they apply to certain types of products and specific countries and areas of the world. Recent changes in the governments of various European countries from totalitarian to democratic forms of government is bringing about changes in the Bureau of Export Administration's guidelines and will bring further changes with time and evaluation. A judicial rather than a regulatory group is the United States International Trade Commission. Nongovernment organizations who disseminate helpful information, data, and publications—usually on a fee or a membership basis—are the International Chamber of Commerce, Export-Import Bank's Foreign Credit Insurance Association, National Association of Credit Management's Foreign Credit Information Bureau, Dun & Bradstreet International Ltd., etc.

Prepared or Unprepared to Enter Export Trade?

The following examples offer a comparison between a company that has prepared itself to enter the business of Export and one that has not. You would have no difficulty fitting them into their proper category, even if I had not done it.

Prepared: The Billington Company is a corporation, has been in business for eight years, and has attained goals of annual growth to current sales of $25 million a year. The company is well-managed, profitable, generates enough cash flow internally to meet all but an occasional short-term (10 to 15 days) need for bank borrowing. The company's product requires no changes for the foreign market and there is enough surplus production capacity to sustain an increase of $5 to $6 million in foreign and domestic sales. The company has recently hired a person with a background in export trade who will oversee administrative matters such as applications for export licenses, Department of Commerce regulations, the preparation and forwarding of documents packages, etc. The company credit manager is experienced in handling letters of credit and ensuring that the requirements for payment are incorporated into the documents package.

This company has personnel experienced in international trade, is positioned to sustain an adequate level of cash flow with no major changes in its pattern of bank borrowing, has a product that incorporates no dual-purpose baggage, has several importers who are interested in it, and is a company with a desire to grow in the direction of export sales. Is this company prepared? It is.

Unprepared: The Wompers Company did not do a thorough job of evaluating its position before making the decision to wander off into export. Started six years ago as a partnership, Wompers was incorporated at the end of the fourth year, lost money for each of those four years, has been borderline profitable for the past two years on sales that have stalled between $25 and $30 million a year. Projections for annual growth have not been achieved in any one of the six years and sales that were projected in the business plan to be at $40 million by the end of the sixth year are $12 to $15 million below that figure.

Thirty percent of the company's production capacity is not being used, but the offset is that the company has no one with the experience necessary to handle applications for licensing, to understand what the Department of Commerce does and does not allow, and to prepare, forward, and monitor the documents package. The company's credit manager? A person who has had no experience in getting and monitoring letters of credit or ensuring that the documents package for each contains everything necessary to meet the requirements for payment. It should come as no surprise that internally generated cash flow is well below monthly requirements, which necessitates a monthly level of bank borrowing that is fairly substantial. The loan balance is not zeroed from one month to the next and the open balance is getting bigger.

It is obvious that The Wompers Company is not prepared to go into the business of export, certainly not at this time. It is currently borderline profitable, falls far short of generating internally enough cash for its monthly needs, goes to the bank too frequently and for too much, and has a product that incorporates the probability that it could be converted to a second, warfare-oriented purpose. The fact that most of the interest has come from importers whose credentials might be found to be inadequate or questionable will not go unnoticed or unchallenged by the Department of Commerce. Unless there is interest from importers in countries and areas that can pass the Commerce Department's rigid scrutiny, The Wompers Company may have to defer its plans for export sales to another time and a more acceptable group of prospective customers. Is this company prepared? It is not.

28

Minimizing the Risk

A considerable amount of space has been devoted to the rules of the game as set forth by the Department of Commerce and to the influence exercised by other organizations whose primary purpose it is to gather and disseminate information and data to subscribers or purchasers of services and publications. A company whose goal it is to be a successful exporter must address many concerns and be able to ask questions that will not prompt answers steeped in wishful thinking. The evaluation of the company's capabilities must address honestly the question of whether an assumed capability can be transformed into organized "readiness" to launch an international sales effort, if only on a limited scale.

Decisions have been made, everything is in place, and the company is ready to move forward. At this point, the one element whose presence has drifted in and out of discussions begins to move out of the shadows and into the spotlight. *Risk* begins to come forward to assume its rightful position at center stage—a presence to henceforth become perhaps the dominant factor in the success or failure of the company's venture into export. Other facts are very important and any one or a combination could scuttle the company's fledgling effort to establish an export presence within parameters defined clearly at the outset. Yes, there are other intimidating factors, but *risk*—bold, bad, deceitful, and unforgiving—will be the dominant factor.

There are several organizations whose services can be very helpful to companies who want to be in export, have no international branches or experience, and want to minimize their risk. A few domestic organizations offer services which are directed toward companies that have no international branches, contacts, or experience. It is their role to provide businesses, members, and/or subscribers with information that covers all or specific areas of export sales: assistance in directing companies toward specific markets and market areas, government and nongovernment agencies whose role it is to provide financial assistance to under- or less-developed

595

foreign companies (which may then come back to domestic exporters in the form of orders for products made by domestic manufacturers), and information on overseas buyers helpful to the credit management person who has responsibility to arrange an acceptable form of payment.

Domestic Agencies— International Trade

There are many organizations whose function it is to assist in one way or another with the development of export and import trade by domestic companies. Some of these bureaus and corporations are government-sponsored and government-supported; others have an indirect link to United States Government funding or access to other areas of the bureaucracy.

The following is a supplement to some of the agencies listed in earlier pages:

1. Agency for International Development (*formerly known as AID*)
   Washington, DC 20523

   An agency of the United States International Development Cooperation Agency which provides technical and financial assistance to the less developed countries of Africa, Asia, Latin America, and the Near East. The objective? To help developing countries to achieve self-sustaining economic growth.

2. Overseas Private Investment Corporation (OPIC)
   1615 M Street, N.W.
   Washington, DC 20527

   Authorized in a 1969 amendment to the Foreign Assistance Act of 1961, its purpose is to mobilize and facilitate the participation of United States private capital and skills in the economic and social development of less developed friendly countries and areas. OPIC is also authorized to issue insurance, direct loans, and loan guarantees.

3. Commodity Credit Corporation
   Department of Agriculture
   Washington, DC 20250

   The Commodity Credit Corporation's two programs are an Export Credit Guarantee Program (GSM-102) and an Intermediate Export Credit Guarantee Program (GSM-103).

   These two programs provide payment guarantees to exporters of United States agricultural commodities on credit terms for up to three years under GSM-102, and for more than three years, but not more than ten under GSM-103. Irrevocable commercial letters of credit are the security for these guarantees against the failure of a foreign bank to meet its payment commitment.

International Agencies— International Trade

The following agencies and organizations are not funded solely by the United States Government. Most of them are owned by a great many countries working together to improve living and economic conditions in less-developed countries throughout the world.

1. World Bank (The International Bank for Reconstruction and Development)
1818 H Street, N.W.
Washington, DC 20433

The World Bank is owned by 151 countries. Each country subscribes to the Bank's capital stock in proportion to the country's own economic strength. The World Bank loans money to governments, government agencies, and private enterprises (when there is a government guaranty) in member countries.

Loans are made with the goal of enabling countries to build the foundations for economic growth.

2. International Development Association (IDA)
1818 H Street, N.W.
Washington, DC 20433

The IDA is a World Bank affiliate, established to promote economic development, to increase productivity, and, in so doing, to raise standards of living in the less-developed areas of the world. World Bank members are eligible to join IDA and those who are members have contributed in excess of $1 billion.

IDA relies primarily on the government of its richest member countries for its resources, with assistance concentrated on countries that are very poor. Over 80 percent of IDA's loans go to countries with an annual per capita GNP of less than $580. World Bank supplements IDA's other sources of funding with transfers from its net income.

3. International Finance Corporation (IFC)
1818 H Street, N.W.
Washington, DC 20433

An affiliate of the World Bank, the thrust of IFC's activities is to invest in private industry in developing member countries. IFC's objectives are (*a*) in association with private investors, to provide equity and loan capital for productive enterprises (*b*) to encourage the development of local sources of capital, and (*c*) to increase the flow of private capital from international sources.

4. International Monetary Fund (IMF)
   700 19th Street, N.W.
   Washington, DC 20431

   The IMF, a sister organization of the World Bank, was formed to promote international monetary cooperation and a balanced growth of world trade. Countries must be a member of the Fund before they are eligible to join the World Bank. Funds are available only to governments and are used primarily to avoid or correct balance of payment problems.

5. Inter-American Development Bank (IDB)
   1300 New York Avenue, N.W.
   Washington, DC 20577

   The IDB is a hemispheric version of the World Bank, but with a more diversified program of lending. Twenty countries, including the United States, were the organizers; currently more than 40 countries are members, including many from Europe and the Far East. Funding for the bank comes from, one, its ordinary capital and, two, the Fund for Special Operations.

Information on Overseas Buyers

There are several sources that can ease the exporter's mind by adding to the information base that will be used to determine whether a sale can be made, and, if so, under what terms and conditions:

The Exporter's Bank.   Banks which are engaged in a strong volume of overseas business have access to credit information on many foreign companies and businesses. It is in the interest of banks to protect clients in areas where the bank has knowledge, has access to knowledge, and can be helpful. Information regarding overseas companies and businesses is obtained from overseas offices of the bank or from correspondent banks in the country or area of interest.

Dun & Bradstreet.   D & B's reports on overseas buyers follow the format used for its domestic reports. Reports may be obtained by Telex, cable, or airmail.

United States Department of Commerce.   The Department of State's embassies and consulates are used to help Commerce gather information on overseas importers, markets, market conditions, and industries within a country or area. These reports are generally slow to be compiled, because information is forwarded from embassies and consulates on an "as time permits" basis. When information is received by the Commerce Department, it prepares country or industry bulletins and trade reports.

FCIB-NACM.   Foreign Credit and International Business is an association of executives in credit, finance, and international business. The FCIB-NACM Corporation is the international arm of the National Association of Credit Management (NACM), is a member-owned and -operated service organization, and is an excellent source for its members of credit reports and financial services. Now in its 73d year, FCIB publishes a biweekly International Bulletin on finance, credit, collection, and exchange regulations and problems, and an FCIB newsletter, and operates an international collection service department.

An International Round Table Conference meets monthly in New York City to discuss problems in international finance and credit and collections. All FCIB members receive minutes of the New York meetings plus minutes of the three-times a year meetings in the various capital cities of Europe. The FCIB also has many industry export credit groups whose usual format is to hold monthly business lunches during which time information gathered by FCIB and individual members is disseminated to the group.

I recommend NACM's various services and activities (foreign and domestic) to any credit management people who have not experienced the benefits of NACM reports, group meetings, and other services. My years of experience with FCIB-NACM includes many instances of receiving information or report data that enabled me to avoid becoming involved with importers whose questionable integrity, willingness to pay, and ability to pay was brought into sharp focus through the medium of FCIB-NACM reports.

International Trade Publications.   Papers and magazines that are printed in another country can be another helpful source of area or regional information. The problem is that, although many of these publications contain information that would be helpful to an exporter, they are not circulated abroad. Exporters who have offices or representation in an area covered by one of these publications should arrange to have copies forwarded to the exporter's credit office.

The Buyer's Bank.   Unless the bank gives specific information, input received from it may be of questionable integrity and little value. The buyer's bank is interested in helping the customer meet the exporter's requirements; all else is secondary to the goal.

Exporter's Overseas Sales Representative.   This person is in a good position to get solid information for the domestic office.

Export Credit Insurance

Export-Import Bank's credit insurance program helps United States exporters develop and expand their export sales by protecting against losses should a foreign buyer default. When receivables are insured, exporters can afford to arrange more attractive financing and offer more attractive credit terms to their customers.

Export-Import Bank's (Eximbank) credit insurance program is administered for Eximbank by the Foreign Credit Insurance Association (FCIA), an association of leading insurance companies. As Eximbank's agent, FCIA's role is responsible for marketing, servicing, and administering policies and for processing most buyer credit requests and claims.

Several types of policies have been created over the years to fit the needs of all sizes and types of exporters and export situations. There are policies to protect almost any type of credit transaction, although it should be mentioned that the program's protective umbrella changes at various times because of monetary, civil, or economic instability within a country or area. A description of the types of policies follows:

New-to-Export Credit Insurance

This policy is designed to service companies which are new to exporting or those that have only exported occasionally in the past. Insuring their sales of United States products against loss with Eximbank's New-to-Export policy is a safe way to develop an effective export program.

The policy insures export sales of United States products or services on a short-term credit basis, which means that repayment terms may range from payment upon delivery to payment within 180 days from the arrival date of the goods at the port of importation. Repayment terms for capital goods and certain consumer durables may be extended to a maximum of 360 days. The foreign buyer's written obligation to pay is required on all insured transactions. The policy is generally written for one year, but can be cancelled by either party on 30 days written notice. All receivables from shipments made during the policy period are covered. Applicants for this policy must meet export sales volume criteria and may not have held an FCIA policy in two years. (See Figure 28-1 for a summary of this policy.)

Multi-Buyer Export
Policy/Multi-Buyer

The policy provides coverage for exporters' short-term, medium-term, or combined short- and medium-term sales to many different buyers. The policy insures short-term sales with repayment terms of up to 180 days. Sales on terms up to 360 days can be covered for capital goods and certain consumer

Figure 28-1. Policy summary (new-to-export credit insurance).

EXIMBANK NEW-TO-EXPORT CREDIT INSURANCE

A POLICY SUMMARY

Companies new to exporting, or those that have only occasionally exported in the past, can insure their sales of U.S. products against loss and develop an effective export promotion program with the Eximbank New-to-Export policy. The New-to-Export policy protects against failure of a foreign buyer to pay an obligation because of unforeseen commercial or political reasons. It helps increase overseas sales through the use of prudent credit extension practices.

Protected against loss, an exporter is often able to arrange for more attractive financing and, consequently, able to offer foreign buyers affordable and competitive credit terms. To encourage bank financing, a special agreement has been developed for financial institutions taking assignment of a New-to-Export insured's rights to any amount payable under the policy. If the assignee bank complies with its responsibilities, it will be held harmless from many defenses to non-payment of a claim which ordinarily would be asserted.

WHAT IS COVERED

The New-to-Export policy insures export sales of U.S. products or services on a short-term credit basis. Products of less than 50 percent U.S. content and certain defense products are not eligible for cover. Short-term sales involve repayment terms ranging from payment upon delivery to payment at 180 days from the date of arrival of the goods at the port of importation. For capital goods and certain consumer durables, repayment terms may be extended up to 360 days. A valid written obligation of the foreign buyer to pay is required on all insured transactions.

The policy is generally written for one year, but is cancellable by either party on 30 days written notice. Receivables from shipments made during the policy period are covered.

TYPES OF LOSSES COVERED

The New-to-Export policy provides coverage on the insured percentage of a loss that exceeds the amount of any applicable deductible resulting from a default by a buyer. The default may be the result of one of the political risks defined in the policy, such as war, revolution, cancellation of an import or export license, or currency inconvertibility, or it may be for commercial reasons. Commercial risks under the policy are considered to be losses arising out of defaults for reasons other than the specifically defined political reasons.

HOW TO QUALIFY

Because the New-to-Export policy is a special program for small or new exporters, all companies applying for the policy must meet certain requirements. The applicant, together with its affiliates, must have:

- average annual export credit sales during the preceding two fiscal years not exceeding $750,000. If the preceding fiscal year was the firm's first year of export sales, sales on credit terms may not have exceeded $1,000,000; and

- not been a policyholder under any other export credit insurance policy, under which Eximbank was an insurer during the last two years, either directly or through an affiliated entity.

In addition, all of the following information is required to be submitted along with an application for quotation:

- a current (not older than six months) credit agency report on the applicant, or $35 to cover Eximbank's cost of ordering the report;

- references from two of the applicant's suppliers and one from its bank;

- audited or signed financial statements for the applicant's latest fiscal year.

The New-to-Export policy is a limited-life program that remains in force for up to five policy periods. Under this policy, whenever the exporter's insured shipments exceed $1 million during any policy year, the applicant no longer will qualify for renewal. Instead, the applicant will be considered for one of Exmbank's regular multi-buyer policies, as will those applicants who have completed the fifth and final year of coverage under the New-to-Export policy.

HOW THE POLICY WORKS

The New-to-Export policy insures an exporter's sales to creditworthy buyers in most countries throughout the world. Eximbank generally requires a company to insure all eligible credit sales under the policy. This ensures a reasonable spread of risk for Eximbank and prevents an exporter from insuring only transactions considered marginal.

PERCENTAGES OF COVER

Political risks are covered at 100 percent throughout the life of the policy. The following table summarizes some of the key commercial coverage variables during each of the five possible years of a New-to-Export Policy:

Policy Year	Maximum Commercial Coverage Percentage	Commercial Loss Deductible
1	95%	$0
2	95%	$0
3	90%	$2,500
4	90%	$5,000
5	90%	$7,500

CREDIT LIMITS

There are two types of insured credit limits under the New-to-Export policy.

The first is the Special Buyer Credit Limit (SBCL). In addition to having an Eximbank policy in full force, the insured must submit an SBCL application for coverage on each eligible buyer, requesting Eximbank to establish a revolving credit limit. Once approved, this limit is endorsed to the policy.

(Continued)

Figure 28-1. (*Continued*) Policy summary (new-to-export credit insurance).

When an SBCL is in effect, the insured may ship to that buyer repeatedly and be insured as long as the conditions of the SBCL, and the policy as a whole, are met and the outstanding amount does not exceed the authorized credit limit. For higher amounts, the insured may either request an increase in its SBCL or hold shipment until the buyer pays the outstanding amount. Each SBCL issued carries a final shipment date that limits the length of time Eximbank's coverage on the buyer is in force.

At least two current credit reports on the buyer must be submitted with each application for an SBCL. When requests exceed $100,000, current financial statements on the buyer should also be submitted. All credit and financial information should be dated within one year of the transaction dates.

Although not applicable to most New-to-Export policyholders, the second type of limit is the Discretionary Credit Limit (DCL). The DCL allows an exporter to exercise credit authority for creditworthy buyers up to a specific limit without seeking prior approval from Eximbank. Several conditions must all be met:

- the transaction must meet the conditions of the country limitation schedule;
- the amount of discretionary credit extended may not exceed the amount per buyer specified in the policy;
- the insured is required to obtain credit reports that justify the amount of credit being extended;
- the amount extended may not exceed the amount justified by the reports or the amount per buyer specified in the policy, whichever is less.

Eximbank generally will consider a DCL only after the policyholder has developed a satisfactory track record.

WHAT THE INSURED AGREES TO DO

Among other things, the insured agrees to submit monthly premium reports to Eximbank listing all reportable transactions.

The insured also agrees to all of the following:

- not to further insure sales of goods or services to buyers already 90 days or more past due;
- to make written demand for payment upon the buyer no later than 30 days prior to submission of a claim;
- to exercise reasonable care to minimize or prevent losses;
- to generally refrain from rescheduling due dates without prior Eximbank approval.

Other agreements are specified in the policy.

PREMIUM RATES

All New-to-Export policies are endorsed with a rate schedule that states the appropriate premium rate applicable to each eligible shipment. Rates are determined by the length of the credit terms and type of buyer.

Each year prior to the issuance of the New-to-Export policy or its renewal, payment of an advance premium equivalent to the minimum premium of $500 is required.

PREMIUM PAYMENT

All eligible shipments must be reported by the 30th of the month following the date of shipment.

Premium is not required to be paid until the month in the policy period when the actual premium due for the policy year-to-date exceeds the amount of the advance premium already paid. After that, the appropriate premium must be paid with each report form for the remainder of the policy period. If the insured fails to file any premium report, to declare any shipment or to pay any premium when due, Eximbank may at its option, terminate or continue the policy and hold the insured liable for payment of premium.

OVERDUES AND CLAIMS

Exporters must report all insured buyers that fall into late payment situations on a monthly basis after obligations in excess of $100,000 become 90 days past due. In all cases, these reports should continue for as long as the overdue situation exists, or until proof of loss claim forms are submitted.

When claims are submitted, copies of all documents pertaining to the transaction, such as invoices, bills of lading, debt instruments and guarantees, should also be included for review. Claims may be filed 90 days after default and must be filed within 240 days of default. Eximbank will process claims within 60 days of receiving a satisfactorily completed and documented proof of loss.

WHO TO CONTACT:

For more information, contact or ask your insurance agent or broker to contact:

FCIA MANAGEMENT COMPANY, INC., 40 RECTOR ST., 11th FLOOR, NEW YORK, N.Y. 10006   Tel.: (212) 306-5000

Or call one of the regional offices in Chicago (312/641-1915), Houston (713/589-8182), the Los Angeles area (310/322-1152), Miami (305/372-8540) and New York (212/227-7020).

FCIA Management Company, Inc. is a New York corporation operating as an independent servicing company for the Export-Import Bank of the United States ("Eximbank").

FCIA Management Company, Inc. administers insurance policies underwritten by Eximbank.

This is not a solicitation by FCIA Management Company, Inc. or its employees. It is a descriptive summary only. The complete terms and conditions of the policy are set forth in the policy, applications and endorsements.

GM-ENBFLY1-10/91

durables. Coverage applies to credit sales for any goods produced in and shipped from the United States during the policy period. Receivables for defense products and for products which are less than 50 percent United States content for short-term sales are not eligible for cover.

The policy offers two coverage options:

Option A: Split coverage, with deductible, provides 100 percent coverage against loss due to specified political events and 90 percent coverage against loss due to most commercial events, with a deductible applying only to commercial risk losses.

Option B: Equalized coverage, with deductible, insures against 95 percent of loss on short-term sales, either political or commercial, and a deductible applies to both political and commercial losses.

Under either option, receivables from sovereign obligors are 100 percent insured without application of a deductible.

(See Figures 28-2 and 28-3 for a summary of this policy.)

Single-Buyer Export Policy

These policies insure short- or medium-term single or repetitive sales to one buyer. Exporters to dealers may insure short-term inventory financing followed by medium-term receivables financing.

The short-term single-buyer policy affords coverage against losses caused by political events such as war, revolution, changes in certain export or import laws, and foreign exchange inconvertibility, or commercial events such as insolvency and protracted default. Equalized coverage for commercial and political risks (comprehensive coverage) or political-only coverage, is available at the following maximum percentages:

	Comprehensive or Political-Only
Sovereign obligors	100%
Private sector and other nonsovereign obligors	90%
Letter of credit transactions	95%
Bulk agricultural transactions	98%

Coverage applies to credit sales to a foreign buyer, or export letters of credit opened by a foreign issuing bank, named in the policy declarations for any goods produced in and shipped from the United States during the policy period. Coverage is generally provided for credit terms up to 180 days for consumer items, parts, and raw materials. On a case by case basis, agricultural commodities, capital equipment, and quasi-capital equipment may be insured on terms up to 360 days. Products which are less than 50 percent United States content of domestic origin and defense products are not eligible for cover. Principal amounts are covered up to the maximum

Figure 28-2. Policy summary (multi-buyer export credit insurance).

EXIMBANK MULTI-BUYER EXPORT CREDIT INSURANCE

A POLICY SUMMARY

> Exporters of U.S. goods and services can reduce their risks of selling abroad by insuring their foreign receivables through Eximbank's Multi-Buyer Export Credit Insurance Policy.
>
> The Multi-Buyer policy is one of the most advantageous of Exmbank's offerings. Multi-Buyer coverage protects against political and commercial risks. Protected against loss, the exporter is usually able to arrange for attractive financing and, consequently, able to offer foreign buyers favorable and competitive credit terms.

WHAT IS COVERED

This policy insures short-term sales with repayment terms of up to 180 days. Sales on terms up to 360 days can be covered for capital goods and certain consumer durables. Coverage applies to credit sales for any goods produced in and shipped from the United States during the policy period. Receivables for defense products and for products which are less than 50 percent U.S. content for short-term sales are not eligible for cover.

Principal amounts are generally covered up to the percentages shown in the options chart. The percentages depend on the options selected by the exporter.

Documented interest is also covered up to rates specified in the interest coverage endorsement. It is covered up to 180 days after the due date (or fewer days when the claim is settled earlier).

For short-term sales, coverage of documented post-maturity interest is limited to the lesser of:

- the rate specified in the obligation
- the rate legally valid in the buyer's country
- the rate below applicable to the approved currency designated in the sales contract:
  - **US Dollars**: *The Wall Street Journal* New York published prime rate minus 0.5 percent ;
  - **Swiss Francs, French Francs, West German Deutsche Marks, UK Pounds Sterling, Canadian Dollars and Japanese Yen**: the six-month Euro-offered rate plus 0.5 percent.

Interest coverage is also available for obligations denominated in an approved foreign currency listed above at varying rates, depending upon the currency involved.

TWO COVERAGE OPTIONS

Both options afford coverage against different categories of risk. Degree of coverage and amount of deductible vary. Risk categories include losses caused by war, revolution, seizure of goods, revocation of license, foreign exchange inconvertibility, insolvency and protracted default.

Option A: Split coverage, with deductible, provides 100 percent coverage against loss due to specified political events and 90 percent coverage against loss due to most commercial events, with a deductible applying only to commercial risk losses.

Option B: Equalized coverage, with deductible, insures against 95 percent of loss on short-term sales, either political or commercial, and a deductible applies to both political and commercial losses.

Under either option, receivables from sovereign obligors are 100 percent insured without application of a deductible.

INSURED PERCENTAGES OF COVERAGE OPTIONS

	OPTION A Split Coverage*		OPTION B Equalized Coverage
	"Political" Risks	"Commercial" Risks	All Risks
Sovereign Obligors	100%	100%	100%
Approved Agricultural Commodities	100	98	98
Letters of Credit	100	90	95
All Other	100	90	95

* Deductible applies to commercial risks only.

For an additional premium, the insured may request pre-shipment coverage. This is valuable in cases where goods are special ordered, or there is a long manufacturing run prior to shipment. By obtaining this option, the insured locks in coverage conditions for a specified period of time, generally up to 180 days from contract signing. Endorsements for non-acceptance cover and other specialized cover are also available.

THE PERIOD COVERED

The policy is written for one year, but is cancellable by either party on 30 days written notice. Receivables arising from shipments made during the policy year are covered.

THE DEDUCTIBLE AMOUNT

A deductible applies per policy year and is negotiated separately with each insured.

Figure 28-2. (*Continued*) Policy summary (multi-buyer export credit insurance).

CREDIT LIMITS

There are two types of credit limits. The first is the discretionary credit limit. It permits you to extend insured credit without prior approval from Eximbank. To use your DCL, several conditions must be met prior to shipment:

- The transaction must meet the conditions of Eximbank's country limitation schedule, *and*
- you must obtain at least two pieces of credit information on the buyer dated within 12 months prior to shipment:

  1. either a domestic or foreign credit agency report or a "World Traders Data Report", *and*
  2. either a domestic or foreign commercial bank report *or* two written trade references, or for letter-of-credit transactions, you must obtain at least one favorable written bank report or written bank reference on the foreign bank issuing the letter of credit.

- The credit amount extended may not exceed the amount justified by the credit information, or the per-buyer amount listed in the policy declarations, whichever is less.

The second type of limit is the special buyer credit limit or issuing bank credit limit. Insureds must apply for these limits, typically when the discretionary credit limit is too low or constrained by the country limitation schedule.

Other limitations on Eximbank's liability are specified in the policy. The aggregate limit of liability represents the maximum amount Eximbank will pay with respect to shipments during any one policy year. The buyer credit limits noted above are not cumulative.

Eximbank is not liable for expenditures made by the insured to minimize loss unless prior approval is obtained.

WHAT THE INSURED AGREES TO DO

The insured agrees to submit reports periodically, listing all eligible shipments and buyers, with payment of the appropriate premiums (which will vary from month-to-month, with the level of activity).

The insured also agrees:

- to report monthly all past due insured buyers with overdue balances exceeding $100,000 to FCIA monthly, for both insured and uninsured transactions;
- not to further insure sales of goods or services to buyers already 90 days or more past due;
- to make written demands for payment upon the buyer no later than 30 days prior to submission of a claim;
- to exercise reasonable care to minimize or prevent losses;
- to refrain from altering due dates unless specifically approved by the policy or unless prior written approval is obtained from Eximbank.

CLAIMS AND PAYMENTS

Claims may be filed 90 days after the due date and must be filed within 240 days. The insured also agrees to file a release and assignment form with Eximbank, transferring any rights to the defaulted receivables and any security when the claim is paid, so that Eximbank may attempt recovery.

Eximbank will pay claims within 60 days of receiving a satisfactorily completed and documented proof of loss.

PREMIUM RATES

Premiums are based on many factors, including length of terms offered, buyer type, spread of country risk, transaction type, and previous export experience.

A minimum annual premium of $500 is paid for each policy period. An advance premium generally equal to one month's estimated premium is collected when the policy is issued.

WHO TO CONTACT:

For more information, contact or ask your insurance agent or broker to contact:

FCIA MANAGEMENT COMPANY, INC., 40 RECTOR ST., 11th FLOOR, NEW YORK, N.Y. 10006   Tel.: (212) 306-5000

Or call one of the regional offices in Chicago (312/641-1915), Houston (713/589-8182), the Los Angeles area (310/322-1152), Miami (305/372-8540) and New York (212/227-7020).

FCIA Management Company, Inc. is a New York corporation operating as an independent servicing company for the Export-Import Bank of the United States ("Eximbank").

FCIA Management Company, Inc. administers insurance policies underwritten by Eximbank.

This is not a solicitation by FCIA Management Company, Inc. or its employees. It is a descriptive summary only. The complete terms and conditions of the policy are set forth in the policy, applications and endorsements.

GM-ESCFLY1-10/91

insured percentages stated previously or as specified in the policy declarations. (See Figure 28-4 for a summary of this policy.)

Medium-Term Export Credit Insurance

Eximbank's medium-term policies cover two types of losses:

Figure 28-3. Multi-buyer export credit insurance (extending credit under your policy).

EXIMBANK MULTI-BUYER EXPORT CREDIT INSURANCE

EXTENDING CREDIT UNDER YOUR POLICY

Being able to extend credit terms to foreign buyers gives you an advantage in doing business abroad and is a major benefit of your Eximbank policy.

The Export-Import Bank of the United States (Eximbank) offers exporters two types of credit limits:

1. a Discretionary Credit Limit (DCL) which is included in many Eximbank Multi-Buyer policies, and
2. a Special Buyer Credit Limit (SBCL), for which you need to apply when your policy doesn't include a DCL, when your DCL is too low for a particular buyer, or when your DCL is restricted by Eximbank's country limitation schedule.

1. YOUR DCL

A DCL is a per-buyer limit included in many Multi-Buyer policies which enables you to extend credit terms, up to a specified amount, without prior Eximbank approval, provided that you first obtain certain information that justifies the credit amount you're extending.

There are two types of DCLs:

1. A "credit information" DCL requires you to obtain current credit information on the buyer before making shipment.

2. A "ledger experience" DCL authorizes you to extend credit terms to a buyer, or foreign bank issuing letters of credit on your buyer's behalf, based on your past favorable trading experience on comparable amounts and similar repayment terms. This allows you to act quickly on customer orders and save time and expenses associated with ordering credit information.

The amount of your "credit information" and "ledger experience" DCLs and terms for their use are set forth in the policy declarations and DCL endorsement. Please read them carefully.

The "Credit Information" DCL

To use your "credit information" DCL several conditions must be met prior to shipment:

• The transaction must meet the conditions of Eximbank's country limitation schedule, *and*

• you must obtain at least two pieces of credit information on the buyer dated within 12 months prior to shipment:

1. either a domestic or foreign credit agency report or a "World Traders Data Report", *and*

2. either a domestic or foreign commercial bank report *or* two written trade references, *or* for letter-of-credit transactions, you must obtain at least one favorable written bank report or written bank reference on the foreign bank issuing the letter of credit.

• The credit amount extended may not exceed the amount justified by the credit information, or the per-buyer amount listed in the policy declarations, whichever is less.

The "Ledger Experience" DCL

To use the "ledger experience" DCL, your payment experience with your buyer, the repayment terms and the credit amount you're extending must meet certain conditions:

• Your customer must have a record of paying you promptly on *all* shipments made on similar terms during the previous 12 months.

• For sight-draft-documents-against-payment and cash-against-documents transactions, payment must have been received within 20 days of arrival of the products at the port of importation.

• For all other transaction types, payment must have been received within 60 days of the due date.

• Shipments under your "ledger experience" DCL must be made on terms equivalent to those made on shipments within the prior 12 months.

• Shipments made on secured terms (such as letter-of-credit or sight-draft-documents-against-payment) can be used only to justify other secured-term shipments.

• Prior shipments made on draft or open account terms must be used to justify "ledger experience" DCL shipments made on draft or open account terms.

• You can't use sales made on secured terms to justify using your "ledger experience" DCL for unsecured sales.

• The credit limit extended under a "ledger experience" DCL must be comparable to previous credit limits extended.

• The credit amount must not exceed 125% of the highest amount owed and paid promptly, as defined above, by the buyer or issuing bank at any one time within the 12-month period prior to shipment.

• For example, let's assume that your policy has a "credit information" DCL of $20,000 and a maximum "ledger experience" DCL of $50,000. Based on written credit information you obtained in accordance with your policy, you shipped an $18,000 order to a buyer who paid you promptly. Under your "ledger experience" DCL, you are now able to increase the credit limit for that buyer to $22,500 ($18,000 x 125%). You then ship a $22,500 order to the buyer on similar terms, and the buyer again pays the full amount promptly. Now you can increase the credit for that buyer to $28,125 ($22,500 x 125%). The "ledger experience" DCL may be increased in this way up to $50,000.

Claim Filing on a "Ledger Experience" Transaction

If a claim arises on a "ledger experience" DCL transaction, you must be able to substantiate your favorable trading experience with the buyer or the bank issuing the letter of credit. To avoid claim denials, make sure that your "ledger experience" DCL is properly monitored and calculated for each buyer or issuing bank.

Figure 28-3. (*Continued*) Multi-buyer export credit insurance (extending credit under your policy).

---

2. YOUR SBCL

An SBCL establishes a revolving credit limit and is used in place of a DCL for a particular buyer. You must apply for an SBCL when:

- your policy doesn't include a DCL, or
- your DCL is too low for a particular buyer, or
- your DCL is restricted in a particular market by the country limitation schedule.

Eximbank Coverage Under an SBCL

With an SBCL in effect, Eximbank will cover shipments to a particular buyer as long as the outstanding amount doesn't exceed the credit limit specified in the SBCL endorsement and conditions of the SBCL and the policy are met. If you need a higher credit amount for the buyer, you may either request an increase in the SBCL or hold shipment until the buyer pays the outstanding amount.

Each SBCL indicates a final shipment date that limits the length of time Eximbank coverage is in effect for a buyer. You may request an SBCL renewal by submitting an application.

Applying for an SBCL

To apply for an SBCL do the following:

- Complete an SBCL application form. These are included in your policy documents folder and may also be obtained from your broker or FCIA Management Company, Inc.
- On the application, complete all items, including the credit limit and payment terms you're requesting and a summary of your credit experience with the buyer during the current year and the past two years, including uninsured experience. The credit experience summary must include any amounts past due from the buyer with maturity dates and an explanation.
- With your application submit credit agency and bank reports obtained on the foreign buyer dated within one year prior to the shipment date. Credit requests for more than $100,000 also require the last two or three years of the buyer's financial statements.

Helpful Hints for Expediting SBCL Processing

With your help, an SBCL application can usually be processed within five business days. To assist us you can:

- Make certain you complete all items on the application.
- Provide all necessary credit and financial information on the buyer. You are responsible for putting credit procedures in place so that you can provide us with the required information. On an occasional basis, if you need to expedite a rush order, you may check with FCIA to see if it has any of the required credit information already on file. You may have to supplement this information.
- Check the latest country limitation schedule for special conditions that may affect information requirements in a particular market. For example, the schedule may specify that short-term transactions can only be insured on a letter-of-credit basis. In that case, you should be sure that you can obtain the letter of credit.
- Set up a reminder system for renewable credit limits that will alert you three to four months before the limit expires. This will give you sufficient time to order the necessary credit information for the renewal. If you use a broker, they may be able to assist you with this. Eximbank generally sets the expiry dates of SBCLs at up to a maximum of 12 months from the approval date, or for a shorter period coinciding with the availability of new information, such as current financial statements on the buyer.

WHO TO CONTACT:

For more information, contact or ask your insurance agent or broker to contact:

FCIA MANAGEMENT COMPANY, INC., 40 RECTOR ST., 11th FLOOR, NEW YORK, N.Y. 10006   Tel.: (212) 306-5000

Or call one of the regional offices in Chicago (312/641-1915), Houston (713/589-8182), the Los Angeles area (310/322-1152), Miami (305/372-8540) and New York (212/227-7020).

FCIA Management Company, Inc. is a New York corporation operating as an independent servicing company for the Export-Import Bank of the United States ("Eximbank").

FCIA Management Company, Inc. administers insurance policies underwritten by Eximbank.

This is not a solicitation by FCIA Management Company, Inc. or its employees. It is a descriptive summary only. The complete terms and conditions of the policy are set forth in the policy, applications and endorsements.

GM-ESCDCL1-10/91

---

1. Commercial losses resulting from nonpayment for such reasons as a buyer's insolvency or failure to pay an obligation within six months of the due date.

2. Political losses resulting from certain specifically defined risks, such as war, revolution, cancellation of import or export licenses, and currency inconvertibility.

Figure 28-4. Short-term single-buyer export credit insurance.

EXIMBANK SHORT-TERM SINGLE-BUYER EXPORT CREDIT INSURANCE

A POLICY SUMMARY

Exporters of U.S. goods can reduce their risks of selling abroad and expand their worldwide market by selectively insuring foreign receivables under a Short-Term Single-Buyer Export Credit Insurance Policy.

The coverage protects against export credit risks, both political and commercial. Exporters may cover single or multiple shipments under a sales contract. Because there is no requirement to insure a spread of business, Exmbank's Short-Term Single-Buyer policy provides new opportunities for exporters to insure transactions selectively with or without linking them to bank financing.

Exporters may obtain Eximbank's export credit insurance either for multi-buyer *or* selective coverage. In general, however, policyholders may have only one type of coverage at a time.

PERCENTAGES OF COVER

The Short-Term Single-Buyer policy affords coverage against losses caused by political events, such as war, revolution, changes in certain export or import laws, and foreign exchange inconvertibility, or commercial events, such as insolvency and protracted default. Equalized coverage for commercial and political risks (comprehensive cover), or political-only cover, are available at the following maximum percentages:

	Comprehensive or Political-Only
Sovereign obligors	100%
Private sector and other non-sovereign obligors	90%
Letter of credit transactions	95%
Bulk agricultural transactions	98%

WHAT IS COVERED

Coverage applies to credit sales to a foreign buyer, or export letters of credit opened by a foreign issuing bank, named in the policy declarations for any goods produced in and shipped from the United States during the policy period. Cover is generally provided for credit terms up to 180 days for consumer items, parts and raw materials. On a case-by-case basis, agricultural commodities, capital equipment and quasi-capital equipment may be insured on terms up to 360 days. Products which are less than 50% U.S. content and defense products are not eligible for cover. Principal amounts are covered up to the maximum insured percentages stated above or as specified in the policy declarations.

Documented interest is covered at the applicable rate specified in the interest coverage endorsement up to 180 days after the due date (fewer days when the claim is settled earlier). Coverage of interest is capped at the lowest of:

- the rate specified in the debt instrument or invoice,
- the rate legally valid and enforceable in the buyer's country, or

- the rate below applicable to the payment currency specified:

  — for **U.S. dollars**: *The Wall Street Journal* New York published prime rate minus 0.5 percent

  — for **Swiss Francs, French Francs, West German Deutsche Marks, UK Pounds Sterling, Canadian Dollars and Japanese Yen**: the six month Euro offered rate plus 0.5 percent

WHAT PERIOD IS COVERED

Since the policy is structured for single-sale transactions, the standard policy period during which shipments can be made is three months. Eximbank will consider requests to issue a policy for up to 12 months to accommodate multiple shipments under a sales contract.

RISK RETAINED BY THE INSURED

There is no first loss deductible provision in the policy; however, the policyholder must stay at risk for the amount exceeding the insured percentage of coverage specified in the policy declarations.

COVERAGE LIMITS

In addition to the insured percentage of coverage, some other limitations should be noted.

- The shipment volume limit indicates the maximum value which may be insured under the policy and represents principal charged to the buyer. The first shipment(s) made to the buyer under the coverage terms and after the coverage effective date are insured until this shipment volume is reached. Any further shipments are not covered.

- The claim payment limit (principal) is the maximum amount Eximbank will pay for all claims for principal amounts resulting from all insured shipments made while the policy is in effect. Eximbank will also pay the insured percentage of interest owing under the terms specified in the interest coverage endorsement.

Figure 28-4. (*Continued*) Short-term single-buyer export credit insurance.

WHAT THE INSURED AGREES TO DO

The insured agrees to:
- pay the premium in full before the policy is issued;
- report to Eximbank in writing, if the buyer has not paid any insured amount for 90 days after it was due;
- cease shipments if the buyer is insolvent or has any debts, insured or uninsured, payble to the insured, which are 90 days or more past due;
- make a written demand for payment on the buyer and any guarantor at least 30 days before filing a claim;
- do everything reasonable to collect from the buyer any amounts owing;
- obtain Eximbank's written approval **before** rescheduling any insured transaction.

CLAIMS AND PAYMENTS

Claims may be filed 90 days after the due date and must be filed within 240 days. Upon payment of a claim, the insured agrees to sign a release, and to transfer the covered debt obligations to Eximbank and notify the buyer to make future payments to Eximbank.

Eximbank pays properly submitted and documented claims within 60 days of receipt.

RISK-BASED PREMIUM RATES

A risk-based pricing system is utilized. A disciplined formula provides a premium rate that reflects the major risk elements of each transaction. The pricing system does not provide for published rates; exporters or their insurance brokers may obtain a *non-binding* rate indication by contacting the Buyer Underwriting unit of FCIA Management Company, Inc. with specifics of the proposed transaction. Changing conditions may result in a different rate being finally offered than is initially indicated.

Premium is paid on the total principal volume amount to be insured. If requested, additional premium rates for preshipment coverage will be added to the premium rate for the transaction resulting in a final rate per $100 of invoice value.

MINIMUM PREMIUMS

The following minimum premiums apply:

Sovereign buyers and political-only coverage	$ 2,500
Letters of credit, other transactions with bank obligors and non-sovereign government-owned obligors	$ 5,000
Private buyers	$10,000

Special lower minimum premiums apply for "New-to-Export" exporters at 30% of the above amounts. ("New-to-Export" exporters are those entities which, together with their affiliates, have had average annual export credit sales not exceeding $750,000 for the preceding two fiscal years. Export credit sales are those exports made on terms other than cash in advance or confirmed irrevocable letters of credit.)

POLICY APPLICATION PROCEDURE

The application form is completed by the exporter outlining the specifics of the transaction. Information about the exporter and the buyer, including a credit agency report and financial statements on each entity, must be submitted to support the request.

Upon review and approval of the application, Eximbank issues a commitment notice on the transaction, stating the parameters of coverage. These parameters include Eximbank's limit of liability for the transaction, the insured percentage, shipment volume limit, payment currency, premium, policy period and any special conditions required.

The commitment notice is effective for a maximum of 90 days and locks in the coverage as outlined. This assures the exporter that all policy conditions will remain unchanged for the commitment period. Commitment periods in excess of 90 days are not available. The policy is issued upon receipt of the premium (the policy coverage effective date), which must be received within the commitment period. The policy coverage expiration date is set at 90 days after the effective date unless a longer period was requested of, and approved by, Eximbank.

POLICY PROCEEDS ARE ASSIGNABLE

By submitting the appropriate notification form to Eximbank, the policy proceeds may be assigned to a commercial bank or other lender. Thus, the policyholder can realize greater financial liquidity and flexibility in administering its foreign receivables portfolio.

WHO TO CONTACT:

For more information, contact or ask your insurance agent or broker to contact:

FCIA MANAGEMENT COMPANY, INC., 40 RECTOR ST., 11th FLOOR, NEW YORK, N.Y. 10006   Tel.: (212) 306-5000

Or call one of the regional offices in Chicago (312/641-1915), Houston (713/589-8182), the Los Angeles area (310/322-1152), Miami (305/372-8540) and New York (212/227-7020).

FCIA Management Company, Inc. is a New York corporation operating as an independent servicing company for the Export-Import Bank of the United States ("Eximbank").

FCIA Management Company, Inc. administers insurance policies underwritten by Eximbank.

This is not a solicitation by FCIA Management Company, Inc. or its employees. It is a descriptive summary only. The complete terms and conditions of the policy are set forth in the policy, applications and endorsements.

GM-ESSFLY1-10/91

Eximbank normally indemnifies an exporter for up to 90 percent of the financed portion in the event of a commercial loss, and for 100 percent on a political loss.

Medium-term policies cover credit sales in which payment terms range between 181 days and five years after the goods arrive at the port of importation. Policies are available to accommodate three types of transactions:

1. *Single sales*—one-time transactions
2. *Repetitive sales*—ongoing relationships, generally with a dealer or distributor
3. *Combination short-term/medium-term sales of capital equipment and related spare parts to dealers and distributors*

Under all of the medium-term policies, it is required that the insured obtain a cash-down payment from the buyer in an amount equal to at least 15 percent of the contract price. The remaining financed portion is then insured at the applicable percentage of cover. The buyer's obligation to pay the financed portion must be evidenced by a promissory note. The financed portion may be payable in equal installments of principal on a monthly, quarterly, or semiannual basis. (See Figure 28-5 for a summary of this policy.)

Bank Letter of Credit Insurance

This policy protects banks against losses on irrevocable letters of credit issued by foreign banks in support of United States exports. It applies to irrevocable letters of credit which conform with the Uniform Customs and Practice for Documentary Credits (UCP), 1983 revision, publication number 400 of the International Chamber of Commerce where the insured has a relationship with the foreign issuing bank. The policy is not applicable to revocable, back to back, red clause or conditional letters of credit.

Coverage applies to irrevocable letter of credit sales of goods produced in and shipped from the United States during the policy period, and for services performed by United States personnel in a host country. Receivables for products which are less than 50 percent United States content of domestic origin and certain defense products are not eligible for cover.

Terms of up to 180 days from the date of first presentation of documents may be extended for consumer items, parts, and raw materials. On a case by case basis, agricultural commodities, capital equipment, and quasi-capital equipment may be insured on terms up to 360 days.

Principal amounts are covered up to the maximum insured percentages stated here or as specified in the policy declarations. Documented interest is covered up to 180 days after the date of the issuing bank's default (or fewer days when the claim is settled earlier). On letters of credit that are

Figure 28-5. Policy summary (medium-term export credit insurance).

EXIMBANK MEDIUM-TERM EXPORT CREDIT INSURANCE

A POLICY SUMMARY

Exporters of U.S. capital and quasi-capital equipment can insure their foreign receivables against certain losses with Eximbank medium-term policies.

Eximbank medium-term policies protect a U.S. company's sales to a single foreign buyer against the buyer's failure to pay an obligation because of unforeseen commercial or political reasons. The policies can often help U.S. exporters obtain financing and, therefore, compete in selling overseas through the use of prudent credit extension practices.

There is no requirement to insure all capital equipment sales under the medium-term policies since each policy covers only an exporter's transactions with one particular buyer.

WHAT IS COVERED

Eximbank's medium-term policies cover *two types of losses*:

1. *Commercial losses* resulting from nonpayment for such reasons as a buyer's insolvency or failure to pay an obligation within six months of the due date.

2. *Political losses* resulting from certain specifically defined risks, such as war, revolution, cancellation of import or export licenses, and currency inconvertibility.

Normally, Eximbank indemnifies an exporter for up to 90 percent of the financed portion in the event of a commercial loss, and for 100 percent on a political loss.

Eximbank's medium-term policies cover credit sales in which payment terms range between 181 days and five years after the goods arrive at the port of importation. Policies are available to accommodate *three types of transactions*:

1. *single sales* - one-time transactions;

2. *repetitive sales* - ongoing relationships, generally with a dealer or distributor, and

3. *combination short-term/medium-term sales* of capital equipment and related spare parts to dealers and distributors.

Under all of the medium-term policies, it is required that the insured obtain a cash down payment from the buyer in an amount equal to at least 15 percent of the contract price. The remaining financed portion is then insured at the applicable percentage of cover. The buyer's obligation to pay the financed portion must be evidenced by a promissory note. The financed portion may be payable in equal installments of principal on a monthly, quarterly or semi-annual basis.

INFORMATION REQUIRED FROM APPLICANTS

- Applicant information - The following information is required:

  1. Completed application for approval as a medium-term exporter

  2. Financial statements for the most recent fiscal year.

- Buyer Information - The applicant must also provide information about the buyer. In general, the following guidelines apply:

  - for transactions up to $50,000, two credit reports (one from a credit reporting agency and the other from a commercial bank) which contain some financial information on the foreign buyer;

  - for transactions from $50,001 to $100,000, one year of financial statements on the buyer, in addition to the two credit reports;

  - for transactions above $100,000, three years of financial statements on the buyer, in addition to the two credit reports.

SINGLE-SALE POLICY

The exporter submits an application for coverage of a single-sale transaction with a foreign buyer.

If the transaction is approved, Eximbank issues a commitment notice stating the parameters on which we would be willing to issue coverage. Those parameters include Eximbank's limit of liability, the amount of the contract price, the down payment and the financed portion, the payment terms, the premium amount, the policy period, and any special conditions required. The policy will be issued upon receipt of the quoted premium amount.

Although the Single-Sale Policy covers only one specific transaction with a particular buyer, more than one shipment can be made to complete the transaction.

REPETITIVE SALES POLICY

The exporter submits an application for coverage on a series of transactions with a particular buyer. In place of a commitment notice, Eximbank issues a policy with a transaction endorsement stating the parameters of coverage.

Following shipment, the exporter submits a monthly shipment report form, accompanied by the appropriate premium check, stating the shipments made during the prior month.

THE COMBINED POLICY

The Combined Policy insures, on a revolving basis, U.S. exports of capital goods, parts and accessories sold on credit terms to a particular dealer or distributor. "Combined" refers to the payment terms being offered for different types of products. Capital goods may be sold on payment terms between 181 days and three years, while spare parts carry terms of up to 180 days. The application and shipment report requirements are the same as for the Repetitive Policy.

The Combined Policy allows a flexible arrangement between the exporter and the dealer in the form of a floor plan period for inventory financing of capital goods.

Buyers under medium-term policies are required to make a down payment of at least 15 percent of the contract price of a transaction on or before delivery of the capital goods. With the Combined Policy's floor plan arrangement, the dealer may forego this down payment for either 180 or 270 days while the goods remain in the dealer's inventory. In essence, the capital goods are insured on a short-term basis during the floor plan period.

(Continued)

Figure 28-5. (*Continued*) Policy summary (medium-term export credit insurance).

At the end of the floor plan period, the dealer may:
- make payment in full for capital equipment sold during the floor plan period;
- roll its obligation to pay into a medium-term note after a 15 percent down payment, for goods which remain unsold or which have been resold by the dealer on extended credit terms,
- extend the floor plan an additional 90 days.

If the option to extend the floor plan period is taken, at the end of the extension period one of the following must happen:
- if the products have been resold by the dealer on terms requiring payment in full by the buyer prior to the end of the floor plan period, the dealer must pay in full, or
- if the units remain unsold at the end of the floor plan period, or have been resold by the dealer on extended terms, the obligation of the dealer to pay may be rolled into a medium-term note after payment of a 15 percent down payment.

ELIGIBLE REPAYMENT TERMS

The length of payment terms available under Eximbank medium-term policies depends on the total value of sales and, to some extent, upon the unit value of capital goods. The following table shows the maximum terms for specified dollar amounts:

Contract Price of Transaction	Maximum Payment Term
less than $75,000	two years
$75,000 - less than $150,000	three years
$150,000 - less than $300,000	four years
$300,000 or more	five years

Capital equipment sales to dealers are generally limited to maximum credit terms of three years.

PREMIUM RATES AND PAYMENT

Under single-sale policies, a policy and transaction endorsement are issued when the appropriate premium is received. Repetitive and Combined policies require premium payment by the 15th day of the month immediately following each insured shipment. For each policy type, premium is calculated on the financed portion of the medium-term shipments made during the period. For short-term sales under the Combined Policy, premium is calculated based upon the gross invoice value.

INTEREST COVERAGE

On short-term shipments, the insured interest rate is either the per annum rate set forth in the contract of sale between the insured and the buyer *or* a fixed rate equal to one percent in excess of the six-month U.S. Treasury borrowing rate on the day of shipment, whichever is less.

The interest rate on medium-term transactions is determined on the due date of each installment in default. It is either the rate provided in the note *or* one percent in excess of the U.S. Treasury borrowing rate in effect on the due date of each installment having the same maturity as the remaining repayment term of the note, whichever is less. The remaining repayment term is the period commencing on the due date of the installment in default and ending on the due date of the final installment. To be covered, post-maturity interest must be stipulated by the insured in the promissory note.

Coverage of interest charges may extend to the date of claim payment, or 90 days beyond the minimum required waiting period before a claim can be filed, whichever is earlier.

OVERDUES AND CLAIMS

Insureds must report all buyers which fall into default on a monthly basis after they reach 60 days past due. In all cases, these monthly reports of overdue situations should continue for as long as the overdue exists, or until a claim is submitted.

When claims are submitted, copies of all documents pertaining to the transaction, such as invoices, bills of lading, promissory notes and guarantees, should be forwarded in conjunction with proof of loss forms for review.

For commercial default claims, there is a 180-day waiting period after the date of default before a claim can be filed. For claims resulting from the insolvency of the buyer or for one of the political risks defined in the policy, there generally is no waiting period for filing a claim. The latest date for filing any type of claim is 240 days after the date of default.

WHO TO CONTACT:

For more information, contact or ask your insurance agent or broker to contact:

FCIA MANAGEMENT COMPANY, INC., 40 RECTOR ST., 11th FLOOR, NEW YORK, N.Y. 10006   Tel.: (212) 306-5000

Or call one of the regional offices in Chicago (312/641-1915), Houston (713/589-8182), the Los Angeles area (310/322-1152), Miami (305/372-8540) and New York (212/227-7020).

FCIA Management Company, Inc. is a New York corporation operating as an independent servicing company for the Export-Import Bank of the United States ("Eximbank").

FCIA Management Company, Inc. administers insurance policies underwritten by Eximbank.

This is not a solicitation by FCIA Management Company, Inc. or its employees. It is a descriptive summary only. The complete terms and conditions of the policy are set forth in the policy, applications and endorsements.

GM-MTFLY1-10/91

payable in United States dollars, the insured interest rate is generally prime rate minus one-half percent or the rate stated in the credit agreement, whichever is less. Eximbank uses the prime rate published in the *Wall Street Journal* under the table "Money Rates."

The policy specifically excludes coverage for those transactions in which there is an unresolved documentary dispute between the insured and the issuing bank. Additionally, coverage is specifically excluded in situations in which the issuing bank refuses documents at the time of presentation and seeks a refund from the insured bank to whom a reimbursement has already been made. (See Figure 28-6 for a summary of this policy.)

It should be noted that the Bank Letter of Credit Policy is not available to exporters. The exporter's position is protected by the guarantee of the domestic bank which issues an irrevocable letter of credit for a specific sum of money, subject to the fulfillment of certain terms and conditions which have been provided by the foreign bank. When a bank or a country is known to have a potential for problems in the monetary system, in the economy, and perhaps in the government itself, the domestic bank might elect to protect itself against the possibility of the foreign bank's nonpayment with an Eximbank Letter of Credit Insurance Policy.

What is the message to the domestic bank if the Foreign Credit Insurance Association declines the risk? If FCIA will not issue a policy it is because, one, the country is too unstable; two, the monetary system is tottering; and three, the government of the customer country will authorize the transfer of United States dollars for a very limited number of products and purposes. The domestic bank (and the exporter) are put on alert that the transaction embraces a high level of danger. A situation whose best offer to the exporter is a high risk of nonpayment is not an acceptable transaction.

Operating and Financing Lease Insurance

These policies insure both operating and financing leases. An eligible lessor is any leasing company, manufacturer, bank, trust, partnership, or other entity, foreign or domestic, that leases or participates in the financing of leases of United States manufactured equipment and services outside the United States.

1. Lease coverage can apply to new or used equipment and related services.

2. As a general rule, no more than 15 percent of the value of the leased products, exclusive of price mark-up, may consist of labor, raw materials, component parts, or any combination thereof, originating or manufactured outside the United States. Any foreign content in the leased products must be specifically approved by Eximbank.

3. The transaction must be subject to a lease agreement between the lessee and lessor which is valid and enforceable in the United States and in the lessee's country at the time the policy becomes effective.

Eximbank's coverage for operating leases was designed around a general lease transaction concept in which:

Figure 28-6. Policy summary (letter of credit insurance).

EXIMBANK BANK LETTER OF CREDIT INSURANCE

A POLICY SUMMARY

The Eximbank Bank Letter of Credit policy can reduce your risks on confirmations and negotiations of irrevocable letters of credit issued by overseas financial institutions for the financing of U.S. exports.

This policy affords commercial and political coverage against the failure of an overseas financial institution (issuing bank), whether sovereign or private, to make payment or reimbursement to the insured bank on an irrevocable letter of credit. Coverage is also provided for the insured bank's refinancing of payments under a sight irrevocable letter of credit of the issuing bank.

WHAT IS COVERED

The policy applies to irrevocable letters of credit which conform with the Uniform Customs and Practice for Documentary Credits (UCP), 1983 revision, publication number 400 of the International Chamber of Commerce where the insured has a relationship with the foreign issuing bank. The policy is not applicable to revocable, back-to-back, red clause or conditional letters of credit.

Coverage applies to irrevocable letter of credit sales for goods produced in and shipped from the United States during the policy period, and for services performed by U.S. personnel in a host country. Receivables for products which are less than 50% U.S. content and certain defense products are not eligible for cover.

Terms up to 180 days from the date of first presentation of documents may be extended for consumer items, parts and raw materials. On a case-by-case basis, agricultural commodities, capital equipment, and quasi-capital equipment may be insured on terms up to 360 days.

Principal amounts are covered up to the maximum insured percentages stated below or as specified in the policy declarations. Documented interest is covered up to 180 days after the date of the issuing bank's default (or fewer days when the claim is settled earlier). On letters of credit that are payable in U.S. dollars, the insured interest rate is generally prime rate minus 0.5% or the rate stated in the credit agreement, whichever is less. Eximbank uses the prime rate published in the Wall Street Journal, under the table "Money Rates."

The policy specifically excludes coverage for those transactions in which there is an unresolved documentary dispute between the insured and the issuing bank. Additionally, coverage is specifically excluded in situations in which the issuing bank refuses documents at the time of presentation and seeks a refund from the insured bank to whom a reimbursement has already been made.

PERCENTAGES OF COVER

The Bank Letter of Credit policy provides coverage against losses caused by events such as war, revolution, expropriation or confiscation by a governmental authority, cancellation of import or export licenses, and foreign exchange inconvertibility, and commercial losses caused by events such as insolvency of the foreign issuing bank, and failure to reimburse or to pay for other reasons. Equalized coverage for commercial and political risks (comprehensive cover), or political-only cover are available at the following maximum percentages:

	Comprehensive or Political-Only
Sovereign Financial Institution	100%
Non-Sovereign Financial Institution	95%
Approved Agricultural Commodities	98%

RECOURSE

The insured may arrange recourse or "pass back" to a third party of all or any part of any uninsured amount.

ELIGIBLE INSURED BANKS

The policy may be issued to any bank doing business in the United States in accordance with applicable federal or state banking laws and regulations. The insured bank must act under the terms of the UCP as either the paying, accepting, or negotiating bank for the insured transaction.

HOW THE POLICY WORKS

The policy affords coverage for eligible issuing banks as determined by Eximbank based on the insured's submission of an issuing bank credit limit (IBCL) application for the overseas financial institution and issuance by Eximbank of a written credit approval in the form of a policy endorsement. The application requires disclosure of all relevant financial information on the issuing bank.

High credits may be extended up to the amount specified in the IBCL, which generally remains valid for a maximum period of 12 months. Once issued, the IBCL becomes a revolving credit approval limited only to the approved issuing bank with specified terms and tenor.

Figure 28-6. (*Continued*) Policy summary (letter of credit insurance).

The insured bank is required to obtain an exporter certificate certifying, among other things, that a letter of credit has been established in support of the described transaction and that the goods are manufactured or produced in and shipped from the United States. If the beneficiary of the letter of credit is an entity other than the U.S. exporter, additional certificates are required.

PRE-PRESENTATION AGREEMENT

Prior to the presentation of documents on the insured bank under a letter of credit and at the time an insured bank commits to finance or pay, the insured may obtain a pre-presentation agreement under which Eximbank agrees not to withdraw coverage, add, delete, or amend any policy condition, credit limit or other limitation, including the country limitation schedule for a period of 90 days. The policy also sets forth a method by which this optional agreement may be extended for additional time.

WHAT THE INSURED AGREES TO DO

The insured agrees:

- to submit reports to Eximbank, listing appropriate bank commitments and insured transactions, with payment of the corresponding premiums (which will vary from month to month with the level of activity);

- to report all amounts past due (insured and uninsured) from the foreign issuing bank;

- not to enter into an insured transaction with an issuing bank which is 30 days or more past due;

- to obtain Eximbank's prior written approval for rescheduling or accelerating any insured transaction;

- to make written demands for payment on the foreign issuing bank within 30 days after default;

- to exercise reasonable care to minimize or prevent loss.

CLAIMS AND PAYMENTS

Claims may be filed no earlier than 60 days and no later than 120 days after the date of default. Prior to claim submission, the insured is required, within 30 days of default, to make written demand for payment on the issuing bank. The insured is required to file a release and assignment form with Eximbank, transferring any rights to the defaulted receivables and any security when the claim is paid, so that recovery may be attempted.

Eximbank will pay claims within 60 days of receiving a satisfactorily completed and documented proof of loss.

RISK-BASED PREMIUM RATES

A risk-based pricing system is utilized that reflects the major risk elements of each transaction. The pricing system does not provide for published rates; banks or their insurance brokers may obtain a nonbinding rate indication by contacting the Buyer Underwriting unit of FCIA Management Company, Inc. with specifics of the contemplated transaction. Changing conditions may result in a different rate being finally offered than is initially indicated.

A minimum annual premium of $2,000 is paid for each one-year policy period. This premium is collected upon issuance of the policy.

WHO TO CONTACT:

For more information, contact or ask your insurance agent or broker to contact:

FCIA MANAGEMENT COMPANY, INC., 40 RECTOR ST., 11th FLOOR, NEW YORK, N.Y. 10006   Tel.: (212) 306-5000

Or call one of the regional offices in Chicago (312/641-1915), Houston (713/589-8182), the Los Angeles area (310/322-1152), Miami (305/372-8540) and New York (212/227-7020).

FCIA Management Company, Inc. is a New York corporation operating as an independent servicing company for the Export-Import Bank of the United States ("Eximbank").

FCIA Management Company, Inc. administers insurance policies underwritten by Eximbank.

This is not a solicitation by FCIA Management Company, Inc. or its employees. It is a descriptive summary only. The complete terms and conditions of the policy are set forth in the policy, applications and endorsements.

GM-ELCFLY1-10/91

- payments total less than full value of leased products.

- there is residual value of the leased products.

- there is usually an intention of the lessor to repossess the leased products and release, sell, or otherwise dispose of them.

- the lessor keeps the risk that the leased products will decline in market value at a greater rate than expected.

The Operating Lease Policy divides coverage into two parts which may be purchased together or separately:

1. *Coverage for Stream of Payments*
   (The policy provides coverage for the "stream of payments" falling due during the repossession-efforts period after default of the lessee.)

2. *Coverage against Governmental Prevention of Repossession (GPR)*
   (As a second part of the coverage, Eximbank will insure the political risk of prevention of repossession of the leased products due to specific government actions, including, but not limited to, expropriation, confiscation, and cancellation of export license. This coverage, usually provided at 100 percent for all lessee types, comes into effect only after the end of the repossession-efforts period. It is limited to the fair market value of the leased products at the time of claim. (See Figure 28-7 for a summary of this policy.)

Most FCIA policies cover 90 to 95 percent of commercial risk and 95 to 100 percent of political risks. In addition, the exporter may be required to absorb a first-loss deductible. Certain agricultural commodities may be covered at 98 percent of commercial risk and 100 percent of political risk (if equalized coverage is selected, cover is 98 percent).

Exporters also may obtain special endorsements to cover sales into or out of consignment, sales made from an overseas warehouse, nonacceptance of shipments, preshipment payments in a foreign currency, sale out of foreign trade fairs, used equipment sales, and sales of dairy/breeding cattle.

Premiums vary with the credit terms, the exporter experience, the quality and number of buyers insured, and the importing countries. Most policies require a minimum premium to be paid at the beginning of every policy year.

Eximbank is prohibited from financing sales to certain countries and is closed in markets where it cannot find reasonable assurance of repayment. Special conditions and restrictions are outlined in a Country Limitation Schedule, which is revised every six months. Policies toward individual countries may be revised when conditions change significantly.

Support for Small Business

Eximbank is especially interested in supporting exports by small- and medium-sized companies. In FY 1990 (figures are not available for 1991), the Bank authorized $2.1 billion in support for exports by small businesses, 22 percent of all the authorizations approved in the year. This small business support included $1.6 billion in export credit insurance, $89 million in working capital guarantees, $291 million in export loan guarantees, and $106 million in direct and intermediary loans.

Figure 28-7. Policy summary (operating and financing lease insurance).

EXIMBANK OPERATING AND FINANCING LEASE INSURANCE

A POLICY SUMMARY

Companies leasing products of U.S. origin outside the United States can reduce their risks by insuring stream-of-lease payments and the fair market value of the leased products through Eximbank's lease policies. The coverage protects against credit risks, both political and commercial. Coverage is available for a cross-border lease (a lease in which the lessor and lessee are in two different countries) or an international lease (a lease in which both the lessor and lessee are in the same country, other than the United States).

Eximbank offers two credit insurance policies for the leasing industry: an Operating Lease Policy and a Financing Lease Policy. Each provides a unique system of coverage described below. The choice of the Operating Lease Policy or Financing Lease Policy is solely the lessor's and is based upon an evaluation of which coverage structure fits the specific transaction.

ELIGIBLE LESSORS

An eligible lessor is any leasing company, manufacturer, bank, trust, partnership or other entity, foreign or domestic, that leases or participates in the financing of leases of U.S.-manufactured equipment and services outside the United States.

ELIGIBLE LEASE TRANSACTIONS

- Lease coverage can apply to new or used equipment and related services.

- Generally, no more than 15% of the value of the leased products, exclusive of price mark-up, may consist of labor, raw materials, component parts, or any combination thereof, originating or manufactured outside the United States. Any foreign content in the leased products must be specifically approved by Eximbank.

- The transaction must be subject to a lease agreement between the lessee and lessor, which is valid and enforceable in the United States and the lessee's country at the time the policy becomes effective.

OPERATING LEASE POLICY

Eximbank's coverage for operating leases was designed around a general lease transaction concept in which:
- payments total less than full value of leased products;
- there is residual value of the leased products;
- there is usually an intention of the lessor to repossess the leased products and release, sell or otherwise dispose of them;
- the lessor keeps the risk that the leased products will decline in market value at a greater rate than expected.

The Operating Lease Policy divides coverage into two parts which may be purchased together or separately:

1) **Coverage for Stream of Payments**: The policy provides coverage for the stream of payments falling due during a repossession-efforts period after default of the lessee. This part of the overall cover-age is intended to maintain the insured's stream of pay-ments while action is taken to repossess the leased pro-ducts. Although the length of the repossession-efforts period is underwritten on a case-by-case basis, it will generally extend to cover those periodic and non-periodic payments which fall due for up to five months after default.

Under the lease, periodic payments, representing the rental portion of the lease, must be due from the lessee to the insured at regular intervals. The amounts of such payments may, however, be unequal. Periodic payments can be insured at face amount whether or not that amount includes imputed interest, profit or any other component.

The non-periodic payment concept is intended to include those payments which are obligations of the lessee under lease contingencies. Such obligations might include service or maintenance payments payable by the lessee to the insured lessor. Coverage of non-periodic payments will be specifically underwritten by Eximbank and a credit limit will be entered for each approved non-periodic payment.

Coverage for the stream of payments is provided at a maximum of 100% for sovereign lessees and 90% for all others.

2) **Coverage Against Governmental Prevention of Repossession (GPR)**: As a second part of coverage, Eximbank will insure the political risk of prevention of repossession of the leased products due to specific government actions, including, but not limited to, expropriation, confiscation and cancellation of export license. This coverage, usually provided at 100% for all lessee types, comes into effect only after the end of the repossession-efforts period. It is limited to the fair market value of the leased products at the time of claim.

- Under risks on the stream of payments, Eximbank's maximum claim payment would be the insured percentage of the loss up to the actual amount of the limited number of periodic and non-periodic payments specified in the policy declarations.

- Under GPR, the lessor may purchase insurance up to the Eximbank-approved credit limit to cover the value of the leased products should governmental intervention, as set forth in the policy, prevent repossession. The claim payment would be the insured percentage of the fair market value at the time of claim, limited by the credit limit coverage purchased. Prior to policy issuance, the lessor must make the final decision on the credit limit, taking into consideration whatever factors are deemed appropriate, including the possibility of default and prevention of repossession occurring very early in the life of the lease.

(Continued)

Figure 28-7. (*Continued*) Policy summary (operating and financing lease insurance).

FINANCING LEASE POLICY

This policy was designed around a lease concept in which there is generally little residual value remaining in the leased products and ownership is transferred to the lessee at the end of the lease. Eximbank views the structure as similar to a medium-term sale transaction and requires a 15% advance payment from the lessee to the lessor on or before delivery of the leased products. Eximbank will insure only the remaining 85% of the lease transaction. Generally, the advance payment may not be financed by the insured, by a financial institution which requires any share of the leased products as security against the loan.

Should the lessee default, coverage is provided for the insured percentage of each lease payment as it falls due until the end of the lease term. Coverage is usually provided at a maximum of 100% for sovereign lessees and 90% for all others. Eximbank's maximum claim payment for risks 1, 2, 3 and 4 is the insured percentage of the loss on approved non-periodic payments and on the principal and covered interest of each actual periodic payment, as set forth in the policy declarations.

Accrued regular interest and post-default interest coverage is provided on the outstanding principal balance, subject to duration and rate limitations specified in the policy declarations.

RISK RETAINED BY THE INSURED

There is no first-loss deductible provision in the policy However, the policyholder must stay at risk for the amount exceeding the insured coverage percentage specified in the policy declarations.

POLICY ISSUANCE

Both the Operating Lease and Financing Lease policies cover single transactions. A separate policy is issued for each lease insured with Eximbank. Upon review and approval of an application, Eximbank will issue a commitment notice for 90 days, reflecting coverage parameters, including credit limits and premium due, for the specific lease transaction. The policy is issued if the premium is paid in full prior to the expiration of the commitment notice.

Both policies require that the lease documentation set forth certain obligations. Before Eximbank can underwrite a transaction, we need to review a complete draft of the lease documentation.

CLAIMS AND PAYMENTS

Under the Operating Lease Policy:
- Stream-of-payments claims for risks 1, 2, 3 and 4 may be filed no earlier than the date the leased products are repossessed or the end of the repossession-efforts period, and no later than 120 days after this period.
- Governmental-prevention-of-respossession claims under risk 5 may be filed no earlier than the end of the repossession-efforts period and no later than 120 days after this period.

Under the Financing Lease Policy:
- Claims may be filed from 120 to 240 days after default.

Under both policies, the insured is obligated to transfer the lessee's lease obligations to Eximbank at time of claim payment. It is also obligated to transfer title to the leased products to Eximbank for claims paid under risk 5 of the Operating Lease Policy or any Financing Lease Policy claim.

Eximbank pays properly submitted and documented lease policy claims within 60 days of receipt.

RISK-BASED PREMIUM RATES

A risk-based pricing system is utilized. The premium rate reflects the major risk elements of each lease and is determined by the length of the lease, the country involved and the type of lessee (sovereign, nonsovereign public sector, or private sector).

Under the Operating Lease Policy, premium is payable per $100 of:
- the specified stream-of-payments coverage credit limit;
- the fair market value liability limit specified in the policy for governmental-prevention-of-repossession coverage.

Under the Financing Lease Policy, premium is payable per $100 of:
- the specified stream-of-payments coverage credit limit (representing principal only).

Due to the different structures of the policies, premium for a single transaction could vary greatly, depending upon the policy chosen.

The pricing system does not provide for published rates. Lessors or their insurance brokers may obtain a non-binding rate indication by contacting the Buyer Underwriting unit of FCIA Management Company, Inc. with specifics of the transaction. Changing conditions may result in a different rate than is initially indicated.

ASSIGNMENT OF PROCEEDS

Subject to Eximbank approval, policy proceeds may be assigned to a commercial bank or other lender. Thus, the policyholder can realize greater financial liquidity and flexibility in administering its foreign receivables portfolio.

WHO TO CONTACT:

For more information, contact or ask your insurance agent or broker to contact:

FCIA MANAGEMENT COMPANY, INC., 40 RECTOR ST., 11th FLOOR, NEW YORK, N.Y. 10006   Tel.: (212) 306-5000

Or call one of the regional offices in Chicago (312/641-1915), Houston (713/589-8182), the Los Angeles area (310/322-1152), Miami (305/372-8540) and New York (212/227-7020).

FCIA Management Company, Inc. is a New York corporation operating as an independent servicing company for the Export-Import Bank of the United States ("Eximbank").

FCIA Management Company, Inc. administers insurance policies underwritten by Eximbank.

This is not a solicitation by FCIA Management Company, Inc. or its employees. It is a descriptive summary only. The complete terms and conditions of the policy are set forth in the policy, applications and endorsements.

GM-LSEFLY1-10/91

Working capital guarantees encourage commercial lenders to make loans to small companies that have exporting potential, but need funds to produce or market goods or services for export (see Figure 28-8). Export loan guarantees provide repayment protection for commercial lenders extending loans to foreign buyers of United States exports. Direct and intermediary loans provide competitive, fixed interest rate financing to foreign buyers of United States exports.

Eximbank provides information on the availability and use of its programs through a toll-free Export Financing Hotline, (800) 424-5201.

Contacting Eximbank

Mail: 811 Vermont Ave., N.W., Washington, D.C., 20571
                 (or West Coast Office at 11000 Wilshire Blvd., Suite 9103,
                 Los Angeles, California 90024)

Telephone: (202)566-2117   Los Angeles—(213)575-7425

Telefax: (202)566-7524   Los Angeles—(213)575-7428

Telex: TRT 197681 (EXIM UT)

Cable: "EXIMBANK"

TDD: (202)535-3913

Export Financing Hotline: (800)424-5201

Electronic Bulletin Board: (202)566-4699

Program Contacts

For information pertaining to Direct Loans, Intermediary Loans, and Guarantees contact the appropriate area division, based on the buyer's country:

Africa and Middle East Division   (202)566-8011

Asia Division   (202)566-8885

Europe and Canada Division   (202)566-8813

Latin America Division   (202)566-8943

For information pertaining to Working Capital Guarantees, contact the following:

United States Division   (202)566-8819

Export Credit Insurance

For information or answers to questions pertaining to Export Credit Insurance, contact the FCIA at these offices:

New York: 40 Rector Street
                 New York, New York 10006
                 (212)227-7020

Figure 28-8. Facts about the California Export Finance Program.

CALIFORNIA STATE WORLD TRADE COMMISSION

EXPORT FINANCE OFFICE

107 South Broadway   San Diego Representative
Suite 8039   P.O. Box 3694
Los Angeles, CA 90012   Rancho Santa Fe, CA 92067
213/620-2433   619/759-1153

CALL 415-557-9812

FACTS ABOUT THE CALIFORNIA EXPORT FINANCE PROGRAM

STATUTORY AUTHORITY: California Government Code, Sections 15390-15396 (Enabling Legislation SB 1196, Vuich, Chapter 1693, Statutes of 1984); Effective January 1, 1985

FRAMEWORK: The Program is administered by the California Export Finance Office (CEFO), a unit of the California State World Trade Commission (CSWTC). Governing CEFO's affairs is the Export Finance Board, consisting of seven members as follows: the director of Food and Agriculture or a designee; the executive director of the Office of Small Business Development, or a designee; one Governor's appointee, knowledgeable and experienced in affairs and the export finance needs of California agriculture; two appointees from export firms, one each by the CSWTC and the Speaker of the Assembly; two appointees from financial institutions, one each by the CSWTC and the President pro Tempore of the Senate. Current board members are:
  Cassandra S. De Berge, First Interstate Bank
  Stanley W. Epstein, American Export Trading Company
  Richard Nelson, California Office of Small Business Development
  Jack Pandol, Sr., Pandol Brothers, Inc.
  Richard Patterson, California State University, Stanislaus
  Marilynn Bonin, California Department of Food and Agriculture
  Herbert Hawkins, Agriculture/International Financial Consultant
  CEFO director, L. Fargo Wells, owned and operated an export company for 15 years. Mr. Wells is a former president of both the Foreign Trade Association of Southern California and the Export Managers Association of California, and currently serves on the Southern California District Export Council. He is also co-author of the recently-published *EXPORTING: FROM START TO FINANCE.*
  The deputy director, Irene L. Fisher, was a senior loan specialist with SBA, with special emphasis on export-related loans, and is well known in

Figure 28-8. (*Continued*) Facts about the California Export Finance Program.

the Southern California financial community. She currently serves on the Board of Directors of the Foreign Trade Association of Southern California and the Southern California Coordinating Council.

Loan officer William Jimenez functioned in that capacity 14 years with Security Pacific Bank in the international department, and prior to joining CEFO, owned and operated an export company.

Manager of the Northern California region, J. H. "Ham" Dethero, brings over 30 years of international banking and trade experience. He is a past president of the California Council for International Trade, and currently chairs the District Export Council of Northern California.

Serving the San Diego area is field representative Hugh Grigsby who was a senior trade finance officer with Bank of America for 18 years. Grigsby has been an officer and director of many international trade associations in the San Francisco Bay area, and is a former CEFO board member.

RESOURCES: A $4 million Export Finance Fund (EFF) is continuously appropriated to secure loan guarantees. Outstanding loan guarantees must not exceed four times the current value of the EFF, including accrued interest and fee income. After a special claim reserves accrual, a major portion of CEFO's net income is contributed to the current operational budget.

LOCATION: The main office is located in the State Office Building in Los Angeles. The Northern California regional office is situated in the World Trade Center in San Francisco. An experienced CEFO representative serves as a field loan officer in the San Diego area. The staff makes field trips to all key areas of the State and services have been expanded with the establishment of satellite offices throughout California.

PURPOSE: The purpose of the law is to make it easier for California's small- and medium-sized businesses to increase their export sales through financial and informational assistance. The program is designed to provide loan guarantees secured by the EFF to commercial lenders on behalf of exporters. CEFO also assists exporters in the utilization of existing state and federal programs, such as the Export-Import Bank of the U.S. (Eximbank) and the Foreign Credit Insurance Association (FCIA). Counselling is provided to assist exporters in qualifying for the most appropriate channel of financial support. In addition, general guidance is available to help make export transactions occur that otherwise would not materialize.

(*Continued*)

Figure 28-8. (*Continued*) Facts about the California Export Finance Program.

HOW THIS IS ACCOMPLISHED:

Financial Assistance—Through loan guarantees, CEFO can help exporters secure loans. Guaranteed loans must be used for export transactions, the majority of which must be California goods or services, exported by small- and medium-sized industrial, commercial, or agribusiness enterprises. CEFO guarantees may help finance the purchase of materials, services, and labor to prepare for the export sale. The guarantees may also secure loans to allow qualified California exporters to extend post-export payment terms to insured foreign buyers. Requests for guarantees may be initiated by the exporter or by the lending institution.

The maximum guarantee amount is $350,000 per export transaction. The maximum term for repayment of pre-export loans is 360 days. Repayment terms for individual post-export loans are limited to 180 days. Adequate collateral or security is required by CEFO to ensure full repayment of each loan. The guarantee fee usually equals one percent of the guaranteed amount, but may range from .5 to 1.5 percent, depending on the degree of risk. A non-refundable processing fee of $100, which will be applied to the guarantee fee, must accompany each eligible application.

The present financial programs are briefly described below:

CEFO Pre-shipment Exporter Risks Guarantee—Up to 85 percent of a working capital (pre-shipment) loan to an exporter is guaranteed by this program. A firm export order with some form of credit insurance or guarantee, *or* a letter of credit is required. CEFO must be satisfied that the transaction is credit worthy and that the exporter can fulfill the responsibilities leading to the export sale.

When working capital requirements exceed $411,000, the Small Business Administration (SBA) may co-guarantee with CEFO to allow for a loan of up to $822,000. The process will originate through CEFO. Upon receipt of the application from CEFO, SBA will then process its portion of the guarantee of a "fast track" basis, using the standard SBA procedures.

When appropriate, CEFO may also co-guarantee working capital loans with Eximbank or other appropriate organizations.

CEFO Post-shipment Exporter Risks Guarantee—To help the exporter extend terms to a foreign buyer for the purchase of California goods, this program guarantees up to 85 percent of post-shipment financing. CEFO's Post-shipment Guarantee is usually extended in conjunction with FCIA, private credit insurance, or an Eximbank guarantee. CEFO's

Figure 28-8. (*Continued*) Facts about the California Export Finance Program.

guarantee covers post-shipment risks pertaining to exporter performance not normally covered by Eximbank, FCIA, or private insurers.

When an exporter is shipping on open account and does not have a foreign credit insurance policy, CEFO may provide FCIA insurance through a state held umbrella policy. The exporter would need only to qualify the foreign buyer and pay the corresponding insurance premiums on the transaction.

CEFO Combination Exporter Risks Guarantee—This program applies when pre-shipment financing is required, but the nature of the transaction allows some post-shipment exposure through on-site inspection or extended use of the goods, prior to the buyer's obligation to pay. Otherwise, the guarantee conditions are similar to those stated for the Pre-shipment and Post-shipment Guarantees.

Informational Assistance

CEFO may avoid the need for financial guarantee assistance in a prospective export transaction through direct counselling of the exporter in structuring the particular transaction.

Some or all of the following steps are often appropriate to assist a prospective exporter:

a. a review of the export potential;

b. a study of the proposed transaction;

c. an examination and analysis of the company's financial presentation;

d. a determination of the most appropriate state or federal financial programs available, including those of CEFO; and,

e. assistance in sourcing potential private financial institutions, services and programs.

In addition to the above assistance, CEFO will offer other informational programs:

- Foreign country creditworthiness information to warn of economic or political conditions that may confront California exporters as they consider credit arrangements.

- Export finance seminars and meetings to disseminate information or finance opportunities on the many assistance programs available.

- A resource library of financial material and country information is available for exporter research and reference.

EF0-89-001 (10/89)   89   54618

Chicago:	20 North Clark Street, Ste. 910, Chicago, IL 60602 (312)641-1915
Houston:	Texas Commerce Tower 600 Travis, Ste. 2860 Houston, Texas 77002 (713)227-0987
Los Angeles:	222 N. Sepulveda Blvd., Ste. 1515, El Segundo, California 90245 (213)322-1152 (*This is the FCIA's only West Coast office*)
Miami:	World Trade Center 80 Southwest 8th Street Miami, Florida 33130 (305)372-8540 (*see Figures 28-9 and 28-10*)

The United States International Trade Commission

The Commission is a quasi-judicial, independent, and bipartisan agency established by Congress with broad investigative powers on matters of trade. In its role as an adjudicator, the Commission determines the extent of injury and the threat of injury by imports to United States industry. As the governments's think tank on trade, the Commission is a natural resource that gathers and analyzes trade data, information that is then provided to the President and Congress as part of the information on which United States trade policy is based. Perhaps the Commission's best known public role is the determination of domestic injury from dumped or subsidized imports. Its least known role? Investigative work in the areas of unfair trade practices in pharmaceuticals and a variety of integrated circuit technologies. Other investigations include alleged misappropriation of trade secrets, violations of the antitrust laws, passing off, and false advertising.

The role of the United States International Trade Commission is growing in importance and complexity. Some of its offices and their activities are:

1. Office of the Administrative Law Judges (Hears and decides unfair trade practice cases brought under section 337 of the Tariff Act of 1930)

2. Office of Congressional Liaison (Coordinates activities between the Commission and Congress and responds to inquiries from congressional offices)

FOREIGN CREDIT INSURANCE ASSOCIATION

APPLICATION FOR QUOTATION – EXPORT CREDIT INSURANCE

MULTIPLE BUYER COMPREHENSIVE INSURANCE POLICY

(All questions must be fully answered. If question is not applicable, please so indicate. Use continuation sheets as necessary)

THIS DOCUMENT WILL BE A MATERIAL BASIS OF THE INSURANCE IF QUOTATION IS MADE AND ACCEPTED, AND INFORMATION SUBMITTED WILL BE TREATED AS CONFIDENTIAL.

Date _____

1. Name and Address of the Applicant: _____

_____

2. Name and Address of Insurance Broker or Agent: _____

_____

3. Summary of background of the Applicant:
   Date established: _____ Years exporting on credit terms: _____

   Total number of employees engaged in international credit evaluations: _____

   Name of any parent, subsidiary or affiliate also engaged in exporting _____

_____

4. Additional Insureds: The following domestic subsidiaries and affiliates of the Applicant are to be considered as Additional Insureds named under the Policy and the figures and statistics herein include their total exports. Each Additional Insured must sign separate Certification to the Foreign Credit Insurance Association and to the Export-Import Bank of the United States.

Name	Address
_____	_____
_____	_____

5. Names and Address of the Applicant's principal banks _____

_____

6. Please attach to this form your most recent annual report or financial statement.

7. Name and title of individual responsible for export credit decisions

_____

   The following sources of credit information are normally used before approving a line of credit.

   a) Credit agency ☐   d) World Trade Directory Report ☐
   b) Commercial bank in the United States ☐   e) Trade references ☐
   c) Commercial bank in country of buyer ☐   f) Financial statements ☐

8. Products to be exported: _____
   (Please attach descriptive literature)

9. Type of buyers: _____
   (Indicate percent of total exports by buyer type, e.g. manufacturers, dealers or distributors, retailers, end-users, government departments or agencies, etc.)

10. Export Sales and Losses during the last 5 years. Please explain any unusual losses and any losses resulting from political causes. Describe steps taken to prevent recurrence:

	19___	19___	19___	19___	19___
Export Sales	$_____	$_____	$_____	$_____	$_____
Export Losses	$_____	$_____	$_____	$_____	$_____

11. Aging of Receivables (current and overdue) as of _____ (Date)
    Note: If any obligations have been rescheduled during the last 12 months, attach a separate sheet giving details. Also provide explanation of receivables past due for more than 180 days, including amounts collected to date, any security held and potential for recovery. Indicate whether this amount of overdues is normal ☐ or unusually large☐. If unusually large, describe steps taken to prevent recurrence.

$_____	$_____	$_____	$_____	$_____
Current	30 – 120 days Past Due	120 – 180 days Past Due	180 – 360 days Past Due	Over 360 days Past Due

Form FCIA 6-800 A (Rev. 6/73)

Figure 28-9. Application for quote—export credit insurance (FCIA).

FCIA

FOREIGN CREDIT INSURANCE ASSOCIATION

SUMMARY OF TOTAL EXPORT SALES SHORT TERM

FOR THE LAST TWELVE MONTHS (OR LAST CALENDAR YEAR)

(Please indicate any substantial variation in markets or terms anticipated during the next 12 months)

Unrelated Buyers ☐   Subsidiaries or Affiliates ☐   (Use separate sheet for each category)

———————————— Show figures in $ THOUSANDS – 000 omitted ————————————

| Country of Destination | Total Sales 12 Months | Unconfirmed L/C | | CAD or SD/DP | 30 days | 60 days | 90 days | 120 days | 150 days | 180 |
		Sight to 90	91 to 180 days							
	$	$	$	$	$	$	$	$	$	$
Short Term Totals										

(Use additional sheets as necessary)

Form FCIA 6–800A-1 (10/72)

Figure 28-10. Summary of total export sales short-term (12 months).

3. Office of the Secretary (Compiles and maintains the Commission's official records and receives petitions and briefs)

4. Office of the General Counsel (The Commission's principal legal advisor, responsible for litigation, input on investigations, and reports on proposed legislation)

5. Director of Operations (Supervise all substantive work of the Offices of Investigations, Industries, Economics, Tariff Affairs and Trade Agreements, Unfair Import Investigations, and Trade Remedy Assistance Office)

6. Office of Economics (Provides economic analyses to help the Commission investigate the effects of United States foreign trade on domestic production, employment, and consumption and to provide expert advice to Congress and the President on international economic issues)

7. Office of Industries (Provides technical and economic information and assessments of United States industries and merchandise trade)

8. Office of Investigations (Coordinates the Commission's countervailing duty, antidumping and review investigations, escape clause and market disruption investigations, and investigations under Section 22 of the Agricultural Adjustment Act)

9. Office of Tariff Affairs and Trade Agreements (Prepares reports on tariff legislation, publishes United States tariff schedule, chairs import-export statistical committee, and participates in Harmonized System Committee)

10. Trade Remedy Assistance Office (Provides information to the public on remedies and benefits available under United States trade laws and offers technical assistance to eligible small businesses seeking relief under the trade remedy laws)

11. Office of Unfair Import Investigations (Participates in all investigations conducted under section 337 of the Tariff Act of 1930)

12. Director of Administration (Supervises support services of the Commission, which include Library Services and the Offices of Finance and Budget, Management Services, Information Resources Management, and Personnel)

13. Office of Finance and Budget (Responsible for the budget, payroll, and accounting functions)

14. Office of Information Resources Management (Provides information services and resources through the ongoing activities of its three division: Computer Services, Statistical Services, and Applications Development)

15. Office of Management Services (Coordinates mail, supply, and building maintenance services and editorial, design, printing, and procurement functions)

16. Office of Personnel (Recruits, places, and trains employees and administers position classification, benefits, employee relations, and labor relations programs)

17. Library Services (Provides library services—other than law—through
    the National Library of International Trade)

The United States International Trade Commission plays an important
role in the structure that protects domestic manufacturers.

Although there is a higher level of credit risk in export sales than in
credit sales to domestic accounts, a good credit manager can lengthen the
odds against loss. It is his or her responsibility to ensure that no product
leaves the company's warehouse for shipment to a foreign customer until
the payment arrangement is satisfactory and the document is in hand (a
properly executed letter of credit, a sight draft, etc.), the documents package is complete and conforms to requirements for payment set forth in the
letter of credit, and the shipment is put aboard the designated ship or air
cargo line in plenty of time to arrive at the port of entry within the time
frame prescribed for delivery to the buyer/importer.

The credit manager/administrator is not off the hook until the documents package has been delivered to the issuing or the correspondent
bank, as prescribed in the instructions, and the letter of credit (or other
instrument) has been accepted and paid. It is a sequence of events that
demands of the credit manager/administrator a broad knowledge in the
area of export sales. If the person who has credit responsibility for foreign
accounts does not meet that criterion, the company's export program
could be the victim of some costly experiences.

29

Methods of Payment for International Credit Sales

The objective of this chapter is to familiarize readers with the various financial instruments—the payment options—that are available to pay for export credit sales. They are several in number and do not offer a uniform level of safety for the seller/exporter or a uniform level of attractiveness for the buyer/importer, but each has something that might be used to bring an otherwise stalemated situation into the category of a "done deal."

The federal government frequently gives the impression that it has few qualms when offering loans—frequently long-term and almost never secured—to nations and companies whose ability to repay at some future date is dim to nonexistent. Conversely, your company is a profit-making organization, which means that the credit decisions must be good—consistently good. Whether the federal government can ever be diverted into a path of fiscal responsibility is a major concern, but it is not a responsibility or the subject of this chapter. Protecting the assets of your company when it ventures into export sales is the subject, and a knowledge of which payment arrangements are or are not in the best interest of your company is imperative to the success of the company's effort in the international marketplace.

First-time foreign buyers will generally offer payment terms that are the most advantageous to themselves, but they should be negotiable. Your company is the one that will be at risk and if what is being offered does not provide the degree of security appropriate for the proposed transaction, the credit manager must so advise the person who is working with the buyer. That person must follow the credit manager's guideline suggestions for the one or two preferred methods for the buyer to pay for product(s). Because these payment options will be less favorable to the buyer than what the buyer has offered, there should be negotiations in which the credit manager will participate. This serves to draw any irritation on the buyer's part away from the person in export sales or administration and move it onto the credit manager.

When the credit manager becomes a visible participant in negotiations over a method of payment, he or she can react immediately to suggestions and fine-tune the exporting company's requirements to what is perceived to be the best the importer can offer. If the two are close, a sale can be consummated.

The Granting of Credit

When an exporter extends credit to a foreign buyer, the seller/exporter's primary concern is that the buyer/importer will pay for the goods within the time frame specified in their agreement. The exporter must do everything possible to avoid having all or part of the payment withheld or delayed because the carrier did not deliver the goods within the time frame specified in the letter of credit, the goods arrived on time, but were damaged in transit, the goods arrived on time and in good shape, but the government's monetary policy changed during the time the goods were in transit and the buyer refuses to authorize the release of dollars to pay for the goods, or the carrier supplied reliable transport to the border of the buyer's country, but the shipment disappeared between the port of entry and the province, area, or city in which the buyer is located. When any of the foregoing problems occur and the freight forwarder in the buyer's country is not a branch of the domestic forwarder, the exporter may be dealing with internal channels of transport that have little system, dependability, or responsibility.

A key indicator as to how conditions are within the importer's country is when the exporter applies for insurance to protect the shipment and no insurer will touch the risk. If the application is denied because the importer's country is on a list of high-risk or unstable areas and countries (unstable government, unstable monetary system, and a government that will not authorize the release of dollars to pay for products in your company's category), there is almost no chance that a deal can be cut between the exporter and importer. There is, however, the slim possibility that an agency of the United States Government might be able to help put together a guaranty of payment.

Exporters must be aware of the risks inherent in each type of payment process before they select one or before they allow the importer to talk them into accepting one that incorporates too many factors of risk. The following list of credit terms includes most of those worthy of an exporter's consideration, and even includes some that are unsatisfactory in virtually any export sale circumstance (see Figure 29-1).

1. *Cash in Advance:* A shipment that is prepaid by the buyer/importer offers the maximum amount of security for the seller/exporter. Most buyers will resist this form of payment, citing the financial burden that it places on them, the long period of time between prepayment and the arrival of the goods, etc. If, however, the exporter is unsure that any of the other terms of sale will provide an appropriate level of security, he or she must insist that the buyer prepay the shipment.
2. *Letter of Credit:* Letters of Credit come in three forms: Confirmed Irrevocable L/C, Unconfirmed Irrevocable L/C, and Revocable L/C.

   The least acceptable of the three options is the Revocable L/C. It is a form of payment that should not be entered into unless the conditions under which the L/C might be revoked are very narrow, are spelled out in the payment agreement, and leave no room for misinterpretation or abuse on the part of exporter or importer.

   An Unconfirmed Irrevocable L/C protects the exporter against what is referred to as the "commercial risk," a risk caused by the the insolvency of the buyer or the risk that the buyer might refuse to make payment after the goods have been shipped or are ready for shipment, thereby breaching the contract between exporter and importer.

   A Confirmed Irrevocable L/C is the best and safest of the category of Letters of Credit. It protects the exporter against risks previously mentioned plus the risk of a foreign government intervening to block the transfer of foreign exchange (in this example United States dollars) to

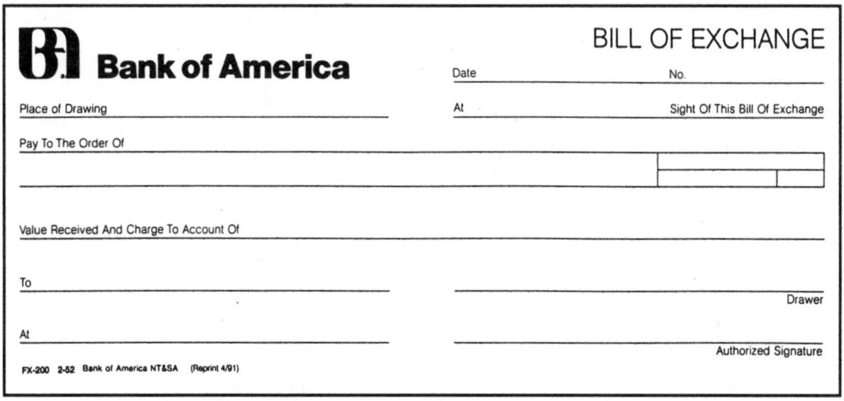
Bank of America
BILL OF EXCHANGE
Date No.
Place of Drawing
At Sight Of This Bill Of Exchange
Pay To The Order Of
Value Received And Charge To Account Of
To
Drawer
At
Authorized Signature
FX-200 2-52 Bank of America NT&SA (Reprint 4/91)

Figure 29-1. Bill of exchange (Bank of America).

the United States. Upon shipment of the goods, the exporter is able to obtain payment because he or she can negotiate drafts with the domestic bank.

3. *Sight Drafts (documents against payment):*   These include shipping documents such as commercial invoices, insurance certificates, bills of lading, and other documents that are attached to the draft as support documents and deposited for collection at the bank. The importer does not receive the documents, which are the title to the goods, until the draft has been paid.

4. *Time Draft (documents against acceptance):*   The procedure for collection is similar to the Sight Draft, except that the importer has a longer time frame in which to pay for the shipment. A draft is accepted when it is presented to the buyer and the word "accepted" is either stamped or written across the draft above the buyer's signature. This is the buyer's acknowledgment that the draft is acceptable and will be paid when due. When the importer accepts the draft, controlling documents for the shipment are released to the importer. The exporter does not receive payment before title passes, but the exporter receives the signed obligation of the importer, which is the acceptance.

5. *Clean Drafts:*   "Clean" in this context refers to the absence of any attached documents. A clean draft may be used to collect an outstanding balance for goods shipped previously. In some circumstances, it may be used to elevate the obligation to the written form which would have advantages in a formal collection effort or proceeding.

6. *Open Account:*   This can be an especially high-risk type of sale. There is agreement between exporter and importer as to when the first payment or the total amount of the obligation is payable, but the exporter loses all control of the situation when the shipment crosses the border of the importer's country. If the buyer defaults, it may be impossible to collect the money.

7. *Consignment:*   This is not a term of sale that is used in the normal course of export-import trade. It should be used exclusively to transfer goods or product between branches or subsidiaries of a company, but not when dealing with agents or importers unrelated to the exporting company.

Letters of Credit—Notification

The process of notification is used by banks to notify customers, other banks, and all parties involved in a transaction of its intentions and/or what it can and cannot do under the terms of the L/C, or under the Article of the Uniform Customs and Practice For Documentary Credits (1983 Revision), The International Chamber of Commerce Publication Number 400.

1. When a credit does not indicate whether it is revocable or irrevocable, it is deemed to be revocable.

2. A credit may be advised to a beneficiary through another bank (the advising bank) without engagement on the part of the advising bank, but that bank shall take reasonable care to check the apparent authenticity of the credit which it advises.

3. Revocable credits may be amended or cancelled by the issuing bank without prior notice to the beneficiary.

4. The issuing bank must reimburse a branch or bank when a revocable credit has been made available for sight payment, acceptance or negotiation, for any payment, etc., prior to receipt by it of notice of amendment or cancellation.

5. An irrevocable credit imposes definite obligations on the issuing bank, provided that the required documents are presented and the terms and conditions are complied with:

   The L/C provides for sight payment? Issuing bank pays.

   The L/C provides for deferred payment? Issuing bank pays or arranges to have payment made in accordance with payment date(s) stated in the credit.

   The L/C provides for acceptance? Issuing bank accepts drafts drawn by the beneficiary if credit stipulates they are to be drawn on the issuing bank, or to be responsible for their acceptance and payment at maturity if the credit stipulates they are to be drawn on the applicant for the credit of any other drawer stipulated in the credit (L/C).

   The L/C provides for negotiation? Issuing bank to pay without recourse to drawers and/or bona fide holders, draft(s) drawn by the beneficiary, at sight or at tenor, on the application for the credit or on any other drawee stipulated in the credit other than the issuing bank itself, or to provide for negotiation by another bank and to pay, as previously stated, if such negotiation is not effected.

   The L/Cs must clearly indicate whether they are available by sight payment, by deferred payment, by acceptance or by negotiation.

   The L/Cs must nominate (name) the paying bank to accept drafts (accepting bank) or to negotiate (negotiating bank), unless the credit allows negotiation by any bank (negotiating bank).

The act of an issuing bank nominating another bank to perform any or all of the functions and services enumerated in the preceding paragraphs does not relieve the issuing bank of the responsibility to reimburse the nominated bank(s) in accordance with the provisions of Articles under Uniform Customs and Practices For Documentary Credits (1983 Revision), The International Chamber of Commerce Publication Number 400.

(As mentioned earlier in this chapter, there are 55 Articles under Uniform Customs and Practices. What has been included in the preceding paragraphs illustrates the scope of the guideline material contained in Articles 7, 8, 9, 10, and 11.)

Liabilities and Responsibilities

Banks take on both liability and responsibility when they become involved with letters of credit: with L/Cs they issue themselves, with credits they did not issue, but to which they added their confirmation, and when they are called upon to pay letters of credit for other banks on the basis of documentation that appears to be authentic and correct but might be flawed, in error, or fraudulent. A few examples of those liabilities and responsibilities follow:

1. Banks must exercise reasonable care in examining all documents to determine whether they appear on their face to be in accordance with the terms and conditions of the credit. Documents which appear on their face to be inconsistent with each other will be considered as not appearing on their face in accordance with the terms and conditions of the credit.

2. If an authorized bank effects payment, incurs a deferred payment arrangement, etc., the party giving such authority is bound to reimburse the bank which has effected payment, incurred a deferred payment undertaking, etc.

3. If the issuing bank considers, after receiving the documents, that they appear not to be in accordance with the terms and conditions of the credit (L/C), the bank must determine, on the basis of the documents alone, whether to take up such documents (accept and pay them), or to refuse them and claim that they appear not to be in accordance with the terms and conditions of the credit.

4. Banks assume no liability or responsibility for the form, genuineness, etc. of any documents, or for the general or particular conditions stipulated in the documents or superimposed therein. They also do not assume any liability or responsibility for the description, weight, quality, condition, packing, delivery, etc., or for the good faith or acts and/or omissions, solvency, performance, or standing of the consignor, the carriers, the insurers of the goods, or any other party to the transaction.

5. Banks assume no liability or responsibility for the consequences arising out of delay and/or loss in transit of messages, letters or documents, or for delay, mutilation, or other errors arising in transmission or any telecommunication; they also assume no liability or responsibility for

errors in translation or interpretation of technical terms, and reserve the right to transmit credit terms without translating them.

(The preceding paragraphs are examples of what is contained in Articles 15 through 18 of Uniform Customs and Practice for Documentary Credits. It is intended to acquaint the reader with the contents of ICC's Publication Number 400 and to encourage any reader whose company is in export-import to obtain a copy of the publication.)

Documents

Instructions for issuance of L/Cs and/or amendments thereto must name the documents against which payment, acceptance, or negotiation is to be made.

Letters of credit should stipulate by whom transport documents, insurance documents, and commercial invoices shall be issued, and state their wording and content. Banks will accept documents that make it possible for them to relate goods or services referred to therein as those referred to in the commercial invoices presented, or to those referred to in the credit.

Insurance Documents

These documents must be stipulated in the letter of credit and must be issued and signed by insurance companies, underwriters, or their agent(s). Cover notes issued by insurance brokers are not acceptable unless specifically allowed by the credit (L/C).

Unless it is stipulated in the credit and addressed in the insurance document(s), banks will refuse insurance documents which bear a date later than the date of loading on board, dispatch, or taking control of goods as indicated by the transport document(s).

Credits must state the type of insurance required and whether additional risks are to be covered. Terms such as "usual risks" or "customary risks" are imprecise and should not be used.

When a letter of credit requires "insurance against all risks," banks will accept an insurance document with an "all risks" notation or endorsement.

Commercial Invoice(s)

Unless there is a stipulation in the credit to the contrary, commercial invoices are made out in the name of the credit applicant.

Banks may refuse invoices issued for amounts in excess of the amount of the credit unless it is otherwise noted in the credit.

Descriptions of goods in the commercial invoice must agree with the description in the letter of credit. When the goods are referred to in other documents, the reference may be in terms consistent with the description in the credit.

Certification of Weight

If goods will be transported other than by sea, the credit may call for the weight of the goods to be certified or attested (by signature, etc.). A weight stamp or a declaration of weight which appears to have been superimposed on the transport document by the carrier or agent is acceptable to banks. In some instances, however, the credit may require that certification or attestation must be done on a separate document.

Expiry Date—Letter(s) of Credit

The possibility that a letter of credit might expire before goods or services can be delivered to its destination, and the required documents assembled and presented for payment to the issuing or confirming bank, is one of the more nightmarish fears of exporters. Every exporter must monitor carefully the time frame for each of the stages in the proposed shipment to ensure that the time allotted to make the delivery, gather the documents, and present them for payment to the issuing or confirming bank is an adequate time frame—and incorporates an additional margin to cope with the unexpected.

The expiry date is the last date for presentation of documents for payment, acceptance, or negotiation. All documents must be presented to the issuing or confirming bank on or before that date.

What is the guideline when an issuing bank states that the credit is to run for a specific number of months, but does not specify the date from which the time period is to start? The starting date will be the date of issuance of the issuing bank.

An extension of the expiry date by the issuing bank does not extend the original date for loading goods on board, dispatch, or taking in charge. Banks will reject documents which indicate a date of issuance later than the expiry date stated in the attached credit or amendments.

Date Terms

Terms should be clearly understood between exporter and importer, and should be stated clearly and precisely in the credit itself.

When words such as "to," "until," and "till" are applied to any date term in the credit, it will include the date mentioned. The word "after" will exclude the date mentioned.

The terms "first-half" and "second-half" of the month shall be construed to mean respectively "1st to the 15th" and "16th to the last day of the month" inclusive.

The terms "beginning," "middle," or "end" of a month shall be construed respectively as from the 1st to the 10th, the 11th to the 20th, and the 21st to the last day of the month inclusive.

Transferable Credit

A credit is transferable when the credit gives the beneficiary the right to request the bank that will effect payment (or acceptance or negotiation) to make the credit available in whole or in part to one or more other parties (known as "second beneficiaries").

A credit must be designated as transferable by the issuing bank.

The transferring bank is not obligated to go beyond the limitations placed upon the credit by the issuing bank.

A transferable credit cannot be transferred more than once.

Unless specifically forbidden in the credit, the first beneficiary of a transferable credit may request that it be transferred to a second beneficiary in the same or another country.

Terms Applicable to the Shipment of Goods

ExShip: Seller must make the goods available to the buyer on board the ship at the destination named in the sales contract. The seller bears the full cost and risk of bringing the goods to the ship.

ExQuay: Seller makes the goods available to the buyer on the wharf (quay) at the destination named in the sales contract. The seller bears the full cost and risk of bringing goods to the ship.

Delivered at Frontier: Seller's obligations are fulfilled when the goods arrive at the frontier, but before "the customs border" of the country named in the sales contract.

Delivered Duty Paid: This term involves the seller's maximum obligation to the buyer. The seller must do all the work of clearing the goods for import. Value Added Tax (VAT) may or may not be excluded from this responsibility.

FOB Airport: This term differs from other uses of "FOB" in that the seller's responsibility terminates with the next word following FOB.

Free Carrier: The seller fulfills his obligation when the goods are delivered to the carrier at the designated point. "Carrier" covers every type of transport: rail, road, sea, air, or a combination of those modes of transport.

Freight Carriage Paid to: Seller pays the freight for the carriage of goods to the named destination. Responsibility for the goods passes from seller to buyer when the seller delivers to the first carrier and not at the ship's rail.

Freight Carriage and Insurance Paid to: Same as "Freight."

Miscellaneous Information— Letters of Credit

There are several pieces of information which are relevant to Letters of Credit, but which do not fit into any of the major subsections of the subject. Under this title and this subsection, they have found a home.

1. A "letter of credit" is a designated method of payment for goods or services.
2. A "standby letter of credit" is the name applied when it is used as a guarantee.
3. A "letter of credit" becomes payable when the person or company in whose favor the letter is drawn fulfills the terms of the letter.
4. A "standby letter of credit" does not become payable unless the party defaults.

A letter of credit is a document that has three contractual arrangements, each containing provisions that must be fulfilled as specified if the whole of the letter is to meet the requirements for payment. The beneficiary's money is riding on the premise of all parties to the three contractual arrangements fulfilling their obligations.

1. *Customer and the seller (beneficiary).* The beneficiary agrees to accept payment for goods, etc., under the letter of credit.
2. *Customer and the bank (issuer).* The bank issues a letter of credit and the customer promises to reimburse the bank (issuer) for the amount of the letter plus a fee and/or commission.
3. *Letter of credit and the bank.* The bank agrees to pay the letter of credit upon presentation by the beneficiary of the documents required for payment.

Third Party Attaches Beneficiaries' Interest

In the worst of scenarios for the beneficiary of a letter of credit, his or her interest is attached by a third party. The immediate question is, "Can the beneficiary's interest be attached, and if it can, what effect will the attachment have on the payment process?"

In the event of attachment, the beneficiary will receive the amount of the letter of credit less the amount of the attachment obtained by the third party. If the beneficiary does not have access to all of the funds, another problem could occur; it might be impossible for the beneficiary to complete shipments, etc. as required by the contract between himself/herself/a company and the customer. It could also be a major problem for the bank that confirmed the letter of credit. The confirming bank might not receive reimbursement if the beneficiary had been paid in full before the confirming bank received notice from the issuing bank that the letter of credit had been attached. How can the confirming bank be victimized for an attachment of which it had no knowledge? This is a controversial area and the object of mixed rulings regarding the legality of a third-party attachment of a beneficiary's interest. To this point, circumstances have been the factor that has weighed most heavily in decisions for or against the beneficiary.

A company, whose commitment to the highly specialized business of export trade is firm, must be constantly alert to the potential for collusion between buyers whose primary reason for existing is to funnel goods and products to areas and countries denied the right to those goods, products, or services by the United States Department of Commerce and other international regulatory authorities. Domestic exporters must be aware also of the potential for fraud and deceit in other areas, areas that not only fly against Department of Commerce rules and regulations, but would pose a high risk in the area of a timely and satisfactory payment arrangement.

Most international traders are reputable people and companies. They pay for their shipments as agreed, do not make frivolous or unreasonable claims, and are interested generally in developing strong ties to dependable sources of goods, products, or services. There are, however, enough buyers in the international marketplace who do not meet those criteria to turn the term "buyer beware" into "seller beware." Although it is the responsibility of the seller/exporter to get as much information about a prospective customer as the exporter's resources for acquiring information will permit, it is the Bureau of Export Administration's Office of Export Licensing that will scrutinize the would-be importer. When the application for an export license is forwarded by the exporting firm, the Office of Export Licensing will scrutinize the prospective buyer/importer and validate or reject the proposed sale.

There is no reason why a company, whose preparations for entering export trade have been sound, cannot be successful. It is well to remember, however, that conditions in many of the foreign countries can change dramatically and suddenly. You do not want your company to be exposed to financial risks that can be or should have been avoided. Negotiate payment arrangements from the position of a willing seller, but from the position of strength that a strong domestic sales base provides for your company. If your company is willing to take risks in the international marketplace that it would be unwilling to take in the domestic marketplace, there is some convoluted thinking that had better be promptly adjusted before the losses become excessive. Any attempt to utilize the court systems of many countries to force a customer to pay—or to force an extension of a letter of credit when (*a*) the customer has suffered no loss or damage and (*b*) events were beyond the control of the seller—is usually costly and unsuccessful. Add to the high costs of litigating a case in a foreign country (attorneys, depositions, company representatives, etc.) the cost of having the freight forwarder repackage the goods and return them to the United States, thereby incurring a second round of shipping costs.

Credit management people whose responsibilities include an overview of the export documents package must be familiar with or have access to rules and regulations put out by the Department of Commerce. If within your company there is no International Trade Services Department and the Export Department is one or two people, neither of whom is especially knowledgable, the credit manager or administrator must know enough about the total process of export to recognize the potential for violations, to recognize individual violations, and to take the steps necessary to avoid being in violation of rules and regulations published by the Bureau of Export Administration, Office of Export Licensing (Department of Commerce).

Any company whose interest in export sales motivates it to find a customer, then apply for a license to sell that customer, has assumed a serious responsibility. There are rules and regulations; ignorance of them is no excuse.

Licenses

Three types of export licenses are issued by the Office of Export Licensing (OEL), Bureau of Export Administration: General, Individual Validated, and Special Procedure. The Commerce Control List (CCL), known as the "core list," categorizes and assigns numbers to commodities and provides one of the key sources for determining which of the three types of licenses is applicable to a specific situation. Reports are forwarded to the Office of Export Licensing for processing, but are returned to the sender if required data (drawings, descriptive data, etc.) is omitted or the request has been prepared improperly (see Figure 29-2).

The categories and subcategories of licenses follow.

General Export License

These are licenses that certain companies are authorized to issue to themselves and generally do not require validation from the United States

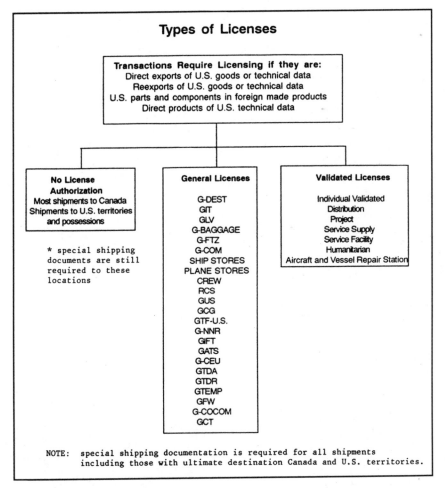

Figure 29-2. Types of licenses.

Government. If your company has permission to issue General Export Licenses to itself, it must first make sure that the commodity to be shipped and all of the specifics pertinent to that shipment fall within the parameters defined within the United States Export Regulations Manual.

IVL

IVLs are licenses that are approved individually in Washington, D.C. These licenses are usually approved by the United States Department of Commerce, Bureau of Export Administration, but may have to go to another department or even to the Committee for Multilateral Export

Controls (COCOM) for approval. This license can be obtained in as short a period of time as three days or as long as several months. The length of time depends on the product and the country of ultimate destination.

Each export controlled commodity has an assigned number. Each assigned number has certain parameters which are listed to advise you when making your application. To apply for IVL, you must always follow the procedures set forth in the Export Regulations Manual, and you must use both the product and order specifications. IVLs are:

- good for one customer only.
- acceptable for multiple shipments.
- valid for two years.
- good for a specific number of dollars.
- good for specific quantities.
- good for specific model numbers.
- must be amended in writing.

Special Procedure Export License

The Distribution License (DL) is in this category. It allows the license holder to make more than one shipment to more than one customer, and there is no limit to the dollar amount or the quantity. Products are listed by category and not by specific model number.

It usually takes approximately three months to collect the data and make out the application for a Special Procedure Export License, and another three months for the United States Government to approve it. Getting a DL is considered a privilege, and to maintain it requires a great deal of effort.

Distribution License Holder (DLH)

If your firm is a Distribution License Holder (DLH), it means that the Bureau of Export Administration (United States Department of Commerce) has licensed it to make multiple exports of eligible commodities, without restriction on quantity or value, under one license which is valid for four years. Your company's approved foreign consignees (FC) may re-export products among themselves or to other approved destinations under the license. These benefits enable the company to provide better service to its customers, giving it a competitive edge in the export business environment.

These benefits do not come without responsibilities. With the acceptance of benefits comes the agreement to comply with Export Administration Regulations (EAR), adopt an internal program of control to monitor the administration of the DL, and undergo periodic reviews by the Office of Export Licensing (OEL) to ensure that the procedure is applied properly. Reviews and review procedures are described in the United States Department of Commerce booklet titled "Distribution License—Systems Review." Familiarity with the procedure will enable your company to protect the national security and foreign policy interests of the United States while maintaining its eligibility to continue operating under this special license.

The Office of Export Licensing (OEL) evaluates firms that apply for a DL, checking carefully into the background of the business, whether business volume warrants a license, and whether the business has a solid record of compliance with United States export controls. It must also demonstrate the requisite technical expertise and adopt the controls necessary to ensure compliance with regulations governing the DL. Nothing is overlooked; nothing is taken for granted. The OEL grants licenses only to firms it considers reliable, but it continues to monitor the company's compliance with Export Administration Regulations (EAR). To ensure that each license holder meets the required levels of compliance, OEL conducts one- or two-day on-site reviews to monitor performance of DLH and FC. From these on-site reviews, the OEL is able to determine whether the licensed company has an adequate internal control system in place and functioning.

The OEL review process consists of four phases: notification, planning, site visit, and report of findings. The process of notification and review is outlined in the Bureau of Export Administration's booklet "Distribution License—Systems Review," and includes objectives the OEL feels are necessary to offer as liberal a marketing climate as considerations of national security will permit.

The Review Objectives

1. Evaluate the operation of the Internal Control Program (ICP).

2. Determine general attitudes within the firm, especially those of upper management regarding the importance of export controls.

3. Review corporate policies regarding compliance with export requirements and controls.

4. Examine the organization structure and delegation of responsibility for administering the export program.

The Site Visit

1. Check compliance with export control guidelines.
2. Check the training of personnel.
3. Check the effectiveness of record keeping.
4. Check distribution and verification of the Table of Denial orders and updates to the United States Export Administration Regulations.
5. Check the order processing system.
6. Check individual validated licenses.

Persons likely to be interviewed by two Export Compliance Specialists are:

1. Export Control Administrator
2. Export Control Administrator's Supervisor
3. Individuals involved in order processing
4. Individuals involved in shipping
5. Individuals who evaluate foreign consignees
6. Internal audit staff

Documents to Be Examined

1. Corporate and export activity organization charts
2. Export policies and procedures manuals
3. Job descriptions for individuals with export control responsibilities
4. Validated forms BXA-622, 685, and 6052P
5. Product technology matrix, if one is available
6. Applicable certificates (Swiss Blue Import, Yugoslavia End Use Certificates, etc.)
7. Table of Denial orders
8. Shipping documents, purchase orders, invoices, destination control statements
9. Internal audit or review programs

The Review Process

It is usually performed by two Export Compliance Specialists and follows a review process that entails:

1. Entrance conference to make introductions and to explain the purpose of the review
2. Interviews with key personnel
3. Examination of documents
4. Tests of selected export transactions

The Exit Interview

Reviewers will, at the completion of the review, discuss their preliminary findings with the Export Control Administrator and other key management personnel. Suggestions for improvement will be provided for areas where deficiencies were identified.

Report of Findings

Findings noted during the review will be documented, entered in the Department's file for the firm, and presented in a letter prepared and sent within 45 to 60 days of the review. The letter will also inform the company of recommended enhancements or mandatory corrective actions the business must make to improve its export controls. The letter may provide target dates for expected improvements and the name and telephone number of the reviewer who may be contacted for clarification and assistance.

The types of deficiencies will determine whether the firm will be required to respond to the letter.

The Internal Review of Export Controls

Distribution License Holders (DLH) must develop an Internal Control Program (ICP) to ensure that their export procedures are in compliance with requirements of the Distribution License and the Export Administration Regulations (EAR), section 773.3 (e)(1). Each DLH must also review its program periodically to:

- verify compliance with the DL and EAR.
- educate personnel regarding the necessity of proper controls.
- ensure that actual procedures reflect the written Internal Control Program (ICP).

These requirements apply regardless of the characteristics of the DL: product types, export destinations, or numbers of foreign consignees.

The EAR does not specify the control system that must be used by each firm. Instead, it provides elements that must be included in each firm's control system. Firms may adapt the general control elements described in the EAR to their own business environment.

There is no specified approach for the required reviews. Firms may tailor the Department of Commerce's general review approach to their own operations.

The Department of Commerce guidelines are not intended to be all-inclusive. Most firms will find it appropriate to supplement the Department's guidelines with some additional procedures. A well-rounded program of controls will ensure that necessary corrective actions are taken to assure full compliance with all applicable regulations.

Who Should Perform the Internal Review?

Reviewers should have objectivity, which means that they should not be involved in the day to day export process. Reviewers with no direct responsibility for export activities are less likely to ignore problems for the sake of convenience.

Reviewers with Objectivity

Persons who might meet the criteria of objectivity for reviewing the DLH are:

1. The Export Control Administrator's Supervisor

2. Corporate auditing personnel or legal counsel

3. Independent auditors or consultants

4. Other internal personnel with appropriate training

(The Export Control Administrator is likely to be sufficiently objective and knowledgeable enough to perform the reviews of Foreign Consignees [FC].)

Reviewers with Proper Qualifications

Reviewers should have the following knowledge or training:

1. Knowledge of the firm's products

2. Knowledge of the firm's export procedures

3. Thorough knowledge of the DL program and EAR, and the applicable restrictions

4. Good communication skills, both oral and written

5. Adequate authority to ensure acceptance of the findings and recommendations by upper management

Reviewers whose qualifications match these requirements should be able to analyze the procedures, evaluate the functioning of the controls, document the findings, develop feasible recommendations, and persuade upper management to make necessary changes.

When Should the Review Be Performed?

If monitoring of export activities is not adequate, there is danger that the Distribution License Holder (DLH) will overlook an Export Administration Regulations (EAR) violation. If a problem arises, the Department of Commerce will make its decision on the basis of frequency (and adequacy) of the reviews.

Internal Reviews

Distribution License Holders (DLH) who receive or ship large quantities of commodities under their DL should do a complete review annually of their export controls, and periodically spot check the functioning of key controls.

Review of Foreign Consignees

The guideline for determining the frequency of these reviews is the nature of the Distribution License Holder's activities and the characteristics of its Foreign Consignees (FCs). If exported products are very sophisticated or there is a high volume of business, a semiannual or annual review may be necessary. FCs that present little risk may need to be reviewed no more frequently than every other year.

Alternatives to On-Site Reviews by the DLH

1. A written agreement among DLHs having a common consignee that one DLH will conduct the review

2. A checklist completed by the FC and submitted for review to the DLH

(To ensure compliance with the DL procedure and the EAR, these alternatives should be discussed in advance with OEL.)

How to Conduct Internal Reviews

The DLH should develop a formal program that ensures a comprehensive review of its internal control procedures. Such a program would do the following:

1. Assure that the reviewers evaluate methodically all essential areas.
2. Provide a logical structure for presenting findings and considering corrective actions.
3. Allow management or the OEL to easily review and evaluate the review module.
4. Increase efficiency by eliminating the need to recreate the process each time a review is performed. (This program could also be adapted and used in reviewing FCs.)

What to Review

1. Corporate policy
2. Organization structure
3. Internal Control Manual
4. Training/knowledge of personnel
5. Licenses and related documents
6. Export transaction records
7. Order processing controls

Review Techniques

1. Read Internal Compliance Procedures (ICP) and other manuals
2. Interview personnel
3. Inspect documents
4. Observe or test actual procedures and compare them to written procedures
5. Analyze transactions
6. Identify deficiencies and required enhancements
7. Recommend corrective actions

Documenting the Review

Information obtained during the review should be separated into two categories:

1. Interviews acquired through interviews or the review of documentation
2. Information acquired through test procedures

(The DLH should maintain records for reviews already performed. Procedures must be established to report results and required follow-up actions to upper management, giving management a valuable tool plus a record of oversight activities.)

The Commerce Control List

The Bureau of Export Administration (BXA) maintains the Commerce Control List (CCL) which includes all items (commodities, software, and technical data) subject to BXA export controls. The CCL does not include those items controlled exclusively for export by another department or agency of the United States Government. For example, arms, ammunition, and implements of war are controlled by the Office of Defense Trade Controls, United States Department of State. Another subchapter of the Commerce Department's Federal Register lists exports controlled by other United States Government departments and agencies.

The CCL and related information are contained in supplements to part 799 of the Federal Register. Supplement Number 1 is the CCL. Supplement Number 2 includes the General Technology and Software Notes. Supplement Number 3 contains definitions, and Supplement Number 4 is a cross reference from pre-September 1, 1991 entries on the CCL to post-September 1, 1991 entries.

Structure of the CCL

Before a person can identify specific controls on a product, it is necessary for the person to understand how the CCL is structured.

The CCL is divided into 10 general categories with numbers from 1 to 0. The list follows:

1. Materials
2. Materials Processing
3. Electronics
4. Computers

 5. Telecommunications and Cryptography

 6. Sensors

 7. Avionics and Navigation

 8. Marine Technology

 9. Propulsion Systems and Transportation Equipment

10. Miscellaneous

There are five groups of products within each category which are identified by the letters *a* through *e* and follow this explanation:

a. Equipment, Assemblies, and Components

b. Production and Test Equipment

c. Materials

d. Software

e. Technology

Within each of the preceding five groups, paragraphs are numbered using a two-digit format. Although each set of digits represents a particular type of control, there may also be other controls that affect the same items. For example, a COCOM-controlled item may also be controlled for missile or foreign policy reasons. The basic paragraph numbering system is as follows:

01–19—COCOM Controls

20–39—Missile technology controls

40–59—Nuclear nonproliferation controls

60–79—Chemical and biological weapons controls

80–99—Other controls

The four-digit number will be followed by a code letter. This code letter is a key to the documentation requirements of part 775 of this subchapter, and is used by many exporters as a data processing code to indicate the country group level of control for CCL entries. The letters used and the respective letter country controls are as follows:

A—QSTVWYZ (COCOM)

B—QSTVWYZ (non-COCOM)

C—QSTVWYZ, except specified countries

D—QSTVWYZ and Canada

E—SZ, South African military and police, and countries
   listed in certain Supplements to the EAR

F—SZ, South African military and police, and certain other specified countries

G—SZ, South African military and police

H—Z, South African military and police

I—None

Export Control Classification Number (ECCN)

Using this numbering system leads to a five-character ECCN for each entry. For example, the first subparagraph in group A category 1 would have been an ECCN of 1A01A. When that entry is followed by a unilateral missile control entry, the ECCN would be 1A21B, and a related nuclear entry might be 1A41E. The next multilateral entry would be 1A02A.

The list is subdivided into a requirements list and a list of items that are controlled (see Figures 29-3 thru 29-9).

The requirements for each category tell why and where the ECCN is controlled, including the following:

Validated license requirements by country group and, at times, special country lists or individual destinations; by identifying the countries subject to validated license, this also tells the exporter when General License G-DEST is available

The unit of quality or value to use on the application for export license

Reason for Control

The following symbols are used to identify key reasons for control:

NS—National Security

MT—Missile Technology

NP—Nuclear Proliferation

CB—Chemical or Biological Warfare

FP—Other Foreign Policy Controls

SS—Short Supply

General Licenses

For commodities, there are descriptions of eligibility for General Licenses GCT, GFW, and GLV. For software and technical data, the descriptions of

The Commerce Control List

On September 1, 1991, the Bureau of Export Administration implemented the new Commerce Control List (CCL), which replaced the former Commodity Control List. The new CCL incorporates not only the national security controlled items agreed to by COCOM (commonly known as the "Core List"), but also items controlled for foreign policy and other reasons. The list adopts a totally new method of categorizing commodities, and for the first time includes all software and technology within the list.

Within the CCL, each type of item is given an Export Control Classification Number (formerly called the Export Control Commodity Number), which consists of a five character number including both digits and letters (e.g. 1A01A, 2B96G, etc.) For those of you familiar with the old CCL, BXA added Supplement 4 to Part 799.1 of the Export Administration Regulations (EAR), which gives a cross reference to the old and new numbering system. However, this supplement should be used with caution. The cross reference is only meant to be used as a general guide for re-classifying your commodity, and should not be relied upon as the sole guide to locating items on the new CCL.

In addition to the cross reference supplement mentioned above, two other supplements have been added to the new CCL. Supplement 2 to Part 799.1 contains the General Technology Note and the General Software Note, which are necessary to understanding certain technology and software entries on the CCL. Supplement 3 contains definitions of terms enclosed by quotation marks on the CCL. These definitions are no longer included in the individual entries.

Defining an ECCN

Using the Commerce Control List

You should refer to the Commerce Control List, Supplement No. 1 to Section 799.1 of the Regulations, to determine which Export Control Classification Number (ECCN) your product is controlled under. Every product has an Export Control Classification Number. To classify your item, you must review the product's technical specifications against the Commerce Control List.

Figure 29-3. Commerce department control list (defining an Export Control Classification Number [ECCN]).

First, identify which of the ten category groups your item falls within. Review the individual entries within that group to locate the proper ECCN for your product. The CCL is divided into 10 general categories, numbered 1 to 0, as follows:

Category Groups

Category Number	Category Groups
1	Materials
2	Materials Processing
3	Electronics
4	Computers
5	Telecommunications and Cryptography
6	Sensors
7	Avionics and Navigation
8	Marine Technology
9	Propulsion Systems and Transportation Equipment
0	Miscellaneous

Second, review the individual ECCNs under the category group to determine which entry your product is controlled under. Review all possible category groups that the product may fall under.

Each CCL entry is preceded by a five-digit Export Control Classification Number (ECCN).

Example ECCN

1A01A

Figure 29-4. Category groups (ECCN).

eligibility for general licenses are set forth as GTDR, which means General License GTDR with written assurance, and GTDU, which is used to indicate General License GTDR without written assurance. The General License indicators in the list of items controlled provide only information specific to each particular entry. It is the exporter's responsibility to read part 771 of this subchapter before making any shipment under a General License, to ensure that each export conforms to all country and item restrictions, as

The first digit relates to the **Category Number.**

1A01A

↑

The second digit relates to one of the 5 different **Product Groups.**

1A01A

↑

Product Groups

A	**Equipment, Assemblies, and Components**
B	**Production and Test Equipment**
C	**Materials**
D	**Software**
E	**Technology**

Figure 29-5. Product groups (ECCN).

The third and fourth digits relate to the **Level of Control.** Within each group, paragraphs are numbered using a two-digit format. Although each set of digits represents a particular type of control, there may also be other controls that affect the same items. For example, a COCOM controlled item may also be controlled for missile technology reasons. The basic paragraph numbering system is as follows:

1A01A

Level of Controls

Digits	Level of Control
01-19	COCOM Controlled
20-39	Missile Technology Controls
40-59	Nuclear Non-Proliferation Controls
60-79	Chemical and Biological Weapons Controls
80-99	Other Controls

Figure 29-6. Level of controls (ECCN).

well as other limits of the General License (see Figures 29-10 thru 29-13). It is important that the exporter knows what countries are eligible for General Licenses GLV, GFW, and GCT, and all other rules applicable to each general license before applying the entry-specific information to a given export. It is equally important to read part 779 of this subchapter and understand the limits of GTDR before exporting software or technology.

(The following is of special interest to companies contemplating an entrance into the world of export sales. The preceding information, and what follows, is from pages 42826, 42827, and 42828 of the Federal Register/Volume 56, Number 168/Thursday, August 29, 1991/Rules and Regulations—Part VI, Bureau of Export Administration, Department of Commerce—Revision of Commodity Control List; Interim Rules with Request for Comments.)

The fifth digit identifies the **Country Groups** to which a license is required as well as support documentation requirements as described in Section 775.1.

1A01<u>A</u>

↑

Code Letter	Destinations for which a Validated License is Required
A	QSTVWYZ (COCOM Controlled)
B	QSTVWYZ (non-COCOM Controlled)
C	QSTVWYZ, except specified countries
D	QSTVWYZ, and Canada
E	SZ, South African military and police and other countries listed in certain Supplements
F	SZ, South African military and police and certain other specified countries
G	SZ, South African military and police
H	Z, South African military and police
I	None

Figure 29-7. Country groups (ECCN).

Export Control Classification Requests—Identifying the Proper CCL Entry

The exporter must first attempt to identify which ECCN covers the commodity proposed for export. The general characteristics of the commodity, software, or technical data will usually guide the exporter to the appropriate category. Once the appropriate category is identified, the particular characteristics and functions of the item should be matched to a specific ECCN. The index to the CCL may also help to match the general descrip-

Composition of Each Export Control Classification Number

The previous information results in a five character ECCN. For example, the first subparagraph in Group A under Category 1 would have an ECCN of 1A01A. Before the list of commodities controlled under each ECCN, you will find the following information:

ECCN: Export Control Classification Number

Title: Description of Items covered by this particular entry.

Validated License Required: Lists which country groups and individual countries require a validated license. This information will help you determine if your commodity is eligible for general license G-DEST.

Unit: Indicates how an item is licensed, i.e. number, pounds dollar value, etc..

Reason for Control: Tells why the particular commodity is controlled. The following symbols are used.

NS	**National Security**
MT	**Missile Technology**
NP	**Nuclear Non-Proliferation**
CB	**Chemical or Biological Warfare**
FP	**Other Foreign Policy Controls**
SS	**Short Supply**

General Licenses: Indicates if the particular commodity is eligible for general license GCT, GFW, or GLV. For software and technology, two versions of the same general licenses may be applicable. GTDR means General License GTDR with written assurance, and GTDU is used to indicate General License GTDR without written assurance. Before you use any general license, however, you should consult Section 771 of the Export Administration Regulations.

Group W Favorable Consideration: Favorable consideration license processing applies to all exports of "A" level commodities to civil end-users in Country Group W, except those commodities specifically excluded by this paragraph.

Notes: Here you will find any additional restrictions or exemptions that apply.

Following the above "Requirements" section is a list of the specific items which are controlled under your particular ECCN.

Figure 29-8. Composition of ECCNs.

```
┌─────────────────────────────────────────────────────────────┐
│   ┌──────────────────────────────────────────────────┐      │
│   │      Summary of Core List Numbering Systems       │      │
│   └──────────────────────────────────────────────────┘      │
```

First Digit Indicates the Category

       1 - Materials
       2 - Materials Processing
       3 - Electronics
       4 - Computers
       5 - Telecommunications and Cryptography
       6 - Sensors
       7 - Avionics and Navigation
       8 - Marine Technology
       9 - Propulsion Systems and Transportation Equipment

Second Digit (first letter) Indicates the Type of Product

       A - Equipment, Assemblies, and Components
       B - Production and Test Equipment
       C - Materials
       D - Software
       E - Technology

Third and Fourth Digits Indicate Type of Controls

       01 - 19 COCOM controlled
       20 - 39 Missile technology controls
       40 - 59 Nuclear non-proliferation controls
       60 - 79 Chemical and biological weapons
       80 - 99 Other controls

Last Digit (letter) Indicates Level of Control

       A - QSTVWYZ (COCOM)
       B - QSTVWYZ (Non-COCOM)
       C - QSTVWYZ, except specified countries
       D - QSTVWYZ and Canada
       E - SZ, South African military and police and countries
           listed in certain Supplements to the EAR
       F - SZ, South African military and police and certain
           other specified countries
       G - SZ, South African military and police
       H - Z, South African military and police
       I - None

Figure 29-9. Summary of core number listing systems.

EXPORT LICENSE
GTDA
GENERAL LICENSE
TECHNICAL DATA
"AVAILABLE"

* TECHNICAL DATA THAT IS AVAILABLE TO THE GENERAL PUBLIC, UNRESTRICTED EXPORTS TO ANY DESTINATION

* INFORMATION HANDED OUT AT TRADE SHOWS

* EDUCATIONAL MATERIALS OR TECHNICAL INFORMATION AVAILABLE IN A PUBLIC LIBRARY.

* "FREE" AT NO COST TO THE RECIPIENT

* INFORMATION LEADING UP TO A SALE. THE INFORMATION CAN NOT SHOW HOW TO DESIGN, PRODUCE, CONFIGURE, MAINTAIN, OR OPERATE AN OTHERWISE LICENSABLE PRODUCT.

* FUNDAMENTAL RESEARCH THAT HAS BEEN PUBLISHED OR SHARED IN AN OPEN CONFERENCE.

* CATALOG COURSE MATERIALS THAT ARE AVAILABLE IN A COLLEGE BOOK STORE

* PATENTED ITEMS - AVAILABLE FOR REVIEW IN A PUBLIC PATENT OFFICE.

* ANYTHING DEEMED - PUBLIC DOMAIN

LOS 1/92

Figure 29-10. Export license General License Technical Data "Available" (GTDA).

GTDU
GENERAL LICENSE
TECHNICAL DATA
"UNRESTRICTED"
NO LETTER OF ASSURANCE
REQUIRED

* COMPANY BUSINESS DOCUMENTS NOT AVAILABLE TO THE GENERAL PUBLIC

* ACCOUNTING INFORMATION

* COMPANY CONFIDENTIAL MATERIAL - FINANCIAL, STATISTICAL, OR PERSONNEL (NON-TECHNICAL)

* PROPRIETARY TECHNICAL INFORMATION ABOUT THE COMPANY, OR ITS PRODUCTS THAT DOES NOT SHOW HOW TO DESIGN, PRODUCE, MAINTAIN OR OPERATE LICENSABLE PRODUCTS.

* MASS MARKETED SOFTWARE FOLLOWING THESE SPECI-FICATIONS:
  1) DESIGNED FOR NORMAL COMMERCIAL PRACTICE
  2) RELEASED FROM THE U.S. DEPARTMENT OF STATE FOR INTERNATIONAL DISTRIBUTION'
  3) OVER-THE-COUNTER PURCHASE IN MOST RETAIL COMPUTER SOFTWARE OUTLETS
  4) INSTALLATION BY THE USER WITHOUT TECHNICAL ASSISTANCE
  5) TELEPHONE SUPPORT IS PERMITTED

LOS 1/92

Figure 29-11. Export license General License Technical Data "Unrestricted" (GTDU)—no letter of assurance required.

GTDR
GENERAL LICENSE
TECHNICAL DATA
"RESTRICTED"
LETTER OF ASSURANCE
<u>REQUIRED</u>

* TECHNICAL DATA (INSTRUCTIONAL MATERIALS) SHOWING HOW TO OPERATE AND MAINTAIN LICENSABLE COMMODITIES. THE COMMERCE CONTROL LIST, IN THE U. S. EXPORT ADMINISTRATION REGULATIONS MANUAL, MUST SPECIFY USE OF THE GTDR, AS PERMISSABLE, UNDER THE COMMODITY NUMBER GOVERNING THE TRANSACTION.

  OPERATIONAL TECHNICAL DATA IS DEFINED AS EXPLICIT DATA IN SUCH FORMS AS MANUALS, INSTRUCTION SHEETS, BLUEPRINTS, OR SOFTWARE (INCLUDING OBJECT CODE).

* AN INDIVIDUAL VALIDATED LICENSE IS REQUIRED AND A GTDR CAN NOT BE USED FOR LICENSING TECHNICAL DATA TO ANY PROSCRIBED OR U. S. EMBARGOED DESTINATIONS.

* SEE THE SAMPLE GTDR IN THIS PACKET FOR PROSCRIBED DESTINATIONS, AT THE TIME OF THIS WRITING. THIS LIST WILL CHANGE FROM TIME TO TIME AND SHOULD BE ADJUSTED ACCORDINGLY

* SEE ATTACHED THE FULL EXPLANATION OF GTDR, ITS ADVANTAGES AND LIMITATIONS.

LOS 1/92

Figure 29-12. Export license General License Technical Data "Restricted" (GTDR)—letter of assurance required.

HOW TO USE A GENERAL LICENSE GTDA, GTDU, OR GTDR

* GTDA - WHEN YOU ARE SHIPPING SMALL QUANTITIES OF GTDA MATERIAL, YOU ARE NOT REQUIRED TO NOTIFY BTNA'S INTERNATIONAL TRADE SERVICES DEPARTMENT. JUST WRITE THE SYMBOL "GTDA" IN THE BOTTOM LEFT HAND CORNER OF THE ENVELOPE. THIS WILL ADVISE THE MAIL ROOM THAT THE CONTENTS OF THE ENVELOPE HAVE BEEN LICENSED UNDER GTDA.

* GTDU - WHEN SHIPPING SMALL QUANTITIES OF GTDU MATERIAL, YOU FOLLOW THE SAME INSTRUCTIONS AS LISTED IN GTDA, EXCEPT, USING THE "GTDU" SYMBOL .

* GTDR - RESTRICTED MATERIAL WILL ALWAYS REQUIRE ASSISTANCE FROM INTERNATIONAL TRADE SERVICES OR SOMEONE AUTHORIZED TO ACT IN THEIR STEAD. BEFORE ANY GTDR TRANSACTION CAN TAKE PLACE, THE RECIPIENT MUST SUBMIT A WRITTEN GTDR LETTER OF ASSURANCE TO THE SHIPPER. THE ORIGNIAL, OR A COPY, MUST BE SENT TO THE INTERNATIONAL TRADE SERVICES DEPARTMENT FOR PERMANENT RECORD. THE GTDR SYMBOL IS WRITTEN IN THE LOW LEFT HAND CORNER OF THE ENVELOPE.

NOTE: LARGER QUANTITIES OF TECHNICAL DATA OR GTDR TRANSACTIONS MAY REQUIRE ADDITIONAL DOCUMENTATION PLEASE CONTACT THE INTERNATIONAL TRADE SERVICES DEPARTMENT FOR ASSISTANCE WITH DOCUMENT PREPARATION AND SHIPPING.

los 1/92

Figure 29-13. How to use a general license GTDA, GTDU, or GTDR.

tion to a specific entry. All items subject to licensing jurisdiction are included in the CCL, either in a specific item listing or in any "other, n.e.s." entry at the end of each category. (The abbreviation "n.e.s." appearing in various CCL entries means "not elsewhere specified." If an item you intend to export appears to be covered by a CCL entry and the description carries the limitation "n.e.s.," you should not use the CCL entry until you determine whether another CCL entry covers specifically that item.)

BXA Classification Requests

The Bureau of Export Administration (BXA) will respond to properly submitted requests for verification of the proper ECCN within 10 working days after receipt of the request. To insure that the explanation will be acted upon expeditiously, it will be necessary for the requester to do the following:

1. The requester must submit a recommended classification for the item(s) and explain the reason for this classification. This explanation must contain an analysis of the classified item(s) in terms of the technical control parameters specified in the appropriate ECCN. If the requester cannot determine the appropriate classification, then the requester must explain the reason for failing to recommend an appropriate classification. This explanation should include an identification of ambiguities or deficiencies in the regulations that precluded making a classification.

2. The requester must attach descriptive literature, brochures, technical papers, or specifications that provide sufficient technical detail to enable BXA personnel to verify or correct the classification.

3. The item(s) to be classified must be clearly listed by model number in the request. No more than five items will be considered in a single request. Exceptions may be made on a case by case basis for several related products if the relationship between these products is satisfactorily substantiated and documented.

4. The request must be mailed to the following address: Bureau of Export Administration, P.O. Box 273, Washington, DC 20044.

5. Request(s) must be clearly marked at the top of the first page and on the lower left-hand corner of the envelope "Commerce Classification Request." Any request that omits essential information, or is otherwise incomplete, will be returned to the requester specifying the reasons for the return.

(The preceding pages—beginning with "The Commerce Control List"—contain verbatim excerpts from the Rules and Regulations [Federal Register] that must be followed by every exporter. To willfully or carelessly flaunt or violate these rules is to risk fines, possible criminal charges, and the loss of the export privilege.)

International Transactions

There are several questions that, when answered properly, help to acquaint the newcomer or the relative newcomer with a few of the basics of export trade. The questions that follow may seem overly simplistic to the person whose experience and knowledge is levels above this segment of material, but not every reader has been exposed to the complexities of sales to foreign markets. Here are a few basic building blocks:

What Is an Export?

An export is the transfer of information across international borders. This can include, but is not limited to, using the telephone or fax, placing equipment orders, speaking to a visitor from a foreign country, traveling to another country, mailing a document, etc. Contrary to the definition held by many, "export" is not limited to the transfer of goods across international borders.

The Proforma Invoice

A "Proforma Invoice" is issued to a customer as a formal quotation of a coming order. It spells out specific terms of sale and payment. It can be used by the customer to obtain an International Import Certificate, when one is required. It is used also as the instrument to set up the terms of a letter of credit. The "Proforma Invoice" includes the same terms that are in the contract. "Proforma Invoices" prepared for either of these reasons should be done only with approval from your International Trade Services Department or the person in charge of export.

Which Transactions Require Export Assistance and Licensing?

The answer is "All Transactions!" The United States Government controls the export and re-export of all United States origin technical data, software, hardware, technology, and information that is not classified as public domain. There are different types of licenses available for different circumstances. It is true, however, that all transactions involving United States origin technology require some type of export authority when shipping across international borders.

What Determines which Export License Should Be Used?

United States laws govern the transfer of all United States origin commodities (technical data, technology, software, firmware, and hardware) for the life of the product. There are many different types of export licenses. The license that is selected must fit the specific circumstances of the international business transaction.

Technical Information in the Public Domain

Technical information that is available at trade shows, public libraries, technical publications, and technical seminars to which the public is invited is considered "public domain." There are no licensing restrictions on the exporting of this type of information from the United States. Is your company shipping anything more than an envelope full of documents or brochures? Your company would be wise to have a "commercial shipping invoice" to cover the shipment (see Figure 29-14). The classification of material for entry into more than one country will vary slightly from one country to another. There may be taxes or duties that are applicable in the receiving country, a situation governed usually by the type or category of goods being moved into the country. It is good business practice to have a commercial shipping invoice provide details of any transaction and to establish the value of the shipment. This is true whether there is or is not to be a charge.

Shipping and Shipping Documentation

The type of shipping documentation needed for a specific shipment is determined by the terms of sale, terms of payment, other terms written into the contract, and government regulations applicable to all parties involved in the transaction. Because requirements vary from order to order, this will also explain how the order is to be shipped.

Every international transaction which carries a classification other than public domain requires at least one shipping document. If documents appropriate for the transaction are not prepared, it could result in a lost shipment, the assessment of incorrect duties or taxes, and the possibility of administrative or criminal penalties.

Figure 29-14. Technical data details.

```
┌─────────────────────────────────────────────────────────────────┐
│  ┌───────────────────────────────────────────────────────────┐   │
│  │                  TECHNICAL DATA DETAILS                    │   │
│  └───────────────────────────────────────────────────────────┘   │
│                                                                   │
│  A GTDR Letter of Assurance is a United States Government         │
│  requirement when certain types of technical data and software   │
│  are transferred from a United States entity to a non-United     │
│  States entity.  This transfer can occur not only through the    │
│  actual shipment of materials, from one party to another, but    │
│  when technical information is transferred verbally or visually,  │
│  by any means.  This transfer requires a written Letter of       │
│  Assurance from the recipient to the shipper before the          │
│  technical data transfer can be licensed for export under        │
│  "GTDR".                                                          │
│                                                                   │
│  The "GTDR" Letter of Assurance serves two purposes.  It is:     │
│                                                                   │
│       1) notification from the exporter to the recipient that    │
│       the technical data they are about to receive is            │
│       licensable, and controlled, by the United States           │
│       Government; and,                                            │
│                                                                   │
│       2) assurance from the recipient that they will follow U.S. │
│       Export Regulations with regard to this transfer, paying    │
│       special attention to proscribed countries.  The technical  │
│       data received will not be transferred, in any form, to     │
│       any other foreign entity, without obtaining the            │
│       appropriate U. S. Government authority.                     │
│                                                                   │
│  COMPANY BUSINESS INFORMATION, is a specific type of technical   │
│  data, that does not show how to design, maintain, manufacture,  │
│  or operate otherwise licensable commodities, does not require   │
│  a supporting Letter of Assurance.  However, this information    │
│  is not Public Domain and is transferred under export license   │
│  "GTDU".                                                          │
│                                                                   │
│  PUBLIC DOMAIN Technical data, readily available to the general  │
│  public through public libraries, university libraries, trade    │
│  journals, technical magazines/publications, open public         │
│  classrooms, trade shows, patent offices, etc.  This type of     │
│  technical data is transferred under export license "GTDA" and   │
│  no supporting documents are required from the recipient.        │
│                                                                   │
│  How to Use the Symbol "GTDA", "GTDU", or "GTDR" to license      │
│  export of technical data.  The licensing method should be       │
│  specific to the terms of the technical transfer as defined      │
│  above.                                                           │
│                                                                   │
│  Verbal and Visual transfers of technical data, without written  │
│  documentation that the transaction has taken place, does not    │
│  relieve the exporter from licensing the transaction.  We should │
│  keep personal notes on technical data transfers regarding what  │
│  was transferred, how, to whom, and when the transfer took       │
│  place.  This is good practical business sense.                  │
│                                                                   │
└─────────────────────────────────────────────────────────────────┘
```

Export Import Agents

Your company's International Trade Services Department should select an agent or agents with the experience and qualifications to be effective in the company's geographic area of interest. When the consignee expresses a preference for another agent, have the consignee furnish the name and complete address. You might have arranged for better shipping rates with another agent, but you do as the customer asks.

Figure 29-14. (*Continued*) Technical data details.

Technical Data Details Continued(2)

Shipping technical data material: The appropriate symbol should be written on the lower left hand corner of the envelope, or shipping container. The appropriate symbol should also be indicated on all shipping documents and invoices used in the transaction. Anyone can use these symbols, and license their exports, as long as you are only transferring small amounts of qualified technical data (such as: 10 brochures or one computer tab run of information, etc.). You should request assistance from the BT North America Inc, International Trade Services Department, when you are shipping anything in a box. Although technical data may not require additional assistance for reasons of licensing restrictions, larger quantities of technical data may require additional export documentation to ensure it reaches its destination the fastest most economical way, without being delayed in customs. The International Trade Services Department specializes in shipping and export documentation to all parts of the world. We will be happy to assist you. Documentation requests require a forty-eight hour lead time. The exception being to supply documents in less time for emergencies.

<u>Submit GTDR Letters of Assurance</u>, as required, to the shipper or person transferring the technical data, prior to the actual transaction. GTDR Letters of Assurance should be collected from:

    1) Other BT Offices and Employees outside the U.S. Although BT Offices are covered under a general statement, made at the time BT acquired the U. S. business, the International Trade Services Department is responsible to collect GTDR Assurances, and raise the level of awareness, from all offices and individual employees that are receiving technical data, by direct shipment or through special training.

    2) Beginning January 1991, all BT North America Inc employees were required to sign a GTDR Letter of Assurance. Each "new" employee is require to sign one during employee orientation. The Letter of Assurance is held, in the employees personnel file, in Human Resources. BT North America is required to notify each employee of its export policies and procedures to support one of its special licensing privileges authorized by the United States Government.

    3) A GTDR Letter of Assurance should be obtained prior to any technical conversations outside "Public Domain" information. Due to the type of business we are in technical information is passed freely by telephone, demonstration, etc. One customer may communicate with several BT employees from different parts of the world, one GTDR Letter of Assurance will license all of the communications. We need to make sure BT Corporation is fully

---

(*Continued*)

Distribution License for Export

A United States validated Distribution License for Export brings with it a special mix of advantages and responsibilities. The goal of compliance with guideline regulations is the primary responsibility of the United States exporter, but it must be the guideline also for the consignee.

The United States Exporter must do and manage the following:

Figure 29-14. (*Continued*) Technical data details.

---

protected for transfer of all information that could be deemed
licensable.

Technical Data Details(3)

---

4)   Non-U.S. citizens visiting BT facilities that will receive
BT demonstration involving U. S. technology, factory tour, or
participating in technical discussions must sign a GTDR Letter of
Assurance.   This usually takes place at the BT North America Inc
reception desk with little inconvenience to the visitor.

5)   Individuals receiving detailed product training will be ask
to sign individual GTDR Letters of Assurance.

SPECIAL NOTE: Foreign nationals from proscribed countries (listed on
the GTDR Letter of Assurance) are not permitted to receive technical
data of U. S. origin under the GTDR License.   Additional authority is
required from the United States Department of Commerce prior to any
transfer of technical data, including visits to a U. S. facility owned
by BT North America Inc.   Please contact Linda Smith, Manager
International Trade Services, BT North America Inc, telephone: 408-
922-6073,   or Rita Gormley, Supervisor Export, telephone: 408-922-
7156, for guidance on <u>potential visitors</u>, employees, students, or
shipments.   A licensing authority must be received from the United
States Department of Commerce prior to any transaction.

<u>RESPONSIBLE TO OBTAIN GTDR LETTERS OF ASSURANCE:</u>   Technical data
transfers can take place in many different forms, therefore, there are
various individuals and departments responsible for collecting the
GTDR Letter of Assurance.

1)   The Human Resources Department will collect the Letter of
Assurance from BT North America Inc employees and contractors.

2)   BT North America Inc, Security Department is responsible to
provide and instruct each reception desk for outside visitors.
The visitors log will have the GTDR Letter of Assurance in the
right hand corner.   When a visitor signs in on the log, the
receptionist will point out the GTDR statement and provide the
visitor with a copy of the statement, for their reference.

3)   Technical training instructors are responsible to collect
Individual GTDR Letters of Assurance from each non-U.S. student
participating in the training course.

4)   Each BT salesperson that is providing U. S. technical
information, to a customer, is responsible to inform the customer
that the technical data is controlled by the U. S. Government.
If the customer is a non-U.S. citizen, the salesperson must
collect a GTDR Letter of Assurance and forward it to the export
person responsible for the region.

---

1. Manage the Distribution License for Export within defined parameters

2. Serve as liaison between the exporter's consignees and the United States Government

3. Initiate and implement an export program

4. Provide the training necessary to conduct the type of business authorized by the Distribution License

The Consignee must do and be aware of the following:

1. Know the customers, know who the end-user will be (if it is not the customer), and take whatever additional measures may be necessary to ensure compliance with guidelines imposed by the Department of Commerce's Bureau of Export Administration (BXA)

2. Provide customer information and screens to the distribution license holder
   a. Table of Denial orders
   b. High-risk diversion
   c. Nuclear end-use
   d. GTDR Letter of Assurance

3. Initiate and implement an export program

4. Monitor customer activities

Distribution License Advantages

The advantages that a Distribution License can give to an exporter are several and important. When used properly, they offer a competitive advantage that is difficult to offset.

1. *Immediate Delivery:* There is no waiting for an export license. It is already available for shipments to most free-world countries.

2. *Temporary Exports:* With the assistance of an ATA Carnet, shipments can be made in and out of free-world countries temporarily without paying duty.

3. *Drop Shipments:* With permission, it allows a seller to use the license for drop shipments to approved customers.

4. *No Limit to Quantity or Dollar Amounts:* With individual export licenses there is a fixed dollar amount. There is no fixed amount of dollars or quantity on the Distribution License.

5. *Third-Party Sourcing:* The seller is not restricted to shipping only the products manufactured by the seller. It is possible for the seller to buy products from another source to operate a system.

The disadvantages that a Distribution License brings to a company or business have importance, but they are greatly overshadowed by the advantages. Nothing in export should be considered to be of small or limited consequence, but the advantages are overwhelming and obvious.

1. *More Paperwork:* There is much more work involved when exporting is done under a Distribution License.

2. *Screens and Checklist:* High-risk Diversion Profile Nuclear End-Use Screen; Table of Denial Orders; Product country matrix; GTDR Letter of Assurance

3. *Approved Export Customer List:* The seller should devise a system to limit the duplications of screens. When a customer has passed all of the screens and checklists, the name should be listed on an "Approved List of Export Customers." If the company has international business units, the list is then distributed to them.

If a customer fails to pass the screen, it does not mean the seller cannot export to that customer; it means that the seller cannot use the Distribution License to export to the customer. The situation would demand that an Individual Validated License should be used instead of the Distribution License.

The United States Government's "Love Rule"

It may come as a shock to business people who have had less than pleasant contact with various government agencies to learn that in the area of Export, the United States Government's "love rule" lasts from now to forever. That's correct—*forever!*

1. All products and technology of United States origin are governed by United States laws as well as the laws of the receiving country.

2. No matter how many times a product is sold, the United States Government claims rights *forever.*

3. Re-exports from one country to another are governed by the laws of the United States Government, the re-exporting country, and the receiving country.

Illegal Exports

There have been times, particularly in the high-tech industries, when manufacturers have felt that the Office of Export Enforcement of the Department of Commerce's Bureau of Export Administration has been too restrictive. Manufacturers of mainframe computers, laser beam products and technology, and various other "dual use" products or technologies have been outspoken in their opposition to some of the restraints that have been imposed. Some of the comments may have been justified, some may not.

The Department of Commerce solicits the participation of exporters in the effort to identify customers who might plan to redirect illegal shipments of controlled products to terrorist nations or other proscribed destinations. The following are some possible indicators that an illegal diversion is being planned by a customer:

1. The customer or purchasing agent is reluctant to offer information about the end use of a product.

2. The product's capabilities do not fit the buyer's line of business; for example, an order for several sophisticated computers for a small bakery.

3. The product ordered is incompatible with the technical level of the country to which the product is being shipped. Semiconductor manufacturing equipment would be of little use in a country without an electronics industry.

4. The customer is willing to pay cash for a very expensive item when the terms of the sale call for financing.

5. The customer has little or no business background.

6. The customer is unfamiliar with the product's performance characteristics, but still wants the product.

7. Routine installation, training, or maintenance services are declined by the customer.

8. Delivery dates are vague, or deliveries are planned for out of the way destinations.

9. A freight forwarding firm is listed as the product's final destination.

10. The shipping route is abnormal for the product and destination.

11. Packaging is inconsistent with the stated method of shipment or destination.

12. When questioned, the buyer is evasive and especially, unclear about whether the purchased product is for domestic use, export, or re-export.

(Example: Government agents can point to a long string of arrests of individuals and companies on charges of illegally diverting equipment with potential nuclear and missile uses to Iran, Iraq, Syria, and other countries. The owner and operations manager of a California computer consulting company were recently arrested for allegedly diverting to Iran portable oscilloscopes, which measure and analyze electrical impulses and can be used in missile guidance systems. Federal law requires exporters of these types of equipment to obtain licenses from the Commerce Department before they can ship high-tech items to Iran and various other countries.)

Coordinating Committee (COCOM) Member Countries

An informal agreement was readied in 1950 between 17 western industrial nations to control the export of strategic products and technical data to the eastern bloc and the People's Republic of China. The policy body is called the Consultive Group and the working body is called the Coordinating Committee (COCOM). Day to day responsibilities of COCOM include reviewing items to be included in the International List of embargoed items, as well as reviewing specific transactions proposed by member countries for exception to the embargo.

The 17 COCOM member countries are:

United States	Italy	Japan
United Kingdom	Australia	Luxembourg
Belgium	Netherlands	Canada
Norway	Denmark	Portugal
Germany	Spain	France
Greece	Turkey	

COCOM has agreed to a total revision of the International Industrial List, which describes the dual-use items subject to COCOM control. As a result of this agreement, the Bureau of Export Administration (BXA) is publishing an entirely new Commerce Control List (CCL), which will replace the former Commodity Control List. (Products with the potential for dual use include nuclear material used to generate power or make bombs for nuclear warfare, super computers used to control business activities missiles during warfare, germs to make vaccines to improve health conditions and prolong life for humans and animals used in biological warfare.

The new COCOM list, commonly known as the "core list," adopts a totally new method of categorizing commodities, and for the first time it includes all software and technology. Because the list has used the COCOM numbering system as a base, the extensive change in the Industrial List has required the Bureau of Export Administration (BXA) to develop a totally new Commerce Control list (CCL). This rule describes the new format and sets forth the complete new CCL and related information. The BXA maintains the CCL, which includes all items (commodities, software, and technical data) subject to BXA export controls. The CCL does not include those items exclusively controlled for export by another department or agency of the United States Government. For example, arms, ammunition, and implements of war are controlled by the Office of Defense Trade

Controls, United States Department of State. Other exports are controlled by other United States Government departments and agencies.

The new CCL will benefit exporters because it removes national security controls on many items, allowing exports without the previously required validated export licenses. The rule became effective September 1, 1991 and will be monitored by the COCOM to ensure that it is both effective and equitable.

30
Coexisting with the Bureaucracy

Much negative comment has over the years been heaped upon the heads of policy-makers at the Department of Commerce. High-tech industries have been especially caustic in their comments regarding the Department's hard-nosed approach to classifying computer and other dual-purpose technology to make it unavailable to countries and areas that were formerly communist-dominated. The Department's attitude has remained consistent from the early beginnings of the high-tech industries to the present date, yielding only recently some minor adjustments and some slight relaxation of controls that have prevailed through the belligerent years of communism to and through the present date.

The Berlin Wall is down, European countries are trying to understand and apply the mechanics of democracy, and the USSR has become an unexpected example of a badly split personality. Has this breaking up of communist states caused the Department of Commerce to revise some of its regulations in favor of encouraging the sale of high-technology products, goods, and services? It has indeed. National security control has been removed on many of the Commerce Control List items, allowing export of those items without the previously required validated export licenses. That is not to say, however, that the Department of Commerce has loosened the reins to the point where it has a bandwagon approach to these changes.

Until stable governments have been established, high-tech and other companies will have great difficulty selling their products in many of these countries, and, quite unexpectedly, the damper on sales may not come from the Department of Commerce. The problem for those who would try to establish export trade with former communist countries and businesses in those countries is the sorry state of their financial condition. None of them has an internationally acceptable money system and there is no supply of dollars, marks, pounds, or francs that might be used to fund letters of credit or other instruments of payment. Export administrators and credit managers have no common monetary basis upon which to establish and fund a trade relationship and, until there is some discernible level of monetary stability within the various countries, the potential for selling large quantities of product will remain largely unfulfilled.

The Role of the Credit Department

Companies of moderate to large size whose percentage of international sales is high enough to be a significant part of the annual sales total usually have adequate depth in their International Trade Services Department, depth in numbers and knowledge. Credit managers and administrators in these companies should not have to concern themselves with the integrity of an export documents package. The credit department's involvement should be limited to approving an order, establishing the method of payment (letter of credit, etc.), and monitoring the presentation for payment (with required documents of delivery) of the letter of credit.

In the smaller companies, there is a much closer working relationship between Credit and the International Trade Services Department; there may, in fact, be no such department. Credit Department responsibilities include the approval of individual sales and approval of the payment process (as in larger companies), but in smaller companies the Credit Department may have active overview responsibility to ensure that the export package (documents, contents of letter of credit, shipping and arrival/delivery dates, etc.) is in compliance with the customer's instructions.

When a shipment of goods is turned over to a freight forwarder and is subsequently delivered to the customer, there is, in many countries, very little that a credit manager or administrator can do to retrieve the goods. If the customer is unhappy and uncooperative, the seller has a real problem.

Uniform Customs and Practice for Documentary Credits

The International Chamber of Commerce (ICC) wrote the first edition of the Uniform Customs and Practice for Documentary Credits in 1933. Since that date there have been many dramatic changes in the way international trading is conducted, but the UCP (Uniform Customs and Practices) is used by an ever increasing number of banks and company executives who must know what to use each day, and how to use it.

Sellers need to know now, as they did 59 years ago, that they are going to be paid for goods they release for overseas shipment. The creditworthiness of an overseas account is of primary importance in such a transaction, so it is the bankers who play the key role in allowing these transactions to take place. Bankers assure their customer that they will pay against presentation of documents and when there has been compliance with the buyer's conditions. These transactions could not be made to work as effectively as they do if it were not for documentary credits.

The periodic changing and upgrading of the UCP has kept them contemporary with the needs and requirements of the international trading community. International trade has proliferated to the point where something new and meaningful is occurring with alarming frequency; the frequency and magnitude of the changes within countries and regions of the world offers international traders wonderful opportunities, but little peace of mind, were it not for organizations such as the International Chamber of Commerce and its Uniform Customs and Practice for Documentary Credits.

The International Chamber of Commerce works to promote more freedom of trade between countries, to bring business and trade practices within common parameters, and to represent the business communities of all member countries at international levels. It offers, through Uniform Customs and Practice (UCP), guidelines prepared by the ICC's Commission on Banking Technique and Practice. Although the ICC's 43-page booklet costs an eyebrow-raising $11.95 ($8.95 plus a $3.00 shipping charge), it is the only source for the specialized (and copyrighted) material covered in its 55 articles.

Adhering to the copyright reservations, it is still possible to mention some of the major topics: Articles 1 thru 6 give an overview of general provisions and definitions of the material to follow; Articles 7 thru 14 describe the form, notification, and processing of letters of credit; Articles 15 thru 21 examine the bank's liabilities and responsibilities as they relate to a transaction; Articles 22 thru 42 examine the various types of documents that are involved, from the initial instructions for the issuance of credits through the documents involved in invoicing, insuring, certification(s), transporting, etc.; Articles 43 thru 53 pick up on important items not included in any of the preceding Articles, such as expiry date and presentation of letters of credit, partial shipments, quantity and/or amount, etc.; Articles 54 and 55 cover the transfer of a credit and the right of a beneficiary to assign proceeds.

The following list includes some other services offered by ICC to the International Business Community:

1. *The ICC Court of Arbitration* (It is recognized as the leading body in international commercial arbitration. Founded in 1923, it has a well-deserved reputation in the community of international trade for impartiality in its

decisions and judgments. An average activity year for the Court of Arbitration will total more than 250 new cases and involve parties in 80 or more countries. Arbitration hearings are held throughout the world and conducted under the ICC's Rules of Arbitration. This brings to the Court an immediacy in presence and actions that have been rewarded with the recognition of integrity and sound judgment in all arbitrations.)

2. *International Centre for Technical Expertise* (The purpose of the Centre is to offer parties involved in international contracts the possibility of recourse to independent experts.)

3. *Standing Committee for the Regulation of Contractual Relations* (At first reading, the title seems to employ an excessive number of words, but when gauged against the Committee's objective—to offer facilities for nomination of independent experts qualified to adjust a contract— every word seems to have a purpose.)

4. *ICC/CMI International Maritime Arbitration Organization* (The purpose of this organization is to administer rules prepared specifically for the needs of the maritime transport sector.)

5. *Institute of International Business Law and Practice* (The Institute is active in organizing seminars on international commercial arbitration and other subjects that have their roots in Business Law and Practice. The Institute also conducts research projects into the background of legal judgments pertaining to international trade usages, arbitration and state enterprises, etc.)

6. *International Maritime Bureau* (The Bureau was formed in 1981 to aid in countering the problem of maritime fraud. Member companies and organizations may obtain information and advice about trading partners, specific ports, and other questions relative to the concerns of shippers. It also undertakes investigations, negotiations, authentication of documents, monitoring of ships, and other services.) For specific information, including costs, address inquiries to the following address:

> The Director
> International Maritime Bureau
> Maritime House, 1 Linton Road
> Barking, Essex 1G118HG, United Kingdom
> Tel: 01-591 3000 - Telex: 8956492 IMB LDNG
> Cables Marbureau Barking

7. *ATA Carnets* (These are international Customs documents which enable travellers to take value goods across national boundaries for short periods of time, as in exhibitors at trade fairs, samples, etc.) Carnets enable business travellers to take their items of value into a country for a short period

without paying duty taxes or experiencing problems or delays with customs. Carnets are issued through a 40-country guarantee chain that was organized by the ICC's International Bureau of Chambers of Commerce.

The ICC offers several publications pertaining to letters of credit which expand on information contained in the booklet Uniform Customs and Practice for Documentary Credits. The charge for publications of interest may be ascertained at the time inquiry is made regarding availability.

1. *Case Studies on Documentary Credits* (Publication Numbers 459–166—case studies and problems/answers unique to letter of credit transactions)

2. *Documentary Credits:* UCP 1974/1983 Revisions, Compared and Explained (Publication Number 411—detailed comparative study on the 1974/1983 revisions with explanation of changes and the necessity for them)

3. *Guide to Documentary Credit Operations* (Publication Number 415—commercial transactions explained with visual material from the points of view of buyer and seller)

4. *Standard Documentary Credit Forms* (Publication Number 416—model forms and guidance notes of aid to applicants in the issuance of documentary credits)

5. *Standard Form and Guidance Notes for Credit Applicants* (Publication Number 416A—designed to assist applicants in the issuance of documentary credits)

These publications will help an individual or a company learn more about the various forms of letters of credit.

Agency assistance (government or other) is available to companies interested in becoming exporters of goods or products to every area of the world where such shipments are permitted. Whether the assistance is needed for a specific area or as a global effort to target prospective customers for your company's product(s), is needed for agency financing to supplement the resources of your own company to finance its effort to become active, or more active, in export trade or is just a call for specific or general information, agency help is available for those who go after it.

31

The Necessary Shipping Documents

A package of shipping documents that has been properly prepared is essential to acceptance of the shipment at the port of entry of the buyer's country, to arrival at the "ship to" address within that country, and to subsequent processing of the instrument of payment (letter of credit, bill of exchange, sight draft, etc.). Does the documents package not conform to the customs requirements of the importer's country? There is a dual possibility: the shipment will be held in customs beyond delivery date while the exporter and/or the exporter's representative tries to satisfy the requirements of customs *or* the shipment will be rejected at the port of entry and returned to the exporter/shipper. A sale has been lost, two-way freight and other expenses incurred, and an exporter/importer relationship damaged or destroyed.

Export and shipping documents carry the weight of the entire transaction on their several pages and if one or more of the documents contains errors or deviations from the format prescribed by the United States Department of Commerce, United States Customs, or the counterpart agencies of the buyer's country, the probability that it will become a long and well-remembered shipment will loom larger and larger. Too many companies are sending and receiving too many shipments for export and import authorities to devote an unusual amount of time to the problem(s) of any one shipment. Every exporter is expected to be familiar with what is required by the Department of Commerce and the Customs Authorities of both (or more than two) countries. Exporters or their representatives are expected to adhere to the rules and requirements set forth by each of these control centers.

The Export License

An application for an export license is the first step a company must take after it has received a firm order for products/goods/commodities (synonymous terms in the context of these pages) (see Figures 31-1 and 31-2). The appropriate form is the Application for Export License, United States Department of Commerce, Bureau of Export Administration (Form BXA–622P—Rev. 6–89). When completed, it should be mailed to the Office of Export Licensing, P.O. Box 273, Washington, D.C. 20044.

Instructions for completing the Application for Export License are more complex than the general instructions that follow, but they are indicative of what is required:

1. *When to Use This Form*—Use this form to apply to the United States Department of Commerce for a validated license, when required, as authorization to export commodities or technical data.

2. *Who May Apply*—A license application may be made only by a person subject to the jurisdiction of the United States who is in fact the exporter, or by his or her duly authorized agent. An application may be made on behalf of a person not subject to the jurisdiction of the United States by an authorized agent in the United States, who then becomes the applicant.

3. *What to Submit*—Submit everything in this package except the cover sheet and the last page. Do not separate the remaining parts of the packet.

4. *Duplicate Applications*—Do not submit an application for export license if a pending application covers the same transaction.

5. *Compliance with Regulations*—Instructions for filling out and filing an application for export license, and information on other export control matters, may be found in the Export Administration Regulations. An applicant must comply with the provisions relating to individual or other validated licenses and special provisions of the Export Administration Regulations relating to the desired export. These regulations are codified at 15 C.F.R. 768 et seq. Changes to the regulations are published in the Federal Register. The Department of Commerce also publishes a loose leaf version of the Regulations. Supplements to the Regulations are issued as Export Administration Bulletins. Subscription to the Export Administration Regulations, including the Bulletins may be placed with the Superintendent of Documents, United States Government Printing Office, Washington, D.C. 20402.

6. *Licensee*—The applicant to whom the license is issued becomes the licensee and will be held strictly accountable for the use of the license. Exports under a validated license may be made only for the account of the licensee.

FORM BXA-622P
(REV. 6-89)
FORM APPROVED: OMB No. 0694-0005

U.S. DEPARTMENT OF COMMERCE
Bureau of Export Administration

Application for Export License

GENERAL INSTRUCTIONS

Public reporting for this collection of information is estimated to average 45 minutes per response, including the time for reviewing instructions, searching existing data sources, gathering and maintaining the data needed, and completing and reviewing the collection of information. Send comments regarding this burden estimate or any other aspect of this collection of information, including suggestions for reducing this burden, to Office of Security and Management Support, Bureau of Export Administration, U.S. Department of Commerce, Washington, D.C. 20230; and to the Office of Management and Budget, Paperwork Reduction Project (0694-0005), Washington, D.C. 20503.

A.   WHEN TO USE THIS FORM. Use this form to apply to the U.S. Department of Commerce for a validated license, when required, as authorization to export commodities or technical data.

B.   WHO MAY APPLY. A license application may be made only by a person subject to the jurisdiction of the United States who is in fact the exporter, or by his duly authorized agent. An appliction may be made on behalf of a person not subject to the jurisdiction of the United States by an authorized agent in the United States, who then becomes the applicant.

C.   WHAT TO SUBMIT. Submit everything in this packet except this cover sheet and the last page. Do *not* separate the remaining parts of the packet.

D.   DUPLICATE APPLICATIONS. Do not submit an application for export license if a pending application covers the same transaction.

E.   COMPLIANCE WITH REGULATIONS. Instructions for filling out and filing an application for export license, and information on other export control matters may be found in the Export Administration Regulations. An applicant must comply with the provisions relating to individual or other validated licenses and special provisions of the Export Administration Regulations relating to the desired export. These regulations are codified at 15 C.F.R. 768 et seq. Changes to the regulations are published in the Federal Register. The Department of Commerce also publishes a looseleaf version to the Regulations. Supplements to the Regulations are issued as Export Administration Bulletins. Subscription to the Export Administration Regulations, including the Bulletins may be placed with the Superintendent of Documents, U.S. Government Printing Office, Washington, D.C. 20402.

F.   LICENSEE: The applicant to whom the license is issued becomes the licensee and will be held strictly accountable for the use of the license. Exports under a validated license may be made only for the account of the licensee.

G.   ASSISTANCE AND COPIES OF APPLICATION. For assistance regarding export matters, consult with the Exporter Assistance Staff on (202) 377-4811 or any District Office of the International Trade Administration. You can obtain small quantities of this form from a District Office. To order large quantities write to the following address and include a completed address label.
Operational Support Staff, P.O. Box 273, Washington, D.C. 20044.

MAIL APPLICATION TO:	COURIER DELIVERIES TO:
OFFICE OF EXPORT LICENSING P.O. BOX 273 WASHINGTON, D.C. 20044	OFFICE OF EXPORT LICENSING ROOM 2705 14TH ST. & PENNSYLVANIA AVE., N.W. WASHINGTON, D.C. 20230

INCOMPLETE APPLICATIONS WILL BE RETURNED FOR THE NECESSARY INFORMATION AND/OR DOCUMENTATION.
DETACH THIS SHEET AT PERFORATION. SEE SPECIFIC INSTRUCTIONS ON REVERSE SIDE.

Figure 31-1. Application for export license (Department of Commerce).

1. CONTACT PERSON

Name _____ Telephone Number _____

Information furnished herewith is subject to the provisions of Section 12(c) of the Export Administration Act of 1979, 50 U.S.C. app. 2411(c), and its unauthorized disclosure is prohibited by law.

| 2a. FORMS ATTACHED | BXA-622P-A | BXA-622P-B | BXA-6031P | TECH. SPEC'S. |

APPLICATION CONTROL NUMBER
This is NOT an export license number.

| 2b. DOCUMENT(S) ON FILE WITH APPLICANT | BXA-629P | LETTER OF ASSURANCE | OTHER |

C 508465

4. SPECIAL PURPOSE

I.C. and/or END-USE CERTIFICATE(S) COUNTRY # ___ COUNTRY # ___

3. RESUBMISSION OF CASE NUMBER

5. APPLICANT	7. PURCHASER	Same as Item #6
ADDRESS	ADDRESS	
CITY	CITY	POSTAL CODE
STATE	ZIP CODE	COUNTRY	TELEPHONE NO.

6. ULTIMATE CONSIGNEE	8. INTERMEDIATE CONSIGNEE	Same as Item #7
ADDRESS	ADDRESS	
CITY	POSTAL CODE	CITY	POSTAL CODE
COUNTRY	TELEPHONE NO.	COUNTRY	TELEPHONE NO.

9 (a) QUANTITY	(b) COMMODITY PDR	MANUFACTURER'S DESCRIPTION OF COMMODITY (Place model # before description, followed by a colon. End description with ECCN Paragraph Reference)	PROCESSING CODE	(c) ECCN	(d) NET VALUE U.S. DOLLARS	
					UNIT PRICE	TOTAL PRICE
					TOTAL OF ENTIRE TRANSACTION $	

10. PARTY OTHER THAN APPLICANT AUTHORIZED TO RECEIVE LICENSE

11. MANUFACTURER(S)

ADDRESS _____ TELEPHONE NO. _____

13. END-USER if different from Item #6
NAME

CITY ___ STATE ___ ZIP CODE ___

ADDRESS

12. SPECIFIC END-USE OF COMMODITIES OR TECHNICAL DATA BY CONSIGNEE IN ITEM #6 ABOVE

| CITY | POSTAL CODE |
| COUNTRY | TELEPHONE NO. |

15. ADDITIONAL INFORMATION

14. FOREIGN AVAILABILITY SUBMISSION ATTACHED | YES | NO |

16. APPLICANT'S CERTIFICATION: I hereby make application for a license to export, and I certify that (a) to the best of my knowledge, information and belief all statements in this application, including the description of the commodities or technical data and their end-uses, and any documents submitted in support of the application are correct and complete and that they fully and accurately disclose all the terms of the order and other facts of the export transaction; (b) this application conforms to the instructions accompanying this application and the Export Administration Regulations; (c) I obtained the order from the order party who has completed item 17, or I negotiated with and secured the export order directly from the purchaser or ultimate consignee, or through his or their agent(s); (d) I will retain records pertaining to this transaction and make them available as required by §787.13 of the Export Administration Regulations; (e) I will report promptly to the U.S. Department of Commerce any material changes in the terms of the order or other facts or intentions of the export transaction as reflected in this application and supporting documents, whether the application is still under consideration or a license has been granted, and (f) if the license is granted, I will be strictly accountable for its use in accordance with the Export Administration Regulations and all the terms and conditions of the license.

SIGN HERE IN INK _____ (SIGNATURE of person authorized to execute this application)

Type or Print _____ (NAME and TITLE of person whose signature appears on line to the left)

DATE OF APPLICATION

17. ORDER PARTY'S CERTIFICATION (See §772.6 (b) of the *Export Administration Regulations*.) - The undersigned order party certifies to the truth and correctness of item 16(a) above, and that he has no information concerning the export transaction that is undisclosed or inconsistent with representations made to the Department of Commerce and agrees to comply with items 16(d) and 16(e) above.

Type or Print _____ (Order Party)

SIGN HERE IN INK _____ (Signature of Person authorized to sign for the order party)

Type or Print _____ (NAME and TITLE of person whose signature appears on line to the left)

BB

ORIGINAL

USCOMM-DC 89-24379

Figure 31-2. General instructions.

7. *Assistance and Copies of Application*—For assistance regarding export matters, consult with the Exporter Assistance Staff at (202)377-4811 or any District Office of the International Trade Administration. You can obtain small quantities of this form from a District Office. To order larger quantities write to the following address and include a completed address label: Operational Support Staff, P.O. Box 273, Washington, D.C. 20044.

When a Buyer Is Not the Ultimate Consignee

As it is with domestic shipments of commodities, not every foreign buyer is the ultimate consignee. Commodities may be shipped to the buyer as consignee and the buyer may then send the shipment to the ultimate consignee, without opening or disturbing the contents of the package.

This is something that must be documented before the application for an export license is submitted to the Office of Export Licensing. If an export license is issued on the basis of data which indicates that the buyer is the ultimate consignee, any deviation from that position after the export license has been granted would be an unlawful situation, if not reported before time for the shipment to be released.

Statement by Foreign Consignee in Support of Special License Application

Any form whose title or description is as long as this one should be in a position of importance, respect, or ridicule. Fortunately for this form, it is one of considerable importance in the scheme of the Office of Export Licensing's consideration of export licensing applications (see Figure 31-3).

It is the responsibility of the consignee to complete and to submit this form to the exporter named on line two of the document. The intention of the form is to assure the licensing body that the product(s) or commodities will be used for one or a combination of the purposes listed on the form:

1. If capital equipment, it will be used in the form in which it is received in a manufacturing process in the country named in Item 1 and "will not be re-exported or incorporated into an end product." (The in-quotes statement can be very important to the granting of an export license.) National security items (NS—National Security, MT—Missile Technology, NP—Nuclear Nonproliferation, CB—Chemical or Biological Warfare,

Request for Export Documentation

(Please print or type the following information)

Request Submitted by: _____ Date of Request: _____

Department: _____ Mail Stop: _____ Phone Number: _____

Sales Order Number: _____ Required Ship Date: _____

Shipping to: _____

_____

_____

_____

_____

Attention of: _____ Phone Number: _____

Part Number/Description   New/Used   Quantity   Unit Price

Check One: Repair_____   Replacement_____   New Sale_____

Temporary Export_____

Other_____

Complete the Following:

No Charge to the Customer:_____ Value/Customs Purpose Only:_____

Freight, Duty & Taxes—Responsibility: Shipper____ Receiver____

Is Inner Office Billing Required?____ If Yes, Which One?_____

Comments:

Manager's Signature: _____

Dept. Name: _____

Figure 31-3. Request for export documentation.

FP—Other Foreign Policy Controls, and SS—Short Supply) will not be licensed for export to various countries whose stability is questionable or who have pursued or might pursue a pattern of aggression.

2. If the exported commodity is to be processed or incorporated into another commodity, the product and country in which the manufacturing process is to occur must be named.

3. If the commodity will be used to service another commodity (computers, aircraft, etc.), the final destination of the exported commodity(ies) must be stated.

4. If the commodity is to be resold by the foreign consignee in the condition in which it is received, the end use by the consignee's customer must be stated if known. If not known, or alleged not to be known, the type of commodity and the country to which it will be resold will have considerable influence on whether the application for an export license is approved or rejected.

5. If the customer checks the line which states that the commodity will be re-exported by the foreign consignee to an ultimate consignee located in one or more countries, and if the nature of the exported commodity could have a dual purpose or application, there could be additional difficulty to the exporter in getting an export license.

Statement by Ultimate Consignee and Purchaser

When the purchaser and ultimate consignee will not be the same individual or company, the Department of Commerce (Bureau of Export Administration) has a form that must be completed by the importer/purchaser and returned to the United States seller/exporter with whom the commodities order has been placed. The completed order is then submitted in support of one or more applications for export licenses to the Bureau of Export Administration's Office of Export Licensing (see Figures 31-4, 31-5, and 31-6).

The form asks for the following information and statements to which the consignee/buyer and the ultimate consignee/purchaser must certify as to accuracy:

1. Name and address of the ultimate consignee plus one reference

2. Requests that the Statement be considered as a part of the application for export license being filed OR as a part of every export license filed by (name of United States exporter or "order party" in United States with whom order was placed)

Figure 31-4. Statement by foreign consignee in support of special license application (Department of Commerce).

Form BXA-6052P (Rev. 5-89)	**STATEMENT BY FOREIGN CONSIGNEE IN SUPPORT OF SPECIAL LICENSE APPLICATION**	**U.S. DEPARTMENT OF COMMERCE** BUREAU OF EXPORT ADMINISTRATION

	1. NAME AND ADDRESS OF CONSIGNEE	
No shipment may be made under the Special Licenses procedure unless a completed Form BXA-6052P has been received. (50 U.S.C. 2401 et seq.; 15 C.F.R. Part 773.	Name	
	Street and Number	
	City	Country

INSTRUCTIONS: This form must be submitted by the consignee, in three copies, to the exporter named in item 2, below. Only items 1 through 9, inclusive, are to be completed by the consignee. Item 10 is to be completed by the U.S. exporter. In all cases, the signatures required must be those of responsible officials who are authorized to bind the firms for which they sign. If more space is needed, attach an additional copy of this form or sheet of paper signed as required in items 9 and 10. The information furnished herewith is to be used in connection with an application for a license from the U.S. Government for the export of U.S. commodities. In the case of a Project License, technical data may also be included. Information furnished herewith should not be published or disclosed except in accordance with the provisions of Section 12(c) of the Export Administration Act of 1979, 50 U.S.C. app. 2411(c), and its unauthorized disclosure is prohibited by law. Public reporting for this collection of information is estimated to average 10 minutes per response, including the time for reviewing instructions, searching existing data sources, gathering and maintaining the data needed, and completing and reviewing the collection of information. Send comments regarding this burden estimate or any other aspect of this collection of information, including suggestions for reducing this burden, to Office of Security and Management Support, Bureau of Export Administration, U.S. Department of Commerce, Washington, D.C. 20230; and to the Office of Management and Budget, Paperwork Reduction Project (0694-0050), Washington, D.C. 20503.

2. Request

I (We) request that this statement be considered a part of the ☐ Distribution)
☐ Service Supply) License Application
☐ Project)

filed by _____
(Name and address of exporter with whom we have placed or may place an order.)

for export to us of the commodities/technical data shown in Item 3 below during the validity period of the relevant export license issued to the exporter.

3. Description of commodities/technical data

I (We) expect to use, sell, install, or reexport the following commodities/technical data: *(Describe briefly)*

4. Consignee's business and relationship with exporter named in Item 2

a. Nature of business is: Distributor, broker, sales agent, manufacturer, etc. *(Specify)*

b. Our business relationship with the exporter is: Franchise, exclusive sales agency, authorized sales agency, customer, etc. *(Specify)*

c. We have had this business relationship for _____ years.

5. Disposition or use of commodities by ultimate consignee named in Item 1 *(check and complete the appropriate box(es))*

I (We) certify that the commodities listed in Item 3 will be:

☐ Used by us (as capital equipment) in the form in which received in a manufacturing process in the country named in Item 1 and will not be reexported or incorporated into an end product.

b. ☐ Processed or incorporated by us into the following products(s) _____
(Specify)

to be manufactured in the country named in item 1 for distribution in _____
(Name of country or countries)

c. ☐ Used to service the following commodities _____
(Specify computers, aircraft, etc.)

in the following destinations _____

d. ☐ Resold by us in the form in which received in the country named in Item 1. The specific end-use by our customer will be

_____
(Specify, if known)

e. ☐ Reexported by us in the form in which received to _____
(Name of country or countries)

f. ☐ Other *(Describe fully)* _____

6. Disposition or use of commodities/data by Project License ultimate consignee name in Item 1

I (We) certify that the ☐ commodities ☐ technical data listed in Item 3 will be used soley for the purposes described in the project description included as an attachment to this form.

USCOMM-DC 89-24223

Figure 31-4. (*Continued*) Statement by foreign consignee in support of special license application (Department of Commerce).

7. Additional Information (*Any material facts which will be of value in considering this statement.*)

8. Assistance in preparing statement (*Name of persons other than employees of firm named in Item 1, who assisted in preparing this statement.*)

9. CERTIFICATION OF CONSIGNEE

I (We) certify that all of the facts contained in this statement are true and correct to the best of my (our) knowledge and belief and I (we) do not know of any additional facts which are inconsistent with the above statement. I (We) shall promptly send a supplemental statement to the exporter named in Item 2, disclosing any change of facts or intentions set forth in this statement which occurs after the statement has been prepared and forwarded, except as specifically authorized by the U.S. Export Administration Regulations. I (We) (a) will not use, reexport, sell, distribute, install or otherwise dispose of any commodities/technical data covered by this statement contrary to U.S. Export Administration Regulations; and (b) will not sell or otherwise dispose of any of these commodities to any person or firm listed on the U.S. Department of Commerce Table of Denial Orders or where there is reason to believe that the commodities will be reexported to a destination not authorized by the Office of Export Licensing.

Signature of official of firm named in Item 1 (*See instructions on front of form*) (*Sign here in ink*)	Date signed
Name of person signing this document (*Print or type*)	Title

10. Request and Certification of U.S. Exporter

We request that the firm named in Item 1 be approved as a consignee to whom we may export commodities/technical data, under the special license specified in Item 2. We understand that all undertakings, commitments, obligations, and responsibilities under the applicable special licensing procedure, and the Export Administration Regulations related thereto, are fully applicable to any export to the above mentioned consignee if this form is validated by the Office of Export Licensing. No corrections, additions, or alterations were made on this form by us after the form was signed by the official named in Item 9 above. We certify that we will not export or otherwise dispose of any commodities/technical data covered by the special license issued to use for the consignee names in Item 1, until this form has been validated or after it has expired or been revoked.

Signature of person authorized to certify for exporter (*Sign here in ink*)	Date signed
Name of exporter firm (*Print or type*)	Name of and title of person signing this document

The making of any false statement or the concealment of any material fact or failure to file required information may result in denial of participation in U.S. exports. Notarial or Government certification is not required.

DO NOT WRITE BELOW THIS LINE—FOR DEPARTMENT OF COMMERCE USE ONLY

NOT APPROVED UNLESS THE OFFICIAL VALIDATION STAMP APPEARS HEREON	Approval of this form by the U.S. Government does not remove the need to obtain authorization from any other government for the proposed use or disposition of the commodities/technical data covered. If authorization for the use or disposition of these commodities is required under the laws of any other government, such authorization should be obtained in additional to that of the U.S. Government.
Validation	☐ Approved ☐ Not Approved
	Expiration Date: _____
	U.S. Department of Commerce Bureau of Export Administration Office of Export Licensing P.O. Box 273 Washington, D.C. 20044 (Date)

FORM BXA-6052P (5-89)   USCOMM-DC 89-24223

Figure 31-5. Statement of ultimate consignee and purchaser.

OMB NO. 0625-0136

| FORM BXA-629P (REV. 1-90) | | U.S. DEPARTMENT OF COMMERCE BUREAU OF EXPORT ADMINISTRATION |

STATEMENT BY ULTIMATE CONSIGNEE AND PURCHASER

GENERAL INSTRUCTIONS—This form must be submitted by the importer (ultimate consignee shown in Item 1) and by the overseas buyer or purchaser, to the U.S. exporter or seller with whom the order for the commodities described in Item 3 is placed. This completed statement will be submitted in support of one or more export license aplications to the U.S. Department of Commerce. All items on this form must be completed. Where the information required is unknown or the item does not apply, write in the appropriate words "UNKNOWN" OR "NOT APPLICABLE." If more space is needed, attached an additional copy of this form or sheet of paper signed as in Item 8. Submit form within 180 days from latest date in Item 8. Information furnished herewith is subject to the provisions of Section 12(c) of the Export Administration Act of 1979, 50 USC app. 2411(c), and its unauthorized disclosure is prohibited by law.

Public reporting for this collection of information is estimated to average 45 minutes per response, including the time for reviewing instructions, searching existing data sources, gathering and maintaining the data need, and completing and reviewing the collection of information. Send comments regarding this burden estimate or any other aspect of this collection of information, including suggestions for reducing this burden, to Office of Security and Management Support, Bureau of Export Administration, U.S. Department of Commerce, Washington, D.C. 20230; and to the Office of Management and Budget, Paper Reduction Project (0694-0005), Washington, D.C. 20503.

1. Ultimate consignee name and address

Name

Street and number

City and Country

Reference *(if desired)*

2. Request *(Check one)*

a. ☐ We request that this statement be considered a part of the application for export license filed by

_____

U.S. exporter or U.S. person with whom we have placed order (order party)

for export to us of the commodities described in item 3.

b. ☐ We request that this statement be considered a part of every application for export license filed by

_____

U.S. exporter or U.S. person with whom we have placed our order (order party)

for export to us of the type of comodities described in this statement, during the period ending June 30 of the second year after the signing of this form, or on _____

3. Commodities

We have placed or may place orders with the person or firm named in Item 2 for the commodites indicated below:

COMMODITY DESCRIPTION	*(Fill in only if 2a is checked)*	
	QUANTITY	VALUE

4. Disposition or use of commodities by ultimate consignee named in Item 1 *(Check and complete the appropriate box(es))*

We certify that the commodity(ies) listed in Item 3:

a. ☐ Will be used by us (as capital equipment) in the form in which received in a manufacturing process in the country named in Item 1 and will not be reexported or incorporated into an end product.

b. ☐ Will be processed or incorporated by us into the following product(s)_____
to be manufactured in the country named in Item 1 for distribution in _____
(Name of country or countries)

c. ☐ Will be resold by us in the form in which received in the country named in Item 1 for use or consumption therein.

The specific end-use by my customer will be _____

d. ☐ Will be reexported by us in the form in which received to _____ *(Specify, if known)* _____
(Name of country(ies)

e. ☐ Other *(Describe fully)*_____

NOTE: If Item (d) is checked, acceptance of this form by the Office of Export Licensing as a supporting document for license applications shall not be construed as an authorization to reexport the commodities to which the form applies unless specific approval has been obtained from the Office of Export Licensing for such reexport.

(Reproduction of this form is permissible, providing that content, format, size and color of paper are the same)

Please continue form and sign certificate on reverse side.

Figure 31-5. (*Continued*) Statement of ultimate consignee and purchaser.

5.	Nature of business of ultimate consignee named in Item 1 and his relationship with U.S. exporter named in Item 2.

a. The nature of our usual business is _____
(Broker, distributor, fabricator, manufacturer, wholesaler, retailer, etc.)

b. Our business relationship with the U.S. exporter is _____
(Contractual, franchise, exclusive distributor, distributor

_____
wholesaler, continuing and regular individual business, etc.)
and we have had this business relationship for _____ years.

6.	Additional information *(Any other material facts which will be of value considering applications for licenses covered by this statement.)*

7.	Assistance in preparing statement *(Names of persons other than employees of consignee or purchaser who assisted in the preparation of this statement.)*

8.	CERTIFICATION OF ULTIMATE CONSIGNEE AND PURCHASER (This item is to be signed by the ultimate consignee shown in item 1 and by the purchaser where the latter is not the same as the ultimate consignee. Where the ultimate consignee is unknown, this item should be signed by the purchaser.)

We certify that all of the facts contained in this statement are true and correct to the best of our knowledge and belief and we do not know of any additional facts which are inconsistent with the above statement. We shall promptly send a supplemental statement to the person named in Item 2, disclosing any change of facts or intentions set forth in this statement which occurs after the statement has been prepared and forwarded. Except as specifically authorized by the U.S. Export Administration Regulations, or by prior written approval of the U.S. Department of Commerce, we will not reexport, resell, or otherwise dispose of any commodities listed in Item 3 above: (1) to any country not approved for export as brought to our attention by means of a bill of lading, commercial invoice, or any other means; or (2) to any person if there is reason to believe that it will result directly or indirectly, in disposition of the commodities contrary to the representations made in this statement or contrary to U.S. Export Administration Regulations.

Ultimate Consignee   **Purchase:**

Signature
in ink _____   Signature
(Signature of official of ultimate consignee)   in ink _____
(Signature of official of purchaser firm)

Type or
print _____   Type or
(Name and title of official of ultimate consignee)   print _____
(Name and title of official of purchaser firm)

Date _____

Type or
print _____
(Name of purchaser firm)

Date _____

9.	CERTIFICATION FOR USE OF U.S. EXPORTER in certifying that any correction, addition, or alteration on this form was made prior to the signing by the ultimate consignee and purchaser in Item 8.

We certify that no corrections, additions, or alterations were made on this form by us after the form was signed by the (ultimate consignee) (purchaser).

Type or
print _____   Type or
(Name of exporter)   print _____
(Signature of person authorized to certifiey for exporter)

_____   _____
(Date signed)   *(Name and title of person signing this document)*

The making of any false statement, the concealment of any material fact, or failure to file information may result in denial of participation in U.S. exports. Notarial or governmental certification is not required.

USCOMM-DC 90-24114

FORM BXA-629P (REV. 1-90)   ☆ U.S.GPO:1990-0-258-500

TO:
BT NORTH AMERICA INC.
ATTN: INTERNATIONAL TRADE SERVICES DEPARTMENT
M/S F-27 P.O. BOX 49019
SAN JOSE, CA 95161-9019 USA
FAX NUMBER: 408-922-7962

RE: INDIVIDUAL GTDR TECHNICAL DATA LETTER OF ASSURANCE

I may be receiving from BT North America Inc. technical information, technical training to operate a system, and/or software relating to BT products. I agree not to disclose or reexport, directly or indirectly, the software or technical data, or any direct product thereof, received from BT North America Inc. to any of the countries listed below without the prior consent of the United States Government. I understand that exporting or diverting BT technology contrary to United States Law is prohibited.

COUNTRY LIST: AFGANISTAN, ALBANIA, BULGARIA, CUBA, CZECHOSLOVAKIA, ESTONIA, HAITI, HUNGARY, IRAN, IRAQ, KAMPUCHEA (CAMBODIA), LAOS, LATVIA, LIBYA, LITHUANIA, MONGOLIAN PEOPLE'S REPUBLIC, NORTH KOREA, PEOPLE'S REPUBLIC OF CHINA, POLAND ROMANIA, SYRIA, THE FORMER UNION OF SOVIET SOCIALIST REPUBLIC, VIETNAM, AND/OR MILITARY, POLICE, ENTITIES OF REPUBLIC OF SOUTH AFRICA. I UNDERSTAND THAT THIS LIST MAY CHANGE FROM TIME TO TIME. ANY ADDITIONAL COUNTRIES THAT ARE EMBARGOED OR PROHIBITED BY THE UNITED STATES GOVERNMENT WILL BE AUTOMATICALLY INCLUDED.

PRINT NAME:_____ DATE:_____

SIGNATURE:_____ CITIZENSHIP:_____

TITLE:_____

COMPANY NAME:_____
ADDRESS:_____
CITY:_____ COUNTRY:_____
POSTAL CODE:_____ TELEPHONE:_____

to be completed by BT North America Inc:	The Original Document is retained on file with:
_____at	_____los 1/92

Figure 31-6. Re: individual GTDR technical data letter of assurance.

3. Description of commodity(ies) ordered, also quantity and value

4. Multiple choice pertaining to disposition or use of commodity(ies) by the ultimate consignee (see explanation of items on preceding Statement)

5. Nature of ultimate consignee's business and the relationship with United States exporter

6. Additional information if needed

7. Names of persons who assisted in preparation of the Statement

8. Certification of Ultimate Consignee and Purchaser: statement in which facts are represented as true and correct, etc., signed by the Purchaser (individual or official of the company) and the Ultimate Consignee (individual or official of the company)

Shipper's Export Declaration

This and related forms (Export Declaration for In-Transit Goods, etc.), such as joint forms of the Bureau of the Census and the International Trade Administration, are used for compiling the official United States export statistics and administering requirements of the Export Administration Act as provided for in the Foreign Trade Statistics Regulations and the Export Administration Regulations (see Figure 31-7).

SEDs are required to be filed for virtually all shipments including hand-carried merchandise, although there are some exemptions if the shipment is valued at $1500 or less. SEDs must also be filed for shipments from the United States or Puerto Rico to the United States Virgin Islands.

Information and statements required on the SED are as follows:

1. Name and address of exporter

2. Names of the intermediate and ultimate consignees

3. Forwarding agent, name of vessel, and pier at which it will be docked

4. Name of the exporting carrier

5. Date and port of export

6. Whether shipment will be containerized (vessel only)

7. Port of unloading and country of ultimate destination

8. A description of the commodity(ies), packaging, quantity, value, and export license (Validated License Number or General License Symbol)

9. Export Control Classification Number (ECCN) when required, and signature and title of person authorized to certify that statements contained therein are true and correct

Request for Amendment Action

When an application for an export license has been forwarded by the exporter (or if a license has been granted based upon statements and facts thought to be correct at the time the application was forwarded and pro-

---

TO:
BT NORTH AMERICA INC.
ATTN: INTERNATIONAL TRADE SERVICES DEPARTMENT
M/S F-27 P.O. BOX 49019
SAN JOSE, CA 95161-9019 USA
FAX NUMBER: 408-922-7962

RE: CORPORATE GTDR TECHNICAL DATA LETTER OF ASSURANCE

I (We) may be receiving from BT North America Inc. technical information, technical training
to operate a system, and/or software relating to BT products. I (We) agree not to disclose or
reexport, directly or indirectly, the software or technical data, or any direct product thereof,
received from BT North America Inc. to any of the countries listed below without the prior
consent of the United States Government. I understand that exporting or diverting BT technology
contrary to United States Law is prohibited.

COUNTRY LIST: AFGANISTAN, ALBANIA, BULGARIA, CUBA, CZECHOSLOVAKIA,
ESTONIA, HAITI, HUNGARY, IRAN, IRAQ, KAMPUCHEA (CAMBODIA), LAOS,
LATVIA, LIBYA, LITHUANIA, MONGOLIAN PEOPLE'S REPUBLIC, NORTH KOREA,
PEOPLE'S REPUBLIC OF CHINA, POLAND ROMANIA, SYRIA, THE FORMER
UNION OF SOVIET SOCIALIST REPUBLIC, VIETNAM, AND/OR MILITARY,
POLICE, ENTITIES OF REPUBLIC OF SOUTH AFRICA. I UNDERSTAND THAT THIS
LIST MAY CHANGE FROM TIME TO TIME. ANY ADDITIONAL COUNTRIES THAT ARE
EMBARGOED OR PROHIBITED BY THE UNITED STATES GOVERNMENT WILL BE
AUTOMATICALLY INCLUDED.

I certify that I am a responsible employee of the corporation listed in this assurance. I have the
authority to sign this document on behalf of the corporation and its employees. Any other
corporate locations authorized to receive technical data under this assurance will be individually
listed on company letterhead, by name and address, and attached to this assurance.

PRINT NAME:_____DATE:_____
SIGNATURE:_____CITIZENSHIP:_____
TITLE:_____
COMPANY NAME:_____
ADDRESS:_____
CITY:_____COUNTRY:_____
POSTAL CODE:_____TELEPHONE:_____

to be completed by BT North America Inc:	The Original Document is retained on file with:
	_____at_____ los 1/92

Figure 31-7. Re: corporate GTDR technical data letter of assurance.

---

cessed), and it is found subsequently that the license as requested or as
issued does not reflect changes in the facts upon which the application was
based, this is the form that must be completed by the seller/exporter and
forwarded to the Office of Export Licensing, Washington, D.C.
Information to complete the form should be readily available from other
documents and sources (see Figure 31-8).

FORM **7525-V** (1-1-88)

U.S. DEPARTMENT OF COMMERCE — BUREAU OF THE CENSUS — INTERNATIONAL TRADE ADMINISTRATION

SHIPPER'S EXPORT DECLARATION

OMB No. 0607-0018

1a. EXPORTER *(Name and address including ZIP code)*

ZIP CODE

2. DATE OF EXPORTATION

3. BILL OF LADING/AIR WAYBILL NO.

b. EXPORTER'S EIN (IRS) NO.

c. PARTIES TO TRANSACTION
☐ Related ☐ Non-related

4a. ULTIMATE CONSIGNEE

b. INTERMEDIATE CONSIGNEE

5. FORWARDING AGENT

6. POINT (STATE) OF ORIGIN OR FTZ NO.

7. COUNTRY OF ULTIMATE DESTINATION

8. LOADING PIER *(Vessel only)*

9. MODEL OF TRANSPORT *(Specify)*

10. EXPORTING CARRIER

11. PORT OF EXPORT

12. PORT OF UNLOADING *(Vessel and air only)*

13. CONTAINERIZED *(Vessel only)*
☐ *Yes* ☐ *No*

14. SCHEDULE B DESCRIPTION OF COMMODITIES
15. MARKS, NOS., AND KINDS OF PACKAGES
(Use columns 17-19)

D/F (16)	SCHEDULE B NUMBER (17)	CHECK DIGIT	QUANTITY — SCHEDULE B UNIT(S) (18)	SHIPPING WEIGHT *(Kilos)* (19)	VALUE (U.S. dollars, omit cents) *(Selling price or cost if not sold)* (20)

21. VALIDATED LICENSE NO./GENERAL LICENSE SYMBOL

22. ECCN *(When required)*

23. Duly authorized officer or employee

The exporter authorizes the forwarder named above to act as forwarding agent for export control and customs purposes.

24. I certify that all statements made and all information contained herein are true and correct and that I have read and understand the instructions for preparation of this document, set forth in the **"Correct Way to Fill Out the Shipper's Export Declaration."** I understand that civil and criminal penalties, including forfeiture and sale, may be imposed for making false or fraudulent statements herein, failing to provide the requested information or for violation of U.S. laws on exportation (13 U.S.C. Sec. 305, 22 U.S.C. Sec. 401, 18 U.S.C. Sec. 1001; 50 U.S.C. App. 2410).

Signature

Confidential - For use solely for official purposes authorized by the Secretary of Commerce (13 U.S.C. 301 (g)).

Title

Export shipments are subject to inspection by U.S. Customs Service and/or Office of Export Enforcement.

Date

26. AUTHENTICATION *(When required)*

This form may be printed by private parties provided it conforms to the official form. For sale by the Superintendent of Documents, Government Printing Office, Washington, D.C. 20402, and local Customs District Directors. The **"Correct Way to Fill Out the Shipper's Export Declaration."** is available from the Bureau of the Census, Washington, D.C. 20233.

Figure 31-8. Shipper's export declaration (Department of Commerce).

1. Export license number, date of expiration, and application control number

2. Country of ultimate destination, ECCN, dates of any previous extensions, and whether a request for extension has been declined

3. Name and address of the applicant

4. Space for the applicant to describe the commodity, number or amount, ECCN, unit price, and total price (The information in this section may differ from that included on the application for export license because the buyer/importer has increased the size of the order, opted for a smaller or larger model of the product, etc.)

There is a section in which the exporter is asked to state specifically the way the license should read (which part of the license has been issued or application is pending that should be amended), and a summation of the facts or reasons why an amendment is necessary.

The form is to be signed by an authorized agent/employee of the licensee, dated, and forwarded to the Office of Export Licensing for review, change, and issuance of an amended export license.

Request for Re-export Authorization

When the importer/consignee is not the ultimate consignee, this form must accompany the application for an export license if the consignee is to have the permission required to re-export the shipment (see Figure 31-9). The United States government retains control over a shipment licensed for export to and through the ultimate consignee and/or destination. Does an "ultimate consignee" receive a shipment from an exporter in the United States and re-export it to a firm or country which is not approved to receive the commodity being shipped? The United States can move through international control organizations to impose restrictions upon the company or country that does not abide by the certified and sworn statements that enabled the exporting company to obtain the export license. The renegade foreign firm or country will be banned from consideration for import sales by member nations; the weight of such a sanction can destroy an import firm.

The form has space for the following information:

1. Names and addresses of applicant and ultimate consignee

2. Resubmission of case number, special purpose, and whether the commodity or technical data was previously exported (and if so, under what Validated License Number or General License)

MM FORM BXA-685P (REV. 6-89)
FORM APPROVED OMB No. 0694-0007

U.S. DEPARTMENT OF COMMERCE
Bureau of Export Administration

DATE RECEIVED
(Leave Blank)

1. CONTACT PERSON

Name

**REQUEST FOR
AMENDMENT ACTION**

Telephone Number

2. LICENSE NUMBER

Consult 772.11 & 772.12 of the Export Administration regulations for information regarding amendment procedures.
Public reporting for this collection of information is estimated to average 15 minutes per response, including the time for review-ing instructions, searching existing data sources, gathering and maintaining the data needed, and completing and reviewing the collection of information. Send comments regarding this burden estimate or any other aspect of this collection of information, including suggestions for reducing this burden, to Office of Security and Management Support, Bureau of Export Administration, U.S. Department of Commerce, Washington, D.C. 20230; and to the Office of Management and Budget, Paperwork Reduction Project (0694-0007), Washington, D.C. 20503.

3. LICENSE EXPIRATION DATE

4. APPLICATION CONTROL NUMBER
(Insert from the original BXA-622P or BXA-699P)

5. EXPORT CONTROL COMMODITY NUMBER

6. PROCESSING CODE

7. COUNTRY OF ULTIMATE DESTINATION

8. DATE OF PREVIOUS EXTENSIONS
(If any)

9. HAS THIS REQUEST BEEN PREVIOUSLY REJECTED OR IS IT PENDING IN ANY COMMERCE DEPARTMENT OFFICE? (If yes, explain here)

10. APPLICANT

ADDRESS

CITY

STATE

ZIP CODE

11. QUANTITY	(b) COMMODITY PDR	MANUFACTURER'S DESCRIPTION OF COMMODITY (Place model # before description, followed by a colon. End description with ECCN Paragraph Reference)	(c) ECCN	(d) NET VALUE U.S. DOLLARS	
				UNIT PRICE	TOTAL PRICE

(Additional information should be submitted on the BXA-622P-A COMMODITY DESCRIPTION SUPPLEMENT FORM).

TOTAL OF ENTIRE
TRANSACTION $

12. STATE SPECIFICALLY THE WAY THE LICENSE SHOULD READ. (Identify that portion of the license upon which amendment is required.)

13. FACTS NECESSITATING AMENDMENT

14. SIGNATURE

Signature of Licensee   By Authorized Agent   Title   Date

When request is submitted by an officer or agent authorized by the licensee, said person must sign the request by entering licensee's name and thereafter his/her own signature prefixed with the word "By" and followed by his/her title and date signed.

MM

Information furnished herewith is subject to the provisions of section 12(c) of the Export Administration Act of 1979, 50 U.S.C. app. 2411(c) and its unauthorized disclosure is prohibited by law.

NO EXPORT LICENSE WILL BE AMENDED UNLESS THIS FORM IS COMPLETED AND SUBMITTED IN ACCORDANCE WITH EXPORT ADMINISTRATION REGULATION 772.11(h) (50 U.S.C. app. Sec. 2401, et seq., 15 CFR Part 772).

ORIGINAL

Figure 31-9. Request for amendment action (Department of Commerce).

3. Name of the original ultimate consignee

4. List of commodities involved, ECCN, and value of shipment

5. Name of intermediate consignee and request for authorization to re-export, sell, or other

6. Applicant's certification as to truth of statements (best of knowledge), and signature of person authorized to execute the request

Exporter's Certificate of Origin (Canada)

Under the Free Trade Agreement between Canada and the United States, this form identifies the origin of goods being shipped to a customer in Canada. The form seeks to establish whether goods or commodities being shipped were wholly produced or obtained in the United States (or Canada) and whether they were transformed, which would make them subject to a change in tariff classification (see Figure 31-10).

There is a section for a description of the goods, tariff classification, gross weight or other quantity, invoice numbers and dates. The form concludes with a Certificate of Origin in which it is stated that all goods have been produced in the United States or Canada and that they comply with the origin requirements specified for those goods in the Canada-United States Free Trade Agreements; it is stated also that further processing or assembly in a third country has not occurred subsequent to processing or assembly in Canada or the United States.

Canadian Customs Invoice

This invoice is a form of Canada's Department of National Revenue—Customs and Excise (see Figure 31-11). It is a declaration for Canada's Customs and Excise Tax people of the goods being shipped from the United States to a purchaser, consignee, or lessee in Canada. It includes information such as names and addresses of vendor, consignee, and purchaser (if other than consignee), the place of direct shipment to Canada and mode of transportation to be used, country of transshipment (if there is one), origin of goods (if a country other than the United States), conditions of sale and the currency (United States, Canadian, etc.) to be used to pay for the goods. Commodities being shipped are identified as to number of packages, kinds of packages (crates, containers, etc.), marks and numbers, quantity in units, unit, and total price.

NN FORM BXA-699P (REV. 3-88) FORM APPROVED: OMB No. 0625-0009	U.S. DEPARTMENT OF COMMERCE Bureau of Export Administration	DATE RECEIVED (Leave Blank)
	REQUEST FOR REEXPORT AUTHORIZATION	

1. CONTACT PERSON

Name	Telephone Number

2a. FORMS ATTACHED	BXA-622P-A	BXA-622P-B	ITA-6031P	TECH SPEC'S

No reexport requiring authorization from the Office of Export Licensing may be authorized unless a complete Form BXA-699P has been received (50 U.S.C. 2401 et seq., 15 CFR Part 374).

APPLICATION CONTROL NUMBER
This is NOT an export license number.

H148644

2b. DOCUMENT(S) ON FILE WITH APPLICANT	ITA-629P	LETTER OF ASSURANCE	OTHER

I.C. and/or END-USE CERTIFICATE(S) COUNTRY #	COUNTRY #	3. RESUBMISSION OF CASE NUMBER	4. SPECIAL PURPOSE

5. APPLICANT	7. COMMODITIES OR TECHNICAL DATA PREVIOUSLY EXPORTED UNDER
ADDRESS	VALIDATED LICENSE NO.
	GENERAL LICENSE *(SPECIFIC TYPE)*

CITY	STATE/COUNTRY	ZIP/COUNTRY CODE

6. ULTIMATE CONSIGNEE	8. ORIGINAL ULTIMATE CONSIGNEE
ADDRESS	ADDRESS

CITY	POSTAL CODE	CITY	POSTAL CODE
COUNTRY	TELEPHONE NO.	COUNTRY	TELEPHONE NO.

9 (a) QUANTITY	(b) COMMODITY PDR	MANUFACTURER'S DESCRIPTION OF COMMODITY *(Place model # before description, followed by a colon. End description with ECCN Paragraph Reference)*	PROCESSING CODE	(c)ECCN	(d) NET VALUE U.S. DOLLARS	
					UNIT PRICE	TOTAL PRICE
					TOTAL OF ENTIRE TRANSACTION $	

10. PARTY OTHER THAN APPLICANT AUTHORIZED TO RECEIVE AUTHORIZATION	11. SPECIFIC END-USE OF COMMODITIES OR TECHNICAL DATA BY NEW ULTIMATE CONSIGNEE IDENTIFIED IN ITEM #6 ABOVE
ADDRESS	

CITY	STATE	ZIP CODE	TELEPHONE NO.

12. INTERMEDIATE CONSIGNEE *(IF NONE - STATE NONE)*	TELEPHONE NUMBER
ADDRESS	CITY	POSTAL CODE	COUNTRY

13. I (WE) HEREBY REQUEST AUTHORIZATION TO REEXPORT_____ SELL_____ OTHER *(SPECIFY)*_____ THE COMMODITY(IES) OR TECHNICAL DATA STATED IN ITEM #9. If this request is being submitted on behalf of another firm or individual, explain in item # 14 below)

14. ADDITIONAL INFORMATION

15. APPLICANTS CERTIFICATION - I (We) certify that the above statements are true to the best of my (our) knowledge and belief. If authorization is granted, I (we) will be strictly accountable for its use in accordance with the Export Administration Regulations and all terms and all conditions specified on the authorization.

SIGN HERE IN INK	TYPE OR PRINT	
(Signature of person authorized to execute this request)	(Name and title of person whose signature appears on line to left)	Date of Application

NN

Submit the original, and the OEL copy to the Office of Export Licensing

MAIL APPLICATION TO: OFFICE OF EXPORT LICENSING
P.O. BOX 273
WASHINGTON, D.C. 20044

COURIER DELIVERY TO: OFFICE OF EXPORT LICENSING
ROOM 2705
14th ST. & PENNSYLVANIA AVE., N.W.
WASHINGTON, D.C. 20230

Information furnished herewith is subject to the provisions of Section 12(c) of the Export Administration Act of 1979. 50 U.S.C. app. 2411 (c), and its unauthorized disclosure is prohibited by law.

ORIGINAL

Figure 31-10. Request for re-export authorization (Department of Commerce).

Figure 31-11. Exporter's certificate of origin (Canada).

Revenue Canada Customs and Excise — Revenu Canada Douanes et Accise

CONTINUATION SHEET FOR THE CANADA — U.S. FREE TRADE AGREEMENT

FEUILLE DE CONTINUATION ACCORD DE LIBRE-ÉCHANGE ENTRE LE CANADA ET LES ÉTATS-UNIS

EXPORTER'S CERTIFICATE OF ORIGIN

CERTIFICAT D'ORIGINE DE L'EXPORTATEUR

1. Goods consigned from (Exporter's business name, address, country, tax identification number)
Marchandises en provenance de (nom ou raison sociale, adresse, pays et numéro d'identification aux fins de l'impôt de l'exportateur)

3. Goods consigned to (consignee's name, address, country)
Marchandises expédiées à (nom, adresse et pays du destinataire)

4. Producer's name, address, country, tax identification number (if different from exporter)
Nom, adresse, pays du producteur et son numéro d'identification aux fins de l'impôt (s'il est différent de ceux de l'exportateur)

7 Origin criterion (see fields 5 or 6) Critères d'origine (voir les zones 5 et 6)	8 Description of goods Désignation des marchandises	Tariff classification (to six digits) Classement tarifaire (6 premiers chiffres)	9. Gross weight or other quantity Poids brut ou autre quantité	10 Invoice Number(s) and Date(s) Numéro et date de la ou des facture(s)

Note: This continuation sheet is to be considered part of the Exporter's Certificate of Origin and the signed certification on the latter applies to statements made on this sheet.
Cette feuille de continuation est partie intégrante du Certificat d'origine de l'exportateur et la déclaration signée qu'il contient s'applique aux énoncés de sa ou de ses feuilles de continuation.

DEPARTMENT OF NATIONAL REVENUE — CUSTOMS AND EXCISE — MINISTÈRE DU REVENU NATIONAL — DOUANES ET ACCISE

B 181-1 (11/88)

Canada

There is a space for the exporter's name and address (if other than the vendor), originator's name and address, any applicable ruling(s) by the Department of National Revenue, transportation charges, commissions, and sundry other charges. It is a clean and a relatively hassle-free approach to trade between two neighboring countries who enjoy a relationship that is virtually without parallel in any other area of the world.

Figure 31-11. (*Continued*) Exporter's certificate of origin (Canada).

Airbill (Air Express International)

The airbill contains space for a description of goods to be shipped by air (see Figure 31-12). On receipt of the shipment described in the airbill, Air Express International will prepare and issue the air waybill, sign such waybill in the name of the exporter, consign the shipment for carriage to destination or to onward carriage and delivery by any other transportation organization in accordance with terms and conditions contained in the air waybill, traffic rules, and regulations, and to prepare and execute in shipper's name any documents required for export.

The airbill form includes the following list of documents which Air Express International is specifically requested and required to prepare under authority granted AEI by the exporter.

Proforma Invoice

Consular Invoice

Certificate of Origin

Insurance Certificate

Banking (sight draft) (If the instrument of payment is to be a letter of credit, this would not be applicable.)

Other Documents (Documents such as Commercial Shipping Invoice, Billing Invoice, Shipper's Export Declaration, etc., will be prepared by the exporter.)

Commercial Shipping Invoice

Prepared by the manufacturer/exporter/shipper and including information such as shipping to, invoice number and date, type of carrier (air, vessel, rail, etc.), terms of sale, description of item or goods, quantity, unit price and extended price, total value (F.O.B. factory in United States dollars), certification (the sample form) that commodities are of United States origin and licensed for export under listed license number, certification as to truth and correctness of information contained therein, and the signature and title of person signing for the shipper (see Figure 31-13).

Every document in a chain that begins when an application for an export license is forwarded, with supporting documents, to the Office of Export Licensing in Washington, D.C., must be scrupulously truthful and accurate to the best of the applicant's knowledge and belief. Any less truthful or

Revenue Canada Customs and Excise	CANADA CUSTOMS INVOICE	Page of

1. Vendor (Name and Address)	2. Date of Direct Shipment to Canada
	3. Other References (Include Purchaser's Order No.)

4. Consignee (Name and Address)	5. Purchaser's Name and Address (If other than Consignee)
	6. Country of Transhipment
	7. Country of Origin of Goods — IF SHIPMENT INCLUDES GOODS OF DIFFERENT ORIGINS ENTER ORIGINS AGAINST ITEMS IN 12.

8. Transportation: Give Mode and Place of Direct Shipment to Canada	9. Conditions of Sale and Terms of Payment (I.e. Sale, Consignment Shipment, Leased Goods, etc.)
	10. Currency of Settlement

11. No. of Pkgs	12. Specification of Commodities (Kind of Packages, Marks and Numbers, General Description and Characteristics, I.e. Grade, Quality)	13. Quantity (State Unit)	Selling Price	
			14. Unit Price	15. Total

18. If any of fields 1 to 17 are included on an attached commercial invoice, check this box ☐ Commercial Invoice No. _____	16. Total Weight	17. Invoice Total
	Net	Gross	

19. Exporter's Name and Address (If other than Vendor)	20. Originator (Name and Address)

21. Departmental Ruling (If applicable)	22. If fields 23 to 25 are not applicable, check this box ☐

23. If included in field 17 indicate amount:	24. If not included in field 17 indicate amount:	25. Check (If applicable):
(i) Transportation charges, expenses and insurance from the place of direct shipment to Canada $_____	(i) Transportation charges, expenses and insurance to the place of direct shipment to Canada $_____	(i) Royalty payments or subsequent proceeds are paid or payable by the purchaser ☐
(ii) Costs for construction, erection and assembly incurred after importation into Canada $_____	(ii) Amounts for commissions other than buying commissions $_____	(ii) The purchaser has supplied goods or services for use in the production of these goods ☐
(iii) Export packing $_____	(iii) Export packing $_____	

DEPARTMENT OF NATIONAL REVENUE—CUSTOMS AND EXCISE REV. 7/84

Figure 31-12. Canadian customs' invoice.

FOR TERMS, CONDITIONS AND LIMITATIONS OF LIABILITY, SEE REVERSE.

SHIPPER - CHECK ONE: PREPAID, COLLECT
SHIPPER - CHECK ONE: REGULAR, ECONOMY, INTERPAK, DIRECT AIRLINE SERVICE

DATE | SHIPPER REFERENCE NUMBER

1a. EXPORTER (Name and address including ZIP code)
ZIP CODE

AEI AIRBILL NUMBER
48997605

Air Express International **AEI**
PANDAIR

EXECUTIVE OFFICES:
120 TOKENEKE ROAD - P.O. BOX 1231 - DARIEN, CT. 06820
PHONE: 203-655-7400 TELEX: 475 6148
FAX: 203-655-5779

b. EXPORTER'S EIN (IRS) NO. | c. PARTIES TO TRANSACTION ☐ Related ☐ Non-related

4a. ULTIMATE CONSIGNEE

SHIPPER'S LETTER OF INSTRUCTION
ON RECEIPT OF THE SHIPMENT DESCRIBED BELOW, AIR EXPRESS INTERNATIONAL IS REQUESTED AND AUTHORIZED TO PREPARE AND ISSUE THE NECESSARY AIR WAYBILL, SIGN SUCH AIR WAYBILL IN THE NAME OF THE UNDERSIGNED, CONSIGN SUCH SHIPMENT FOR CARRIAGE TO DESTINATION OR FOR ONWARD CARRIAGE AND DELIVERY BY ANY OTHER TRANSPORTATION ORGANIZATION IN ACCORDANCE WITH THE TERMS AND CONDITIONS CONTAINED IN THE AIR WAYBILL, TARIFFS, RULES AND REGULATIONS, AND TO PREPARE AND EXECUTE IN SHIPPER'S NAME ANY DOCUMENTS REQUIRED FOR EXPORT.

b. INTERMEDIATE CONSIGNEE

THESE COMMODITIES ARE LICENSED BY THE US FOR
7. COUNTRY OF ULTIMATE DESTINATION
DIVERSION CONTRARY TO U.S. LAW PROHIBITED

IF THIS IS A SHIPMENT OF HAZARDOUS GOODS, U.S. LAW REQUIRES THE SHIPPER TO PREPARE R.A. STATEMENT.
6. POINT (STATE) OF ORIGIN OR FTZ NO.

CONSIGNEE REFERENCE NUMBER

DOCUMENTS ATTACHED

AEI'S LIABILITY FOR LOSS OR DAMAGE IS LIMITED TO $9.07 PER POUND PER PIECE. IN NO EVENT WILL AEI'S LIABILITY EXCEED $250,000. CARRIAGE: THE SHIPPER MAY INCREASE AEI'S LIABILITY BY DECLARING A HIGHER VALUE IN THE CARRIAGE BOX AND PAYING THE ADDITIONAL CHARGE. INSURANCE: THE SHIPPER MAY ALSO PURCHASE INSURANCE ON THE GOODS COVERED BY THIS AIR WAYBILL BY INDICATING THE VALUE IN THE INSURANCE BOX AND PAYING THE ADDITIONAL PREMIUM. THE TERMS, CONDITIONS AND LIMITATIONS OF LIABILITY ON THE REVERSE SHOULD BE READ BEFORE ELECTING ADDITIONAL COVERAGE.

DOCUMENTS FOR AEI TO PREPARE
☐ PROFORMA INVOICE ☐ OTHERS:
☐ CONSULAR INVOICE
☐ CERTIFICATE OF ORIGIN
☐ INSURANCE CERTIFICATE
☐ BANKING (SIGHT DRAFT)

☐ COMMERCIAL INVOICE   ☐ EXPORT LICENSE
☐ CERTIFICATE OF ORIGIN ☐ LETTER OF CREDIT
☐ PACKING LIST   ☐ R.A. STATEMENT
☐ BANKING-SIGHT DRAFT ☐ IMPORT LICENSE
☐ GBL (GBL NO.:)
☐ OTHERS:

CARRIAGE VALUE | INSURANCE AMOUNT
$ | $

14. SCHEDULE B DESCRIPTION OF COMMODITIES, (Use columns 17-19)
15. MARKS, NOS., AND KINDS OF PACKAGES

VALUE (U.S. dollars, omit cents)
(Selling price or cost if not sold)
(20)

D/F (16)	SCHEDULE B NUMBER (17)	CHECK DIGIT	QUANTITY-SCHEDULE B UNIT(S) (18)	SHIPPING WEIGHT (Kilos) (19)

NEW FORMAT
U.S. DEPT. OF COMMERCE NOW REQUIRES THE SHIPPING WEIGHT (19) BE REPORTED IN WHOLE UNIT KILOS.

IF YOU HAVE ANY QUESTIONS, PLEASE CONTACT YOUR LOCAL AEI STATION.

Thank You!

PIECES | L | W | H | SPECIAL INSTRUCTIONS | AEI QUOTE NO.
DIMENSIONS

ONE MUST BE CHECKED
☐ NDR ☐ G-DEST ☐ GLV
☐ OTHER

21. VALIDATED LICENSE NO. / GENERAL LICENSE SYMBOL | 22. ECCN (When required)

THE SIGNATURE OF THE EXPORTER AUTHORIZES AEI TO EFFECT THE EXPORT WHEN AEI DOES NOT HAVE FORMAL POWER OF ATTORNEY.

23. Duly authorized officer or employee
SHIPPER - IMPORTANT
◆ SIGN HERE & ORIGINAL EXPORT DEC.

24. I certify that all statements made and all information contained herein are true and correct and that I have read and understand the instructions for preparation of this document, set forth in the "Correct Way to Fill Out the Shipper's Export Declaration." I understand that civil and criminal penalties, including forfeiture and sale, may be imposed for making false or fraudulent statements herein, failing to provide the requested information or for violation of U.S. laws on exportation (13 U.S.C. Sec. 305; 22 U.S.C. Sec. 401; 18 U.S.C. Sec. 1001; 50 U.S.C. App. 2410).

We have forwarded to you, the shipment described above via:
☐ Your Truck, or ☐ OTHER CARRIER (SHOW BELOW)
TRUCK LINE NAME
RECEIPT (PRO) NUMBER

Signature FOR
Title AEI USE
Date ONLY

Confidential - For use solely for official purposes authorized by the Secretary of Commerce (13 U.S.C. 301 (g)).
Export shipments are subject to inspection by U.S. Customs Service and/or Office of Export Enforcement.
25. AUTHENTICATION (When required)

GOODS RECEIVED IN APPARENT GOOD ORDER AT:
☐ SHIPPER DOOR ☐ RESIDENCE DOOR ☐ CITY TERM. ☐ AIRPORT TERM. ☐ CARRIER ADVANCE ☐ OTHER CARRIER DOOR

TIME | DATE | NO. OF SHIPMENTS | SIGNED FOR BY:

AEI ORIGIN STATION

Figure 31-13. Air Express International airbill.

accurate approach carries with it the possibility of being denied the export privilege, facing charges of attempting to evade export laws and regulations of the United States Government, plus fines and possible jail time. It is not an area for individuals or companies whose approach to doing business at the international level is less than truthful, is less than watchful of the background and reputation of potential buyers, and is geared morally and ethically to an all-out, no-holds-barred pursuit of the dollar.

Export sales represent an excellent growth area for a company whose sales goals are or are not being fulfilled by domestic sales at the area, regional, or national marketing levels. For the company with a desire to grow more rapidly and a domestic sales program that is not delivering at the projected growth rate, exporting a commodity or commodities to a specific area or country is a possibility for sales limited primarily by the type of commodity or goods being offered. When the exporting company's interests are more global, the goods or commodities are not subject to any sales-inhibiting restrictions, and the need for the goods in numerous areas of the world is unquestioned, the exporter is in a position to have a sales experience that can add an unexpected layer of success to the company's growth effort.

Incoterms, Invoices, Abbreviations, and Common Terms

If this has the look of a group of important items that somehow do not fit into what might have been other and perhaps more effective locations or sequences, then the explanation has served its purpose.

Their appearance in this area is, however, appropriate and should make a worthwhile contribution to the whole of the chapter.

Incoterms

Prior to 1980, United States exporters and importers were governed by a set of definitions known as the American Foreign Trade Definitions. These definitions have been replaced by an amended version of Incoterms: the international rule for the interpretation of trade terms recognized by the world's other international trading countries.

The International Chamber of Commerce first published Incoterms in 1953 with revisions made subsequently in the years 1967, 1976, and 1980. A guide to Incoterms and the 1980 text may be purchased from the ICC Publishing Company, 156 Fifth Avenue, Suite 820, New York, New York 10010.

The terms FOB, C&F, and CIF have been retained unchanged in the present version of Incoterms and conform with the practice of delivering the goods on board the transporting vessel. Current practice leans more frequently toward the seller delivering the goods to a carrier before shipment on board takes place. In this more current context, shippers are advised to use new and amended terms such as Free Carrier (named point), Freight/Carriage paid to, or Freight/Carriage and Insurance paid to. A definition of "carrier" has been inserted as a footnote to the term Free Carrier (named point).

These terms and definitions are important to the clarity of the contract or arrangement between shipper and buyer. There must be no ambiguity in the spoken or written arrangements which might lead one or the other to misinterpret the agreement or arrangement in such a way as to adversely impact the interests of the other party. A misunderstanding could result in a delay or a refusal on the part of the buyer to accept the shipment. The refusal to pay for it could lead to a mutually costly attempt to arrive at what each party perceives to be justice.

There are 13 terms (Incoterms) which are used in international sales contracts, terms that are revised periodically to conform with current requirements and practices. These terms were last revised by the Vienna Congress of International Chamber of Commerce and combined in *Incoterms 1980*. The ICC is currently offering a guide to Incoterms which is a companion piece to ICC's *Incoterms 1990*. It defines the 13 trading terms, but also specifies the rights and obligations of the buyer and seller in an international transaction.

EXW—Ex Works

FCA—Free Carrier

FAS—Free Alongside Ship

FOB—Free on Board

CFR—Cost and Freight

CIF—Cost, Insurance, and Freight

CPT—Carriage Paid to

CIP—Carriage and Insurance Paid

DAF—Delivered at Frontier

DES—Delivered Ex Ship

DEQ—Delivered Ex Quay

The Arbitration of International Commercial Problems

Arbitration clauses are present in most international trade agreements because of the complex nature of these transactions. There are so many factors involved over which shipper/exporter and importer/buyer have only limited control. When that limited control breaks down to the point where one party or the other suffers injury or claims to have been injured or damaged, arbitration is a far more viable approach than an expensive and relationship-terminating session in the courts. Importers and exporters do not like to drag their disputes on and on; they are interested perhaps more than most other types of traders in prompt and practical solutions and decisions. Also, because many firms are in the position of being forced to work constantly with the same firms or individuals or not do any business in an area or country, solutions and settlements via the medium of arbitration offers the least traumatic way to a speedy solution of the problem.

As international commercial arbitration has increased, reliance on good-will to enforce awards has decreased. It is no longer enough for participants in a commercial arbitration to receive the decision of an arbitration board as an automatic prelude to prompt compliance with the board's decision. Several international groups are available now to enforce the agreement to go to arbitration, and to enforce the decision when it is rendered. The United Nations Convention on the Recognition and Enforcement of Foreign Arbitral Awards (1958) is, with 170 countries and territories, party to this primary force for enforcing decisions handed down from arbitration.

There are other arbitration groups that are respected and active, including the ICC's Court of Arbitration and the Inter-American Commercial Arbitration Commission for trade with the western hemisphere. Failure to abide by decisions made in international arbitration could bring penalties (trading and monetary) onto the head of the exporter or importer who is tempted to challenge the rules of civilized commercial international trade.

Invoices

Commercial Shipping Invoices and Commercial Billing Invoices are intertwined so completely that one is not effective without the support of the other. If a Commercial Shipping Invoice is the most important document for any international shipping transaction, then a Commercial Billing Invoice is at a value level almost equal to the CSI.

The following illustrates what role each document plays in a shipment that has been prepared for export:

Commercial Shipping Invoice

1. Contents of the Shipment
2. Terms and Conditions of the Transaction
3. Total Value for Customs
4. Origin of the Product (What percentage of the product was made in the United States?)

5. Special Government Regulations Governing the Transaction

6. Parties Who Have Transaction Responsibility

7. Harmonized Numbers for Calculation of Applicable Duty

8. Certification from the Exporter Signed in Ink

A Commercial Shipping Invoice must explain in detail each of the listed items. No shipment can cross the border from one country to another unless this information is on the CSI.

The items on the Commercial Billing Invoice should match information on the Commercial Shipping Invoice plus the addition of freight and insurance if the shipment went to the ultimate consignee "prepaid and bill." If the Commercial Billing Invoice and the Commercial Shipping Invoice do not match (any difference in contents, terms, value, origin, etc.), the recipient of the shipment may not be allowed to pay for it. (Example: There is the risk of United States Government fines for evasion of Duties and Taxes if items pertinent to the determination of these charges are not stated similarly on the CSI and CBI.)

Anti-Boycott Laws

The rule to be remembered is that boycotts are against United States law. Some of the more flagrant violations of these laws are listed here:

1. Refusals to do business with Israel or any blacklisted companies

2. Discrimination based on race, religion, sex, national origin, or nationality

3. Furnishing information about relationships with Israel or blacklisted companies

4. Furnishing information about race, religion, sex, or national origin

5. Implementing letters of credit that include prohibited boycott terms and conditions

6. Accepting customer contracts that include prohibited boycott terms and conditions

Violations can be costly in fines and penalties.

Invoices—Types and Descriptions

The invoices that are involved in the preshipment and shipment phases of a transaction are important instruments in the process of shipping and receiving products or goods. They are equally important to the process of being paid for those goods, products, or services.

Several of the types of invoices used in international trade, with explanations of their purposes, are listed here:

1. *Proforma Invoice:* This is an invoice that is sent to a customer as a quotation before shipment takes place. It is also used to request an import certificate or, when they are required, to set up letters of credit.

2. *Commercial Billing Invoice:* It is an invoice that does not accompany the shipment, but goes from the supplier to the customer.

3. *Commercial Shipping Invoice:* It is issued by the shipper/seller and accompanies the shipment from factory shipping point to the receiving site. The invoice provides both countries (exporting and importing) with details of the order (description of merchandise, export license number, quantity, unit price, how shipped, terms of sale and payment, and shipper's certification as to accuracy of information contained therein).

4. *Canada Customs Invoice:* All of the information that is essential for the importing country's customs department to identify every meaningful detail of the transaction is included.

Abbreviations Used Frequently in Export

COCOM—Committee for Multilateral Export Controls

BXA—Bureau of Export Administration

CCL—Commerce Control List

OEL—Office of Export Licensing

ECCN—Export Control Classification Number

ECCR—Export Control Classification Request

ICP—Internal Compliance Procedures

PDR—Processing Data Rate

MTCR—Missile Technology Control Regime

DL—Distribution License

DLH—Distribution License Holder

CL—Core List

EAR—Export Administration Regulations

GTDA—General License Technical Data "Available"

GTDU—General License Technical Data "Unrestricted" (No Letter of Assurance Required)

GTDR—General License Technical Data "Restricted" (Letter of Assurance Required)

CTP—Composite Theoretical Performance

GLV—General Limited Value

G-Dest—General License Destination

FC—Foreign Consignee

GTE—General Temporary Export

IVL—Individual Validated License

TDO—Table of Denial Orders

"n.e.s."—not elsewhere specified

Common Terms Used in Foreign Trade

It is important for sellers and buyers to agree that contracts are subject to the "Revised American Foreign Trade Definitions—1941" and that the points outlined are acceptable to both parties. There must be complete agreement and understanding of credit and sales terms, the products to be purchased and shipped, and the prices, packaging, quotas, territories, delivery dates, miscellaneous expenses, and other factors that enter into the transaction. If the facts of the transaction are clear, the chances of a mutually unsatisfactory problem at some point in the flow of the transaction should be minimized. Abbreviations in contracts or quotations are not a good policy. Misunderstanding can occur, which could prove disruptive to both the seller and the buyer.

The following terms are used frequently in international trade. They differ from those used in domestic business and care should be taken to ensure their proper usage.

1. E.X. (point of origin)

2. F.O.B. (Free on Board)
   F.O.B. (named inland carrier at named inland point of departure)

3. F.O.B. (named inland carrier at named inland point of departure plus freight prepaid to named point of exportation)

4. F.O.B. (named inland carrier at named inland point of departure plus freight allowed to named point of exportation)

   F.O.B. Vessel (named port of shipment)

   F.O.B. (named inland point in country of importation)

5. F.A.S. (Free Along Side)

   F.A.S. Vessel (named port of shipment)

6. C. & F. (Cost and Freight)

   C. & F. (named point of destination)

7. C.I.F. (Cost, Insurance, Freight)

   C.I.F. (named point of destination)

8. EX DOCK

   Ex Dock (named port of importation)

Add to the above listed foreign trade terms some others that are used at times:

a. Free Harbour

b. C.I.F. & I. (Cost, Freight, Insurance, and Interest)

c. C.I.F. & C. (Cost, Insurance, Freight, and Commission)

d. C.I.F. Landed (Cost, Insurance, Freight, Landed)

It must be noted again that these terms and the list that preceded them should not be used unless the seller and buyer have a clear understanding of their meaning in the context of the contract, deal, or arrangement. Anything less than that level of understanding is unacceptable.

Although the following are not terms used in foreign business or trade, they are an essential part of any shipment your company may make to an international customer. The items are Insurance, Freight, Duty, and VAT (Value Added Tax).

Export is a complex area of business, but it offers an attractive potential for the company whose product(s) can be priced attractively, can be marketed effectively, and is in short supply in a marketplace that is acceptable to the Department of Commerce. An exporter must, however, have the in-house level of experience that will allow it to cope successfully (marketing, permits to export, documents packages, letters of credit, etc.) with the intricacies of international sales.

Is export a viable option for your company? Think about what you have just read, and about your company's financial, production, and marketing capabilities, and relate the whole to your company's short- and long-term goals. Does export seem to be a fit? Then why not give it a limited trial? The experience could introduce to your company a new contributor to the good health of the company's bottom line.

Index

About the Author

Cecil J. Bond has more than 30 years of experience as a corporate credit and business manager and consultant to manufacturers in the semiconductor, computer, rubber, floor coverings, and food processing and packaging industries. He has also served on court-appointed creditor committees to help rescue failed and failing companies. Mr. Bond is a former director of the National Association of Credit Management/Northern and Central California, has been chairman of the NACM's Regional Credit Management Conference, and was chairman of the NACM South Bay Credit Executives Committee. He is the author of *Credit and Collections for Your Small Business* (1989) and *Hands-On Financial Controls for Your Small Business* (1991).